THE PEOPLING OF
A TIMELINE OF EVENTS THAT HELPED
SHAPE OUR NATION

A Historical Perspective

Compiled by Allan S. Kullen
Editorial Coordination by Martha J. Burney
Programmatic Design by Gail C. Christopher

Americans All A National Education Program
Teacher Resources and Student Materials, No. 12

This publication is dedicated to the memory of two people without whose assistance it may never have been completed. To my mother, Eunice Kullen, for instilling in me the stubbornness and drive that the world graciously views as tenacity and perseverance, and to my business partner, Ralph C. Williams, Sr., for showing me that a life based on honesty, fairness and trust is a guarantee that nice guys never finish last.

Allan S. Kullen
December 1992

Table of Contents

Editorial Staff

Martha J. Burney is an editorial/research coordinator and publications production specialist in the Washington, D.C., area. She has more than 20 years of experience in prepress composition, research, editing and proofreading, and holds a degree in English literature from the University of New Hampshire.

Dr. Gail C. Christopher, national codirector of the Americans All program, has been an author and human service administrator for 20 years. She is the former executive director of the Family Resource Coalition, a national membership organization that represents thousands of community-based family support and education programs. She began her career as a clinician, providing direct services to individuals and families, but soon specialized in designing programmatic interventions for at-risk population groups. Her programs and related training and curriculum models have been supported by national foundations and recognized in the national media. An award-winning public television documentary, *Crisis on Federal Street,* featured her holistic program design for addressing the effects of institutionalized poverty through family development, self-esteem, stress management and motivational training. She is the author of *Anchors for the Innocent: Inner Power for Today's Single Mothers and Fathers,* and currently serves as the executive director of the Rainbow National Reclaim Our Youth Crusade.

Allan S. Kullen, national codirector of the Americans All program, is the president of a large suburban Washington, D.C.-based commercial printing facility. He was executive editor of the *New American Encyclopedia* and production manager for the *International Library of Afro-American Life and History.* Mr. Kullen was the editorial coordinator and production supervisor of a 700-page *Graphic Arts Guide,* and has taught in the adult education program at the Catholic University of America. A charter member of The Coordinating Committee for Ellis Island, Inc., he has served on many local boards in the Washington area.

Allison I. Porter is a researcher and editor who heads the Washington, D.C.-based Legislative Information Group. Formerly with the American Law Division of the Congressional Research Service at the Library of Congress, Ms. Porter now consults on editorial, legislative and legal projects for trade associations, research consulting firms, publishers, law firms and public relations agencies. She is the author of *Your 1991/92 Guide to Social Security Benefits* and *Porter's Guide to Congressional Roll Call Votes.*

Carole L. Skog is a designer, illustrator and editorial/production coordinator in the Washington, D.C., area. She has worked in fine arts, design, editing, print production and consultation since 1976. Formerly the illustrator and designer of the *League of Michigan Bicyclists' Journal,* she illustrated *Tall Annie,* a young adult biography. She was awarded a grant from the Michigan Council for the Arts for her work in ceramics and the S. E. Lee Scholarship Award for her essays on cross-cultural awareness through the arts.

Biographical information was compiled at the time the individuals contributed to Americans All.

Acknowledgments

We would like to acknowledge the guidance, support and assistance of many of the individuals and organizations that have participated in the direction, collection, translation, verification, writing, editing and production of this edition.

Our thanks go to Gongli Xu for his assistance in the initial organization of this work, which admittedly looks nothing like his original draft manuscript. Although most of the Americans All editorial and advisory staff participated in the work in one form or another, special thanks must be given to the following individuals for their assistance. We are grateful to Carole L. Skog and Gail C. Christopher for suggesting that we make the timeline format a parallel chronology that mirrors our programmatic approach to the historic patterns of diversity within the United States; to Eleanor Sreb for her invaluable contacts within the fields of history and folk culture; and to Cesare Marino with assistance from Robert I. Holden and the Anthropology, Outreach and Public Information Office, National Museum of Natural History, Smithsonian Institution, for the Native American section. Our thanks also go to Robert R. Edgar, Frances J. Powell and Emory Tolbert for original materials, with review assistance from Deidre H. Crumbley, Ronald C. Foreman, Jr., and Walter B. Hill, Jr., for developing the African and African American materials; and to Fred Cordova, Nila Fish, Him Mark Lai and Clifford Uyeda for supplying original materials on Asian Americans, with assistance from Marina E. Espina and Franklin Odo. We thank Frank de Varona, Richard Griswold del Castillo, Janice L. Jayes, Clara Rodríguez, Ricardo Romo and Barbara A. Tenenbaum for supplying original information on Hispanic Americans, with review assistance from Jonathan C. Brown, Millie Garcia, Teresa Grana, Pedro Juan Hernández, Doug Jackson, Everette E. Larson, Deborah Menkart, Maura Toro-Morn and Kal Waggenheim.

Because European American history is so tightly woven into the general history of the United States, special thanks for its availability goes to those individuals and organizations that supplied general historical information: Lawrence H. Fuchs, Charles Keely, Lyn Reese, Joseph M. Petulla, B'nai B'rith, Council for Early Childhood Professional Recognition, Cram Map Company, Houghton Mifflin Company, Mesa Community College/Douglas Conway, National Association for the Education of Young Children, National Women's History Project, the United States Bureau of the Census, the United States Postal Service, Women in the World Curriculum Resource Project and the Women's College Coalition.

Special thanks is also afforded to the Congressional Black Caucus, Constitutional Rights Foundation, the Hispanic Division of the Library of Congress, the Hispanic Policy and Development Project, The Department of the Puerto Rican Community Affairs in the United States, the Palace of the Governors of the Museum of New Mexico, the Simon Wiesenthal Center Museum of Tolerance, the Southwest Museum of the Braun Research Library, the United States Department of State and Georgette Dorn for making specific information available to us.

In addition, we are grateful to The Middle East Institute and to the staffs and services of the embassies and United Nations permanent missions of the following countries for providing materials and support: Afghanistan, Antigua and Barbuda, Australia, Austria, the Bahamas, Bangladesh, Barbados, Belgium, Bulgaria, Burkina Faso, Canada, Cyprus, the Czech Republic, Denmark, Dominica, Fiji, Finland, France, Ghana, Israel, Italy, Japan, Jordan, Kenya, Liechtenstein, Malaysia, Maldives, Mexico, the Mongolian People's Republic, New Zealand, Panama, the Philippines, Poland, Rwanda, Sierra Leone, Singapore, Switzerland, Thailand, Trinidad and Tobago, Tunisia, Turkey, the United Kingdom, Uruguay, Vanuatu, Zambia and Zimbabwe.

Historical societies and cultural offices in the following states have also furnished materials and support: Alaska, Arizona, Arkansas, Colorado, Delaware, Idaho, Iowa, Kansas, Michigan, Missouri, Montana, Nebraska, New Hampshire, North Dakota, Ohio, Pennsylvania, Rhode Island, South Dakota, Tennessee, Vermont and Virginia.

For their care in addressing our specific informational needs and their review of timeline materials, our special thanks go to the State of Arizona Department of Library, Archives and Public Records; State of Louisiana Department of Education; the North Carolina Department of Cultural Resources, Historical Publications Section; the diplomatic staffs of Brazil, Iceland, Jamaica, Luxembourg, Namibia, the Netherlands and Sweden; the German American Chamber of Commerce; and Dr. Henry A. Singer of the American Nobel Committee.

Last, but by no means least, is the staff who devoted more than just time to this work. To Martha Burney who coordinated the editorial project and spent many weekend hours to ensure that whatever had to get done, did — our inadequately spoken appreciation. To Carole Skog, who supervised the internal editorial, typesetting and production staff, which includes Sue Bergoffen, Larry Bradshaw, Jack Feldman, Heidi Fernandez, Todd Kullen, Suzanne Mast, Edna Pohlman, Allison Porter, Mike Shelton, Nancy Tresp and Bill Walker, thanks for a technical job well done.

Preface

Today's students are living in an unprecedented period of change. Complexities of the era include shifts in demographics, social values and family structures, as well as economic and political realities. Understanding their place in both the present and the future lies in history. History is so much more than a collection of facts. When appropriately studied, it is a lens for viewing the motivations, beliefs, principles and imperatives that give rise to institutions and practices of people and their nations. As American schools reform their curricula to reflect the diversity of our nation's school-age population, a major challenge arises. Is it possible to teach United States history as a history of diversity without evoking feelings of anger, bitterness and ethnic hatred? Is it possible to diversify the content of classroom resources without generating feelings of separatism and alienation?

Americans All answers "yes" to both of these questions. The Americans All program has proven that not only is it possible, it is preferable. By choosing to chronicle the history of six groups — Native Americans, African Americans, Asian Americans, European Americans, Mexican Americans and Puerto Rican Americans — the program provides a frame upon which an inclusive approach to multicultural education on a nationwide basis can be built.

Nomenclature, regional differences, language and the demands of interest groups will always challenge an evolving pluralistic approach to education. It is a by-product of the freedoms that we treasure and strive to protect. This reality necessitates a process that becomes part of the product, however. Americans All has integrated feedback from a diverse group of scholars in developing this program and maintains open lines of communication for continuous input from educators, parents and community members. The program's emphasis on six groups is based on historic patterns of migration and immigration. These six groups provide an umbrella under which many other groups fall. By developing 51 additional state-specific resource publications, the continuing saga of diversity in the United States can and will be told.

Americans All has succeeded in avoiding the land mines found in victim/oppressor approaches to our diverse history by using a thematic approach. The theme focuses on how individuals and families immigrated and migrated to and through the United States (voluntarily and by force). Carefully planned learning activities engage teachers and students in comparative critical thinking about all groups simultaneously. These activities assure sensitivity to the previously untold stories of women, the working class and minority and majority groups. Results from the program's implementation in ethnically and culturally diverse school systems confirmed the efficacy of this approach.

We have answered "yes" to the frightening questions about teaching diversity without teaching hate. Our nation's leaders must now answer even more frightening questions: Can we afford not to teach a history that is diverse and inclusive when school dropout rates range from 25 to 77 percent among Native American, African American, Asian American, Hispanic and foreign-born youth? Can we afford to continue preparing so many of our nation's youth for a future of exclusion from the economic mainstream — a future that mirrors a history curriculum that excludes them?

To compound the problem, we must add the very real constraint of urgency. The future of our nation is characterized by computer technology and global interdependence. All students, regardless of their gender or their socioeconomic, ethnic or cultural status, must be helped to see themselves as participants in this human continuum of scientific and mathematical development in order to both visualize and actualize a place for themselves in our future.

Students need to be challenged to think critically and examine how today's technology grew out of yesterday's industrial era, an era spawned by the agricultural accomplishments of prior generations. They need to understand that even the simple tasks of weaving fabric and making dyes from fruits or plants required mathematical and scientific understanding; that today's freeways grew out of yesterday's hand-hewn trails; that ancient tribal herbs (from many cultures) formed the basis of many of today's wonder drugs; and that it took the agricultural skills of many different peoples to produce the nucleus of today's complex farming and food industries. Students must also see the relationship between citizenship responsibilities and privileges and understand their own importance in that dynamic.

The Americans All materials provide diverse and inclusive images of history that can be a catalyst for this type of understanding. Not only is it wise to teach about diversity using an inclusive approach as modeled in the Americans All program, it is essential.

Gail C. Christopher
January 1992

An Improved Approach:
Comparative and Inclusive Chronology

Traditionally, timelines focus on dates from only one nation, cultural group or perspective. This timeline, however, documents a confluence of peoples, cultures and ideologies that make up United States history. This approach is strengthened by de-emphasizing heroes and heroines and eliminating traditionally recognized birth and/or death dates. The emphasis has been redirected toward broader periods, trends and cultural aspects of many groups.

While many groups make up this kaleidoscope we call the United States, this publication focuses on the stories of Native Americans, African Americans, Asian Americans, European Americans and Hispanic Americans. These groups were selected because of their historically important immigration and migration experiences, both forced and voluntary. Each group has a unique history, and each has had a special impact on the development of our nation. We recognize that these groups are not homogeneous and that considerable diversity exists within them; however, from either an historical or demographic perspective, these groupings can serve as organizing themes for an accurate revisiting of United States history.

To provide a general frame of reference for the five specific groups in this chronology, "The Americas" column includes major events in the history of the United States as well as in the history of Canada, Mexico, the Caribbean and the countries of Central and South America. These areas have also been targets of exploration and major sources of immigration to the United States. "The World" column, while in no way inclusive, is intended to show the parallel development of other major countries, and to present discoveries, political conflicts, natural phenomena and other factors that affected the international movement of people. Innovations in communication and transportation are highlighted, and a sampling of accomplishments of individuals is provided for all groups.

In determining placement of entries, particularly with regard to European Americans, who were successful in developing technological communities in the northern and eastern parts of North America, and Hispanic Americans, who were the primary group exploring and colonizing the southern and western parts of North America, and Central and South America, the editors have chosen to place events as follows: If an event involves the government of a country, or interaction between two or more governments in the Americas, the event is listed in the Americas column. If the event relates to a particular ethnic group's coming to the area that is now the United States, the event is listed in its appropriate ethnic group category.

This distinction becomes somewhat less clear, however, when events in question involve the establishment of communities in what will become the United States. Since few American cities remain ethnically homogenous, and since many European and Hispanic communities established in this country were at the expense of older Native American communities on the same sites, it is often inappropriate to credit one specific group with the founding of a city. We therefore have used the following guidelines:

- The establishment of "first" communities by any ethnic group is listed under the appropriate column heading — for instance, the first French community established in the Ohio River Valley is listed in the European American column.
- Communities that are founded by a specific ethnic or religious group are listed in the appropriate ethnic column.
- Events involving the establishment of some major American cities, such as New York, Los Angeles, or New Orleans, are listed in the Americas. In instances where these guidelines overlap, we have chosen to double-list events under both the Americas and their appropriate ethnic group heading.

Development and Purpose

The Peopling of America: A Timeline of Events That Helped Shape Our Nation uses a parallel chronological format, facilitating relational and comparative study. Our researchers and scholars have provided information that may seem new to some. Our developmental approach minimizes the usual delay between the discovery of new information, its publication in scholarly research journals and its appearance in readily available school texts. Producing a black ink, line copy format that provides open columns for student and educator participation enables us to take advantage of continuing feedback from the publication's classroom use as well as our diverse team of authors and writers.

This timeline is a tool that shows the vital role each of these groups has played and gives specific examples of how a community, a family or an individual can impact on our nation's history. "For Classroom Use" columns have been included for use in detailing local histories, accomplishments in other disciplines or the history of groups specifically represented in the classroom.

A Parallel Comparative Chronology

As an acknowledgment that they were the first recorded inhabitants of America, Native Americans are listed first; other groups follow in alphabetical order.

Native American

Entries in the "Native American" category deal specifically with events that occurred among indigenous peoples within the boundaries of what became today's 50 United States. Events relating to other cultures native to the Americas, North and South, such as the Aztecs and Incas, have been listed under either "Hispanic American" or "The Americas."

African American

Early entries under the "African American" heading include some of the events on the African continent that preceded or precipitated both enslavement and forced migration. Much of the history of African Americans, particularly their earlier history, has involved enslavement by European Americans; but it also includes intermingling with other groups, such as Native Americans and Mexican Americans. Equally as strong, but less publicized, is the African Americans' story of resistance to conquest, their ongoing fight for freedom against great odds and their battles for the rights of full citizenship. Events that document the accomplishments of African civilizations are discussed under "The World."

Asian American

In Asia, two powerful empires, China and Japan, officially isolated themselves—particularly from the West—in their earlier history, so the effects of immigration to the United States by these groups are not seen until the late 1700s. Therefore, "Asian American" entries include some of the historical events in Asia that ultimately led to immigration to America. Events that show the development and expansion of Asian cultures are documented in the section on "The World."

European American

The story of European immigration is by far the best documented in readily available sources. Because the early history of European Americans is also the history of certain areas of this country, the story of these groups as separate people tends to be lost. This publication provides information on many of the subgroups that belong to the "European American" category, and on the contributions of individual European Americans. Events in Europe that had a direct impact on immigration to the United States are included both here and in "The Americas."

Hispanic American

Under the heading "Hispanic American," Mexican Americans and Puerto Rican Americans are most heavily represented due to their historical impact on the peopling of the United States. Although these two groups have been represented separately in the Americans All in-school resource materials, this more inclusive heading has been chosen in recognition of and respect for all Hispanic groups, whose histories are also incorporated to the extent that accurate documentation has become available.

Classroom Use

Although a wealth of historical information exists for today's students, much of it is conflicting and generally not offered in comparative format. Therefore, assembling this chronology became a task of collecting, abstracting, prioritizing and arranging data in a manner that would most appropriately tell the story of many groups. Analyzed alone, each separate entry could be viewed in many ways: unique, important, commonplace or peripheral. That is by design. In order to develop the critical thinking skills needed for proficiency in today's world and work environment, students must learn how to analyze and apply the data they receive.

It is not possible for any one publication of a suitable size for classroom use to contain all available historical data. Although this timeline contains a significant amount of American and world history, it is designed to be a representative, rather than an exhaustive, collection of data. It tells the story, in a chronological and comparative format, of the peopling of America. World events are included as they motivated people to come to America; they also establish a context from which the history of the peopling of America emerges. Since people often date events in terms such as "during the Ming dynasty," "Elizabethan England" and "the Kennedy era," the listing of kingdoms, dynasties, and national leaders provides reference points for the relational placement of America's historic events.

While many of the events included are of broad scope and known historical significance, others are selected specifically as human interest events that demonstrate how one person or a handful of people have exercised initiative and made history. They show that a single individual can make a difference, and that history is, after all, the story of people. This chronology works well to springboard students into more specific research; additionally, it illustrates the fact that history is not an isolated field, but the core component of many related subjects.

This Americans All timeline has been designed to accelerate the process of creating in schools and classrooms a developmental learning process that is truly multicultural. By using the information contained in the timeline, teachers and students will increase their awareness of, and appreciation for, the concepts of diversity and democracy that form an integral part of our life in the United States.

The timeline's unique format — columns representing the histories of five ethnic groups, as well as those of the Americas and the World, placed side by side — encourages us to perceive historical facts from multiple perspectives. The scope of the timeline from pre-1500s to 1976 enables us to study in a familiar context the historic experiences of diverse groups who peopled this nation.

This information has been compiled from many sources and reviewed by individuals sensitive to issues of their own ethnic group. Additional data about groups and individuals, particularly regarding their arrival in and movement throughout this country — their conflicts, resistance, victories and achievements — has been incorporated as it has been made available to us.

The Challenges of a Social History

In many ways, this nation was conceived in revolution and battles. Wars were fought between the early European immigrants and the indigenous peoples — Native Americans and Mexicans (later Mexican Americans). Different European nations fought over rights to, and control of, lands and resources on this continent. These territorial struggles involved and adversely affected the indigenous people. The early history of the formation of the United States has, therefore, been filled with documentation about these conflicts, often only described from the viewpoint of the victor. We recognize that there is another face to history, a face that tells of families, communities, day-to-day living and survival in times of war and in times of peace. Since we have gathered much of our information from available primary and secondary historical texts, a portion of the content remains focused in specific time periods. Although history has

been taught from this familiar framework, woven throughout these events of national and international scope are the stories of families and individuals whose singular journeys, battles and triumphs are the fiber and color of this nation's social history.

A Reference Resource

Like any reference text, the timeline must be used at the discretion of teachers and students to help clarify, enhance and augment standard classroom resources. The timeline focuses on events that occurred (and were recorded) during certain time periods. However, history has taught us that each event is not an isolated occurrence. Specific conditions and circumstances create or cause each event; specific consequences follow. While we offer these events for information, we do so only as a catalyst to stimulate research and discussion about the culture and the context in which they occurred. The Americans All background resource books (see page 366) augment data found in standard history textbooks and provide specific information in this area.

Sources

In researching and compiling the timeline, Americans All has consulted the most reliable and most available primary sources. This research presented a recurring challenge, since respected historians often disagree on the exact date or the specific details surrounding an event. Such discrepancies, especially in early recorded history, spring from several causes.

First, sophisticated means of recording data were lacking. Second, because of language difficulties, transmission of information between cultures often involved inaccurate translations. Third, when conquered nations became the conquerors, they often rewrote history in their own best interest, and suppressed other versions. In the case of dynastic changes, for example, sources report varying starting dates because a time of unrest usually accompanied the transition. Often it is not clear whether a source has set the accession date at the unseating of the old dynasty or the seating of the new. In fact, scholars of different backgrounds often interpret historical records and events in very different ways, much as today's newspaper columnists disagree in analyzing the impact of the same current event.

Further discrepancies stem from the fact that, through much of recorded time, no universal calendar existed. When the Common Era dating system was established, Westerners added to the confusion by placing events occurring prior to Anno Domini *backward* on the time continuum for the years preceding the estimated birth date of Jesus of Nazareth.

If scholarly disagreement regarding the date of an event is significant, "c." (*circa*) precedes the year in this text, and we have approximated, within the parameters of the available data, the length of time and numbers of people involved. The *circa* notation has also been used when no reliable source gives a specific date. In reality, most of the pre-1900 entries could have this notation. However, in a comparative format such as this, the important factor is the relative position of events in the historical continuum, rather than the scholarly debate on exact dates.

Most numbers — for example, sizes of armies, casualties of a given battle or natural disaster, or land acreages — are presented as conservative estimates or are expressed in general terms, since sources rarely agree on exact numbers. Population figures, including those from the United States Census Bureau, are also approximated, since accurate census-taking continues to be problematic, as demonstrated by modern-day attempts to gather exact data on America's homeless population.

Another frequent controversy, due primarily to varying translations, lies in the spelling of the names of people and places. We have selected the most common spellings for primary use in this text. If a secondary spelling occurs frequently in reference sources, that variation appears in parentheses. Chinese names appear in the Pinyin transcription, with the Wade-Giles form, where appropriate, in parentheses. Also, for purposes of locating ancient cities and regions, the name at the time of the event appears in the text, followed by either its current name or a modern geographical reference.

In "The Americas" section, we have ordered the information under each date as follows: presidential elections (if appropriate); events and then leaders involved with United States history; events and people involved in state history; accomplishments of individuals as they relate to United States history; events relating to our closest geographic neighbors, Canada and Mexico; events relating to other countries in the Americas and individual accomplishments as appropriate. Events such as major wars are set apart from the rest of the text in a double column format.

Because we recognize the importance of education, we have listed the founding of many of our nation's colleges and universities, including, but not limited to, those that were specifically established for women, Native Americans and African Americans. Out of respect for those institutions, they have not been categorized (except if it remains in their name) by their reason for origin. In identifying their location, if the name of the city or state appears in the name of the school, it has not been repeated in the location, for example: The University of Pittsburgh is founded in Pennsylvania.

In "The World" section, we have ordered the information under each date as follows: events pertaining to countries, accession dates of specific rulers, accomplishments of individuals as they relate to our topics. Span dates are generally used to record dynasties; and certain major events. As in "The Americas," events such as major wars are set apart from the rest of the text in a double column format. Events pertaining to those special sections have not been duplicated under the individual year in which they occurred.

Finally, in the recording of recent or contemporary history, the general rule is to wait a minimum of 20 years to evaluate the significance of an event. Therefore, we have chosen to end this timeline in 1976, which coincides with the 200th anniversary of the United States and also acknowledges and respects the fact that today's teachers have access to databases for current events of the past two decades. To allow for the incorporation of additional information, we have provided empty columns in which to record data from the rest of this century.

This resource publication does not contain a bibliography; the vast number of resources — books, magazines, pamphlets, textbooks, research reports and individuals — used in compiling this timeline make the inclusion of either a comprehensive or representational bibliography impractical. We encourage the use of the bibliographies that are included in each of the Americans All resource books (see page 366) as catalysts for further research and as sources for expansion of the data presented here.

Reader's Guide to Using This Book

The use of B.C. (Before Christ) and A.D. (*Anno Domini*, or Year of the Lord) in counting years was established almost 1500 years ago by Dionysius Exiguus, a Christian monk. He began numbering with the year he believed Jesus was born. However, to avoid favoring any single religious tradition, many people today prefer to use B.C.E. (Before the Common Era) and C.E. (Common Era) to mark dates.

Words in italic are followed by their definitions, which appear in parentheses, after the first use of the word in each section.

"c.," or circa, indicates the date that follows is approximate, either because primary historical references agree that the date is approximate; or because primary references disagree slightly on the exact date an event took place. See "Sources" in the section "An Improved Approach: Comparative and Inclusive Chronology" in the front of this book for a further discussion of dating and numbering challenges.

31 B.C./B.C.E. -
A.D./C.E. **476**

This is the time span generally ascribed to the Roman Empire.

27 B.C./B.C.E.

Octavian is given the title Augustus by the Senate and becomes Rome's first emperor. The *Pax Romana* (a relatively peaceful era in the Mediterranean region during which the area is ruled by Rome) begins. Augustus rules until A.D./C.E. 14.

A.D./C.E. **150**

The Kushans, powerful invaders from central Asia who are dvoted followers of Buddhism, move across Bactria (Afghanistan) to reach the Punjab.

c. 1362

Murad I becomes ruler of the Ottoman Empire after the death of his father, Orkhan (1326). Murad I rules until 1389.

1368-1644

This is the time span generally ascribed to the Ming dynasty that rules in China. It is established by Emperor Taizu (Tai-Tsu), who expels the Mongols. The Ming dragon becomes a symbol of imperial power.

c. 1369

Mongol leader Tamerlane (Timur the Lame) dominates Turkestan from his capital in Samarkand. He began his raids through central Asia with the Russian Mongols (Tartars) of the Golden Horde in the early 1360s. Tamerlane rules until 1405.

A word or phrase that appears in parentheses after a place name is either the modern name for that geographical region, or a locator phrase that will help readers find the region being discussed.

A date that appears in parentheses after a person's name, particularly that of a national leader, refers the reader to a previous timeline entry containing significant information about that person.

A name that appears in parentheses after the name of a person is an alternate spelling or alternate name for that person.

NATIVE AMERICAN	NATIVE AMERICAN	NATIVE AMERICAN	AFRICAN AMERICAN
c. 40,000-10,000 B.C./B.C.E. Modern historians theorize that ancestors of the Inuit (Eskimos) and American Indians begin to arrive in western North America during this period. They migrate across a frozen — and later lost — land bridge through the Bering Strait from Siberia. Some historians place the beginning of this migration as early as 65,000 B.C./B.C.E. While there is some archaeological evidence to support this theory, Native American groups have strong oral, and now written, traditions that detail their origins at different locales and by different methods. **15,000-7000 B.C./B.C.E.** Paleo-Indian hunters spread throughout the North American grasslands into the American Southwest. They manufacture unique projectile points known as Clovis, Folsom and Sandia, named after respective archeological sites in New Mexico. **10,000-7000 B.C./B.C.E.** In the area that is now the United States, the Archaic Tradition develops in the Eastern Woodlands, with hunting, fishing and gathering. In the desert regions, the Southwestern Tradition sees the domestication of corn (maize) and other crops. **c. 5000 B.C./B.C.E.** The Cochise culture develops in what is now southern Arizona. It emphasizes vegetable crops. **c. 2000-1500 B.C./B.C.E.** Natives in what is now the American Southeast first make pottery. **c. 1100 B.C./B.C.E.** The canoe comes into regular use among Native American groups in the eastern and northeastern sections of the area that is now the United States. **c. 1000 B.C./B.C.E.** New vegetable crops, probably from Mexico, are introduced to the Southwest tribes. These crops include beans and squash.	**c. 1000 B.C./B.C.E.-A.D./C.E. 1000** In what is now the United States, mound building characterizes the Eastern and Midwestern native cultures. In the Southwest, Hohokam and Anasazi people build irrigation canals, agricultural villages, roads and complex ceremonial centers. On the Plains, people hunt buffalo on foot and live in fortified, semi-sedentary villages. **c. 100 B.C./B.C.E.-A.D./C.E. 300** Anasazi culture flourishes in the American Southwest. **c. 500-900** The Tchefunte culture represents the beginning of complex material culture in the lower Mississippi Valley. The Tchefunte grow crops and make distinctive pottery. **c. 700-1100** The Anasazi culture evolves into its Pueblo period. This is a developmental stage that sees the use of adobe bricks, stone slabs or mud and sticks in home building. *Kivas* (underground ceremonial chambers) and cotton fabrics come into use. Around 900, the pueblo structures in the American Southwest are constructed. **c. 900-1300** The Copena civilization exists in what is now northern Alabama; advances include pottery, tools, metal and stone ornaments and more sophisticated agriculture. **c. 1100** Hopis in the American Southwest use coal for cooking and heating. **c. 1100-1300** The Pueblo culture in the northern Arizona and New Mexico area reaches its height, with large apartment-type structures, and many material goods. **c. 1150** The pueblo of Oraibi (northeastern Arizona) is founded, the oldest continuously occupied town in the present-day United States.	**c. 1275** Many Southwest pueblos are abandoned due to drought and Athapaskan raiding parties from the north. **c. 1300** Hopis use coal for making pottery. **c. 1300-1600** The great Temple Mound or Middle Mississippi civilization flourishes. This highly agricultural civilization is characterized by separate republics, each having a central city, temple mounds and a chief's house. This is one of the greatest North American native civilizations; several aspects seem to be of Mexican or Middle American origin. **c. 1350** Tuzigoot pueblo, in what is now northern Arizona, is abandoned and the land is occupied by Yavapai and/or Western Apache people. **1390** The Great Binding Law is proclaimed by Huron prophet Deganawidah (Deganawida, Dekanawidah), establishing the Five (later Six) Nations of the Iroquois Confederacy. The five original nations are the Oneida, Onondaga, Mohawk, Seneca and Cayuga. Some sources date the founding of the confederacy in the mid-1500s. **1400** The last pueblo community in southern Arizona, Casa Grande, is abandoned, due in part to Apache raids. **c. 1492** By the time Italian explorer Cristoforo Colombo (commonly anglicized to Christopher Columbus) and his crew arrive in America, more than 300 nations of Native Americans are established in all parts of North America, each with its own name, language, traditions and government. Columbus mistakenly calls them "Indians." This error is continued by later European colonists.	**c. 800 B.C./B.C.E.** Evidence suggests that African travelers may have come to the Americas before Europeans. One indication is the great stone carvings of the Olmec era in Mexico, bearing African facial features. **A.D./C.E. 1442** Antam Gonçalvez, a Portuguese explorer under Prince Henry the Navigator, kidnaps several members of African nobility. He receives as ransom "ten blacks, male and female," whom he sells into slavery at Lisbon. This marks the beginning of the trade in enslaved Africans. **c. 1465** The trade in enslaved Africans grows as a result of Portuguese exploration. **1482** The Portuguese establish the first slave-trading port on the African Gold Coast, São Jorge de Mina. **1492-1493** Africans accompany European explorers in their expeditions to the Americas. The captain of one of Columbus's ships on his first voyage is an African.

Pre-1500

ASIAN AMERICAN	EUROPEAN AMERICAN	HISPANIC AMERICAN	HISPANIC AMERICAN	
Although Chinese seamen have engaged in significant maritime activity from the middle of the seventh century, when Manchus conquer the Chinese people in 1644 and bring the Ming dynasty to an end, a major change in foreign policy occurs. Fearing that Ming loyalists will create a revolutionary force outside the country, officials of the new Qing (Ch'ing) dynasty pass edicts barring emigration. Many Chinese people, especially from the southeastern provinces of Fujian (Fukien) and Guangdong (Kwangtung), continue to travel back and forth between China and the countries of southeast Asia, where sizeable Chinese colonies flourish. However, most of the Chinese people are isolated from the West until early in the nineteenth century. Japan's location off the coast of the Asian mainland keeps its inhabitants relatively isolated from outside visitors. The Japanese people withstand attempted invasions by Kublai Khan in the 1200s, and first encounter Europeans when Portuguese traders arrive off the Asian mainland in the early 1500s. European missionaries follow but, fearing the examples seen in other Asian countries where missionaries were soon followed by military forces, the Tokugawa shogunate issues an effective anti-Christian decree. Japan remains isolated until a United States fleet under Commodore (later Admiral) Matthew Perry sails into Tokyo Bay in 1853.	**C. A.D./C.E. 1000-1004** Norsemen Leif Ericsson and Thorvald Ericsson make separate voyages to the northeast coast of North America (probably Newfoundland and Labrador). They encounter Inuit or other Native Americans. Thorvald attacks a group of natives and is attacked in turn by a second group and fatally wounded. **1007** The first European child born in the Americas, Snorri, is the son of Viking colonists from Iceland. **c. 1010** Norseman Thorfinn Karlsefni lands in North America and takes two native boys to Greenland. **1492** The voyage of Christopher Columbus begins a wave of European exploration of the Americas. **1497-1498** Italian seamen Giovanni and Sebastian Caboto (commonly anglicized to John and Sebastian Cabot) explore the northeastern coast of America for England. **1499** Spanish explorer Alonso de Ojeda sails to the West Indies. While participating in slave raids on the native people there, he is killed with a poisoned arrow.	**c. 2300 B.C./B.C.E.** The native Arcaico people inhabit the island of Borinquen ("Land of the Proud Man"), later known as Puerto Rico. They are nomadic, and different theories exist regarding their origins. **c. 500 B.C./B.C.E.- A.D./C.E. 1500** The Olmec culture in the areas that are now Veracruz and Tabasco, Mexico, is highly developed, especially in art and agriculture. Olmec ruins reveal large sculptured heads, some in excess of 15 tons. **200 B.C./B.C.E.- A.D./C.E. 600** The Igneri culture, known for its ceramics, arises on Borinquen (Puerto Rico). **A.D./C.E. 200** The Mayan civilization arises in the area of southern Mexico and Guatemala. It flourishes for about 500 years. **c. 300-900** At the height of their culture, Mayas attain artistic achievements that surpass those of their Mesoamerican predecessors and their contemporaries. **765** Mayan scientists hold a meeting at Copán (in present-day Honduras) to discuss astronomy and to adjust the calendar. **1000-1500** The island of Puerto Rico is home to the Taino, a native people originally from South America. **1200s-1409** Chichimec tribes invade the Valley of Mexico, gradually intermarry with Toltecs and adopt their language. This combined Chichimec/Toltec culture experiences a brief blossoming. **c. 1325** The Aztecs establish the city of Tenochtitlán (site of present-day Mexico City).	**1494** Christopher Columbus and his crew land on Borinquen. The island's Taino population is estimated at between 20,000 and 85,000. Columbus claims the island for Spain and calls it San Juan Bautista. Columbus's ships bring cattle, sugarcane, wheat and other European animals and plants to Hispaniola (see "The Americas, 1493"). The first Spanish woman arrives in the Americas, sailing with the fleet of Antonio de Floras, who brings supplies to the Spanish colony of Hispaniola.	Pre-1500

THE AMERICAS	THE AMERICAS	THE AMERICAS	THE AMERICAS

Pre-1500

THE AMERICAS

c. 40,000-10,000 B.C./B.C.E.

Modern historians theorize that ancestors of the Inuit (Eskimos) and American Indians begin to arrive in western North America during this period. They migrate across a frozen — and later lost — land bridge through the Bering Strait from Siberia. Some historians place the beginning of this migration as early as 65,000 B.C./B.C.E. While there is some archaeological evidence to support this theory, Native American groups have strong oral, and now written, traditions that detail their origins at different locales and by different methods.

25,000 B.C./B.C.E.

Evidence suggests that early inhabitants of what is now the Yukon Territory are making and using bone tools.

13,000 B.C./B.C.E.

As North America's glacial covering melts and retreats northward, Niagara Falls is formed.

10,000-5000 B.C./B.C.E.

Villages emerge in the Andes and Mexican highlands. Early inhabitants cultivate corn, squash and beans to supplement their hunting and gathering.

c. 9000 B.C./B.C.E.

By this time, early American people have migrated as far south as Patagonia, the southern part of South America.

c. 8000 B.C./B.C.E.

What is now Lake Superior forms from glacial runoff.

c. 5000 B.C./B.C.E.

In the area of southern Ontario province, tobacco comes into use.

c. 4000 B.C./B.C.E.

At several sites in present-day Canada, copper is mined and used for tools.

c. 3700 B.C./B.C.E.

Fishing and early development of agriculture take place in Peru.

THE AMERICAS

c. 3500 B.C./B.C.E.

Maize is cultivated as far north as present-day New Mexico among the indigenous people.

c. 3200 B.C./B.C.E.

Early forms of pottery are used in the area that is now Ecuador.

3111 B.C./B.C.E.

This is the first year of the Mayan calendar. In one dating method, modern historians call this year 1 A.C. (American Civilization). It is not historically clear what happened in the Mayan culture in this year.

c. 3000 B.C./B.C.E.

Seafaring Archaic Indians, presumed to be the ancestors of the Beothuks, inhabit the island of Newfoundland.

c. 2800 B.C./B.C.E.

Inhabitants of modern-day Wisconsin use copper for making tools and jewelry.

c. 2500-1500 B.C./B.C.E.

Permanent towns are established in Central America, with farming-based economies. One of the earliest villages is established in Guatemala at the site of Ocós. Irrigation, pottery, weaving and ritual religions appear. Small villages band together in mini-states.

c. 2400 B.C./B.C.E.

Inhabitants near the area that is now Georgia make the earliest pottery found in North America.

c. 2000 B.C./B.C.E.

The Olmec civilization emerges at the La Venta site in Veracruz, Mexico.

Inuit people begin to move onto the Arctic coast from Siberia east to Greenland.

c. 1800 B.C./B.C.E.

Inhabitants of northern Peru weave designs into cotton cloth.

c. 1200-50 B.C./B.C.E.

The Olmec civilization flourishes in much of Central America. The Olmec are the first American society to have solidified communities, established trade routes, highly developed art and architecture and a form of writing.

THE AMERICAS

c. 700 B.C./B.C.E.

The Chavín culture begins to dominate in northern Peru. The chief ceremonial center is Chavín de Huantar. Its power begins to decline c. 200 B.C./B.C.E.

Pottery comes into use for cooking and storage among the people of the area that is now North Dakota.

c. 300 B.C./B.C.E.-A.D./C.E. 500

The Hopewell Territory (Illinois and Ohio) develops rapidly after receiving maize and beans from Mexico.

c. 200 B.C./B.C.E.

The Zapotecs, an agricultural and city-dwelling people of Mexico, have their religious center at Mitla and their chief city at Monte Albán.

c. 100 B.C./B.C.E.

The Mochica civilization in northern Peru is highly developed and militarily strong. Sometimes referred to as early Chimu, it exists for approximately 1,000 years.

c. A.D./C.E. 35-1100

The first Arawaks make their homes in the Antilles, beginning at Indian Creek (now in Antigua and Barbuda). This village supports about 50 people.

c. 100-900

This is the classic era of pre-Columbian civilizations, from the Hohokam and Anasazi civilizations in present-day Arizona and New Mexico, to Zapotecs, Toltecs and people of Teotihuacán in central Mexico, Mayas in the area that is now Guatemala, and Mochica and Nazca civilizations in Peru. Developments include construction of religious ceremonial centers, irrigation ditches, terraced fields, warrior classes, astronomy, metallurgy and writing.

THE AMERICAS

c. 200-900

This is the time span generally ascribed to the Mayan Empire in the Mexican regions of Tabasco and Chiapas, and Guatemala and Honduras. At the height of their culture, the Mayas attain artistic achievements that surpass those of their meso-American precedessors and their contemporaries. Among the Mayas, as well as the Aztecs and Incas, there are female priests and several female gods are worshipped.

c. 500-600

The golden age of the Mayas in the Yucatán is reflected in their preoccupation with complex calculations.

The city of Chichén Itzá (central Yucatán, Mexico) flourishes during this period.

c. 600

The city of Teotihuacán (in Mexico), a commercial and cultural center, covers eight square miles, with a population of more than 100,000.

c. 700

The Anasazi culture has evolved into its later period, known as the Pueblo period.

c. 750

Teotihuacán is destroyed, probably through a combination of drought, internal unrest and conquest by other groups.

c. 765

The city of Copán in the Honduras area becomes the center for Mayan scientific discovery.

850-900

The Toltecs gain control of central Mexico and begin building cities.

c. 850

In Bolivia near the Peruvian border, the pre-Inca community of Huari becomes the center of Tiahuanaco culture and masonry craftsmanship.

c. 900

The Mayas migrate from the lowlands of Mexico to the Yucatán peninsula.

THE AMERICAS	THE AMERICAS	THE AMERICAS	FOR CLASSROOM USE	

The Mixtec people in Mexico move south, taking control of the Oaxaca Valley. They fight constantly with the Zapotecs until the two groups join forces against a strong common enemy, the Aztecs. The Mixtecs are defeated when the Zapotecs ally with the Aztecs and later with the Spanish conquistadors.

c. 900-1000

A nomadic group, ancestors of today's Inuit, migrates to Canada's arctic area from Alaska.

968

Topiltzin, a priest to the god Quetzalcóatl, becomes the Toltec leader and founds the city of Tula (central Mexico). He rules until 987.

c. 984

Norseman Eric the Red sails to Greenland.

c. 986

Norse merchant Bjarne Herjulfsson, blown off course on a voyage from Iceland toward Greenland, sights the northeast coast of North America, probably Newfoundland or Labrador.

987

In Central America, Mayas found the cities of Uxmal and Mayapán.

987-1224

The city of Chichén Itzá (Central Yucatán, Mexico) reaches its height.

c. 1000

The Zapotecs at Monte Álban and the Chavín culture in Peru have well-developed societies and governmental organizations.

c. 1001

Norsemen Leif Ericsson and Thorvald Ericsson make separate voyages to North America (probably Labrador, now part of Newfoundland Province, Canada), an area they call Vinland. The groups encounter Inuit or other Native Americans. Thorvald attacks a group of natives and is attacked in turn by a second group and fatally wounded.

1040

The Toltec princess Guerillera leads an army to defeat the enemies of her father.

c. 1050-1300

The Anasazi civilization reaches its greatest level of sophistication during this period.

c. 1100

The development of the Inca civilization begins when the legendary Manco Capac leads bands of Andean mountain nomads to establish a community in Peru's Cuzco Valley.

c. 1125

The Chibacas are the most highly developed of the Indian tribes of Colombia. They flourish until defeated by conquistadors in the sixteenth century.

1156-1168

The Toltecs suffer droughts, crop failures and internal dissension, and the empire crumbles. Tula is sacked by invaders, and nomadic tribes move into central Mexico.

1194

Chichén Itzá is destroyed by the League of Mayapán. The Itzás, a strong Mayan tribe originally from the Yucatán, are forced to move and ultimately make their homes at Lake Petén in the area that is now Guatemala. They remain an independent people until conquered by Spanish forces in 1697.

c. 1200

The Caribs, a South American Indian group, have come up through the islands with a warlike nature, greedy for power. They establish strongholds in Dominica and St. Kitts, and make raids on Antigua, plundering the peaceful Arawak communities.

c. 1200-1533

This is the time span generally ascribed to the Inca Empire in South America.

c. 1200-1500

The Aztec and Incan Empires emerge, building on the remnants of collapsed classic civilizations.

c. 1300

Aztecs (Mexica tribes) migrate from the north to join other small city states in the Valley of Mexico.

1300-1460

This is the time span generally ascribed to the Chimu Empire in South America. The Chimu people are gradually absorbed by the Incas.

c. 1325

The Aztecs found the city of Tenochtitlán (now Mexico City).

1325-1525

This is the time span generally ascribed to the Aztec Empire in Mexico.

1347

Icelandic sagas suggest that a group of Norsemen from Greenland make a trip in this year to an area they call Markland (probably Labrador).

1376

The Aztec state becomes a monarchy under its first king, Acampichtli.

1380-1428

The Tepanec culture flourishes briefly in the Valley of Mexico. This period ends when Aztecs and allied tribes defeat the Tepanecs and divide their territory into three regions.

c. 1400-1450

For reasons still unknown, many Mayan cities are abandoned.

c. 1427

Itzcoatl becomes king of the Aztecs. He rules until 1440.

1430

Aztec ruler Itzcoatl orders all old accounts of Aztec history burned, then writes a new account glorifying the tribe's origins in a mythical northern land called Aztlán.

1440

The various peoples of Central America become unified under Aztec king Moctezuma (Montezuma), who rules until 1469.

Pre-1500

THE AMERICAS	THE AMERICAS	THE AMERICAS	FOR CLASSROOM USE

Pre-1500

c. 1440

Under their ninth emperor, Pachacutec (Pachacuti), the Incas defeat the neighboring Chanca tribe. The Inca Empire eventually grows to include an estimated 16 million subjects and stretches through the Andes from present-day Quito, Ecuador, to Santiago, Chile. The Incas develop a dual political system. The Inca — or emperor — heads government administration, and the Coya — or queen — heads the women's religious hierarchy. The Coya has lands reserved for her use, holds important religious observations and supervises the planting and fertilizing of the fields. Pachacutec rules until 1471; the Inca Empire continues until 1553.

1440s

Aztec king Itzcoatl forms the Triple Alliance with two other city-states and begins the conquest of the Valley of Mexico.

1441

The city of Mayapán, the last centralized Mayan government in the Yucatán, is destroyed.

1450s

King Nezahualcoyotl of the Texcoco kingdom in the Valley of Mexico promotes art, philosophy and law, but the Texcocans are conquered by the expanding Aztec Empire.

Mid-1400s

In Cuzco, King Pachacuti begins to expand the Incan Empire. Eventually stretching through the Andes from present-day Quito to Santiago, the empire attains a population of 16 million.

1466

The Chimu Empire is overrun and seized by the Incas.

1471

Topa Inca Yupanqui begins his reign over an empire that includes large sections of Bolivia, Argentina and Chile. He rules the Incas until 1493.

Portuguese navigators visit the islands of São Tomé e Príncipe, off the west coast of Africa.

1473-1481

Danish and English adventurers conduct explorations of Greenland and the surrounding area.

c. 1480-1500

Carib Indians begin military attacks on Arawak and Ciboney populations of the Antilles Islands.

1486-1502

Ahuizotl expands the Aztec Empire south to present-day Guatemala, west to the Pacific Ocean and north to the Tampico, Mexico, area.

Late 1400s

Carib Indians begin organized attacks on the Arawak and Ciboney peoples of the Antilles Islands.

1492

Italian explorer Cristoforo Colombo (Christopher Columbus), sailing for the Spanish monarchy, arrives in the Americas while attempting to sail to India. He and his crew land on the island of San Salvador in the Bahamas. They explore Cuba and Hispaniola, and Columbus claims these lands for Spain. The ship *Santa Maria* is wrecked off the coast of Hispaniola; Columbus leaves people there to colonize and returns to Spain. He makes three more voyages before his death in 1506, still seeking lands that resemble Japan or the Asian coast. Arawak Indians welcome the Spanish and warn them of fierce Carib warriors.

At the time of Columbus's landing, estimates of the population north of Mexico range from 2 or 3 million to as high as 10 million.

Columbus and his crew build the fort of La Navidad in Haiti, which stands for only a few months.

1493

Columbus's second expedition to the Americas includes miners, colonists, Hispanicized Africans in bondage and conquistadors. This time the group's first landfall is in the Lesser Antilles, and Columbus explores the Leeward Islands and Puerto Rico. On returning to the Hispaniola colony, the expedition finds it destroyed, probably by Caribs. The colonists establish the community of La Isabela nearby, where they unload the cattle, sugarcane, wheat and other European animals and plants they have brought with them. La Isabela is one of the earliest European communities in the Americas. Columbus continues to explore the islands.

1494

Christopher Columbus sights Jamaica.

The first Spanish woman arrives in the Americas, sailing with the fleet of Antonio de Flores, who brings supplies to the Spanish colony of La Isabela.

1496

Spanish colonists led by Bartholomew Columbus, brother of Christopher Columbus, establish a community on the southwestern shore of Hispaniola. Called Santo Domingo, it is the earliest continuously inhabited European community in the Americas.

1497

Italian explorers Giovanni and Sebastian Caboto (John and Sebastian Cabot) lead an exploratory expedition to North America. Italian seamen sailing under the English flag, they bring a single ship and a crew of approximately 20 people to Newfoundland, and claim the region for England.

1498

By the time of Columbus's third voyage, word has gotten back to Spain's king and queen of horrible conditions in the new colony; and Columbus is forced to take convicts as crew and colonists. The expedition first lands at Trinidad, then explores the Orinoco River. These are the first Europeans to see Venezuela. They are also the first Europeans to view the Guiana coast. Columbus gives Guiana its name.

1499

Spanish conquistador Alonso de Ojeda, accompanied by Amerigo Vespucci, explores the coast of South America, landing in an area where they see huts on poles above the water. They name the area Venezuela (Little Venice). Ojeda continues along the coast, rounds Cape de la Vela and becomes the first European to see what is now Colombia.

1499-1500

The area that is now Colombia is explored by Spanish navigators.

FOR CLASSROOM USE	FOR CLASSROOM USE	FOR CLASSROOM USE	FOR CLASSROOM USE	
				Pre-1500
FOR CLASSROOM USE	FOR CLASSROOM USE	FOR CLASSROOM USE	FOR CLASSROOM USE	

THE WORLD	THE WORLD	THE WORLD	THE WORLD

Pre-1500

THE WORLD

3,000,000 B.C./B.C.E.

Early humans hunt animals and gather wild plants on the plains of East Africa.

2,500,000 B.C./B.C.E.

Early humans create stone tools, which make hunting and gathering easier.

850,000 B.C./B.C.E.

Groups of hunter-gatherer people begin to appear in Europe during the Paleolithic period. In hunting-gathering societies, women contribute most to the total food supply by gathering a wide variety of plants. Men generally hunt for meat. Women and men have separate, equally important domestic responsibilities.

500,000 B.C./B.C.E.

The earliest known human in China, "Peking Man," or *homo erectus pekinensis*, dates from this time.

110,000 B.C./B.C.E.

The first inhabitants of the Philippines, "Dawn Man" or Pygmies, walk through the Malay Peninsula, Borneo, and a now-submerged land bridge to the Philippines.

70,000 B.C./B.C.E.

Great ice sheets cover large areas of the earth. Early humans learn to make fires.

40,000-10,000 B.C./B.C.E.

According to modern historians, ancestors of the Inuit (Eskimos) and American Indians begin to arrive in western North America during this time. They migrate across a frozen — and later lost — land bridge through the Bering Strait from Siberia. Some historians place the beginning of this migration as early as 65,000 B.C./B.C.E.

30,000 B.C./B.C.E.

Rice cultivation apparently begins in Southeast Asia.

30,000-10,000 B.C./B.C.E.

People from the areas that are now southern India, Sri Lanka and southeast Asia begin to migrate to Australia.

22,000 B.C./B.C.E.

Stone-age man is present in the Philippines.

THE WORLD

15,000 B.C./B.C.E.

Evidence exists of the first agricultural development in Egypt.

10,000-2000 B.C./B.C.E.

Africa's fertile Sahara region becomes a barrier desert between north and south Africa.

10,000-1800 B.C./B.C.E.

Stone Age people in Denmark are making and using tools and weapons of flint, including swords, axes, arrowheads, and others.

c. 8500 B.C./B.C.E.

Groups of hunter-gatherers live along the Tigris River in the Middle East and begin farming.

c. 8000 B.C./B.C.E.

During the Stone Age, the area that is now Zimbabwe is inhabited by the San and Khoi people.

8000-300 B.C./B.C.E.

This era in Japan's history is called the Jōmon period. "Jōmon" means "cord-marked" and refers to the decorative pottery from this time.

c. 7500-1500 B.C./B.C.E.

During the Stone Age, humans make their homes as far north as the Arctic circle in the area that is now Finland.

c. 6500 B.C./B.C.E.

In the Balkan and Aegean regions, sheep and goats are domesticated; and farming of cereal grains begins.

Rising sea levels gradually separate the British land mass from the European mainland.

c. 6000 B.C./B.C.E.

Prototypes of today's cities exist at Jericho in the Jordan Valley and Catal Hüyük in Anatolia.

Among many early societies, goddess worship is as important as the worship of male gods. Groups that worship particularly powerful goddesses often practice matriliny, a system whereby family name and inheritance pass to future generations through the female line.

People migrate from Anatolia across the Aegean Sea to the Greek Isles.

THE WORLD

c. 5450-2500 B.C./B.C.E.

Saharan people create intricate cave and rock paintings.

c. 5200 B.C./B.C.E.

People in the area that is now the Netherlands begin farming.

c. 5000-3000 B.C./B.C.E.

This is the time span generally ascribed to the Yangshao culture in northern China. Although they are primarily hunters and fishermen, Yangshao farmers grow crops similar to cabbage.

4241 B.C./B.C.E.

This is the earliest recorded date in the Egyptian calendar.

c. 4000 B.C./B.C.E.

People begin to make their homes along the Nile River.

The Cordedware civilization, named for the distinctive markings of its pottery, arises in the southeast Netherlands.

4000-3000 B.C./B.C.E.

Population and agriculture grow rapidly in western Europe (present-day France, northern Germany, northern Poland, southern Scandinavia, the Netherlands, England and Spain).

3760 B.C./B.C.E.

This is the first year of the Jewish calendar.

c. 3500 B.C./B.C.E.

Small cities, the beginnings of the world's first organized civilization, begin to appear in southern Mesopotamia (Sumer), in the lower Tigris-Euphrates Valley. The Sumerians invent the wheel and the sailboat. Among the Sumerians, women have important roles as priestesses. The most powerful goddess is Inanna, whom the king of Sumer ritually "marries" every year. One famous high priestess is Enhduanna, who writes moving poems to the goddess Inanna.

Semitic nomads called Akkadians migrate northward, probably from the Arabian peninsula, into Upper Mesopotamia. They form trade and political alliances with the Sumerians to their south.

THE WORLD

c. 3100 B.C./B.C.E.

As small farming villages consolidate, the Egyptian civilization develops. King Menes, founder of Dynasty I, unites the kingdoms of Upper and Lower Egypt, locating his capital at Memphis. Scholars differ on the names of this region: Memphis is located in Northern Chem or Lower Egypt; Northern Ethiopia or Upper Egypt contains the localities of Thebes and Aswan; Southern Ethiopia or Nubia becomes the area located south of the First Cataract, thus making the First Cataract the dividing line between the ancient regions of Chem and Nubia.

c. 3100-2258 B.C./B.C.E.

This is the time span generally ascribed to the Old Kingdom or Old Empire that rules ancient Egypt. It is comprised of Dynasties I through VI. Precise dates for the dynasties of ancient Egypt are a source of scholarly debate.

c. 3000 B.C./B.C.E.

Canaanites, inhabitants of what is now Lebanon, come to be called Phoenicians (from the Greek word for purple) when merchants among them trade purple cloth with Greece.

Horse-drawn chariots are used in Mesopotamia.

An early form of cotton is produced in India.

3000-2000 B.C./B.C.E.

In the areas that are now the Ukraine, western Europe and the Balkans, invasions by peoples from the steppes bring about a serious decline in both agriculture and population growth.

Seafaring Indonesians migrate to the Philippines.

c. 2680 B.C./B.C.E.

The Great Pyramid of Khufu or Cheops, at Gizeh near Cairo, is the largest ever built. It is considered one of the Seven Wonders of the Ancient World.

c. 2650-2190 B.C./B.C.E.

In Egypt, the "Age of the Pyramids" takes place during Dynasties III through VI.

c. 2500 B.C./B.C.E.

The first Ur dynasty is founded by Mesannepadda in Sumeria.

The Indus Valley civilization begins to flourish in the area that is now Pakistan; Harappa is a major Indus city.

The Assyrian people make their homes on the Upper Tigris River.

A Babylonian clay tablet contains the oldest known map.

The Amorite people migrate from the Arabian desert into what is now northern Syria.

2300s B.C./B.C.E.

Sargon of Akkad conquers the Sumerians, unites all of Mesopotamia and creates the world's first empire. It collapses due to internal strife and attacks from Zagros Mountains tribes.

2258-1786 B.C./B.C.E.

This is the time span generally ascribed to the Middle Kingdom or Middle Empire that rules ancient Egypt. It is comprised of Dynasties VI through XII.

c. 2230 B.C./B.C.E.

The Akkadian empire is defeated by the Gutians.

2205-1766 B.C./B.C.E.

This is the time span generally ascribed to the Xia (Hsia) dynasty that rules China. This early Bronze Age dynasty sees improvements in farming, including irrigation, and China's first known writing.

c. 2200 B.C./B.C.E.

Greek civilization begins as the first Greek-speaking people migrate into present-day Greece, an area occupied by the Helladic, Cycladic and northeast Aegean regional civilizations.

Copper from Cyprus is used throughout the Mediterranean; it is believe that the island's name is from *kypros*, the Greek word for copper.

c. 2060 B.C./B.C.E.

The third dynasty of Ur is founded by King Ur-Nammu who defeats the Gutians. In c. 1960 B.C./B.C.E. the dynasty ends when it is conquered first by the Elamites and then by the Babylonians.

Egypt is reunited under King Mentuhop of Thebes.

c. 2000 B.C./B.C.E.

The Jōmon appears to be the earliest indigenous culture recorded in Japan; it continues for approximately 1800 years.

Amenemhet founds Dynasty XII in Egypt, centralizes the government and rules until his death 1971 B.C./B.C.E.

The second wave of Indonesian migration takes place in the Philippines.

Fortified communities begin to appear in Europe and Minoan Crete.

c. 2000-1425 B.C./B.C.E.

This is the time span generally ascribed to the Minoan civilization that arises on the island of Crete. It ends with the destruction of the city of Cnossus (Knossos) by the Mycenaean people.

1971 B.C./B.C.E.

Sesostris I, who has served as coregent since 1980, becomes pharaoh of Egypt after the death of his father, Amenemhet (c. 2000 B.C./B.C.E.). Sesostris I rules until 1935 B.C./B.C.E.

1935 B.C./B.C.E.

Amenemhet II becomes pharaoh of Egypt after the death of his father, Sesostris I, with whom he served as coregent since 1938 B.C./B.C.E. Amenemhet II rules until 1903 B.C./B.C.E. and increases trade during his reign.

1903 B.C./B.C.E.

Sesostris II becomes pharaoh of Egypt after the death of his father, Amenemhet II (1935 B.C./B.C.E.), with whom he served as coregent since 1906 B.C./B.C.E. Sesostris II rules until 1887 B.C./B.C.E.

c. 1900 B.C./B.C.E.

Hieroglyphic Cretan writing is invented.

1887 B.C./B.C.E.

Sesostris III becomes pharaoh of Egypt after the death of his father, Sesostris II (1903 B.C./B.C.E., with whom he served as coregent since 1878 B.C./B.C.E. Sesostris III establishes Egypt's southern borders, invades Canaan (Palestine) in 1860 B.C./B.C.E. and rules until 1849 B.C./B.C.E.

1849 B.C./B.C.E.

Amenemhet III becomes pharaoh of Egypt after the death of his father, Sesostris III (1887 B.C./B.C.E.), with whom he served as coregent. Amenemhet III develops irrigation systems and rules until 1801 B.C./B.C.E.

1801 B.C./B.C.E.

Amenemhet IV becomes pharaoh of Egypt after the death of his father, Amenemhet III (1849 B.C./B.C.E.). Amenemhet IV's death in 1792 B.C./B.C.E. ends the peaceful and technologically advanced Dynasty XII.

c. 1792-1750 B.C./B.C.E. **or c. 1728-1686** B.C./B.C.E.

Hammurabi the Great rules Babylonia for 42 years. His code of laws is generally humanitarian but carries the concept of retribution with the literal meaning of "an eye for an eye." Modern historians dispute the exact dates of his reign.

1786-1570 B.C./B.C.E.

This is the time span generally ascribed to the Hyksos, an Asiatic people who arrive in horse-drawn carriages and rule ancient Egypt. It is comprised of Dynasties XIII through XVII.

c. 1766-1122 B.C./B.C.E.

This is the time span generally ascribed to the Shang dynasty that rules China. Metalwork, particularly in copper and bronze, develops in China. The first Chinese calendar is invented.

c. 1750 B.C./B.C.E.

In India's Rig-Vedic period, Indian women have the right to be educated, to move about freely and to participate in religious functions. Some women are among the composers of the hymns of the Veda, the sacred text of Hinduism.

c. 1600 B.C./B.C.E.

Cush (Kush), the ancient kingdom of Nubia in what is now Sudan, Africa, is established.

c. 1595 B.C./B.C.E.

The Hittites, from the area that is now central Turkey, conquer Babylonia.

Pre-1500

THE WORLD	THE WORLD	THE WORLD	THE WORLD

Pre-1500

c. 1575-1070 B.C./B.C.E.

Egyptian leaders conquer neighboring peoples and expand trade.

1570 B.C./B.C.E.

Amasis I, founder of Dynasty XVIII, becomes king of ancient Egypt. He drives the Hyksos back to Syria and Canaan and begins to reunite Upper and Lower Egypt. Amasis I rules until 1545 B.C./B.C.E.

1570-332 B.C./B.C.E.

This is the time span generally ascribed to the New Kingdom or New Empire that rules ancient Egypt. It is comprised of Dynasties XVIII through XXX.

c. 1550 B.C./B.C.E.

The Aryans, an agricultural people believed to have come from southern Russia, begin to migrate into the Indus Valley, India.

1545 B.C./B.C.E.

Amenhotep I becomes king of ancient Egypt after the death of his father, Amasis I (1570 B.C./B.C.E.). Amenhotep I rules until 1525 B.C./B.C.E.

c. 1541 B.C./B.C.E.

The Hittites under Mursilis I raze the city of Babylon.

1525 B.C./B.C.E.

Thutmose I becomes king of ancient Egypt after the reign of Amenhotep I (1545 B.C./B.C.E.). Egyptian forces under Thutmose I conquer Cush. Thutmose I rules until c. 1510 B.C./B.C.E.

c. 1510 B.C./B.C.E.

Thutmose II becomes king of ancient Egypt after his father, Thutmose I (1525 B.C./B.C.E.), is removed from the throne. Thutmose II rules with his wife and half sister, Queen Hatshepsut, until c. 1500 B.C./B.C.E.

c. 1500 B.C./B.C.E.

The Israelites move into Canaan.

Stonehenge is completed on what is now Salisbury Plain in southern England. Modern archaeologists and astronomers still debate its function, but agree that work on the structure was probably begun c. 2000 B.C./B.C.E.

In Europe, bronze replaces stone as the utensil material of choice. Inhabitants of the Netherlands begin the practice of cremating their dead. Tombs dating from this period contain metal, amber and beads as well as earthenware. The use of bronze, and then copper, moves north to the regions that are now Denmark and Sweden.

Egypt extends trade into the African continent. As a child, Thutmose III becomes king of ancient Egypt after the death of his father, Thutmose II (1510 B.C./B.C.E.). Thutmose III rules under his regent, Queen Hatshepsut until her death, and then as sole ruler until 1450 B.C./B.C.E.

c. 1500-500 B.C./B.C.E.

After major population movements in Europe and the Near East, societies become more stable and the population begins to increase again.

1486 B.C./B.C.E.

Queen Hatshepsut comes to power in Egypt. The only woman to rule as pharaoh, she encourages peace, trade and the building and restoration of temples throughout Egypt. She rules until 1468 B.C./B.C.E.

c. 1450 B.C./B.C.E.

Amenhotep II becomes king of ancient Egypt after the death of his father, Thutmose III (1500 B.C./B.C.E.). Amenhotep II rules until c. 1420 B.C./B.C.E.

Myceneans take control of Crete.

c. 1425-1100 B.C./B.C.E.

The Mycenaeans conquer the Minoans and rule the Aegean region.

c. 1420 B.C./B.C.E.

Thutmose IV becomes king of ancient Egypt after the death of his father, Amenhotep II (1450 B.C./B.C.E.). Thutmose IV rules until c. 1410 B.C./B.C.E.

c. 1410 B.C./B.C.E.

Amenhotep III becomes king of ancient Egypt after the death of his father, Thutmose IV (c. 1420 B.C./B.C.E.) Amenhotep III rules until c. 1379 B.C./B.C.E.

---

c. 1400 B.C./B.C.E.

The Assyrian kings become the first rulers to develop extensive rules regarding life within the royal household. The women of the palace live in secluded quarters. This practice continues among other dynasties that follow.

c. 1379 B.C./B.C.E.

Amenhotep IV (Ikhnaton) becomes king of ancient Egypt after the death of his father, Amenhotep III (c. 1410 B.C./B.C.E.). Amenhotep IV rules until 1358 B.C./B.C.E.

c. 1358 B.C./B.C.E.

As a child, Tutankhamen becomes the last king of ancient Dynasty XVIII in Egypt after the death of his father, Amenhotep IV (1379 B.C./B.C.E.). Tutankhamen rules until 1350 B.C./B.C.E.

c. 1304 or c. 1292 B.C./B.C.E.

Ramses II becomes king of Egypt. He is responsible for creating peace by obtaining a friendship treaty with the Hittites in c. 1280 B.C./B.C.E. Ramses II rules for 67 years. Historians dispute the date of his reign.

c. 1300 B.C./B.C.E.

People from New Guinea colonize the islands of Melanesia (Fiji, New Hebrides) and move on to Polynesia (Samoa and Tonga).

c. 1250 B.C./B.C.E.

Moses leads the Hebrews out of Egyptian captivity.

c. 1200 B.C./B.C.E.

The Sea People who make their homes on the Canaanite coast become known as Philistines.

c. 1193 B.C./B.C.E.

Although the events are surrounded in myth, Greek forces are said to destroy the city of Troy during the Trojan War.

c. 1100-c. 950 B.C./B.C.E.

Dorian Greeks invade Peloponnesus. The Dorians later develop Greek city-states, the two most powerful being Athens and Sparta.

---

c. 1100 B.C./B.C.E.- **612** B.C./B.C.E.

This is the time span ascribed to the Assyrian Empire in Mesopotamia.

c. 1080 B.C./B.C.E.

Tiglath-Pileser I, king of Assyria, invades Asia Minor. He rules until c. 1074 B.C./B.C.E.

c. 1066-221 B.C./B.C.E.

This is the time span generally ascribed to the Zhou (Chou) dynasty that rules China. Written laws appear during this period as do the teachings of Confucius. During this time, China's feudal system collapses in political chaos, though philosophy and written laws develop, as do the use of iron and money. The "Warring States" era at the end of the Zhou dynasty divides the country into small local kingdoms.

c. 1020 B.C./B.C.E.

The Hebrews found a kingdom in the Palestine region with Saul as their king.

c. 1000 B.C./B.C.E.

David becomes king of the Hebrews and makes Jerusalem their capital. He rules until 961.

The development of iron manufacturing enables the Celts to expand their conquests in central Europe.

The nomadic Aramaean people migrate into Syria and found the city of Damascus.

Early inhabitants of the Malay peninsuls, the Proto-Malays, have established communities by this time.

Early hill forts are constructed in western Europe. Iron is in use in the Aegean area and central Europe.

c. 1000-500 B.C./B.C.E.

The Veda, a series of Aryan writings of verying styles and sources, is compiled. It later becomes the basis of the Hindu faith.

THE WORLD	THE WORLD	THE WORLD	*FOR CLASSROOM USE*	

c. 1000-400 B.C./B.C.E.

In the area that is now Austria, Illyrians from the Balkan Peninsula migrate into present-day Austria and develop a sophisticated civilization.

961 B.C./B.C.E.

Solomon succeeds David as king of the Hebrews. He rules until 932 B.C./B.C.E.

c. 960 B.C./B.C.E.

Hebrew King Solomon orders and oversees the construction of the first temple at Jerusalem.

c. 950 B.C./B.C.E.

Sparta is created by combining four small villages into a single community.

Etruscans immigrate, possibly from Asia Minor, to Italy.

932 B.C./B.C.E.

The Hebrew kingdom is divided into Israel in the north and Judah in the south.

c. 900-650 B.C./B.C.E.

The Assyrian Empire expands with the conquest of neighboring lands.

c. 900 B.C./B.C.E.
A.D./C.E. 400

This is the time span generally ascribed to the kingdom of Kush or Meroe in the Sudan.

c. 884 B.C./B.C.E.

Ashurnasirpal II becomes king of Assyria. He rules until his death, c. 860 B.C./B.C.E.

c. 860 B.C./B.C.E.

Shalmaneser III becomes king of Assyria after the death of his father, Ashurnasirpal II (c. 884 B.C./B.C.E.). Shalmaneser III rules until c. 824 B.C./B.C.E.

841-477 B.C./B.C.E.

Zhou authority declines in China. Feudal lords contend with one another for hegemony. This is known as the "spring and autumn" period.

776 B.C./B.C.E.

This is the traditional date of the first Olympic games, held in Greece.

c. 770-500 B.C./B.C.E.

Greek explorers and merchants migrate and establish trade centers around the Mediterranean and Black Seas.

760 B.C./B.C.E.

The first Greek colony in Italy, Cumae (near Naples), is established.

c. 753 B.C./B.C.E.

This is the traditional date for the founding of Rome.

c. 745 B.C./B.C.E.

The rulers of the Nubian kingdom of Cush conquer Upper Egypt. The Nubian dynasty (XXIII) of Egypt, with its capital at Napata, rules until 718 B.C./B.C.E.

Tiglath-Pileser III becomes king of Assyria. He rules until his death in 728 B.C./B.C.E.

c. 741 B.C./B.C.E.

Piankhi becomes king of Nubia. He rules until c. 715 B.C./B.C.E.

728 B.C.

Shalmaneser V becomes king of Assyria. He dies in battle in 722 B.C./B.C.E. and is succeeded by Sargon II.

c. 722 B.C./B.C.E.

Sargon II conquers the Hittites in Syria and destroys Samaria, the capital of Israel, making it a province of Assyria. Many Israelites migrate to Media and Mesopotamia. Sargon II rules until 705 B.C./B.C.E.

c. 721 B.C./B.C.E.

Nubian forces under King Piankhi defeat Tefnakhte and conquer Lower Egypt. Upper Egypt is already under Nubian control at the time.

705 B.C./B.C.E.

Sennacherib becomes king of Assyria after the death of his father, Sargon II (c. 722 B.C./B.C.E.). He devotes his career to military battles to maintain his father's empire and conquers Babylonia, Egypt and Elam. He rules until 681 B.C./B.C.E.

c. 700 B.C./B.C.E.

During the Scythian conquest of Asia, the technique of fighters on horseback, using short bows with arrows of stone and iron is first used.

People in the area that is now the Netherlands begin to use iron.

c. 690 B.C./B.C.E.

Cimmerian nomads conquer the kingdom of Phrygia in Asia Minor.

c. 688 B.C./B.C.E.

Tirhakah (Taharka), the son of Piankhi, becomes the last king of Dynasty XXV of ancient Egypt. Tirhakah rules until 663 B.C./B.C.E.

681 B.C./B.C.E.

Sennacherib, king of Assyria (705 B.C./B.C.E.), is assassinated by two of his sons. A third son, Esar-Haddon, takes the throne, and rules until 668 B.C./B.C.E.

671 B.C./B.C.E.

Assyrian forces under Esar-Haddon conquer the Cushites under Tirhakah. The Cushites lose control of Egypt in 663 B.C./B.C.E.

668

Ashurbanipal (Assurbanipal) comes to power in Assyria. His forces capture Thebes in 660 B.C./B.C.E. Ashurbanipal rules until c. 633 B.C./B.C.E. Two of his sons succeed him briefly; however, the height of the Assyrian culture has passed.

660 B.C./B.C.E.

Japanese oral tradition sets this year as the founding of the Japanese Empire; the first emperor, Jimmu, is said to be a direct descendant of the Sun Goddess.

650 B.C./B.C.E.

Sparta becomes a major military power in Peloponnesus.

c. 640 B.C./B.C.E.

The Greek trading city of Naucratis is established in the Nile delta.

c. 625 B.C./B.C.E.

Cyaxares rules as king of Media, and makes his kingdom into a powerful nation.

Pre-1500

THE WORLD	THE WORLD	THE WORLD	THE WORLD
612 B.C./B.C.E. With the destruction of the Assyrian capital city of Nineveh by the Babylonians, Medes and Scythians, the Assyrian Empire comes to an end. **c. 600** B.C./B.C.E. The hanging gardens and walls of Babylon are built by Nebuchadnezzar. They are recognized as one of the Seven Wonders of the Ancient World. Sisunaga founds a new dynasty in the kingdom of Magadha in India. The religion of Zoroastrianism, founded by Zarathustra, arises in Persia. **c. 591** B.C./B.C.E. The city of Meroë is founded, in the region that is now northern Sudan. Meroë serves from 530 B.C./B.C.E. until A.D./C.E. 350 as the capital of the empire of Kush (Cush). **586** B.C./B.C.E. Babylonian troops under Nebuchadnezzar destroy Jerusalem, forcing the Hebrews into exile. **c. 560** B.C./B.C.E. Sparta forms the Peloponnesian League to consolidate support from its allies in the same manner as Athens, which formed the Delian League. **550** B.C./B.C.E. After conquering Lydia and the Medes, Cyrus II (the Great) becomes king of the Medes and Persia. Cyrus II rules until 529 B.C./B.C.E. Persia is a major empire until c. 335 B.C./B.C.E. **c. 550** B.C./B.C.E. The highly developed cities of Harappa and Mohenjo-Daro flourish in India until their destruction by the Aryans in A.D./C.E. 1550. Jainism, the religion of Jina, arises in India as a reaction against Hindu ritualism. It gradually spreads from India, and takes on some Hindu aspects, such as certain deities and the caste system.	**c. 544** B.C./B.C.E. The Temple of Diana, recognized as one of the Seven Wonders of the Ancient World, is built at Ephesus. **c. 540** B.C./B.C.E. Greek forces are defeated by Carthaginians and Etruscans off the coast of Corsica. **539** B.C./B.C.E. Babylonia is conquered by Cyrus II and Palestine becomes part of the Persian Empire, which during its early days tolerates the religious beliefs of captured peoples. In 536 B.C./B.C.E. Cyrus II aids Jews in their return to Israel. **535** B.C./B.C.E. Carthaginian forces defeat Greek warriors and begin their domination of southern Spain. Carthaginian rule continues until the Roman victory in the Second Punic War (218-201 B.C./B.C.E.). **c. 530** B.C./B.C.E. The ancient city of Meroë succeeds Napata as the capital of the Cushite empire and remains as such for 850 years. **c. 528** B.C./B.C.E. Siddhartha Gautama achieves supreme enlightenment and becomes the Buddha (enlightened one). He spends the rest of his life teaching and establishing a community of monks to continue his work. **525** B.C./B.C.E. King Cambyses II of Persia, son of Cyrus the Great, conquers Egypt and declares himself pharaoh. Cambyses rules from 529 B.C./B.C.E. to 521 B.C./B.C.E. **521** B.C./B.C.E. Darius I becomes king of Persia and establishes a uniform currency and military reforms. He and his army are defeated by Greek forces under Miltiades at Marathon in 490 B.C./B.C.E. Darius rules until 486 B.C./B.C.E.	**520** B.C./B.C.E. Construction begins on the Second Temple at Jerusalem. The edifice is finished five years later. **c. 511** B.C./B.C.E. Confucius establishes a new system of ethical behavior. Under Confucianism, the ideal woman is seen as one who is secluded within the home and submissive to the authority of the males in her family. **509** B.C./B.C.E. Rome becomes a republic after overthrowing its Etruscan king. **c. 500** B.C./B.C.E. People move into the North African area that is now Nigeria and begin making iron tools. The use of iron spreads across Africa. The Greek city-state of Athens, named after Athena, the goddess of warfare and wisdom, develops the world's first democracy. The Maldive Islands in the northern Indian Ocean, and Sri Lanka to the southeast, are colonized at approximately the same time by migrating Aryans. By this time much of Europe is under Celtic control. The relative freedom that women in India have experienced is reduced as the religious leaders begin to impose restrictions on women and on other social groups. The knowledge of the Veda is restricted to men, and women are assigned the same low status as the caste directly above "untouchables." **c. 483** B.C./B.C.E. Vijaya, a descendant of the migrating Singhalese tribe from northern India, is chosen king in Ceylon and establishes the capital at Anuradhapura. **480** B.C./B.C.E. Forces under King Xerxes of Persia defeat Spartan troops under King Leonides at Thermopylae and capture and burn Athens. Xerxes rules from 486 B.C./B.C.E. to 465 B.C./B.C.E.	**479** B.C./B.C.E. Greek forces destroy the Persian navy at the Battle of Salamis and defeat the Persians at the Battle of Plataea. Thus, the age of Athenian democracy under Pericles begins. During the "Golden Age" of Athens men enjoy considerable political liberties, but the activities of female citizens are severely restricted. Most freeborn females are confined to their homes and their domestic duties. **476-221** B.C./B.C.E. Stronger states in China conquer weaker and smaller states. This is known as the "warring states" period. **c. 450** B.C./B.C.E. The kingdom of Magadha defeats the kingdom of Kosala and becomes the main power in northern India. Hippocrates of Cos (Kos, an island off the southwestern coast of Turkey) carefully records his studies of human anatomy. **c. 433** B.C./B.C.E. The Statue of Olympus is built by Phidias in the Temple of Olympia, near the Alpheus River in Greece. The statue is considered one of the Seven Wonders of the Ancient World. **431-404** B.C./B.C.E. The Peloponnesian War begins with Sparta's demand for autonomy for all the cities in the Delian League and concerns over the ambitions of Pericles, and ends when the Spartans conquer Athens. **c. 430** B.C./B.C.E. Athens experiences a severe outbreak of the plague. **c. 400** B.C./B.C.E. Sporadic trade develops between China and the Philippines. The Greek philosopher Democritus theorizes that all things are composed of tiny particles, which he calls atoms ("not divisible" in Greek). Hippocrates acknowledges the natural causes of disease.

Pre-1500

387 B.C./B.C.E.

Rome is sacked by invading Gauls.

365 B.C./B.C.E.

Chinese astronomers observe the moons of the planet Jupiter.

350 B.C./B.C.E.

The mausoleum at Halicarnassus is built by Artemisia for her dead husband Mausolus, King of Caria. This is recognized as one of the Seven Wonders of the Ancient World.

c. 350 B.C./B.C.E.

Celts from France and Spain migrate into what is now Ireland. They conquer the native people, and establish five kingdoms.

Greek philosopher Aristotle details a basic philosophy of the biological sciences and a theory of evolution.

341 B.C./B.C.E.

Egypt's last native dynasty is ended by invading Persian forces.

338 B.C./B.C.E.

Macedonians under Philip invade from the north and defeat Greek forces. Philip rules from 359 B.C./B.C.E. to 336 B.C./B.C.E.

336 B.C./B.C.E.

Philip II of Macedon is assassinated by a Spartan general named Pausanias.

Alexander III (the Great) becomes king of Macedon, ends uprisings in Thrace and Illyria, sacks Thebes and thereby wins dominance over all of Greece. In 334 B.C./B.C.E. he begins his eastward conquest, taking Persia, Tyre, Gaza, Egypt, Mesopotamia, northern India and Bactria (present-day Afghanistan). Alexander III rules until 323 B.C./B.C.E.

Darius III becomes king of Persia. He rules until 330 B.C./B.C.E.

320 B.C./B.C.E.

Ptolemy I (Ptolemy Soter), the first king of the Macedonian dynasty of ancient Egypt, leads an invasion of Syria. He rules until 284 B.C./B.C.E.

Chandragupta of Magadha defeats the Nanda dynasty and founds the Maurya dynasty. He begins to unite India by conquest. Chandragupta rules until c. 297 B.C./B.C.E.

c. 320-64 B.C./B.C.E.

The Seleucid Empire, which loosely controls states in Asia Minor, rules for more than 250 years. The empire is ended by Pompey during the Roman conquest of Syria.

c. 320 B.C./B.C.E.- **A.D./A.C.E. 50**

The kingdom of Axum (Aksum) in Ethiopia experiences its first flourishing.

311 B.C./B.C.E.

The Roman Empire organizes the world's first permanent navy, with navy commissioners to protect the empire's trade ships and those of its allies from pirates and trade rivals.

c. 300 B.C./B.C.E.

Aristarchus of Samos, a Greek astronomer, is said to be the first person to suggest that the sun, and not the earth, may be the center of the solar system.

The Iron Age comes to Ireland.

300s-200s B.C./B.C.E.

Taoism, which arises in China, is generally attributed to the mystic Laozi (Lau Tse). Its teachings are collected into a book, the Daodejing (Tao-te-ching).

c. 295 B.C./B.C.E.

Macedonian forces under King Demetrius I capture Athens. Demetrius I rules until 285 B.C./B.C.E.

c. 290 B.C./B.C.E.

The Colossus at Rhodes — a statue of Apollo — is built. It is recognized as one of the Seven Wonders of the Ancient World.

285 B.C./B.C.E.

King Demetrius I of Macedonia is removed by an army revolt and replaced by Pyrrhus, king of Epirus, who is then succeeded by Lysimachus, a former general of Alexander the Great.

Ptolemy II becomes king of Egypt. He rules until his death in 246 B.C./B.C.E.

c. 285-282 B.C./B.C.E.

The Etruscans and Gauls are defeated by Romans.

c. 275 B.C./B.C.E.

The Pharos (lighthouse) at Alexandria, recognized as one of the Seven Wonders of the Ancient World, is built by Ptolemy Philadelphus.

264-241 B.C./B.C.E.

The First Punic War between Rome and Carthage is fought mostly in Sicily and at sea.

260 B.C./B.C.E.

Asoka, Chandragupta's grandson, conquers Kalinga. This conquest brings all of India, with the exception of the southernmost section, under one rule. Asoka rules from c. 274 B.C./B.C.E. to c. 236 B.C./B.C.E.

257 B.C./B.C.E.

The kingdom of Au Lac, extending from Guangdong province in China to what is now northern Vietnam, is established.

256 B.C./B.C.E.

The Great Wall of China, actually a union of several lesser walls, is begun as a defense against the Xiongnu (Huns). The entire wall, approximately 1,500 miles long, runs mostly along the southern edge of the Mongolian plain. Much of it is constructed during the Qin (Ch'in) Dynasty. Later invasions by northern nomadic peoples will show the wall to be of little defensive value.

c. 250 B.C./B.C.E.

Aryan Hindus begin the conquest of Ceylon.

Buddhism arrives in Ceylon from India.

246 B.C./B.C.E.

Ptolemy III becomes king of ancient Egypt after the death of his father, Ptolemy II (285 B.C./B.C.E.). Ptolemy III rules until 221 B.C./B.C.E.

223 B.C./B.C.E.

Antiochus III becomes king of Syria. He rules until 187 B.C./B.C.E.

221 B.C./B.C.E.

Ptolemy IV becomes king of ancient Egypt after the death of his father, Ptolemy III. Ptolemy rules until 205 B.C./B.C.E. The Ptolemy line rules Egypt until c. 31 B.C./B.C.E.

221-206 B.C./B.C.E.

Qin Shihuangdi (Ch'in Shih-huang-ti) unifies China by conquering the separate states in the Yellow River and Yangzi River basin. He limits the power of the feudal lords and establishes an orderly government. Canals and roads are built and Qin Shihuangdi furthers construction of the Great Wall.

218-201 B.C./B.C.E.

During the Second Punic War, Carthaginian General Hannibal makes a surprise attack, crossing the Alps and Pyrenees with foot soldiers, cavalry and elephants to attack Italy from the north. Roman General Scipio and his army decisively win the Battle of Zama in 202 B.C./B.C.E. and the war ends in Roman victory the following year.

214 B.C./B.C.E.

Qin armies conquer Guangdong.

208 B.C./B.C.E.

Forces under Zhao Tuo, a Qin official in Guangdong, attack and conquer Au Lac.

207 B.C./B.C.E.

A peasant uprising overthrows the Qin emperor; Zhao Tuo establishes the state of Nanyue (Nam Viet) in Guangdong and North Vietnam.

206 B.C./B.C.E.- **A.D./C.E. 220**

This is the time span generally ascribed to the Han dynasty that rules China. It begins after several years of fighting between Xiang Yu (Hsiang Yu) and Liu Bang (Liu Pang). The writing brush, paper and ink come into wide usage, and the first dictionary is compiled. Liu Bang is the first emperor, but the greatest cultural development occurs under Wudi (Wu Ti).

Pre-1500

THE WORLD	THE WORLD	THE WORLD	THE WORLD

Pre-1500

THE WORLD

c. 206 B.C./B.C.E.

Malay people navigate the Pacific Ocean, traveling, trading and colonizing as far north as Korea and Japan, east to Polynesia, and west to Africa and Madagascar. They colonize in the mountains of the Philippines and introduce agriculture, iron smelting, weaving and pottery. The extensive system of mountain rice terraces of Banaue stretches for hundreds of miles and is still used late into the twentieth century.

195 B.C./B.C.E.

Masses of Roman women hold a public demonstration in front of the Forum to persuade the Senators to repeal the Oppian Law, which forbade women from wearing bright jewelry or riding in chariots. The law is rescinded.

191 B.C./B.C.E.

Roman forces under Glabrio defeat Seleucid King Antiochus III at Thermopylae.

185 B.C./B.C.E.

Antiochus IV becomes king of Syria. He rules until 163 B.C./B.C.E.

c. 185 B.C./B.C.E.

Pushyamitra founds the Sunga dynasty in India, bringing the Maurya dynasty to an end.

167 B.C./B.C.E.

Albania becomes part of the kingdom of Illyria after Roman forces invade.

The Maccabeans engage in a religious revolt against the Seleucids under King Antiochus IV.

149-146 B.C./B.C.E.

In the Third Punic War, Carthage and Corinth are destroyed by Roman forces. Macedonia, Achaea and Africa are made provinces of Rome.

After defeating Greek forces, the Romans rule the Mediterranean area.

c. 141 B.C./B.C.E.

Simon Maccabee's forces remove the Syrians from Jerusalem. Judean independence lasts until 63 B.C./B.C.E.

THE WORLD

140 B.C./B.C.E.

Wudi becomes emperor of China. He rules until 87 B.C./B.C.E.

136 B.C./B.C.E.

Chinese authorities begin planning a series of highways to reach Burma and India.

133 B.C./B.C.E.

Asia Minor becomes a province of Rome, joining Sicily, Sardinia and Corsica, the two Spains, Gallia, Africa and Macedonia. In the Mediterranean area, only Egypt is not ruled by Rome.

128 B.C./B.C.E.

Chinese forces begin the conquest of Manchuria and Korea.

115 B.C./B.C.E.

Under Han Emperor Wudi, the Chinese army crosses the Lop Nor Desert and occupies the Tarim Basin, imposing Chinese authority on the inhabitants.

112 B.C./B.C.E.

War in Africa occurs between Roman forces and troops led by Jugurtha, king of Numidia. Jugurtha rules from c. 118 B.C./B.C.E. to 106 B.C./B.C.E..

111 B.C./B.C.E.

The Han dynasty brings all of Nam Viet under its control.

c. 109 B.C./B.C.E.

Huns invade China.

108 B.C./B.C.E.

Chinese explorers begin to make expeditions into central Asia.

105 B.C./B.C.E.

Roman forces under Marius and Sulla defeat Jugurtha of Numidia and his military ally, Bocchus of Mauritania.

101 B.C./B.C.E.

Romans under Marius defeat the Cimbri at the Battle of Vercellae. Marius is elected consul for the sixth time the following year.

c. 100 B.C./B.C.E.

The Andhara dynasty begins in northern India.

THE WORLD

Traders and colonists from India travel as far as Malaya, the Philippines, Formosa and the Celebes.

In the arid regions of Asia and the Middle East, camels are domesticated and used to transport goods. Camels are then brought to Africa, making trade across the Sahara Desert possible.

The "Silk Route" carries goods from Asia to Europe. This trade route runs from western China, on both sides of the Takla Makan Desert to Kashgar, crosses the Pamir Mountains and on to Bactria; it connects to the Kushan and Persian trade routes.

The island of Cyprus is conquered by Roman forces and becomes part of the Roman Empire.

90 B.C./B.C.E.

Civil war erupts in Italy following central Italy's creation of a separate state. Marius and his army overpower Sulla's forces but Sulla and the Roman army regain control in 89 B.C./B.C.E. However, they are forced to grant the rights of Roman citizenship to all Italians.

82 B.C./B.C.E.

Sulla, after returning from victories in Asia, makes himself dictator of Rome but resigns the lifetime position three years later due to old age.

71 B.C./B.C.E.

A revolt of slaves and gladiators led by Spartacus is crushed by Consuls Crassus and Pompey.

63 B.C./B.C.E.

Forces of Roman General Pompey conquer Jerusalem.

60 B.C./B.C.E.

The First Triumvirate, comprised of Pompey, Crassus and Julius Caesar, rules Rome.

THE WORLD

59 B.C./B.C.E.

Roman leader Julius Caesar arrives in Alexandria and helps Cleopatra, queen of Egypt, to defeat her brother and retain her throne. Cleopatra is one of Egypt's most active queens. She has romances with both Julius Caesar and Mark Antony, and unsuccessfully fights to keep the country independent from Rome.

58 B.C./B.C.E.

Caesar's army enters Gaul and western Germany and in 49 B.C./B.C.E., crosses the Rubicon River and conquers Rome. They defeat Pompey and take control of North Africa and Spain.

57 B.C./B.C.E.

The Rhine, whose main course at the time flows near the city of Leiden, marks the northern border of the Roman Empire as the first imperial forces arrive. The inhabitants of Frisia to the north retain their autonomy. The Roman invaders actually colonize only in the southernmost part of what is now the Netherlands.

c. 50 B.C./B.C.E.

In Africa, Meroë is a major center for iron smelting.

44 B.C./B.C.E.

Roman leader Julius Caesar is murdered through a conspiracy led by Brutus and Cassius.

31 B.C./B.C.E.

At the Battle of Actium, the Roman fleet of Octavian defeats the combined fleet of Marc Antony and Cleopatra. Egypt becomes a Roman province and Antony and Cleopatra commit suicide.

31 B.C./B.C.E. - A.D./C.E. **476**

This is the time span generally ascribed to the Roman Empire.

27 B.C./B.C.E.

Octavian is given the title Augustus by the Senate and becomes Rome's first emperor. The *Pax Romana* (a relatively peaceful era in the Mediterranean region during which the area is ruled by Rome) begins. Augustus rules until A.D./C.E. 14.

6 B.C./B.C.E.

Judaea is annexed by Palestinian King Herod. After his death two years later, the region is divided among his sons.

A.D./C.E. **c. 1-50**

The Kushans, powerful invaders from central Asia who are devoted followers of Buddhism, move across Bactria (Afghanistan) to reach the Punjab.

2

An early census shows more than 57 million people residing in China.

c. 5

Cymbeline, king of the Catuvellauni, is recognized by Rome as the king of England. He rules until 40.

6

Judaea becomes a Roman province.

Wang Mang usurps the Han throne. His drastic measures to improve the economy cause chaos in the country, and Wang Mang is killed by rebels, c. 23.

9

The Roman army led by Varus is solidly defeated by the Cherusci under Arminius at the Battle of the Teutoburg Forest, ending Roman efforts to colonize beyond the Rhine River.

c. 23

The later (or Eastern) Han dynasty is established by Liu Xiu (Liu Hsiu).

c. 27

Jesus, a Jew from Nazareth, begins his ministry.

c. 30

On the orders of Pontius Pilate, Jesus of Nazareth is crucified.

Roman forces annex the Celtic kingdom comprising the Alpine and Danube regions in the area that is now Austria.

37

Caligula becomes Roman emperor. Though ill and probably insane, he rules until 41, when he is assassinated by an officer of his guard.

c. 37

Christianity is introduced to north Africa, particularly in Egypt, Cyrene and Carthage, by the apostle Philip.

39

The Annamese (Nam Viet, now Vietnam) under sisters Trung Trac and Trung Nhi stage a successful rebellion against Chinese domination. The Trung sisters lead an army that includes female officers and win independence for Vietnam. However, three years later, Chinese forces retake the lost territory; the Trung sisters commit suicide.

41

Claudius becomes Roman emperor after the death of Caligula (37). Claudius rules until 54.

43

Claudius and his Roman forces conquer England. Roman influences are seen in the Celtic culture of this time.

50

A Gothic kingdom appears on the Lower Vistula River.

54

Nero becomes emperor of Rome. He rules until 68.

58

Mingdi (Ming-Ti) becomes emperor of China and introduces Buddhism there. He rules until 75.

64

A great fire sweeps through Rome. Emperor Nero blames Christians for the fire and orders them killed.

70

The Jews revolt against Rome. Roman military leader Titus (later emperor) takes Jerusalem and destroys the Second Temple.

79

The eruption of Mount Vesuvius destroys the cities of Pompeii and Herculaneum.

93

Mesopotamia is annexed to the Roman Empire.

96

Roman dictator Domitian is assassinated.

98

Trajan becomes Roman emperor. The empire reaches its greatest geographical extent during his reign. He rules until 117.

The first recorded mention of the Swedish people is in the works of Tacitus, a Roman historian.

c. 100

The Funan kingdom is founded in what is now Cambodia.

100s

Greco-Egyptian scientist Ptolemy compiles his 13-volume *Almagest*, a collection of the scientific inquiry and ideas of his time. Ptolemy's complex theory of a geocentric planetary system, a theory he credits largely to the work of Greek astronomer Hipparchus, is detailed in the text. Ptolemy's writings serve for several hundred years as a major astronomy and science text.

c. 109

The first trade caravan of silk is taken from China to Persia. Evidence also exists of paper manufacturing in China at this time.

115

Roman Emperor Trajan and his troops conquer Macedonia.

115-117

Jews on the island of Cyprus stage a violent rebellion against Roman persecution. As a result of this failed revolt, Jews are banned from the island and those who fail to leave are put to death.

117

Hadrian becomes emperor of Rome. He rules until 138.

c. 120

Kanishka, founder of the second Kushan dynasty, becomes king of northern India.

Pre-1500

Pre-1500

122

Emperor Hadrian orders his soldiers to begin construction of a wall in England to protect the Roman Empire's borders. Fragments of the wall, completed in 126, remain today.

132-135

After a major revolt led by Bar Kochba against Rome under Hadrian, Jews are forbidden to live in Jerusalem. This begins the Great Diaspora.

161

Marcus Aurelius becomes Roman emperor. He rules until his death in 180.

c. 175

In his many writings, the Greek physician Galen establishes basic principles for the field of anatomy and physiology. His work is so respected that it remains unquestioned and actually hampers further inquiry until the 1500s.

180

The *Pax Romana* (a relatively peaceful era in the Mediterranean region during which the area is rule by Rome) ends with the death of Emperor Marcus Aurelius.

192

The kingdom of Champa is founded in the southern part of what is now Vietnam.

200

Afghanistan is invaded by the White Huns, who rule the country for more than 300 years.

c. 200

West African people called Bantu migrate into central and southern Africa.

The regions that are now Austria are overrun by Germanic tribes.

200s

The structure of the Christian church is established in Rome. In the early practice of Christianity, women assumed full roles in the new religion. With church laws, known as canons, being codified, and with an established power structure in place, women's roles become subordinated to the authority of men.

212

The Edict of Caracalla provides Roman citizenship to every freeborn person in the empire.

220

The end of China's Han dynasty is accompanied by fighting and unrest. China divides into three kingdoms: Wei in North China, Wu in the middle and lower Yangzi River valley and Shu in Sichuan. Confucianism is superseded by Buddhism and Taoism. Glass is introduced.

Goths invade Asia Minor and the Balkan peninsula.

c. 224-640

This is the time span generally ascribed to the Sassanid dynasty that rules Persia. Zoroastrianism, which declined when Alexander conquered Persia, sees a revival under Ardashir I, the first Sassanid ruler. This period also sees recurring conflict between Rome and Persia over control of Armenia. Ardashir I rules until 241.

c. 230

Japan's Empress Jingu puts on men's clothing to lead her army in an invasion of Korea after her husband's death. Empress Jingu becomes so venerated by the Japanese that she is seen as second only to the female goddess Amaterasu.

241

Shapur I takes the throne of Persia after the death of his father, Ardashir I (224). Shapur I rules until 272.

c. 250

Widespread persecution of Christians occurs in the Roman Empire.

The Traikutaka dynasty in southern India begins.

c. 257

Goths invade the Black Sea area and are divided into two groups, the Visigoths and the Ostrogoths.

265-280

In China, the Jin (Chin) depose the Wei, which had conquered the Shu in 263. The Jin army captures Nanjing (Nanking), capital of Wu, to reunify China.

265-420

This is the time span generally ascribed to the Jin (Chin) dynasty that rules southern China. Much of northern China is ruled by Xiongnu (Hun) invader groups.

268

Goths sack Athens, Sparta and Corinth.

270

Aurelian becomes emperor of Rome. Early in his reign, the Roman army defeats the Marcomanni and Alemanni, and the emperor orders the walls of Rome rebuilt. Aurelian rules until 275.

285

Carausius, the Roman commander of the English fleet, declares himself the independent emperor of England.

Emperor Diocletian partitions the Roman Empire into eastern and western sections. Diocletian became emperor in 284, and rules until 305.

300

Iceland is visited by Picts and Celts from Ireland and Scotland.

A second migratory wave of seafaring Malays seeking freedom from despotic rule in Borneo, a tributary state of the Malayan Empire, arrives in the Philippines. They are led by Datu Puti.

c. 300

German peoples begin to solidify into five separate powers: Alemanni, Franks, Goths, Saxons and Thuringians.

The influence of Buddhism increases in China.

Christianity is introduced in Armenia and Austria.

The Marquesas Islands are colonized by people from Samoa and Tonga.

In northern Africa, the kingdom of Axum (Aksum) accepts Christianity.

Lombards begin migrating from the Lower Elbe River southward towards Italy.

c. 300-900

This is the time span generally ascribed to the Axum Empire in Ethiopia.

c. 300-1500

This period marks the rise of several major African states: Ghana, Mali, Songhai, Benin, Ife, and the culture of Great Zimbabwe.

c. 304

The Xiongnu (Huns) who were allowed to make their homes inside the Great Wall of China rebel and establish a kingdom. They were driven northward by the Han dynasty during the first century.

309

Shapur II, a child, becomes Sassanid king of Persia after the death of his father, Hormuz II. During his reign, Shapur II's army regains lost Persian lands and conquers Armenia. Shapur II rules until his death in 379.

313

Constantine sees a vision of the cross before battle, and becomes a convert to Christianity. His Edict of Milan establishes tolerance for all religions within the Roman Empire.

317

In China, the Jin (Chin) court retreats south of the Yangzi to Nanjing. Rebellion of Xiongnu and invasion by other people in the north cause political chaos. There is a mass migration south to the Yangzi River valley. China is split into north and south empires. During this period of fighting and unrest, Confucianism gives way to Buddhism and Taoism. Central to the practice of Buddhism in China is the worship, particularly among women, of Guan Yin, the goddess of mercy. While Buddhist beliefs about women's status are restrictive, women play an important part in the religion and can become nuns.

THE WORLD	THE WORLD	THE WORLD	FOR CLASSROOM USE	

c. 320-c. 544

Chandragupta I establishes the Gupta dynasty in northern India and becomes its emperor. He rules until c. 380. During the Gupta dynasty, India has established trade relations with the Eastern Roman Empire, China and Persia. The Hindu religion prospers with the writing of great poems, including an epic about a hero named Rama. The Laws of Manu, compiled during India's Gupta period, further restrict the freedom of Indian women. They severely reduce women's property rights, advocate the early marriage of women, and ban widows from remarrying — thus encouraging the practice of *sati* (the burning of widows upon their husband's death.)

324

Troops under Emperor Constantine defeat the forces of Licinius, thus for a time reuniting the Roman Empire. The empire divides again after Constantine's death.

325

The first Council of Nicaea denounces Arianism, a doctrine that Jesus of Nazareth was neither human nor divine.

330

Byzantium is renamed Constantinople (now Istanbul, Turkey) and becomes the Roman capital.

Cyprus is annexed to the Byzantine Empire.

350

Ethiopian emperors from Axum conquer the Cushites at Meroë.

c. 350

Huns invade Persia.

360

Picts and Scots break through Hadrian's Wall and invade England, but are driven out at the end of the decade by forces under Theodosius. Theodosius rules as Roman emperor of the east from 379 to 395 and of the west from 392 to 395.

Japanese forces invade and conquer Korea.

c. 360

The Hun invasion of Europe begins.

The Palava dynasty comes into power in southern India and fights with the Chalukyas. It remains in existence for approximately 400 years.

376

Huns invade Russia.

378

At the Battle of Adrianople in Thrace, Emperor Valens is defeated and killed by the Visigoths.

379

Ardashir II becomes Sassanid king of Persia after the death of his brother, Shapur II (309). Ardashir II rules until 383.

383

Shapur III becomes Sassanid king of Persia after the reign of his uncle, Ardashir II (379). Shapur III rules until his death in 388.

395

Albania is annexed to the Byzantine Empire.

Malta becomes part of the Western or Byzantine Empire.

Alaric becomes king of the Visigoths. He rules until 410.

395-1453

This is the time span generally ascribed to the Byzantine Empire. The will of Theodosius I officially splits the Roman Empire into the Eastern Roman, or Byzantine, and the Western Roman Empires.

400-900

Several kingdoms develop on the African continent, including the Jenne, Gao, Yoruba, Hausa and Igbo-Ukwu.

c. 400

This is the traditional date for the beginning of Japan's recorded history.

The Celts begin to move from the Rhine and the Danube toward the British Isles, France, Spain and Italy.

Sporadic trade between China and the Philippines begins.

c. 400-c. 1100

This is the time span generally ascribed to the kingdom of Ghana (Mali) in West Africa.

407

Roman forces withdraw from England. The English culture, a combination of Roman and Celtic, comes under attack by various nomadic invaders.

410

Visigoths under King Alaric conquer Rome.

415

The Visigoths under Ataulf conquer Spain and force the Vandals into Africa.

Hypatia, a well-known pagan mathematician, philosopher and scientist, is murdered in Alexandria by a Christian mob. Fanatic Christian monks see evil and heresy in her work. Since no significant advances in the sciences are made in the West for the ensuing 1000 years, Hypatia's death comes to symbolize the end of ancient science.

419-711

This is the time span generally ascribed to the Visigothic Empire of Toulouse.

420-751

This is the time span generally ascribed to the Merovingian dynasty (the first Frankish dynasty). This span overlaps with the Carolingian (second Frankish dynasty) due to conflicting territorial claims in France.

c. 428

Gaiseric establishes a Vandal kingdom in north Africa, and in 443 removes the last part of Roman control and creates a monarchy. Gaiseric rules until 477.

432

A Catholic boy from England is captured by Irish Celts and forced into slavery in Ireland. He later escapes. Returning this year to Ireland, he makes converts and establishes Christianity on the island. He is later canonized as Saint Patrick.

433

Attila becomes ruler of the Huns.

Pre-1500

THE WORLD	THE WORLD	THE WORLD	THE WORLD

Pre-1500

444

Taoism becomes the official religion of China's Northern Wei Empire.

c. 450

Huns led by Attila begin to invade India, Gaul and Italy.

England, abandoned by the Romans 50 years ago, is inhabited by Jutes, Angles and Saxons.

451

At the Battle of Chalon, Attila's invasion into Gaul is stopped by an alliance of Franks, Alemanni and Romans under Aetius. Attila's death in 453 ends Hun attacks into Europe.

455

Vandal forces under King Gaiseric sack Rome.

c. 455

In northwest India, the Hephthalites (or White Huns), invaders from beyond the Oxus River, are defeated by Skandagupta when they attack. Skandagupta rules as emperor of India until 467.

456

The Visigoths conquer the Iberian peninsula and rule until the Moorish invasion in 711.

460-481

Pope Leo I serves for 21 years and is credited with greatly strengthening the papacy.

c. 470

Nomadic Hungarian tribes begin to move into the Black Sea area from the Ural Mountains.

471

Theodoric (the Great) is chosen king of the Ostrogoths. He rules until 526.

476

Germanic chieftain Odoacer overthrows Romulus Augustulus. This event ends the Western Roman Empire. Odoacer rules as patrician in Italy until 493.

c. 480-534

This is the time span generally ascribed to the kingdom of Burgundy, which runs from southeastern France to west Switzerland.

481

During the reign of Frankish King Clovis I the Franks defeat the Alemanni, kill Visigoth King Alaric II in the Battle of the Campus Vogladensis and annex the Visigothic kingdom of Toulouse. Clovis, son of Childeric and grandson of Meroveus, is credited with the founding of the Merovingian dynasty, and converts to Christianity in 496. Clovis I rules until his death in 511.

484

In northern India, the Gupta dynasty is overthrown by White Hun invaders. The Guptas continue to rule Bengal until 544.

The first schism between eastern and western churches begins. It continues until 519.

486

Syagrius, the last Roman governor of Gaul, is defeated by Clovis I at Soissons.

493

Ostrogothic King Theodoric (the Great), in league with the Byzantine emperor, leads an assault on Odoacer's Italian kingdom. Theodoric kills Odoacer at Ravenna in north central Italy; he then founds the Ostrogothic kingdom in Italy.

c. 500

Dionysius Exiguus creates the Christian calendar.

Babylonian cartographers produce the earliest known map of the world.

Christianity takes root in the kingdom of the Franks.

Four groups claim areas of Scotland: Picts, Scots, Welsh Britons and Angles.

c. 500-800

Bavarian tribes overrun the area that is now Austria. Toward the end of this time, Charlemagne establishes a border province (part of modern-day Hungary) to defend his empire in the east. This province is seized by the Magyars in 880.

500s

The kingdom of Kush emerges, combining Egyptian and African traditions.

511

After the death of Clovis, the Frankish kingdom is divided among his four sons, Childebert, Chlodomer, Lothair and Theodoric.

519

Reconciliation of the eastern and western churches ends the schism of 484.

525

The Ethiopians defeat the Himyarites in the area that is now Yemen. The Himyarites came to power during the fourth century by conquering the kingdom of Saba (also called Sheba).

527

Justinian becomes Byzantine emperor. He rules until 565. His wife, Theodora, who rules until 545, is considered the most powerful woman in Byzantine history. Theodora sometimes countermands her husband's orders and is so powerful it is later said of her that she "made and unmade popes."

531

Khosru I becomes Sassanid king of Persia after the death of his father, Kavadh (Kobad) I. Khosru I rules until 579.

533

Belisarius, a Byzantine general under Justinian, and his army defeat the Vandals of North Africa. In 535 Belisarius begins the occupation of the Ostrogothic kingdom of Italy.

538

Buddhism is introduced in Japan. Some scholars place this event in 552.

c. 540

A Chinese book is written about methods of cultivation.

541

Totila becomes the last king of the Ostrogoths. In 546 his army takes Rome. Totila rules until 552.

542

A pandemic, later described by Gildas as a "plague of boils," hits Constantinople and spreads through Europe. It is believed to have been carried by rats from Syria and Egypt.

c. 550

Japanese rulers permit the practice of Buddhism; the first monastery is erected in 587.

c. 553

Byzantine emperor Justinian sends missionaries to smuggle silkworms out of China, thus beginning the European silk industry.

568-774

This is the time span generally ascribed to the Lombard kingdom in northern Italy.

581-618

In the Sui dynasty, Yang Jian (Yang Chien) rules China. During this time, China is unified, the Great Wall is rebuilt and Turk invasions from the north are stopped.

593

Prince Shōtoku, son of Empress Suiko, becomes prime minister of Japan. He serves until 622.

590

Pope Gregory I, the Great, rejects forced baptism and tries to convert his conquered people with diplomacy. He is regarded as the first monastic pope. He serves until 604.

600

Christianity is brought to England.

c. 600

Slavic warriors, uprooted by the invasion of the Avars, move into Greece and the Balkans.

Tibet begins to develop into a unified state.

The Bulgars take control of the western shore of the Black Sea.

c. 600-1100

The Shrividjaya Empire in Sumatra and later the kingdom of Madjapahit invade the Philippines and set up colonies on the islands.

602

Sui reimpose Chinese rule on Nam Viet.

603

The Lombards convert to Christianity.

604

Prince Shotoku issues Japan's Seventeen Article Constitution.

606

Harsha (Harshavardhana) of Thanesar founds an empire in northern India in the area of the Ganges. Although he later assumes the title of Emperor of the Five Indies (Bengal, Darbhanga, Kana Uj, Orissa and Punjab), he is unable to defeat the powerful Chalukya kingdom in southern India. Harsha rules until 647.

610

Muhammad (Mohammed) begins preaching a new religion to be called Islam. Muhammad's first wife, the twice-widowed Khadijah, supports him through her import-export business. Khadijah eventually bears Muhammad six children; she is his first and strongest supporter when the call comes to his prophetic mission. His followers later compile the Koran, the book of his teachings.

Heraclius becomes Byzantine emperor. He rules until 641.

c. 618-907

During the reign of the Tang (T'ang) dynasty, resistance to Chinese control in Nam Viet is eliminated and the region's name is changed to Annam, which means "conquered South" in Chinese.

Under Tang leadership, China's government becomes more sophisticated and centralized. Artistic endeavors flourish again, and trade expeditions travel regularly between China and the Byzantine and Islamic Empires.

622

Muhammad's flight to Medina, called the Hegira, begins the Islamic era.

627

The army of Byzantine Emperor Heraclius soundly defeats the Persians at Nineveh and thus halts the seizure of Byzantine lands by the Sassanid dynasty.

c. 627

The Khmer state of Chenla (now northern Cambodia and southern Laos) overtakes the Malay state of Funan.

628-987

This is the time span generally ascribed to the Carolingian dynasty (second Frankish dynasty). This and the Merovingian (first Frankish dynasty) overlap due to conflicting territorial claims in France.

630

Olaf Tratelia, after being expelled from Sweden, sets up a colony in Vermeland (present-day Norway).

Chinese forces gain a major victory over the Turks.

632

Muslim armies begin to build an empire under Omar, the Great Caliph. By 750, lands from Spain in the west to India in the east are a part of the Muslim Empire.

c. 637

Muslim Arabs capture Jerusalem.

640

Islam spreads in north, east and central Africa.

643

Muslims capture Tripoli and complete their conquest of Persia. As a result, the Zoroastrian religion virtually disappears.

646

The Taika Reforms are begun in Japan, and are completed by the publication of codes based on those of China's Tang dynasty.

650

The official version of the Koran is compiled under Othman, 24 years after Muhammad's death.

656

During the "Battle of the Camel" Muhammad's favorite wife Aisha becomes the rallying point for rebel soldiers in a battle against the Calif Ali. Ali is the fourth leader of the Muslims after Muhammad's death. Aisha remains unharmed during the battle, though her camel is killed and her litter filled with arrows. This event, among others, establishes Aisha as a major female figure in the Islamic world.

c. 661-751

The murder of Ali and the succession of Muawiyah begin the Muslim Omayyad (Umayyad) dynasty, which governs from Damascus.

c. 668

Korea begins a decade under Chinese rule.

c. 673

"Greek fire," a flammable mixture believed to contain sulphur and quicklime, is invented by Kallinikus (Callinicus) and is used by the Byzantines.

679

The Bulgars cross the Danube River from central Asia and begin to establish communities in the Balkans, an area under Byzantine authority.

680

Tibetan armies continue to encroach into China and central Asia.

c. 680

Egypt is conquered by Arab forces who introduce their language and the Muslim faith.

c. 681-1018

This is the time span generally ascribed to the first Bulgarian Empire.

687

Pepin the Younger's victory at Testry (now Tertry, in northern France) unites the Frankish Kingdom and begins the rise of the Carolingian dynasty. Pepin rules all of the Franks except the Aquitaine region until 714.

Pre-1500

THE WORLD	THE WORLD	THE WORLD	THE WORLD

Pre-1500

c. 690-1590

This is the time span generally ascribed to the Songhai (Songhay) Empire in Niger.

694

Chinese forces are victorious in battles with the Turks and Tibetans.

c. 697

The Arabs conquer and destroy Carthage.

c. 700

The maritime empire of Shrividjaya in Indonesia, which evolved from the Palembang Kingdom in Sumatra, serves as an early center of Buddhism.

c. 700s-965

The Khazars, a Turkic people, reach the peak of their imperial power, with holdings from the Black and Caspian Seas to the city of Kiev. Khazar nobles accept Judaism, and are believed to be the ancestors of many modern European Jews. The Khazars practice complete religious tolerance. This empire falls in 965 with their defeat by the duke of Kiev.

701

The Japanese government issues the Taiho Code which binds its subjects to very rigid moral laws based on Confucian and Buddhist philosophy. Women are severely restricted. They can no longer head their households; and a woman must completely obey first her father, then her husband, then, when aged, her son.

c. 710

Japanese and Chinese legal codes are written down, including the Tang (T'ang) code in China.

711

Following their victories in the east, Muslim Arab forces defeat the Berbers in Africa and cross the Strait of Gibraltar to enter Spain. Roderick, the last Visigothic king of Spain, is defeated.

712

Muslim forces under Muhammad ibn Kasim invade and conquer Sind in northern India.

720

Muslim armies cross the Pyrenees into France and take Narbonne. They also occupy Sardinia.

732

Christian forces in France under Charles Martel defeat Muslim (Saracen) invaders at the Battle of Poitiers (between Poitiers and Tours), thus preventing Muslim armies from overrunning Europe.

740

An earthquake hits Asia Minor.

749

Abu-l-Abbas (as-Saffah) becomes the first Abbasid *caliph* (spiritual and civil head of a Muslim state). He rules until 754.

749-1258

This is the time span generally ascribed to the Abbasid *caliphate* which governs from Baghdad.

751

In Europe the Franks are united under Pepin III (the Short) who rules until 768. He is the first Carolingian king, son of Charles Martel and father of Charlemagne.

Lombard King Aistulf captures Ravenna.

The Chinese lose control of western Asia to the Arabs, with a solid defeat at the Talas River. Arabs learn the art of papermaking from captured Chinese artisans, and establish the first paper mill outside of China at Samarkand in Russia.

754

Mansur becomes the Abbasid *caliph* after the death of his brother, Abu-l-Abbas (749). Mansur rules until 775.

Hostility against Frankish rule and the royal alliance with the church comes to a head in Friesland when a teacher, St. Boniface, and several of his students are murdered in Dokkum, Friesland's northernmost city. Frisians interpret the missionary's presence as a threat to the region's independence, believing that where missionaries arrive, the king's army soon follows.

756-1031

This is the time span generally ascribed to the Arab *emirate* (the jurisdiction of an *emir,* an independent Muslim prince or commander) of Córdoba that governs Moorish Spain.

757

Offa is crowned king of Mercia (in England). He rules until 796.

765

The armies of Tibet invade China.

768

Charlemagne, the Germanic leader, becomes king of the Franks. Under his rule, Saxons and Frisians are conquered and converted to Christianity. The punishment for resisting conversion is banishment or death. Charlemagne rules until 814.

774

The alliance between the Carolingian Franks and the papacy leads to Charlemagne's conquest and annexation of the Lombard kingdom.

778

Charlemagne and his forces are defeated by Basques at Roncesvales Pass in the Pyrenees.

779

Having already defeated Wessex and Kent, Offa defeats the West Saxons and is now considered king of all England.

c. 786

The accession of Harun al-Rashid as Abbasid *caliph* begins the golden age of Arab culture. Harun al-Rashid's queen is Zubaidah. Owning vast estates in her own name, Zubaidah creates a luxurious, cultured court, and roads and way stations for pilgrims going to Mecca. She plays a conciliatory role in settling affairs in Baghdad. Zubaidah is one of a series of queens who become powers "behind the throne" during the height of the Islamic Empire. Harun al-Rashid rules until 809.

787

Vikings from Scandinavia begin their raids on England.

789-926

This is the time span generally ascribed to the Idrisids who govern Morocco.

c. 790-1306

This is the time span generally ascribed to the Przemyslids who govern the area of Bohemia.

793

Danes sack the monastery at Lindisfarne (peninsula/island off northern England). In the next few years they attack other missionary communities, including Iona, off the coast of Scotland.

c. 794

Arabs in Baghdad begin making and using paper.

795

Vikings land in Ireland.

c. 795

There is evidence that Irish monks travel to Iceland to live in seclusion there.

797

Irene begins her five-year reign as Byzantine empress. She refuses to recognize the authority of Charlemagne at his coronation in 800.

800

Charlemagne is crowned Emperor of the West by Pope Leo III. This coronation paves the way for the later development of the Holy Roman Empire. The "West" or Carolingian Empire Charlemagne rules includes the areas that are now France, Belgium, the Netherlands, western Germany, Austria, Switzerland and parts of Italy.

c. 800

New writing systems are developed. As a result, the Carolingian, Byzantine and Chinese "renaissances" take place.

The Hawaiian Islands are colonized by people from the Marquesas Islands.

Aotearoa (present-day New Zealand) is colonized by people from the Marquesas Islands. Their travel route includes the Cook Islands.

In northern India, the Rajputs, descendants of various invading peoples, occupy Kana Uj and set up a powerful kingdom from Bihar to the Sutlej River.

800-909

This is the time span generally ascribed to the Aghlabids who rule northern Africa (modern-day Tunisia and Algeria) and Sicily.

c. 800-1050

The kingdom of Ghana controls western Africa's rich trade; villagers use cowry shells for money.

c. 800-c. 1808

This is the time span generally ascribed to the kingdom of Kanem (later Bornu) in present-day Chad.

800s

Gunpowder is invented in China.

The Catholic Church becomes the center of life in Europe.

802-1016; 1042-1066

England is ruled by Saxon kings.

809

Bulgarian Khan Krum captures Sofia and in 811, defeats Byzantine Emperor Nicephorus I. Krum rules from 803 to 814.

813

Al-Mamun becomes Abbasid *caliph* of Baghdad after the reign of his brother, Al-Amin. Al-Mamun rules until 833.

Charlemagne names his son Louis I (the Pious) as coemperor of the Carolingian Empire. On Charlemagne's death in 814, Louis I becomes emperor.

817

Emperor Louis I names his son Lothian I as coemperor of the West. He also gives parts of the empire to his sons Pepin I and Louis (the German). Rebellion is later sparked when Louis I tries to create a kingdom for Charles, his son by a later marriage.

821

Tibetan forces occupy China's Kansu region.

825

Dicuil, an Irish monk in Charlemagne's court, writes a geographical description of a land called "Thule," based on the testimony of three Irish monks who visited that land. Dicuil's account accurately describes Iceland.

826-827

Arab forces conquer Crete, Sicily and Sardinia.

829

Sweden receives its first Christian missionary, St. Ansgar.

All the small kingdoms of England are united at least nominally for the first time under Egbert (Ecgberht) of Wessex.

c. 840

Rurik, a Swedish Varangian, starts to consolidate the Slavic and Finnish tribes into the beginning of the modern Russian state. Rurik rules until 879.

843

The Treaty of Verdun formally divides Charlemagne's Carolingian Empire into three sections: France to Charles II (the Bald), Germany to Louis (the German) and the central portion (Lorraine, Alsace, Burgundy and most of Italy) to Lothair I. Louis (the German) rules as king of the Eastern Franks from 817 to 876; Lothair I rules as Holy Roman Emperor from 840 to 855 and Charles II rules as king of the Western Franks from 843 to 877 and as emperor of the West from 875 to 877. This division marks the end of political unity in western Europe.

c. 844

Picts and Scots unite under Kenneth MacAlpin, king of the Scots, and proclaim the new kingdom of Albyn. England at this time is a cluster of separate kingdoms.

846

Arab forces sack Rome.

851

A major earthquake occurs in Rome.

852

Boris I becomes Khan (ruler) of Bulgaria. In 864, he accepts Christianity, and forces it on his subjects; he also makes Slavonic the official language of the realm. Boris I rules until 889.

855

After the death of Lothair I, the lands given him by the Treaty of Verdun (843) are divided between Louis II and Lothair II, king of Lotharingia (Lorraine). Lothair II rules until 869 and Louis II rules until 875.

868-905

This is the time span generally ascribed to the Tulunids who govern in Egypt and Syria.

870

The Treaty of Mersen (in the Netherlands) redivides the Carolingian Empire between Charles II (the Bald) of France and Louis the German. Although the "Middle Kingdom" is eliminated, the southern portion of Lothair's kingdom remains, governed by Louis II.

Arab forces seize Malta.

871

Alfred (the Great) becomes king of Wessex. He rules until 899.

874

Scandinavians establish their first community in Iceland. Sources vary regarding the leader of this expedition, who is either chieftain Arnarson or Ingolf Vilgerdarsson.

c. 874

It is estimated that by 930, the combined Norse and Celtic population of Iceland is approximately 30,000.

878

King Alfred (the Great) defeats the Danes under Guthrum at the Battle of Edington. He then cedes parts of northern and eastern England to the Danes, but manages to hold Wessex.

879

Nepal wins its independence from Tibet.

Pre-1500

c. 880-1303

This is the time span generally ascribed to the Arpad dynasty that rules Hungary. Arpad rule begins with the conquest of the Frankish border province that Charlemagne established.

c. 883-1047

During this time, Viking rulers govern Denmark.

888

The Chola dynasty begins in southern India and Ceylon building on scattered remnants of earlier Chola landholdings. It lasts until the accession of Sundara Pandya in 1251.

889

Vladimir becomes ruler of Bulgaria after his father, Boris I (852), retires to a monastery. Vladimir attempts to reintroduce paganism into the Christianized kingdom. He is deposed in 893 through the combined efforts of his father and Simeon I, his brother.

c. 890

Magyar people migrate in large numbers to the Danube River basin in the region that is now Hungary.

893

The first Bulgarian Empire reaches its height under Simeon I, who takes the title czar after deposing his brother, Vladimir (889). Simeon I rules until 927.

c. 895

After being expelled from southern Russia, the Magyars under Arpad migrate to Hungary. Arpad rules until c. 907. Arpad's life is cloaked in legend, and it is not clear who succeeded him.

900

Córdoba, the largest city in western Europe, is the center of western Islam.

c. 900

The first significant kingdoms in Scandinavia are established. Much of Norway is united under King Harold I. Over time, the kings of Denmark, Norway and Sweden use their conversion to Christianity to increase their power.

The Premyslid dynasty solidifies Bohemia into an autonomous state.

c. 907

The Magyars, having destroyed the Moravian Empire, begin raids into Germany and Italy.

907-960

China is in civil turmoil during this period known as the Five Dynasties and Ten Kingdoms. Qidans (Khitans, Liao) from Manchuria enter North China.

907-1125

This is the time span generally ascribed to the Liao dynasty established by the Khitans in northern China.

909-1171

This is the time span generally ascribed to the Fatimid *caliphate* that rules Egypt, Syria and northern Africa.

911

The dukedom of Normandy is established by the Treaty of St. Claire-sur-Epte, with Rollo as first duke.

912

Abdu-r-Rahman III becomes *emir* of Córdoba, and first *caliph* of Córdoba in 929. He rules until 961.

914-1014

Viking invaders take and hold the Irish kingdoms.

916-1125

This is the time span generally ascribed to the kingdom of the Khitan in eastern Mongolia and Manchuria.

919 or 936-1024

Though sources vary, this is the general time span of the Saxon rule in Germany. Henry I comes to power in 919, but is not crowned. Otto I becomes king of Germany in 936. He rules until 973.

925

The first Slavic kingdom in southern Europe is established when Tomislav is crowned king of Croatia.

926

Athelstan, king of Wessex, removes Guthfrith of Northumbria and annexes his kingdom. The kings of Strathclyde, and Wales, and of the Picts and Scots submit to his control. Athelstan thus comes to rule all of England. He retains control until his death in 939.

c. 930

The Commonwealth of Iceland is formed. The Althing, the oldest parliamentary assembly in Europe, is convened at Thingvelli. Christianity is made the state religion in 1000.

939

In Japan, the challenge to imperial rule by the Taira and Minamoto clans triggers a civil war that lasts almost 250 years.

Edmund becomes king of Wessex after the death of his half-brother, Athelstan (926), inheriting as well the regions the late king annexed. Unable to hold all his lands, Edmund dies in 946 while trying to retake Strathclyde.

946

Edred (Eadred) becomes king of the English after the death of his brother, Edmund (939). Edred rules until his death in 955.

c. 950

The Heian Era begins in Japan. This period of peace and refined courtly life encourages scholarship among upper class men and women. Women become Japan's major writers. The Heian Era lasts until 1050.

955

At the Battle of Lechfeld, near Augsburg, Germany, imperial troops under Otto I defeat Magyar forces.

c. 960

Eirik the Red emigrates to Iceland from Norway with his exiled father.

960-1279

The Song (Sung) dynasty begins in China. It produces a period of cultural stability and artistic creativity. Toward the end of this time, the Song neglects its northern and western borders, and Mongols invade.

962-1155

These are the traditional dates of the Turkish Ghaznivid dynasty that rules in Afghanistan. The dynasty maintains control of a smaller territory until 1186.

962-1370

This is the time span generally ascribed to the Piast dynasty that rules Poland. The first leader of this dynasty is Mieszko I, who rules until 992.

962-1806

This is the time span generally ascribed to the Holy Roman Empire, which rules the German states plus Austria, Bohemia and Moravia and has limited control at various times over other parts of Europe. The empire is loosely formed under German King Otto I.

963

Count Sigefroi founds Luxembourg.

965

Harold Bluetooth, king of Denmark, converts to Christianity. Harold became king in 935, and rules until his death, c. 985.

The nomadic Khazars, a Turkic people who in the eighth century converted to Judaism, are defeated by Sviatoslav, duke of Kiev.

966

The Polish people under Mieszko I convert to Christianity.

967

Boleslav, duke of Bohemia, converts to Christianity.

967-1068

The Fujiwara family dominates Japan.

969

The Fatimids conquer the Rostamids of Tahir, Idrisids of Fez and Aghlabids of Kairouan (in Tunisia), expanding the area under their power.

972

The Hungarian people are first visited by a Catholic missionary, a Bavarian called Wolfgang.

973

Otto II, son of Otto I (962-1806), becomes Holy Roman Emperor. Otto II has served as coemperor since 967, and rules until 983.

974

An earthquake in England is the first to be accurately recorded in this area.

976

Leopold von Babenberg is named as the Holy Roman Empire's prince of Austria.

978

Aethelred becomes king of England after the death of his brother, Edward (the Martyr). Aethelred rules until 1016.

977-1186

This is the time span generally ascribed to the Ghaznivids who govern northern India.

c. 980

Dynastic power struggles take place in Russia. Vladimir I, son of Sviatoslav (965) and grandson of Prince Ivor of the house of Rurik, is victorious over his brothers and becomes grand duke of Kiev. Vladimir I rules until 1015.

c. 981 or 982

Eirik the Red spends three years exploring Greenland. He returns to Iceland, assembles an expedition of several hundred would-be colonists, and returns to Greenland in 985 or 986.

982

Viking invaders renew raids on England.

986

Sweyn I becomes king of Denmark after his forces defeat and kill his father, Harold Bluetooth (965). Sweyn I rules until 1014.

987-1328

The ascension of Hugh Capet to the throne of France ends the Carolingian reign. Hugh Capet rules until 996. The House of Capet rules France for over 340 years.

988

The eastern form of Christianity is introduced into Russia by the baptism of Prince Vladimir, resulting in the practices of the Eastern rather than the Roman church.

992

Boleslaus I becomes ruler of Poland on the death of his father, Mieszko I (962). A strong leader, Boleslaus further loosens German control of his countries, and strengthens Poland's ties with the church. The pope crowns him king in 1025, shortly before his death.

c. 993

Olaf Skötkonung becomes the first Christian king of Sweden. He rules until 1024.

995

Olaf I (Olaf Tryggvesson), a convert to Christianity, defeats Haakon, becomes king of Norway and forces his new religion on his people. Olaf I rules until 1000.

996

Robert II becomes king of France after the death of his father, Hugh Capet (987). Robert II rules until 1031.

c. 997

Stephen I of the Arpad dynasty becomes duke of the Magyars (Hungary). He is crowned king in 1001, rules until 1038 and is later canonized.

Ghasnivid ruler Mahmud (the Great) becomes ruler of Hindu Kush (Afghanistan), the Punjab in India and large tracts of land beyond the Oxus River, thus ending the Samanid kingdom. Mahmud rules until 1030.

1000

Sweyn I of Denmark defeats and kills King Olaf I of Norway to bring Norway and Sweden under Danish control.

King Rajaraja of the Chola dynasty conquers Ceylon.

King Stephen I's coronation marks the beginning of the kingdom of Hungary. Stephen I rules until 1038.

c. 1000

The making of gunpowder is perfected in China.

The area that is now the Netherlands is divided into several regions governed by barons (particularly the eastern provinces), the bishop of Utrecht, the dukes of Brabant and Gelderland, and several counts. Friesland continues to be self-governing.

Several provinces of Sweden, formerly independent states, become united.

1002

Danish people in England are killed by order of King Aethelred. This attack, known as the Massacre of St. Brice's Day, marks the beginning of 10 years of strife between England and Denmark.

1006

Muslims migrate to northwest India.

1009

Muslims destroy the Church of the Holy Sepulchre in Jerusalem. As a result, the demand for a Crusade to recapture the Holy Lands begins to grow.

1010

The Li dynasty in Annam (now Vietnam) defeats the Chinese, takes control of part of Champa and provides stability in the region for approximately 200 years.

1013-1035

Denmark experiences a brief rise as a European power, beginning with the Viking conquest of England in 1013.

1014

Ireland ends Viking rule when Brian Boru succeeds at the Battle of Clontarf. Brian Boru rules, by power of conquest, as king of Ireland from 1002 to 1014.

Harold II becomes king of Denmark after the death of his father, Sweyn I (986). Harold II rules until 1018.

1015

King Olaf II regains Norwegian independence and reaffirms the practice of Christianity. He rules until 1028.

Pre-1500

THE WORLD	THE WORLD	THE WORLD	THE WORLD

Pre-1500

Scotland's Malcolm II conquers the Lothian region.

1016

Edmund Ironside is declared king of England after the death of his father, Aethelred. However, most of the English nobility support Danish King Canute to rule England. After months of fighting the two rulers agree to partition the country, but Edmund dies, leaving all of England to Canute. Canute governs England until 1035, Denmark from 1018 to 1035 and Norway from 1028 to 1035.

1018

The Byzantines regain control over Macedonia and defeat the Bulgarian Empire.

The Treaty of Bautzen ends the war between Germany and Poland. Boleslaus I (Boleslav the Brave), ruler of Poland since 992, obtains control of Lusatia.

Canute becomes king of Denmark after the death of Harold II (1014). He rules until 1035. After his death, Denmark experiences nearly 140 years of turmoil, marked by power struggles, short reigns and civil wars.

1019

Yaroslav, the son of Vladimir I, becomes the grand duke of Kiev after defeating his brother, Sviatopulk. Yaroslav rules until 1054.

c. 1020

The city of Goa in India adopts Islam.

1024-1137

This is the time span generally ascribed to the Franconian (Salian) dynasty that rules an area that is now eastern Germany.

1025

Mieszko II becomes king of Poland after the death of his father, Boleslaus I (992). Mieszko II rules until 1034.

The Cholas, a powerful dynasty in southern India, attack the Shrividjaya Empire in the Malay Peninsula and sack the Sumatran city of Palembang.

Lothian is formally ceded to Scotland by Northumbria; Malcolm II, king of Albyn, becomes the first monarch of an area that approximates modern Scotland.

1028

Canute, king of Denmark and England, defeats Olaf II, and conquers Norway.

1031

Henry I becomes king of France after the death of his father, Robert II (996). Henry I rules until 1060.

1035

Upon the death of Canute, his kingdom is divided among his three sons: Harold Harefoot receives England which he rules as regent until 1037 and king until 1040; Sweyn obtains Norway for a brief period; and Hardicanute rules Denmark as king until 1042 and England from 1040 until 1042.

1038-1194

This is the time span generally ascribed to the Seljuk Turks who govern in Persia.

1040

King Duncan is murdered by his military commander, Macbeth, who seizes the throne and rules until 1057.

1042

Edward the Confessor, son of Aethelred, becomes the last Anglo-Saxon king of England after the death of Hardicanute. Edward rules until 1066.

Constantine IX Monomachus becomes Byzantine emperor. He rules until 1054.

1044

Anawratha establishes Burmese control over the Irrawaddy delta and Thaton, thus establishing the Talaing-Pyu Pagan Empire. Hinayana Buddhism is introduced in Burma during Anawratha's reign.

1047-1375

This is the time span generally ascribed to the Estrith dynasty that rules Denmark.

c. 1050

The astrolabe, an instrument of navigation, reaches Europe from the East.

1054

Continuing differences between the church in Rome and the church in Constantinople cause the churches to separate, creating the Roman Catholic Church and the Eastern Orthodox Church, respectively.

Almoravid Berbers begin the Islamic conquest of western Africa.

1055

The Seljuk Turks, having conquered Persia, enter Baghdad, found a new dynasty and begin conquests of Syria, Palestine and large sections of Asia Minor. Their threat to take Constantinople begins the Holy Crusades.

1056

Henry IV becomes Holy Roman Emperor. He rules until 1105.

Michael VI becomes Byzantine emperor after the death of Theodora. This ends the Macedonian dynasty begun by Justinian in 527.

1056-1147

This is the time span generally ascribed to the Almoravids who govern in Spain and northern Africa.

1057

Malcolm III becomes king of Scotland after the death of Macbeth. Malcolm III rules until 1093.

1060

Philip I becomes king of France after the death of his father, Henry I (1031). Philip I rules until 1108.

1061

Normans forces conquer Messina (a northeastern province of Italy) and begin the conquest of Sicily.

1066

The Normans, under William of Normandy (The Conqueror), subdue the English. King Harold II is killed at the Battle of Hastings, and William takes the English throne and rules until 1087.

1066-1135

This is the time span generally ascribed to the Norman rule of England.

1071

By winning the Battle of Manzikert (now Malazkirt, Armenia) against Romanus IV, the Seljuk Turks significantly weaken the Byzantine Empire's hold on Asia Minor.

The Normans conquer Bari and Brindisi, the last Byzantine possessions in southern Italy.

1072

Norman forces under Robert Guiscard conquer Palermo, Sicily. Guiscard joined his brothers in c. 1045 to help remove the Byzantines from Italy.

1073-1085

Pope Gregory VII attempts to assert church authority over Holy Roman Emperor Henry IV. This sparks a divisive power conflict between the religious and secular heirs of the empire, which leads to Henry's excommunication and civil strife in Germany, weakening the monarchy.

The Almoravids sack Kumbi, the capital of Ghana, and spread Islam to Africa.

1077

Ladislas I (later Saint Ladislas) becomes king of Hungary. He rules until 1095.

1081-1118

Alexius I rules as Byzantine emperor.

1083

Anna Comnena, the eldest daughter of Byzantine Emperor Alexius I, establishes a medical school. Anna is a doctor, who also writes histories of her family and the Byzantine courts.

1086

The Domesday Book is compiled. An early census of England, it contains information about population, economy and land use, and is compiled for tax purposes.

Almoravids defeat Alfonso VI, king of Leon and Castile, near Badajoz and keep parts of Spain under Muslim control.

THE WORLD	THE WORLD	THE WORLD	FOR CLASSROOM USE

1087

William II inherits the throne of England on the death of his father, William I (1066). William II rules until 1100.

1089

Hungarian forces overrun Slavonia. Hungary's borders are further enlarged by the conquest of Croatia in 1091.

1090

Norman forces drive the Muslims out of Malta.

1094

Spanish soldier El Cid (Rodrigo Díaz de Vivar) captures Valencia from the Moors. He rules until 1099.

1095

At the Council of Clermont, Pope Urban II demands a war to rescue the Holy Land from the Muslims. The first Crusade begins the following year. Jerusalem is taken from Muslim forces in 1099.

Anti-Jewish *pogroms* (organized attacks) begin as part of religious intolerance in Europe.

1100

Henry I seizes the throne of England after the death of his brother, William II (1087). Henry I rules until 1135.

c. 1100

Runic characters, a written alphabet which spreads from southern and central Europe to the Nordic countries, is replaced by Latin script.

1100s

Styria and a region roughly equal to present-day Lower Austria are proclaimed a duchy of the Holy Roman Empire.

The trading city of Awda-ghost in northwest Africa reaches its high point.

1108

Louis VI (the Fat) becomes king of France after the death of his father, Philip I (1060). Louis IV rules until 1137.

1109

Urraca becomes queen of Castile and Leon. She rules until 1126.

1115-1234

This is the time span generally ascribed to the Jurchen Jin dynasty that rules Manchuria.

1122

In the Concordat of Worms in Germany, a compromise agreement is reached in which Holy Roman Emperor Henry V is forced by the German princes to accept the spiritual authority of the pope over church officials.

1124-1211

This is the time span generally ascribed to the Western Liao dynasty established by the Khitans in northern China.

1125

The Almohads conquer Morocco.

The Qidans (Khitans, Liao) are conquered by Nüzhens (Nuchen, Jin) from Manchuria. The Nüzhens enter North China.

1126

Alfonso VII becomes king of Castile and Leon after the death of his mother, Urraca (1109). In 1135 he is crowned emperor in Leon and rules until 1157.

1127

In northern China, the Northern Song dynasty is overrun by the Jin.

**1130-1269
or 1140-1250**

Although sources vary, this is the time span generally ascribed to the Almohads who govern Spain and northern Africa.

1133-1266

Sweden is governed by the Sverker and Eric dynasties.

1135

Though England's King Henry I has done much to secure succession for his daughter, Matilda, upon his death a struggle ensues, and Stephen usurps the throne. Though he receives papal approval, Stephen's reign is marked by nearly constant turmoil as Matilda and her supporters attempt to regain the throne. Stephen rules until 1154.

1136

Hildegarde of Bingen becomes a convent abbess in Germany and begins work on the first of many books. In her writings she demonstrates broad knowledge of science, theology and philosophy. Hildegarde acquires a wide reputation as a prophet and an intellectual, and corresponds with heads of state such as Holy Roman Emperor Frederick Barbarossa.

1137

Louis VII becomes king of France after the death of his father, Louis VI (1108). Louis VII rules until 1180.

1138-1273

This is the time span generally ascribed to the Hohenstaufen dynasty that rules as monarchs of Germany and as Holy Roman emperors.

1139

Moorish invaders are defeated at the battle of Ourique and driven out of Portugal. The count of Portugal, Alfonso Henriques of the house of Burgundy, declares himself king as Alfonso I. He is officially recognized by the pope in 1179.

1146

In China, the Nüzhens force the Song to retreat southward to the Yangzi valley.

1147

The Second Crusade is led by emperor and German king Conrad III and Louis VII of France. It is considered a failure and ends in 1149.

Eleanor of Aquitaine joins her husband, Louis VII of France, on the second Crusade. Later she separates from Louis and marries Henry II of England, joining her French Aquitaine lands with his. Eleanor's court in southern France is known for its sophistication. She encourages the troubadour tradition in Europe and the ideal of male chivalry, which she promotes in England when she rules as regent for her son, Richard I (the Lion Heart, 1189), during his absence on the Crusades.

Almohad forces capture Marrakesh from the Almoravids.

Pre-1500

Pre-1500

Portuguese forces retake Lisbon from the Moors.

c. 1150

Ghazni is destroyed by Persian forces from Ghor and the Yamini flee to the Punjab.

1152

Frederick I (Barbarossa) becomes king of the Germans.

1153-1154

The king of the Maldive Islands officially accepts Islam, thus reducing the practice of Buddhism in his country.

1154-1399

This is the time span generally ascribed to the Plantagenet rule of England. Henry Plantagenet becomes King Henry II and rules until 1189. His marriage to Eleanor of Aquitaine brings over half of French landholdings under English control.

1155

King Frederick I (Frederick Barbarossa) of Germany becomes Holy Roman Emperor. He rules both domains until his death in 1190.

1156

Japan's Minamoto and Taira clans struggle for power.

1157

Valdemar I (The Great) becomes king of Denmark. A strong and popular monarch, he brings some measure of stability to the country. Valdemar I rules until 1182.

1162

Stephen III becomes king of Hungary. He rules until 1172.

1168

Andrei Bogolyubsky, ruler of Suzdal, sacks Kiev and takes the title of grand prince. He shifts the center of Russian politics from southern to central Russia.

1169

Forces of King Henry II of England invade Ireland. Henry II has been granted lordship over Ireland by the pope, who is eager to have the full submission of the Irish church.

1170

Thomas á Becket, who became the Archbishop of Canterbury in 1162, is murdered by agents of Henry II.

"Strongbow" de Clare, Norman earl of Chepstow, invades Ireland.

1171

Muslim leader Saladin ends the Fatimid dynasty and founds the Ayyubid dynasty in Egypt. He rules until 1189.

1171-1250

This is the time span generally ascribed to the Ayyubids who govern in Egypt and Syria.

1172

Béla III becomes king of Hungary after the reign of Stephen III (1162). He rules until 1196.

1176

Forces of Holy Roman Emperor Frederick I are defeated by the Lombard League at Legnano.

Muhammad of Ghor becomes ruler of the Delhi sultanate. He rules until 1206.

1178

Emperor Frederick I is crowned king of Burgundy.

1180

Philip II (Philip Augustus) becomes king of France after the death of his father, Louis VII (1137). Philip II rules until 1223.

1182

France expels its Jewish population and, although religious intolerance eases, Jews are expelled again in 1252 by Louis IX.

Canute IV, Valdemar's (1157) son, becomes king of Denmark. He rules until 1202.

c. 1185

The first shogunate is established when Minamoto Yoritomo becomes leader of Japan.

c. 1186-1396

This is the time span generally ascribed to the second Bulgarian Empire, which includes the entire Balkan Peninsula except Greece.

1187

Saladin defeats Christian forces at the Battle of Hittin and later captures Jerusalem.

Muhammad of Ghor and his forces conquer the Punjab.

1189

After the death of England's King Henry II (1154-1399), Richard I (the Lion Heart) takes the throne. He rules until 1199.

The Third Crusade takes place following Egyptian sultan Saladin's capture of Jerusalem. The Crusaders capture Acre and Cyprus, but fail to retake Jerusalem. Richard I of England and Saladin reach an agreement that allows Christians to visit the holy city. Frederick I (Barbarossa) drowns in Cilicia, Turkey, in 1190. The Crusade ends in 1192.

1190

Henry VI assumes the thrones as king of Germany and Holy Roman Emperor after the death of his father, Frederick I (Barbarossa, 1155). He is officially crowned by the pope in 1191. Henry VI rules both domains until 1197.

1191

Cyprus, part of the Byzantine Empire until this year, is captured by Crusaders under England's King Richard I.

1192

English King Richard I is captured by Duke Leopold of Austria (South Austria), and imprisoned by Holy Roman Emperor Henry VI. Richard I is released after payment of ransom and an acknowledgement of the emperor's authority over England.

1192-1398

This is the time span generally ascribed to the Delhi sultanate, the first Muslim kingdom in India. Afghan ruler Muhammad of Ghor defeats the Hindu forces of Prithvi Raj and captures Delhi, Bihar and Bengal, establishing the sultanate.

1192-1333

The Kamakura shogunate governs Japan. The Minamoto family rules until 1219 and the Hojo family until 1333.

1197

Ottocar I becomes duke and then king (1198) of Bohemia. He rules until his death in 1230.

1200

Slavery no longer exists in Bohemia.

c. 1200

The compass, probably a Chinese invention, comes into regular use among European mariners.

c. 1200-1450

In Africa, intensive population growth occurs in the Great Zimbabwe area; there are indications of its political dominance of the region and its extensive trade routes.

1200-1600

The city of Ife asserts political, technical, artistic and religious dominance in Yorubaland on Africa's southwest coast.

1202

The Fourth Crusade is marked by political rivalries. At the urging of the Venetians, Constantinople is stormed. This Crusade ends in 1204.

Valdemar II (The Victorious) becomes king of Denmark after the reign of Canute IV (1182). He rules until 1241.

1203

Forces of Muhammad of Ghor complete the conquest of norther India.

1205

Andrew II becomes king of Hungary. He rules until 1235.

1206

Genghis Khan (Temujin) becomes chief of the Mongols. He rules until 1227.

1206-1290

During this time, the Delhi sultanate is led by former slaves, beginning with Qutb-ud-din. This period is known as the Slave dynasty.

THE WORLD	THE WORLD	THE WORLD	*FOR CLASSROOM USE*	

1208

Theodore Lascaris (Laskaris) founds the empire of Nicaea, Asia Minor.

1209

Jews are expelled from England.

1212

The Children's Crusade ends in failure as young French and German people perish crossing the Alps; the survivors are sold into slavery.

1213-1214

Genghis Khan and his Mongol forces invade and conquer much of northern China. Wives of the great Mongol khans play an active role in the internal politics of the state and participate in the deliberations of the highest council in the choice of the ruler.

1214

The victory of Philip II of France over King John of England releases French lands from English rule. Philip II rules from 1180-1223.

1215

At Runnymede, English barons force King John to ensure feudal rights and not encroach on their privileges. The document created at this time, the Magna Carta, lays the foundation for political and civil rights, and demonstrates that the king's authority is not absolute. After John's death in 1216, a second version of the Magna Carta, weakened by omissions, is issued.

1217

The Fifth Crusade is directed against Egypt. It ends in defeat in 1221, in a battle for Cairo.

Haakon IV becomes king of Norway on the death of King Inge. Haakon IV rules until 1263.

King Andrew II of Hungary leads a Crusade to the Holy Land.

1220

Frederick II becomes Holy Roman Emperor. He rules until 1250.

1222

Hungarian King Andrew II (Andreás II) issues a Golden Bull (the Hungarian Magna Carta) that guarantees the rights of nobility and prevents foreigners and Jews from holding land or office without permission of the monarchy.

1223

Russian forces are defeated at the Kalka River by Mongol invaders.

Louis VIII becomes king of France after the death of his father, Philip II (Philip Augustus, 1180). Louis VIII rules until 1226.

Afghanistan begins a period of approximately 100 years under Mongol domination.

1225

England's Magna Carta, issued for the third time, takes final form.

1226

Louis IX becomes king of France after the death of his father, Louis VIII (1223). Louis IX rules until 1270.

1227

Genghis Khan, ruler of the Mongols, the largest empire in history, dies in battle in northern China. His empire is divided among his sons and grandsons.

1228

The Sixth Crusade, led by Emperor Frederick II, is a non-military expedition that results in a truce between Muslims and Crusaders. The Crusade ends in 1229.

1228-1574

This is the time span generally ascribed to the Hafsids who govern northern Africa (Tunisia and Algeria).

1230

Wenceslaus I becomes king of Bohemia on the death of his father, Ottocar I (1197). Wenceslaus I rules until 1253.

1230-1492

This is the time span generally ascribed to the Nasrid dynasty that rules in Granada (southern Spain).

c. 1230-c. 1550

This is the time span generally ascribed to the Mali Empire in West Africa.

1233

Pope Gregory IX assigns responsibility to the Dominicans for combating heresy, thus beginning the Inquisition. Instruments of torture are first used by the Inquisition in 1252.

1236

Ferdinand III, king of Castile, captures the Moorish capital of Córdoba. Ferdinand III rules as king of Castile from 1217 to 1252 and king of Léon from 1230 to 1252.

Sultana Razia, the daughter of Suntan Shamsuddin Iltutmish, is accepted as ruler of Delhi, according to her father's wishes. An outstanding military leader, she appears in public without a veil.

1237

The second Mongol invasion of Russia begins.

1237-1368

Most of China's provinces are under Mongol rule.

1238

The T'ai people migrate down the Valley of the Menam, capture Sukhotai from the Khmers and establish an independent kingdom.

1240

The destruction of Kiev by Mongol forces effectively breaks apart the Russian state.

In Africa, the empire of Ghana falls to Mali forces under Sundiata Keita.

1241

The fall of Hungary to the Mongols marks the decline of the Arpad dynasty. Arpad's dynasty rule ends with the death of Andrew III (Andreás III), in 1301.

Mongols defeat German forces at the Battle of Liegnitz in Silesia and invade Poland. They withdraw after Ughetai, the Mongol leader, dies.

Pre-1500

THE WORLD	THE WORLD	THE WORLD	THE WORLD

Pre-1500

The Hanseatic League is formed by Baltic trading towns. It will reach its height in 1370.

1242

Batu Khan, grandson of Genghis Khan, founds the warlike "Golden Horde" (also called the Kipchak Empire) at Sarai, on the Lower Volga River, in southern Russia.

Gunpowder, probably from China, is first seen in Europe.

1244

Jerusalem falls to the Khwarazmi (Khorezmi), a people from what is now Uzbekistan. The city remains under Egyptian control for nearly 300 years.

1246

The last of the ruling Austrian Babenberg family, Friedrich the Quarrelsome, is killed in a battle against the Magyars. Since Friedrich is childless, Austria (now the province of South Austria) passes to Ottokar II, king of Bohemia, and Styria (now a province of Austria) goes to King Béla of Hungary.

1248

The Seventh Crusade, led by Louis IX of France, is against Egypt. Although the city of Damietta falls, a force against Cairo is defeated. The Crusade ends in 1254.

1250-1318

This is the time span generally ascribed to the Folkung dynasty in Sweden.

1250-1517

This is the time span generally ascribed to the Mamelukes (Mamluks) who govern in Egypt and Syria.

c. 1250

Sundiata becomes king of Kangaba (Mali) in Africa.

The Malay people establish a three-district alliance called the Confederation of Madya-as. The oldest known pre-Spanish code of laws in the Philippines, the Maragtas Code, is written.

Malay elders are required to teach the young. The rudiments of reading and writing (in Sanskrit) are taught, as well as basic arithmetic.

1251

Kublai Khan governs China and becomes the Mongol ruler in 1260.

1252

The Ahom kingdom is founded in Assam, India.

1253

Ottocar II becomes king of Bohemia after the death of his father, Wenceslaus I (1230). Ottocar II rules until 1278.

1256-1258

Mongols move decisively into Persia and conquer and destroy Baghdad, ending the Abbasid *caliphate*.

1256-1349

This is the time span generally ascribed to the Ilkhan dynasty that rules Persia. The first Mongol ruler, Hülegü, governs until 1265.

1257

Mongol invaders are unable to conquer Annam, now ruled by the Tran dynasty. Mongol invasions are also defeated in 1284 and 1287.

1260-1368

The dawn of the Yuan (Yüan) dynasty marks the beginning of Mongol rule in China under Kublai Khan. He rules until 1294. Major revolts throughout China help bring the dynasty to an end.

1261

Norway annexes Greenland. The king of Norway agrees to send two supply ships annually to Greenland, and forbids trade with any other country. Over the next two centuries, the European communities in Greenland are largely ignored, and European inhabitants virtually disappear, either through death or through absorption into the native Inuit (Eskimo) culture.

1261-1453

Greek forces capture Constantinople and form a new dynasty, the Palaeologus. The first Byzantine emperor of this family, Michael VIII, rules until 1282.

1263

Haakon IV, king of Norway, is defeated at the Battle of Largs by troops under Scotland's Alexander III. Haakon is forced to surrender the Hebrides Islands and the Isle of Man.

1265

Eleanor de Montfort, sister of England's King Henry III, commands Dover Castle, the Montfort castle, during a revolt of nobility against the king. She pursues her own property claims in France with such obstinacy that an important peace treaty between France and England is delayed for two years.

1270

The Eighth Crusade begins. It ends the same year when French King Louis IX dies.

Philip III (the Bold) becomes king of France after the death of his father, Louis IX (1226). Philip III rules until 1285.

A new dynasty in Ethiopia proclaims legitimate descent from Solomon.

1271

Marco Polo, at age 16, makes his first trip to India and China. He accompanies his father, a Venetian merchant.

The Ninth Crusade, led by Prince Edward of England, ends in a truce with the Muslims in 1272.

1272

Edward I becomes king of England. He rules until 1307.

Ladislas IV becomes king of Hungary. He rules until 1290.

1273

Count Rudolf von Habsburg is named Holy Roman Emperor. He serves until 1291.

1274 and 1281

Mongol attempts to invade Japan fail.

1275

Marco Polo enters the service of Kublai Khan. He serves until 1292.

1277

The English army under Edward I invades Wales and builds castles to fortify its positions.

1285

The Mongols gain political control over Champa and Cambodia and, in 1288, over Vietnam.

Philip IV (the Fair) becomes king of France after the death of his father, Philip III (1270). Philip IV rules until 1314.

1287

Kublai Khan and his Mongol forces invade Burma.

c. 1288-1918

This is the time span generally ascribed to the Ottoman Empire which includes Turkey, parts of western Arabia, Syria, Egypt and parts of northern Africa. Osman I (Othman I) becomes the first sultan and rules until 1326.

1290-1320

This is the time span generally ascribed to the Khalji dynasty that rules Delhi, India.

1291

The "Everlasting League," the beginning of the Swiss Confederation (now Switzerland), is established as a defensive alliance. The cantons of Schwyz, Underwalden and Uri reject Hapsburg rule following the death of Emperor Rudolf I, and unite to form the confederation.

The fall of Acre to the Mamelukes ends Christian rule in the East.

1292

English King Edward I, in an attempt to annex Scotland, grants the Scottish throne to John de Baliol. Baliol returns the crown four years later. Though Scotland is nominally under English control, open rebellion continues into the 1300s.

1295

Marco Polo returns to Italy. His stories of China's wonders start Europeans thinking about exploration.

King Edward I of England summons the Model Parliament, the first truly representative English parliament.

THE WORLD

1296

John de Baliol surrenders the crown of Scotland, which he gained in 1292, to England's Edward I.

1300

A third wave of Malay travelers brings Islam to the Philippines. The calendar, laws and literacy of Islam are introduced.

1300s

Many European countries experience social upheaval as groups of peasants agitate for better conditions, and as members of nobility vie among themselves for power and land.

The city of Mogadishu on the east coast of Africa sees its boom years as a trade center.

1301

Osman I defeats Byzantine forces at Baphaion and begins to unite conquered territories.

1302

Forces of Malik Kafur, a former Hindu slave, conquer southern India.

1306

Jews are expelled from France by King Philip IV, beginning a century of religious persecution by the French. Although Jews are allowed to return in 1315, they are banished again in 1322, allowed to return in 1359 and are expelled yet again in 1394.

After years of open fighting, Scottish rebels are successful in driving British forces out of Scotland. Robert Bruce is crowned king of Scots. In 1314 Robert leads Scottish forces in a successful battle against English troops at Bannockburn. Robert rules Scotland until 1329.

1307

Edward II becomes king of England after the death of his father, Edward I (1272). Edward II rules until 1327.

1308

Henry VI, count of Luxembourg becomes king of Germany and Holy Roman Emperor.

THE WORLD

1308-1437

This is the time span generally ascribed to the house of Luxembourg's rule as monarchs of Germany and as Holy Roman Emperors.

c. 1312

Mansa Musa becomes king of Mali. He rules until 1332.

1313

Berthold Schwartz, a German friar, is credited with the invention of the cannon.

1314

Louis X becomes king of France after the death of his father, Philip IV (the Fair, 1285). Louis X is a weak ruler whose reign is dominated by Charles of Valois, the king's uncle. Louis X rules until 1316.

1315

At the Battle of Morgarten, the army of Leopold of Austria is defeated by Swiss forces. As a result, the prestige of the Hapsburgs is damaged and the Swiss Confederation's power expands. In 1318 a truce is declared between the Swiss Confederation and the Hapsburgs.

A famine hits Europe.

1316

John I, the posthumous infant son of Louis X (1314) is born king of France. He survives for only five days. Philip V, son of Philip IV (1285) and uncle of the infant king, serves as regent during those five days, and becomes king of France upon the child's death. Philip IV is officially recognized as king in 1317 and rules until 1322.

1317

Salic Law, which bars women from succession to the throne, is adopted in France.

1320

Christopher II becomes king of Denmark. He rules until 1326.

1322

Charles IV becomes king of France after the death of his brother, Philip V (1317). Charles IV is the last of the Capetian dynasty, and rules until 1328.

THE WORLD

1323

A treaty between Sweden and Novgorod (Russia) grants eastern Finland to Novgorod. Southern and western Finland remain under Swedish control. Karelia province is ceded to Novgorod. In this way, the Karelian tribe is divided into two kingdoms.

1325

Alfonzo IV becomes king of Portugal after the death of his father, Denis (1279). Alfonzo IV rules until 1357.

1325-1415

This is the time span generally ascribed to the Tughluq (Tughlak) dynasty, rulers of the Delhi sultanate in India. Although the dynasty loses its power in 1398, local rulers continue until 1415.

1326

Orkhan becomes sultan of the Ottoman Empire after the death of his father, Osman I (c. 1288-1918). Orkhan rules until 1362.

Valdemar III becomes king of Denmark after the reign of Christopher II (1320). Valdemar III rules until 1330.

1328

Ivan I gains control over other Russian princes and makes Moscow his capital. Ivan I rules until 1341.

Scottish independence is recognized by English King Edward III in the Treaty of Northampton. Edward III rules from 1327 to 1377. The countries remain separate for almost 400 years.

Philip VI becomes king of France after the death of his cousin, Charles IV (1322). Philip VI rules until 1350.

1328-1589

This is the time span generally ascribed to the House of Valois, which rules France.

1329

The Compact of Pavia creates the separate states of Bavaria and the Palatinate.

1332

Lucerne becomes a member of the Swiss Confederation.

Pre-1500

Pre-1500

c. 1332

The bubonic plague (Black Death) probably originates in India.

1332-1353

The cantons of Zurich, Zug, Bern, Glarus and Luzern join the Swiss Confederation.

1333

With the rise of Yusuf I as *caliph* of Granada, Muslim power reaches its peak in Spain.

Observing that shogunate power is declining, the court of Emperor Godaigo in Kyoto, Japan, begins a rebellion to overthrow the shogunate. The rebels finally succeed, and full power is restored to the emperor.

1335

In Japan, Ashikaga Takauji, leader of the samurai guard, opposes Emperor Godaigo and forces him to flee. Takauji establishes a rival emperor and creates a new shogunate, the Muromachi. This situation of two rival courts, the northern and southern, exists for almost 60 years. The southern court finally surrenders authority.

1337

Portuguese explorers have reached the Canary Islands.

1337-1453

A series of battles between England and France begins when English King Edward III claims the French throne. Although England is successful in the early years, France prevails. Only Calais is under English control at the end of the war. This struggle is now known as the Hundred Years War. One outcome of this fight is that England's monarchy is weakened as its parliament gains strength.

1340

At Fabriano, Italy, the first paper mill in Europe is established.

Valdemar IV becomes king of Denmark. He rules until 1375.

1342

Louis I becomes king of Hungary. He rules until 1382.

1346

In one significant battle of the Hundred Years War, French forces led by King Philip VI are defeated at Crécy by Edward III of England and his army. English longbows prove more successful than the French armed cavalry.

Charles IV, count of Luxembourg, becomes king of Germany and Holy Roman Emperor.

1347-1351

A bubonic plague (Black Death) occurs. In 1349 the Black Death is blamed for destroying almost a third of the population of England. The plague spreads throughout Europe. Estimates are that between 25 and 75 million people worldwide die during this time.

1349

Jews are expelled from Hungary.

1350

John II becomes king of France after the death of his father, Philip VI (1328). John II rules until 1364.

c. 1350

Polynesians, ancestors to the present-day Maoris, migrate to New Zealand.

Swedish provincial laws are collected into a national code of laws during the reign of Magnus Eriksson (1319-1364).

The Madjapahit Empire, a loosely organized group of states, rules Indonesia.

The T'ai kingdom of Ayuthia is founded in Siam (Thailand) by Rama Tibodi, prince of Utong.

1351

Zurich becomes part of the Swiss Confederation. Glarus, Zug and Bern join the Confederation by 1353.

1353

Under the leadership of Mouong Swa chief Fa Ngum, many independent states established by migrating bands of people from China unite into a single Laotian kingdom.

1354

Turkish forces capture the Gallipoli peninsula (now part of Turkey), and the Turks thus become a force in Europe.

1356

At the urging of the German princes, Emperor Charles IV of Luxembourg issues an edict (the Golden Bull) establishing the procedure for the election of German kings. It remains in effect until 1806.

1357

Peter I becomes king of Portugal after the death of his father, Alfonzo IV (1325). Peter I rules until 1367.

1358

After a series of military defeats at Zurich, the Hapsburgs make peace with the Swiss Confederation.

The Hanseatic League is officially organized. A loosely-formed trade league formed in c. 1241, it provides its members, mostly German cities, protection against pirates.

1359

Dmitri Donskoi becomes grand duke of Moscow as Dmitri IV. He rules until 1389.

c. 1362

Murad I becomes ruler of the Ottoman Empire after the death of his father, Orkhan (1326). Murad I rules until 1389.

1364

Charles V (the Wise) becomes king of France after the death of his father, John II (1350). Charles V rules until 1380.

1367

Ferdinand I becomes king of Portugal after the death of his father, Peter I (1357). Ferdinand I rules until 1383.

1368

Ashikaga Yoshimitsu becomes shogun of Japan.

1368-1644

This is the time span generally ascribed to the Ming dynasty that rules in China. It is established by Emperor Taizu (Tai-Tsu), who expels the Mongols. The Ming dragon becomes a symbol of imperial power.

c. 1369

Mongol leader Tamerlane (Timur the Lame) dominates Turkestan from his capital in Samarkand. He began his raids through central Asia with the Russian Mongols (Tartars) of the Golden Horde in the early 1360s. Tamerlane rules until 1405.

1370

A monopoly on trade with Scandinavia is granted to the German cities of the Hanseatic League by the Treaty of Stralsund with Denmark.

King Louis I of Hungary also becomes king of Poland after the reign of his uncle, Casimir II. Louis I rules both regions until his death in 1382.

1371

The reign of the Stuart family begins in Scotland with Robert II. He rules until 1390.

1375

Mamelukes (Mamluks) capture Sis, the capital of Armenia, and thus end Armenian independence.

c. 1375

Songhai begins to rival Mali as the major power in the central Sudan region in Africa.

1376

Olaf III (Håkonsson) becomes king of Denmark. He rules until his death in 1387.

1377

Richard II becomes king of England after the death of his grandfather, Edward III (1328). Richard II rules until 1399.

c. 1377

Catherine of Sienna, a Dominican nun, uses her fame as a mystic to convince Pope Gregory XI to return to Rome from Avignon, France, where he has created a second holy seat. In her many letters to him she urges him to replace priests who are too worldly and to organize a crusade aimed at capturing the Holy Lands from the Turkish Muslims.

Pre-1500

1378

The Great Schism in the Roman Catholic Church divides church loyalties between Avignon and Rome. It ends the hope of a united Europe under the Roman Catholic church, weakens the grip of the church on European thought and custom; and opens the door for the dissent that will set the Reformation in motion. The Schism ends in 1414.

1380

Muslim missionary Karimal Mahdum builds the first mosque in Sulu (southwestern Philippines).

Russian forces under Dmitri IV (Dmitri Donskoi) defeat Mongol troops at Kulikov.

Norway and Iceland submit to Danish rule.

Charles VI becomes king of France after the death of his father, Charles V (1364). Charles VI rules until 1422.

1381

Acute labor and food shortages in England lead to the Peasants' Revolt, led by Wat Tyler. Mobs of angry peasants sack and burn buildings in Canterbury and London. Tyler is killed in a brawl with the mayor of London, and the mob disperses. After this incident, the rebellion is brutally suppressed by royal forces.

Venice gains a military victory over Genoa.

1385

John I, illegitimate son of Ferdinand I (1367), becomes king of Portugal following a popular revolt. John I rules until 1433.

1386-1572

This is the time span generally ascribed to the Jagiello dynasty that rules Poland and Lithuania. It also rules Hungary from 1440 to 1444 and later from 1490 to 1526, and Bohemia from 1471 to 1526.

1387

Margaret (Margrethe) becomes queen of Denmark and Norway after the death of her son, Olaf III (1376). Margaret rules until 1412.

Sigismund, husband of Queen Mary of Hungary, is crowned king of that country. In 1410 he becomes king of Germany. He signs the order in 1417 for the execution of religious reformer John Huss, thus earning the continued hatred of the Czech people. Sigismund becomes king of Bohemia in 1415 and begins a religious war against the Hussites. The pope crowns him Holy Roman Emperor in 1433. Sigismund rules all his domains until his death in 1437.

1388

Shah Ruka, Tamerlane's (c. 1369) more peaceful son, marries Guahar Shad. After Shah Ruka comes to power in c. 1409, the two move the capital of the Mongol Empire from Samarkand to the city of Herat. Here they establish a center of culture and learning. Guahar builds mosques and colleges. Shah Rukh does his best to heal the wounds inflicted on western and central Asia by his father's harsh wars and raids.

1389

Noblemen of Sweden, displeased with the rule of King Albert, offer the Swedish throne to Margaret (Margrethe), queen of Denmark and Norway. She has Albert imprisoned, and rules the three countries until 1412.

A combined army of Serbs, Albanians and Bosnians under Prince Lazar is defeated by Ottoman forces under Murad I at Kosovo (Kossovo). As a result, Serbia is annexed to the Ottoman Empire. Murad I is killed in battle. Bajazet (Beyazid I) becomes the new Ottoman sultan and rules until 1402.

The Turks conquer all of Serbia.

1390

Robert III becomes king of Scotland after the death of his father, Robert II (1371). Robert III rules until 1406.

1392

Korea becomes a vassal state of China.

Ashikaga Yoshimitsu resolves the conflict between the Northern and Southern courts. This is the only major dynastic schism in Japanese history.

1393

The population of China is approximately 60 million.

Bulgaria is absorbed into the Ottoman Empire. It remains under Turkish rule for almost 500 years.

1394

Austria renounces its claims to the Swiss cantons of Luzern, Glarus and Zug.

1396

At Nicopolis, Ottoman sultan Bajazet leads Turkish forces to victory over the Christian army led by Sigismund of Hungary. The second Bulgarian kingdom also is absorbed by the Ottoman Empire. Bajazet rules until 1402.

1397

An agreement called the Union of Kalmar, which would formally unite Sweden, Denmark and Norway, is written up but not signed. Eric of Pomerania is crowned king of Norway, Denmark and Sweden, but his mother Margaret, queen since 1389, continues to rule the three countries until her death in 1412.

1398

Tamerlane and his Mongol forces invade and conquer northern India. They already dominate Persia, Mesopotamia and Afghanistan.

1399

Richard II, king of England, has become increasingly despotic and self-serving during his reign, and has murdered or banished several nobles who oppose him. In this year, remaining nobles unite and force Richard II to abdicate the throne in favor of the duke of Hereford, who becomes Henry IV. He rules until 1413.

1399-1461 and 1470-1471

During these time spans, the House of Lancaster rules England.

Pre-1500

1400

Trade flourishes between Japan and the Philippines.

Le Qui Li takes power in Annam (Vietnam) and founds a new dynasty, which ends in c. 1406 with a Chinese invasion.

c. 1400

A local Welsh revolt against English rule grows into a national rebellion. Rebel leader Owen Glendower (Owain Glyndŵr) essentially rules Wales until 1410, when English forces regain control.

The Middle East and eastern Africa are visited by Chinese trading ships.

1402

Tamerlane and his Mongol forces defeat and capture Ottoman sultan Bajazet (1389).

1405

Zheng He (Cheng Ho) leaves China with more than 300 vessels on a mission to make the seas between China and India safe for merchant trade. His later voyages are for diplomatic purposes.

1406

James I becomes king of Scotland after the death of his father, Robert III (1390). James I rules until 1437.

c. 1406

Chinese armies occupy Annam (Vietnam).

1410

English forces reconquer Wales and force Owen Glendover to surrender control.

1412

Margaret, queen of Norway, Denmark and Sweden, dies. Eric of Pomerania, Margaret's grandnephew and puppet king under her for several years, battles with Swedish nobles, and the three kingdoms enter a period of turmoil.

1413

Muhammad I becomes sultan of the Ottoman Empire after winning over his brothers in a power struggle. Muhammad I rules until 1421.

Henry V becomes king of England after the reign of Henry IV (1399). Henry V rules until 1422.

1414

Parameswara, a prince from Palembang in Sumatra and founder of the kingdom of Malacca, accepts the Muslim faith and helps spread Islam in both Malaya and Sumatra.

The Council of Constance (in western Germany) secures the election of a pope — Martin V — and thus ends the Great Schism in the Roman Catholic Church.

1415

Portuguese forces conquer Ceuta and gain a foothold in Africa.

Bohemian preacher Jan Hus (John Huss) is burned at the stake as a heretic at Constance, Germany. This incident sparks the Hussite Wars between Bohemia and Germany.

King Henry V of England and his army defeat French forces at the Battle of Agincourt.

c. 1418

Portuguese Prince Henry the Navigator establishes a naval exploration base at Sagres on Cape Saint Vincent and begins to sponsor explorations of Africa's coasts.

c. 1419

Portuguese navigators reach the Madeira Islands.

1420

The Treaty of Troyes establishes peace between England and France. King Henry V of England marries Catherine of France's ruling Valois family.

c. 1420

Spanish and French fishermen, mostly Basques, visit the waters around Greenland and the Labrador Sea.

1421

Murad II becomes sultan of the Ottoman Empire after the death of his father, Muhammad I (1413). Murad II rules until 1451.

1422

A document, "Overall Survey of Ocean's Shores," is compiled and published in China.

Charles VII becomes king of France after the death of his father, Charles VI (1380). Charles VII rules until 1461.

1427-1431

A Portuguese fleet under Diogo de Seville reaches and explores the Azores island group, off the coast of Portugal.

1428

The Le dynasty is established in Annam by Le Loi, following the decisive victory of his forces over the Chinese at Hanoi.

The Treaty of Delft brings peace between England and Flanders.

1429

During the Hundred Years War, Joan of Arc, believing that she has been called by God, leads French forces in a victory over English troops at Orléans.

1430

A large cast-iron gun, 16 feet in length, is introduced at Ghent. This new weapon is called "Mad Marjorie."

1431

The Khmer Empire in Indochina collapses.

Joan of Arc is burned at the stake as a witch in Rouen, France. One of the charges against her is that she dressed and acted like a man.

Duarte becomes king of Portugal after the death of his father, John I (1385). Duarte is a brother to Prince Henry the Navigator, and rules until 1438.

1434

Portuguese sailor and explorer João Diaz rounds Africa's Cape Bojador.

Zara Yakob reigns in Ethiopia. He is a warrior leader and spirited reformer. He rules until 1468.

Ladislaus III becomes king of Poland. He rules until his death in 1444.

1435

The Treaty of Arras between King Charles VII of France and Philip (the Good), duke of Burgundy, ends Burgundy's alliance with England.

1436

The Compact of Iglau between the Hussites and the Council of Constance ends the Hussite Wars with the recognition of Holy Roman Emperor Sigismund (1387) as king of Bohemia.

1437

James I (1406) of Scotland is assassinated in his home by a group of nobles led by Sir Robert Graham. James II, son of James I, succeeds to the throne. He rules until 1460.

Albert becomes the first Hapsburg king of Hungary. He rules until 1439.

1438-1745

During this time, each Hapsburg leader rules as both German monarch and Holy Roman Emperor.

1439

The Swiss Confederation officially breaks from the Holy Roman Empire.

1440

Polish King Ladislaus III becomes King Uladislaus I of Hungary. He rules both regions until his death in 1444.

Christopher III becomes king of Denmark. He rules until 1448.

1441

Portuguese forces capture Africans near Cape Blanc, south of Morocco, and sell them into slavery.

1442

The Mali Empire has an established trading system along the Niger River. The Yoruba and Hausa peoples of Nigeria have city-states ruled by royal families with nobility, court systems and militias.

Christopher III, king of Denmark, becomes king of Norway, beginning a period of almost 400 years during which Norway is ruled by Danish kings.

The duchy of Luxembourg falls to the troops of Philip (the Good) of Burgundy.

1444

Ottoman sultan Murad II defeats and kills Ladislaus III, king of Poland and Hungary, at Verna.

Skanderbeg (George Castriota) unites feuding Albanian nobles and declares himself prince of Albania. He rules until his death in 1468.

1445

Portuguese sailor Diniz Diaz sights Cape Verde, on Africa's west coast.

1447

Skanderbeg of Albania and his army defeat Ottoman forces under Murad II. India, Persia and Afghanistan gain their independence as a result of the break-up of Tamerlane's vast empire.

1448

The Ottoman army led by Murad II defeats forces of János Hunyadi at the Battle of Kosovo (Kossovo) in Serbia.

Portuguese forces build a fort at Argvin on the west coast of Africa.

Constantine XI Palaeologus becomes the last Byzantine emperor after the death of his brother, John VIII Palaeologus.

Christian I becomes king of Denmark. Two years later he also becomes king of Norway, and in 1457 takes the throne in Sweden as well. Christian I rules Denmark and Norway until his death in 1481, but retains the Swedish throne only until c. 1464.

1448-1975

This is the time span generally ascribed to the Portuguese Empire, which includes colonies in Africa.

1450

Jack Cade's rebellion in England is caused by high taxation and anger at how the war with France is being conducted.

1451

Bahlol Lodi becomes the first Pathan king of Delhi.

Muhammad II becomes Ottoman sultan after the death of his father, Murad II (1421). Muhammad II rules until 1481.

1452

Ladislav V is chosen king of Hungary. He gains the title of king of Bohemia in 1453. However, John Hunyadi rules as regent in Hungary and George of Podebrad is regent in Bohemia. Ladislav V never actually rules, but he holds these titles until his death in 1457.

1453

The Byzantine (or Eastern Roman) Empire ends when Constantinople falls to the Ottoman Turks.

Jewish merchants and artisans in the Ottoman Empire are given preferential status.

1454

Johann Gutenberg invents a printing process with movable type, at Mainz, Germany.

1455

Cadamosto, a Venetian sailor, explores the Senegal River.

Johann Gutenberg prints the Mazarin Bible. This is called the 42-line Bible because it has 42 lines on each page. It is probable that the actual production carried over into 1456.

1455-1485

The Wars of the Roses, a series of battles between the rival houses of York and Lancaster, begin in England. During these conflicts, Edward IV defeats and kills Richard, earl of Warwick. Edward IV then defeats Margaret, queen consort to Henry VI, and kills Prince Edward of Wales at Tewkesbury, and thus establishes the ascendancy of the House of York.

1456

The verdict given at the trial of Joan of Arc is annulled.

Ottoman forces capture Athens and begin almost 400 years of rule over Greece and the Balkans. János Hunyadi defeats the Turks at Belgrade, thus keeping Hungary free from Ottoman rule for 70 years. Hunyadi dies later this year.

1458

Matthias Corvinus, son of János Hunyadi, is elected king of Hungary. He rules until 1490.

1459

The Bill of Attainer is first used in England. This document enables the government to imprison its subjects, seize their property and put them to death without listing charges or having a trial.

1460

James III becomes king of Scotland after the death of his father, James II (1437). James III rules until 1488.

1461

Louis XI becomes king of France after the death of his father, Charles VII (1422). Louis XI rules until 1483.

1462

Portuguese sailor Pedro de Cintra sights Sierra Leone (Lion Mountains) in western Africa.

Ivan II (the Great) comes to power in Moscow and begins to establish the Russian state. He becomes grand duke in 1472 and rules until 1505.

1464

Sonni Ali becomes ruler of the Songhai Empire. His army captures Timbuktu in 1468 and he rules until 1492.

1467

In Japan, a dispute over succession to the shogunate in the Ashikaga family leads to the Onin War. The country divides in support of the candidates and the ensuing battles in and around Kyoto virtually destroy the city and enable local vassals to control sections of the country. This conflict begins almost a century in Japanese history known as "the age of warring states."

Charles (the Bold) becomes duke of Burgundy.

1468

Ferdinand (the Catholic) becomes King Ferdinand II of Sicily, a domain given him by his father, John II. Ferdinand II rules Sicily until his death in 1516.

Pre-1500

THE WORLD	THE WORLD	THE WORLD	THE WORLD

Pre-1500

1469

Ferdinand II (the Catholic), king of Sicily, marries Isabella I, queen of Castile. In 1474 Ferdinand II inherits Leon. He and Isabella begin to consolidate the Spanish state.

1470

Spain acknowledges Portugal's monopoly on the trade in enslaved Africans.

c. 1470

Portuguese sailors reach the Gulf of Guinea, on Africa's west coast.

1471

Swedish troops under Sten Sture defeat Danish forces under Christian I at the Battle of Brunkeberg, Norway. Sture rules as regent from 1470 to 1497 and again from 1501 to 1503.

1477

Charles the Bold, duke of Burgundy, is defeated and killed by French and Swiss forces at Nancy.

1478

The city of Lang Chang in Laos is taken by the Annamese people.

Ivan the Great's conquest of Novgorod gives Russia access to the sea.

1479

Ferdinand II (the Catholic), king of Sicily, inherits Aragon on the death of his father, John II. Ferdinand II rules Aragon until his death in 1516.

c. 1479

Ferdinand II (the Catholic) and Isabella of Castile jointly establish the Spanish state. They are authorized by Pope Sixtus IV to appoint inquisitors to prosecute heresy; this marks the beginning of the Spanish Inquisition under the control and direction of both state and church. Isabella travels across Spain on horseback helping raise an army to drive out the last of the Islamic Moors. Ferdinand II and Isabella rule Castile and León from 1474 to 1504.

1480

Ivan III, generally regarded as the founder of the modern Russian state, refuses to pay tribute to the Mongols of the Golden Horde. He begins to draw other Russian territories away and establishes a capital at Moscow. Ivan III came to power in 1462, became grand duke of Moscow in 1472, and rules until 1505.

1481

Bajazet II becomes Ottoman sultan after the death of his father, Muhammad II (1451). Bajazet II rules until 1512.

Two additional cantons, Fribourg and Solothurn, become part of the Swiss Confederation.

John I (Hans) becomes king of Denmark after the death of Christian I (1448). John I rules until 1513.

1482

Portuguese forces build Fort Elmina on the Gold Coast of Africa.

A second Treaty of Arras between the Hapsburgs under Archduke Maximilian and France under Louis XI partitions Burgundy.

1483

A map of the world drawn by Ambrosius Macrobius appears in *Commentary on the Dream of Scorpio,* published in Brescia, Italy.

Russians begin to explore Siberia.

Charles VIII becomes king of France after the death of his father, Louis XI (1461). Charles VIII rules until 1498.

Richard III, brother of King Edward IV, usurps the throne of England on his brother's death. Richard III rules until 1485.

c. 1484

Portuguese navigator Diego Cam explores the mouth of the Congo River in Africa.

1485

Henry VII becomes king of England after defeating Richard III (1483) in a York-Lancaster battle for the crown. Henry VII (Lancaster/Tudor) then marries Elizabeth (York). The Hundred Years War ends with this marital union of the two houses. Henry VII rules until 1509. His reign is marked by a policy of suppression of the Irish people.

1485-1683

During this time, the House of Tudor rules England.

1486

Portuguese navigators explore Angola.

In Africa, the kingdom of Benin begins trade with Portugal and Portuguese navigators explore Angola.

The *Malleus Maelficarum* (Hammer of Witches) is written by two Catholic Church inquisitors. Describing the habits and characteristics of witches, it is widely consulted during the obsessive witch-hunts that continue in Europe until 1650. During this time over a million people are put to death; at least 80 percent of those tried and condemned as witches are women.

Portuguese explorer Bartholomeu Diaz (Bartholomew Dias) sails around the Cape of Good Hope and arrives in Mussel (Mossel) Bay, South Africa; this journey opens an eastern sea route to India.

1489

Yasuf Adil Shah, a former slave, becomes the first independent ruler of Bijapur, India.

1490

Uladislaus II becomes king of Hungary. He rules until 1516.

1492

The Moorish kindgom ends when Granada falls to Spanish forces.

The Spanish Inquisition reaches its peak under Tomás de Torquemada. Spanish Jews are given three months to either convert to Christianity or be expelled. Along with the Moors, most Jews leave Spain.

Consistent European exploration of the Americas begins with the expedition of Italian navigator Christopher Columbus and his three-ship fleet (*see* "The Americas, 1492 ").

1493

Pope Alexander VI divides the non-Christian world between Spain and Portugal, granting Spain the larger portion.

The Songhai Empire reaches its height under Askia Muhammad I, who succeeded Sonni Ali (1464). Muhammad I rules until 1528.

Maximilian becomes Holy Roman Emperor. He rules until 1519.

Through the Treaty of Senlis between France and the Holy Roman Emperor, France cedes the Netherlands to Burgundy.

Husain Shah becomes the king of independent Bengal.

Poland's first constitution creates a two-house parliament, presided over by the king.

1494

French forces led by King Charles VIII invade Italy and march into Rome.

After a revolt expels the Medici family from power, Savonarola Girolamo makes Florence an independent republic. His support of Charles VIII's invasion of Italy angers the pope. Girolamo is excommunicated in 1497 and burned as a heretic one year later.

Passage of the Poynings Laws gives the English parliament legal authority over the Irish parliament and makes laws passed in England applicable in Ireland as well.

THE WORLD	THE WORLD	FOR CLASSROOM USE	FOR CLASSROOM USE	

In the Treaty of Tordesillas, signed at Tordesillas, Spain, emissaries of the Portuguese and Spanish crowns "divide" the non-Christian world between the two countries along a line similar to that of the papal bull issued a year earlier. Under that edict, Spain controls all of the Americas and Portugal receives Africa and Asia. The new treaty moves the dividing marker just enough to give Portugal "legal" right to colonize Brazil. Since much of the world is unknown or only partially known to those making this agreement, it comes to carry little weight as exploration by several European countries increases.

1495

King Charles VIII of France is forced to withdraw his troops from Italy by an alliance created to free Italy from foreign control.

Manuel I succeeds to the throne of Portugal. He rules until 1521.

1496

Jews are expelled from Portugal.

1497

Portuguese explorer Vasco da Gama sails around southern Africa's Cape of Good Hope.

The Yorkist revolts of feudal nobles in England are repressed by forces of King Henry VII. This effectively breaks the power of feudalism.

1498

Vasco da Gama reaches Calicut, India. He becomes the first European to use this sea route around Africa's southern tip.

Portuguese explorers make Goa, India, a center for trade and Catholic missionary activity.

Louis XII becomes king of France after the death of his cousin, Charles VIII (1483), who left no male heir. Louis XII rules until 1515.

1499

Swiss forces soundly defeat Maximilian I's imperial troops. The result of this fighting is the Treaty of Basel, which acknowledges the independence of the Swiss Confederation.

The attempt by the Spanish Inquisition to force mass conversion on the remaining Moors causes a major revolt in Granada.

1499-1501

Cesare Borgia, younger son of Pope Alexander VI, conquers the cities of the Romagna, and becomes duke of Romagna in 1501.

Pre-1500

	NATIVE AMERICAN	AFRICAN AMERICAN	ASIAN AMERICAN	EUROPEAN AMERICAN
1500 through **1519**	**c. 1500** Native Americans in the Florida and Mississippi areas attain high artistic skill in wood carvings, ceramics and ornaments of sheet mica. Part of the Ojibwa (Chippewa) tribe migrates from the Atlantic coast to the southern shore of Lake Superior. At about this time, the Ojibwa, Potawatomi, Algonquin and Ottawa become separate tribes. European diseases begin ravaging natives of North America. **1500-1509** Indian tribes on the southern Atlantic coast begin to hear about a strange people with beards and white skin. **1513** On his first voyage to what is now Florida, Spanish explorer Juan Ponce de León explores the coast but is driven away by Calusa natives in war canoes.	**1501** The Spanish monarchy sanctions the introduction of enslaved Africans into the Spanish colonies. **1511** The first enslaved Africans arrive in Hispaniola. **1513** Thirty Africans accompany Vasco Núñez de Balboa on his trip to the Pacific Ocean. **1516** Cardinal Cisneros, regent of Spain, bans the importation of enslaved Africans to Spain's American colonies. **1517** Bishop Bartolomé de Las Casas petitions Spain to allow the importation of 12 enslaved Africans for each household immigrating to America's Spanish colonies. De Las Casas later regrets this plea, and becomes a strong opponent of slavery. **1518** King Charles I of Spain begins granting licenses to import enslaved Africans to the Americas. The first shipload of enslaved Africans directly from Africa arrives in the West Indies. Prior to this time, Africans were brought to Europe first.	Although Chinese seamen have engaged in significant maritime activity from the middle of the seventh century, when Manchus conquer the Chinese people in 1644 and bring the Ming dynasty to an end, a major change in foreign policy occurs. Fearing that Ming loyalists will create a revolutionary force outside the country, officials of the new Qing (Ch'ing) dynasty pass edicts barring emigration. Though many Chinese people, especially from the southeastern provinces of Fujian (Fukien) and Guangdong (Kwangtung), continue to travel back and forth between China and the countries of southeast Asia, where sizeable Chinese colonies flourish, most of the Chinese people are isolated from the West until early in the nineteenth century. Japan's location off the coast of the Asian mainland keeps its inhabitants relatively isolated from outside visitors. The Japanese people withstand attempted invasions by Kublai Khan in the 1200s, and first encounter Europeans when Portuguese traders arrive off the Asian mainland in the early 1500s. European missionaries follow but, fearing the examples seen in other Asian countries where missionaries were soon followed by military forces, the Tokugawa shogunate issues an effective anti-Christian decree. Japan remains isolated until a United States fleet under Commodore (later Admiral) Matthew Perry sails into Tokyo Bay in 1853.	**1506** Norman captain Jean Denys leads an expedition along the North American coast in the vicinity of the Gulf of St. Lawrence, from the Strait of Belle Isle to Bonavista. The voyage is privately financed, and is primarily a fishing expedition. **1507** German cartographer Martin Waldseemüller publishes a map in which the name "America" appears for the first time; the Western Hemisphere is thus named after Italian navigator Amerigo Vespucci. **1513** Juan Ponce de León's group explores the coast of what is now Florida. They explore the Gulf Current and Ponce de León gives the name to the Tortugas islands.

HISPANIC AMERICAN	HISPANIC AMERICAN	FOR CLASSROOM USE	FOR CLASSROOM USE	

1502-1520

Under Moctezuma (Montezuma) II, the Aztec Empire expands southward, conquering most of Oaxaca.

1505

Vincente Yáñez Pinzón, a Spanish navigator who piloted the Niña, one of the ships of the 1492 Columbus expedition, in named governor of San Juan Bautista (Puerto Rico). He sends a herd of pigs and goats to the island as part of a colonization attempt.

1508

Spanish explorer Juan Ponce de León meets with Taino chief Abueybaná in Puerto Rico; they hold the ceremony of "Guiatios" — or Alliance.

Gold mining begins in Puerto Rico.

1508-1519

Caparra, the first Spanish community in Puerto Rico, is established.

1509

Juan Garrido is the first African identified in Puerto Rico. A free man, he arrived with the Ponce De León expedition. Garrido later participates in the colonization of Florida and serves with Spanish explorer Hernàn (Fernando) Cortés in the conquest of Mexico. Also in this year, a few enslaved Africans arrive in Puerto Rico to provide assistance in domestic chores for isolated individuals.

1513

Ponce de León and his expedition sail from Puerto Rico and explore what is now Florida. They ride the Gulf Current, and Ponce de León gives the name to the Tortugas islands.

Alonso Manso, the first bishop to arrive in the Americas, establishes his archbishopry in the city of Puerto Rico.

On the east side of San Juan Bautista (Puerto Rico), a Taino rebellion takes place under the leadership of the Cacique of Vieques, Cacimar.

The Spanish government approves special licenses permitting the trade in enslaved Africans in San Juan Bautista. By 1518 extensive traffic in enslaved Africans takes place on the island.

1514

Juan Ponce de León divides the island of San Juan Bautista into two political/administrative districts: Puerto Rico (today San Juan) and San Germán.

1518

An expedition led by Juan de Grijalva explores the coast of the Yucatán and Mexico.

Hernàn (Fernando) Cortés is commissioned to undertake trade with Mexico, but decides to conquer the country.

Cortés sails from Cuba to the coast of Mexico. He lands near the site of modern-day Veracruz and marches against the Aztecs. By 1521 that empire falls to him.

The Cortés expedition brings Arabian horses from Spain to North America.

Alonso Álvarez de Piñeda explores the west coast of Florida and the Gulf of Mexico. He is the first European to reach the Mississippi River.

1519-1521

The community of Caparra is moved to the city of Puerto Rico (present-day San Juan).

1500

through

1519

THE AMERICAS	THE AMERICAS	THE AMERICAS	THE AMERICAS

1500 through 1519

1500

Portuguese navigator Pedro Álvares Cabral leads an expedition that explores the coast of Brazil.

1500s

In many of Spain's American colonies, Europeans compel Indians to live in villages to facilitate christianization, tribute payment and labor drafts. *Obrajes* (workhouses where Native Americans are forced to produce textiles, pottery and furniture as tribute) are established.

1501

Portuguese explorer Gaspar Corte-Real makes his second trip to Greenland. Harsh winter weather forces him off course, so he also explores Hamilton Inlet (Labrador). According to one legend, Corte-Real inadvertently gives Canada its name by remarking, "Ca, nada," (Here, nothing), after a failed attempt to find a northwest passage to Asia. One of Corte-Real's ships, with the explorer on board, is lost at sea while attempting to return to Portugal.

Italian Amerigo Vespucci and Spaniard Alonso de Ojeda — and in a separate expedition Vincente Yañez Pinzón — explore the coast of Brazil. Each is credited with the early sighting of the Amazon River.

1502

The earliest Portuguese map of North America shows Greenland, the Corte-Real voyages to Labrador and an expedition to Florida antedating Juan Ponce de León's trip of 1513. The map also records the Cabral trip to Brazil in 1500.

Italian explorer Cristoforo Colombo (Christopher Columbus) is the first European to sight the island now called Martinique, inhabited at the time by the Arawak and Carib peoples. He is also credited with being the first European to visit the area that is now Nicaragua.

Moctezuma (Montezuma) II becomes emperor of the Aztecs. At this time, his empire extends from the Caribbean to the Pacific.

1502-1504

On Columbus's fourth voyage to America, many members of his crew are prisoners and criminals. They explore what is now Honduras, Panama and Jamaica. Columbus and his crew spend a year in St. Ann's Bay, Jamaica. Their ships are so worm-eaten they can go no farther, and they must wait a full year before help arrives. This is the longest time Columbus ever spends in any one location in America.

1502-1508

Nicolás de Ovando, the new governor of Hispaniola, entices colonists to migrate from Spain with promises of *encomiendas* (grants of Indian labor). War soon breaks out as the native people resist Spanish attempts to enslave them.

1503

The House of Trade in Seville is founded to regulate and license commerce between Spain and its American colonies, thus initiating a mercantilist economic relationship with America.

The name "Newfoundland" is used in a formal English document. It is the first recorded use of a European name in Canada.

1504

This year marks the beginning of commercial fishing off the Grand Bank south and east of Newfoundland, as the first Norman fishing boat arrives. Soon French vessels are making two trips annually to fill their holds with fish. In the early years of this cycle, the catch — primarily codfish — is cleaned, heavily salted and stacked below deck. The discovery is soon made that cod can be sun-dried, which makes it not only easier to store and transport, but improves the taste as well. Following this discovery, French fishermen begin to build communities along Newfoundland's coast, where they can sun-cure their catch. Portuguese, English and Dutch fleets soon follow. In modern times, the Grand Banks area still has a reputation as the best cod-fishing region in the world.

On Easter, a giant wooden cross is erected in Canada by French sailors from the ship *Espoir*. The cross is engraved with the name of the pope, King Louis XII, Admiral de Graville and the crewmen.

1507

Martin Waldseemüller of Germany is the first mapmaker to call the Western Hemisphere "America," named after Amerigo Vespucci, the Italian navigator who explored the northern and eastern coasts of South America.

1508

Thomas Aubert of Dieppe explores the Gulf of St. Lawrence. He probably brings several natives on his return to Rouen, France.

By this time there are 15,000 Spanish colonists on Hispaniola. A growing shortage of Indian labor leads to slave raids on surrounding islands and coastal Central America.

Spanish explorer Sebastián de Ocampo proves that Cuba is an island by circumnavigating it.

African Juan de Garrido participates in the conquest of Puerto Rico.

1508-1511

Spanish colonists establish communities on Puerto Rico, Jamaica and Cuba. They plant wheat, sugar and tobacco, and use the land to graze pigs and cattle. In 1509 Jamaica's first town, Sevilla Neuva, is built by the Spanish near St. Ann's Bay on the island's north coast.

1509

Diego de Nicuesa leads a fleet of six ships and crew in the exploration of the Caribbean coast of Panama. In 1510 this group establishes a colony at Nombre de Dios (Panama), the site of Columbus's landfall in 1502.

Alonso de Ojeda leads the exploration of the coast of Colombia and founds the city of San Sebastián.

1510

A Spanish colony is established at Nombre de Dios (Panama), and Panama City is founded.

1511

"Brazil" first appears as a place name on a map. The name comes from brazilwood, used as a dye, and found along the country's coasts.

Spanish colonists and forces under Diego de Velázquez de Cuellar begin the colonization of Cuba.

Nicolás de Ovando, Spanish governor of Hispaniola, has royal authorization to bring enslaved Africans to the island, and the first ones arrive.

Dominican priest Antonio de Montesinos argues in a sermon that Hispaniola Indians are humans who have souls, and should not therefore be forced into slavery. He tells the Spanish colonists that they will "go to hell" for their treatment of the Indians.

In Puerto Rico, Taino natives rise up against Spanish colonists for the first time.

Eighteen shipwrecked Spanish adventurers land on the Yucatan coast of Mexico. Two survivors, Jeronimo de Aguilar and Gonzalo de Guerrero, live among the Mayas. Guerrero's marriage to the daughter of Chief Nachan Can is believed to mark the beginning of the intermarriage of European and native people in the Americas.

1512

The Laws of Burgos, Spain, give Spanish colonists the right to enslave American Indians found living on granted lands and regulate the treatment of enslaved people.

Pope Julius II decrees that Indians are descended from Adam and Eve.

Civil war rages in Guatemala between Quiché Indians and the Cakchiquel people, allies of the Aztecs.

Spanish explorer Juan Díaz de Solís sails up the Rio de la Plata in what is now Uruguay. He is the first European to explore this area. He is killed by Indians.

1513

Juan Ponce de León claims Florida for Spain.

THE AMERICAS	THE AMERICAS	FOR CLASSROOM USE	FOR CLASSROOM USE	

Spanish conquistador Vasco Núñez de Balboa, after his mutiny of a ship commanded by explorer Enciso, crosses the isthmus of Panama and reaches the Pacific Ocean, claiming the area for Spain.

Inca leader Huayna Capac establishes Quito (Ecuador) as the northern capital of the Inca Empire.

1514

Pedro Arias Dávila, called Pedrarias, begins to explore the Pacific coast of Central America.

1515

Pérez de la Rua, a Spanish explorer, leads an expedition along the coast of Peru.

A community called Havana is founded in Cuba by Spanish colonists.

1516

Cardinal Francisco Jiménez de Cisneros serves as regent of Castile (Spain) during Ferdinands's absence in Italy. During his regency, Cisneros bans the importation of enslaved Africans to Spanish America.

1517

Francisco Hernández de Córdoba leads an expedition into Florida. These are the first Europeans to sight and explore Yucatán.

More than 50 European ships, from Spain, Portugal, France and England routinely fish the waters off the coast of Newfoundland.

1518

Baron de Léry makes an abortive attempt to establish a French colony at Sable Island off modern-day Canada. Cattle left on the island when the colony fails multiply and provide food for later expeditions.

The first known smallpox outbreak in the Caribbean islands begins. Within 100 years European disease epidemics of smallpox, measles and influenza exterminate more than 90 percent of the indigenous population throughout the Americas.

Spain initiates the *asiento* system, the granting of official licenses to merchants for importation of African people as slaves into the colonies. Over the next 300 years, five million enslaved Africans are brought to the Caribbean, and an equal number die en route. Conditions for enslaved Africans worsen as slavery becomes a permanent rather than a temporary condition, and as the mobility they enjoyed in early colonial times disappears.

Aztec Emperor Moctezuma II learns that foreign men are exploring the coast of Veracruz.

1519

Hernán (Fernando) Cortés and conquistadors with him travel from Cuba to the Mexican mainland, landing at a place they call Veracruz. With the aid of Malinche (Malintzin), an enslaved Aztec woman in their company who serves as interpreter and guide, they gather Indian allies for an assault on the Aztec city of Tenochtitlán. In the city, Cortés speaks with Emperor Moctezuma through Malintzin, but war breaks out and Moctezuma is killed. A smallpox outbreak begins among the Aztecs. Two years later Aztec Emperor Cuauhtemoc surrenders Tenochtitlán — a city broken by the conquistadors and by disease — to Cortés. The Spaniards destroy the Aztec buildings and build the European-style Mexico City.

The community of Havana, Cuba, established by Spanish colonists in 1515, is moved to its new location. One of the best natural harbors in the Western Hemisphere, the port of Havana, gradually becomes the center of Spanish shipping in the Caribbean.

Panama City (Panama) is established by a group of Spanish colonists under the leadership of Pedrarius Dávila.

Balboa (1513) is beheaded in Panama after accusations of treason. His father-in-law, Dávila (1514), is his chief accuser.

1500 through 1519

THE WORLD	THE WORLD	THE WORLD	THE WORLD

1500 through 1519

THE WORLD

Summary

In the early 1500s, the world's leading powers are the Ottoman Turkish Empire under Suleiman the Magnificent, China under the Ming dynasty and the Holy Roman Empire under Charles V. In addition, the Muslim world produces two major powers, the Mogul Empire under Babur and Akbarand Safavid Persia under Ismail Safavi and Abbas I. Conflict erupts between Sunnite Turkey and Shi'ite Persia, while in Europe, Martin Luther's list of church abuses loosens the political hold of the papacy and sets the Protestant Reformation in motion. In Japan, warring clans are conquered by Oda Nobunaga and Toyotomi Hideyoshi, preparing the way for the Tokugawa shogunate. In Africa, Portuguese merchants seek to share the Muslim-controlled gold trade. However, the development of sugar plantations in the Americas shifts Portuguese attention to the profitable trade in enslaved people. As the century ends, the Muslim Empires are beginning to weaken. Power shifts to nations that control the seas, as exploration and foreign trade gain in importance.

Once Europeans find a need to sail to Asia, Portuguese seamen sail east and establish trading colonies around the Indian Ocean. Spanish mariners generally sail west seeking that elusive route to the Spice Islands, and inadvertently come upon the Americas. Although Ferdinand Magellan and his crew reach the Philippines, the length of this route makes it unfeasible for trade.

Several civilizations flourish in Africa before the European intrusion. They include Ghana in the eleventh century; Mali in the fourteenth century; Kongo, Swahili and Monomotapa in the fifteenth century; and Songhai (Songhay), Kanem-Bornu, Bunyoro and Luanda in the sixteenth century. The Mali Empire has a trading system that reaches as far as China. In Hausaland, the concept of a constitutional monarchy predates the Europeans.

THE WORLD

In America, the Aztec, Inca and Maya Empires see a rapid decline through European weapons and diseases.

1500

The Council of Regency is established by the Diet of Augsburg to administer the Holy Roman Empire and subdivide Germany into six regions.

Pope Alexander VI initiates a crusade against the Turks.

Spanish cartographer Juan de la Cosa produces the first world map to include the areas visited by Italian explorer Christoforo Colombo (Christopher Columbus).

Portuguese explorer Pedro Álvares Cabral is the first European to explore the area that is now Brazil. He claims this land for Portugal. Cabral then sails around the Cape of Good Hope and establishes trade colonies on India's west coast.

c. 1500

According to oral tradition, Tutsi cattle farmers begin migrating from the Horn of Africa into the area that is now Rwanda, and gradually subdue the Hutu people.

1501

At the Peace of Trent, French conquests in northern Italy are recognized by Holy Roman Emperor Maximilian I.

Albania again comes under Turkish rule.

A Portuguese colony is established at Cochin (in southwest India) under the leadership of Vasco da Gama.

Portuguese navigator João de Nova sights the islands of Ascension and St. Helena (in the Atlantic Ocean, some 1200 miles west of Africa).

The cantons of Basel and Schaffhausen become part of the Swiss Confederation.

c. 1501-1736

This is the time span generally ascribed to the Safavid dynasty that governs in Persia (Iran).

c. 1502

Ismail I becomes shah of Persia. He rules until 1524.

THE WORLD

1503

Portuguese merchants establish a trading post at Zanzibar in eastern Africa.

Bavaria and Palatinate engage in a war over Bavaria's right of succession.

Svante Sture becomes regent of Sweden. He rules until 1512.

1504

Moguls conquer Afghanistan.

Babur (Baber, Babar) leaves the principality of Ferghana (northern India) and captures Kabul.

Through the Treaty of Lyons, Louis XII cedes Naples to Ferdinand II of Aragon. Louis XII rules France from 1498 to 1515. Ferdinand rules Aragon from 1479 to 1516. He also rules as king of Sicily from 1468 to 1516 and king of Naples from 1504 to 1516.

Oba Esigie assumes leadership of the Benin Empire (now Nigeria).

c. 1504-1821

This is the time span generally ascribed to the Funj Empire in Nubia (modern-day Sudan).

1505

Established Portuguese communities exist on both the east and west coasts of the southern peninsula of Africa.

Portuguese explorer Francisco de Almeida becomes the first European to reach Ceylon (now Sri Lanka).

Portuguese forces led by Francisco de Almeida destroy the African city-state of Kilwa when its leader Ibrahim refuses to pay tribute.

The Diet at Rákos decrees that future kings of Hungary must be native Hungarians.

Vasily III (Vasily Ivanovich) becomes grand duke of Moscow after the death of his father, Ivan III (the Great, 1480). Vasily III rules until 1533.

1505-1545

Affonso comes to power in Africa's Kongo (Congo) kingdom. He rules until 1545.

THE WORLD

1506

Philip I (the Handsome) becomes king and joint ruler of Castile with his wife, Joanna. Philip dies and Joanna's father, Ferdinand II (the Catholic) of Aragon, becomes regent, marries Geremaine de Foix, niece of Louis XII of France and rules Castile until 1516 as Ferdinand V.

Sigismund I becomes king of Poland. He rules until 1548.

1507

The unity of the Holy Roman Empire is recognized by the Diet of Constance.

1508

Pope Julius II formally decrees that the king of Germany will automatically become the Holy Roman emperor.

Forces led by Safavid Shah Ismail I capture Baghdad, making Iraq a Persian province.

In a world map published this year, American lands explored by Giovanni Caboto (John Cabot) are drawn as if connected to Asia.

1509

Jews are persecuted in Germany.

Pope Julius II joins the League of Cambrai (made up of Emperor Maximilian I, Louis XII of France, Ferdinand V of Castile and others). Their combined forces defeat the Venetians at Agnadello (northern Italy).

A Portuguese expedition establishes a community in Sumatra.

Henry, prince of Wales, becomes King Henry VIII of England after the death of his father, Henry VII (1485). Henry VIII rules until 1547.

1509-1515

Portugal's governor of India, Afonso d'Albuquerque, oversees and expands Portugal's trade interests in India. When Portuguese forces take Goa in 1510, Muslims lose their trade monopoly in the region. The seizure of Malacca by Portuguese forces marks the beginning of European colonization of the Malay Peninsula.

Pope Julius II reconciles with Venice and with Aragon, and forms the Holy League to emove French influence from Italy.

1512

Algiers becomes the principal center of Ottoman pirate activity against Christian shipping in the Mediterranean.

Safavids make Shi'ism the state religion in Persia.

A Portuguese expedition led by Antonio d'Abreu explores New Guinea. Portuguese explorers sight Amboina (Amboyna), an island in the Moluccas.

At the Battle of Ravenna (northern Italy), the French army under Gaston de Foix defeats Spanish and papal forces.

A territorial war erupts between Russia and Poland; it continues for 10 years.

Selim I becomes sultan of Turkey after the abdication of his father, Bajazet II (1481). Selim I rules until 1520.

Sten Sture becomes regent of Sweden after the death of his father, Svante Sture (1503). Sten Sture rules until 1520.

By this year the unification of Spain, which began with the marriage of Ferdinand and Isabella and the resultant joining of Aragon and Castile, is completed.

1513

In the Treaty of Mechlin, Maximilian I, Henry VIII, the pope and Ferdinand II of Aragon agree to invade France.

Christian II becomes king of Denmark and Norway after the death of his father, John I. Christian II rules until 1523.

The infant James V becomes king of Scotland after the death of his father, James IV (1488) James V comes of age in 1524 and rules until 1542.

The canton of Appenzell joins the Swiss Confederation.

c. 1513

Portuguese explorer Jorge Alvarez reaches Canton, China.

1514

Silver mines are opened in Yunnan, China.

Selim I, Ottoman sultan, begins a series of conquests by declaring war on Persia. Successful in this campaign, he later takes eastern Anatolia, Kurdistan, Moldavia and Syria. In 1517 he ends the Arab Mameluke dynasty and governs Cairo and Arabia.

1515

Portuguese forces capture Hormuz, on the Persian Gulf.

The Treaty of Vienna creates an alliance between the Hapsburg and the Jagiello (Jagello) families regarding mutual succession.

Francis I becomes king of France after the death of his father-in-law and cousin, Louis XII (1488). Francis I rules until 1547.

In Hungary, marriage agreements are made between the Hapsburg and Jagiello families, with engagements between Louis Jagiello and Maria Hapsburg, and Ferdinand Hapsburg and Anna Jagiello.

1516

Ottoman forces defeat the Mamelukes near Aleppo and annex Syria.

A Jewish ghetto is established in Venice.

Louis II becomes king of both Hungary and Bohemia after the death of his father, Uladislaus II (1490). Louis II rules until 1526.

At age 16, Archduke Charles becomes Charles I, king of Spain after the death of his grandfather, Ferdinand II (the Catholic, 1468). Charles I also inherits the lands of his late father, Philip I of Castile (1506), which include Luxembourg and the Netherlands.

The port city of Macau (Macao, new Heungshan in southeast China) is home to the oldest European community in the Far East. Portuguese merchant seamen use the port as a stopover for their trade with Japan.

1516-1700

During this time, the House of Hapsburg governs Spain.

1517

Martin Luther posts his 95 theses denouncing church abuses on the door of the Palast Church in Wittenberg, thus beginning the Reformation in Germany.

Portugal's king authorizes a trade mission to Canton (China).

Selim's army takes Cairo and Ottoman forces capture Mecca, Arabia.

1518

In an agreement called the Peace of London, Cardinal Thomas Wolsey arranges for England, France, Spain, the Holy Roman Empire and the papacy to join forces against the Ottoman Empire.

In the service of King Charles I of Spain, Portuguese explorer Ferdinand Magellan sets sail from Sanlúcar de Barrameda, Spain, to travel around the world.

Ulrich Zwingli begins the Swiss Reformation by lecturing in Zurich against the Catholic church.

1519

Ferdinand Magellan sets sail from Seville, Spain, for an expedition to the East.

King Charles I of Spain, grandson to Emperor Maximilian (1493) becomes Holy Roman Emperor Charles V. He is forced to issue an edict outlawing Martin Luther and his followers. He attempts to show the German princes, many of them tolerant toward the Reformation, that they must remain in submission to the Holy Roman Empire and the Catholic church. Charles V rules until 1556.

1500

through

1519

NATIVE AMERICAN	NATIVE AMERICAN	AFRICAN AMERICAN	ASIAN AMERICAN
1523 A Spanish expedition to America's southern coast (South Carolina) returns to Spain with a captured American Indian they call Francisco de Chicora. **1524** Giovanni da Verrazano, an Italian navigator sailing for France, visits the Atlantic coast from the Carolinas to Newfoundland. Of the Algonquan Indians of Rhode Island Verrazano writes: "These people are the most beautiful and have the most civil customs we have found on this voyage." Still, his crew kidnap an Indian child and attempt unsuccessfully to abduct a young Indian woman. **1525** Esteban Gomez, a Spanish-Portuguese explorer, travels the coasts of Nova Scotia and Maine. He kidnaps Native Americans as slaves. **1528** The Karankawa Indians of what is now Texas capture Álvar Núñez Cabeza de Vaca and other survivors of a Spanish shipwreck. The captives eventually escape overland to California. **1535-1536** French explorer Jacques Cartier sails to America and visits Indian villages on the St. Lawrence River. During his exploration, Cartier is received by Chief Donnacona of the St. Lawrence River Iroquois. Donnacona and nine other Indians are kidnapped by Cartier and taken to France where they all die before Cartier's return trip to America in 1541. **1537** The bull *Sublimis Deus* of Pope Paul III recognizes that Native Americans are "truly men" with the right to freedom and property.	**1539** Priest Marcos de Niza and the African guide Estevanico, in search of the legendary Seven Cities of Cibola, contact the Zuni tribe of what is now New Mexico. The Zunis kill Estevanico; de Niza returns to Mexico and continues the legend of the existence of rich cities to the north. Spanish governor Hernando de Soto begins his lengthy exploration of the Southeast and Texas; he establishes the first contacts with several Muskogean tribes, and with the powerful Cherokees. De Soto leads the first armed conflict of Europeans against Native Americans, in what is now Alabama. Lectures of Francisco de Vitoria in Spain advocate that Native Americans are free men exempt from slavery.	**1520s** Enslaved Africans are used as laborers in Puerto Rico, Cuba and Mexico. **1526** Spanish colonists led by Lucas Vásquez de Ayllón attempt to build a community in what is now Georgia. They bring along enslaved Africans, considered to be the first in the present-day United States. These Africans flee the colony, however, and make their homes with local Indians. **1527-1536** Álvar Núñez Cabeza de Vaca and Estevanico, the African guide, are credited with being the first to explore the territory that is now Arizona and New Mexico. African scout and explorer Estevanico is later killed by Zuni tribesmen.	Although Chinese seamen have engaged in significant maritime activity from the middle of the seventh century, when Manchus conquer the Chinese people in 1644 and bring the Ming dynasty to an end, a major change in foreign policy occurs. Fearing that Ming loyalists will create a revolutionary force outside the country, officials of the new Qing (Ch'ing) dynasty pass edicts barring emigration. Chinese people, especially from the southeastern provinces of Fujian (Fukien) and Guangdong (Kwangtung), continue to travel back and forth between China and the countries of southeast Asia, where sizeable Chinese colonies flourish. However, most of China is isolated from the West until early in the nineteenth century. Japan's location off the coast of the Asian mainland keeps its inhabitants relatively isolated from outside visitors. The Japanese people withstand attempted invasions by Kublai Khan in the 1200s, and first encounter Europeans when Portuguese traders arrive off the Asian mainland in the early 1500s. European missionaries follow but, fearing the examples seen in other Asian countries where missionaries were soon followed by military forces, the Tokugawa shogunate issues an effective anti-Christian decree. Japan remains a feudal nation until a United States fleet under Commodore (later Admiral) Matthew Perry sails into Tokyo Bay in 1853.

1520

through

1539

EUROPEAN AMERICAN	HISPANIC AMERICAN	HISPANIC AMERICAN	HISPANIC AMERICAN	

EUROPEAN AMERICAN

1527

Observer John Rut counts 14 European fishing vessels in the Bay of St. John, Newfoundland — 11 from Normandy, two from Portugal and one from Brittany.

1528

The first Catholic bishop in the area of the United States arrives in Florida.

HISPANIC AMERICAN

1520

Tribal warriors under the leadership of Cuitlahuac hold off a Spanish attack at present-day Mexico City.

The great Mayan civilization in Mexico, Guatemala, Belize, Honduras and El Salvador comes to an end.

1521

The colony of New Spain is founded, consisting of Spain's holdings in North and Central America and the West Indies. Mexico City becomes the center of colonial rule.

Borinquen's capital city is renamed San Juan, and the island takes the name of the capital — Puerto Rico.

Juan Ponce de León again sails for Florida from Aguada, Puerto Rico, with three large sailing vessels; he is fatally wounded in Florida.

c. 1521

Spanish colonists in Mexico and the native peoples begin intermarrying. The offspring of these marriages are the first *mestizos,* ancestors of today's Mexicans and Mexican Americans.

1523

The first sugar refinery, owned by Tomás de Castellón, is established in Añasco, Puerto Rico.

1525

Esteban Gómez explores the east coast of North America from Florida to Canada.

1526

Lucas Vásquez de Ayllón secures permission from the Spanish crown to colonize Florida. He founds the first European city in the present-day United States, San Miguel de Gualdape. Ayllón's expedition left from Hispaniola with five ships, 89 horses and about 600 people. Among his expedition are Dominican missionaries, enslaved Africans and women. The colony of San Miguel de Gualdape, located on the coast of North Carolina, fails after six months. Allyón's death prompts the colonists to return to Hispaniola.

HISPANIC AMERICAN

1527

A revolt against enslavement takes place on Puerto Rico.

1528

San Germán, Puerto Rico, is attacked by the Corsican French.

Carib and Taino natives in Puerto Rico attack a Franciscan monastery in Aguada.

1528-1536

Pánfilo de Narváez lands in Tampa Bay in 1528 and explores Florida. Alvar Núñez Cabeza de Vaca is the treasurer of the expedition. Narváez dies. Later, Cabeza de Vaca's expedition is shipwrecked on the Gulf coast of Texas. He finds 80 survivors of an earlier shipwreck. Of these two groups, only Lopez de Oviedo and Cabeza de Vaca remain together. They encounter three later shipwreck survivors: African Estevanico and two Spanish adventurers. All are taken prisoner by native tribes, but escape through Texas, across the Rockies to the Gulf of California. Cabeza de Vaca's report to Mexican viceroy Antonio de Mendoza confirms three important facts: 1) several native tribes speak of the Seven Cities of Cibola; 2) there are vast herds of bison; and 3) turquoise is available in the lands they have traveled. Upon his return to Spain, Cabeza de Vaca writes a book called *La Relación* explaining his adventures in Florida and the Southwest. It is probably the first book written by a European about North America.

1530

With Puerto Rico's gold supply exhausted, many colonists move to other parts of the Spanish Empire, for example, Mexico and Peru; others turn to agriculture.

Puerto Rico experiences an economic crisis. The island's economy is based on agriculture, with sugarcane and cattle as principal products.

Puerto Rican Governor Francisco M. Lando orders the island's first census.

HISPANIC AMERICAN

1533

Construction begins on *La Fortaleza* (the Fortress) in Puerto Rico. It is the oldest government residence still in use in the Americas. Construction is completed in 1542.

1537-1544

Puerto Rico is governed through a political system of municipal judges.

1538

A Portuguese slaver — the first in the Caribbean — reaches Puerto Rico.

1539

The first printing press in the Americas is established by Antonio de Mendoza, the first viceroy of Mexico.

De Mendoza authorizes a land expedition northward. Fray Marcos de Niza is appointed to lead the expedition, and he recruits the African Estevanico as his guide. They reach the presumed site of the city of Cibola. Estevanico is killed and Marcos de Niza returns to Mexico with turquoise and tales of riches.

Construction is begun on the castle of San Felipe del Morro, Puerto Rico.

1539-1542

Francisco Vásquez de Coronado and his men reach the Grand Canyon. They march into the area that is now Arizona, New Mexico and western Oklahoma. His forces massacre the Pueblo tribes they encounter.

Hernando de Soto becomes governor of Cuba and La Florida. He sails from Spain to Havana and leaves his wife, Isabel de Bobadilla, as governor of Cuba. Isabel becomes the first woman to govern a territory in the Western Hemisphere. De Soto and his expedition, which includes Cuban-born soldiers, land in Tampa Bay and explore 10 southern states. De Soto reaches the Mississippi River in 1541, and later dies of a fever. The survivors of the expedition sail down the Mississippi River and reach New Spain (Mexico). His expedition spreads diseases throughout the southern United States causing the deaths of thousands of Native Americans.

1520

through

1539

43

THE AMERICAS | THE AMERICAS | THE AMERICAS | THE AMERICAS

1520

Chocolate is brought from Mexico to Spain.

Aztec leader Cuauhtemoc is briefly successful in driving Spanish forces from Tenochtitlán. The Spaniards withdraw to the area of Tlaxcala (between Veracruz and Mexico City).

1520s

Smallpox devastates the over-extended Inca Empire and leads to the death of Emperor Huayna Capac. Civil war breaks out between his two sons.

1521

Francisco de Gordillo explores the American Atlantic coast up to what is now South Carolina.

Portuguese immigrants begin the colonization of Brazil.

Cortés and Indian allies from Tlaxcala join forces against the Aztecs. They retake Tenochtitlán, and the Spaniards destroy the city. One year later, Spanish colonists begin to build Mexico City atop the ruins of the Aztec capital city.

The Church of San Fernando in Tlaxcala is, built this year, is still standing today. It is though to be the oldest church in North America.

1522

There is a slave revolt in Hispaniola.

Spanish conquistadors come in contact with the Inca Empire.

Pascual de Andagoya leads an expedition from Panama into Peru. He goes on to explore to the north, in what is now Colombia.

Spanish forces conquer Guatemala.

1522-1523

Spanish conquistadors led by Gil González de Ávila conquer Nicaragua and establish the colony of New Spain.

1522-1563

Spanish explorations cover much of South and Central America, and cities are established at Guatemala City, Santa Marta, Guadalajara, Cartagena, Lima, Asunción, Bogotá, Santiago and Acapulco.

1523

An expedition under Hernández de Córdoba establishes the cities of Granada and León, both in what is now Nicaragua.

1524

The Council of the Indies is established in Madrid by the Spanish monarchy to administer Spain's American colonies. Viceroys reside in Mexico City (after 1527) and Lima (after 1542) as representatives of Spain.

Spanish explorer Francisco Pizarro leads an expedition from Panama to the Colombian coast.

The last Aztec king, Cuauhtemoc, held prisoner by the conquistadors for about three years, is hanged for treason.

Italian navigator Giovanni da Verrazano explores the Atlantic coast of North America. He gives the name, "Rhode Island," to one of the regions he visits.

1525

Esteban Gómez, of Oporto, Portugal, Magellan's chief pilot, is commissioned by Holy Roman Emperor Charles V to find a northwest passage across North America. He enters the Gulf of St. Lawrence, sights Prince Edward Island and follows the coasts of what are now Nova Scotia and Maine. He sails up the Penobscot River looking for the elusive strait.

Inca Emperor Huayna Capac dies. His sons, Huascar and Atahualpa, divide the empire.

A group led by Spanish explorer Rodrigo de Bastidas establishes a community, Santa Marta, in the region that is now Colombia. De Bastidas forbids exploitation of the native people.

Honduras becomes the first area in Central America to be acknowledged by Spain as a colonial territory.

The cities of Trujillo (now a Honduran port city) and San Salvador are established by Spanish expeditions in Central America.

1525-1545

Mexico City becomes a central departure point for Spanish expeditions to other parts of the Americas. Pedro de Alvarado leads conquistadors in defeating the divided Cakchiquel and Quiché peoples in the region that is now Guatemala. Francisco Vásquez de Coronado and Father Marcos de Niza explore present-day Arizona and New Mexico. Hernando de Soto and Alvar Núñez Cabeza de Vaca explore Florida, the Carolinas, Mississippi and Texas.

1526

The first Dominican monks in Mexico arrive from Spain.

Spanish explorer Lucas Vázquez de Ayllón attempts to establish a colony in present-day North Carolina. After Ayllón's death, the group returns to Hispaniola.

1527

The Spanish captaincy-general of Guatemala is established. It includes the areas that are now Guatemala, Honduras, Nicaragua, Costa Rica and El Salvador. A group of Spanish colonists led by Pedro de Alvarado establishes a community at Santiago de los Caballeros, a site that later becomes Guatemala City.

Pánfilo de Narváez sails from Spain with five ships and a crew of approximately 600 men. He has royal authority to colonize and explore from Florida to Mexico.

After several years of fierce fighting against Spanish conquistadors, the Pipil Indians (in modern-day El Salvador) are conquered by forces under Pedro de Alvarado.

1528

Narváez and 400 survivors of the voyage from Spain arrive at what is now Tampa Bay. Many die of starvation, thirst and exposure. The last 150 make their way to an island in the Gulf of Mexico. Narváez is lost at sea.

1528-1536

An expedition under Alvar Núñez Cabeza de Vaca explores the area that is now the American Southwest, and lives among Indian tribes there.

1529

In Spain, Francisco Pizarro is given the titles of governor and captain-general over Peru, a land not yet conquered by the Spanish.

1530s

Enslaved Africans brought from Spain and fluent in Spanish accompany the conquistadors on their South American expeditions. Many are rewarded for their service with grants of freedom, land and Native American labor. In Peru and Mexico such Hispanicized Africans work as drivers, farmers, miners and artisans.

1531

Culiacán (Mexico) is founded by an expedition under Don Nuño de Guzmán. It becomes the capital of the state of Sinaloa.

A peasant named Juan Diego reports that the Virgin Mary has appeared to him and requested that a shrine be built. Constructed to the Virgin of Guadalupe, the shrine becomes a force for converting the native peoples of the Americas to Catholicism. The Virgin Mary becomes a central, emotional focus for Latin American Catholicism.

1532

Portuguese colonists make their homes at São Vicente, near present day São Paulo, Brazil. Within a year, Brazil's first sugar mill is in operation.

1533-1572

Pizarro leads a Spanish expedition through the Andes to the already crumbling Inca Empire. Conquistadors capture Cuzco in 1533 and establish their capital at Lima in 1535. The fine metalworks of the Incas are looted, and Chief Atahualpa is killed. Other Incas flee to remote mountain regions with their last emperor, Tupac Amaru. Spanish forces conquer the last Inca stronghold in 1572.

1520 through 1539

1534

French explorer Jacques Cartier leads his first expedition to North America, landing at Newfoundland. The group explores the Strait of Belle Isle and travels along the St. Lawrence River. Cartier and his expedition build a small fort on the site of the present-day city of Quebec. Since their location is about two degrees south of the latitude of Paris, Cartier and his men are shocked by the severity of the winter, with heavy snows in mid-November. The group also is ravaged by scurvy until local Native Americans show them a remedy of a tea made with white cedar needles and bark.

1534-1536

The area that is now Argentina is explored by Pedro de Mendoza, under a commission from Emperor Charles V. His expedition establishes a community on the Río de la Plata. The city of Buenos Aires is founded.

Portugal's King John (Joao) III grants 12 large tracts of land in Brazil, called captaincies, on the condition that the recipients colonize their lands at their own expense. Most of these captaincies fail when the land recipients refuse to keep their side of the agreement, but two — São Vicente and Pernambuco — are colonial and commercial successes.

1535

Cartier's expedition sails up the St. Lawrence River, establishing French land claims in Canada.

The *Codex Mendoza,* a compilation of Aztec Indian work and rituals, is compiled by Mexican people and presented to King Charles I of Spain.

1535-1538

Gonzalo Jimenez de Quesada leads conquistadors against the Muisca and Chibcas Indians in the area that is now Venezuela and Colombia. Bogota is founded in 1538. During this time Francisco de Orellana also leads an expedition along the Amazon River.

1536

More than 1,000 Spanish colonists under the leadership of Pedro de Mendoza establish the community of Santa María del Buen Aire (Buenos Aires), in what is now Brazil. However, within three years conflicts with the indigenous people cause the Spaniards to flee, and the community is abandoned. A few survivors establish Asunción, Paraguay, and soon miscegenate with the Guaraní people there. The site of the abandoned community is used later for the establishment of Buenos Aires (1580).

1536-1537

Spaniard Diego de Almagro and forces under his command take the region that is now Chile. After losing much of his army to starvation and thirst while traveling across the desert, de Almagro retreats from the native Araucanian tribe. These Indians are not conquered until 1550.

Despite the rebellions of Manco Capac, the Incas are dominated by the Spanish.

1536-1540

Enslaved Indians from Nicaragua are taken to Peru by Spanish colonists.

1537

The city of Comayagua is established in the area that is now Honduras.

c. 1537

Some Amerindians, probably Caribs, are on the island of Barbados when Portuguese mariners stop there on their way to Brazil.

1538

Flemish cartographer Gerardus Mercator uses the terms America and North America on a map.

Spanish forces under half-brothers Gonzalo and Hernando Pizarro take control of Bolivia.

The first known shipment of enslaved Africans arrives in Brazil. By the 1550s, people from the Dahomey, Yoruba, Hausa and Bantu groups are working sugar plantations in Brazil.

Spanish colonists establish a community, Spanish Town, on the south coast of Jamaica.

1539

The first printing press in the Americas is established in Mexico by Viceroy Antonio de Mendoza.

Marcos de Niza, a Franciscan monk, explores the southwestern part of the United States.

Spanish forces under Pedro de Valdivia battle Araucana indians to the south of Lima, and establish a community at Santiago. An Indian revolt threatens the community, but is finally put down by troops under the military leadership of Inés Suárez, a woman who dons armor and fights while Valdivia is away.

1539-1543

Spanish adventurers explore the areas of Mississippi, New Mexico, Colorado and California.

1520

through

1539

THE WORLD	THE WORLD	THE WORLD	THE WORLD

1520
through
1539

1520

Pope Leo X issues a papal bull excommunicating Martin Luther.

The Anabaptist movement begins in Germany under Thomas Münzer, a Saxon pastor.

Portuguese traders build communities on the China coast.

King Christian II of Denmark and Norway defeats the Swedes at Lake Asunden and is crowned king of Sweden. In an event that comes to be called the Stockholm massacre, he orders the execution of approximately 80 prominent supporters of Sweden's separation from the Union of Kalmar. Christian II rules Sweden until 1521.

Suleiman (the Magnificent) becomes Ottoman sultan after the death of his father, Selim I (1512). He begins four decades of conquest, seizing Hungary, Rhodes and Tripoli. He also tries unsuccessfully to take Austria, makes peace with Persia and destroys the Spanish fleet commanded by the duke of Medina. Suleiman rules until 1566.

1520s

The Kongo (Congo) kingdom in central West Africa becomes Portugal's primary source of enslaved Africans for trade.

1521

Martin Luther, after cross-examination before the Diet of Worms, is banned from the Holy Roman Empire. While imprisoned in Wartburg, he begins his German translation of the Bible.

The Sinhalese kingdom is founded at Avissawella (in present-day Sri Lanka).

Ferdinand Magellan's fleet lands in the Philippines. At first they are welcomed, but Magellan is later slain by chieftain Lapu-lapu, for interference in local wars.

John (Joao) III (the Pious) becomes king of Portugal after the death of his father, Manuel I (1495). John III rules until 1557.

Rebellion in Sweden leaves that country's government in the hands of Gustavus Vasa, a member of the nobility. Vasa proclaims Sweden's separation from the Union of Kalmar, and in 1523 becomes King Gustavus I. He rules until 1560.

1522

Under the command of Sebastian del Cano, one of the ships of the Magellan expedition, the *Victoria,* completes the first circumnavigation of the world.

1523

Portuguese are expelled from China.

Christian II (1513) is deposed in Denmark and Norway and replaced by Frederick of Holstein, who becomes King Frederick I. He rules until 1533.

1523-1654

This is the time span generally ascribed to the Vasa dynasty that rules Sweden.

1524

The Peasants' Revolt takes place in southern Germany under the leadership of radical reformer Thomas Münzer. It is suppressed the following year.

The Diet of Pest, Hungary, decrees that Lutherans are to be burned at the stake.

Reformer Ulrich Zwingli abolishes Catholic mass in Zurich.

Tahmasp I becomes shah of Persia after the death of his father, Ismail I (c. 1502). Tahmasp I rules until 1576.

1525

German and Spanish forces under Holy Roman Emperor Charles V defeat Francis I of France and Swiss troops at Pavia (Italy).

The potato, which probably originated in Chile, is brought to Europe.

1526

Ottoman forces, outnumbering Hungarian troops almost 10 to one, deliver a bloody and crushing defeat to Hungary at the Battle of Mohács. Hungarian King Louis II and most of his army are killed in the fighting; the rest of his troops are captured and slaughtered. This battle marks the beginning of Ottoman domination of Hungary, and splits the country into three regions or factions. One area is held by Austrian Archduke Ferdinand, chosen king of Hungary by members of the nobility; another is held by John Zápolya, chosen king of Hungary by a competing group of nobles; a large region between them is under Ottoman control. John Zápolya rules as John I until 1540. Ferdinand takes the throne in Bohemia, beginning Hapsburg rule over this kingdom.

Babur and his army invade India and defeat Ibrahim Lodi, the last sultan of Delhi, at Panipat to secure Agra and Delhi. Babur becomes the first Mogul emperor of India, and rules until 1530.

1526-1761

This is the time span generally ascribed to the Mogul rule of India.

1527

The Le dynasty, in what is now Vietnam, is overthrown by Mac Dang Dung, who establishes a new dynasty.

The imperial army under Charles V attacks Rome and takes Pope Clement VII prisoner. This event is considered the end of the Renaissance in Italy.

Sweden's King Gustavus I makes Lutheranism the state religion, and lays the foundation for the government's confiscation of all property of the Roman Catholic Church.

Mogul Emperor Babur and his forces defeat the Rajput Confederacy under Rana Sanga of Mewar.

Hernandarius (or Hernando Arias de) Saavedra finds a route from Mexico across the Pacific Ocean to the Molucca (Spice) Islands.

1528

Austrian Anabaptist Balthasar Hubmair is burned at the stake in Vienna for heresy.

The Reformation begins in Scotland.

In Africa, Askia Mohammed I's rule of the Songhai (Songhay) Empire ends.

1529

Turkish forces lay siege to Vienna, but are held off by Austrian forces. An army made up of 3,000 women fights in three regiments during the defense of Vienna against the Ottoman Turks.

Sir Thomas More succeeds Cardinal Wolsey as lord chancellor to England's King Henry VIII. More serves until 1535.

The Treaty of Cambrai ends the war between France and Spain. Also called the Ladies Peace, it is signed by Francis I's mother, Louise of Savoy, and Charles V's aunt, Margaret of Austria.

1530

Humayun (Homayun) becomes Mogul emperor of India after the death of his father, Babur (1526). Humayun rules until 1556.

The Confession of Augsburg, the official creed of the Lutheran church, is signed by the German Protestant princes.

The Reformation comes to Denmark when King Frederick I permits Lutheran preaching.

Sultan Suleiman I (Suleyman) the Magnificent marries his favorite slave, the Russian Harrem, who exerts significant influence over him. This marks the beginning of the so-called "reign of women." For about 150 years, harem women of the Ottoman sultans, in particular their mothers, play active roles in state affairs.

1531

During civil war in Switzerland, the Catholic cantons defeat Protestant Zurich and kill reformer Ulrich Zwingli at the Battle of Kappel.

THE WORLD	THE WORLD	FOR CLASSROOM USE	FOR CLASSROOM USE	

The Schmalkaldic League is formed by the German Protestant princes and representatives of the free cities to counter an earlier threat of Charles V to destroy Lutheranism. Its leaders are Philip of Hesse and John Frederick I of Saxony. The German Reformation spreads because of the league's protection.

The "Great Comet," appears in the sky. It is later named after Edmund Halley who will observe it in 1682 and will accurately predict its future appearance.

1532

The Reformation begins in France as a result of John Calvin's ministry there.

Ottoman forces from central Hungary are unable to subdue Croatia.

1533

Lehna, who took the name Angad, becomes the second guru of the Sikh faith after the death of Nának. Angad holds this position until 1552.

As a child, Ivan IV becomes grand duke of Moscow. He later becomes the first Russian ruler to take the title "czar." Ivan IV rules until 1584.

1533-1612

This is the time span generally ascribed to the Rurik family rule of Russia.

1534

The first Act of Supremacy in England makes King Henry VIII the supreme head of the Church of England, and severs ties with Rome. A later act passes this supremacy on to Elizabeth I.

Christian III becomes king of Denmark after the death of his father, Ferdinand I (1523). Christian III's election as king is delayed because as a Lutheran, he faces strong opposition. German princes loyal to the Roman Catholic Church launch an unsuccessful invasion of Denmark; this prompts Danish nobility to place Christian III on the throne to ensure that their monarch is a Dane. Christian III rules until 1559.

Ignatius Loyola founds the Society of Jesus (the Jesuit Order).

1535

Forces of Holy Roman Emperor Charles V capture Tunis.

Catholic humanist Sir Thomas More refuses to swear to the supremacy of England's King Henry VIII, and is tried for treason and executed.

1536

The Reformation begins in Norway as Luther's teachings take root there.

An act of Parliament declares the authority of the pope void in England. Hundreds of religious houses are dissolved by royal decree.

In England the Act of Union and later legislation abolishes Welsh customary legal codes, and brings Wales under full English control.

The Pilgrimage of Grace, an uprising of Roman Catholics in northern England, is led by Robert Aske. Its repression in 1537 quiets opposition to the government's religious policies.

King Henry VIII of England has his second wife, Anne Boleyn, executed on a charge of adultery.

1536-1546

The Indian and Ottoman Empires form an alliance against Portuguese encroachment.

1537-1542

The Jerusalem wall, which surrounds the Old City, is built by Suleiman (the Magnificent).

1520

through

1539

	NATIVE AMERICAN	AFRICAN AMERICAN	ASIAN AMERICAN	EUROPEAN AMERICAN
1540 **through** **1559**	**1540** Reports from Spanish explorations in the American Southwest mention "Querechos," "Teyas" and "Paducahs," Indian tribes who, unlike the pueblo dwellers, have homes of skin tents and hunt buffalo. **1540-1542** Francisco Vásquez de Coronado explores the Southwest in search of the Seven Cities of Cibola, encountering the Hopi, Apache, Pawnee, Zuni and Wichita tribes. **1550-1559** Pensacola Indians of western Florida resist a Spanish attempt led by Tristan de Luna to establish a colony at what is now Pensacola Bay.	**1540** The second immigrant to make his home in what is now Alabama is an African from Hernando de Soto's expedition. He likes the countryside and lives among the Native Americans there. Africans serve in the New Mexico expedition of Coronado and Hernando de Alarcón. **1543** King Charles I of Spain (who is also Holy Roman Emperor Charles V) gives permission for the importation of enslaved Africans to Spain's American colonies. **1551** Spanish laws prohibit Africans from using Native Americans as servants or slaves. Laws also forbid them to carry any type of weapon.	Although Chinese seamen have engaged in significant maritime activity from the middle of the seventh century, when Manchus conquer the Chinese people in 1644 and bring the Ming dynasty to an end, a major change in foreign policy occurs. Fearing that Ming loyalists will create a revolutionary force outside the country, officials of the new Qing (Ch'ing) dynasty pass edicts barring emigration. Chinese people, especially from the southeastern provinces of Fujian (Fukien) and Guangdong (Kwangtung), continue to travel back and forth between China and the countries of southeast Asia, where sizeable Chinese colonies flourish. However, most of China is isolated from the West until early in the nineteenth century. Japan's location off the coast of the Asian mainland keeps its inhabitants relatively isolated from outside visitors. The Japanese people withstand attempted invasions by Kublai Khan in the 1200s, and first encounter Europeans when Portuguese traders arrive off the Asian mainland in the early 1500s. European missionaries follow but, fearing the examples seen in other Asian countries where missionaries were soon followed by military forces, the Tokugawa shogunate issues an effective anti-Christian decree. Japan remains a feudal nation until a United States fleet under Commodore (later Admiral) Matthew Perry sails into Tokyo Bay in 1853.	**1540** By this year, French vessels dominate the fishing waters off the coast of Newfoundland. The first known European visitors to the area that is now Tennessee are part of a Spanish expedition led by Hernando de Soto. Over the next year, the group follows the Arkansas River into the regions that are now Arkansas and Oklahoma.

HISPANIC AMERICAN				

1540-1542

Coronado leads the first Spanish expedition into the northern borderlands of New Spain. Alarcón, who arrives from Acapulco to support the expedition in 1540, sights the Colorado River as it empties into the Gulf of California.

1542

In their drive to put down the Mixton Rebellion (*see* "The Americas, 1540-1542"), the Spaniards give horses to their Indian allies.

La Fortaleza (The Fortress), begun in Puerto Rico in 1533, is completed this year.

1544-1564

The political-administrative system of the Learned/Lawyer Governors is established in Puerto Rico.

1546

Spanish forces crush a Mayan revolt in the Yucatán.

1550

The mural of San Telmo in the Church of San Jóse in Puerto Rico is painted. It is the oldest surviving church wall mural in America.

1559

Tristán de Luna Arellano becomes governor of La Florida. He brings 500 soldiers, 1,000 colonists and 240 horses to Ochuse, near present-day Pensacola. De Luna also tries unsuccessfully to establish a colony at Santa Elena, in present-day South Carolina. He explores present-day Georgia. The expedition fails and he returns to New Spain (Mexico).

1540

through

1559

	THE AMERICAS	THE AMERICAS	THE AMERICAS	THE AMERICAS
1540 **through** **1559**	**1540** An American Indian guide accompanying Hernando de Soto is the first person baptized in the Americas. The rite is performed by priests who are also part of the de Soto expedition. García López de Cárdenas is the first European to see the Grand Canyon in Arizona. **1540-1542** Francisco Vásquez de Coronado leads an expedition that travels from New Mexico to Arizona, and then north to the area that is now Kansas. San Diego Bay and Alta California are explored by Juan Rodríguez Cabrillo, a Portuguese seaman sailing for Spain. In the Mixton Rebellion, Indians led by Tenamaxtli in what is now west central Mexico revolt against particularly brutal treatment by Spanish authorities under Nuño de Guzmán. **1540-1561** Spaniards led by Pedro de Valdivia conquer Chile. They establish the city of Santiago in 1541. Valdivia is killed in 1554 by the Araucanian Indians led by Lautaro. Lautaro dies in 1557 fighting for Chilean independence. **1540s** Fisheries are established at Tadoussac (Canada), located at the confluence of the Saguenay and St. Lawrence Rivers. **1541** De Soto's group sights and explores the Mississippi River. Jean-Francois de la Rocque de Roberval is appointed first viceroy of Canada, Newfoundland and Labrador. He is authorized to bring convicts to Canada. A group of French people led by Jacques Cartier disembarks near what is now Quebec, Canada. Cartier has orders to set up a permanent colony. The de Soto expedition completes two years of exploration west of the Mississippi River.	Santiago de los Caballeros, in what is now Guatemala, is destroyed by a flood. After the death of Guatemala's governor, Pedro de Alvarado, the council appoints his widow, Beatriz de la Cueva, to serve as governor of the colony. **1541-1542** Francisco de Orellana leads the first European expedition down the Amazon River in Brazil. **1542** After an unsuccessful inland excursion in search of mythical cities of gold, Coronado returns to Mexico. Francisco de Orellana explores the Amazon River. The "New Laws" are established in Spain's American colonies. Bartolomé de Las Casas, a priest and missionary, is mainly responsible for these laws, which require the humanitarian treatment of South American Indians in Spanish possessions. Indians are still subject to forced temporary labor. Conditions worsen for enslaved Africans as they become the primary labor force on the islands. An expedition led by Cabrillo reaches upper California and claims the area for Spain. **1544** Inca ruler Manco Capac II is killed by conquistadors after a bloody, 10-month battle. **1544-1545** Silver deposits are discovered at Potosi, Bolivia, and mines are opened under Spanish control. **1545** Bartolomé de Las Casas begins his office as bishop of Chiapas, Mexico. He is met with some hostility from Spanish colonists, because he seeks equitable treatment for the native peoples. A serious epidemic, possibly typhus, occurs in Cuba and New Spain, resulting in almost 500,000 deaths. After 20 years of fighting, Spanish forces finally establish a community in the Maya-controlled Yucatán.	**1546** Silver deposits are discovered at Zacatecas, Mexico. Two years later, the first mining operation is established there. The mining operation attracts colonists and creates the need for a steady labor supply. Increasingly, Indians are used as rotating labor in the mines. In 1548 a gold rush in this area raises the need for new mining techniques, which are then developed by the native miners. **1548** The forces led by Pedro de la Gasca gain a victory over the troops of Gonzalo Pizarro at the Battle of Xaquixaguane, Peru. **1549** Brazil's government is centralized in Bahia under Tomé de Sousa. The first Jesuit missionaries arrive in that country. The Spanish colony of New Granada (present-day Colombia) is given official recognition and some self-government by King Charles I of Spain (who is also Holy Roman Emperor Charles V). Portuguese communities are established in Bahia, Brazil. **1550s-1580** The semi-nomadic Chichimeca tribes of north central Mexico acquire horses. Their fierceness in battle against Spanish encroachment seriously delays the expansion of Spain's colonial empire in the Americas. **1551-1553** The Spanish monarchy charters universities in Lima and Mexico City. As a result, the National University of Mexico and the University of San Marcos at Lima are founded this year. Different historians credit each with being the oldest university in the Western Hemisphere. **1552** The city of Sonsonate is established in the area that is now El Salvador. **1555** Tobacco is brought to Spain from America for the first time.	Viceroy Andrés Hurtado de Mendoza arrives in Peru with authority from the Spanish crown to organize the colony. Peru becomes the center of Spain's colonial empire in the Americas. French colonists under Vice-Admiral Durand de Villegagnon establish a community on Guanabara Bay (now the site of Rio de Janeiro, Brazil) where a thick stand of valuable brazilwood is located. **1557** Viceroy Mendoza of Peru names his 21-year-old son García Hurtado de Mendoza as the governor of Chile. Caupolicán, an Araucano Indian, rises in revolt against the Spaniards in Chile. He is captured and put to death. **1559** A Spanish colony is established at Pensacola, Florida.

FOR CLASSROOM USE	FOR CLASSROOM USE	FOR CLASSROOM USE	FOR CLASSROOM USE	
				1540 through **1559**
FOR CLASSROOM USE	FOR CLASSROOM USE	FOR CLASSROOM USE	FOR CLASSROOM USE	

THE WORLD	THE WORLD	THE WORLD	THE WORLD

1540

England begins casting cannons.

John II (John Sigismund Zápolya) becomes king of Hungary after the death of his father, John I (Zápolya, 1526). John II rules until 1571.

1541

John Calvin's teachings bring the Reformation to Geneva. In Scotland, John Knox leads the Calvinist movement.

Ottoman forces annex Hungary. The Ottoman Empire controls the city of Buda for almost 150 years.

England's King Henry VIII takes the titles of king of Ireland and head of the Irish church.

The Bible is translated into Swedish. The New Testament is translated into Hungarian.

1542

Portuguese merchants, probably led by Antonio da Mota, enter Japan as the first Europeans.

The Papal Inquisition (different from and less harsh than the Spanish Inquisition) is reintroduced in Europe to combat "heresy," as a result of rising Protestantism.

The infant Mary Stuart becomes Queen of Scots after the death of her father, James V (1513). Her mother, Mary of Guise, rules as regent until 1560.

1543

The Spanish Inquisition begins sentencing Protestant "heretics" to be burned at the stake.

A Portuguese ship drifts ashore on Tanegashima (a small Japanese island). The ship's cargo includes the first guns the Japanese people have seen.

1544

Witch hunts in Denmark result in approximately 50 executions.

1545

Holy Roman Emperor Charles V and Ottoman Sultan Suleiman I agree to a truce at Adrianople (or Edirne), Turkey.

India's first print shop is established.

1545-1563

The Council of Trent is established. This group meets intermittently for the next 18 years to define Catholic doctrine, as well as review the Reformation and papal authority.

1546

In Germany, civil war erupts between Charles V and the Schmalkaldic League.

1547

Charles V and his forces defeat the Schmalkaldic League at Mühlberg, but the Protestant princes keep some of their independence.

Henry II becomes king of France after the death of his father, Francis I (1515). Henry II rules until 1559.

Edward VI becomes king of England after the death of his father, Henry VIII (1509). Edward VI rules until 1553.

Ivan IV (the Terrible) takes the title of czar, and tightens Moscow's dominion over other areas of Russia. Ivan IV rules until 1584.

1548

Ottoman forces occupy Tabriz, Persia.

Sigismund II becomes king of Poland after the death of his father, Sigismund I (1506). Sigismund II rules until 1572.

The New Testament is translated into Finnish by the Bishop of Turku, Mikael Agricola, who is the first to produce the language in writing. Agricola brings Reformation teachings to Finland.

1548-1549

Holy Roman Emperor Charles V coerces the German princes to agree on standards of succession in all northern and southern Netherlands provinces. The Netherlands is then annexed to the Holy Roman Empire as the "Burgundian District."

1549

The first national assembly in Russia is convened by Ivan IV.

Maximilian becomes king of Bohemia. He rules until 1576.

Spanish Jesuit priest Francis Xavier reaches the Japanese island of Kyushu and begins to preach Christianity. This is one of the earliest instances of contact between Japanese and European people.

c. 1549-1654

This is the time span generally ascribed to the Saadi dynasty that rules in Morocco.

1551

Jews suffer persecution in Bavaria.

1551-1581

King Bayinnaung of Toungoo reunites Burma and conquers Siam (Thailand) and Laos.

1552

Russian forces conquer the khanates of Kazan and Astrakhan. The taking of Kazan provides access to Siberia; Astrakhan gives Russia frontage on the Caspian Sea.

After the death of Angad (1533), Kashatri Amãr Dãs becomes guru of the Sikh faith. Amãr Dãs holds this position until 1574.

1553

English merchants arrive in Benin (now Nigeria).

After the death of Edward VI (1547), Lady Jane Grey rules England for less than two weeks. Mary Tudor, daughter of Henry VIII and Catherine of Aragon, takes the throne of England from Lady Jane Grey and restores Roman Catholicism. Her actions against English Protestants earn her the name "Bloody Mary." Mary I rules until 1558.

1555

The Peace of Augsburg is signed by the German princes, in which each prince determines whether his domain will be Catholic or Protestant. Most southern princes remain Catholic, while most northern rulers choose Lutheranism. The Peace of Augsburg brings a temporary halt to religious fighting in the German states.

Japanese pirates attack Hangchow, China.

William I (William of Orange, William the Silent) becomes *stadtholder* (governor or viceroy) of Holland, Zeeland and Utrecht under Philip, son of Charles V. William I rules until 1584.

1555-1556

Mogul authority is restored in northern India under Humayun (Homayun).

c. 1555-1600

Large numbers of English and Scottish Protestants migrate to Ulster, in northern Ireland.

1556

A severe earthquake hits Shaarod, China (Shensi province), causing more than 800,000 deaths.

Charles V surrenders control of the Holy Roman Empire to his brother Ferdinand I. Charles's son Philip takes the throne as King Philip II of Spain, Naples and Sicily and the Hapsburg rule in Europe splits into two branches — Austrian, ruled by Ferdinand I, and Spanish. Philip II reigns as king of Spain until 1598.

Akbar (the Great), son of Humayun (1530), conducts a campaign of conquest and becomes Mogul emperor of India. His forces take Afghanistan, Baluchistan (now eastern Iran and southwestern Pakistan) and northern India. Akbar rules until 1605.

1557

The Livonian War begins as forces from Moscow invade Poland and the Swedes capture Estonia. The fighting continues for 14 years.

Jesuit priests from Portugal enter Ethiopia; they later win favor with Emperor Susneyos, who embraces Roman Catholicism and tries to convert the country by force.

At age three, Sebastian becomes king of Portugal after the death of his grandfather, John (Joao) III. His grandmother and later his uncle serve as regents. Sebastian is declared to be of age in 1568, and rules until 1578.

1540 through 1559

THE WORLD	FOR CLASSROOM USE	FOR CLASSROOM USE	FOR CLASSROOM USE	

The Chinese government agrees to let Portuguese traders establish a community at Macau (Macao, Heungshan), but requires that they pay taxes.

1558

French forces under the Duke of Guise retake the city of Calais from the English, who have held it for 200 years.

Ferdinand I, who has ruled the Holy Roman Empire for two years, is formally crowned. He rules until 1564.

Elizabeth I, daughter of Henry VIII and Anne Boelyn, becomes queen of England after the death of her half-sister, Mary I (1553). Elizabeth I restores Protestantism, and the English Renaissance peaks during her reign. Elizabeth I rules until her death in 1603.

1559

The Acts of Uniformity and Supremacy create a national religion in England, later called Anglicanism, and make England independent of Rome.

The Treaty of Câteau-Cámbresis ends the conflict between France and Spain.

Frederick II becomes king of Denmark and Norway after the death of his father, Christian III (1534). Frederick II rules until 1588.

Emmanuel Philibert, duke of Savoy, regains the lands lost by his father to Francis I (1515) of France and the Swiss. Philibert rules until 1580 as duke of Savoy.

Francis II becomes king of France after the death of his father, Henry II (1547). Francis II, married to Mary, Queen of Scots, rules France until his death in 1560.

Margaret of Parma, half-sister of Philip II, becomes Spain's governor of the Netherlands. She rules until 1567.

1540

through

1559

	NATIVE AMERICAN	AFRICAN AMERICAN	ASIAN AMERICAN	EUROPEAN AMERICAN
1560 **through** **1579**	**c. 1560-1570** The leaders of the Seneca, Cayuga, Onondaga, Oneida and Mohawk tribes, after a period of internal warfare, unite and establish the Iroquois Confederacy (League of the Iroquois, or Five Nations). Some sources indicate the Confederacy was founded with The Great Binding Law of 1390. **1568** Jesuits organize a school in Havana, Cuba, for Native American children brought from Florida. This is the first missionary school for Native North Americans. **1578-1579** English adventurer (Sir) Francis Drake explores the California coast, where he encounters the Coast Miwok, a Penutian tribe of north-central California, who occupy a large part of the region that is now Marin and Sonoma counties.	**1562** An expedition to Hispaniola led by (Sir) John Hawkins, the first English slave trader, sparks English interest in that activity. Hawkins' travels also call attention to Sierra Leone. Hawkins is knighted in 1588 for his service in England's victory over the Spanish Armada. **1565** African farmers and artisans accompany Pedro Menendez de Aviles on the expedition that establishes the community of San Agustín (St. Augustine, Florida). **1573** Professor Bartolomé de Albornoz, of the University of Mexico, writes against the enslavement and sale of Africans.	**1571** Spanish forces defeat the Muslim kingdom around Manila and establish the city as capital of the Philippine colony. **c. 1575-1585** Filipinos begin to arrive in Mexico.	**1562** A group of French Protestants (Huguenots) attempt to colonize near the Florida-South Carolina border. Their presence prompts King Philip II of Spain to increase colonization of this area. **1578-1583** Englishman Sir Humphrey Gilbert obtains a patent from Queen Elizabeth I to explore and colonize in North America. He makes two voyages, but lacks the financial support to establish colonies.

HISPANIC AMERICAN	FOR CLASSROOM USE	FOR CLASSROOM USE	FOR CLASSROOM USE	

1564-1582

The island of Puerto Rico is ruled by a system of military governors.

1565

Five ships, with approximately 500 soldiers, 200 sailors and 100 colonists under the leadership of Pedro Menéndez de Avilés, sail from Spain for America. This expedition establishes San Agustín (St. Augustine, Florida), the oldest continuously occupied European community in the United States. Spanish forces then capture the French community of Fort Caroline, execute Huguenot colonists and rename the community the Fort of San Mateo.

Father Martín Francisco López de Mendoza Grajales becomes the first priest of the first Catholic parish of San Agustín.

1569

French forces attack near San Germán, Puerto Rico.

1570

Construction is begun on Porta Coeli in San Germán, Puerto Rico. It is one of the oldest churches in the Americas.

1570-1600

Spaniards in Chihuahua begin to raid the native peoples to the north, capturing slaves to work the silver mines.

1573

Construction is begun on the Mexico City Cathedral (finished in 1813).

1574

Gaspar Ferreira, a native of Oporto, Portugal, who immigrated to Guadalajara, New Galicia, is condemned by the Mexican Inquisition as a "Lutheran heretic."

1560

through

1579

THE AMERICAS	THE AMERICAS	THE AMERICAS	*FOR CLASSROOM USE*

1560 through 1579

THE AMERICAS

1560

On the island of Hispaniola, the ratio of Africans to Europeans is 15 to one.

1562

Englishman John Hawkins tries to end Portugal's monopoly on the sale of enslaved Africans; he begins to sell slaves in Hispaniola.

1563

The city of Durango, in what is now north central Mexico, is founded by Spanish colonists.

1564

Fort Caroline is built by French Huguenots on the St. Johns River in Florida.

1565

Spanish troops drive the French people out of Florida destroy the Huguenot's Fort Caroline and establish the first permanent European community, San Agustín (St. Augustine), in Florida, founded by Menéndez de Avilés.

After a 10-year war against Tupinambas and other Indian tribes in southern Brazil, Governor Mem de Sà leads a Portuguese expedition in the founding of Rio de Janeiro.

1566

The Jesuit Order founds its first mission in Florida.

1567

Spanish colonists begin to make their homes on the coast of Venezuela.

Mem de Sa's Portuguese soldiers drive the French colonists out and establish the city of Rio de Janeiro, Brazil.

The city of Caracas, Venezuela, is established by a Spanish expedition under Diego de Losada.

1568

A typhoid fever epidemic hits South America, killing over 1 million Indians.

c. 1568

King Sebastian I of Portugal forbids the enslavement of Indians in its American colony of Brazil.

THE AMERICAS

1569

The Inquisition arrives in the Americas to enforce religious orthodoxy. It particularly opposes Indian religions and Judaism.

1570

(Sir) Francis Drake makes his first voyage to the West Indies.

To encourage colonization and to discourage miscegenation, the Spanish monarch forbids married men from travelling to the Americas for more than six months without their wives and families. The edict is ignored.

1570s

In Brazil, missionaries and colonists dispute the fate of Indians. Missionaries seek peaceful converts to the faith, and colonists generally seek slave labor. In 1570 Portugal's King Sebastian I, a devout Catholic, proclaims that Indians other than those taken as prisoners of war may not be enslaved. This continuing dispute encourages the enslavement and sale of African people.

c. 1570s

A cobblestone roadway called Las Cruces Trail is constructed in Panama, to ease transportation of precious metals to the Spain-bound galleons at Portobelo. Portions of the highway can still be found today.

1572

(Sir) Francis Drake leads an attack on Spanish colonies in Central America. He crosses the isthmus of Panama and is credited with being the first Englishman to see the Pacific Ocean. Drake also leads a raid against a Spanish mule train carrying gold out of Peru.

1573

Jesuits attempt to establish a mission in the Chesapeake Bay area, but Indians slaughter the priests.

1574

Spanish explorer Juan Fernández sights the islands off the west coast of South America near Chile that will carry his name.

THE AMERICAS

1576-1578

(Sir) Martin Frobisher, an English explorer, makes three attempts to find a northwest passage through America to Asia. He discovers a bay in Canada that now bears his name, and explores Baffin Island. He kidnaps three Inuit (Eskimos) and takes them back to Europe.

1579

An expedition led by (Sir) Francis Drake explores the territory of upper California (New Albion) and claims it for Queen Elizabeth I.

Silver is discovered in Potosí (Bolivia). By 1650, Potosí is the largest city in South America; the area is the world's leading silver producer until the nineteenth century.

1560

through

1579

THE WORLD	THE WORLD	THE WORLD	THE WORLD
1560	Maximilian II, the son of Ferdinand I, is crowned king of Bohemia. The following year, he also becomes king of Hungary. Maximilian II rules until 1576.	An Ottoman attack on Malta is repelled by the Knights of St. John under Jean de La Valette.	The Diet of Torda (today Turda) in Transylvania (one of three regions of divided Hungary) establishes freedom of religion by allowing preachers to offer their own interpretations of the Bible.

1560

The Puritanism movement begins in England.

The Treaty of Edinburgh removes French troops from Scotland.

At age 10, Charles IX becomes king of France after the death of his brother, Francis II (1559). His mother, Catherine de'Medici, is regent until 1563 and Charles rules until 1574.

Eric XIV becomes king of Sweden after the death of his father, Gustavus I (1523). Eric XIV rules until 1568.

John Knox plays a major role in drawing up the constitution of the newly formed Church of Scotland.

Mary of Guise, regent of Scotland for her daughter, Mary, Queen of Scots, dies. The following year, Mary, Queen of Scots, returns from France and takes the throne in Scotland. Her reign is one of constant turmoil, through romantic intrigues and incessant plotting to gain the throne of England. Mary rules Scotland until 1567, when she is imprisoned in England and forced to abdicate.

1561

Early Calvinists flee persecution in Flanders and make new homes in England.

In France, persecution of Huguenots is suspended by the Edict of Orléans.

After gaining control of Estonia, Sweden attains its objective, at least partially, of limiting Russia's trade in the Baltic area.

1562

An expedition to Hispaniola by (Sir) John Hawkins, the first English slave trader, begins English interest in that activity. Hawkins's travels also bring attention to Sierra Leone.

The massacre of more than 1,000 Huguenots by the Spanish at Vassy marks the beginning of the French Wars of Religion between Catholics and Protestants.

Holy Roman Emperor Ferdinand I enters an eight-year truce with Ottoman Sultan Suleiman I.

Maximilian II, the son of Ferdinand I, is crowned king of Bohemia. The following year, he also becomes king of Hungary. Maximilian II rules until 1576.

1563

Europe suffers an outbreak of the plague.

The Anglican Church is established in England.

The Peace of Ambroise ends the first War of Religion between Protestants and Catholics in France.

Calvinism takes root in the Netherlands.

1564

The Peace of Troyes ends the conflict between England and France.

Russian Czar Ivan IV (the Terrible) battles the *boyers* (nobles) for power.

Spanish King Philip II sends Miguel Lopez de Legazpi to colonize and Christianize the islands that will bear the king's name, Filipinas (the Philippines).

Maximilian II, king of Bohemia and Hungary, becomes Holy Roman Emperor after the death of his father, Ferdinand I (1556, 1558). Maximilian II rules until 1576.

c. 1564

The printing press first appears in Russia.

1565

The Legazpi expedition lands in Cebu and establishes the first Spanish community in the Philippines at this site. Some natives are converted to Christianity. The establishment of this community marks the beginning of the Manila galleon trade.

The Hindu kingdom of Vijayanagar, led by warrior Ramaraja, is defeated at Talikot by an alliance of the Muslim sultans Ahmadnager, Bidar, Bijapur and Golconda. After the fall of the Vijayanagar Empire, Madura, Tanjore and Kancheepuram become independent Hindu states. Golconda remains a Muslim state.

An Ottoman attack on Malta is repelled by the Knights of St. John under Jean de La Valette.

Spain first receives potatoes from Peru.

1566

Reinforcements for Legazpi arrive from Mexico. Legazpi establishes a second community on Panay (Philippines) and defeats Muslims who raided the villages.

Selim II begins his reign as Ottoman sultan following the death of his father, Suleiman I (1520). Selim II rules until 1574.

1567

After a rebellion against Queen Elizabeth I, Irish revolutionary leader Shane O'Neill is slain by men hungry for the bounty on him.

Lord Darnley, husband of Mary Queen of Scots, is assassinated in an explosion near Edinburgh. The Earl of Bothwell is the suspected assassin.

James VI, son of Mary, Queen of Scots (1560), becomes king of Scotland. He also gains the English throne in 1603 as James I, and rules both domains until his death in 1625.

Spanish navigator Alvaro de Mendaña de Neyra, sailing from Peru, discovers what are now the Solomon, Marshall and Ellice Islands.

Protestant uprisings occur in the Spanish Netherlands. Fernando Álvarez de Toledo, the Spanish Duke of Alba (Alva) is quick and harsh when he puts down these revolts.

1568

The Treaty of Longjumeau ends the second War of Religion between Catholics and Protestants in France.

Protestant provinces of the Netherlands revolt against Catholic Spain, causing the Spanish Inquisition to condemn the Dutch as heretics. Culturally, this period is a high point of the Dutch Renaissance.

John III becomes king of Sweden after his brother, Eric XIV (1560), is deposed. John III rules until 1592.

The Diet of Torda (today Turda) in Transylvania (one of three regions of divided Hungary) establishes freedom of religion by allowing preachers to offer their own interpretations of the Bible.

1568-1580

Oda Nobunaga, the son of a *daimyo* (Japanese feudal lord), becomes dictator of central Japan. He restores the shogunate but maintains real power with the assistance of his general, Hideyoshi Toyotomi, and his chief ally, Ieyasu Tokugawa. The triumvirate unifies all of Japan except for sections of the north and west. They weaken the power of the militant Buddhists but allow Jesuit missionaries to preach. Nobunaga rules until his assassination in 1582. Hideyoshi and Ieyasu complete the unification of Japan after Nobunaga's death.

1569

Poland and Lithuania are united under Sigismund II by the Union of Lublin.

The Mercator projection chart is developed by Flemish geographer Gerardus Mercator (Gerhard Kremer) as a device to assist in navigation.

The earls of northern England rise against Queen Elizabeth I and her Protestant rule.

1570

Japan allows foreign trade ships into the port of Nagasaki.

Ivan IV engages in a reign of terror over Novgorod for more than a month because of that city's alleged support of Poland in the Livonian War.

Queen Elizabeth I is excommunicated by Pope Pius V.

(Sir) John Hawkins, probably at the direction of Lord Burghley, offers to assist the king of Spain in uncovering a plot to kill Queen Elizabeth I.

The Peace of Stettin ends a seven-year war between Sweden and Denmark and recognizes Swedish independence.

Idris Aloma becomes leader of the empire of Kanem-Bornu in Africa. He rules until 1603.

THE WORLD

The Pact of Speyer is concluded between John Sigismund Zapolya, prince of Transylvania, and Holy Roman Emperor Maximilian II, a Hapsburg. By its terms, Hungary comes under Hapsburg rule after Zapolya's death.

c. 1570

Portuguese colonists establish communities in Africa around Luanda and in the Zambezi valley.

The first modern world atlas, published by Abraham Ortelius of Antwerp, contains the work of Gerardus Mercator.

1570-1571

Cyprus, annexed by Venice in 1489, is seized by Turkish forces; the island remains under Ottoman rule until 1878.

1570-1617

The African empire of Kanem-Bornu (Lake Chad area) is at the peak of its power.

1571

Stephen (István) Báthory becomes prince of Transylvania.

A Spanish expedition to the Philippines destroys the existing Muslim kingdom under Raja Suleiman. Manila becomes the capital.

The Ottoman fleet is defeated at the Battle of Lepanto by a combined fleet from the Mediterranean sea, led by Don John of Austria. This is one of the last naval battles in which oar-propelled vessels are used as warships.

1572

The St. Bartholomew's Day Massacre occurs in France. Thousands of Huguenots are murdered by Roman Catholics at the wedding festivities of Henry of Navarre (later Henry IV) to Margaret of Valois.

Continued uprisings of Dutch Protestants against Spanish Catholic rule begin to solidify into an organized fight for independence.

THE WORLD

Sigismund II, king of Poland, dies childless. The country experiences three years without a stable sovereign, until the election of Stephen Báthory in 1575.

1573

Emperor Wanli (Wan-Li) of the Ming Dynasty begins his reign in China. Wanli rules until 1620.

The Netherlands city of Haarlem falls to Spanish troops after a seven-month siege.

The Treaty of Constantinople between Venice and the Ottomans stops Turkish attacks on Europe.

Henry of Valois, the duke of Anjou, is elected king of Poland. He rules for one year and leaves to become king of France.

Muhammad Thakurufaan liberates the Maldive Islands from Portuguese rule, and begins the ruling house of Utheemu.

The Ashikaga shogunate, which has ruled parts of Japan since 1336, is ended when Oda Nobunaga (1568-1582) defeats Yoshiake.

1574

Henry of Valois, king of Poland, becomes King Henry III of France after the death of his brother, Charles IX (1560). Henry III rules until 1589.

Rām Dās becomes the fourth guru of the Sikh faith after the death of his father-in-law, Amār Dās (1552). Rām Dās holds this position until 1581.

Murad III becomes Ottoman sultan after the death of his father, Selim II (1566). Murad III rules until 1595.

1575

Portuguese merchants establish a permanent community at Luanda (northwest Angola), on the western coast of Africa, in a vain attempt to locate salt and silver mines; instead, they begin to build the trade in enslaved Africans. Angola supplies most of Brazil's enslaved Africans for the next 250 years.

Stephen (István) Báthory, prince of Transylvania, is elected king of Poland. Báthory rules until 1586.

THE WORLD

1575-1591

During this time, more than 50,000 enslaved Africans are exported to Brazil from Angola.

1576

Akbar captures Bengal in northern India.

Miguel Lopez de Legazpi dies. His successors expand Spanish control over most of Luzon and Visayan islands, in the Philippines.

Ismail II becomes shah of Persia after the death of his father, Tahmasp I (1524). Ismail II rules until 1578.

John of Austria becomes governor of the Netherlands. He holds this office until 1578.

Rudolf II becomes Holy Roman Emperor after the death of his father, Maximilian II (1562, 1564). Rudolf II rules until 1612.

1577

(Sir) Francis Drake leaves England to sail around the world via the Cape Horn route.

John of Austria, in his capacity as governor of the Netherlands, attempts to end the dispute between the Netherlands and Spain. His attempt is rejected by William I (William of Orange, William the Silent), chief spokesman for the Dutch rebels.

1578

King Sebastian (1557) of Portugal is killed at Alcazar as he leads a crusade against the Moors in Morocco. Philip II of Spain gains the crown of Portugal. He rules both domains, plus Naples and Sicily, until 1598.

Alessandro Farnese becomes governor of the Netherlands.

Muhammad Khudabanda becomes shah of Persia after the death of his brother, Ismail II (1576). Muhammad Khudabanda rules until 1587.

THE WORLD

1579

In the League of Arras, the Catholic provinces of the Netherlands, mainly the southern provinces, form a mutual defense union. Very soon after this, the northern provinces form a single political entity through the Union of Utrecht. The Netherlands is effectively split in half, the northern, Protestant half calling itself the United Provinces.

The Portuguese establish a trading station in Bengal.

Protestants are expelled from Bavaria.

1560

through

1579

NATIVE AMERICAN	AFRICAN AMERICAN	ASIAN AMERICAN	EUROPEAN AMERICAN
1581 Pueblo tribesmen of New Mexico kill three Franciscan friars who came to convert them. In their exploration of New Mexico, Spaniards Augustín Rodríguez and Francisco Sánchez Chasmuscado visit Zuni and Piro pueblos. Rodríguez is killed by the Zunis. **1585-1586** Manteo and Wanchese, two Algonquin Indians from North Carolina, are taken to England and eventually serve as interpreters for British colonists. **1587** The first Native American is baptized in the Church of England. **1590-1599** Despite Indian resistance, Juan de Oñate's expedition takes possession of the Pueblo region of New Mexico.	**c. 1582** King Philip II of Spain sends some of his enslaved Africans to work in San Agustín (St. Augustine, Florida).	**1580-1599** Filipino and southeast Asian migrants arrive in Mexico on the Manila galleon.	**1583** The first known Hungarian visitor to America is Stephen Parmenius. A humanist and writer from the city of Buda, he is employed to chronicle English explorer Sir Humphrey Gilbert's colonizing expedition. **1584** (Sir) Walter Raleigh explores and annexes Virginia. **1585-1586** An expedition consisting of seven ships and approximately 100 men under the command of Sir Richard Grenville and Ralph Lane arrives at Roanoke Island, off the coast of North Carolina. Though the colony lasts only one year, it is significant because it is the first English colony in North America. **1586** As part of his warfare against Spanish communities along the Florida coast, Sir Francis Drake destroys St. Agustín. **1587** An English expedition under John White returns to the Roanoke Island colony and finds no survivors. White leaves a new group of colonists on the island and sails for England. Virginia Dare is the first child of English parents to be born in America. **c. 1590** John White again returns to the Roanoke Island colony, but finds no trace of the colonists. Their disappearance remains a mystery. **1597** An act of Parliament in England orders sentences of transportation to the colonies for convicted criminals.

1580

through

1599

HISPANIC AMERICAN	HISPANIC AMERICAN	FOR CLASSROOM USE	FOR CLASSROOM USE	
1580 Ginger becomes a principal crop of Puerto Rico. **1582** Puerto Rico is made a "Capitanía General" (General Captaincy) and the governors of the island are Captain-Generals. A shipment of money is sent to Puerto Rico from the colony of New Spain for development, defense and administration of the military. **1590s** By this time, native tribes of Nuevo León, Mexico — approximately 50 miles south of the present Texas border — have acquired horses. **1593** A contingent of Portuguese soldiers arrives toward the end of the year in San Juan, Puerto Rico. Many of the men bring their wives, others marry on the island. From these men descend the many Puerto Rican families with Portuguese surnames. **1595** Sir Francis Drake fails in his attack on San Juan, Puerto Rico. **1598** A group of Spanish, *mestizo* (people of mixed Indian and European ethnicity) and native Mexicans establish a capital on the Rio Grande. De Oñate and a group of Spanish colonists found a capital city, San Juan de los Caballeros, about 25 miles north of present-day Santa Fe. De Oñate also establishes the colony of San Gabriel del Yunque, known today as San Juan Indian Pueblo in New Mexico. A successful revolt of miners from Tepic (capital of Nayarit) occurs against Spanish colonists in Mexico. George Clifford, the Count of Cumberland, captures San Juan, Puerto Rico, with 4,000 men and holds it for three months.	**1598-1610** Spanish forces and their native Tlaxcaltecos allies invade New Mexico, seize the Tiwa pueblo and others and demand tribute. Many Indians flee north and east to the Navajos and Apaches.			**1580** through **1599**

THE AMERICAS	THE AMERICAS	THE AMERICAS	THE AMERICAS

1580 through 1599

THE AMERICAS

1580

The city of Buenos Aires, Argentina, is permanently established by a group of *mestizo* (people of combined Indian and Spanish ethnicity) from Paraguay, under the direction of Spanish conquistador Juan de Garay.

c. 1580

As Spanish colonists move into the region that is now Paraguay, they find it inhabited by the Guarini Indians.

c. 1580-1600

In the Spanish colonies of America, agriculture begins to replace the taking of tribute as a primary source of wealth. Products include sugar, wheat, wine, olives, silk, tobacco, indigo, cattle and sheep.

c. 1580s-1600

This period marks the rise of racial categories or classes in Spain's American colonies. *Gachupines* (pure blooded Spaniards born in Spain) receive the most desirable political posts. *Creoles* (people of solely European descent born in America) are gaining economic and local political influence. Indians are socially and legally isolated within separate villages and courts. *Mestizos, mulattoes* (people of combined African and European ethnicity), *zambos* (people of combined African and Indian ethnicity) and enslaved Africans face respectively increasingly legal, professional and social restrictions.

1581

Spanish explorers Augustín Rodríguez and Francisco Sánchez Chasmuscado travel in New Mexico.

Juan de Oñate leads 300 colonists to the Rio Grande Valley of New Mexico to establish Franciscan missions. However, colonization is limited by constant opposition from Apaches, Navajo and Comanches. Those colonists who do stay remain in close proximity to missions or presidios (military forts).

1582

Antonio de Espejo discovers silver deposits in Arizona.

The first Jesuit missionaries arrive in Central America.

THE AMERICAS

1582-1583

Sir Humphrey Gilbert, half-brother of Sir Walter Raleigh, is credited with founding the first English colony in Newfoundland.

1584

The first printing press is established in Peru.

Queen Elizabeth I grants Sir Walter Raleigh the first patent to lands including the present state of Tennessee.

1585

On the orders of Queen Elizabeth I, Sir Francis Drake leads attacks on Spanish communities in the West Indies.

Thomas Cavendish leaves Plymouth on a voyage of circumnavigation; he returns in 1588.

1585-1586

An expedition consisting of seven ships and approximately 100 men under the command of Sir Richard Grenville and Ralph Lane arrives at Roanoke Island, off the coast of North Carolina. Though the colony lasts only one year, it is significant because it is the first English colony in North America.

1585-1587

Englishman John Davis makes three attempts to find a northwest passage across Canada's arctic lands. On one of these trips, he discovers the strait between Canada and Greenland that bears his name.

1585-1616

Colonization in northern coastal Brazil by French, Dutch and English groups motivates Portuguese groups to begin northward "defensive colonizing," with communities at Filipéia (modern day João Pessoa) in 1585; Natal in 1599; Fortaleza in 1611; São Luís in 1614; and Belém in 1616.

1587

An English expedition under John White returns to the Roanoke Island colony and finds no survivors. White leaves a new group of colonists on the island and sails for England.

THE AMERICAS

1590

Portuguese explorer Gaspar Castano de Sosa explores the American Southwest and the Pecos River for Spain.

c. 1590

John White again returns to Roanoke Island and again frinds the colony abandoned, with no survivors. Their disappearance remains a mystery.

1591

The Portuguese government closes Brazil to all non-Portuguese immigrants except enslaved Africans to work on its plantations.

1592

Juan de Fuca explores the area that is now British Columbia.

1594

The *Audiencia* (High Court) in Santo Domingo declares that "more than half the people on the island are Portuguese."

A Spanish colonial report from this year states that the Central American community of Sonsonate has more than 300 inhabitants and is a major cocoa producer.

1596-1597

Dutch navigator Willem Barentz makes three arctic trips in search of a northwest passage. His charts and descriptions are the most accurate of the time.

1597

The city of Portobelo (Panama) is established.

1598

French King Henry IV commissions the Marquis de la Roche to establish a colony in North America. La Roche organizes 200 men and 50 women, many from French prisons, to colonize Sable Island, a small island off Nova Scotia's coast. Five years later, in 1603, 11 survivors are rescued and returned to France.

De Oñate establishes a colony at San Gabriel (present-day Chamita, New Santa Fe).

THE AMERICAS

1599

Vicente, Cristóbal, Francisco and Juan, the Zaldívar family, explore the New Mexico region for Spain.

FOR CLASSROOM USE	FOR CLASSROOM USE	FOR CLASSROOM USE	FOR CLASSROOM USE	
				1580 through **1599**
FOR CLASSROOM USE	FOR CLASSROOM USE	FOR CLASSROOM USE	FOR CLASSROOM USE	

1580
through
1599

1580

The potato is introduced in Ireland.

Spain's army invades Portugal, bringing the country under Spanish rule until 1640. Philip I (King Philip II of Spain) becomes king of Portugal. Philip I rules until 1598.

(Sir) Francis Drake becomes the first Englishman to circumnavigate the earth. He is knighted by Queen Elizabeth I upon his return.

Charles Emmanuel I becomes duke of Savoy after the death of his father, Emmanuel Philibert (1559). Charles Emmanuel rules until 1630.

Chinese porcelain arrives in Europe.

1580-1640

Brazil is taken from Portugal by Spanish forces, but several powers continue to struggle for control of this area.

1580s

Maravi warriors sweep up the east coast of Africa in an apparent challenge to Portuguese dominance.

1581

The Dutch proclaim their independence from Spain.

Russian people begin to migrate into Siberia.

Forces under Mogul Emperor Akbar conquer Afghanistan.

Arjan Dev, after the death of Rām Dās (1574), becomes the fifth guru of the Sikh faith. Arjan Dev holds this position until 1606.

1582

Russia begins the conquest of Siberia.

Russia makes peace with Poland and Sweden, releases claims to Livonia and Estonia to Poland and loses its access to the Baltic Sea.

The Gregorian calendar is adopted in the Papal States, Spain, Portugal, France, the Netherlands and Scandinavia. England does not accept the Gregorian calendar until 1752 and Russia does not until 1918.

A Jesuit mission is founded in China.

Japanese leader Oda Nobunaga (1568-1582) is assassinated by one of his generals. The unification of Japan is completed under Hideyoshi and Ieyasu.

1583

English merchants begin to travel to India and the Persian Gulf.

1584

A Dutch trading post is established at Archangel, Russia.

William I (William of Orange, William the Silent, 1555), *stadtholder* of the United Provinces (Netherlands), is assassinated by Balthazar Gérard at the request of King Philip II of Spain who considers William I a traitor.

Fyodor I becomes czar of Russia after the death of his father, Ivan IV (the Terrible, 1547). Fyodor I rules until 1598.

Maurice of Nassau becomes *stadtholder* of the Netherlands after the death of his father, William the Silent (1555). He also becomes *stadtholder* of Utrecht in 1588, and rules both regions until 1625.

1585

Hideyoshi Toyotomi becomes shogun in Japan. He rose from a peasant background to a position of respect, and becomes one of Japan's most admired leaders.

1586

Mary, Queen of Scots is implicated in the Babington Plot to kill Queen Elizabeth I. Mary is executed in 1587.

1587

Mogul forces under Akbar annex Kashmir.

Sir Francis Drake and his men destroy the Spanish fleet at Cadiz.

Hideyoshi Toyotomi banishes all missionaries from Japan but allows merchants and traders to stay.

Abbas I (the Great) becomes shah of Persia after the death of Muhammad Khudabanda (1578). Abbas I rules until c. 1629.

Sigismund III becomes king of Poland after the death of Stephen Báthory (1575). Sigismund III rules until 1632.

1588

King Philip II of Spain orders the launching of the Spanish armada in an attempted invasion of England. Queen Elizabeth I gives a stirring speech to her troops at Tilsbury, England, as they prepare for the threatened invasion by the Spanish. More than 100 ships and 30,000 men strong, the armada, led by Alonso Pérez de Guzmán, the duke of Medina Sedonia, is attacked by English warships and fireships under the command of Lord Charles Howard. Spain's armada is badly crippled in the fighting. This battle marks England's rise as a naval power. English slave trader John Hawkins is knighted for his service in this victory.

Christian IV becomes king of Denmark and Norway after the death of his father, Frederick II (1559). Christian IV rules until 1648.

The Guinea Company is founded and obtains a monopoly from the English Crown to trade in enslaved Africans.

1589

Dom João da Gama, who serves as captain of the Portuguese outpost of Malacca, sails via Macao for Mexico across the Pacific Ocean. This is the first recorded voyage across the Pacific by a Portuguese ship.

Henry of Navarre, a Protestant leader, becomes King Henry IV of France after his father, Henry III, is stabbed to death. Henry IV rules until 1610.

1589-1792; 1814-1848

The House of Bourbon rules France during these time spans.

1590

Shah Abbas I of Persia and Murad III of Turkey end hostilities.

Hideyoshi Toyotomi unifies Japan, and encourages foreign trade.

Akbar's Modul forces conquer Orissa, India.

Portuguese mariners explore the island of Taiwan and give it the name Formosa.

King Henry IV of France, a Huguenot, commands an attack on the Catholic League's stronghold of Paris. Though the attack fails, Henry IV is able to win over the Catholic leaders by eventually rejecting Protestantism with the statement that "Paris is well worth a mass."

The first print shop is established in Japan.

1590s

African tribes attack Portuguese forts at Sena and Tete, in eastern Africa.

1591

James Lancaster's expedition sets sail via the Cape of Good Hope and becomes the first English fleet to reach the East Indies.

Moroccan fighters rout forces of the Songhai (Songhay) Empire in two battles: Tondibi, near the capital city of Gao, and Banba, near Timbuktu.

1592

A Portuguese colony is established at Mombasa, east Africa.

Akbar's Mogul forces conquer the Sind, India.

Trinh Tong reunites most of Vietnam. The Le dynasty is restored in Annam, but a power struggle ensues.

Japanese forces invade Korea. Korean Admiral Yi Sung Si invents and uses ironclad warships, and the Japanese attack is thwarted. Japan continues to press the war for six years.

King Sigismund III (1587) of Poland becomes king of Sweden after the death of his father, John III (1568). His staunch support of Catholicism and extended absences create strong Swedish opposition. Sigismund III unites the houses of Vasa and Jagiello and rules until 1599.

James Lancaster sails around the Malay peninsula.

John Davis sights the Falkland Islands.

THE WORLD	THE WORLD	FOR CLASSROOM USE	FOR CLASSROOM USE	

1593

The Khmer capital of Lovek is overrun by Thai forces, and Cambodia becomes a vassal state.

Chinese troops cross the Yalu River into Korea and force the Japanese to leave Seoul.

1594

King Henry IV of France is accepted in Paris and is crowned at Chartres.

The Portuguese trade monopoly in India is stopped by the English.

1595

Dutch seamen establish trading posts in Africa, on the eastern coast of Guinea.

Álvaro de Mendaña sights Marquesas and Santa Cruz Islands.

King Henry IV of France declares war on Spain in retaliation for Spanish interference in France's Wars of Religion.

Peasants begin a revolt in upper Austria.

Dutch explorer Cornelis de Houtman reaches Bantam in Java.

Muhammad III becomes Ottoman sultan after the death of his father, Murad III (1574). Muhammad III rules until 1603.

Irish rebel leader Hugh O'Neill fights for political and religious freedom from England.

1596

Dutch traders establish a post at Palembang in Sumatra.

English forces capture Cadiz (southwestern Spain).

1597

The second Spanish Armada sent by Philip II against England is destroyed by storms.

The Dutch establish Batavia in Java and begin trading with Bali.

Serfdom is established in Russia. Peasants may not change residences or masters.

1598

Dutch colonists build communities on the island of Mauritius (named for Maurice of Nassau) in the Indian Ocean and maintain control of it for more than 100 years.

Korea and China are severely damaged by their six-year war with Japan.

In the Edict of Nantes France's King Henry IV grants religious freedom to the Huguenots.

The Peace of Vervins ends the war between France and Spain.

Russia's national assembly formally elects Boris Godunov as czar after the death of Fyodor I (1584). Godunov rules until 1605.

Philip III becomes king of Spain, Naples and Sicily after the death of his father, Philip II (1556, 1580). He rules until 1621. Philip III also rules Portugal as Philip II until 1621.

Dutch navigator Oliver Van Noort begins his circumnavigation of the globe.

The Tokugawa shogunate begins in Japan.

1599

The Earl of Essex, who is also Lord Lieutenant of Ireland, fails to stop the rebellion started five years earlier and signs a truce with Irish rebel Lord Tyrone. On his return to England, he is banished by Queen Elizabeth I.

Charles (Karl) IX deposes his nephew, Sigismund III (1592), as king of Sweden. Charles IX refuses to formally take the crown, however, until Sigismund's brother, John, renounces it in 1604. Charles IX rules until 1611. Sigismund III continues to rule Poland until 1632.

1580

through

1599

NATIVE AMERICAN	AFRICAN AMERICAN	ASIAN AMERICAN	EUROPEAN AMERICAN
1600 Franciscans from Spain establish missions in Hopi areas of what is now Arizona. **c. 1600** In the area that is now North Dakota, several Native American groups begin migrating to new homes. The Cheyenne move to the Sheyenne River valley; the Hidatsa migrate westward to the Missouri River; and the Sioux migrate out of the Minnesota woodlands onto the Plains. **c. 1600-1770** Use of horses spreads from Indian tribes in Mexico through the Southwest into America's Great Plains. **1608** A visitor to Durango, Mexico, reports that Native Americans there all have horses. **1609** Samuel de Champlain, with a party that includes two Frenchmen and about 60 Native Americans, heads down the St. Lawrence River. Near Ticonderoga, his group encounters approximately 200 Iroquois. The Iroquois, who have never seen firearms, flee. French forces accompany a war party of Wyandots (Hurons) and Algonquins to Lake Champlain for an attack against the Mohawks. The Wyandot and Algonquin party is successful, and several Mohawk leaders are killed.	**1600** Records indicate there are approximately 900,000 enslaved Africans in Latin America. **1602** By Spanish law, *mulattos* (people of combined African and European ethnicity), convicts and "idle" Africans may be shipped to Latin America and forced to work in the mines there.	Although Chinese seamen have engaged in significant maritime activity from the middle of the seventh century, when Manchus conquer the Chinese people in 1644 and bring the Ming dynasty to an end, a major change in foreign policy occurs. Fearing that Ming loyalists will create a revolutionary force outside the country, officials of the new Qing (Ch'ing) dynasty pass edicts barring emigration. Many Chinese people, especially from the southeastern provinces of Fujian (Fukien) and Guangdong (Kwangtung), continue to travel back and forth between China and the countries of southeast Asia, where sizeable Chinese colonies flourish. However, most of the Chinese people are isolated from the West until early in the nineteenth century. Japan's location off the coast of the Asian mainland keeps its inhabitants relatively isolated from outside visitors. The Japanese people withstand attempted invasions by Kublai Khan in the 1200s, and first encounter Europeans when Portuguese traders arrive off the Asian mainland in the early 1500s. European missionaries follow but, fearing the examples seen in other Asian countries where missionaries were soon followed by military forces, the Tokugawa shogunate issues an effective anti-Christian decree. Japan remains isolated until a United States fleet under Commodore (later Admiral) Matthew Perry sails into Tokyo Bay in 1853.	**1607** The first permanent English community in North America is established by the London Company under Captain Christopher Newport at Jamestown (Virginia). Three German colonists, the earliest known in the Americas, are part of the Jamestown colony. **1608** Skilled Polish and German glass makers arrive in Jamestown, Virginia, to establish the first manufacturing operation in the colonies. Polish immigrants to the colony later demand — and receive — the right to vote. **1609** John Smith leaves the Jamestown colony. Lord Thomas De la Warr heads the colony, creating unrest. The colonists also experience a food shortage known as the "starving-time."

1600

through

1609

HISPANIC AMERICAN	FOR CLASSROOM USE	FOR CLASSROOM USE	FOR CLASSROOM USE	

1600

Seven Franciscan missionaries and 70 colonists migrate to San Gabriel in New Mexico from Mexico City.

Governor De Oñate of New Mexico moves colonists from San Juan de los Caballeros to San Gabriel on the Rio Grande.

c. 1600

Spanish colonists introduce sheep into the southwestern area of what is now the United States. Native Americans there learn about wool and the loom.

1600s

The majority of colonists in Puerto Rico during this time come from the Canary Islands; near the turn of the century, some also come from Portugal.

1602

Sebastián Vizcaíno explores the California coast, and gives San Diego its name.

1608

The bridge of San Antonio and the fort at Cañuelo are erected in Puerto Rico.

1609

The city of Santa Fe is established by an expedition under Pedro de Peralta, governor of New Mexico. Santa Fe is the third permanent European community in what is now the United States, and it is the oldest state capital.

1600

through

1609

THE AMERICAS	THE AMERICAS	THE AMERICAS	THE WORLD
1600 A fortified trading post is built at Tadoussac (northeast of the modern-day city of Quebec) by French merchants François Gravé du Pont and Pierre Chauvin de Tonnetuit. A few colonists are left at Tadoussac when the fleet returns to France with a load of furs. Only five survive the winter; they are rescued in the spring of 1601. Juan de Oñate, the first governor of New Mexico, moves colonists from San Juan de los Caballeros to San Gabriel on the Rio Grande. Oñate serves as governor until 1607. Portuguese navigator Pedro Teixeira reaches the coast of what is now California north of Cape Mendocino. **c. 1600** Brazil and Angola, both Portuguese colonies, develop a strong trade alliance; in fact, in the mid-1660s, two governors of Angola are Brazilians. A strong triangular trade develops with European manufactured goods going to Africa, Africans being sold into slavery in Brazil, and Brazil supplying sugar, tobacco, beans and flour to Europe. **1602** English explorer Bartholomew Gosnold sails the coast of what is now Massachusetts and gives Cape Cod and Martha's Vineyard their names. Portuguese navigator Pedro Fernandes de Quieros sails from Callao, Peru, crosses the Pacific Ocean, explores Tahiti and the New Hebrides and eventually sails to Mexico. **1603** French explorers Samuel de Champlain and François Gravé du Pont travel to the Indian village of Stadacona (site of present-day Toronto) and find it abandoned. Later this year, de Champlain travels to Hochelaga (now Montreal) and likewise finds no trace of the village. Gravé du Pont and Champlain return to Tadoussac with two ships. De Champlain explores the Saguenay and St. Lawrence Rivers.	The Sieur de Roberval returns to Sable Island (off what is now Nova Scotia) to rescue the 11 survivors of the colony he established in 1598. Martin de Aguilar explores the coast of Alaska. Pierre du Gua, Sieur de Monts, a Huguenot, is commissioned as lieutenant-governor of Canada, and receives a 10-year fur trade monopoly in Acadia (Nova Scotia, New Brunswick and eastern Maine) and a commission to colonize this area. **1604** French colonists led by de Gua and de Champlain arrive in Acadia, and winter at St. Croix Island. Nearly half of de Champlain's expedition dies of scurvy. The community is moved to Port Royal in 1605. This is the first permanent European community in Canada. **1604-1626** European colonists, first English, then Dutch and French establish communities on the South American coast in the area that later becomes the Guianas. **1605-1606** George Weymouth explores the northeastern American coast (Maine) for England. He trades for furs with the Native Americans there. **1606** A Virginia charter is granted to the Plymouth Company and the London Company by England's King James I to establish separate colonies in America. The French North American colonies experience a relatively mild winter. De Champlain remarks that "only a quarter of the people died." **1607** The first permanent English colony in North America (named for King James I) is established by the London Company under Captain Christopher Newport at Jamestown (Virginia). More than half of the colonists die during the first few months due to famine, disease and poor leadership.	When Captain John Smith becomes president of the Jamestown colony's governing council, he emphasizes agriculture. Conditions improve under his leadership. Sir Ferdinando Gorges, a key figure in the founding of the Plymouth Company in 1606, is a chief sponsor of the Sagadahoc community at the Kennebec River, Maine. The colony fails in 1608. Pedro de Peralta becomes governor of New Mexico. He serves until 1614. **1607-1776** This is the time span generally ascribed to the British colonial empire in North America. Women generally are not legally allowed to enter professions or businesses. In actual fact they do so because of critical labor shortage. A few women become practicing doctors, nurses, midwives, lawyers, etc. Training is through apprenticeship and study. **1608** A French expedition led by de Champlain builds a fortified trading center at Quebec. Captain John Smith journeys from Virginia up the Susquehanna River, visiting the Susquehannock Indians. **1608-1759** This is the time span generally ascribed to France's colonial empire in North America. **1609** Santa Fe is established in what is now New Mexico. De Champlain, traveling with a Huron war party, explores the lake that now bears his name. Englishman Henry Hudson, hired by the Dutch East India Company, explores Delaware Bay and the river named after him. The English vessel *Sea Venture*, under the command of Admiral Sir George Somers, is destroyed at sea while transporting colonists to Jamestown. The passengers reach Bermuda and establish a community called Somers Island.	**Summary** In the arena of exploration, Portugal is a merchant empire while Spain's interests lie more in conquest and colonization. Both England and France refuse to recognize the division of the newly discovered Western Hemisphere between Spain and Portugal, and try unsuccessfully to find a northern water route across America to Asia. In this process, they begin the European colonization of the Americas. At the same time, the Netherlands, England and France are unwilling to relinquish the profitable trade with Southeast Asia to Spain and Portugal. In Africa, the Atlantic coastal kingdoms of Ashanti (Asante), Benin and Dahomey expand as trade centers. Portuguese — and later Dutch — slave traders enourage fighting among African kingdoms or factions in order to increase the number of Africans for sale into servitude in Europe and the Americas. In South Africa, the Dutch Boers (Afrikaners) come into power and expand their territory. --- **1600** Religious intolerance persists in Europe, and Giordano Bruno, who angered the Roman Catholic church by supporting the Copernican theory of the universe, is burned as a heretic in Rome. Protestants are expelled from the Austrian province of Styria. By this time most of the Philippines is under Spanish dominion. The British East India Company is chartered by Queen Elizabeth I to acquire a share of the Asian spice trade for England. The company eventually oversees trade and political affairs in India. Ieyasu defeats his rivals at the Battle of Sekigahara, Mino Province. He later becomes ruler of Japan. William Adams, the first Englishman to visit Japan, serves as Ieyasu's advisor on shipbuilding.

1600

through

1609

c. 1600

Tantric Buddhism spreads in Mongolia.

1600-1601

The regions of Walachia, Moldavia and Transylvania are united briefly under Romanian prince Michael (the Brave). Michael rules from 1593 until his assassination in 1601. After his death the Ottoman Empire reasserts its authority over Walachia and Moldavia, while Austria takes control of Transylvania.

1600s

Despite the Qing (Ch'ing) dynasty's official opposition, several Chinese cities begin trade with European nations.

Dahomey becomes a center of the trade in enslaved Africans.

1601

Jesuit missionary Matteo Ricci arrives in Peking, China.

1601-1604

The Great Siege of Ostend, Belgium, ends in a Spanish victory.

1602

The Dutch East India Company is founded to protect and expand Dutch trade and colonization interests abroad.

The Spanish army, after landing in Ireland in support of Hugh O'Neill, earl of Tyrone, at the end of 1601, surrenders to English forces at Kinsale. Tyrone makes peace with the English the following year.

c. 1602

Portuguese colonists establish a base at Syriam near Rangoon, in what is now Burma.

1603

England is severely affected by an outbreak of the plague.

Siam (Thailand) begins a 15-year conquest of Cambodia (Kampuchea).

James VI of Scotland becomes King James I of England and Scotland after the death of his cousin, Elizabeth I (1558). James VI unites the governments of the two countries and rules until 1625.

Ahmed I becomes Ottoman sultan after the death of his father, Muhammad III (1595). Ahmed I rules until 1617.

Sir Walter Raleigh is arrested for his role in the "Main Plot" to dethrone King James I. He is tried for treason and imprisoned.

The Tyrone Irish Rebellion ends as Hugh O'Neill, earl of Tyrone and O'Neill family chieftain, leads an unsuccessful attack against British forces near Kinsale.

Tokugawa Ieyasu, a *daimyo* (Japanese fuedal lord) based in Edo (present-day Tokyo), establishes himself as the central power of the country. Obtaining appointment as shogun from the imperial court. Building on the social system established by Hideyoshi, the Edo shogunate maintains a stable social order for more than 250 years.

1603-1688

This is the time span generally ascribed to the House of Stuart that rules England.

c. 1603-1868

This is the time span generally ascribed to the Tokugawa family shogunate that rules Japan.

1604

The French East India Company is founded. It remains in existence for 166 years.

Charles IX formally becomes king of Sweden after the title is renounced by Sigismund III's brother, John. Charles IX rules until 1611.

1605

Dutch forces take Amboyna (Amboina), Indonesia, from the Portuguese.

The Gunpowder Plot, led by Guy Fawkes, is uncovered. A conspiracy to blow up England's Parliament and King James I, its exposure serves to worsen the situation for English Catholics.

Czar Boris Godunov (1598) of Russia dies, and the "Time of Troubles" begins. Feodor II becomes czar but a power struggle ensues between him and a pretender to the throne. "False" Dmitri, who claims he is a son of Czar Ivan IV (the Terrible), becomes czar after Feodor II's death. Dmitri is assassinated in 1606.

Jahangir becomes Mogul emperor of India after the death of his father, Akbar (the Great, 1556). Jahangir rules until 1627.

Stephen Bocksay becomes prince of Transylvania. He rules until 1606.

1605-1606

Australia is sighted by Dutch navigator Willem Jansz, who sails close to the northern coast of present-day Queensland; and by Spanish navigator Luis Vaez de Torres who, on a different voyage, sees the northern point of Cape York. Torres later explores the strait between New Guinea and Australia that bears his name.

1606

A peace treaty between the Turks and the Hapsburgs is signed at Zsitva-Torok. By this Treaty, the Holy Roman Emperor stops paying tribute to the Ottoman sultan, and Transylvania becomes independent with Stephen Bocksay recognized as the ruling prince. Bocksay negotiates an agreement in Vienna with Archduke (later Emperor) Matthias that partitions Hungary among the Hapsburgs, the Ottoman sultan and Transylvania. This agreement also provides for freedom of religion in Hungary.

King James I of England gives the Plymouth Company the right to colonize between the 38th and 45th parallels in North America.

The Treaty of Vienna guarantees the independence of Transylvania, the freedom of worship for Protestants and popular election of certain members of the ruling class.

Englishman Guy Fawkes and his fellow conspirators in the Gunpowder Plot are executed.

Punitive laws are established against Roman Catholics in England.

Har Govind becomes guru of the Sikh faith after the death of his father, Arjan Dev (1581). Har Govind holds this position until 1645.

Dmitri (1605) is assassinated by Vasili Shuisky (Basil IV), who is then elected czar of Russia. Shuisky rules until 1610.

c. 1606

Catholics in Sweden are persecuted during the reign of Charles IX.

1606-1632

Suseynos reigns in Ethiopia until he converts to Catholicism and is forced to abdicate.

1607

In Ireland, the "flight of the earls" to avoid suspected British reprisals ends the power of tribal chiefs.

1607-1629

The Acheh kingdom in western Sumatra is at its height.

1608

Pilgrims — separatists from the Church of England — move to the Netherlands to escape religious persecution.

Holy Roman Emperor Rudolf II cedes Austria, Hungary and Moravia to his brother Matthias. Matthias rules as king of Hungary until 1619.

1609

Maximilian of Bavaria forms the Catholic League of German princes as a counter to the newly formed Protestant Union.

Emperor Rudolf II allows religious freedom in Bohemia (a region of what is now Czechoslovakia).

The English Baptist Church is founded in Amsterdam by John Smith and Thomas Helwys.

Polish forces under Sigismund III invade Russia.

Spain and the Netherlands declare a truce in the Eighty Years' War. The war resumes in 1621.

c. 1609

All Moriscos ("Christianized" Moors) are expelled from Spain.

1600

through

1609

69

NATIVE AMERICAN	AFRICAN AMERICAN	ASIAN AMERICAN	EUROPEAN AMERICAN
1613 Pocahontas, daughter of Algonquin Chief Powhatan, marries John Rolfe of the Jamestown colony. French colonists offer the Micmac tribe a bounty on scalps of Beothuk tribesmen. As a result, the Beothuks are virtually annihilated. Samuel de Champlain leads a French expedition along the Ottawa River and promises to assist Hurons and Algonquins against the Iroquois. The policy of French colonists is to include Native Americans in political and economic decisions. **1615** De Champlain's French and Huron forces at Lake Oneida suffer a major defeat, causing many Hurons to question the wisdom of their alliance with the French. **1615-1630s** A small Algonquin group, the Allumettes (Kichesipirini), control an island in the Ottawa River — an important route for the growing fur trade. The Allumettes are able to charge a heavy toll for the passage of trading vessels. The Hurons (Wyandots) have a vast trading network. Graves from this period show goods from Mexico, the Gulf coast and the Minnesota River areas. **1616** A smallpox epidemic devastates the Indian tribes in New England. The missions of Santa Isabel, San Pedro de Athuluteca, San Diego de Santuache and San Felipe de Alabe are established in what is now Georgia for the conversion of Guale Indians. **1618** French forces under de Champlain attack the Iroquois, thus beginning a long-standing animosity between the two. At Plymouth, in what is now Massachusetts, local Algonquin Indians help the Pilgrims overcome initial difficulties. Fifty missions are established in Florida and 16,000 Indians are baptized.	**1619** A Dutch vessel brings approximately 20 enslaved Africans to the Jamestown community. These are the first Africans in the English North American colonies.	**1611** Dominican missionaries establish Santo Tomas University in Manila, Philippines. It is the oldest university in Asia.	**1610-1640s** Italian and French immigrants arrive at the Jamestown colony. **1612** John Rolfe, a colonist at Jamestown, introduces tobacco as a crop. This proves to be a great export. Rolfe marries the Indian princess Pocahontas in 1613. John Smith creates "A Map of Virginia." Dutch merchants use Manhattan as a fur-trading center for the first time. Dutch traders are on the Hudson River, trading with native peoples. **1614** Dutch forces build Fort Nassau (Albany) on the Hudson River. Dutchman Adriaen Block explores Long Island Sound. Jean Vigné, of French Huguenot descent, is the first European child born on Manhattan Island. **1616** John Smith writes *A Description of New England.* **1619** The Virginia Company transports women to Jamestown from England to provide wives for the male colonists and to increase the population.

1610 through 1619

HISPANIC AMERICAN	FOR CLASSROOM USE	FOR CLASSROOM USE	FOR CLASSROOM USE	

1610

A regular supply route runs between Mexico City and Santa Fe.

Captain Gaspar Pérez de Villagra, a member of Juan de Oñate's expedition, writes an epic poem about the exploration of New Mexico, *La Historia de la Nuevo Mexico,* which is published in Spain.

The Inquisition ceases formal operations in Puerto Rico, and moves its American headquarters to Cartagena de Indias (now Cartagena, Colombia).

1612

In Florida, Father Francisco Pareja writes two books on the Timucuan language: *Grammar and Pronunciation in Timucuan and Castillian Languages;* and *Confessional Guide in Timucuan and Castillian Languages.* The books are published in Mexico City.

1616

The missions of Santa Isabel, San Pedro de Athuluteca, San Diego de Santuache and San Felipe de Alabe are established in what is now Georgia, for the conversion of Guale Indians.

1616-1621

Chihuahua and Durango, Mexico are plundered by rebels of the native tribes there. Large numbers of horses and mules are taken and probably brought north.

1617

Spanish colonists establish a community at Taos, New Mexico.

1610

through

1619

THE AMERICAS	THE AMERICAS	THE AMERICAS	THE WORLD

1610

through

1619

THE AMERICAS

1610

Spanish colonists in North America move the government seat to Santa Fe.

Jesuits found missions among the Guaraní Indians in Paraguay and southern Brazil.

1611

English explorer Henry Hudson, his son and several other men are set adrift after a mutiny aboard their ship. They are never seen again. The ship and its crew of mostly convicts sails for England. Only eight survive the voyage.

A Spanish ship sailing up the James River in Virginia is captured by British forces and its crew is held for five years.

French explorer Samuel de Champlain returns to Tadoussac. Within a few days, 13 ships of reinforcements arrive to bolster the colony there.

Charles de Biencourt leads an exploratory party from France aboard the *Grâce à Dieu,* bound for Acadia. Passengers include approximately 50 men and Biencourt's mother, Madame de Poutrincourt, one of the first French women to visit North America.

The first French Jesuits set sail for France's North American colonies.

1612

The Virginia colony harvests its first tobacco crop.

In what is now Colombia, Spanish Jesuit priest Peter Claver brings some 300,000 people into the Catholic church. Claver is known among Catholics as the "Friend of the Blacks."

A group of 60 English colonists from Virginia travels to Bermuda after King James I issues a land grant to the Virginia Company.

Colonists in Brazil establish local "bush captains," militia to protect the interests of slaveholders by suppressing revolts and capturing runaways.

THE AMERICAS

1613

In a surprise attack, an English fleet commanded by Samuel Argall of the Virginia Company sails north, destroys the French St. Sauveur mission (on an island off Maine's southeast coast) and attacks other French communities. This is the first English expedition to challenge French occupation of the area. Port Royal is nearly destroyed, but French colonists soon rebuild. English colonists from Virginia also prevent French colonization of what is now Maryland.

The ship *Le Fleur de May* with 50 French colonists, lands at a place they name Saint-Sauveur, near present-day Penobscot, Maine.

1614

Dutch forces build Fort Nassau (Albany) on the Hudson River.

Dutch explorer Adriaen Block sails through Long Island Sound into the Connecticut River.

By this year, a colony of approximately 60 English people is solidly established at Conception Bay, Newfoundland.

1615

De Champlain and men under him ally themselves with the Huron tribe against Iroquois aggression. Later this year they march against the Iroquois, into what is now New York state. De Champlain and the Hurons are ambushed by Onondagas — members of the Iroquois Confederacy — and withdraw.

It is estimated that more than 500 French vessels sail annually to the fishing and fur-trading areas of France's North American colonies.

The first Catholic mass in New France is celebrated at Quebec.

1616

British arctic explorers William Baffin and Robert Bylot explore and name the area of Baffin Bay, seeking a northwest passage.

THE AMERICAS

1617

Hernando Arias de Saavedra (Hernandarias), Spain's first governor of the River Plate (Uruguay) region, discovers that his domain is rich in pastureland, and introduces cattle and horses.

c. 1617

A serious epidemic, possibly smallpox carried by European explorers, hits New England and moves south to Virginia.

1618

Fifty missions are established in Florida and 16,000 Indians are baptized.

1619

In Virginia, enslaved Africans labor to raise tobacco beside enslaved Native Americans and European indentured servants, whose material conditions are little better. Some Africans are held as indentured servants rather than as slaves.

Leaders of the Pilgrims who migrated to the Netherlands in 1608 set up a joint company to start a community near Jamestown, Virginia.

The first representative assembly in America, the House of Burgesses, is held at Jamestown under Governor Sir George Yeardley.

Enslaved Africans work the sugar plantations in Brazil and in the West Indies.

THE WORLD

1610

Louis XIII becomes king of France as a young boy after Henry IV is assassinated (1589). Louis XIII rules until 1643.

Frederick V becomes Elector Palatine after the death of his father, Frederick IV. Frederick V rules until 1620.

Vladislav IV of Poland becomes czar of Russia after Shuisky (1606) is deposed. Vladislav IV rules until 1612.

1611

King James I dissolves his first English Parliament.

The War of Kalmar begins between Denmark and Sweden.

Masulipatam becomes the first English community on India's Coromandel coast.

The King James version of the Bible is published in England.

Dutch merchants begin trading in Japan, but their operations are officially limited to Deshima Island in Nagasaki Bay.

Nur Jahan, a 34-year-old Persian widow, marries the emperor of Delhi, Jahangir. Because of her outstanding intellect and exceptional political judgement, her husband leaves her virtually in charge of his administration.

Gustavus Adolphus becomes King Gustavus II of Sweden after the death of his father, Charles IX (1604). Gustavus II rules until 1632.

King Matthias of Hungary becomes king of Bohemia. He rules Bohemia until 1617 and Hungary until 1618.

1612

A treaty is signed between the Dutch and the king of Kandy in Ceylon.

The British East India Company establishes a trading station at Surat, India.

The last recorded burning of heretics in England takes place.

Christianity is outlawed in Japan.

King Matthias of Hungary and Bohemia becomes Holy Roman Emperor after the death of his brother, Rudolf II (1576). Matthias holds this title until 1619.

1613

The Treaty of Knärod ends the War of Kalmar; Sweden gives up control of Finland.

Turkish forces invade Transylvania.

Michael I (Michael Romanov) becomes czar of Russia, ending the claims of the false pretenders. Michael I rules until 1645.

c. 1613

A Dutch expedition begins exploration of the coast of what is now Australia.

1613-1917

This is the time span generally ascribed to the House of Romanov that rules Russia.

1614

The second English Parliament (the Addled Parliament) is dissolved by James I for its refusal to discuss financial matters.

The Treaty of Xanten divides the duchies of Jülich and Cleves (both in western Germany) between John Sigismund of Brandenburg, a Calvinist, and William of Neuburg, a Catholic.

Swedish forces under King Gustavus II take Novgorod from the Russians.

1615

Dutch troops capture the Molucca Islands from Portugal.

An English expedition engages and defeats Portuguese forces near the coast of India.

1616

A stern opponent of Christianity, Tokugawa Hidetada becomes shogun of Japan after the death of his father, Ieyasu (1603). Hidetada rules until 1623.

Dutch navigator Willem Cornelis Schouten travels through Le Maire Strait (southern Argentina) to the Pacific Ocean. He names Cape Horn for his birthplace, Hoorn. A group of islands near New Guinea carries his name.

Manchus establish the Dajin dynasty in Manchuria.

Catholicism is restricted in Bohemia.

The Catholic church prohibits Galileo from conducting further scientific research.

1617

The Peace of Stolbovo ends the war between Russia and Sweden. Russia regains control of Novgorod but Sweden obtains Karelia and Ingria.

Ferdinand of Styria (a province of Austria) is elected king of Bohemia as Ferdinand II. Except for one year, 1619-1620, Ferdinand II rules Bohemia until 1637.

Mustafa I becomes Ottoman sultan for less than one year after the death of his brother, Ahmed I (1603). Mustafa I reclaims the sultanate in 1622.

c. 1617

In Africa, Dutch forces take control of the island of Gorée, thus acquiring a base of operations on the Gold Coast.

1617-1629

Poland and Sweden war against each other.

1617-1721

During this time Sweden is a strong European power. It extends its borders to include the Baltic Sea, and increases the size of its province of Finland.

1618

The Peace of Madrid ends the war between Venice and Austria.

The German states of Brandenburg and Prussia are united. The resulting larger state keeps the name "Prussia."

Manchus begin attacks on Ming garrisons in Manchuria.

King James I of England charters the Company of Royal Adventurers in London to trade with African nations south of the Barbary Coast.

Osman II becomes Ottoman sultan after the removal of his brother, Mustafa I (1617). Osman II rules until 1622.

Sir Walter Raleigh is executed for treason in England.

1618-1648

The Thirty Years' War begins in Europe over territorial, dynastic and religious issues between Catholics and Protestants. It starts in Bohemia as a reaction against the Holy Roman Empire's suppression of Protestantism and is ignited by the "Defenestration of Prague." The war spreads to other German provinces, eventually weakening the empire.

1619

Dutch traders establish a fort they call Batavia next to the Javanese community of Djakarta. Djakarta is destroyed in 1620, and the town built on the site is called Batavia until 1949, when it again is renamed Djakarta.

Members of the Czech nobility rebel against Austrian rule in Bohemia. The revolt is suppressed.

Ferdinand II, king of Bohemia and Hungary, becomes Holy Roman Emperor after the death of Matthias (1612). Ferdinand II rules all three domains until 1637.

Elector Palatine Frederick V, son-in-law to King James I of England, rules Bohemia for one year. He obtains the crown after Ferdinand II (1617) is deposed, and is known as the "Winter King" because of his short reign.

1610

through

1619

NATIVE AMERICAN	AFRICAN AMERICAN	ASIAN AMERICAN	EUROPEAN AMERICAN
1620 A school is established by English colonists in Virginia to try to convert Native Americans there to Christianity. The school is destroyed by Native Americans in 1622. **1620s-1636** At its height, the Huron Confederacy has 30,000 to 35,000 people. Two allied tribes, the Wyandot or Tobacco Nation and the Attiwandaronk or Neutral Nation, have 15,000 and 12,000 people, respectively. This alliance dominates the native trade in the Great Lakes-St. Lawrence region. **1621** In New England, Chief Massasoit of the Wampanoag befriends the English and cedes land to the Pilgrims. **1622-1631** In the first Powhatan War, Chief Opechancanough leads the 32 Tidewater-area tribes of the Powhatan Confederacy against European colonists at Jamestown, Virginia. The conflict ravages the area of the Chickahominy tribe and ends without a decisive victory. French Jesuits begin missionary work among the Hurons. The Iroquois react violently to those activities by torturing and killing several missionaries and eventually destroying the Huron Confederacy. **1623-1626** Members of the Jemez Apache (Navajo) tribe war against Spaniards and Tiwas in the area of New Mexico. **1626** Peter Minuit purchases Manhattan Island from the Canarsee tribe for merchandise valued at $24 (60 Dutch guilders). Mahicans and Dutch allies march against the Five Nations of the Iroquois Confederacy and are defeated. Fort Orange (Albany) is subsequently largely abandoned by the Dutch, except for a small military force. **1627** Carib natives, brought to Virginia as slaves, flee to the Powhatan tribes.	**1624** The first African American child born free in the English colonies, William Tucker, is baptized in Virginia. The early Dutch colonists in America import Africans from Angola and Brazil to work on their farms. Under Dutch authority any child of an African who is freed from slavery is born into slavery. **1629** The first enslaved Africans arrive in what is now Connecticut.	Although Chinese seamen have engaged in significant maritime activity from the middle of the seventh century, when Manchus conquer the Chinese people in 1644 and bring the Ming dynasty to an end, a major change in foreign policy occurs. Fearing that Ming loyalists will create a revolutionary force outside the country, officials of the new Qing (Ch'ing) dynasty pass edicts barring emigration. Many Chinese people, especially from the southeastern provinces of Fujian (Fukien) and Guangdong (Kwangtung), continue to travel back and forth between China and the countries of southeast Asia, where sizeable Chinese colonies flourish. However, most of the Chinese people are isolated from the West until early in the nineteenth century. Japan's location off the coast of the Asian mainland keeps its inhabitants relatively isolated from outside visitors. The Japanese people withstand attempted invasions by Kublai Khan in the 1200s, and first encounter Europeans when Portuguese traders arrive off the Asian mainland in the early 1500s. European missionaries follow but, fearing the examples seen in other Asian countries where missionaries were soon followed by military forces, the Tokugawa shogunate issues an effective anti-Christian decree. Japan remains isolated until a United States fleet under Commodore (later Admiral) Matthew Perry sails into Tokyo Bay in 1853.	**1620** Indentured service becomes the dominant means by which the southern colonies of North America get English and Irish laborers. In fact, approximately two-thirds of the European immigrants who travel to colonial America come as indentured servants. **1621** The ship *Flying Harte* arrives at Newport News, Virginia, with a group of Irish colonists under the leadership of Daniel Gookin, a wealthy Irish merchant and Quaker from Cork. **1623** The first English colonists in New Hampshire, led by David Thomas, establish a community at Little Harbor (near present-day Rye). Other English communities soon develop in New Hampshire and Maine. **1624** Dutch colonists arrive in North America and establish communities at Fort Orange (Albany), Fort Nassau (on the Delaware River) and Governor's Island (in New York harbor). **1625** Fort Amsterdam, the beginning of the community of New Amsterdam (New York City), is built by Dutch colonists. The fort was designed by engineer Cryn Frederickzs, to serve as a naval base. The ship *Due Return* arrives at the Jamestown colony, under command of "Symon Turchin, banished out of Ireland and reported strongly affected to Popery." The governor of Virginia forces Turchin to return to England. **1626** Forty English colonists under Roger Conant move to Salem, Massachusetts, and set up a trading post. **1628** By this time New Amsterdam has a population of 270.

1620 through 1629

EUROPEAN AMERICAN	HISPANIC AMERICAN	FOR CLASSROOM USE	FOR CLASSROOM USE	
1629	**1620s**			
Landholders under the Dutch West India Company receive a directive from the company regarding their relationship with Native Americans. One clause of the directive says that "Whosoever shall settle any colony out of the limits of Manhattan Island shall be obliged to satisfy the Indians for the land they shall settle upon."	The native population of Mexico drops to about 1 million from a pre-conquest figure of 25 million people.			**1620** through **1629**
	1625			
	A Dutch fleet attacks San Juan, Puerto Rico, but is rebuffed after its troops sack and burn the city.			
	1629			
	Indians in Texas tell missionaries that a beautiful lady with a blue dress is instructing them in the Catholic faith. Many believe that it is Sister María de Agueda, a nun in Spain with special powers.			
		FOR CLASSROOM USE	*FOR CLASSROOM USE*	

THE AMERICAS	THE AMERICAS	THE AMERICAS	THE AMERICAS

1620

The Pilgrims return to England from the Netherlands. There they join other English separatists and non-Pilgrims and set sail for America aboard the *Mayflower*. The ship sails into Cape Cod Bay, considerably north of its destination.

The Pilgrims sign the Mayflower Compact, an agreement for the government of their colony. They reject the Church of England and practice Congregationalism.

Sir Ferdinando Gorges obtains for the Plymouth Company a grant for "New England," the territory lying between the latitudes 40 and 48 degrees north. The company changes its name to the Great Council of New England.

c. 1620

French explorer Etienne Brulé journeys to the St. Mary's River in the Great Lakes region.

1621

The first grist mill in North America to produce flour from wheat is built in Jamestown, Virginia.

An English expedition attempts to colonize Newfoundland and Acadia (Nova Scotia, New Brunswick and eastern Maine).

The newly established Dutch West India Company lays claim to all land between the Delaware River and Cape Cod, on North America's eastern coast. The company has been granted a trade monopoly, and places its emphasis on furs rather than colonization.

1622

Gorges forms a partnership with Captain John Mason and obtains the rights to lands between the Merrimack and Kennebec Rivers, then part of the territory of Maine.

1623

An expedition of English colonists led by David Thomas establishes the first English community in what is now New Hampshire, at Little Harbor, near Rye.

1624

Dutch traders bring the first Africans into New York's Hudson Valley area.

The London Company goes into receivership. Its Virginia charter is revoked, and Virginia becomes an English royal colony.

Luís Franco Rodrigues, a Portuguese New Christian born in Lisbon, is tried before the Inquisition of Cartagena, New Granada (Colombia).

Bahia (Baía), Brazil, is taken from Spain by Dutch troops led by Piet Hein. It is later known as São Salvador.

Franciscan and Jesuit monks establish several communities in the Uruguayan territory to evangelize and protect the Indians.

c. 1624

Colonists led by Gorges and Mason establish a community at Strawberry Bank (Portsmouth), at the mouth of the Piscataqua River, in what later becomes New Hampshire.

1625

Henri de Lévy becomes the viceroy to New France and bans all but Roman Catholics from the colony. Five Jesuits sent to Quebec are hampered by Huguenot merchants who are upset over the exclusion of Protestants from Canada.

A French expedition occupies the Antilles and Cayenne.

On a return trip from Brazil to England, Captain John Powell lands at Barbados, and claims the uninhabited island in the name of King James I.

Spanish troops under General Ambrogio Spinola recapture Bahia, Brazil, from the Dutch.

1626

Dutch colonists open the first commercial flour mill in North America.

The Plymouth Company sells its land holdings to individual colonists and eight Pilgrims take over the debts of the colony. Plymouth never receives a charter from the English monarchy.

New Amsterdam (New York City) on the Hudson River becomes a center of fur trading for the Dutch West India Company.

Peter Minuit purchases Manhattan Island from the Canarsee Indian chiefs for merchandise valued at $24 (60 guilders). Minuit becomes governor of New Netherland.

Five Jesuits come to Acadia to evangelize among the Indians.

1627

Dutch colonists make their homes in Connecticut.

The Company of New France, also called the One Hundred Associates, is incorporated by Cardinal Armand Jean du Plessis Richelieu. The company is required to move 300 colonists annually into New France and provide them with agricultural equipment.

English Admiral Sir David Kirke and his fleet capture French fishing and supply ships — more than 35 vessels in all — off the coast of New France.

The British colony of Barbados is established, with a governor appointed by the island's proprietors, and a council chosen by the governor. A group of approximately eighty colonists arrives from England at the site now called Holetown. Local tradition, however, sets the founding of Barbados at 1650.

1628

An English expedition acquires Nevis, one of the Leeward Islands.

The New France colonies of Acadia and Quebec are besieged by English forces led by Sir David Kirke.

1629

The Massachusetts Bay Company receives its royal charter and sends its first fleet of English colonists (Puritans) to North America. They land at Salem (originally called Naumkeag), a colony founded in 1626 by Roger Conant. John Endecott (Endicott) serves from 1628 to 1630 as the first governor of the colony at Salem.

Captain John Mason claims the area between the Piscataqua and Merrimack Rivers and calls it New Hampshire.

Frenchman Samuel de Champlain surrenders Quebec to Kirke's English forces. Kirke's men occupy the city until 1632.

A hundred Scottish colonists arrive in Acadia. They build Charles Fort about five miles from Port Royal, and remain there until Acadia is returned to France in 1632 through the Treaty of Saint-Germain-en-Laye. Most then return to Scotland, but a few households remain under French government in Acadia.

1620
through
1629

1620

Spanish forces capture Valtelline and overrun the Palatinate region of western Germany. This initiates a war of almost two decades between Catholics and Protestants in this region.

The Catholic League of German princes under Johannes Tserklaes, Count of Tilly, defeats the army of King Frederick V (1619) of Bohemia at the Battle of White Mountain, near Prague. Ferdinand II is reinstated as king of Bohemia.

1620-1623

More than 100,000 Protestants are driven from Bohemia.

1621

Persian forces invade and occupy Mesopotamia (Iraq).

The Dutch West India Company is chartered. It remains in business for 170 years.

The Great Commons Protestation occurs in England.

Forces under Sweden's King Gustavus II capture the Latvian city of Riga.

After a 12-year truce, war resumes between Spain and the Netherlands.

In France, Huguenots rebel against King Louis XIII.

Philip IV becomes king of Spain after the death of his father, Philip III (1598). Philip IV rules Spain until 1665. He also rules Portugal as Philip III from 1621 until 1640.

1622

King James I dissolves the English Parliament again.

As part of the Thirty Years War, Count Tilly and his army are defeated by Protestant forces under Count Peter Ernst Mansfeld II at Weisloch. However, Tilly and his troops capture Heidelberg and Mannheim, defeat the forces of George Frederick of Baden at Wimpfen and are victorious over the Protestant army of Christian of Brunswick at Höchst.

The city of Montpellier, a Huguenot stronghold in southern France, is invaded by the army of King Louis XIII. The treaty signed to end this conflict forces Huguenot acceptance of Catholic rule.

Persian and English forces retake the Strait of Hormuz from the Portuguese.

Mustafa I is reinstated as Ottoman sultan after the execution of his nephew, Osman II (1618). Mustafa I is removed a second time and another nephew, Murad IV, becomes sultan. He rules until 1640.

1623

Dutch governor Herman van Speult of Amboyna (Amboina) executes 12 Englishmen on charges of conspiracy. This event, called the Massacre of Amboyna, results in England's changing its colonization focus to India.

Baghdad is captured from the Ottoman Turks by Persian forces under Shah Abbas I.

Iemitsu becomes shogun of Japan after the abdication of his father, Hidetada (1616). Iemitsu rules until 1651.

1624

Dutch communities are established in southern Formosa (Taiwan), while Spanish people colonize in the north.

The first English colony in eastern India is established.

Japan discontinues trading with the Philippines.

Cardinal Armand Jean du Plessis Richelieu becomes chief minister to King Louis XIII. He solidifies France's monarchy by weakening both the Huguenot faction and the French nobility. Cardinal Richelieu supports the German princes against Austria and Sweden. He serves until 1642.

The first submarine is built by Dutch inventor Cornelis Drebbel.

1624-1625

Spanish forces under General Ambrogio Spinola capture Breda (southern Netherlands).

1624-1656

Nzinga, queen of the Matamba people (in Angola), disrupts the Portuguese trade in enslaved Africans. This extraordinary woman transformed herself from a palace slave into a queen as a result of her resistance to Portuguese expansion. In 1656 she negotiates a treaty with the Portuguese which protects her land and people.

1625

England begins a five-year war against Spain and France. The Treaty of Southampton allies England and the Netherlands against Spain.

Charles I becomes king of England and Ireland after the death of James I (1603), and dissolves his first parliament. Charles I rules until 1649.

1626

Charles I dissolves his second Parliament.

Holy Roman Emperor Ferdinand II's army, led by General Albrecht Wenzel Eusebius von Wallenstein, defeats Count Ernst von Mansfield and his Protestant army at the Bridge of Dessau, and moves against Hungary.

The Treaty of Monzon between Spain and France ensures the independence of Grisons (a region of Switzerland).

French colonies are established in Senegal and Madagascar.

1627

Catholic forces under Wallenstein capture the Prussian province of Silesia and Mecklenburg, a region of Germany; they then invade Jutland. Count Tilly captures Brunswick, also in Germany.

Shah Jahan becomes Mogul emperor of India after the death of his father, Jahangir (1605). Shah Jahan rules until 1658.

1628

Richelieu gains control over the Huguenot seaport of La Rochelle for France. The residents, plagued by critical food shortages, are forced to surrender.

The Treaty of Stuhmsdorf is signed between Gustavus II of Sweden and Christian IV of Denmark for the defense of Stralsund (part of Mecklenburg). This brings Sweden into the Thirty Years War.

The English Petition of Right is passed by Parliament. It denies King Charles I the right to quarter soldiers in civilian homes, to levy taxes without parliamentary approval or to arbitrarily arrest and imprison people.

1629

Charles I dissolves his third English Parliament.

The Edict of Restitution in Germany returns property to the Catholic church that was secularized by the Peace of Augsburg in 1555.

By the Treaty of Lübeck, Denmark's Christian IV and Holy Roman Emperor Ferdinand II make peace. Christian IV retains his territorial claims by agreeing not to interfere in Germany's war.

The Treaty of Altmark is signed between Sweden and Poland.

c. 1629

Safi I becomes shah of Persia after the death of his grandfather, Abbas I (the Great, 1587). Safi I rules until 1642.

1620

through

1629

	NATIVE AMERICAN	AFRICAN AMERICAN	ASIAN AMERICAN	EUROPEAN AMERICAN
1630 through **1639**	**1631** English colonial leader Roger Williams argues that the royal charter for Massachusetts illegally seizes Indian tribal lands; he urges a more humane policy. **1633** In New England, a smallpox epidemic kills hundreds of members of the Narragansett tribe. **1635** By this date, beaver are virtually eliminated in Huron country. **1637-1638** The Pequot Indians (Connecticut) resist encroachment by European colonists. The Pequot War ends with the near destruction of the tribe. The Reverend John Davenport and merchant Theophilus Eaton, both from England, establish a community at New Haven, in what is now Connecticut. Land is reserved there for the Quinnipiac tribe. **1637-1641** Spaniards in New Mexico raid Ute villages for the purpose of acquiring slave labor. Many Utes escape, bringing Spanish horses with them.	**1634** Slavery is introduced in Maryland. **1636** The first enslaved Africans arrive in the Delaware colony. **1637** The first enslaved Africans arrive in New Amsterdam (New York City). **1638** Trade begins in enslaved Africans to France's North American colonies.	**1635** Local barbers in Mexico City complain to the municipal council about competition from Chinese barbers.	**1630** John Billington is the first English colonist to be executed in America. One of the signers of the Mayflower Compact, he is hanged for murdering a fellow Pilgrim. **1631** The first European village in what is now Delaware is a Dutch coastal community at Lewes. **c. 1633** Windsor, founded by Puritans from Massachusetts, becomes the first English colony in what is now Connecticut. **1634** The Roman Catholic colony founded at St. Mary's, Maryland, soon becomes home to Irish immigrants who come as indentured servants. Frenchman Jean Nicolet arrives at Green Bay and explores what is now Wisconsin for France. **1635** English colonists led by John Winthrop (the Younger) establish a community at Fort Saybrook, Connecticut. **1636** Hartford, on the west bank of the Connecticut River, is established by colonists led by Thomas Hooker and Samuel Stone. The original community, called Newtown, is built on the site of a former Dutch trading post. A group of Puritan colonists under the leadership of William Pynchon establishes the town of Springfield, Massachusetts. **1638** Fort Christina is built by Swedish colonists on the Delaware River, on the site that is now Wilmington, Delaware. Margaret Brent arrives from England in St. Mary's, Maryland, with her sister and two brothers. She becomes the first woman in Maryland to own land in her own name.

EUROPEAN AMERICAN	HISPANIC AMERICAN	FOR CLASSROOM USE	FOR CLASSROOM USE	
1639 Groups of English Puritans migrate to the Dutch colony of New Netherland (now New York and New Jersey) to escape persecution.	**1630** Portuguese Franciscan Afonso de Benavides publishes his *Memorial,* a mission chronicle of New Mexico, in Madrid. By this date Spanish immigrants have established at least 25 missions in New Mexico, with workshops and schools for teaching Native Americans. Santa Fe has a population of approximately 1,000 people, 200 Spaniards and 800 *mestizos* (people of combined Native American and Spanish ethnicity). **1631** Construction begins on the massive El Morro Fortress to protect the city of San Juan, Puerto Rico. **1632** Zunis kill a Franciscan priest and the Zuni pueblos (modern-day Arizona-New Mexico border region) are independent of Spanish control for a short time. **1633** In Florida, construction begins on the "Camino Real" (Royal Road) between St. Augustine on the Atlantic coast and St. Mark on the Gulf coast. By the end of the century, the road is completed and several missions are established along it. **1635-1782** Construction continues on the thick walls around the city of San Juan, Puerto Rico. **1637-1641** Spaniards in New Mexico raid Ute villages for the purpose of taking slaves. Many Utes escape, taking Spanish horses with them.			**1630** **through** **1639**

1630 through 1639

1630

Pirates establish a community in Tortuga, off the northwest coast of Hispaniola.

English Puritan leader John Winthrop arrives in Massachusetts with 1,000 colonists. Winthrop founds Boston and becomes the first governor of Massachusetts.

By this year there are trading posts established in Acadia (Nova Scotia, New Brunswick and eastern Maine) in addition to Port Royal — at Pentagouet, also in the Cape Sable area, and on the St. John River, and at Cape Breton.

The silver mines of Cerro de Pasco in central Peru are opened.

c. 1630

Spanish and Portuguese supremacy in the Caribbean islands is challenged by British, French and Dutch mariners. Dutch forces capture Curaçao and Guiana. French colonists occupy western Hispaniola. British forces seize uninhabited islands, including St. Kitts, Barbados and Antigua, and begin the cultivation of sugar.

1631-1633

English expeditions to Central America establish communities on Providencia Island, approximately 130 miles off the east coast of present-day Nicaragua, and on Cape Gracias a Dios on the eastern border of Honduras and Nicaragua.

1632

George Calvert, the first lord of Baltimore, secures a grant from England's King Charles I of territory north of the Potomac River.

France's King Louis XII and England's King Charles I sign the Treaty of St. Germain-en-Laye which, among other things, returns to France the control of all territories in North America that the English took by force, including Quebec, Acadia (Nova Scotia, New Brunswick and eastern Maine) and Port Royal. Samuel de Champlain is commissioned as governor of Quebec.

Louis XII confirms the Jesuits' right to carry on missionary work in New France, and forbids foreigners and Huguenots from immigrating to the colonies.

Antigua is colonized by an English expedition led by Captain Edward Warner.

1633

The Dutch build a fort, called the House of Hope, in what is now Hartford, Connecticut.

Plymouth Colony administrators send William Holmes to establish a trading center at Windsor (now in Connecticut).

1634

Representative government is established in the Massachusetts Bay colony, when each town gains the right to send deputies to the General Court, the body that passes all laws for the colony.

One export product from the New Hampshire colony is timber. In this year, the first pine masts are sent to British ports.

The community of Trois-Rivières (in Quebec province) is established by a group of colonists under de Champlain.

While permanent English residents in Massachusetts alone number about 4,000, all of Canada probably has fewer than 100 permanent French residents. French travel to North America tends to be cyclical and seasonal, with people involved primarily in fur trapping and fishing. Many visitors return to France or travel back and forth.

Jesuit missionaries expand their activities from Acadia into Huron territory, establishing three missions.

The English royal grant to George Calvert, first Lord of Baltimore, is established as the Maryland colony, a refuge for Roman Catholics.

The island of Curaçao is taken from Spain by Dutch forces.

1635

Dutch colonists occupy the English Virgin Islands and French Martinique; Dutch forces invade northern Brazil.

Puritans establish the first English communities in what is now Connecticut. The following year, Thomas Hooker and his congregation leave Massachusetts Bay to seek less restrictive laws and better land.

c. 1635

General Henrique Diaz, born a slave in Recife, Brazil, plays an important role in helping Brazil gain its independence from the Dutch.

1635-1636

Roger Williams is banished from the Massachusetts Bay colony for preaching the separation of church and state, and for suggesting that the English crown has no authority to give away Native American lands. He and his followers secure land from the Narragansett chiefs and establish Providence in Rhode Island, the first colony to practice full religious freedom.

1636

Hartford is founded in what is now Connecticut.

Springfield is founded in Massachusetts.

Harvard College is founded at Cambridge, Massachusetts.

1637

Anne Hutchinson is banished from the Massachusetts colony after she voices a woman's right to speak and participate in church, and begins to teach the Scriptures. After her banishment, she leads in the establishment of a community at Portsmouth, Rhode Island.

Pequod Fort in Connecticut is destroyed.

c. 1637-1638

Puritan leaders Theophilus Eaton and John Davenport establish the colony of New Haven.

1638

The Reverend John Wheelwright, after being banished from Massachusetts, establishes Exeter, New Hampshire. Another Puritan group builds a community at Hampton, also in New Hampshire.

Wilmington is founded by Swedish colonists in what is now Delaware.

The first Baptist congregation in England's North American colonies is established at Providence, Rhode Island.

French explorer Jean Nicolet leads an expedition to Lake Michigan, then down Green Bay to the Fox River. The expedition develops a trading relationship with the Winnebagos, and tries to make peace between the Winnebagos and the Hurons. This journey greatly expands the French fur trade.

1639

Sir Ferdinando Gorges receives title to Maine but is financially unable to colonize the area.

Hartford, Windsor, and Withersfield are loosely united into the Connecticut colony after the three towns vote to accept the Fundamental Orders of Connecticut, an early constitution which establishes popular consent to govern and suffrage for free males. John Hayes is chosen as Connecticut's first governor.

The first printing press in the English North American colonies is established at Cambridge. The following year, *The Whole Book of Psalms,* is published.

Canada's first hospital, Hotel-dieu of Quebec City, opens its doors.

The Barbados Parliament opens its first session.

THE WORLD

1630

England's King Charles I makes separate peace treaties with France and Spain.

Count Tilly replaces General Wallenstein as head of Holy Roman Emperor Ferdinand II's military.

George I (George Rakoczy) becomes prince of Transylvania after the death of Gabriel Bethlen. George I rules until 1648.

Victor Amadeus I becomes duke of Savoy after the death of his father, Charles Emmanuel I (1580).

1630-1632

Sweden's King Gustavus II intervenes in Germany to protect German Protestants from aggression by the Holy Roman Emperor's army.

1630s

England's textile industry suffers a depression, and farmers in the eastern part of the country experience crop failures.

Japan's Edo shogunate government outlaws Christianity; Portuguese trade ships are banned, as is travel abroad by Japanese people. However, the port of Nagasaki remains open to limited trade with Dutch merchants.

1631

The Netherlands, the Protestant German princes and Elector of Saxony John George align with Sweden's Gustavus II against Holy Roman Emperor Ferdinand II.

Gustavus II and Count Tilly each lead successful military campaigns but after Gustavus II defeats Tilly at the Battle of Breitenfeld, Wallenstein replaces Tilly as head of Ferdinand's imperial forces. Tilly is killed at the Battle of the Lech River (Germany) the following year.

A severe earthquake hits Naples, Italy.

1632

Jesuits are evicted from Ethiopia.

THE WORLD

At the Battle of Lützen, Swedish forces are victorious against imperial troops under General Wallenstein, but King Gustavus II (1611) of Sweden is killed.

As a child, Christina becomes queen of Sweden after the death of her father, Gustavus II (1611). Chancellor Axel Oxenstierna serves as regent until Christina comes of age in 1644. Christina rules until 1654.

Vladislav IV becomes king of Poland after the death of his father, Sigismund III (1587). Vladislav IV rules until 1648.

1633

After publishing his observations supporting the Copernican theory that the sun, and not the earth is the center of the solar system, Galileo is condemned by the papal inquisition.

Portuguese colonists and traders are expelled from Ethiopia.

King Charles I of England becomes king of Scotland. He rules until 1649.

1634

King Vladislav IV of Poland renounces his claim to the Russian throne by the Treaty of Polianov but receives Smolensk in exchange from Michael I of Russia.

General Wallenstein is dismissed from command of imperial forces and is later murdered after being accused of treason.

English trading begins in Bengal (India).

Episcopacy — civil government by church officials — is abolished in Scotland.

1635

France forms an alliance with Sweden and declares war on Spain.

The Treaty of Stuhmsdorf provides for a 20-year truce between Poland and Sweden.

The Peace of Prague is signed between Holy Roman Emperor Ferdinand II and Elector of Saxony John George. The Thirty Years War now becomes chiefly an alliance of France and Sweden against the Hapsburgs of the Holy Roman Empire.

THE WORLD

1636

The Dutch, through a treaty with the king of Kandy, begin to colonize in Ceylon (Sri Lanka).

The Manchus establish a base in Mukden and proclaim the start of an imperial dynasty, the Qing (Ch'ing).

1637

Russian explorers in Siberia reach the Pacific Ocean.

Dutch forces take the city of Elmina (in southern Ghana) from the Portuguese and dominate Africa's Gold Coast.

Ferdinand III becomes king of Hungary and Holy Roman Emperor after the death of his father, Ferdinand II (1619). Ferdinand III rules until 1657.

1638

Japanese rulers suppress a revolt of peasants seeking economic and religious freedom.

Ottoman troops under Murad IV retake Baghdad from the Persians.

Dutch colonists form a community on Mauritius, and name the island after Prince Maurice.

1639

The First Bishops' War takes place in Scotland. Although no blood is shed, Protestant opposition to the English episcopacy remains strong.

Russian explorers travel east and reach the Sea of Okhotsk.

1630

through

1639

NATIVE AMERICAN	AFRICAN AMERICAN	ASIAN AMERICAN	EUROPEAN AMERICAN
1640 The beaver population is decimated in Iroquois country, and the Five Nations do not have enough furs to trade for what they need from the Dutch. **1641** In response to the killing of a farmer by Raritan Indians, Dutch authorities in New Amsterdam (New York City) offer bounties for Raritan scalps or heads. Dutch forces attack and massacre more than 100 Indians in a surprise night raid. **1642** Virginia Governor Sir William Berkeley forces Native Americans to cede all lands between the York and James Rivers. **1643** Roger Williams's book, *Key into the Language of America,* is published. This is a guide to the Native American languages to which Williams has been exposed. The Narragansett War against the New England colonies ends with the capitulation of the Narragansett Indians. The first Protestant mission school for American Indians is established on Martha's Vineyard, Massachusetts, by the Reverend Thomas Mayhew, Jr. **1644-1646** In the Second Powhatan War, Opechancanough, aged chief of the Powhatan Confederacy, again leads his warriors against English colonists. Initially successful, the Powhatans are eventually driven back by superior English numbers and weapons. Opechancanough is captured and killed. **1646** Iroquois war parties begin assaults that virtually destroy the Huron nation by 1649. The Reverend John Eliot begins to gather Indian converts into so-called praying towns, the most successful being Natick; each of the 14 praying towns has a school for American Indians.	**1641** Mathias De Sousa, an African indentured servant who came from England with Lord Baltimore, is elected to Maryland's General Assembly. **1642** Virginia passes a fugitive slave law. Offenders helping runaway slaves are fined in pounds of tobacco. An enslaved person is branded with a large "R" after a second escape attempt. **1643** The New England Confederation reaches an agreement that makes the signature of a magistrate sufficient evidence to convict a person of being a fugitive slave. **1645** In Boston, merchant ships arrive from Barbados, where they traded their cargoes of enslaved Africans for sugar and tobacco. The profitability of this action encourages the slave trade in New England. **c. 1645** Dutch colonists transfer some of their landholdings in New Amsterdam to their former enslaved Africans as compensation for their support in battles with Native Americans. A condition of the land transfer, however, is the guarantee of a specified amount of food from those lands to their former owners.	**1640-1660** Despite the separation of Portugal from Spain, enslaved people are sent from Portuguese colonies in India to Mexico via Acapulco. Filipinos are included in these cargoes.	**1640** By this year, approximately 20,000 English people have immigrated to New England. A large group of English immigrants arrives in Maryland. They are mostly Protestant, and are upset by the prominence of Catholics in the colony. Irish scout Darby Field is sent on a northerly expedition by Governor Winthrop of Massachusetts. During his exploration, Field is probably the first European to see New Hampshire's White Mountains. The Reverend John Eliot's *Bay Psalm Book,* printed this year, is the oldest surviving book printed in America. **1640s** One early contribution of Swedish immigrants to America is their introduction of the dovetailing technique used to build log homes. **1641** French colonists arrive in Michigan. **1642** Thousands of involuntary Irish Catholic immigrants — political and military prisoners and their dependents — are sold into servitude. Johannes Megapolensis, a Dutch Reformed clergyman, leads in the establishment of two Reformed congregations in northern New Netherland (New York, New Jersey and Deleware). Megapolensis learns the Mohawk language, and makes converts among the Indians. **1643-1654** New Sweden, on the Delaware River, establishes Lutheranism as its official religion, but also tolerates Calvinism. **1649** The colonial legislature of Virginia pledges its allegiance to the Stuart family after England's King Charles I is executed. The Virginia colony becomes a refuge for prominent Cavaliers who come to America.

1640

through

1649

EUROPEAN AMERICAN	HISPANIC AMERICAN	FOR CLASSROOM USE	FOR CLASSROOM USE	
During the administration of colonial Maryland's Deputy Governor William Stone, a Protestant, a Toleration Act is passed. The Calverts, proprietors of the colony and Catholics, recognize that the majority of Maryland residents are Protestants, and agree to this legislation to keep the peace.	**1640-1650** A gradual recovery and increase of the Indian population begins in Mexico. **1641-1642** Disputes break out between Spanish groups in New Mexico. The Pueblo tribes suffer from both sides. **1642** A Franciscan monastery is established in Puerto Rico by friars, mostly Portuguese, who reached the island in 1641. **1643** King Philip IV of Spain emphasizes the strategic and military importance of Puerto Rico. **1644** Members of the Toboso tribe revolt against Spanish dominion in Chihuahua and seize 3,500 head of livestock. They are soon joined by other Indians in the Texas border area in raiding the herds of Spanish colonists. **1646** A small shrine, the Ermita of the Virgin of Monserrate, is built in Puerto Rico at the site of her reported appearance. The town of Hormigueros develops around the shrine. **1647** The memoir of Diego Torres Vargas indicates the development of a creole class in Puerto Rico.			**1640** through **1649**

THE AMERICAS	THE AMERICAS	THE AMERICAS	THE WORLD

1640 through 1649

THE AMERICAS

1640

By this time, four European communities have been established in the New Hampshire colony. They are Strawberry Bank (which later becomes Portsmouth), Exeter, Hampton and Hilton's Point (which later becomes Dover).

Pirates inhabit Barbados.

Tadoussac (in Quebec province) becomes a significant fur-trading post for French merchants, and the site of a Jesuit mission.

An unofficial census lists the population of New France at under 400.

1641

The Massachusetts Body of Liberties is passed by the citizens of Massachusetts. Many of the concepts listed in the document, such as the protection of free men to own property without fear that the government can seize it without compensation, later make up the core of the Bill of Rights.

1642

Jewish colonists arrive in Brazil.

French colonists led by Paul de Maisonneuve immigrate to New France and establish a community they call Ville-Marie de Montreal (now Montreal, in Quebec province).

The Massachusetts colony passes a law requiring that each town educate its children.

1643

A visitor to New Amsterdam (New York City) reports hearing 18 different languages spoken in that community.

The first Lutheran congregation in the North American colonies is established by Swedish Lutherans at Tinicum Island, Pennsylvania.

A woolen mill, the first in North America, opens for business at Rowley, Massachusetts. In this same year, the earliest significant ironworks establishment also opens, in Lynn, Massachusetts.

THE AMERICAS

Deborah Moody, banished from Massachusetts for her adherence to Anabaptist beliefs, seeks and receives permission from Dutch authorities to establish a community in New Netherland. Her Gravesend community (now part of Brooklyn, New York) is granted religious freedom, and is the first town chartered to a woman.

The Confederation of New England is formed when the colonies of Massachusetts Bay, Plymouth, Connecticut and New Haven make a pact for "mutual safety and welfare."

Dutch forces raid Trujillo (in present-day Honduras). This attack causes Spain to abandon the port city for almost 150 years.

1643-1644

In Acadia (Nova Scotia, New Brunswick and eastern Maine), long-standing trade competition and territorial fighting continues between the Iroquois and Hurons on one side, and French and Algonquins on the other. Losses are heavy and neither side gains a clear victory.

1645

By this winter smallpox has killed more than half of Acadia's 15,000 Huron residents.

British colonists on Barbados export sugar to Britain for the first time.

1646

Explorer Darby Field and two guides with him climb the tallest mountain in New England, which is later named Mount Washington.

Margaret Brent, a prosperous landowner, is appointed administrator of the Maryland colony as executor of the estate of Governor Calvert. The following year, she asks for the right to vote, but is refused. Brent, who came from England in 1638, is the first woman in Maryland to own land in her own name.

English colonists occupy the Bahamas.

1647

Barbados experiences an outbreak of yellow fever.

THE AMERICAS

c. 1648

Puritans from Virginia establish a colony known as Providence, later named Annapolis (Maryland) in honor of England's Queen Anne.

The Maryland colonial assembly turns down attorney and landowner Margaret Brent's request for a seat in the assembly. Although she maintains her property in Maryland, she later moves to Virginia.

1649

A toleration act is passed in the Maryland colony to sustain peace between Catholics and Protestants and guarantee freedom of worship to all Christians.

The government of Virginia announces its allegiance to England's Stuart family after King Charles I is executed. The colony provides refuge to English Cavaliers who immigrate to America.

Enslaved Africans on Barbados stage their first revolt.

THE WORLD

1640

The Second Bishops' War between England and Scotland ends with the Treaty of Ripon.

For the next two decades, often with French support, rebellions occur against Spanish rule in Catalonia, a northeast region of Spain.

Because diplomatic ties are strained after Portugal gains its independence and because trade relations with the Dutch were stopped earlier in the decade, for two decades Spain does not issue an *asiento* (an exclusive license to control the transport of enslaved Africans to Spain's colonies in the Americas).

English colonists establish Fort St. George in Bengal.

Portugal regains its independence from Spain, and John Braganza takes the throne as King John IV. He rules until 1656.

Ibrahim I becomes Ottoman sultan after the death of his brother, Murad IV (1623). Ibrahim I rules until 1648.

Frederick William (the Great Elector) rules Brandenburg after the death of George William. Frederick William rules until 1688.

1640-1641

Dutch forces capture Malacca from the Portuguese.

1641

Irish Protestants are massacred by Catholics in Ulster. Catholics rebel throughout Ireland.

c. 1641

Spaniards in Formosa (Taiwan) are expelled by the Dutch, who then claim the whole island.

1641-1648

Dutch forces occupy Angola.

1642

Cardinal Jules Mazarin succeeds Cardinal Richelieu (1624) as chief minister of France. Mazarin is confirmed in 1643 by Anne of Austria, the queen mother of Louis XIV and wife of Louis XIII.

Tasmania is explored by a Dutch expedition led by Abel Janszoon Tasman. This land mass is originally named Van Diemen's Land in honor of Anton van Diemen, governor general of the East Indies. Tasman also explores the area that is now New Zealand.

The Bible is first translated into Finnish.

The British East India Company establishes a community in Bengal (East Pakistan).

The Portuguese government cedes the African Gold Coast to the Netherlands.

Abbas II becomes shah of Persia after the death of his father, Safi I (1629). Abbas II rules until 1667.

1642-1648

The English Civil War begins as a conflict between Royalists and Parliamentarians. Royalist supporters include the nobility and Anglican and Catholic officials. Parliamentarians include the merchant and trades classes, and Scottish Protestants called Covenanters. King Charles I dissolves Parliament twice by royal decree before fighting begins. Early battles are indecisive, but Protestant/Parliamentary forces under Oliver Cromwell win two significant battles against Royalist soldiers. The Royalists, also called Cavaliers, are eventually defeated, and Charles I is forced to surrender. A second, short-lived war commences when Charles I escapes and attempts to retake the throne. He is quickly defeated and recaptured, and is beheaded in 1649.

1643

Abel Tasman explores Tonga and skirts Fiji and New Guinea. His tales of treacherous reefs keep other European vessels away.

As a child, Louis XIV becomes king of France after the death of his father, Louis XIII (1610). Anne of Austria, the queen mother, acts as regent, but relies heavily on Cardinal Mazarin. Louis XIV comes of age in 1661 and rules until 1715.

1643-1646

A Russian expedition led by Poyarkhov explores the Amur River in northeast Asia.

1644

Tasman charts parts of the northern and western coasts of Australia, then called New Holland.

Dutch and Portuguese colonists establish sugar plantations in Surinam (Dutch Guiana).

The Ming dynasty ends when peasant rebels capture Peking and the emperor hangs himself. A Ming general invites the Manchus from the northeast to enter China to fight the peasant rebels. The Manchu Qing (Ch'ing) dynasty occupies China's throne. Manchu women are less restricted than Chinese women: they do not bind their feet, they have some voice in marriage arrangements, and Manchus do not practice female infanticide. Ming rule continues in southern China and Formosa for a few years. The Qing dynasty rules China until 1911.

1645

The Dutch occupy St. Helena, in the South Atlantic Ocean.

Capuchin monks sail up the Congo River.

The Ottoman army begins a two-decade war with Venice over the Island of Crete.

Har Rai becomes guru of the Sikh faith after the death of his grandfather, Har Govind (1606). Har Rai holds this position until 1661.

Alexis I (Alexis Mikhailovich) becomes czar of Russia after the death of his father, Michael I (1613). Alexis I rules until 1676.

1646

Manchu forces occupy Zhejiang (Chekiang) and Sichuan (Szechuan), and one year later take Canton, China.

1646-1680

The Mahrattas gradually gain power in India.

1647

Russia's peasants revolt against Czar Alexis I in Moscow.

1648

The Peace of Westphalia, which ends the Thirty Years War, produces many changes. It reduces the power of the Holy Roman Empire and the Hapsburg family; the sovereignty of the German states is recognized; France and Sweden obtain new territory; Prussia gains new lands in western Germany; Lutherans and Calvinists retain lands held before 1624; local rulers may still determine the religion of their domains, but citizens are free to worship as they did in 1624; and the independence of the United Provinces (modern-day Netherlands) and the Swiss Confederation is recognized.

France's first Fronde, the Fronde of the Parlement (a revolt against the Mazarin administration), ends with the Treaty of Rueil in 1649.

By the Treaty of Münster, Spain recognizes the independence of the Netherlands.

Bohdan Chmielnicki leads Ukranian Cossacks, Russian warriors of the peasant class, in a rebellion against Polish rule.

The population of Germany sees a dramatic drop, from approximately 17 million in 1618 to approximately eight million, due to the Thirty Years War, famine and plague. Sources vary on the exact figure.

Frederick III becomes king of Denmark and Norway after the death of his father, Christian IV (1588). Frederick III rules until 1670.

John II (John Casimir) becomes king of Poland after the death of his brother, Vladislav IV (1632). John II rules until 1668.

Muhammad IV becomes Ottoman sultan after the death of his father, Ibrahim I (1640). Muhammad IV rules until 1687.

George II (George Rakoczy) becomes prince of Transylvania after the death of his father, George I (1630). George II is deposed in 1657.

1648-1658

Jews are persecuted in Poland and in the Ukraine.

1649

England's new government is a Puritan Commonwealth, with Oliver Cromwell as virtual dictator. Cromwell leads a merciless punitive raid into Ireland, massacres a Royalist garrison at Drogheda, and begins a policy of placing Irish lands in the possession of English nobles. Cromwell rules England until 1660.

English emigration virtually ceases as Puritans gain influence at home. In fact, more educated men return to England than leave it.

Charles II is proclaimed king of Scotland after Charles I (1633) is beheaded. Charles II is crowned in 1651.

1640

through

1649

NATIVE AMERICAN	AFRICAN AMERICAN	ASIAN AMERICAN	EUROPEAN AMERICAN
1650 The first European traders reach Ojibwa (Chippewa) territory on the southwest shore of Lake Superior. Five hundred Huron survivors of the Iroquois attacks of 1646-1649 flee to Quebec, where they later are the only group to maintain Huron tribal identity. After defeating the Hurons the Iroquois, backed by the Dutch, wage war against the French. **1651** The defeat of the Neutral tribe, which is friendly toward French colonists, is complete when a large village of 1,600 Neutrals is captured by the Iroquois and all adult males are killed. **1653-1656** The Erie tribe is virtually annihilated by the Iroquois. **1656** Ottawa and Huron traders, accompanied by two Frenchmen, bring a large canoe fleet of furs to Montreal, thus angering the Iroquois tribes, who are their competitors in the fur trade. **1656-1658** Laws passed by the Virginia House of Burgesses state that: lands granted to Native Americans by the assembly cannot be taken away except by consent of the assembly; no land grants can be issued to Europeans until every tribe receives 50 acres for each "bowman"; Native Americans have hunting rights on all unclaimed land; and any tribal lands included in grants at Rappahannock must either be purchased from, or returned to, the tribe. Late in 1658, the assembly admits that English colonists are still intruding on native lands. **1657** Following a peace treaty with the Iroquois, a group of French colonists leaves Montreal and winters in Onondaga country (upstate New York).	**1650** Connecticut legalizes slavery. Rhode Island has large plantations worked by enslaved Africans. In New Netherland, the Dutch West India Company introduces slavery in a form similar to indenturing. Even after gaining freedom, former slaves have to give fixed amounts of their crops to the company. After the English capture of the colony, traditional enslavement is introduced and even the limited freedoms are curtailed. **1651** Anthony Johnson, a free African American, imports several enslaved Africans and is given a grant of land on Virginia's Puwgoteague River. Other free African Americans follow this pattern.	Although Chinese seamen have engaged in significant maritime activity from the middle of the seventh century, when Manchus conquer the Chinese people in 1644 and bring the Ming dynasty to an end, a major change in foreign policy occurs. Fearing that Ming loyalists will create a revolutionary force outside the country, officials of the new Qing (Ch'ing) dynasty pass edicts barring emigration. Many Chinese people, especially from the southeastern provinces of Fujian (Fukien) and Guangdong (Kwangtung), continue to travel back and forth between China and the countries of southeast Asia, where sizeable Chinese colonies flourish. However, most of the Chinese people are isolated from the West until early in the nineteenth century. Japan's location off the coast of the Asian mainland keeps its inhabitants relatively isolated from outside visitors. The Japanese people withstand attempted invasions by Kublai Khan in the 1200s, and first encounter Europeans when Portuguese traders arrive off the Asian mainland in the early 1500s. European missionaries follow but, fearing the examples seen in other Asian countries where missionaries were soon followed by military forces, the Tokugawa shogunate issues an effective anti-Christian decree. Japan remains isolated until a United States fleet under Commodore (later Admiral) Matthew Perry sails into Tokyo Bay in 1853.	**1652** Approximately 30 Scottish Royalists and Covenanter prisoners are transported to Virginia after the Battle of Dunbar. **1654** When Recife, Brazil, falls to Portuguese forces, 23 Jewish people who went there to escape the Spanish Inquisition flee again — this time to New Amsterdam (New York City). These are the first recorded Jewish immigrants to British North America. Seventy orphan boys and girls are sent from Amsterdam to New Netherland as apprentice workers and future colonists. **1655** The first Jewish congregation in what is now the United States, Sheareth Israel, is established in New Amsterdam. **1656** English Quakers begin arriving in Massachusetts Bay. Two Quaker women are banished, however, for religious nonconformity. Later Quakers are also persecuted. **1658** The death penalty is established at Massachusetts Bay for banished Quakers who return to the colony. Two violators are hanged. **1659** A Huguenot church is founded in New Amsterdam.

1650 through 1659

HISPANIC AMERICAN	FOR CLASSROOM USE	FOR CLASSROOM USE	FOR CLASSROOM USE	

1650

Sugar becomes Puerto Rico's most important export crop.

Puerto Rican privateer Miguel Enriquez, a *mulatto* (a person of combined African and European ethnicity), is honored for his achievements.

1655

There are by this time more than 40 missions in Florida. The chain of missions extends west from St. Augustine to present-day Tallahassee, and north from St. Augustine to Santa Elena, in what is now South Carolina.

1659

Franciscan missionaries establish a community at what is now Juárez, Mexico, on the west bank of the Rio Grande.

1650

through

1659

THE AMERICAS	THE AMERICAS	THE WORLD	THE WORLD

1650 through 1659

THE AMERICAS

1650

A two-year civil war begins in Barbados.

1651

The first English Navigation Act limits the types of goods that can be imported to England and its colonies on Dutch ships.

1652

Maine becomes part of the Massachusetts Bay Company.

1653

Portsmouth, established c. 1624, is incorporated by Massachusetts. It is the colonial capital until the Revolutionary War.

The first permanent European community in what is now North Carolina is established at Albemarle Sound by colonists from Virginia.

1654

Portuguese forces expel Dutch colonists from Brazil and gain control of the region.

1655

English forces under William Penn capture Jamaica from Spain. The island becomes a base for British smuggling and piracy activities against Spain.

A fleet of four ships and 500 men out of Boston attacks Acadia (Nova Scotia, New Brunswick and eastern Maine), capturing Port Royal and several French trading posts.

A Dutch fleet lands at and conquers Fort Christina (site of Wilmington, Delaware). New Sweden (Delaware) becomes part of New Netherland (most of present-day New York, New Jersey and Delaware).

THE AMERICAS

c. 1655

One result of the British conquest of Jamaica is that many Africans formerly held in slavery by Spanish colonists flee to the mountain regions and form communities and military units to protect themselves from reenslavement. These Africans are called Maroons. They are so skilled at their guerilla-style warfare that British colonists sign treaties with them, granting autonomy and the right to lands that the Maroons hold.

1656

Two women — Ann Austin and Mary Fisher — are the first Quakers to come to the Massachusetts Puritan colony. They are imprisoned and deported. Quakers who arrive later also are driven away.

The fur trade in Canada is carried on by the Ottawas, who have taken the place of the Hurons. Iroquois Confederacy members are enraged, and send war parties against French communities from Quebec to Montreal, burning crops and homes and killing colonists.

1658

French trader Médard Chouart Groseilliers and his brother-in-law Pierre Esprit Radisson explore the area of Minnesota.

THE WORLD

1650

The second French Fronde, the Fronde of the Princes, occurs. Mazarin arrests Louis II, prince of Condé (Great Condé), and the leaders of the Second Fronde.

Charles II arrives in Scotland. Oliver Cromwell and his forces defeat the Scots at the Battle of Dunbar (Firth of Forth), thus enabling the Commonwealth to control Scotland south of the Forth.

The first Catholic church is built in Peking, China.

c. 1650

The Quaker religion is founded in England by George Fox. Quakers resist the state-dominated church and practices they believe are too much like those of the Roman Catholic Church. The homes of women become the first meeting places for Quaker worship.

Dahomey becomes a powerful region under leader Wegbaja.

1651

Cardinal Mazarin flees Paris and goes to Germany after the Frondeurs gain the support of the queen mother, Anne of Austria, who is also regent of France.

The English Navigation Act requires that goods produced for England's American colonies be shipped on English vessels or those of the manufacturing countries. The act is designed to eliminate competition from the Dutch merchant fleet in foreign trade.

Charles II is crowned king of Scotland. He marches into England to take the English throne as well, but is defeated at Worcester by Oliver Cromwell and flees to France.

Ietsuna becomes shogun in Japan after the death of his father, Iemitsu (1623). Ietsuna rules until 1680.

1652

Louis XIV enters Paris and reinstates the monarchy.

The English Parliament passes the Act of Pardon and Oblivion to reconcile with the Royalists.

THE WORLD

The Dutch East India Company establishes a station for its ships at the Cape of Good Hope in South Africa. This is the beginning of the Dutch colonization of the area.

England and the Netherlands (United Provinces) become commercial rivals; as a result, a series of sea battles takes place between the two countries. The battles end in 1654 with England gaining compensation for its war damage and official respect for its ships in English waters. Both parties agree to use arbitration to settle disputes over territorial claims.

1653

Cardinal Mazarin returns to Paris and the Fronde is ended with the surrender of the city of Bordeaux.

Oliver Cromwell takes the title of Lord Protector of England, Scotland and Ireland.

Reports from shipwrecked Dutch sailors are the first eyewitness accounts of Korea and its people.

1654

The Treaty of Westminster brings peace between England and the Netherlands and the Dutch recognize the authority of the Navigation Act of 1651.

Polish rebel Bohdan Chmielnicki requests military aid from Russia's Czar Alexis I. As a result, the Ukraine becomes a Muscovite protectorate. Russian troops take the city of Smolensk, opening a thirteen-year territorial war between Poland and Russia.

By this time approximately 50,000 Scots have immigrated to Ulster, Ireland. They are the ancestors of the Scotch-Irish who later play a big part in American immigration history.

Charles X becomes king of Sweden after the abdication of his cousin, Queen Christina (1632). Christina's abdication is considered scandalous, especially because she converts to Catholicism. Charles X rules until 1660.

1654-1751

This is the time span generally ascribed to the Palatinate dynasty that rules Sweden.

THE WORLD	THE WORLD			

1655

Swedish armies invade Poland and capture Warsaw and Krakow (Cracow). This act begins the first Northern War.

Oliver Cromwell dissolves Parliament and divides England into military districts.

1656

The Treaty of Köningsberg is signed between Sweden and Brandenburg. Sweden later recognizes Frederick William of Brandenburg as ruler of East Prussia.

Dutch merchants begin trading with China.

Dutch forces take the Ceylonese strategic port city of Colombo from the Portuguese.

Jews are readmitted to England by Oliver Cromwell.

Alfonso VI becomes king of Portugal after the death of his father, John IV (1640). Alfonso VI rules until 1683.

The appointment of Albanian Muhammad Kiuprili as grand *vizier* (minister of state) to Ottoman Sultan Muhammad IV begins a Turkish revival. Kiuprili serves until 1661.

1657

Brandenburg and Poland form an alliance against Swedish aggression. Denmark declares war on Sweden to protect Danish fishing interests in the Baltic Sea.

The English monarchy transfers the trade monopoly in enslaved Africans from the Guinea Company to the East India Company.

The pendulum clock is invented by Christian Huygens, a Dutch physicist.

The Dutch expand their station at the Cape of Good Hope into a permanent colony.

Narai becomes king of Siam (Thailand). He rules until 1688.

George II (Rákóczy), prince of Translyvanis, is deposed after he leads an unsuccessful invasion of Poland.

Leopold I becomes king of Hungary and Holy Roman Emperor after the death of his father, Ferdinand III (1637). Leopold I rules until 1705. He is also king of Bohemia from 1656-1705.

1658

The Treaty of Roskild (Roskilde) ends a territorial war between Sweden and Denmark. However, troops under Danish King Charles X make an unsuccessful attempt to seize Copenhagen.

Portuguese rule in Ceylon (Sri Lanka) ends.

In the Battle of the Dunes, Henri de La Tour d'Auvergne, vicomte de Turenne uses a French and English force to defeat Spanish troops under Louis II de Bourbon, prince de Condé and Don John of Austria. D'Auvergne's troops take Dunkirk.

Aurangzeb defeats his brother, Dara Shikuh, at the Battle of Samugarh and deposes his father, Shah Jahan (1627), to become Mogul emperor of India. A devoted follower of Islam, he rules until 1707.

Richard Cromwell becomes lord protector of England after the death of his father, Oliver Cromwell (1642, 1649). A weak leader, Richard Cromwell resigns in 1659 and the protectorate collapses.

1659

The Treaty of Pyrenees ends a long conflict between France and Spain and provides France with territorial gains.

Senegal becomes a French colony.

1650

through

1659

NATIVE AMERICAN	AFRICAN AMERICAN	ASIAN AMERICAN	EUROPEAN AMERICAN
1660 The Ojibwa (Chippewa) now have firearms and migrate west into the Mississippi Valley, driving the Sioux south and west. **1660-1670** Wyandots and Ottawas establish a trading center at Chegnamegon Bay on Lake Superior and trade with French colonists. By 1670 there are 50 tribal villages on the bay. **1661** The first American edition of the Bible, translated by the Reverend John Eliot with Native American assistance, is in the language of the Indians of Massachusetts. Spanish posts in what are now Georgia and South Carolina are attacked by Indians. Missions north of the Savannah River are subsequently abandoned. **1662** A Virginia law mandates that Native Americans are to be "protected in their property as if they were Englishmen." **1665** Caleb Cheeshateaumuck is the first Native American to earn an A.B. degree at Harvard College. **1667-1680** Apache and Navajo groups begin continuous warfare against Spanish forces in New Mexico. One valuable commodity is horses, which the Native Americans capture and trade to tribes to the north and east.	**1660** A Connecticut law prohibits African Americans from serving in the militia. **1662** Virginia enacts a law that makes the free or enslaved status of children dependent on the status of the mother. **1663** Maryland slave laws provide that all imported Africans are slaves; that free European American women who marry enslaved men lose their freedom; and that the children of these unions are enslaved. Other North American colonies have similar laws. A planned revolt of enslaved Africans is uncovered in Virginia. **1664** In Virginia, the enslaved African's status is clearly differentiated from the indentured servant's when colonial laws decree that enslavement is for life and is transferred to the children through the mother. Black and "slave" become synonymous, and enslaved Africans are subject to harsher and more brutal control than other laborers. **1667** England enacts strict laws regarding enslaved Africans in its colonies. An enslaved African is forbidden to leave the plantation without a pass, and never on Sunday; and may not possess weapons or signalling mechanisms such as horns or whistles. Punishment for an owner who kills an enslaved African is a 15-pound fine.	Although Chinese seamen have engaged in significant maritime activity from the middle of the seventh century, when Manchus conquer the Chinese people in 1644 and bring the Ming dynasty to an end, a major change in foreign policy occurs. Fearing that Ming loyalists will create a revolutionary force outside the country, officials of the new Qing (Ch'ing) dynasty pass edicts barring emigration. Many Chinese people, especially from the southeastern provinces of Fujian (Fukien) and Guangdong (Kwangtung), continue to travel back and forth between China and the countries of southeast Asia, where sizeable Chinese colonies flourish. However, most of the Chinese people are isolated from the West until early in the nineteenth century. Japan's location off the coast of the Asian mainland keeps its inhabitants relatively isolated from outside visitors. The Japanese people withstand attempted invasions by Kublai Khan in the 1200s, and first encounter Europeans when Portuguese traders arrive off the Asian mainland in the early 1500s. European missionaries follow but, fearing the examples seen in other Asian countries where missionaries were soon followed by military forces, the Tokugawa shogunate issues an effective anti-Christian decree. Japan remains isolated until a United States fleet under Commodore (later Admiral) Matthew Perry sails into Tokyo Bay in 1853.	**1660** Two Norwegian immigrants to New Netherland (New York, New Jersey and Delaware) establish the first successful sawmills in North America. In Yarmouth, Massachusetts, Irish immigrant Teague Jones is fined for refusing to swear allegiance to Britain. **1662** Peter Cornelisz Plockhoy brings 25 Mennonite families to a spot on the Delaware River where they establish a communal town. This is one of the first communal groups in America, and the only organized Dutch group migration to New Netherland. This small community is over-run by British forces in 1664, and many of its inhabitants are sent to Virginia as domestics and laborers. **1664** At this time, New Netherland has about 10,000 people, primarily Dutch, but also English, French Huguenots, Walloons (Celtic people from France and Belgium) and Germans. English forces under the command of Colonel Richard Nicolls capture New Netherland from the Dutch and divide it into two regions, New York and Jersey (later New Jersey). A land grant to Sir George Carteret and Lord John Berkeley (the area that is now New Jersey), includes provisions for a governor appointed by the proprietors, a council appointed by the governor, an elected assembly and religious freedom. Governor Philip Carteret brings about 30 English colonists to the area in 1665. **1665** English law is introduced in New York. **1666** Puritans from Connecticut make their homes in the area that what is now Newark, New Jersey.

1660 through 1669

HISPANIC AMERICAN	FOR CLASSROOM USE	FOR CLASSROOM USE	FOR CLASSROOM USE	

1660

Disputes become so bitter between religious and civil authorities in New Mexico that the Franciscans threaten to leave.

Governor Pérez de Guzmán of Puerto Rico writes King Philip IV of Spain that "eleven years have passed since the last ship came to this island."

1662-1668

A community is established at El Paso del Norte (Juárez, Mexico). The presidio there is built in 1683.

1663

Spanish conquistadors raid the sacred *kivas* (underground ceremonial chamber) of the Pueblo tribe and destroy artifacts in an attempt to suppress the native religion.

1664

In an effort to prevent a Pueblo-Apache alliance, Governor Peñalosa of New Mexico limits the number of Native Americans in the Spanish-held towns at any time and the length of time they may stay.

Fugitives who have escaped slavery in the Lesser Antilles are granted their freedom in Puerto Rico.

1668

Pirate John Davis sacks St. Augustine, Florida, and burns the town.

1660

through

1669

1669

through

1669

1660

Land grants in (South) Carolina are given to European colonists, who bring in enslaved Africans.

The Virginia colony recognizes England's King Charles II.

Mary Dyer, a former follower of Anne Hutchinson (1637) who later converted to the Quaker faith, is hanged in Boston.

In early attempts to legislate a man's familial responsibilities, Connecticut law requires a man to live with his family, and Massachusetts law declares a man responsible for supporting his own children, even those born out of wedlock.

An early census of Canada shows slightly more than 3,200 Europeans in New France, while the European population of New England numbers just under 80,000.

Iroquois attack Montreal, but are held off outside the city by a small group of French colonists and Huron and Algonquin warriors.

Under an agreement signed this year between French and British officials, the government of Dominica is left to its Carib Indian inhabitants.

Guatemala has its first printing press.

c. 1660

While most colonial church organizations believe that women should keep silent in church, the Quaker faith allows the participation of both genders. Many future women's rights activists are rooted in the Quaker church.

1660-1675

With the restoration of the House of Stuart in England, the Virginia colony suffers hard times. The Dutch Wars and British Navigation Acts dampen the colony's economy by severly limiting trade; and conditions further deteriorate as a result of servant unrest, an epidemic that kills many cattle and the reinstatement of the poll tax.

1661

The first American edition of the Bible, translated by the Reverend John Eliot, is in the native language of the Indians of what is now Massachusetts.

Unrest in the Maryland colony is due to raids by Native Americans, the restriction of the vote to landholders and continued anti-Catholic sentiment.

c. 1661

Persecution of Quakers is suspended in the American colonies.

1661-1664

English forces conquer New Netherland.

1662

Governor John Winthrop, Jr., obtains a royal charter for the colony of Connecticut that also includes the acquisition of New Haven.

The first English colony in Belize is established.

1663

New France is organized into a province with the city of Quebec as its capital.

The governor of New France issues an edict prohibiting the sale of liquor to Indians.

England's King Charles II grants land in the Carolinas to eight of his supporters, the foremost being Lord Anthony Ashley Cooper. Religious freedom is allowed. Charles II also grants a charter to Rhode Island, but lets it continue under independent rule.

England passes a second Navigation Act specifying that all goods shipped to English colonies in America must be shipped on English vessels and prohibiting colonists from trading with other European countries. This act is opposed by colonists and also by traders, notably from France and the Netherlands.

1664

English forces take New Amsterdam and Fort Orange from the Dutch, renaming them New York and Albany, respectively.

James, the duke of York, takes land from the Dutch New Netherland colony that stretches between the Delaware and Hudson Rivers. He issues a grant to Sir George Cartaret and Lord John Berkeley who become proprietors of the area called Jersey (New Jersey). Richard Nicolls, acting for James but unaware that he has issued a land grant, enables those seeking religious freedom to obtain portions of these same lands in the Elizabethtown and Monmouth purchases. Although the colony is established to ensure religious freedom, East Jersey is plagued by confusion in land ownership. Early opposition to slavery by Dutch and Swedish colonists keeps Jersey from becoming a major slaveholding colony.

French colonists establish a city, Port-de-Paix, in the western part of Hispaniola.

1665

The ratio of males to females in New France is approximately five to one. The intendant, Jean Baptiste Talon, petitions King Louis XIV for prospective brides. The first shipload of "Filles du Roi" (the king's girls) comes from the Royal Orphanage in Paris.

Dutch forces attack the English community at St. Johns, Newfoundland.

1666

Troops from New France march south to force peace on the Mohawk people. They unexpectedly encounter an English outpost outside of what is now Schenectady, but both sides part after a peaceful exchange.

Tobago falls to English pirates.

English forces overrun the Dutch community at Tortola, Virgin Islands, making it an English possession.

French forces capture Antigua and Montserrat.

French explorer René Robert Cavelier, sieur de La Salle (La Salle), receives a land grant to explore along the St. Lawrence River.

1667

Under the Treaty of Breda, France regains permanent title to Acadia (Nova Scotia, New Brunswick and eastern Maine) from England.

1668

Pirate John Davis sacks St. Augustine, Florida, and burns the town.

The first Jesuit mission in Michigan is established at Sault Ste. Marie, under the direction of Father Jacques Marquette.

1660

The Treaty of Oliva ends the five-year Northern War between Poland and Sweden; Livonia comes under Swedish control and Poland's King John II gives up claims to the Swedish throne.

The Treaty of Copenhagen ends the second war between Sweden and Denmark. Denmark retains Bornholm and Trondheim but surrenders some of its southern territory.

The Royal African Company is founded.

West New Guinea is claimed by the Netherlands.

Dutch peasants (Boers) make their homes in South Africa.

Bambara kingdoms reach their peak in the upper Niger River region of Africa.

The monarchy is restored in England. Parliament invites Charles II to return to England and he is crowned king in 1661. Charles II rules until 1685. Emigration is officially discouraged.

Charles XI becomes king of Sweden after the death of his father, Charles X (1654). Charles XI rules until 1697.

1661

The Treaty of Kardis brings peace between Russia and Sweden.

Portugal cedes Ceylon, Malacca and the Moluccas to the Netherlands; the Dutch withdraw all claims in Brazil.

Famine is widespread in India due to a two-year drought.

King Louis XIV assumes total control and begins his formal reign in France after the death of Cardinal Mazarin.

Mawlay al Rashid is proclaimed sultan of Morocco and begins to reestablish the Moroccan Empire.

As a child, Hari (Har) Krishan becomes guru of the Sikh faith after the death of his father, Har Rai (1645). Hari Krishan holds the position until 1664.

Ahmed (Achmet) Kiuprili becomes grand *vizier* (minister of state) of the Ottoman Empire after the death of his father, Muhammad Kiuprili (1656). Ahmed Kiuprili holds this office until 1676.

1662

Dutch colonists are expelled from Taiwan (Formosa) by forces under Zheng Chenggong (Koxinga), a supporter of the Ming dynasty. Taiwan, however, remains independent of mainland China until 1683 when it falls to the Manchus.

In England, the Law of Settlement requires that a person who falls under the Poor Law must return to his or her parish of birth from his or her parish of residence.

The marriage of England's Charles II and Portugal's princess Catherine da Braganza unites the two nations and transfers control of the Port of Tangier, Morocco, and the Island of Bombay to England.

Kangxi (K'ang hsi) becomes emperor of China after the death of his father, Shunzhi (Shun Chih). Kangxi rules until 1722. The last Ming pretender to the throne is pursued and captured by the Qing (Ch'ing) in Burma.

1662-1683

The Manchu conquest of southern China and Taiwan (Formosa) takes place.

1663

Ottoman forces under Ahmed Kiuprili attack Austria, Hungary and Transylvania.

The English Parliament passes a second Navigation Act to control shipping and commerce to its American colonies.

1664

The Treaty of Vasvar between Holy Roman Emperor Leopold I and the Ottoman Empire follows the Austrian victory under Raimondo Conte di Montecucculi at St. Gotthard on the Raab River.

A three-year war breaks out between England and the Netherlands.

Territorial conflicts in India begin between England and France.

The first Russian mission goes to Isfahan, Persia.

Tegh Bahādur becomes guru of the Sikh faith after the death of Hari Krishan (1661). Tegh Bahādur holds the position until 1675.

1665

The Great Plague of London kills almost 70,000 people.

Portugal gains its independence after English and Portuguese forces defeat the Spanish army at Montes Claros and Villa Viciosa.

Charles II becomes king of Spain after the death of his father, Philip IV (1621). Charles II rules until 1700.

1666

France and the Netherlands declare war on England.

An alliance is formed between Brandenburg, Brunswick, Denmark and the Netherlands to protect the Dutch position against the French.

The Great Fire occurs in London.

In order to escape the death penalty issued by grand *vizier* (minister of state in the Ottoman Empire) Ahmed Kiuprili for his revolutionary activities, Sabbatai Zevi converts to Islam at Adrianople (Edirne, Turkey) and takes the name Mehmed Effendi.

1667

The Treaty of Breda ends the conflict between England, France and the Netherlands. The treaty improves the Dutch position in the East Indian and West African slave trades and allows them to keep Surinam, while the English gain control of the North American colony of New Netherland (New York, New Jersey and Delaware); France, which did not participate much in the war, and England agree on mutual compensation for damage done during the fighting.

The War of Devolution begins as France attacks the Netherlands.

An earthquake in Shemaka (Caucasia, now eastern Azerbaidzhan) kills 80,000 people.

The army of France's King Louis XIV attacks the Spanish Netherlands.

The Treaty of Andrusovo ends the war between Russia and Poland, and partitions the Ukraine between the two countries; Kiev and Smolensk become part of Russia.

Suleiman I becomes shah of Persia after the death of his father, Abbas II (1642). Suleiman I rules until 1694.

1668

The British East India Company receives Bombay from England's King Charles II and founds Fort William (Calcutta).

By the terms of the Treaty of Aix-la-Chapelle, the war between France and Spain ends. France retains most of its territory in Flanders and Spain receives back conquered lands and has its holdings in the Spanish Netherlands guaranteed by the Triple Alliance of England, the Netherlands and Sweden.

Manchuria is closed to the Han-Chinese and reserved for the Manchus.

Portuguese troops kill the king of the Kongo in the Battle of Ambuila. The kingdom soon declines.

Spain recognizes Portugal's independence by the Treaty of Lisbon.

Mogul ruler Aurangzeb destroys Hindu temples and prohibits freedom of religion in India. His suppression of Hinduism further encourages the rise of the Mahrattas — Hindu warriors — led by Sivaji Bhonsla.

Michael Wisniowiecki becomes king of Poland after John II (1648) abdicates. Wisniowiecki rules until 1673.

1669

A cholera epidemic breaks out in China.

A severe famine is experienced in India.

The Hanseatic League, a German trade league formed in 1358, is dissolved.

The fall of the island of Candia, Venice's last colonial possession, yields all of Crete to the Ottoman Turks, who govern it until 1898.

1660
through
1669

	NATIVE AMERICAN	AFRICAN AMERICAN	ASIAN AMERICAN	EUROPEAN AMERICAN
1670 through **1679**	**1670** The first Protestant Indian Church is established on Martha's Vineyard, Massachusetts, by Thomas Mayhew, Jr. **c. 1670** A Mohawk girl, Catherine Tekakwitha, converts to Catholicism and becomes the first known Native American nun. **1672** Colonial postal clerks use Native American couriers between New York City and Albany due to their endurance in cold weather. **1672-1680** Apache and Navajo warriors continue to fight Spanish colonists in New Mexico. **1675** In New Mexico, tension grows between Pueblo Indians and Spaniards, who accuse the Pueblos of using witchcraft to kill several friars and colonists. Three Indians are hanged by the Spaniards. **1675-1676** In King Philip's War, Metacomet (also called King Philip) attempts to unite the New England tribes against English encroachment. The war ends with the defeat of the Indians. Metacomet is killed and dismembered, and his wife and son are sold as slaves. The Susquehannock tribe of Maryland retaliates for the murder of their chiefs by attacking English communities. Nathaniel Bacon, Jr., a young planter, leads unauthorized attacks on friendly Indians in Virginia. Bacon's Rebellion lasts several months until its leader suddenly dies. His followers are caught and 23 are hanged. In 1677 a treaty of peace is signed with the local Indians.	**1670** A law is enacted in Virginia that all non-Christians who arrive by ship are to be enslaved. Those children who enter by land must serve until they are 30, or for 12 years if they are adults. A French royal decree brings French shippers into the slave trade, with the rationale that the labor of enslaved Africans helps the growth of France's island colonies. The Massachusetts legislature passes a law that enables its citizens to sell the children of enslaved Africans into bondage. **1671** A Maryland law states that the conversion of enslaved African Americans to Christianity does not affect their status as enslaved people. **1672** King Charles II of England charters the Royal African Company, which dominates the slave trade to North America for the next half century. **1673** The Massachusetts legislature passes a law that forbids European Americans from engaging in trade with any African American.	**1672** Enslaved Filipinos are given their freedom in Spain's American colonies.	**1670** English and Irish colonists under William Sayle establish a community at Charles Town (Charleston), South Carolina. **1670-1715** Many European traders in South Carolina take Native American wives and learn the native languages. **1677** Huguenot colonists purchase a tract of land from Native Americans and establish what is now the town of New Paltz, New York. A group of Portuguese Jews from Barbados comes to Newport, in what is now Rhode Island. A group of approximately 50 Irish colonists establishes the community of East Grenwich, in Rhode Island. The group is led by Charles McCarthy, from Cork.

HISPANIC AMERICAN				

1670

The *Ermita* of Nuestra Señora de Guadalupe (Our Lady of Guadalupe), a small shrine, is established at what later becomes Ponce, Puerto Rico.

1671

After being on a wagon train to Albuquerque during an Apache raid, the new Spanish governor of Mexico mounts a campaign to exterminate the Apache tribe.

1672

Construction begins on the Castillo de San Marcos in St. Augustine, Florida, the largest masonry fort in what is now the United States. Cuban-born Ignacio Daza is the engineer on the project. After its completion, the structure becomes a refuge for the people of St. Augustine during attacks by British soldiers from the Carolinas and Georgia.

1675

Four Native Americans are hanged and more than 40 are whipped and enslaved after a Spanish tribunal convicts them of bewitching the superior of the San Ildefonso (New Mexico) Franciscan monastery.

1676-1677

The Spanish-held pueblos in New Mexico are abandoned after repeated Apache raids.

1670

through

1679

THE AMERICAS	THE AMERICAS	THE AMERICAS	THE WORLD

1670 through 1679

THE AMERICAS

1670

William Sayle and a group of colonists make their homes at Albemarle Point, South Carolina. Seven years earlier, this land was granted by King Charles II to eight of his supporters, led by Lord Anthony Ashley Cooper. John Locke wrote the Fundamental Constitutions to govern the area in 1669.

France's King Louis XIV declares Acadia (Nova Scotia, New Brunswick and eastern Maine) a crown colony, and names Hector d'Andigny, Chevalier de Grandfontaine as the new governor. Grandfontaine arrives at what is now Penobscot, Maine.

Hudson's Bay Company is incorporated by an English royal charter.

1670-1789

Hudson's Bay Company colonizes a large tract of Canadian territory known as Rupert's Land, named after Prince Rupert, the company's first governor. The area, sold to Canada in 1789, is made up of large sections of the present-day provinces of Ontario, Quebec and Alberta as well as all of Manitoba and Saskatchewan.

1671

A second mission in the region that is now Michigan is established under Jesuit Father Jacques Marquette. This new mission, St. Ignace, and the community at Sault Ste. Marie, become central contact points for traders, missionaries, French Canadian officials and Indians.

The ship *l'Oranger* from La Rochelle, France, arrives in Acadia with about 50 colonists.

English forces led by Henry Morgan destroy Panama City, Panama.

1672

Father Marquette explores the area north of the Missouri River.

A Danish colony is established on St. Thomas, in the Virgin Islands, under the Danish West India Company.

THE AMERICAS

Louis de Buade de Frontenac et de Palluau (Louis de Frontenac) becomes governor of New France.

1673

Father Marquette and Louis Joliet explore the upper Mississippi River area.

Dutch forces regain control of New York and Delaware.

Separate French and British expeditions explore the region that is now Tennessee.

Fort Frontenac is constructed on Lake Ontario.

Sir Henry Morgan is made lieutenant governor of Jamaica by King Charles II. Morgan becomes acting governor between 1680-1682.

1674

Under the Treaty of Westminster, the Netherlands returns its North American holdings to England.

Sir Christopher Codrington comes to Antigua and begins the first large-scale sugar crop on this island.

French Guiana is declared a crown colony of France.

1676

The English colony of Jersey is divided into East and West Jersey.

In Virginia, a popular revolt against low tobacco prices, high taxes and lack of protection against Indian attacks is led by Nathaniel Bacon. Bacon opposes Governor Sir William Berkeley and is successful in several expeditions against the Indians; however, his sudden death brings an end to the rebellion. Bacon's actions make the region safer against Indian attacks and Berkeley is removed from office. He is succeeded by Thomas Culpeper who pardons all participants in the rebellion.

1677

Massachusetts buys title to Maine from the heirs of Sir Ferdinando Gorges.

A revolt against Thomas Miller, acting Carolina governor, occurs. It is commonly called Culpeper's Rebellion.

THE AMERICAS

1678

French Jesuit missionary Father Louis Hannepin explores Niagara Falls, New York.

By this time, half of Antigua's residents are enslaved Africans, imported to work the booming sugar plantations.

1679

New Hampshire separates from Massachusetts and becomes an independent royal colony.

King Charles II urges Huguenots in England to emigrate to (South) Carolina.

French explorer Daniel Greysolon Dulhut, explores Lake Superior.

Robert Cavelier, Sieur de la Salle directs the building of the *Griffin* — the first Great Lakes sailing ship. This same year, La Salle leads the construction of Fort Miami — the first European community in the lower peninsula of what is now Michigan.

La Salle explores the Great Lakes for France and reaches the mouth of the Mississippi River in 1682. He names the Louisiana Territory in honor of Louis XIV.

THE WORLD

1670

The Ukrainian Cossacks' rebellion against Polish rule is put down by Jan Sobieski.

The secret Treaty of Dover is signed between King Charles II of England and King Louis XIV of France. It ends England's official opposition to France.

The Bambara kingdoms defeat the Mandingo Empire in western Africa.

Jews are expelled from Vienna.

Christian V becomes king of Denmark and Norway after the death of his father, Frederick III (1648). Christian V rules until 1699.

1671

The Ottoman Empire declares war on Poland in support of the Ukrainian Cossacks.

Russian peasants take part in a revolt led by Stenka Razin. The disturbance is crushed.

The first Arabic edition of the Bible is printed in Rome.

In Hungary, Protestant schools are seized at Sárospatak and Eperjes (present-day Prešov, Czech Republic).

1672

A combined force of Ottomans and Cossacks invades Poland.

The Royal African Company, founded in 1660, is chartered and granted a monopoly for almost two decades to trade in enslaved Africans.

After securing support from England, Sweden and some of the German states, Louis XIV declares war on the United Provinces of the Netherlands to reduce the Dutch threat to French commerce and to gain revenge on the Dutch for aiding his political enemies.

Englishman Isaac Newton formulates the law of gravitation.

1673

The Test Act in England, directed mainly against Catholics, excludes from public office anyone who does not swear allegiance to the Church of England.

Holy Roman Emperor Leopold I declares war on France.

The Polish army under Jan Sobieski defeats Ottoman forces at Khoresm.

William of Orange saves Amsterdam from a French attack by opening the sluice gates to cause flooding. As a result, he gains the support of Frederick William, elector of Brandenburg.

1674

French troops under Henri de La Tour d'Auvergne, vicomte de Turenne, overrun the Palatinate. Spain, the Holy Roman Emperor and the Netherlands create an alliance against Louis XIV.

The Mahratta (Maratha) state is formed by Sivaji Bhonsla after he declares independence from Mogul Emperor Aurangzeb.

John III (Jan Sobieski) becomes king of Poland after the reign of Michael Wisniowiecki (1669). John III rules until 1696.

1675

Denmark declares war on Sweden.

The armies of Spain, Austria and Brandenburg defeat Swedish troops at Fehrbellin, Brandenburg.

Sikh guru Tegh Bahādur is executed by Mogul ruler Aurangzeb for refusing to accept Islam.

Victor Amadeus II becomes duke of Savoy after the death of his father, Charles Emmanuel II. Victor Amadeus II holds this position until 1713. He later rules as king of Sicily from 1713 to 1720, and king of Sardinia from 1720 to 1730.

1676

Govind Rai, who took the name Singh, becomes guru of the Sikh faith after the death of his father, Tegh Bahādur (1664). Govind Rai, the last guru, holds the position until 1708 and makes the Sikhs into a militant order in northern India.

Feodor III becomes czar of Russia after the death of his father, Alexis I (1645). Feodor III rules until 1682.

Kara Mustafa becomes grand *vizier* (minister of state) under Ottoman Sultan Muhammad IV after the death of his brother-in-law, Ahmed Kiuprili (1661). Kara Mustafa holds this position until his death in 1683. After several military setbacks, the sultan orders Kara Mustafa to commit suicide.

1677

A French army led by the duke of Orleans defeats Dutch troops under William III of Orange at Cassel.

Swedish forces are defeated at Oland by a combined Dutch-Danish fleet.

French troops capture Dutch ports on the Senegal River in Africa.

Anthony van Leeuwenhoek makes major functional improvements to the microscope, and views spermatozoa and microorganisms.

1678

The "Popish Plot" is fabricated in England by Titus Oates and Israel Tonge. Rumored to be a Jesuit-planned scheme to assassinate King Charles II and have James, the duke of York and a Roman Catholic, take the throne, the plot's discovery stirs intense persecution. Roman Catholics are excluded from seats in both Houses of Parliament.

War breaks out between Russia and Sweden.

The Peace of Nijmegen ends the conflict between France and the Netherlands, giving the town of Maastricht to the Dutch, an improved trade position to the French and an agreement that the Netherlands will remain neutral in European affairs. In a related treaty with Spain, who entered the war to assist the Netherlands, France keeps a series of border posts but pulls out of the Spanish Netherlands. France also maintains control over portions of Lorraine in a subsequent treaty with the Holy Roman Empire.

1678-1680

Hungary is devastated by a plague epidemic.

1679

A revolt of Covenanters is stopped by the duke of Monmouth at Bothwell Bridge.

The Treaty of St. Germain-en-Laye is signed between Sweden and Brandenburg and grants to Sweden territory in Pomerania captured by Brandenburg.

Denmark and France make peace at Fontainbleau.

The treaty of Lund establishes peace between Denmark and Sweden.

The English Habeas Corpus Act is passed by Parliament and is designed to deter unlawful imprisonment.

1670

through

1679

NATIVE AMERICAN	AFRICAN AMERICAN	ASIAN AMERICAN	EUROPEAN AMERICAN
1680-1683 English forces in South Carolina attack the Westos to gain slaves for trade and to get better access to interior areas. By 1683 only 50 Westos remain. They later join the Creek tribe. **1680-1684** English colonists in South Carolina and their Indian allies attack Spanish outposts in Georgia. Spanish control in Georgia crumbles after English and Indian attacks. **1680-1688** Popé, a Pueblo Indian and medicine man, leads a successful revolt against Spanish colonists in New Mexico. About 2,000 Spanish and *mestizo* (a person of combined European and Native American ethnicity) colonists flee to El Paso and 800 are killed by Indians. Popé dies in 1688. **1681-1682** Nanagoucy, a Mahican leader, travels among the Ohio country tribes advocating an intertribal confederacy. **1682** William Penn's treaty with the Delawares begins a time of cooperation between Quakers and Native Americans. **1683-1690s** The Shawnee of the Savannah River (Georgia) dominate trade with European American colonists in South Carolina, acquiring firearms in exchange for furs and enslaved Indians captured in raids on other tribes. **1687** Members of the Yamasee tribe revolt against Spanish rule in Florida and Georgia and flee north.	**1681** Maryland laws mandate that children of European servant women and African men are free. **1682** A harsher slave code in Virginia requires passes, prohibits weapons for slaves and forbids even self-defense by African Americans. **1688** Mennonite Quakers in Germantown, Pennsylvania, denounce slavery in the first recorded formal protest in North America against the enslavement of Africans.	**1680-1689** Migration from the Philippines to Mexico continues, and includes artisans, merchants and nobles. Convict exchanges also take place between Mexico and the Philippines.	**1680** Huguenots begin large-scale migration to Charleston, South Carolina. Explorer Father Louis Hennepin and his expedition establish a French colony called Minneapolis at St. Anthony Falls, in what is now Minnesota. **1682** Robert Cavelier, sieur de La Salle, takes possession of the Mississippi Valley for France, calling it Louisiana. **1683** The first German Protestant colonists arrive in Pennsylvania seeking freedom of worship. These first Germantown residents work as weavers, artisans and farmers; many are Mennonites who originate from Krefeld, Germany. Those who follow want both religious toleration and economic opportunities. A Scottish colony under Henry Erskine is established at Port Royal, South Carolina, but is overrun by Spanish forces in 1686. William Rittenhouse, of the German Mennonite colony, builds a papermill in Germantown, Pennsylvania, the first of its kind in America. **1684** A small group of Scots is brought to America by the proprietor of the Carolinas, to establish Stuart's Town in what is now South Carolina. **1685** Thousands of Huguenots flee France and come to America, especially to New York and South Carolina. Most are artisans or skilled farmers. An expedition under La Salle builds Fort St. Louis on the La Vaca River, the first French community in Texas. **1688** Anne Glover is hanged as a witch in Boston. Originally a native of Ireland, she was sold into slavery in Barbados and later brought to Massachusetts.

1680 through 1689

HISPANIC AMERICAN	FOR CLASSROOM USE	FOR CLASSROOM USE	FOR CLASSROOM USE	

1680

The city of Ponce is founded on the south coast of Puerto Rico.

1680-1688

Popé, a Pueblo Indian and medicine man, leads a successful revolt against Spanish colonists in New Mexico. About 2,000 Spanish and *mestizo* (a person of combined European and Native American ethnicity) colonists flee to El Paso and 800 are killed by Indians. Popé dies in 1688.

1682

In Sonora, two rebellions by the Opata tribe are suppressed by Spanish forces.

1683

The first permanent European community in Texas is established by Spanish missionaries.

1687-1711

Jesuit priest and explorer Eusebio Francisco Kino arrives in New Mexico. Over the next several years Father Kino leads the establishment of missions in Arizona, among them San Xavier del Bac south of Tucson. Father Kino travels along the Gila and Colorado Rivers to the Gulf of California in 1702. He maps thousands of miles in the Southwest before his death in 1711.

1688

Wars between Spaniards and Indians take place from Sonora to Coahuila.

1680

through

1689

THE AMERICAS	THE AMERICAS	THE AMERICAS	THE WORLD

1680 through 1689

THE AMERICAS

1680

During the great Pueblo revolt in the Santa Fe area, Indians destroy 21 Franciscan missions and drive all 2300 Spanish colonists out of New Mexico and Arizona. The area is slowly reconquered by Spanish forces during the 1690s.

By this time France's North American colonial empire extends from Quebec to the mouth of the Mississippi River, much of the exploration due to the efforts of Robert Cavelier, sieur de La Salle.

French colonists and soldiers under La Salle build Ft. Crévecoeur (near present-day Peoria, Illinois).

Minneapolis is established in what is now Minnesota.

Sir Henry Morgan becomes acting governor of Jamaica. He serves until 1682.

1680s-1690s

Sara Sands, the first woman doctor in the English colonies, practices on Block Island, Rhode Island. She is principal surgeon and physician on the island for many years.

1681

King Charles II grants William Penn a tract of land. Penn envisions a refuge for English Quakers, but advertises generally for colonists. This tract is eventually called Pennsylvania and is colonized by German as well as English immigrants.

Guatemala's University of San Carlos is opened.

1682

Philadelphia is established as a Quaker community by William Penn.

In the Virginia colony, conversion to Christianity does not give freedom to enslaved Native Americans, African Americans or *mulattos* (people of combined European and African ethnicity).

James, the duke of York, annexes present-day Delaware and transfers it to William Penn. Although the inhabitants (Dutch, Swedish and Finnish colonists) object to being part of the Quaker colony, they remain affiliated with Pennsylvania until the American Revolution.

THE AMERICAS

Norfolk, Virginia, is established.

La Salle claims the entire Mississippi River drainage basin for France, from North Dakota to the Gulf of Mexico. He names Louisiana Territory for King Louis XIV. La Salle's expedition builds Fort Prud'homme on the Hatchie River at Chickasaw Bluff (now in Tennessee).

Authorities of New France declare it illegal, under penalty of death, for any French person to relocate to England's North American colonies.

c. 1683

Bermuda becomes an English colony.

1685

La Salle and an expedition under him establish Fort St. Louis on the Lavaca River. He and his party become the first French immigrants in Texas. La Salle is assassinated two years later, and several survivors of his expedition, including Jean Hueri, make homes and families with the Native Americans of the area.

1686

Spanish forces, aided by Timucua and *mulatto* allies, attack and destroy a Scottish community in (South) Carolina.

Arkansas Post, the oldest European town in present-day Arkansas, is established as a trading center by Henri de Tonti, a member of La Salle's party.

Fort Abitibi is established in present-day Ontario province and serves as an important station for the French fur trade.

1688

The administrators of New France petition France's King Louis XIV to allow importation of enslaved Africans to cover an acute labor shortage. The king finally gives his approval.

1689

The ascension of William III of Orange and Mary II to the English throne brings about reforms in the Virginia colony. The changes prompt a new wave of English immigrants.

THE AMERICAS

Jacob Leisler, a German immigrant and staunch Protestant, raises a private militia and seizes a portion of southern New York, in a show of anti-Catholic sentiment as Protestants William and Mary take the throne of England. An offcial force is promptly dispatched against Leisler, who is caught, convicted of treason, and hanged. This brief insurrection is known as Leisler's Rebellion.

Louis de Frontenac is reappointed governor of New France.

A force of 1,500 Iroquois overruns and destroys the French community at Lachine on Montreal Island, killing 200 people and abducting 90.

Captain Alonso de Len is sent to Texas by the viceroy of New Spain to find and destroy French communities. He comes upon the ruins of the La Salle expedition's Fort St. Louis, but sees no current French presence.

1689-1763

The French and Indian Wars take place in North America. These campaigns correspond with territorial conflicts occurring in Europe, and have the end result that France loses virtually all of its North American holdings to England. The first, King William's War, from 1689 to 1697, corresponds in Europe to the War of the Grand Alliance, 1688 to 1697. It ends with the Treaty of Ryswick. The second war, Queen Anne's War from 1702 to 1713, corresponds to the War of the Spanish Succession in Europe, 1701 to 1714. It ends with the Peace of Utrecht. King George's War, from 1744 to 1748, corresponds to the War of the Austrian Succession, 1740 to 1748, which is resolved by the Treaty of Aix-la-Chapelle. The final conflict in the colonies is generally called the French and Indian War, from 1754 to 1763 and occurs during the Seven Years' War in Europe, 1756 to 1763. These are ended with the Treaty of Paris.

THE WORLD

1680

Charles XI increases his powers in Sweden at the expense of the aristocratic class.

Sunayoshi (Tsunayoshi) becomes shogun of Japan after the death of his brother, Ietsuna (1651). Sunayoshi rules until 1709.

c. 1680

Osei Tutu consolidates the Ashanti (Asante) people into a single political state (modern Ghana).

1681

Russia's Czar Feodor III reduces the power of the boyars (Russia's noble class).

The troops of France's King Louis XIV occupy Strasbourg.

In Hungary, the Diet of Sopron strengthens the rights of nobility and limits those of Protestants.

1682

Russia and the Ottoman Empire reach a peace agreement.

Dutch forces expel the British from Bantam (Java).

King Louis XIV of France moves his court and government to Versailles.

Austrian and Turkish forces fight each other, primarily for control of Hungary.

Ivan V and Peter I (the Great) become joint czars of Russia after the death of their brother, Feodor III (1676). Ivan V, who is mentally retarded, rules in name only until 1689; Peter I rules until 1725.

The "Great Comet" seen in the sky in 1531 returns. It is observed by and named after English astronomer Edmund Halley, who accurately predicts that the comet will reappear in 1759.

1683

The Rye House Plot to murder England's King Charles II and James, Duke of York, is discovered.

Dutch merchants gain entry to Canton.

Spain declares war on France.

The Ottoman siege of Vienna is lifted by the troops of Poland's King John III (Jan Sobieski). Pest is liberated from Ottoman control and Hungary is gradually reunited over the next 16 years, after being under three separate governments since 1547.

Manchu forces conquer Taiwan (Formosa), and the island comes under the reign of the Qing (Ch'ing) dynasty.

Many French Huguenots are forced to convert to Catholicism.

Peter II becomes king of Portugal after the death of his brother, Alfonso VI (1656). Peter II rules until 1706.

1685

Foreign merchants trade at a number of Chinese ports.

Jews in England are granted religious freedom.

The Edict of Nantes, which granted religious freedom to French Protestants in 1585, is revoked. This begins a second wave of Huguenot immigration to England and to North America, mostly to New York and South Carolina.

Frederick William I, the Great Elector of Prussia, issues the Edict of Potsdam, giving French Huguenots refuge in the Prussian province of Brandenburg.

James II becomes king of England, Scotland and Ireland after the death of his brother, Charles II (1660). James II rules until 1688.

James, duke of Monmouth, and nephew of newly crowned King James II of England, claims title to his uncle's throne. The duke is defeated at the Battle of Sedgemoor, captured and beheaded.

1686

Charles, duke of Lorraine, leads an army that captures Buda (Budapest) from the Turks who have controlled the city for almost 150 years. The area is reinhabited, Buda with Germans and Pest with Serbs.

The League of Augsburg is an alliance formed by Holy Roman Emperor Leopold I and several of the German princes (notably from Bavaria and the Palatinate), with the support of Sweden, Spain and the Netherlands. The League's purpose is to block French expansion.

King James II suspends laws against Catholics and dissenters in England and Scotland.

France annexes Madagascar.

Roman Catholics are readmitted into the English army as a result of the case of *Godden* v. *Hales*, which overturns the Test Act.

1687

Ottoman troops under Suleiman are defeated by a combined Austro-Hungarian force under Charles, the duke of Lorraine, at Mohács. This battle effectively ends Turkish expansion into Europe.

The Diet of Pressburg recognizes the crown of Hungary as a hereditary possession of the males of the Hapsburg line.

Venetian troops under Francesco Morosini capture Corinth and Athens; the artillery shelling damages historic monuments, including the Temple of Athena on the Acropolis.

Colonists from Brandenburg (Prussia) establish a community in Arguin (Mauritania, western Africa).

Mogul Emperor Auranzgeb conquers Golconda, India.

Suleiman II becomes Ottoman sultan after his brother, Muhammad IV (1648), is deposed. Suleiman II rules until 1691.

1688

Pirate William Dampier visits the coast of Australia.

The first Huguenots arrive in South Africa.

War between France and the Holy Roman Empire is declared; the forces of Louis XIV invade Palatinate.

Smyrna, Turkey, is hit by an earthquake.

The Glorious Revolution occurs in England. William III of Orange and Mary II, his wife and daughter of King James II (1685), are invited by Parliament to rule England, Ireland and Scotland. James II flees to France. The condition of William and Mary's reign is that they accept the new English Bill of Rights, which establishes the supremacy of Parliament. William officially accepts the throne in early 1689.

The increase of foreign interests in Siam (Thailand) sparks a nationalist coup, and the country is closed to foreign trade for more than 100 years.

Frederick III becomes elector of Brandenburg after the death of his father, Frederick William I (the Great Elector, 1640). Frederick III rules until 1713 as elector, and also as king of Prussia from 1701 to 1713.

1688-1697

In the War of the Grand Alliance, France battles the former League of Augsburg, whose members include the German states, England, the Netherlands and the Holy Roman Emperor. The alliance seeks to stop Louis XIV's territorial advances. The conflict drains both sides and ends with the Treaty of Ryswick, in which France surrenders most of its conquered territory. In the colonies of North America, King William's War takes place (1689-1697).

1689

James II, former king of England, arrives in Kinsala, Ireland.

The Netherlands, England and Savoy join the coalition formed at the League of Augsburg in 1686. The new organization becomes known as the Grand Alliance and is led by William of Orange, the king of England.

France under Louis XIV declares war on Spain and England.

The Treaty of Nerchinsk, a Russian-Chinese border treaty, also enables Russian traders to travel to Peking.

The English Parliament passes the Act of Toleration, granting freedom of worship to all Protestants. A major incentive to leave the country is thus removed and emigration declines for nearly two decades.

Peter I (the Great) becomes sole czar of Russia and attempts to westernize the nation and make it into a strong military power. He rules until 1725.

Mustafa Kiuprili becomes grand *vizier* (minister of state) of the Ottoman Empire. He serves until his death in 1691.

King William III and Queen Mary II unite the houses of Orange and Stuart and rule England, Scotland and Ireland. The combined houses rule until 1802.

1689-1691

In and around Ulster, Irish lands are seized and colonized with Protestant English and Scottish immigrants, who do not assimilate well with the native Irish Catholic population.

1680

through

1689

101

NATIVE AMERICAN	AFRICAN AMERICAN	ASIAN AMERICAN	EUROPEAN AMERICAN

| 1690 through 1699 | | | | |

NATIVE AMERICAN

1690-1720s

The Apache Indians (in Arizona and New Mexico) are weakened by the use of guns by their eastern enemies — the Pawnees, Wichitas and other Caddoan tribes — and raids by Utes and Comanches from the north.

1692

English traders in South Carolina provoke Indian tribes against one another in order to acquire slaves.

1692-1696

Diego de Vargas leads the Spanish reconquest of the Pueblo region of the American Southwest. The Pueblos try again to revolt but are subdued. Only the distant Hopi and non-Pueblo tribes such as the Navajo and Apache continue to elude Spanish rule.

1693

A large party of Iroquois is defeated at the St. Joseph River (central Michigan) by French troops.

The College of William and Mary is founded in Williamsburg, Virginia; its charter contains special provisions for the education of Native Americans.

1695

The first Pima uprising against Spanish dominance takes place in the American Southwest.

Chief Chingcabee of the Ojibwa tribe (Great Lakes region) travels to Quebec seeking French assistance against the Sauk and Fox.

AFRICAN AMERICAN

1690

By this year, all English colonies in America have enslaved Africans.

Enslaved Africans and Native Americans in Massachusetts plan a rebellion.

1692

The Virginia House of Burgesses enacts the Runaway Slave Law making it legal to kill a runaway in the course of apprehension.

1693

All fugitive Africans who have escaped slavery in the British colonies and fled to Florida are granted their freedom by the Spanish crown.

1694

The introduction of rice into the Carolina colony increases the need for cheap labor to work on the new plantations. This adds another factor to the economic justification and rationalization for expanding the slave trade.

1696

American Quakers, at their annual meeting, warn members against holding Africans in slavery. Violators who continue to keep slaves are threatened with expulsion.

1697

As the Royal African Company's monopoly ends, the slave trade expands.

ASIAN AMERICAN

Although Chinese seamen have engaged in significant maritime activity from the middle of the seventh century, when Manchus conquer the Chinese people in 1644 and bring the Ming dynasty to an end, a major change in foreign policy occurs. Fearing that Ming loyalists will create a revolutionary force outside the country, officials of the new Qing (Ch'ing) dynasty pass edicts barring emigration. Many Chinese people, especially from the southeastern provinces of Fujian (Fukien) and Guangdong (Kwangtung), continue to travel back and forth between China and the countries of southeast Asia, where sizeable Chinese colonies flourish. However, most of the Chinese people are isolated from the West until early in the nineteenth century.

Japan's location off the coast of the Asian mainland keeps its inhabitants relatively isolated from outside visitors. The Japanese people withstand attempted invasions by Kublai Khan in the 1200s, and first encounter Europeans when Portuguese traders arrive off the Asian mainland in the early 1500s. European missionaries follow but, fearing the examples seen in other Asian countries where missionaries were soon followed by military forces, the Tokugawa shogunate issues an effective anti-Christian decree. Japan remains isolated until a United States fleet under Commodore (later Admiral) Matthew Perry sails into Tokyo Bay in 1853.

EUROPEAN AMERICAN

1690

A group of French colonists from Virginia migrate to the Pamlico River area in North Carolina and make their homes there.

1691

The Huguenot community at Frenchtown, Rhode Island, is destroyed by a mob of English immigrants. Many Huguenots in Pennsylvania are arrested.

In Virginia, any European American who marries a Native American, an African American or a *mulatto* (a person of combined European and African ethnicity) is banished from the colony.

1694

The first book about North America written in Hungarian is published.

1695

The first Jewish colonists arrive in Charleston, South Carolina.

1698

Scottish colonists organize the first Presbyterian congregation in America at Philadelphia, Pennsylvania.

1699

By this time there are several Welsh communities in Pennsylvania.

The first permanent Swedish Lutheran church in America opens at Cranebrook, Delaware.

Pierre le Moyne, sieur d'Iberville, explores the Gulf Coast with his brother Jean Baptiste Lemoyne, sieur de Bienville. This expedition leads to the establishment of Old Biloxi, the first European colony in the Mississippi Delta region.

The village of Cahokia is established by French colonists in what is now southwestern Illinois. It is the first permanent European community in the region.

HISPANIC AMERICAN	FOR CLASSROOM USE	FOR CLASSROOM USE	FOR CLASSROOM USE	

1690

Alonso de León and Fray Damián Masanet establish the first Spanish mission in East Texas; it is abandoned in 1693.

1690s

The majority of colonists who live on the island of Puerto Rico at the end of the century come from the Canary Islands and Portugal.

1691

Texas is established as a separate Spanish province, with Domingo Terán de los Ríos as its first governor.

1692

Puerto Rico is divided into two administrative districts and the "Partido de Ponce" is separated from San German.

1692-1696

Diego de Vargas leads the Spanish reconquest of the Pueblo region of the American Southwest. The Pueblos try again to revolt but are subdued. Only the distant Hopi and non-Pueblo tribes such as the Navajo and Apache continue to elude Spanish rule.

1693

Mexico's first periodical, *El Mercurio Volante,* is published by Carlos Siguenza y Góngora.

Santa Fé is named a *presidio* (fort or fortified town) and villa, and becomes the capital of New Mexico.

1697

The first mission in Baja California is founded at Laredo by Spanish Jesuits.

1698

The viceroy of Mexico sends Andrés de Arriola of Veracruz to Florida with three ships and 200 men. Arriola lands on the Bay of Pensacola and constructs Fort San Carlos. This is the beginning of the community of Pensacola.

1699-1700

Father Eusebio Kino proves that Baja California is a peninsula.

1690

through

1699

THE AMERICAS	THE AMERICAS	THE WORLD	THE WORLD

1690 through 1699

THE AMERICAS

1690

By this time, Africans are held in slavery in all of England's North American colonies.

Captain Alonso de León returns to East Texas and over the next three years builds several missions, among them San Francisco de los Tejas. In 1693, when no French military have been seen in East Texas, the Spanish government decides to abandon the missions there.

French forces attack English border forts in North America; British troops under Sir William Phips capture Port Royal in Acadia (Nova Scotia, New Brunswick and eastern Maine).

The discovery of gold and diamonds in Minas Gerais, southern Brazil, draws miners and colonists to the area.

1691

The Massachusetts colony grants religious freedom to all free persons except Catholics.

Carolina is divided into North and South Carolina. They do not officially become two separate colonies until 1729.

French forces recapture Port Royal from the English.

Domingo Terán de los Ríos is appointed as the first Spanish governor of Texas. He serves for one year.

1692

When Salem, Massachusetts, girls pretend to be bewitched, Governor Phips, influenced by the Puritan church, creates a special court to try them for witchcraft. As a result, 20 people are executed and more than 100 imprisoned.

The British crown issues a grant to Thomas Neale to set up and maintain a post office in the colonies for a term of 21 years.

Diego de Vargas, governor of New Mexico, restores Spanish rule in the territory. He leads an army of 200 soldiers and, without bloodshed, persuades each of the 77 pueblos in the region to accept Spanish control. Vargas serves as governor until 1697.

THE AMERICAS

An earthquake destroys the community of Port Royal, Jamaica.

1693

The College of William and Mary is founded in Williamsburg, Virginia.

Havana-born Laureano Torres de Ayala becomes governor of Florida. He serves until 1699.

Juana Inés de la Cruz, a brilliant nun who is a poet and intellectual, is ordered by the Archbishop of Mexico to stop writing and turn to "silent prayer." Sister Juana dutifully obeys, but she writes that it is like "putting out a light."

1696

Rice cultivation begins in South Carolina.

1696-1697

Pierre le Moyne, sieur d'Iberville leads French forces in raids against English villages on the Newfoundland coast; his troops capture Fort Pemaquid.

1697

The western part of the island of Hispaniola (Haiti) is ceded by Spain to France.

The Treaty of Ryswick ends King William's War, one of the campaigns of the French and Indian Wars. Under the treaty, Acadia (Nova Scotia, New Brunswick and eastern Maine) returns to French control and England regains Newfoundland and its outposts on Hudson Bay.

1698

Pensacola is established in Florida by an expedition under Andrés de Ariola.

1699

The oldest Quaker meetinghouse in North America is established at Newport, Rhode Island.

An English community develops in Río Tinto, in what is now Honduras.

THE WORLD

1690

The British East India Company establishes a trading station at Calcutta, India, under the direction of Job Charnock.

At the Battle of the Boyne, the army of William III of England defeats former King James II and Irish rebels supported by Louis XIV of France. This is a triumph for the Protestants in Ireland; James II returns to France.

French naval forces defeat a combined English and Dutch fleet at the Battle of Beachy Head.

Southern India, except for Fort Jinji, is under Mogul rule.

The French army under Nicolas Catinat defeats Victor Amadeus II of Savoy and his troops at Staffarda, in northern Italy.

Spain becomes a member of the Grand Alliance against France.

Ottoman forces recapture Belgrade and drive the Austrians out of Bulgaria, Serbia and Transylvania.

c. 1690

Ashanti (Asante) tribes in western Africa become unified, with the city of Kumasi as their capital.

1691

A new East India Company is formed in London.

The army of the Holy Roman Empire under Louis William I, Margrave of Baden, defeats Ottoman forces at Slankamen (Szalankemen, Yugoslavia). Grand *vizier* (minister of state in the Ottoman Empire) Mustafa Kiuprili is killed.

The Treaty of Limerick ends the revolt in Ireland, provides free transportation for Irishmen wanting to go to France and grants religious freedom to Irish Catholics remaining in the area.

A great number of Serbs migrate to southern Hungary.

Ahmed II becomes Ottoman sultan after the death of his brother, Suleiman II (1687). Ahmed II rules until 1695.

THE WORLD

1692

French forces of Louis XIV are successful at Namur and François Henri de Montmorency-Bouteville, duc de Luxembourg, leads his troops to victory over William III and Dutch forces at Steenkerke.

In the naval Battle of La Hogue, a combined English and Dutch force defeats the French navy in the English Channel and stops the attempted invasion of England.

Unrest in the Scottish Highlands is fueled by the Campbell Clan's killing of members of the MacDonald Clan at Glascoe. Rob Roy becomes head of the Macgregor Clan.

1693

An earthquake in Catania, Italy, kills approximately 60,000 people.

The French under Anne Hilarion de Cotentin, comte de Tourville, seriously impair English shipping by winning decisively at Lagos, Portugal (near Cape St. Vincent).

The duc de Luxembourg defeats William III at Neerwinden.

The armies of Savoy, under Victor Amadeus II, are defeated at Marsaglia by French forces under Catinet.

Through the assistance of his wife Madame de Maintenon, Louis XIV begins his peace policy, including reconciliation with the Vatican.

1694

Hussein becomes shah of Persia after the death of his father, Suleiman I (1667). Hussein rules until 1722.

England's Queen Mary II (1689) dies. William III rules alone until 1702.

1695

Namur (Belgium), lost to France in 1692, is captured by forces under William III.

During the Russian war with Turkey, Peter the Great fails to take Azov.

Mustafa II becomes sultan of Turkey after the death of his uncle, Ahmed II (1691). Mustafa II rules until 1703.

THE WORLD	THE WORLD	FOR CLASSROOM USE	FOR CLASSROOM USE	

c. 1695

Portuguese merchants are driven out of the African kingdom of Urozwi.

1696

After building a sailing fleet, Peter the Great's navy takes Azov from the Turks. Russian forces also conquer Kamchatka (northeastern Russia).

The English Parliament suspends the Habeas Corpus Act.

1697

The kingdom of Champa is made part of northern Vietnam.

After a series of defeats, Ottoman Turks are finally forced out of central Europe.

China establishes rule over western Mongolia.

Prince Eugene of Savoy and his army defeat Turkish forces under Mustafa II at the Battle of Zenta (Senta, Yugoslavia).

The British Parliament ends the trading monopoly of the Royal African Company.

The Treaty of Ryswick ends the War of the Grand Alliance and recognizes the independence of Savoy. It also acknowledges William III as king of England and transfers commercial agreements from the French to the Dutch. Louis XIV retains Strasbourg but returns most of the territories he conquered in the past 20 years. This treaty also marks the decline of Spain as a major European power.

Peter the Great, traveling as "Peter Michailoff," sets out on an 18-month journey to Prussia, the Netherlands, England and Vienna to study European customs, often by working in dockyards.

A French expedition under André de Brue attempts to colonize western Africa.

Charles XII becomes king of Sweden after the death of his father, Charles XI (1660). Charles XII rules until 1718.

Augustus II becomes king of Poland after the death of John III (1674). As Frederick Augustus I, he became elector of Saxony in 1694 He rules Poland until 1704, and Saxony until 1733.

c. 1697

In England, partly as a result of the Glorious Revolution, the Royal African Company loses its monopoly and the trade in enslaved Africans is opened to all entrepreneurs.

In Africa, the Ashanti (Asante) Confederacy is formed with Osei Tutu as king.

1698

A new East India trading company called the General Society is created in England.

At the First Partition Treaty, England, the Netherlands, France and the Emperor agree on Spanish succession by designating Joseph Ferdinand, prince of Bavaria, as the main heir to the throne of Spain since Charles II had no children. The treaty gives Naples and Sicily to the French dauphin and Milan to Archduke Charles. Spain and Charles II object, fearing partitioning, and name Joseph Ferdinand sole heir to the entire Spanish empire.

In Africa, the Portuguese are driven out of Mombasa and Oyo warriors invade Dahomey.

Thomas Savery develops the first practical model for a water-rising steam engine. It uses the theory of atmospheric pressure after steam condensation.

1699

The governments of Denmark and Russia sign a mutual defense pact.

By the Treaty of Preobrazhenskoe, the Swedish empire is partitioned among Denmark, Poland, Saxony and Russia.

The Treaty of Karlowitz ends the Austro-Turkish War and gives almost all of Hungary, Transylvania, Croatia and Slovenia to Austria. Poland regains Podolia and part of the Ukraine.

Frederick IV becomes king of Denmark and Norway after the death of his father, Christian V (1670). Frederick IV rules until 1730.

1699-1701

The Ashanti conquer Denkyira and continue expansion in all directions.

1690 through 1699

NATIVE AMERICAN	NATIVE AMERICAN	AFRICAN AMERICAN	ASIAN AMERICAN

1700 through 1709

NATIVE AMERICAN

1700

English traders in the Mississippi Valley urge the Quapaw Indians to raid neighboring tribes to acquire slaves.

1700-1709

War, dispossession and disease cause a considerable decline in the population of Indians along the Atlantic coast.

1700-1724

The Ute and Comanche tribes become allies against Apaches, Pueblos and Spaniards in northern New Mexico. Ute-Comanche raids probably are a factor in splitting the Apache tribe into northern Kiowa and southern Jicarilla-Lipan branches. Utes later become allies to the Jicarilla Apaches.

1702-1703

The Yoa (a branch of Yamasee) tribe withdraws from the coast of Georgia and moves near the Savannah River where other Yamasee live. This leaves the area between St. Augustine and Savannah virtually uninhabited.

1703

English colonists and their Native American allies attack Spanish mission towns among the Apalachee Indians of Florida, and virtually destroy the tribe.

1704

French colonists and Indians attack the town of Deerfield, Massachusetts, at the time the northernmost English community on the Connecticut River. Almost 50 people are killed, and more than 100 are led as prisoners to Canada.

The Tuscaroras raid into the Piedmont Mountains of present-day Virginia from North Carolina. Fear of the Tuscaroras causes European colonists to mistrust other Indian groups as well.

1705

An English and Indian force — mostly Creek — raids the Choctaw tribe (probably in Mississippi) and takes captives to sell into slavery.

NATIVE AMERICAN

The Virginia House of Burgesses enacts laws that restrict the involvement of American Indians in governmental affairs. Native Americans are not allowed to vote, hold public office, testify as witnesses in court or carry dangerous weapons. Native Americans' rights to gather wild foods on English lands — rights granted by treaty in 1658 and 1677 — are restricted.

1707

The enslavement of free Native Americans, the sale of liquor to American Indians and the sale of weapons to hostile tribes are forbidden by South Carolina law.

AFRICAN AMERICAN

1700

A census reports over 27,000 enslaved people, mostly Africans, in the English colonies in North America. The great majority live in the South.

Boston slave traders are involved in selling enslaved Africans in the New England colonies and Virginia.

Massachusetts Chief Justice Samuel Sewall publishes *The Selling of Joseph*, a book that combines both the economic and moral reasons to abolish the trade in enslaved Africans.

1704

French colonist Elias Neau opens a school for enslaved African Americans in New York City.

1705

Virginia passes a law that demands lifelong servitude of all imported African slaves unless they are Christians. A later law makes African Americans' conversion to Christianity irrelevant in determining their freedom. This law also declares that only people of African descent can be enslaved in Virginia.

ASIAN AMERICAN

Although Chinese seamen have engaged in significant maritime activity from the middle of the seventh century, when Manchus conquer the Chinese people in 1644 and bring the Ming dynasty to an end, a major change in foreign policy occurs. Fearing that Ming loyalists will create a revolutionary force outside the country, officials of the new Qing (Ch'ing) dynasty pass edicts barring emigration. Many Chinese people, especially from the southeastern provinces of Fujian (Fukien) and Guangdong (Kwangtung), continue to travel back and forth between China and the countries of southeast Asia, where sizeable Chinese colonies flourish. However, most of the Chinese people are isolated from the West until early in the nineteenth century.

Japan's location off the coast of the Asian mainland keeps its inhabitants relatively isolated from outside visitors. The Japanese people withstand attempted invasions by Kublai Khan in the 1200s, and first encounter Europeans when Portuguese traders arrive off the Asian mainland in the early 1500s. European missionaries follow but, fearing the examples seen in other Asian countries where missionaries were soon followed by military forces, the Tokugawa shogunate issues an effective anti-Christian decree. Japan remains isolated until a United States fleet under Commodore (later Admiral) Matthew Perry sails into Tokyo Bay in 1853.

EUROPEAN AMERICAN	EUROPEAN AMERICAN	HISPANIC AMERICAN	FOR CLASSROOM USE	

1700-1792

Dutch Reformed congregations in the American colonies experience a doubling of congregants during the "Great Awakening."

1701

Antoine de la Mothe, Sieur de Cadillac, and his expedition erect a small wooden fort they call Pontchartrain on the bank of the river between Lakes Huron and Erie. The little fort comes to be called *de troit* (the straits). This develops into an important connecting trade post for the Great Lakes area and later becomes the city of Detroit, Michigan.

1702

French colonists move the original colony of Old Biloxi to Fort Louis on the Mobile River (Alabama).

1704

A census of the French military community at Ft. Louis on the Mobile River reports almost 200 soldiers, 30 families, a handful of clergy and several enslaved Africans.

In the Maryland colony, laws are passed limiting the entry of Irish people – particularly Irish Catholics; similar legislation is repeated in 1715. These laws either exclude Irish immigration altogether or impose heavy duties on the importation of Irish workers.

1706

Charleston, South Carolina, is successfully defended by English colonists against French and Spanish forces.

In Virginia, Reverend Francis Makemie from Donegal, Ireland, and his parishioners establish the first American presbytery. Makemie has been an itinerant preacher since his arrival from Ireland in 1683 and is regarded as the founder of Presbyterianism in America.

1707

Scots establish colonies in America, mostly in the Carolinas. But the movement of Scots across the Atlantic is slow to gain momentum. Most Scottish immigrants are traders, merchants or farmers.

1708

Jean Baptiste le Moyne, Sieur de Bienville, leads in the construction of a fort on Dauphin Island, on the Gulf Coast, to protect the island's French community.

1709

More than half of the colonial Germans, the largest immigrant group after the English, come to America under a system that allows them to pay for their voyages within a certain time after arrival or sold into servitude for a number of years.

Madame Ferree leads the establishment of a Huguenot community in the area that is now Lancaster County, Pennsylvania.

Approximately 14,000 inhabitants of the Palatinate region of Germany immigrate to North America.

1700

Father Eusebio Francisco Kino, Spanish Jesuit priest, leads in the establishment of Mission San Xavier del Bac in Arizona.

1700-1708

The Spanish government plans further colonization of Texas to curtail French expansion.

1700s

Immigration to Puerto Rico continues from the Canary Islands and the Lesser Antilles. Late in the century, many Irish colonists arrive. The trade in enslaved Africans also increases with the growth in the number of sugar plantations.

1702

Antonio de los Reyes Correa distinguishes himself in defending the city of Arecibo, Puerto Rico, against a British attack.

British Colonel James Moore leads a fleet of 12 ships in an attack on the city of St. Augustine, Florida.

Based on explorations and maps, Father Kino proves that California is not an island. Overland explorations to California follow.

1703

An attack on San Germán, Puerto Rico, by Dutch forces fails.

1706

The community of Albuquerque, New Mexico, is established by a group under the leadership of Governor Francisco Cuervy y Valdez.

1700 through 1709

1700 through 1709

1700

French forces led by Pierre Le Moyne, Sieur d'Iberville erect a fort in Louisiana, their second there.

c. 1700

Communities of *Maroons* (Africans who have fled enslavement) in the mountains of Hispaniola, Jamaica, St. Vincent, and other islands, terrify European colonists, and encourage other Africans to flee or rebel.

1700s

Plantation agriculture becomes increasingly important in the Caribbean. The labor of enslaved Africans and Indians produces cotton, coffee, sugar and tobacco. Despite restrictions many people in bondage manage to save money to purchase their freedom by selling crops at local markets or practicing a craft. The growing population of free Africans worries European colonists.

The fortress/community of San Felipe y Santiago de Montevideo is established in what is now Uruguay by Bruno Mauricio de Zabala, the Spanish governor of Buenos Aires. The primary reason for its establishment is to check Portuguese expansion.

1701

Territory north of Lake Ontario and west of Lake Michigan is ceded to England by the Iroquois.

A French community called Fort Ponchartrain du Detroit is established where Lakes Huron and Erie meet. This community develops into a city that is now Detroit, Michigan.

Yale University is founded at New Haven, Connecticut.

1702

Combined forces of approximately 500 English colonists and 300 American Indians attack Spanish and Yoa Indian communities in the St. Augustine, Florida, area. They destroy missions and pressure the Yoa to become allies of the English.

A combined British and Indian force led by British Colonel James Moore attacks the Spanish town of Pensacola.

England declares war on France in the War of the Spanish Succession. The corresponding conflict in North America is called Queen Anne's War, and lasts until 1713. Eventually, English colonial forces prevail over French troops to the north and Spanish forces to the south.

1703

Delaware, formerly part of Pennsylvania, becomes a separate colony.

Jesuit missionaries and American Indians found the village of Kaskaskia on an island near the junction of the Kaskaskia and Mississippi Rivers in what is now Illinois.

1704

The Boston Newsletter, the first regular newspaper in Britain's North American colonies, is founded.

An English raid into Acadia (Nova Scotia, New Brunswick and eastern Maine) ravages French communities there, but is not strong enough to take Port Royal.

French forces and their Indian allies raze the English community at Bonavista, Newfoundland. The French villages of Minas and Beaubassin on the New England/Canada border are destroyed by English colonists.

French forces led by Jean-Baptiste Hertel de Rouville, along with their Indian allies, raid the English community at Deerfield, Massachusetts. More than 50 English colonists are killed and 100 or more are taken to Canada as prisoners.

1705

A group of English people and their Native American allies — mostly Creeks — raid the Choctaw tribe and take captives to sell into slavery.

As a result of raids by Governor Daniel d'Auger de Subercase of Placentia, Newfoundland and a 450-man force under him, all English communities on Conception and Trinity Bays (Canada) are destroyed. The French troops, however, fail to take St. Johns.

1706

When the first presbytery is formed in America, it provides added incentive for Scotch-Irish immigration.

Charleston, South Carolina, is successfully defended by English colonists against French and Spanish forces.

1706

Jean Baptiste le Moyne de Bienville becomes France's governor of lower Louisiana after the death of his brother, Pierre le Moyne, Sieur d'Iberville.

1707

The Act of Union is a push factor for a strong wave of Scottish immigration to the American colonies.

British Colonel John March leads a 1,000-man military expedition against Port Royal in Acadia (Nova Scotia, New Brunswick and eastern Maine). A determined French force under Commander Subercase holds its ground, though outnumbered three to one. British troops try again to take the city-fortress, but are again repelled.

British forces from South Carolina and their Creek allies attack the Spanish fort at Pensacola, in what is now Florida. Eleven Spaniards are killed and about 25 prisoners are taken.

1708

South Carolina reports a population of more than 5,000 free people plus 1,400 enslaved Native Americans and almost 3,000 enslaved African Americans.

A French force of about 170 men leaves Placentia, Newfoundland, to attack the English community of St. Johns. The village is taken by French troops in early 1709, but is abandoned within a few months.

Laureano Torres de Ayala becomes governor of Cuba. He serves until 1711.

Slavery is legalized in Canada.

1700

through

1709

1700 through 1709

Summary

Territorial conflicts in Europe are sparked by succession issues in Spain, and later in Poland and Austria. The War of the Spanish Succession begins when Louis XIV of France seeks to put his grandson, Philip, on the Spanish throne. The Polish succession issue is primarily between Russia and Sweden, both claiming to control the Polish crown. The Pragmatic Sanction in Austria, and Maria Theresa's 1740 ascension as Holy Roman Empress, touch off yet another conflict. European powers exchange lands, and the concept of "balance of power" becomes a stronger force than dynastic ties in regulating international affairs. Two significant results of all these conflicts are that Prussia emerges strengthened, and Sweden's height as a naval power has passed. Corresponding conflicts occur in North America as part of the French and Indian Wars.

Spain's *asiento* (exclusive license to market enslaved Africans in Spain's American colonies) remains a prize in the European conflicts; Britain retains this license. The African kingdoms, particularly those on the west coast, continue to be decimated by this brutal trade.

Russia and China continue a long-standing border dispute. Late in the century, Siam's Chakri dynasty — a dynasty that will continue into the twentieth century — comes to power; and a series of uprisings take place in China against the Qing (Ch'ing) dynasty. Shogunate rule continues in Japan.

The success of the United States in freeing itself from British colonial rule ignites revolutionary movements elsewhere in Europe, and leads Britain to focus its colonization efforts more heavily in India, Malaysia and Australia. As European colonies develop in Australia, the aboriginal population is devastated by smallpox and other European diseases on a scale similar to that suffered by native American civilizations a century and a half earlier. Colonization of India and the regions around it

increases, as British forces drive out first French, and then Dutch, rivals. The native kingdom of Mysore, long a stronghold of resistance, is defeated by British forces; however, Sikh and Mahratta (Maratha) defiance continue throughout the century.

One of the revolutionary fires ignited by America's independence is the French Revolution. Fanned by economic crisis and a reaction against French social class structure, the revolution creates such upheaval that France is ripe for Napoleon Bonaparte's seizure of command. He consolidates his hold on France, and begins lateral conquests that will devastate the economics of Europe.

As the successful harnessing of steam and water for power occurs on a large scale, another type of revolution takes place. With new developments in manufacturing — particularly in textiles and printing — the Industrial Revolution begins in Europe and North America, effecting a fundamental economic change from an agrarian to an industrial base.

1700-1870; 1874-1931; 1975-Present

These are the time spans generally ascribed to the House of Bourbon that governs Spain.

1700

Bavarian prince Joseph Ferdinand dies after having been designated by Holy Roman Emperor Leopold I as heir to the Spanish throne. Under the terms of a new agreement, the Second Partition Treaty, France receives Naples, Sicily and Milan; Charles, Leopold I's son, is to rule the rest of the Spanish Empire. French King Louis XIV agrees to this treaty, but Emperor Leopold I does not.

King Charles XII of Sweden defeats Russia's Peter I at Narva (in Estonia).

The last Hapsburg ruler of Spain, Charles II (1665), dies and a power struggle ensues. Philip V (of Bourbon), grandson of Louis XIV, becomes king. Philip V rules, except for 1724, until 1746.

Guillaume Delisle, often called the father of cartography, creates a world map that corrects the mapwork of Ptolemy.

1700-1721

In the Great Northern War, Denmark, Poland, Russia and Saxony (and later Hanover and Prussia) are successful in weakening Swedish control of the Baltic by taking advantage of the inexperience of King Charles XII. Russia occupies Finland, and Estonia becomes a province of Russia. Losses are heavy, the countries are devastated and, in Estonia in particular, recovery is slow.

1701

At Chiara, Italy, Prince Eugène of Savoy and his troops defeat French forces under François de Neufville, duc de Villeroi.

The Act of Settlement in England provides for Sophia, electress of Hanover and granddaughter of England's King James I, to succeed to the throne of England should King William III and later Queen Anne die childless.

Elector Frederick III of Brandenburg becomes King Frederick I of Prussia. He rules until 1713.

English agricultural reformer Jethro Tull invents a horse-drawn drill for sowing seeds in a row.

1701-1714

The War of the Spanish Succession, caused by King Louis XIV's desire to increase French control over Europe, begins when he accepts the throne of Spain for his grandson, Philip, duke of Anjou. This action is a breach of the Second Partition Treaty. The war aligns Austria, Denmark, England, the Netherlands and most of the German states (the Allies) against Bavaria, France and Spain. It ends with the Peace of Utrecht. In America, the corresponding conflict is known as Queen Anne's War, which ends with the British receiving Newfoundland, Acadia (Nova Scotia, New Brunswick and eastern Maine) and the Hudson Bay Territory from France, and Gibraltar and Minorca from Spain.

1702

The French Guinea Company receives the *asiento* from Spain. It is a license to handle the trade of enslaved people between Africa and the Americas.

Denmark abolishes serfdom.

Anne becomes queen of England, Scotland and Ireland (later Great Britain and Ireland) after the death of her father, William III (1689, 1694). She rules until 1714.

The Netherlands experiences a period of decline after the death of England's King William III.

1703

The Methuen Treaty is signed between England and Portugal to facilitate trade in wool and wine, respectively.

The Ottoman Empire experiences the beginning of a cultural revival that lasts for almost 30 years.

Japan suffers a severe earthquake that causes more than 100,000 deaths.

Ahmed III becomes Ottoman sultan after the death of his brother, Mustafa II (1695). Ahmed III rules until 1730.

1703-1711

Hungary declares its independence. However, the rebel faction is defeated, and Hapsburg rule continues.

1704

French and Bavarian troops are defeated at the Bavarian village of Blenheim by an allied force led by John Churchill, duke of Marlborough, and Prince Eugène of Savoy.

English forces under Captain George Rooke capture Gibraltar from Spain.

Forces of Sweden's King Charles XII invade Poland, depose Augustus II (1697), and place Polish nobleman Stanislaus Leszczynski on the throne as King Stanislaus I. He rules Poland for five years, until Russian forces overrun the country and reinstate Augustus II. Augustus II rules until his death in 1733.

1705

Joseph I becomes Holy Roman Emperor after the death of his father, Leopold I (1657). Joseph I rules until 1711.

English inventors Thomas Newcomen and John Cawley improve Thomas Savery's 1698 steam engine design by separating the boiler from the cylinder.

1706

John Churchill, duke of Marlborough, and his troops defeat French forces under François de Neufville, duc de Villeroi, at Ramillies, Belgium, during the War of the Spanish Succession.

In the Congo (Kongo), Kimpa Vita, or Doña Beatrize, is burned as a heretic by the Capuchin missionaries. This woman of noble birth created a movement against Portuguese encroachment, which also encouraged direct religious experience rather than relying on European Capuchin missionaries or the priestly chiefs.

The victory at Turin of the Holy Roman Empire's troops under Commander Prince Eugène of Savoy drives French forces from Italy.

By the Treaty of Altranstadt, Augustus II formally renounces his claim to the Polish throne and accepts Stanislaus I as king.

John V becomes king of Portugal after the death of his father, Peter II (1683). John V rules until 1750.

1707

Lang Chang, a kingdom formed in 1353 by the union of several Laotian states, is divided into two countries: Vientiane and Luang Prabang.

By the Act of Union, England, Scotland and Wales are joined under the name United Kingdom of Great Britain. This union begins a wave of Scottish immigration to Britain's North American colonies.

Bahadur Shah becomes Mogul emperor of India after the death of Aurangzeb (1658), and the empire begins to decline. Bahadur Shah rules until 1712.

1708

The armies of John Churchill, duke of Marlborough and Prince Eugène defeat French forces at Oudenarde (Belgium).

Russia is divided into eight regional governments by Czar Peter I (the Great).

The British East India Company and the New East India Company merge into the United East India Company.

Jesuit missionaries create an accurate map of China.

The forces of King Charles XII of Sweden invade the Ukraine and attack Poltava but they are unable to hold their conquests.

Govind Singh (1676), the last guru of the Sikh faith, is killed in the Deccan, India.

1708-1715

A plague epidemic breaks out in Hungary.

1709

The armies of Marlborough and Prince Eugène of Savoy defeat French forces at Malplaquet in northern France.

Czar Peter I and his army defeat the forces of Charles XII of Sweden and Mazeppa, *hetman* (Cossack chief) of the Ukraine, at the Battle of Poltava.

A harsh winter in the German states worsens the lives of Germans already devastated during the wars with King Louis XIV of France.

Banda Bairāgi, claiming to be the 11th guru of the Sikh faith, forms a strong military force and secures victories against the Moguls. He finally submits to the *Khalsa* (Sikh military fraternity) and is executed in 1716.

Ienobu becomes shogun of Japan after the death of his cousin, Sunayoshi (1680). Ienobu rules until 1712.

Frederick Augustus I, elector of Saxony, again becomes king of Poland after Stanislaus I (1704, 1706) is deposed. Frederick Augustus I rules until 1733.

1700

through

1709

NATIVE AMERICAN	AFRICAN AMERICAN	ASIAN AMERICAN	EUROPEAN AMERICAN
1710 Three Mohawk chiefs and one Mahican are received in Queen Anne's court as the "Four Kings of the New World." **1711** British authorities establish a school for the purpose of anglicizing and Christianizing Native American youths. Each tribe is forced to send representative young men to this school. British colonists plan a major military campaign against the Choctaw (probably in Mississippi). The British and their Creek and Chickasaw allies raid Choctaw villages, leaving 80 people dead and taking 130 captive. **1711-1713** The Tuscarora War takes place in North Carolina between European colonists and the Tuscarora tribe. The Tuscaroras kill 200 colonists but are eventually defeated; remnants of the tribe migrate north and join the Iroquois Confederacy. **1715-1728** A rebellion of Native Americans against British encroachment occurs in South Carolina when the Yamasees kill the British traders in their territories. The Indians fear British hunger for land and resent exploitation by British traders. This series of battles is generally known as the Yamasee War. **c. 1716** Creek, Coweta, Shawnee, Yuchi, Oconee, Apalachee and several other small tribes — approximately 1,000 people — migrate to the Chattahoochee River (Georgia). This group gradually consolidates into the Creek Confederacy. **1717** Seven chiefs from the Creek and Apalachee tribes travel from Pensacola to Mexico City to visit the viceroy and establish an alliance with Spain.	**Early 1700s** Approximately 20 percent of the inhabitants of New York City are enslaved Africans. **1711** A group of *Maroons* (Africans who have escaped slavery and live primarily in nomadic bands), led by Sebastian, raids European communities in South Carolina. **1712** Several enslaved African Americans are executed and others commit suicide after a failed revolt in New York City in which several European Americans are killed. **1713** The Peace of Utrecht, which ends Queen Anne's War, grants Great Britain a monopoly in the trade of enslaved Africans in America. **1716** The first enslaved Africans are brought into France's Louisiana colony.	Although Chinese seamen have engaged in significant maritime activity from the middle of the seventh century, when Manchus conquer the Chinese people in 1644 and bring the Ming dynasty to an end, a major change in foreign policy occurs. Fearing that Ming loyalists will create a revolutionary force outside the country, officials of the new Qing (Ch'ing) dynasty pass edicts barring emigration. Many Chinese people, especially from the southeastern provinces of Fujian (Fukien) and Guangdong (Kwangtung), continue to travel back and forth between China and the countries of southeast Asia, where sizeable Chinese colonies flourish. However, most of the Chinese people are isolated from the West until early in the nineteenth century. Japan's location off the coast of the Asian mainland keeps its inhabitants relatively isolated from outside visitors. The Japanese people withstand attempted invasions by Kublai Khan in the 1200s, and first encounter Europeans when Portuguese traders arrive off the Asian mainland in the early 1500s. European missionaries follow but, fearing the examples seen in other Asian countries where missionaries were soon followed by military forces, the Tokugawa shogunate issues an effective anti-Christian decree. Japan remains isolated until a United States fleet under Commodore (later Admiral) Matthew Perry sails into Tokyo Bay in 1853.	**1710** Mobile (now in Alabama) is established by an expedition under the French governor of Louisiana, Jean Baptiste le Moyne, Sieur de Bienville. It serves as the capital of Louisiana until 1719. Louisiana Governor Bienville is recalled by the French crown, and replaced by Antoine de la Mothe, Sieur de Cadillac. Paris banker Antoine Crozat becomes financial officer of the colony. **1712** The Palatinate community at New Bern, North Carolina, is nearly destroyed by Native Americans in the Tuscarora War. Consequently, fleeing German colonists migrate to the southeast. **1714-1720** During this time span, more than 50 ships of Scotch-Irish immigrants arrive in the New England region, and a greater number dock at southern harbors. Scotch-Irish communities are soon established in New York, western Massachusetts, New Hampshire and Maine. Scotch-Irish colonists make up the largest group of newcomers to America during the first 65 years of this century, with approximately 250,000 people arriving. One push factor for this group is a series of crop failures in northern Ireland. Some of these Scotch-Irish immigrants bring with them a deep-seated hostility toward England. **1716-1717** French explorer Benard de le Harpe leads an expedition along the Arkansas River. **1717** French colonists build a fort in Alabama territory at the confluence of the Coosa and Tallapoosa Rivers (near present-day Montgomery, Alabama). A small Scotch-Irish community is established in Maine; later, it becomes part of the town of Portland.

1710

through

1719

EUROPEAN AMERICAN	HISPANIC AMERICAN			

EUROPEAN AMERICAN

1718

Approximately 800 French colonists, in three separate voyages, arrive in the Louisiana colony. This group includes le Page du Pratz, Louisiana's first historian. While most of these people make their homes in the French communities already established on the Gulf coast, approximately 100 continue north into the Illnois country.

The first cotton plantation in Louisiana is begun by Emanuel Prud'homme near Natchitoches.

New Orleans, Louisiana, is established by colonists under Bienville. In 1722 it becomes the capital of the French colony of Louisiana.

1718-1729

French colonists expand their holdings on the Mississippi River.

1719

The Pennsylvania colony receives increased immigration from German Brethren, known as Dunkers, who found Germantown under the leadership of Peter Becker. German Mennonites and Moravians also come to Pennsylvania in greater numbers.

Londonderry, New Hampshire, is established by a group of approximately 20 Scotch-Irish families, on a site selected by James McKean. The potato is introduced in the colony.

Several military encounters between Spanish and French forces in Florida result in the Spanish city-fort of Pensacola being surrendered to French forces. The French community at Dauphin Island is attacked by Spanish forces, but is successful in fending off the attack.

HISPANIC AMERICAN

1714

San Mateo de Cangrejos in northeastern Puerto Rico becomes an established population center for *cimarrones* (people from the Lesser Antilles who escaped slavery there) and freed former slaves from Puerto Rico.

1715

The renewed threat of French encroachment into Texas motivates Spanish colonists to plan fortifications and communities among the Tejas tribe.

1716

Captain Diego Ramón and French trader Louis St. Denis are sent by the viceroy of New Spain to establish communities and *presidios* (forts or military posts) in Texas.

Juan de Ayala y Escobar is appointed interim governor of Florida. He serves until 1718.

1718

A Spanish expedition led by Martín de Alarcón establishes a mission, San Antonio de Valero and a *presidio,* San Antonio de Béjar; both are located in what is now San Antonio, Texas. The mission is later renamed the Alamo.

1719

A small group of French soldiers moves into eastern Texas. The new Spanish governor, the Marquis of San Miguel de Aguayo, is sent with 500 soldiers into the area in 1721. His expedition builds 10 additional missions and four presidios. Aguayo sets his capital at Los Adaes, and serves until 1722.

1710

through

1719

THE AMERICAS	THE AMERICAS	THE AMERICAS	THE WORLD

1710 through 1719

THE AMERICAS

1710

A British naval force of approximately 2,000 men under the command of Francis Nicholson leaves Boston to attack the French city of Port Royal. French commander de Subercase and 300 men hold off the British attack for almost two weeks before they are forced to surrender. This British victory ends French rule of Port Royal. Remaining residents of Acadia (Nova Scotia, New Brunswick and eastern Maine) must swear allegiance to Britain's Queen Anne or leave the area.

Mobile is founded in Alabama.

Charleville, a French trader, establishes a trading post at French Lick, now the site of Nashville, Tennessee.

1711

Parliament passes an act that gives immigrants to America who swear allegiance to the Crown most of the rights of British citizens.

British privateers from Jamaica overrun French communities on Dauphin Island.

In an effort to make it impossible for enslaved Africans to earn money and purchase their freedom, Jamaican planters forbid them from owning livestock, or selling meat or sugar.

In an effort later called the "magnificent fiasco," eight of nine ships under the command of Ovenden Walker are lost in the Gulf of St. Lawrence in an ill-fated British attack on Quebec.

North Carolina, separated from the Carolinas in 1691 and ruled by deputy governors from Charleston, South Carolina, get its own governor.

French forces take control of Mauritius from the Dutch.

Rio de Janeiro, Brazil, is captured by French forces under René Duguay-Trouin.

1712

Louis XIV grants the Louisiana colony a charter and the right to establish its own constitution. A governmental body called the Superior Council is established; it includes a governor, commissioner and an appointed local council.

THE AMERICAS

Pennsylvania prohibits the further importation of enslaved people.

French forces build Fort Mackinack, on the northwest shore of Lake Huron (Michigan).

Merchant Antoine Crozat is granted a commercial monopoly by the French residents of Louisiana. He later turns this monopoly over to a company led by Scotsman John Law, whose Mississippi Scheme brings new colonists to the area.

1713

The Peace of Utrecht ends the War of the Spanish Succession in Europe, and the corresponding Queen Anne's War in North America. This treaty's effects in North America are the cession by France of all forts and territories in Newfoundland, Hudson Bay and Acadia (Nova Scotia, New Brunswick and eastern Maine); the continued French possession of the islands of St. Pierre and Miquelon off the coast of Newfoundland, Île Royale (Cape Breton Island) and Île Saint Jean (Prince Edward Island); the retention of French fishing rights in Newfoundland waters; St. Kitts in the Caribbean to England; and the declaration that all Indians in the areas ceded to Britain are British subjects. The Abenakis in Acadia refuse to swear allegiance to the British crown.

Laureano Torres de Ayala again becomes governor of Cuba. He serves until 1716.

1713-1755

An estimated 6,000 Acadians leave Nova Scotia between 1713 and 1755. The plight of those remaining behind worsens under the governorship of Charles Lawrence.

1714

A riot occurs in Quebec over the inflated price of goods.

The first Canadian hospital for the mentally ill opens in Quebec, serving only women patients.

THE AMERICAS

1715

After the failed Jacobite Rebellion in Scotland, the British government banishes several of the rebels to the American colonies.

c. 1715

Virginia colonists led by Alexander Spotswood explore the Shenandoah River Valley. Spotswood is colonial governor of Virginia from 1710 to 1722.

1716

Crop failures in the northern counties of Ireland add to the wave of Scotch-Irish immigration to North America. These Scotch-Irish people carry a deep hostility toward England.

Cuban-born Juan de Ayala y Escobar is appointed interim governor of Florida. He serves until 1718.

The population of Canada exceeds 20,000.

1717

An act of the British Parliament creates a punishment for British criminals of transportation to America. Contractors begin transporting felons regularly.

France annexes the area that is now Illinois to its Louisiana territory.

The colony of New Granada (Colombia) becomes a province of Spain, with the king's deputy as ruler of the province.

1718

Spanish forces occupy Texas and set up a military government.

French colonists on Dauphin Island are attacked by Spanish raiding parties, who abandon the siege after 12 days.

New Orleans is founded in Louisiana.

San Antonio is founded in Texas.

The British Parliament prohibits skilled workers from coming to America.

THE WORLD

1710

The English South Sea Company is founded by Robert Harley.

The Ottoman sultan declares war on Russia.

Dutch colonists and traders abandon the island of Mauritius.

1711

The South Sea Company assumes 9 million pounds in national debt for an interest fee on the debt plus the monopoly of overseas trade in South America and the islands of the South Seas. The British government expands the firm's capital base by exchanging its own debt for stock.

By the Treaty of Pruth, Russia returns Azov and neighboring areas to the Ottoman Empire.

Austria controls Hungary and Transylvania.

Afghanistan gains its independence from Persia with a victory under Mir Vais at Kandahar.

The first public synagogue opens in Berlin.

Charles VI becomes Holy Roman Emperor after the death of his brother, Joseph I (1705). Charles VI rules until 1740.

1712

A war of succession takes place in India among Bahadur Shah's (1707) four sons.

The last execution for witchcraft takes place in Britain.

As a child, Ietsugu becomes shogun of Japan after the death of his father, Ienobu (1709). Ietsugu rules until 1716.

1713

The Treaty of Asiento between Britain and Spain is one of the main causes for the South Sea Bubble. The treaty grants the South Sea Company the right to import enslaved Africans into Spain's American colonies.

The Peace of Utrecht ends the War of the Spanish Succession and Queen Anne's War. In this treaty, as with the Treaties of Rastatt and Baden in 1714, Philip, a Bourbon, is recognized as king of Spain but Gibraltar and Minorca are ceded to Britain, and Austria receives Belgium, Milan and Naples. Britain retains the *asiento*, and the concept of "balance of power" replaces dynastic or national rights in deciding strengths and boundaries of the European powers. Protestant succession is established in Britain.

The Peace of Adrianople is signed between Russia and Turkey.

Under the Hapsburg Pragmatic Sanction, Holy Roman Emperor Charles VI, lacking male heirs, declares that succession to the Hapsburg family empire will pass to his daughter, Maria Theresa. Opposition to this declaration is strong, and Charles's death in 1740 marks the start of the War of the Austrian Succession.

Victor Amadeus II (1675), duke of Savoy, becomes king of Sicily. He rules until 1720. His control of Sicily is strengthened by the Treaties of Utrecht and Rastatt, in which Spain cedes Sardinia and Naples to Austria and Sicily to Savoy. However, the Quadruple Alliance forces him to take Sardinia instead of Sicily for his dominion in 1720. The history of the House of Savoy shifts off the Italian mainland. Victor Amadeus II rules Sardinia until 1730.

Sweden's Charles XII is captured by Ottoman forces at Bender, Hanover, and detained for more than one year.

Frederick William I becomes king of Prussia after the death of his father, Frederick I (1701). Frederick William I rules until 1740.

Frederick William establishes Prussia as a strong military power by the creation of a standing army.

1714

Prussia abolishes the practice of witch trials.

At the Battle of Storkyro, Russian forces dominate the Swedes and gain control of Finland.

By the Treaty of Rastatt, the Hapsburgs gain control of the area that is modern-day Belgium, making the former Spanish Netherlands the Austrian Netherlands.

France annexes Burgundy.

Tripoli gains its independence from the Ottoman Empire.

George I (George Louis, elector of Hanover) becomes king of Great Britain and Ireland after the death of Queen Anne (1702). George I rules until 1727.

The mercury thermometer is invented by Gabriel D. Fahrenheit of Germany.

1714-1901

The House of Hanover (Brunswick) rules Britain.

1715

Jacobites — agitators for the return of the line of James Francis Edward Stuart (the Old Pretender) to the throne of Britain — start a revolt led by John Erskine, earl of Mar. James Stuart has been recognized by Spain and France as James III, heir to the British crown. The Jacobites are defeated at Preston and Sheriffmuir in Scotland, and James III flees to France.

Ottoman forces recapture Peloponnesus (Morea) from the Venetians.

The East India Company establishes a trading station at Canton.

The island of Mauritius, abandoned by the Netherlands in 1710, is claimed by France.

Louis XV, a child, becomes king of France after the death of his great grandfather, Louis XIV (1643). The duc d'Orleans serves as regent. Louis XV comes of age in 1723 and rules until 1774.

Mahmoud (Mahmud) becomes shah of Afghanistan after the death of Mir Vais. Mahmoud rules until 1725.

1716

Chinese Emperor Kangxi (K'ang-hsi) prohibits the teaching of Christianity by repealing the Edict of Toleration.

Prince Eugène and his forces defeat Ottoman troops at Peterwardein (northeastern Yugoslavia).

Holy Roman Emperor Charles VI declares war on Turkey.

Yoshimune becomes shogun of Japan after the death of Ietsugu (1712). Yoshimune rules until 1745.

1717

French merchant Antoine Crozat releases his commercial monopoly in Louisiana and Canada to Scotsman John Law. Law then sets up the Compagnie d'Occident (later expanded and renamed Compagnie des Indes and known as the Mississippi Scheme) to control French colonial trade. The stock company's stories of great opportunities lead to heavy speculation in its shares, and also create a merger with the French national bank in 1720. Overspeculation and poor management lead to the company's financial ruin, but the scheme causes a great influx of colonists into Louisiana.

Lady Mary Wortley Montagu introduces an inoculation against smallpox in Britain.

James III is forced to leave France by an alliance of England, France and Holland.

1717-1724

The Tibetan war ends with the Qing (Ch'ing) conquest of Tibet.

1718

The Treaty of Passarowitz ends the conflict between the Ottoman Empire, Austria and Venice. Austria gains control over the Banat of Temesvar, Northern Bosnia, Lesser Walachia and Northern Serbia (including Belgrade). The Ottomans gain control over Venice's territory on Crete and in the Peloponnesus, except the Ionian Islands and the Dalmatian Coast.

The British Parliament prohibits the emigration of skilled artisans.

Ulrica Leonora becomes queen of Sweden after her brother, King Charles XII (1697), is killed during a battle against Norway. She rules until 1720.

1718-1720

In the War of the Quadruple Alliance, Great Britain, France, the Holy Roman Empire and the Netherlands thwart Spanish King Philip V in his attempt to regain territories lost during the War of the Spanish Succession.

1719

Liechtenstein, by uniting Vaduz and Schellenburg, becomes an independent principality within the Holy Roman Empire.

The British Parliament strengthens its control over Ireland.

Jesuits are expelled from Russia.

France declares war on Spain.

Nizam ul-Mulk, the Mogul viceroy in the Deccan region of India, establishes the state of Hyderabad.

Ali Vardi Khan begins the reign of the *nawabs* (provincial governors) of Bengal.

Muhammad Shah, grandson of Bahadur Shah (1707-1712), becomes Mogul emperor of India after the reign of five ineffective rulers. Muhammad Shah rules until 1748.

1719-1720

The Treaties of Stockholm and Frederiksborg (and Nystadt in 1721) end the Great Northern War with Sweden making peace with all of the countries allied against it except Russia; Poland and Denmark return their conquests; Denmark receives compensation and control over some territory; Prussia keeps Stettin and parts of west Pomerania; and Hanover pays a substantial fee but keeps Bremen and Verden.

1710

through

1719

	NATIVE AMERICAN	AFRICAN AMERICAN	ASIAN AMERICAN	EUROPEAN AMERICAN
1720 through 1729	**1722** Remnants of the Tuscarora tribe who fled north after the Tuscarora War (1711-1713) are officially recognized as part of the Iroquois Confederacy. The Iroquois Confederacy signs a treaty with Virginia, agreeing not to cross the Potomac River or the Blue Ridge Mountains into Virginia. **1722-1726** Native Americans are held in slavery in St. Peter's Parish in Virginia. **1723** The first permanent American Indian school is established in Williamsburg, Virginia, with funds provided by a British scientist. **1726-1727** Yamasees from the St. Augustine area, Creeks under Chief Cherokeeleechee and free African Americans in Florida join forces to raid British communities in South Carolina. **1727** The position of "interpreter" is abolished for the Pamunkey and Chickahominy tribes of Virginia and Maryland, indicating that many in the tribes now speak at least some English. **1728** The Yamasee War against British colonial expansion ends with the defeat and dispersal of the tribe. **1729** The Natchez Revolt occurs when Natchez Indians attack the French outpost of Fort Rosalie in Mississippi, killing 250 colonists. The Natchez are defeated after French colonists call upon the Choctaw for assistance. In a battle fought between the Illinois and Wabash rivers, a force of French and Indians massacres about 500 Fox Indians and captures as many more. This loss devastates the small Fox Nation.	**1721** Marriages of European American women to African American men are outlawed in Delaware. **1724** Enslaved Africans outnumber European Americans two to one in South Carolina. **1725** The Church of Colored Baptists, the first of its kind, is founded in Williamsburg, Virginia. Racial intermarriage is forbidden by law in Pennsylvania. The estimated population of enslaved Africans in the colonies that later become the United States is 75,000. **1729** When North and South Carolina become separate colonies, their position on the issue of slavery is also divided. North Carolina was colonized by less wealthy Virginia farmers, Quakers and Scotch-Irish. Their religious beliefs and lack of plantation-style farming make North Carolina one of the most active antislavery states in the South.	Although Chinese seamen have engaged in significant maritime activity from the middle of the seventh century, when Manchus conquer the Chinese people in 1644 and bring the Ming dynasty to an end, a major change in foreign policy occurs. Fearing that Ming loyalists will create a revolutionary force outside the country, officials of the new Qing (Ch'ing) dynasty pass edicts barring emigration. Many Chinese people, especially from the southeastern provinces of Fujian (Fukien) and Guangdong (Kwangtung), continue to travel back and forth between China and the countries of southeast Asia, where sizeable Chinese colonies flourish. However, most of the Chinese people are isolated from the West until early in the nineteenth century. Japan's location off the coast of the Asian mainland keeps its inhabitants relatively isolated from outside visitors. The Japanese people withstand attempted invasions by Kublai Khan in the 1200s, and first encounter Europeans when Portuguese traders arrive off the Asian mainland in the early 1500s. European missionaries follow but, fearing the examples seen in other Asian countries where missionaries were soon followed by military forces, the Tokugawa shogunate issues an effective anti-Christian decree. Japan remains isolated until a United States fleet under Commodore (later Admiral) Matthew Perry sails into Tokyo Bay in 1853.	**1720** A French military group under Major Pierre Dugue Boisbriant builds Ft. Chartres near the existing community of Kaskaskia (Illinois). French forces also erect Ft. Ouiatanon near the site that is now Lafayette, Indiana. There are now several hundred Scotch-Irish families living in communities along the Kennebec River and in eastern Maine. Residents of Londonderry, New Hampshire, object to being called "Irish," and most declare their allegiance to the British crown. One of the earliest colleges in the Midwest is established at Kaskaskia by Jesuits priests. **1721** Swiss immigrants introduce rifles into America. **1722** The first Capuchin priests come to New Orleans; they open several parish schools. Large-scale planting and harvesting of indigo in Louisiana begins. Nicholas de Beaubois, a Jesuit priest, starts the first commercial dye-making in the area. English merchants and soldiers, trying to attract some of the northern Great Lakes fur trade away from French traders, build a fort and trading post at Oswego, New York. **1723** About 20 percent of the population of Charleston, South Carolina is of French origin. **c. 1725** For two reasons, newer Scotch-Irish immigrants tend to make their homes in Pennsylvania: they have heard of prejudice in the New England colonies; and many of the ships they arrive on are engaged in the flax seed trade out of Philadelphia.

116

EUROPEAN AMERICAN	HISPANIC AMERICAN	FOR CLASSROOM USE	FOR CLASSROOM USE	
1726 The Maryland colony grants special land and tax exemptions to Welsh farmers wanting to come to the colony. Welsh people are considered a positive addition, with a reputation as hard workers. Charles de Beauharnois de La Boische becomes governor of New France. His term is considered the most prosperous era of the New France colony. De La Boische serves until 1747. **1727** By this time, 20,000 German immigrants are living in the Pennsylvania colony. **1728** A group of "filles à la cassette" (casket girls) arrives in the Louisiana colony. Either orphans or the daughters of peasants, they are brought to America to ease the shortage of marriageable women, and are cared for by the Ursuline nuns until they are married. **1729** Animosity between English and Scottish colonists is strong at this time. A nativist mob in Boston blocks the landing of a shipload of Scotch-Irish emigrants. Many Scottish immigrants live in Pennsylvania and South Carolina, since there are few English colonists there.	**1720** Spanish forces under Villasur are killed by Pawnees and Otos on the Platte River. This battle does much to prevent Spanish colonization of the American Plains. **1725** *Presidios* (forts or military posts) are built at San Antonio, Los Adaes and La Bahía in Texas to guard Spanish missions against French encroachment.			**1720** through **1729**

1720 through 1729

1720

The mining of lead begins in Missouri.

Philadelphia's first Catholic parish is organized.

When John Law's Mississippi Company fails, the French communities in Louisiana suffer economic hardships; the French government ignores the colony.

The government of Pennsylvania requires newly arrived immigrants to swear allegiance to the British crown.

The first commercial coal mine in North America opens at Port Morien, in what is now Nova Scotia.

Sebastian Râle, an anti-British Jesuit, incites American Indians to raid British communities in Maine. Britain sends in troops who destroy French missions, kill Râle and weaken the Abenaki tribe.

1721

By this time there is regular postal service between London and New England.

An early form of smallpox inoculation is administered in the Americas by Zabdiel Boylston. He first inoculates his son and two enslaved Africans. When they recover, he inoculates more than 240 colonists, all but six of whom survive.

1722

A combined force of Hurons, Abenakis and other Canadian Indian tribes, numbering about 400 total, raze British communities along Maine's Kennebec River.

1723

In Virginia all American Indians, *mulattos* (people of combined African and European ethnicity) and African Americans over the age of 16, male or female, free or enslaved, are declared taxable.

1724

The convent of Corpus Christi in Mexico is founded to allow Indian women to enter monastic life for the first time. Still, the women accepted into the convent have to be of pure Indian ancestry and legitimate daughters of chieftains.

1725

French forces build a stone structure to replace the log buildings at Fort Niagara, New York.

1726

The population of Louisiana includes almost 2,000 masters of households, approximately 275 hired men and servants, 1,550 enslaved African Americans and 300 enslaved Native Americans.

Spanish colonists establish a community, Montevideo (Uruguay), in South America.

1727

Coffee is first planted in Brazil.

1728

Danish explorer Vitus J. Bering first sails through the strait that now carries his name, the narrow body of water between northeast Asia and northwest America.

The population of New Orleans, Louisiana, is reported at nearly 1,000.

c. 1728

The first public synagogue in America is built in New York City.

1729

The city of Baltimore, Maryland, is founded. It is incorporated in c. 1797.

At the instigation of English traders in the region, Natchez Indians attack the French Fort Rosalie, at the site that is now Natchez, Mississippi. Nearly 300 French colonists and military personnel are killed. In the next two years, French forces conduct a counterattack. Several hundred Natchez Indians are captured and enslaved; the remainder flee to the Choctaws.

The informal 1691 division of Carolina into North and South becomes official and the two become royal colonies.

Benjamin and James Franklin begin publishing *The Pennsylvania Gazette*.

The *Gaceta de Guatemala* (Guatemala Gazette) begins publication.

THE WORLD	THE WORLD	THE WORLD	FOR CLASSROOM USE	

1720

Overspeculation and poor financial management cause both John Law's Mississippi Company and Robert Harley's South Sea Company to fail, creating heavy financial problems for the governments of France and Britain.

Tibet becomes a tributary state of China.

Frederick I becomes king of Sweden after the abdication of his wife, Queen Ulrica Leonora (1718). He rules until 1751.

1721

The Treaty of Nystadt completes the resolution of the Great Northern War. Sweden is weakened, Poland begins to decline, and Russia becomes a major power in Europe. By the terms of the treaty, Sweden retains most of Finland but cedes Livonia, Estonia and part of Karelia to Russia, giving Peter I access to the Baltic Sea. Peter I is proclaimed emperor of "all the Russias."

(Sir) Robert Walpole serves Britain as first lord of the Treasury and chancellor of the Exchequer. He remains in power until 1742.

1722

Dutch navigators visit the islands of Samoa.

Hungary rejects the Hapsburg Pragmatic Sanction that made Maria Theresa Holy Roman Empress. This event sets the stage for the War of the Austrian Succession.

Yongzheng (Yung-cheng) becomes emperor of China after the death of Kangxi (K'ang-hsi, 1662). Yongzheng rules until 1735.

Mahmoud, shah of Afghanistan, becomes shah of Persia (Iran) after the Safavid dynasty ends with the abdication of Shah Hussein (1694). Mir Mahmoud rules until 1725.

1723

The British duty on tea is reduced by Robert Walpole.

Mir Mahmoud engages in a reign of terror in Persia.

1724

Austria accepts the Pragmatic Sanction.

Russia and Turkey invade Persia.

Viceroy Asaf Jah, the nizam (ruler) of Hyderabad, takes control of the Carnatic.

John Carterat, earl of Granville, becomes lord lieutenant of Ireland. He is a successful peacemaker and his support aids in the downfall of Robert Walpole. John Carterat serves until 1730.

Philip V, king of Spain, abdicates in favor of his son, Louis I. However, following his son's death later this year, Philip V reclaims the throne.

1725

The Treaty of Vienna, uniting Spanish Bourbons and Austrian Hapsburgs, guarantees the Hapsburg Pragmatic Sanction.

A map of Europe is created by Guillaume Delisle.

Catherine I becomes czarina of Russia after the death of her husband, Peter I (the Great, 1682). She rules until 1727.

Ashraf, a nephew of Mir Vais, becomes shah of Persia after the death of Mahmoud (1715, 1722). Ashraf rules until 1730.

1726

Holy Roman Emperor Charles VI and Russia form an alliance against the Ottoman Empire.

The first of a series of Miao rebellions occurs in China. Others occur in 1735, 1738, 1793 and 1797.

Charles Albert (later Emperor Charles VII) becomes elector of Bavaria. He holds this position until 1745.

1727

Britain goes to war with Spain following the Spanish attack on Gibraltar.

The Treaty of Kiachta between Russia and China defines the Amur frontier.

Jews expelled from Russia immigrate to Poland.

George II becomes king of Great Britain and Ireland after the death of his father, George I (1714). George II rules until 1760.

Peter II becomes czar of Russia after the death of his grandmother, Catherine I (1725). Peter II rules until 1730.

1728

Danish explorer Vitus J. Bering, working for Peter II of Russia, departs from Kamchatka and sails through the strait that bears his name. It is the body of water that separates northeast Asia from northwest America.

1729

Chinese Emperor Yongzheng forbids the public sale of opium.

The Treaty of Seville is signed between Spain and Britain, France and the Netherlands. By its terms, Britain retains Gibraltar and Spanish succession is preserved in the Italian duchies.

1720

through

1729

	NATIVE AMERICAN	AFRICAN AMERICAN	ASIAN AMERICAN	EUROPEAN AMERICAN
1730 **through** **1739**	**1730** In northern Mississippi and neighboring areas, Chickasaw resistance against French colonists begins when the French and Choctaw unite to interfere with Chickasaw trade to British colonists. The French offer firearms and ammunition for Chickasaw scalps. The Chickasaws remain undefeated when New France is surrendered to Britain. Six Cherokee men are taken to London aboard a British ship. They are treated royally, and create a sensation in London. They are cajoled into signing a treaty of allegiance to the British crown. **1730-1750** Apaches of the southern Plains, under attack from the east and north by Caddoan and Comanche warriors, retreat southward. **1733** A battle is fought between French forces and the Sauk tribe in Wisconsin. Heavy losses occur on both sides. The Sauk abandon the region and join the Fox Nation. The tribes together build a fort on the Wapsipinicon River in Iowa. **1733-1739** Creek Chief Tomochichi establishes friendly relations with Georgia colonists led by James Oglethorpe; in 1734 Oglethorpe takes Tomochichi, his wife, nephew and other Creek Indians to England. After their return, Tomochichi continues to help the English colonists until his death in 1739. **1734** A French expedition marches to the Sauk and Fox fort. The village is found abandoned. Several indecisive skirmishes end when French forces retreat due to hunger. **1738** Separate smallpox epidemics hit the Cherokees of the American Southeast and the tribes in western Canada. Nearly half of the Cherokees die. **1739** War breaks out between the Chippewa and Sioux tribes, with French colonists caught in the middle. The Chippewa drive the Sioux out of central Wisconsin.	**1733** Nantucket Quaker Elihu Coleman publishes *"A Testimony Against That Anti-Christian Practice of Making Slaves of Men."* **1735** John VanZandt of New York City is tried for killing a slave, but a coroner's jury decides that the cause of death was "the visitation of God." **1739** The Stono Rebellion in South Carolina, led by Cato, is one of the largest in the United States. Although precipitated by British mistreatment, it is fueled by Spanish promises of support to the enslaved Africans, most of whom arrived from the Catholic section of the kingdom of Kongo. The severity of the rebellion indicates that many of these men are experienced African warriors. In their organization, deportment, recruiting practices and handling of firearms, the rebels prove themselves to be highly skilled in military tactics. When the rebellion is finally ended, more than 30 European Americans and 40 African Americans are killed, but some enslaved people escape to freedom.	Although Chinese seamen have engaged in significant maritime activity from the middle of the seventh century, when Manchus conquer the Chinese people in 1644 and bring the Ming dynasty to an end, a major change in foreign policy occurs. Fearing that Ming loyalists will create a revolutionary force outside the country, officials of the new Qing (Ch'ing) dynasty pass edicts barring emigration. Many Chinese people, especially from the southeastern provinces of Fujian (Fukien) and Guangdong (Kwangtung), continue to travel back and forth between China and the countries of southeast Asia, where sizeable Chinese colonies flourish. However, most of the Chinese people are isolated from the West until early in the nineteenth century. Japan's location off the coast of the Asian mainland keeps its inhabitants relatively isolated from outside visitors. The Japanese people withstand attempted invasions by Kublai Khan in the 1200s, and first encounter Europeans when Portuguese traders arrive off the Asian mainland in the early 1500s. European missionaries follow but, fearing the examples seen in other Asian countries where missionaries were soon followed by military forces, the Tokugawa shogunate issues an effective anti-Christian decree. Japan remains isolated until a United States fleet under Commodore (later Admiral) Matthew Perry sails into Tokyo Bay in 1853.	**1730** German and Scotch-Irish people from Pennsylvania begin to migrate into the rural South. **1731** The population of Louisiana is reported at 5,000 Europeans and 2,000 Africans. **1732** Conrad Beissel founds the Seventh Day Baptists (Ephrata Community) in Germantown, Pennsylvania. French organizer John Peter Pury acquires 40,000 acres of land on the Savannah River, and leads a group of approximately 300 colonists, both Swiss and French, to make their homes there. The community — Purysburg, South Carolina — grows to 600 residents in the next two years. **1733** Jeremiah Smith, an Irish immigrant, opens the first paper mill in the colonies at Dorchester, Massachusetts. **1734** The new Scotch-Irish Presbyterian church in Worcester, Massachusetts, is destroyed by a nativist mob. Thousands of Salzburg (Austria) Protestant immigrants establish communities in Georgia. **1734-1744** More than 12,000 Swiss-Germans immigrate to America, a majority of them coming to make their homes in the Carolinas. **1735** French colonists found a community at Vincennes, Indiana. **1736** Under the leadership of Samuel Waldo, a German-community of about 40 households is established at Waldoboro, Maine. **1737** On St. Patrick's Day of this year, the Charitable Irish Society is founded in Boston to assist Irish newcomers to the country and to foster Irish unity. This is the oldest Irish society in the United States.

EUROPEAN AMERICAN	HISPANIC AMERICAN	*FOR CLASSROOM USE*	*FOR CLASSROOM USE*	
1739 The Moravian Church in America is founded by Bishop A. G. Spangenberg. The first authentically German newspaper in what is now the United States is published at Germantown, Pennsylvania, by Christopher Saur.	**1730** A group of people from the Canary Islands moves to San Antonio de Béxar (San Antonio, Texas). **1735** Texas serves as a buffer zone between Spanish colonists in Mexico and French encroachment from the Louisiana territory. **1737** Manuel José de Jústiz is appointed interim governor of Florida. He serves for one year and is the region's third Cuban-born governor. **1738** Manuel de Montiano becomes governor of Florida. He establishes the first free African American town in what is now the United States. A former slave, Francisco Menéndez, becomes the leader of the 37 African families in the town of Fort Mose (Gracia Real de Santa Teresa de Mose). When Florida becomes a British possession in 1763, the Spaniards and Africans at Fort Mose move to Cuba. **1739** An epidemic of smallpox and measles breaks out in San Antonio, leading Native Americans to desert the five missions there.			**1730** **through** **1739**

	THE AMERICAS	THE AMERICAS	THE AMERICAS	FOR CLASSROOM USE

1730 through 1739

1730-1739

Spain establishes a third viceroyalty in the Americas. Called New Granada, it includes present-day Colombia, Venezuela, Panama and Ecuador.

1730s

British and Spanish forces battle for control of Central American coastal areas.

1731

French colonists fortify Crown Point on Lake Champlain to block British expansion.

By this year the population of New Orleans, Louisiana is estimated at 7,000.

Barbados has its first newspaper, the *Barbados Gazette*. Its publishers are Samuel Keimer and David Harry.

1732

English philanthropist James Oglethorpe and 19 associates obtain a charter to become trustees of the Georgia colony. Oglethorpe establishes a community at Savannah the next year, building around the existing Indian village of Yamacraw. He and the colonists with him make peace with the neighboring Indian tribes and build fortifications to protect their borders against Spaniards in Florida. One of Oglethorpe's goals is to create a place where debtors from British prisons can start new lives. Georgia becomes Britain's thirteenth colony along North America's Atlantic coast.

Benjamin Franklin publishes the first edition of *Poor Richard's Almanac*.

1733

Britain's Parliament passes the Molasses Act, prohibiting trade between the American colonies and any West Indian islands not held by the British.

Bienville, now 60 years of age, returns to the neglected Louisiana colony. The group is growing, but military and government organization are seriously lacking, and food supplies are low.

1734

St. Thomas Church is built in Bath, North Carolina. It is the area's oldest surviving church.

A road opens between the cities of Quebec and Montreal in Canada.

Enslaved Africans on St. Lucia are prohibited from selling cotton or coffee.

1735

Augusta, Georgia, is established by James Oglethorpe and named for the mother of George III.

John Peter Zenger, publisher of the *Weekly Journal* in New York, is acquitted of libel in a court case that helps establish freedom of the press.

Eliza Lucas Pinckney experiments with, raises and exports large crops of indigo, greatly increasing the economy of the Carolinas.

1736

A massive plot among enslaved Africans on Antigua is betrayed. Nearly 70 of the rebels are hanged over a three-month period to deter further unrest.

1737

Richmond, Virginia, begun as a trading center (Fort Charles) in 1645, is planned and laid out as a town under the direction of William Byrd.

1738

A French expedition establishes Fort La Reine in Manitoba as a fur trading post. The French hold it until Hudson's Bay Company takes control in 1823.

British troops arrive in Georgia to defend the border against Spanish encroachment from Florida.

In the first documented European expedition in the Dakotas, French explorer La Verendrye visits Mandan villages near the Missouri River.

1739

After Britain declares war on Spain, James Oglethorpe leads an unsuccessful expedition against the Spanish in St. Augustine, Florida.

A census of Canada records the population at approximately 42,000.

During the War of Jenkins's Ear, English forces raid several Spanish cities on the Central American coasts. Portobelo (Panama) is destroyed.

A French expedition builds Fort Assumption at the site that is now Memphis, Tennessee.

English officials on Jamaica sign a treaty with Maroon leader Cudjoe, establishing independence for the Maroons.

1730

An earthquake in Hokkaido, Japan, kills more than 137,000 people.

Emperor Yongzheng (Yung-cheng) issues an edict to reduce slavery in China.

Transatlantic shipowners in Europe actively promote emigrant business to fill up their cargo ships on westward voyages.

The shah expels Afghans from Persia (Iran).

Mahmud I becomes Ottoman sultan after his uncle, Ahmed III (1703), is overthrown by the Janissaries, an elite Ottoman military unit. Mahmud I rules until 1754.

Anna becomes czarina of Russia after the death of her cousin, Peter II (1727). She rules until 1740.

Christian VI becomes king of Denmark and Norway after the death of his father, Frederick IV (1699). Christian VI rules until 1746.

Charles Emmanuel III becomes king of Sardinia after the abdication of his father, Victor Amadeus II (1713). Charles Emmanuel III rules until 1773.

Tahmasp II becomes shah of Persia after the death of Ashraf (1725). Tahmasp II rules until 1731.

René Reaumur makes an alcohol thermometer with a graduated scale.

1731

The Treaty of Vienna between Britain, the Netherlands, Spain, Austria and the Holy Roman Empire guarantees the Pragmatic Sanction and dissolves the Ostend East India Company, a major rival of Britain's colonial trade empire.

Due to a labor shortage in Britain, factory workers are not allowed to immigrate to North America.

A minor naval skirmish between Spain and England costs one man his ear and becomes a rallying cry for a later conflict — the 1739 War of Jenkins's Ear.

Protestants in Hungary are barred from holding government positions by the *Carolina Resolutio*.

The sextant is invented by British mathematician John Hadley.

As a child, Abbas III becomes shah of Persia after his father, Tahmasp II (1730) is deposed by Nadir Kuli. Abbas III rules until 1736.

1733

France declares war against Holy Roman Emperor Charles VI.

The death of Poland's King Augustus II (1697, 1704) marks the beginning of the two-year War of the Polish Succession. Augustus III of Saxony, son of Augustus II, receives assistance from Russian and Austrian forces in his bid for the throne. He is opposed by Stanislaus Leszczynski (1704-1709), in alliance with France and Spain. The conflict ends in victory for Augustus III, who takes the throne in 1735. He rules Poland until 1763.

The flying shuttle, a device to speed up production on the hand weaving loom, is developed by British inventor John Kay. The invention, which later helps mechanize the textile industry, is initially viewed as a major threat and the early models are destroyed by mobs, causing Kay to flee to France.

1735

The Treaty of Vienna ends the War of the Polish Succession. By the terms of this agreement, Austria receives Parma and Piacenza and surrenders Naples and Sicily to Spain. The Spanish House of Bourbon establishes the Kingdom of the Two Sicilies and Stainslaus relinquishes the Polish throne.

c. 1735

Potatoes first arrive in Finland and Sweden.

1736

War is declared between Russia and Turkey. Holy Roman Emperor Charles VI enters the war in 1737 to aid Russia.

Qianlong (Ch'ien-lung) becomes emperor of China. He rules until 1796.

Nadir Kuli (Nadir Shah) deposes the infant Abbas III (1731) and becomes shah of Persia. Nadir Kuli rules until 1747.

Baron Theodore von Neuhof, a German soldier and diplomat, becomes King Theodore I of Corsica. He rules until 1738 when the French regain control of Corsica.

1737

An earthquake in Calcutta, India, kills almost 300,000 people.

1738

Ottoman forces take Orsova (southwestern Romania) from Austrian troops.

The Treaty of Vienna, negotiated in 1735, is ratified.

France regains control of Corsica and King Theodore I (1736) is deposed.

The Yoruba people, town-dwelling inhabitants of the area that is now Nigeria, conquer the kingdom of Dahomey.

Excavations begin in Naples on the city of Herculaneum, which was buried in 79 by the volcanic eruption of Mt. Vesuvius.

1739

Forces led by Nadir Kuli of Persia invade the Punjab, sack Delhi, defeat the emperor's forces at Karnal and recover parts of the Indian province from Sikh control.

By the Treaty of Belgrade signed between Emperor Charles VI and Ottoman Sultan Mahmud I, Russia is prevented from keeping a military base at Azov on the Black Sea and Austria gives up control over Serbia and Belgrade.

Vietnam and Cambodia fight for lands along the Mekong River.

1739-1741

Commercial rivalry between Britain and Spain leads to war. The 1731 incident in which Jenkins lost an ear is used to arouse public sentiment and force Robert Walpole to declare war on Spain, popularly known as the War of Jenkins's Ear. Hostilities are limited to minor, inconclusive skirmishes at sea.

1730

through

1739

	NATIVE AMERICAN	AFRICAN AMERICAN	ASIAN AMERICAN	EUROPEAN AMERICAN
1740 through **1749**	**1740-1749** The Plains Indians — Sioux, Crow, Blackfoot, Arapaho, Cheyenne and others — acquire horses from the south and guns from the east through trading and raids. The acquisition of horses marks the beginning of the classic period of Plains tribal life. **1745-1748** The Shawnee tribe, in an effort to unite Native American strength and prevent further intertribal warfare, tries to establish a tribal confederation in the Mississippi Valley.	**1740** South Carolina's slave code forbids enslaved people from raising livestock. There are more than 150,000 enslaved Africans in the British North American colonies: 24,000 in the North and 126,000 in the South. **1741** The New York Conspiracy takes place. A robbery committed by a group of both European and African Americans, coupled with several fires, creates an atmosphere of fear and suspicion in New York City. More than 150 enslaved African Americans and 20 European Americans are brought to trial in this apparent conspiracy. The eventual result of this massive backlash is that 35 people are killed and more than 70 are banished from New York. **1744** A school for African Americans is founded in South Carolina by Anglican missionaries. **1746** Enslaved Africans are sold in the southern colonies of British North America for approximately 100 pounds each. **1747** South Carolina's General Assembly makes a provision for use of enslaved African Americans in the military, based on the observation that African Americans have proven their loyalty in fighting enemies of the British crown.	**1746** An observer notes that numerous "Chinos" have made their homes around Acapulco. These are mostly Filipinos.	**1740** German Moravian colonists and several Norwegian immigrants establish a community at Bethlehem, Pennsylvania. The British Parliament passes a law allowing Jewish colonists to be naturalized citizens after a residency period of seven years. **c. 1740** A Jewish congregation, Mikveh Israel, is established in Philadelphia, Pennsylvania. **1741** A group of Scotch-Irish colonists establishes the community of Blandford, Massachusetts. **1742** Jesuits in Louisiana import large quantities of sugarcane and skilled farm workers from Santo Domingo. **1743** French explorers Pierre and Paul Mallet reach the Rocky Mountains. The first European community in present-day South Dakota is established by a French expedition led by François and Louis Joseph Vérendrye. Animosity between Scotch-Irish and German colonists in Pennsylvania causes the Penn family to direct their agents not to sell land to Scotch-Irish immigrants in areas that are already predominantly German, such as York and Lancaster counties. The Penns also offer to help Scotch-Irish colonists already in these areas if they want to move further north or west. The Sieur de Bienville resigns his position as governor of Louisiana. He is replaced by the Marquis de Vaudreuil. **1744-1754** European Americans from Pennsylvania and Virginia migrate into and colonize the Ohio area. **1745** A British force captures the French fort at Louisbourg, on Cape Breton Island (in Nova Scotia). A number of Germans from Waldoboro, Maine, also take part on the side of the British.

EUROPEAN AMERICAN	HISPANIC AMERICAN	FOR CLASSROOM USE	FOR CLASSROOM USE	

EUROPEAN AMERICAN

1746

The Waldoboro community is virtually destroyed by an Indian raid. Its few remaining inhabitants flee southward.

1748

The Treaty of Aix-la-Chappelle, which ends the War of the Austrian Succession, returns Louisbourg to French control.

1749

A Jewish community is formed in Charleston, South Carolina.

More than 6,000 Germans come to Britain's American colonies this year.

HISPANIC AMERICAN

1740

Governor James Oglethorpe of Georgia leads an expedition against St. Augustine. Additional Spanish militia are sent from Havana, and the attack is repelled.

1741-1742

Colonists in New Spain petition King Philip V for the right to migrate to northern Mexico and the lower Rio Grande area of Texas.

1746

Don Cristobal de los Santos Coy establishes the first non-mission school in Texas, at San Fernando de Béxar.

1746-1759

In Puerto Rico, land reforms during the reign of Spain's King Ferdinand VI lead to an increase in immigration and facilitate inland expansion.

1747-1755

José de Escandón surveys Texas, and the following year leads over 750 soldiers and 2,500 colonists into the area. Over the next seven years, Escandón distributes large parcels of land to colonists. This is the beginning of the cattle industry in Texas.

1749-1760

A Spanish expedition led by José de Escandón explores the Rio Grande and establishes more than 20 towns along the way, including Reynosa, Carmargo, Mier and Laredo.

1740

through

1749

THE AMERICAS	THE AMERICAS	THE WORLD	THE WORLD

1740

Britain's Parliament passes the Naturalization Act, which grants British citizenship to foreign immigrants who come to the North American colonies.

The boundary separating Massachusetts and New Hampshire is settled.

The University of Pennsylvania is founded at Philadelphia.

c. 1740

George Whitefield and Jonathan Edwards lead a religious movement known as the "Great Awakening," which is marked by an appeal to the heart rather than to the mind. This Christian movement marks the infancy of Methodism in North America.

1741

Danish explorer Vitus Bering, under Russian sponsorship, becomes the first European to explore Alaska and the Aleutian Islands.

Russian navigator Alexei Cherikov arrives in California.

c. 1741

French explorers Pierre and Paul Mallet reach the Rocky Mountains.

1742

Jesuits in Louisiana import large quantities of sugarcane and skilled farm workers from Santo Domingo.

Five hundred pine masts for the British navy are shipped from Portsmouth, New Hampshire. This is the largest such shipment on record.

At the Battle of Bloody Marsh, near Fort Frederica on St. Simons Island, James Oglethorpe and his troops defeat the Spanish to give the British control of the Georgia colony.

c. 1743

Benjamin Franklin invents a heating device that fits inside an enclosed fireplace. The Franklin Stove, or Pennsylvania Fireplace, maximizes the principle of heating by warm air.

1743-1763

During this period Alaska's sea otter population is seriously reduced by Russian trappers.

1744

At the Council of Lancaster, delegates from Pennsylvania, Virginia, Maryland and the Iroquois Confederacy sign a treaty which gives a large tract of Iroquois land to the European colonists.

1744-1748

King George's War begins as a series of skirmishes between British and French forces over control of Louisbourg (eastern Cape Breton Island, Canada). The fortified village is eventually surrendered to the British under William Pepperrell and Sir Peter Warren. Through the Treaty of Aix-la-Chapelle in 1748, France receives the town back in exchange for Madras, India. The peace accord accomplishes little else, and the calm is short-lived. British forces retake the site in 1758.

1746

Princeton University is founded in New Jersey.

1747-1748

Colonists from Virginia form the Ohio Company and begin exploration into the Ohio territory. French expeditions are in this area at the same time.

1749

Britain and France both claim control of the Ohio Valley.

Georgia becomes a British crown colony.

Washington and Lee University is founded at Lexington, Virginia.

Fort Rouillé is established on the site of present-day Toronto, Canada.

As Edward Cornwallis takes office as the new governor of Acadia (Nova Scotia, New Brunswick and eastern Maine), the British government begins to consider expelling French Acadians. Cornwallis has instructions to take a census of the French inhabitants, to forbid priests' activities among them, and to provide Protestant instruction for Acadian children.

British Lord Halifax founds the community of Halifax, Nova Scotia with 2,500 colonists.

1740

The Mon Rebellion takes place in Burma.

Maria Theresa invokes the Pragmatic Sanction and becomes Holy Roman Empress after the death of her father, Charles VI (1711). Technically, she rules as Holy Roman Empress for two years, but rules the Hapsburg lands as archduchess of Austria and queen of Bohemia and Hungary until 1780.

Ivan VI becomes czar of Russia as an infant after the death of his great aunt, Anna (1730). He is deposed in 1741.

Frederick II (the Great) becomes king of Prussia (Brandenburg-Prussia) after the death of his father, Frederick William I (1713). Prussia reaches its height as a military power during Frederick II's reign. He rules until 1786.

c. 1740

Ba'al Shem Tov (Israel ben Elizer) moves to Miedzyboz, in the Carpathian Mountains of Poland, and extends his base of orthodox Jewish followers in the Hasidic movement.

1740-1748

Following Maria Theresa's ascension to the throne as Holy Roman Empress, Prussian King Frederick II opens the War of the Austrian Succession by sending forces to invade the contested Silesia region in Poland. France, Spain, Bavaria and Saxony ally themselves with Prussia. England, the Netherlands and Sardinia soon become Austrian allies. The war drags on, spilling into the North American colonies as King George's War (1744-1748). Maria Theresa's husband is elected emperor as Francis I in 1745 and King George II of Britain calls for peace. Prussia emerges from this conflict as a major European power.

1741

After Prussia defeats the Austrians at Mollwitz, Frederick II gains the support of France, Spain, Bavaria and Saxony. The French, Bavarians and Saxons invade Austria and Bohemia and capture Prague.

The infant czar Ivan VI (1740) is deposed and imprisoned. Elizabeth, daughter of Peter I, becomes czarina of Russia and rules until 1762.

1742

The Treaty of Berlin between Austria and Prussia brings to an end the First Silesian War. By its terms, most of the territory of Silesia is ceded to Prussia.

The Mahrattas (Hindu warriors) conquer Bengal.

Charles VII (Charles Albert), elector of Bavaria, becomes Holy Roman Emperor after several European countries reject Maria Theresa's ascension to the throne. Charles VII nullifies the Pragmatic Sanction and rules until 1745.

Swedish astronomer Anders Celsius invents the centigrade (or Celsius) thermometer.

1743

Saxony makes peace with, and becomes an ally of, Austria.

The British army under King George II defeats French forces at Dettingen.

Anti-Jewish *pogroms* (organized attacks) occur in Russia.

1744

Prussia's King Frederick II, worried about increasing military strength in Austria, invades Bohemia to begin the Second Silesian War. His forces capture Prague but troops loyal to Maria Theresa drive the Prussians back to Saxony.

Robert Clive arrives in Madras as a clerk for the East India Company.

A series of wars begins between France and Britain over control of India.

Anti-Jewish *pogroms* are initiated by Maria Theresa in Moravia and Bohemia.

1740
through
1749

1745

French troops under Maurice of Saxony defeat British forces at Fontenoy and attack the Austrian Netherlands (present-day Belgium).

Prussian forces are victorious over Austrian troops at Hohenfriedberg.

The Treaty of Dresden, which follows the Convention of Hanover between Britain's King George II and Prussia's King Frederick II, provides for Prussia to retain Silesia (as guaranteed by the other European powers) and to recognize the Pragmatic Sanction. The war continues in the Americas, Italy and India.

A second Jacobite Rebellion in England and Scotland is led by Prince Charles Edward Stuart (Bonnie Prince Charlie).

Francis I, husband of Maria Theresa, becomes Holy Roman Emperor after the death of Charles VII (1742). Francis I rules until 1765.

Ieshige becomes shogun of Japan after the reign of Yoshimune (1716). Ieshige rules until 1761.

An electrical capacitor is invented independently at both Leyden, Netherlands, and at the Cathedral of Kamin, Pomerania. The Netherlands version is called the Leyden Jar. The work of Edward J. von Kleist is used by Benjamin Franklin when he invents the lightning rod conductor in 1752.

1745-1806

This is the time span generally ascribed to the rule of the Hapsburg-Lorraine family of Holy Roman emperors. In 1806 the Holy Roman Empire is dissolved.

1746

The Jacobites gain a victory at Falkirk, but the rebellion ends in defeat at Culloden Moor. This battle is considered the end of the Jacobite Rebellion in Scotland. Flora Macdonald aids Prince Charles Edward Stuart's escape to the Isle of Skye en route to France. Because of her help, she is imprisoned and Britain prohibits the wearing of the Tartan. The ban on the Tartan is lifted in 1782.

Russia and Austria form an alliance against the rising power of Prussia.

Qing (Ch'ing) imperial edict bans Han-Chinese from migrating to Manchuria.

Ferdinand VI becomes king of Spain after the death of his father, Philip V (1700). Ferdinand VI rules until 1759.

Frederick V becomes king of Denmark and Norway after the death of his father, Christian VI (1730). Frederick V rules until 1766.

1747

In Africa, Oyo forces gain control of Dahomey.

The Shaker Movement (the United Society of Believers in Christ's Second Appearing, or Shaking Quakers) is founded in England by Jane and James Wardley.

William of Nassau, prince of Orange, becomes the hereditary *stadtholder* of the seven provinces of the Netherlands. He rules as William IV until 1751.

Ahmad Shah, a lieutenant of Persia's Shah Nadir Kuli (1736), becomes the first native king of Afghanistan after Nadir Kuli is assassinated by members of his own army. Ahmad Shah builds an empire by conquest and by his popularity. Though unable to unify the fringes of his realm, he is credited with founding the modern Afghan state. Ahmad Shah is the first of the Durani dynasty, and rules until 1773.

1748

The Treaty of Aix-la-Chapelle ends the War of the Austrian Succession. It guarantees the regions of Silesia and Glatz to Prussia; recognizes the Pragmatic Sanction of 1713, and the Protestant succession in Britain; acknowledges Frances I as Holy Roman Emperor; and gives Parma and Piacenza to Spain. The treaty also reinforces Britain's right to transport enslaved people and engage in trade with Spain's American colonies.

Afghan forces under Ahmad Shah invade the Punjab.

Shah Rukh, grandson of Nadir Kuli (Nadir Shah, 1736), comes into power in Persia (Iran).

French governor Joseph François Dupleix successfully defends the French colony of Pondichéry (in India) against British forces under Robert Clive.

The ancient city of Pompeii in southern Italy is rediscovered and large-scale excavation begins.

1749

Maria Theresa removes the last vestiges of Czech self-rule in Bohemia. The Czech people are further Germanized under her son and successor, Joseph II.

Sweden's first official census is completed. The country's population is recorded as 1.8 million.

1740

through

1749

NATIVE AMERICAN	AFRICAN AMERICAN	ASIAN AMERICAN	EUROPEAN AMERICAN
1750 After the death of Chief Red Shoe in a battle with French forces, the Choctaw nation sues for peace. **1750-1800** Some of the Chickahominy of Virginia are gradually pushed off their homelands and are divided into several groups. In Virginia reports of 1768 and 1781, the Pamunkey, Mattaponi and Eastern Shore Indians are mentioned as tribal entities. **1751** Benjamin Franklin cites the Iroquois Confederacy as a model for his Albany Plan of Union. A Pima revolt against Spanish rule occurs in the Southwest. **1754** In Lebanon, Connecticut, Moor's Indian Charity School is founded by the Reverend Eleazer Wheelock. This school is later incorporated into Dartmouth College in Hanover, New Hampshire. **1755** British officials offer a bounty of 40 pounds on the scalp of any American Indian they consider an enemy. **1758** Ojibwas side with French forces against New England colonials at Fort Ticonderoga. One of the first reservations for Native Americans is established in New Jersey.	**1750** Georgia, which originally outlawed the sale or use of enslaved people, relaxes its laws to permit slavery. **c. 1751** The South Carolina General Assembly grants Cesar, an enslaved African American practitioner, his freedom after he develops a cure for the deadly rattlesnake bite. **1754** Benjamin Banneker, an African American who never saw a clock before, constructs the first American-made clock. Quaker minister John Woolman of New Jersey actively opposes the practice of slavery. His work, *Some Considerations on the Keeping of Negros,* is one of the first published attempts to eliminate the institution of slavery. **1758** At the yearly meeting of the Quakers of Philadelphia, a resolution is passed to exclude from church membership anyone who imports enslaved Africans into the city.	Although Chinese seamen have engaged in significant maritime activity from the middle of the seventh century, when Manchus conquer the Chinese people in 1644 and bring the Ming dynasty to an end, a major change in foreign policy occurs. Fearing that Ming loyalists will create a revolutionary force outside the country, officials of the new Qing (Ch'ing) dynasty pass edicts barring emigration. Many Chinese people, especially from the southeastern provinces of Fujian (Fukien) and Guangdong (Kwangtung), continue to travel back and forth between China and the countries of southeast Asia, where sizeable Chinese colonies flourish. However, most of the Chinese people are isolated from the West until early in the nineteenth century. Japan's location off the coast of the Asian mainland keeps its inhabitants relatively isolated from outside visitors. The Japanese people withstand attempted invasions by Kublai Khan in the 1200s, and first encounter Europeans when Portuguese traders arrive off the Asian mainland in the early 1500s. European missionaries follow but, fearing the examples seen in other Asian countries where missionaries were soon followed by military forces, the Tokugawa shogunate issues an effective anti-Christian decree. Japan remains isolated until a United States fleet under Commodore (later Admiral) Matthew Perry sails into Tokyo Bay in 1853.	**1751** Although previously colonized in the mid-1660s, the community of Georgetown is officially formed by British colonists on the west bank of the Potomac River. Now part of Washington, D.C., it is named in honor of King George III. In this year alone, more than 4,000 German immigrants arrive in Philadelphia. Some make their homes in the city, but most move to farmland in the Pennsylvania countryside. **1753** The Marquis Duquesne and French forces occupy the Ohio Valley. Fort Presque Isle is built by the French on the site of present-day Erie, Pennsylvania. A group of Norwegian immigrants comes to the Moravian colony at Bethabara, North Carolina. Among this group is Dr. Hans Martin Kalberlahn, one of the first physicians in the area. **1754** A French expedition led by Pecaudy de Contrecoeur builds a fort on the site that is now Pittsburgh, Pennsylvania. They call the structure Fort Duquesne. **1755** A group of Portuguese Jews sets sail from Lisbon, headed for the Virginia colony. They are apparently forced off course by bad weather, and make their homes in Newport, Rhode Island. **1756** Large numbers of German colonists from Pennsylvania migrate southward into Frederick County, Maryland. Some Germans also migrate northeastward and make their homes in New Jersey. **1759** Scotch-Irish immigrants found a company for the relief of ministers' widows and children. This is probably the first insurance company in America.

1750

through

1759

HISPANIC AMERICAN	FOR CLASSROOM USE	FOR CLASSROOM USE	FOR CLASSROOM USE	

1750

People who fled slavery in other countries are allowed to come to Puerto Rico as free wage earners.

1751

Felipe Ramírez de Estenós, governor of Puerto Rico, promotes coffee cultivation.

A Pima revolt against Spanish domination occurs in the American Southwest.

1752

British forces are driven from the island of Vieques, Puerto Rico.

The *presidio* (fort or military post) and town of Tubac are established, in what is now Arizona, by Captain Juan Bautista de Anza, with 50 soldiers and 400 colonists.

1758

Comanche and Caddoan warriors destroy San Saba, a Spanish mission established in Apache country in northwest Texas.

When Spain joins France against Britain in the Seven Years War, France secretly cedes the Louisiana Territory to Spain. British forces defeat the armies of both countries. Spain loses Florida to Britain in order to regain Havana, which has been captured by the British. Spanish authority in the Louisiana Territory continues until 1803 in New Orleans and 1804 in St. Louis.

1759

Spanish forces under Parilla make a punitive raid against Comanche and Caddoan tribes in retaliation for the destruction of San Saba; the Spanish army is defeated.

1750

through

1759

1750 through 1759

Mid-1700s

Approximately 30,000 enslaved Africans are imported yearly to Saint Domingue to work in the production of sugar. Free *mulattoes* (people of combined African and European ethnicity) become increasingly angry that they have no voice in government; however, many own plantations and slaves.

1750

Dr. Thomas Walker leads an exploratory party through northern Tennessee. This is the first European group to sight and traverse the Cumberland Gap into Kentucky.

1750-1777

Portuguese Minister Marquês de Pombal initiates reforms in Brazil to improve efficiency, and to encourage or even force assimilation of Indians into the colonial population.

1751

Georgetown is founded in present-day Washington, D.C.

North Carolina's first newspaper, the *North Carolina Gazette* is published.

The first printing press in Canada opens for business at Halifax, Nova Scotia, and the *Halifax Gazette* is published the following year.

1752

Based on Edward J. von Kleist's 1745 experiments, Benjamin Franklin invents the lightning conductor rod.

With the purchase of Mount Vernon, George Washington becomes the owner of 18 enslaved Africans. He gradually acquires almost 200 more.

1753

French troops seize the Ohio Valley, and build Fort Presque Isle on the site of present-day Erie, Pennsylvania. Seneca representative Tanaghrisson demands that French militia withdraw. The demand is rejected by French authorities. Tanaghrisson and two other Indian chiefs align themselves with the young George Washington in hopes of ending French presence in the area.

1754

The last of the French and Indian Wars begins, this one corresponding to the Seven Years War in Europe. On orders of Virginia Governor Robert Dinwiddie, George Washington leads Virginia soldiers and Indians under Tanaghrisson against a French force led by Joseph Coulon de Villiers de Jumonville. Washington is victorious and fights again near Uniontown, Pennsylvania, where de Jumonville is killed. Later this year de Jumonville's brother leads 800 French and Indian troops in an attack on Fort Necessity, held by Washington with 350 men. Washington surrenders, leaving the Ohio Valley under French control.

The Albany Congress, a meeting of British colonial representatives, approves Benjamin Franklin's Plan of Union for the colonies and signs an agreement between seven British colonies and the Iroquois Confederacy. Franklin's plan is later rejected, both by colonial legislatures and the British Crown.

French forces defeat a band of Virginia colonists in the Ohio Valley (Pittsburgh, Pennsylvania) and erect Fort Duquesne on the site.

King's College (later Columbia University) is founded at New York, New York.

1755

The European population of New France is recorded at fewer than 70,000, while Britain's colonies to the south — the current United States — have approximately 1,500,000.

The *Connecticut Gazette* is published by James Parker. It is the colony's first newspaper, and is printed in New Haven.

Initial British attempts to capture French forts in the colonies are not successful, especially General Edward Braddock's attempt to capture Fort Duquesne. However, British colonists defeat French forces at Lake George, New York.

British forces capture Acadia (Nova Scotia, New Brunswick and eastern Maine) from the French. The Acadian population is approximately 7,000. Governor Charles Lawrence orders that Acadian lands and property be confiscated. All French Acadians are expelled, and may take only what possessions they can carry. In Beaubassin, approximately 400 French residents assembled to hear the news are arrested and imprisoned. Others, having received warning, hide and eventually flee to Canada. Three hundred of the prisoners are forced onto ships and sent out to sea. The 100 or so that remain, most of them women and children, are abandoned to the elements. They try to reach Canada, but many die of starvation or exposure. Acadians from other communities are also imprisoned, and in the first wave of forced emigration, close to 5,000 people are put aboard ships in the Bay of Fundy, and turned out to sea with limited water and food on board. Governor Lawrence decides to send Acadians to communities along the Atlantic coast of what is now the United States; however, he fails to notify officials of those communities. Smallpox breaks out aboard ship and many Acadians die. Pennsylvania rejects 450 Acadians. Maryland welcomes 1,000 and helps them make new homes. Nearly 1,000 of the exiles who land in South Carolina are forced into indentured servitude in the indigo and cotton growing industries. The majority of Acadians come to Louisana, either initially, or as they become free to migrate from other eastern colonies.

During the first full year of the French and Indian War, the population of New France totals less than 70,000 whereas the English-speaking colonies contain approximately 1 million people.

c. 1755

The Conestoga covered wagon, used to haul freight, is developed in Pennsylvania. It later becomes the primary transportation for westward migrating families.

1756

Comanches and Caddoans destroy San Saba, a mission established for the Apaches in northwest Texas by Spanish missionaries.

French forces drive British troops from America's Great Lakes region.

1758

Approximately 400 indentured or enslaved Acadians in Georgia are given government permission to leave. They buy a ship and sail back toward Canada, but fewer than 100 survive the trip.

French troops and their Ojibwa allies, under General Louis-Joseph de Montcalm, hold Fort Ticonderoga against a British attack led by James Abercromby. A French force defeats a British advance party near Loyalhannon, Pennsylvania, killing more than 300 and taking many prisoners.

George Washington and John Forbes lead British colonial armies against Fort Duquesne. The French army retreats, realizing it is outnumbered, and Forbes's troops take possession of the fort.

Troops led by Jeffrey (Baron) Amherst and James Wolfe capture Louisbourg (in Nova Scotia), providing the British with their first major victory in the war.

French troops at Fort Frontenac (now Kingston, Ontario) surrender the town to British troops under Edward Bradstreet. From this position, the British interfere with French communications with the West and the delivery of supplies to French troops.

The enslavement of native people is outlawed in Brazil.

1759

Jeffrey Amherst and his British forces capture Crown Point and Fort Ticonderoga.

At the Battle of the Plains of Abraham (near Quebec), Montcalm's five French regiments are defeated by six British regiments under General James Wolfe. Both Wolfe and Montcalm are killed, but British forces prevail and Quebec comes under British control.

1750

Joseph I becomes king of Portugal after the death of his father, John V (1706). Joseph I rules until 1777. Sebastião José de Carvalho e Melo, marquês de Pombal, becomes secretary of war and foreign affairs for King Joseph I of Portugal. A powerful statesman, during his tenure Pombal puts the Inquisition under control of the king, removes the Jesuits from Portugal and its colonies, ends slavery and limits the power of the Catholic Church. He holds this position until the death of King Joseph I in 1777.

Ali Bey comes into power in Egypt.

1751

In India, Robert Clive and his British troops capture Arcot, capital of the Carnatic, and defend it against Chanda Sahib and his French allies.

Britain joins the Austro-Russian alliance of 1746 against Prussia.

Tibet becomes a protectorate of China.

Adolphus Frederick becomes king of Sweden after the death of his brother-in-law, Frederick I (1720). Adolphus Frederick's rise to power strengthens French influence in Sweden. He rules until 1771.

As a child, William V becomes *stadtholder* (governor or viceroy) of the Netherlands after the death of his father, William IV (1747). Anne, daughter of King George II of England, becomes regent. William V rules until 1795.

1751-1818

This is the time span generally ascribed to the Holstein-Gottorp dynasty that rules Sweden.

1752

Muhammad Ali, with support from the British East India Company under Robert Clive, gains control of the Carnatic (southern India) from Chanda Sahib, who is supported by the French East India Company under Joseph Dupleix.

Clive's capture of Trichinopoly (in southern India) from the French under Dupleix prevents the French from dominating the Deccan region of the Indian peninsula.

Britain adopts the Gregorian calendar.

The Treaty of Aranjuez is signed between Spain and the Holy Roman Empire.

Alaungpaya unites Burma and begins his invasion of Siam (Thailand).

1752-1951

During this time, Mozambique has no central government structure, but is governed primarily by trading companies.

1753

Luang Prabang (now part of Laos) becomes a vassal state of Burma.

1754

Osman III becomes sultan of Turkey after the death of his brother, Mahmud I (1730). Osman III rules until 1757.

The French government withdraws most of its forces from India.

1755

The Corsican revolt against Genoese rule is led by Pasquale Paoli, who serves as president under a republican constitution.

English author Samuel Johnson's *Dictionary of the English Language* is published.

An earthquake in Lisbon, Portugal, kills more than 30,000 people.

1756

Through the Treaty of Westminster, Britain and Prussia form an alliance.

French troops under Richelieu capture Minorca from the British.

Nawab (provincial governor) Siraj-ud-Daula and his forces capture the English community at Calcutta, India, placing 146 prisoners in the infamous "Black Hole of Calcutta." More than 40 die from their confinement (although some earlier historical estimates place the death toll at 120).

Afghanistan's Ahmad Shah captures Delhi and annexes the Punjab.

1756-1763

The Seven Years War involves virtually all of Europe and all of the colonial holdings of European powers. It is a conflict between Britain and Prussia; Britain and France; and also among Austria, France and Russia. The war begins with the Prussian invasion of Saxony. The two major outcomes of this war are that Britain becomes the world colonial power after France relinquishes almost all of its North American holdings and Prussia further emerges as a major force in Europe.

1757

British forces led by Robert Clive defeat the troops of *Nawab* Siraj-ud-Daula at Plassey. This victory secures Bihar, Orissa and Bengal and is regarded as the traditional beginning of the British Empire in India. Clive is given the title of Baron Clive of Plassey.

Clive and his troops retake Calcutta from Siraj-ud-Daula, even though Siraj-ud-Daula's forces are aided by the French.

Frederick II (the Great) of Prussia and his army win major victories over Austrian forces at Prague and Leuthen and over French troops at Rossbach.

Quakers in Britain and America censure members who hold Africans in slavery.

William Pitt the Elder (later the earl of Chatham) becomes head of a coalition government in Britain. He resigns in 1761 after George III comes into power.

Mustafa III becomes Ottoman sultan after the death of his cousin, Osman III (1754). Mustafa III rules until 1773.

1758

Alaungpaya defeats the Talaings and establishes the Burmese capital at Rangoon.

After the death of the regional Mogul chief, Adína Beg, the Sikhs control central and northeast Punjab.

Russian forces invade Prussia.

Robert Clive becomes Britain's first governor of Bengal (India). In 1760 he returns to England but resumes his duties in Bengal in 1765. Clive serves until 1767.

1759

Britain's position as the dominant European force in India is secured by the victory of Clive and his troops over Dutch forces at Bidar.

Jesuits are expelled from the Portuguese Empire, including Brazil.

The opening of the Brennberg coal pit marks the beginning of Hungary's coal mining industry.

Austrian General Gideon Ernst, baron von Laudon, and his troops defeat the army of Frederick II (the Great) at Kunersdorf during the Seven Years War.

Jacob Frank (Jankiev Lebowicz), founder of the anti-Talmudist Frankist sect, is baptized with his followers into Christianity.

The British navy under Lord Edward Hawke defeats a French fleet in a battle in Quiberon Bay (northern France).

Charles III becomes king of Spain after the death of his half-brother, Ferdinand VI (1746). Charles III rules until 1788.

Shah Alam becomes Mogul emperor of India. Although deposed in 1788 he returns to the throne when the British capture Delhi in 1803. Shah Alam rules until 1806.

1759-1788

Financial reforms under Spain's King Charles III, which dramatically revise tax codes and restructure trade relations with Spanish America, cause violent dissension in South and Central America.

1750

through

1759

	NATIVE AMERICAN	AFRICAN AMERICAN	ASIAN AMERICAN	EUROPEAN AMERICAN
1760 through **1769**	**1761-1766** The Aleut tribe revolts against the Russian presence in what is now Alaska. **1763** In Pontiac's Rebellion, Ottawa Chief Pontiac tries to unite the eastern and midwestern tribes against the British. Pontiac's confederacy launches a surprise attack on British colonists at Detroit. The native force is ultimately defeated. In the aftermath of American Indian attacks on European American towns in Pennsylvania, the Paxton Riots take place, in which peaceful Conestoga Indians are massacred by European colonists. A proclamation by Britain's King George III prohibits displacement of Native Americans without both tribal and crown consent. This is an attempt to keep Europeans east of the Appalachian Divide and provide protected lands for American Indians in the West (the Northwest Territory). European colonists, however, ignore this proclamation. **1766** The Treaty of Oswego ends the three-year Ottawa Indian uprising known as Pontiac's Rebellion. **1768** In the Treaty of Fort Stanwix (in what is now upper New York State) the Iroquois cede portions of their lands to the British crown. **1769** Ottawa Chief Pontiac is killed at Kahokia, Illinois, by a Peoria (some sources say Kaskaskian) Indian.	**1763** The New England region begins to experience a substantial population of free African Americans. Most hold menial jobs as shipyard laborers or domestic servants. **1766** Jenny Slew of Ipswich, Massachusetts, sues for her freedom in court and wins. **1767** The Mason-Dixon Line, drawn by the two English surveyors whose names it bears, marks the boundary between Pennsylvania and Maryland. It later becomes the line of demarcation between free and slave regions. **1769** Thomas Jefferson's first official action after his election to the Virginia House of Burgesses is to introduce a bill to grant freedom to people held as slaves. The House rejects his measure.	**1762** Spain sides with France against Britain in the Seven Years War. Britain retaliates by sending a fleet from India to capture and occupy Manila for two years. **1763** The first Filipino colonists arrive in Louisiana. They are seamen who escape from Spanish ships.	**1760** The tobacco processing firm of P. Lorillard Company is founded by Pierre Lorillard, a young French Huguenot. **1763** In Scotland, poverty, crop failures and cattle illness, along with rent increases and expulsions of tenant farmers from their fields, act as strong push factors to bring Highland Scots to America. Many of these new Scotch arrivals make their homes in northern New York, while a good many more migrate southward to North Carolina. With their unique dress, lifestyle and language, these Highland Scots are less easily assimilated than immigrants from other parts of Scotland. French explorer Pierre Lacléde (Liguest) selects a site for a fur-trading post on the west bank of the Mississippi River in what is now Missouri. The site later becomes the city of St. Louis. Construction is started in 1764 under the direction of Auguste Chouteau. **1763-1775** An estimated 25,000 Scots arrive in North America. At the time of the American Revolution, a majority of Scots are Loyalists who support continued British authority over the colonies. Afterward many of them either relocate to Canada or return to Scotland. **1764** After the Paxton Riots of 1763, Scotch-Irish colonists from Paxton, Pennsylvania, march on Philadelphia in protest of the Quaker failure to protect them against attacks by Native Americans. The first permanent European community in St. Louis is established. **1766** Anthony Benezet, a French colonist, publishes his anti-slavery book, *A Caution and Warning to Great Britain and Her Colonies on the Calamitous State of the Enslaved Negroes*. It is the first publication of its kind in the American colonies.

EUROPEAN AMERICAN	HISPANIC AMERICAN	HISPANIC AMERICAN	FOR CLASSROOM USE	

EUROPEAN AMERICAN	HISPANIC AMERICAN	HISPANIC AMERICAN	FOR CLASSROOM USE	
1768 British colonists receive a charter to found Charlotte, North Carolina. The city's residents soon become some of the most outspoken against the British monarchy. **1768-1769** French colonists living in Spanish-controlled Louisiana revolt against Governor Ulloa. The Spanish crown sends 24 ships, with approximately 2,000 men under command of Alexandro O'Reilly, to end the rebellion. Five rebel leaders are executed and several others sent to prison. **1769** Gaspar de Portolá visits the site of present-day Los Angeles. French Canadian trapper Jacques Timothe Boucher, Sieur de Mont Brun (Timothy Demonbreun) migrates into Tennessee and begins trading with the local Indians.	**1760** The city of Mayagüez is founded on the west coast of Puerto Rico. **1764** Spain establishes a local militia in its American colonies. **1765** Marshall Alejandro O'Reilly inspects the island of Puerto Rico for the Spanish crown and recommends improvements. He publishes *Memoria a SM Sobre la Isla de Puerto Rico.* King Charles III of Spain sends José de Gálvez as "visitador general" to New Spain to reorganize the government and strengthen the northern border. Later, de Gálvez becomes Minister of the Indies, in charge of Spain's American possessions. Under his direction Spain and Spanish America give financial and military aid during the American Revolution to the 13 colonies that will become the United States. The census counts 44,833 people on the island of Puerto Rico; this figure includes 5,037 enslaved people. Trade is permitted between Puerto Rico and other Spanish colonies, and various ports in Spain. Since San Juan is the island's only authorized trade port, contraband trade becomes common in the eighteenth and nineteenth centuries. **1767** A Spanish royal decree expels all Jesuits from New Spain. The total Spanish and *mestizo* (people of combined European and Indian ethnicity) population of New Mexico is 9,550. **1768** A few French officials lead a rebellion against Antonio de Ulloa, the first Spanish governor of Louisiana. Ulloa leaves. **1769** Puerto Rico's Governor Miguel de Muesas encourages the establishment of cities at Rincón, Cabo Rojo, Moca, Cayey, Aguadilla, Vega Baja and Vega Alta.	De Gálvez sends Gaspar de Portolá, named first governor of California, and Franciscan friar Junípero Serra to colonize California. Portolá sets up the first *presidio* (fort) and Father Serra founds the Mission San Diego de Alcalá and 20 others throughout Alta California. A land expedition under Portolá becomes the first European group to reach what is now San Francisco Bay by land. Alexander O'Reilly is named governor of Louisiana and arrives in New Orleans with 24 ships and 2,600 soldiers. Five French leaders of the earlier rebellion are executed, and Spanish rule is restored. O'Reilly serves into 1770.		**1760** through **1769**

133

1760 through 1769

1760

Montreal falls to British forces under the command of Jeffrey Amherst. This event marks the end of the colony of New France.

The population of the British colonies that later become the United States is approximately one million. Almost 20 percent of these are African Americans.

c. 1760

Spain increases its military activity and fortifications around gold and silver mines in northern Mexico to keep British forces away. Spain's standing armies in the colonies and the crown's demand for more revenues anger the Mexican colonists.

1762

The secret Treaty of Fontainebleau between Spain and France cedes portions of Louisiana to Spain. This cession becomes public in the Treaty of Paris in 1763.

In the French and Indian Wars, British and colonial forces under Admiral Sir George Peacock capture Havana, Martinique, St. Lucia and Grenada from the Spanish. Havana is used as a bargaining tool, and is returned to Spain in 1763 in exchange for Florida.

British colonists establish a community at Maugerville, New Brunswick, Canada.

1763

Britain's Proclamation (Edict) of 1763 closes the American frontier by prohibiting colonial expansion west of the Appalachian Mountains (the Northwest Territory). This seriously strains relations with the colonies.

Chief Pontiac, an Ottawa, brings western tribes together in a pan-Indian confederacy to fight British encroachment. In two months, all British forts west of Niagara are captured by the Indians, with the exception of Detroit.

By this time there are reports of thousands of Acadians living in Louisiana.

The Treaty of Paris ends the Seven Years War in Europe and the final French and Indian War in the colonies. The treaty cedes to Britain virtually all of Canada; all French lands east of the Mississippi River, except for New Orleans; the French islands in the West Indies; and India. Spain cedes Florida to Britain but maintains control of Cuba. Britain agrees to dismantle its military installations on Central America's eastern coast, but retains its lumber rights in the area.

British military officials in Canada send nearly 2,500 Acadian prisoners to France, where they make their homes in Aunis, Guyène, Normandy and Brittany.

1763-1775

An estimated 25,000 Scots arrive in North America during this time. At the beginning of the American Revolution, a majority of Scots are Loyalists. After the war, many of them relocate to Canada or return to Scotland.

1764

A large group of Acadians who migrated to the West Indies move again and make their homes in Louisiana. Officials grant them land in the southwestern part of the colony.

Parliament passes the Sugar Act, which places a tax on all sugar, coffee, iron and cloth imported to the colonies from England. This is Britain's first attempt to raise revenues to pay costs of the French and Indian Wars, and to maintain colonial militia.

Scotch-Irish colonists from Paxton, Pennsylvania, march on Philadelphia in protest of the Quaker failure to protect them against attacks by American Indians.

Britain's Currency Act prohibits the colonies from issuing their own paper money and requires the use of gold as payment for all transactions.

The first permanent European community at St. Louis (Missouri) is established.

The newspaper, *Connecticut Courant*, is established at Hartford, by Thomas Green.

Brown University is founded at Providence, Rhode Island.

1763-1783

The United States of America is Formed

1763-1769. In response to British royal edicts limiting western expansion, regulating colonial trade and increasing taxation, conflict deepens between Britain and the American colonies. British acts most offensive to the colonists are the Sugar and Currency Acts of 1764; the Stamp Act, the Quartering Act and the Writs of Assistance of 1765; and the Townshend Act of 1767.

1770-1774. The Boston Massacre and Lord North's attempt at reconciliation take place in 1770. The Boston Tea Party (1773) is followed by the British Parliament's passage of a series of punitive measures called the Intolerable Acts (1774).

1774. The First Continental Congress sends its "Declaration of Rights and Grievances" to the king and urges the colonists to form a continental association.

1775. These grievances and conflicts boil over into overt revolution. Paul Revere's ride and the Battles of Lexington and Concord between the victorious Massachusetts Minutemen and the British follow. The colonists then capture British-held Fort Ticonderoga.

1776. The Second Continental Congress begins to raise an army, appoints General George Washington as commander of the Continental army and seeks an alliance with France. Some colonial legislatures urge their delegates to vote for independence from Britain. British forces are victorious at Bunker Hill, while Quebec withstands an attack by Benedict Arnold and his troops. The colonies officially proclaim their liberty with the signing of the Declaration of Independence on July 4, 1776, and the fighting continues.

1777. British forces under William Howe defeat Israel Putnam's division of Washington's army in Brooklyn Heights, New York, but the Americans escape across the East River. Washington's American army defeats the Hessians at Trenton and the British at Princeton, and spends the winter at Morristown. John Burgoyne surrenders the British army to General Horatio Gates at Saratoga in 1777. Howe's forces winter in Philadelphia and Washington and his men at Valley Forge.

1778-1780. France and the Netherlands recognize American independence. French forces arrive in America and the British are defeated at Monmouth, New Jersey. The war then moves south with the British capturing Savannah in 1778 and occupying Charleston in 1780. American forces carry on successful guerrilla actions under Francis Marion, Andrew Pickens and Thomas Sumter. At the same time, French troops arrive in Rhode Island, Americans lose at Camden and Benedict Arnold's plan to surrender West Point is exposed. In the west, George Rogers Clark and his troops attack Forts Kaskaskia and Vincennes (1778-1779), defeating the British in the region. The British also lose at Cowpens and Eutaw, North Carolina.

1781-1783. In 1781 Britain's General O'Hara, acting for Lord Charles Cornwallis, surrenders 8,000 British troops at Yorktown to a combined Franco-American army under the joint command of General George Washington and Jean Baptiste Donatien de Vimeur, Comte de Rochambeau. The British are now eager for peace because of increasing conflicts with European nations. In 1783 British troops evacuate New York, Britain and America stop armed hostilities and the Treaty of Paris officially recognizes the United States as an independent nation. Parts of the borders between the United States and Canada are established and the official history of United States government action, including immigration policy, begins.

c. 1764

French navigator Louis Antoine de Bougainville and colonists establish a community on the eastern Falkland Islands. However, they lose the colony to Spain in 1766 and the area is renamed Soledad.

1765

The British Quartering Act requires Britain's American colonists to provide for the needs of English soldiers stationed in the colonies, without compensation to the colonists.

The British Stamp Act requires that all legal documents and publications in Britain's American colonies bear a tax stamp. Like the Quartering Act, this measure creates great resentment in the colonies toward the British government.

The British Writs of Assistance (search warrants) enable British officials to enter the homes of American colonists to look for smuggled goods.

The Stamp Act Congress meets in New York and declares that "taxation without representation" — a slogan first used in Boston by James Otis the year before — violates the rights of colonial citizens. The attendees elect to refuse importation of British goods and to officially protest tax laws.

The Daughters of Liberty is established in Boston. The members, primarily working women, demonstrate, parade and organize boycotts against British goods, particularly focusing on replacing British cloth with home spun.

John Morgan founds the first medical school in the colonies at the College of Philadelphia (now the University of Pennsylvania).

1766

The Declaratory Act, passed by the British Parliament when it repeals the Stamp Act, acknowledges Parliament's right to enact any laws necessary to keep Britain and the colonies together and affirms Britain's right to tax its American colonies.

Rutgers University is founded at New Brunswick, New Jersey.

A British expedition establishes a colony on the western Falkland Islands, but it is soon abandoned.

1767

In New York, the colonial assembly refuses to house British troops; the assembly is ordered to disperse.

Two British surveyors, Charles Mason and Jeremiah Dixon, establish the line that bears their names. Originally a dividing line between the colonies of Maryland and Pennsylvania, it later becomes the line of demarcation between the slave and free states.

The Townshend Acts place duties on various goods brought into the British colonies, an attempt by the British government to replace Stamp Act revenues. The Quartering Act requires colonists to feed and house British soldiers. Colonial reaction is strong and negative; a renewal of the agreement of non-importation of British goods is decided upon at a protest meeting in Boston.

American woodsman Daniel Boone leaves North Carolina and begins his explorations west of the Appalachian Mountains, traveling through the Cumberland Gap.

Jesuits are expelled from Spain's American colonies.

1768

Boston citizens refuse to house British troops and the Massachusetts Assembly is dissolved for refusing to help collect taxes.

Charlotte is founded in North Carolina.

Ann Catherine Green publishes the *Maryland Gazette*.

c. 1768

William Bean is the first permanent European colonist in Tennessee. He builds a cabin near the Watauga River.

1769

The Blackstone Commentaries, defining English common law, on which laws in the American colonies are based, declare: "By marriage, the husband and wife are one person in the law...the very being and legal existence of the woman is suspended during the marriage, or at least is incorporated into that of her husband under whose wing [and] protection she performs everything."

In their desire to move west, Virginia colonists ignore Britain's Edict of 1763 and migrate into Tennessee's Watauga River valley and establish a community.

Free Native Americans, African Americans and *mulatto* (people of combined European and African ethnicity) women over the age of 16 are no longer taxable in Virginia, but voting is still prohibited for all non-European colonists.

The Virginia House of Burgesses is ordered dissolved by British authorities after protesting against colonial treason trials held in Westminster.

Dartmouth College is founded at Hanover, New Hampshire.

Prince Edward Island (Canada) becomes a separate British colony.

Spaniards occupy and colonize northern California. Gaspar de Portolá visits the site of present-day Los Angeles.

English explorer Samuel Hearne is the first European to reach the Arctic Ocean from the North American continent.

c. 1769

Daniel Boone begins a two-year exploration of the area that is now Kentucky.

1760

through

1769

THE WORLD	THE WORLD	THE WORLD	THE WORLD

1760

through

1769

1760

British troops led by General Eyre Coote defeat French forces under General Thomas de Lally at Wandiwash (India) during the Seven Years War.

Ahmad Shah's Afghan forces capture Delhi for the second time.

Prussian forces are defeated by Austrian troops at the Bavarian city of Landshut and at Glatz (now in southwestern Poland) but the Austrians are defeated at Liegnitz (Silesia, Prussia); Austro-Russian raiders invade and destroy Berlin.

George III becomes king of Great Britain and Ireland after the death of his grandfather, George II (1727). George III rules until 1820.

Dutch explorer Jakobus Coetsee and his expedition advance beyond the Orange River in southern Africa.

1761

Afghans under Ahmad Shah defeat the Mahrattas at Panipat.

German explorer Karstens Niebuhr leads an expedition sent by Denmark's King Frederick V on a two-year exploration in Arabia.

Ieharu becomes shogun of Japan after the abdication of Ieshige (1745). Ieharu rules until 1786.

1762

Britain declares war on Spain and British naval forces in the Pacific capture Manila.

Jesuits are expelled from France.

Peter III becomes czar of Russia after the death of his aunt, Elizabeth (1741). Catherine II (the Great) this same year becomes czarina of Russia after the death of her husband, Peter III. During her reign, this strong and ruthless woman proves that women can govern as effectively as men. She rules until 1796.

1763

The Treaty of Paris, signed by Britain, France and Spain, and the Treaty of Hubertsburg, involving Prussia, Saxony and Austria, end the Seven Years War. French holdings in North America, except for St. Pierre and Miquelon Islands off Newfoundland, and Guadeloupe and Martinique in the West Indies, are ceded to Great Britain. In India, Britain gains stronger control because the French are not allowed to occupy their forts. The French keep possession of Pondicherry and Chandernagor. In Africa, France retains Gorée but cedes Senegal to Britain. Cuba and the Philippines are returned to Spanish control. Britain receives Minorca and all French troops withdraw from Germany. In the Treaty of Hubertsburg, Prussia retains Silesia and agrees to support Archduke Joseph in his quest to become king of the Romans. Saxony is restored to its prewar boundaries. It is estimated that the war causes more than 850,000 casualties.

Frederick II (the Great) begins a reform movement in Prussia that improves agricultural techniques and land management.

In Hungary, a large number of Szeklers — original Transylvanians — are murdered at Madefalva after they refuse induction into the Austrian military.

British traders construct a small community at Bushire on the Persian Gulf.

1764

Church lands are confiscated in Russia.

The British army under Major Hector Munro defeats a combined force led by Mogul Emperor Shah Alam and *Nawab* Shuja-ud-Daula at the Battle of Buxar. This victory secures British control over Bengal.

Indian military leader Hyder Ali controls the Hindu state of Mysore, India. He rules until 1782.

Stanislaus II (Stanislaus Augustus Poniatowski) becomes king of Poland. He rules until 1795 and is Poland's last king.

1765

Robert Clive returns to India and begins social and economic reforms.

The British Parliament passes the Stamp Act to tax American colonists to pay for boarding soldiers. The Virginia colonists challenge the act. Secret societies called the Sons of Liberty arise, and their actions cause Parliament to cancel the Stamp Act the following year.

China begins a series of invasions into Burma that continue into the early 1770s.

In the Treaty of Allahabad, the British return Oudh to Shuja-ud-Daula, make peace with Mogul Emperor Shah Alam and begin remodeling the government in Bengal, India.

Joseph II becomes Holy Roman Emperor after the death of his father, Francis I (1745), and co-governs with his mother, Maria Theresa, until her death in 1780. He then rules alone until 1790.

c. 1765

Englishman James Hargreaves invents the cotton spinning jenny, which doubles production in the carding process.

1766

The kingdom of Lorraine, ruled since 1737 by dethroned Polish king Stanislaus I, is annexed by France.

Catherine II grants freedom of worship in Russia.

Christian VII becomes king of Denmark and Norway after the death of his father, Frederick V (1746). Christian VII rules until 1808.

1766-1799

In four Mysore wars, the forces of Hyder Ali and his son Tippoo Sahib fight British troops. This series of battles ends with Britain conquering the area and restoring the Hindu dynasty under British protection.

1767

The Sikhs rule part of the Punjab, from the Jamna to the Indus.

Charles III expels the Jesuits from Spain.

Burmese forces are successful in Siam (Thailand) and destroy the Siamese city of Ayuthia.

British navigator Samuel Wallis first sights the Society Islands (Tahiti), named after the British Royal Society.

1768

The Gurkhas, descendants of the Rajputs of northern India, conquer Nepal and establish Hinduism as the state religion.

Genoa cedes Corsica to France.

Catherine II declares war on Sultan Mustafa III, beginning the first of the Russo-Turkish Wars. These wars result in Russia's territorial gains along the Black Sea.

Polish nobles form an anti-Russian union to support Polish independence. Civil war breaks out and Russian troops are sent to suppress the rebellion.

Ali Bey captures Cairo, becomes sultan of Egypt and attempts to restore the Mameluke (Mamluk) Empire. He rules until 1772.

British Admiral Philip Carterat is the first European to sight Pitcairn Island (in the South Pacific Ocean).

French explorer Louis Antoine de Bougainville visits the Solomon Islands (Oceania) and establishes a French claim on parts of the islands.

1769

The Carnatic (now south-central India) is conquered by Hyder Ali of Mysore.

Russian troops invade Moldavia and Walachia.

Austria seizes the Polish territories of Zips and Lvov.

Pasqale Paoli is defeated in his defense of Corsica against the French and escapes to England.

The British Privy Council chooses to keep the duty on tea in the American colonies.

Frenchman Nicholas Joseph Cugnot constructs the first steam road carriage (ancestor to the tractor).

THE WORLD	FOR CLASSROOM USE	FOR CLASSROOM USE	FOR CLASSROOM USE	
Scottish explorer James Bruce begins a series of expeditions into Africa. He reaches the Blue Nile in 1770, and follows it to the White Nile in 1771.

Captain James Cook leads a British expedition to explore and chart what is now New Zealand. His voyages, which reveal an incredible diversity of living species in the Pacific lands, prompt the development of various theories regarding their origins.

English inventor (Sir) Richard Arkwright patents a device to improve the speed of yarn spinning. This water-powered spinning machine helps move yarn manufacturing into factory production and becomes an early ingredient of the Industrial Revolution.

Scotsman James Watt receives a patent for his "separate condenser," invented in 1765. It increases the efficiency of the early steam engine, a major catalyst for Europe's Industrial Revolution.

Prithvi Narayan Shah (the Great), a Gurkha king, conquers the Katmandu region of Nepal, and begins to rule the country. | | | | **1760**

through

1769 |

NATIVE AMERICAN	NATIVE AMERICAN	AFRICAN AMERICAN	AFRICAN AMERICAN
1775 By an act of the Continental Congress, "Indian territory" is divided into three regions: northern, middle and southern. Each region has a commissioner authorized to make treaties with the Indians, and to arrest British agents. At this time, Indian territory is generally defined as the area from the Allegheny-Appalachian mountain range to the Mississippi River, but also refers to any lands occupied by Native Americans. **1775-1779** The Continental Congress controls Native American issues through a committee on Indian affairs. No consistent policy results from this committee, which is disbanded in late 1779. **1775-1783** In the Revolutionary War several tribes, including the Mohawk, Shawnee, Miami, Wyandot and Cherokee, align themselves with British forces against the American colonists. **1776** George Washington's troops at Valley Forge are aided by a gift of medicine, clothing and 300 bushels of corn from Oneida Chief Shenandoah. **1777** The New York constitution declares purchases of Native American territory by European Americans since October 17, 1774 to be invalid, and forbids future land purchases without governmental permission. **1778** The first treaty between the United States government and a Native American tribe, the Delaware, is signed at Fort Pitt. The treaty is for peace, territorial rights for the Delaware and the right for United States troops to pass through Delaware land. The agreement also states that the Delaware will send warriors to help fight British forces. The Delaware are also offered the right to send a delegate to Congress.	**1778-1881** The United States government signs more than 300 treaties with Indian tribes — treaties that generally favor the government's acquisition of Native American property. **1779** The Continental Congress dispatches troops into the Wyoming Valley against Indians who killed colonists there. **1779-1780** The Cree, Chipewyan and Ojibwa tribes are devastated by smallpox. Two thousand die in the Nebo River community in North Dakota.	**1770** Crispus Attucks, *a mulatto* (a person of combined African and European ethnicity), is a leader of the "Boston Massacre." Attucks heads a group of 50 to 60 men, mostly sailors, to harass British soldiers. In the fight that follows, three persons, including Attucks, are killed. The Quakers of Philadelphia establish a school for African Americans and provide for its supervision. Anthony Benezet becomes an instructor at the school in 1782. **1772** Jean Baptiste Pointe du Sable establishes a trading post on Lake Michigan's southern shore. Du Sable, a *mulatto* explorer and adventurer from Haiti, has by this time traveled up the Mississippi River Valley from New Orleans, and has married an American Indian woman. **1774** In his *Thoughts Upon Slavery,* English Methodist John Wesley contrasts the moral relationships and civil behavior among newly enslaved Africans with the harshness and cruelty of slave traders and owners. He says keeping people in slavery is sinful. Trade in enslaved Africans increases dramatically from the following groups or regions: Ashanti, Yoruba, Ibo, Jelofe, Senegal, Dahomey, Angola, Guinea and Minas. **1775** When he becomes commander of the Continental army, George Washington refuses to allow enslaved African Americans to join. Lord John Murray Dunmore, the British Governor of Virginia, offers freedom to enslaved African American males who fight for the British. Because of the overwhelming response, General Washington in 1776 recommends that free African Americans be allowed to serve in the Continental army. African American soldier Peter Salem is responsible for shooting British Major Pitcairn at the Battle of Bunker Hill.	Thomas Paine authors laws that gradually abolish slavery in Pennsylvania. Dr. Benjamin Rush is an organizer in Philadelphia of the first abolitionist society in the United States. **1775-1783** Approximately 9,000 African Americans, both free and enslaved, serve in the American revolutionary army. Also during this time, nearly 25,000 enslaved African Americans from South Carolina and a similar number from Georgia and Virginia escape to join the British. Seamen Joseph Ranger, a free man, and Caesar Tarrant, an enslaved man, are so respected for their wartime service that the Virginia legislature awards large tracts of land to both men after the war. Freeborn James Forten, who later gains fame for both his abolitionist activities and his business skills, works with and is befriended by Commodore Stephen Decatur. Austin Dabney receives a tract of land from the Georgia legislature for his service during the conflict. The Virginia legislature grants James Armistead his freedom and a pension for his work as a spy. Born into slavery, Seymour Burr gains his freedom for service in the Massachusetts militia. **1777** The constitution of Vermont forbids slavery. In Virginia, a young enslaved African woman, whose name is not recorded, runs bullets for the Revolutionary Army. Despite her valor, she is still in bondage after the war; at 80 years of age she finally escapes to Canada. **1778** A resolution passed by the Continental Congress recommends that importation of enslaved people into the United States be stopped.

1770 through 1779

AFRICAN AMERICAN	ASIAN AMERICAN	FOR CLASSROOM USE	FOR CLASSROOM USE	
1779-1782 George Liele, credited as being the first ordained African American minister, preaches in Savannah, Georgia. One of his converts, Andrew Bryant, founds the first Negro Baptist Church in Georgia. Liele later goes to Jamaica as a missionary, paying his passage by indentured service.	**1774-1880** Between these dates, 40 to 60 drifting Japanese sailing vessels make contact with the Pacific coast of North America, between Sitka and Santa Barbara.			**1770** **through** **1779**
AFRICAN AMERICAN	ASIAN AMERICAN	FOR CLASSROOM USE	FOR CLASSROOM USE	

EUROPEAN AMERICAN	EUROPEAN AMERICAN	HISPANIC AMERICAN	HISPANIC AMERICAN
1771 *The Pennsylvania Packet* begins publication as a weekly newspaper. In 1784 it is changed to a daily paper, the United States' first. The publisher/owner is John Dunlap, originally from Ireland. **1772-1773** Almost all the 30,000 immigrants arriving in Britain's North American colonies from Ulster, Ireland, are linen weavers. Some continue their weaving trade; others take up farming instead. **1774** An expedition led by James Harrod establishes the first English colony west of the Allegheny Mountains. In honor of its founder, the Kentucky colony is originally called Fort Harrod, and later renamed Harrodsburg. **1775** Dutch Reformed clergy in the American colonies are so strongly pro-rebel that British troops are permitted to plunder Dutch churches. The Revolutionary War unites various groups in the colonies. Irishmen of all religions serve together in military units on both sides, but most are pro-rebel. Francis Salvador becomes the first Jew elected to public office in America when he serves in the South Carolina Provincial Congress. **1776** By this time, there are approximately 2,000 Jews in America. **1777** Jews in New York are granted equal treatment under the law. **1778** Louisville, Kentucky, is colonized when a group led by George Rogers Clark builds a fort on a site laid out five years earlier. The town is named in 1780 for France's King Louis XVI.	**1779** A severe hurricane destroys the homes of many French Americans in the Louisiana Territory. Nashville, Tennessee, is established on the Cumberland River by North Carolina pioneer James Robertson and a group of colonists who accompany him. Originally a fort called Nashborough, the community is renamed Nashville and incorporated as a town in 1784 and as a city in 1806.	**1770** The mission and town of Monterrey are established in what is now northeastern Mexico. **1771** Friar Iñigo Abbad y La Sierra, the first historian of Puerto Rico, arrives on the island. A census reports the presence of "Indians" in Puerto Rico, but they are not Tainos. They are, in fact, Indians brought to the island from other territories conquered by Spain. Antonio María Bucareli is named viceroy of New Spain by Spanish King Charles III. Bucareli serves until 1779. Mission San Gabriel Archangel is established near present-day Los Angeles. **1771-1776** Apaches seize more than 66,000 head of livestock, including horses, cattle and mules, from Spanish ranches in Chihuahua and Durango. **1772** Dominicans establish missions in Baja California, but the Kamia people of the Baja are effective warriors and difficult to subdue. **1773** Ruins of the ancient Mayan city of Palenque are found in Mexico. **1774** In separate expeditions by sea, Juan Pérez, Bruno de Heceta and Juan Francisco de la Bodega explore the area that is now Oregon, Washington and Alaska. **1775** Puerto Rico's population is 70,250, including 6,467 enslaved Africans. Kamia Indians living at San Diego rebel as anti-Spanish feeling spreads among the native population. San Diego mission is temporarily abandoned.	**1776** A Spanish expedition led by Juan Bautista de Anza establishes the Mission Delores on the site of modern-day San Francisco. Maria Feliciano Arballo y Gutierrez, a young Mexican widow, and her two daughters, travel with De Anza's group and make their new homes in San Gabriel, California. De Anza leads a second expedition into California. More than 200 colonists join him, many of them *mestizos* (people of combined African and European ethnicity) from Mexico. These colonists establish the mission and *presidio* (fort) of Yerba Buena. The community that arises around these structures later becomes the city of San Francisco, California. Two friars, Silvestre Vélez de Escalante and Francisco Atanasio Domínguez, and mapmaker Bernardo Miera, travel 2,000 miles through the area that is now New Mexico, Colorado and Utah. **1777** The city of Mayagüez, Puerto Rico, gives shelter to two United States frigates that are fleeing the British navy. The town of San Jose (California) is established. Bernardo de Gálvez becomes interim governor and then governor of Louisiana. Gálvez sends money and supplies to the American revolutionary armies. He serves as governor until 1785. **1778** Spain is forced to grant the right of private ownership of land in Puerto Rico. Before the eighteenth century, all Puerto Rican land was nominally owned by the Spanish crown. The Royal *Cédula* of January 14 provides for the division and granting of royal lands with the right of individual ownership. Trade is authorized between Puerto Rico and the rebel British colonies in America.

1770

through

1779

HISPANIC AMERICAN	FOR CLASSROOM USE	FOR CLASSROOM USE	FOR CLASSROOM USE	
Juan de Miralles is sent from Havana as a Spanish representative to the United States. He supports independence and urges Spain to enter the war against Britain. Throughout the American Revolutionary War, Spain, Cuba and Mexico send financial aid to the United States.

Historia Geográfica, Civil y Natural de La Isla de San Juan Bautista de Puerto Rico is published in Madrid. Written by Iñigo Abbad y La Sierra, a Benedictine monk, it is one of the most significant historical accounts of eighteenth century Puerto Rico.

1779

Louisiana governor Bernardo de Gálvez raises an army in New Orleans and captures five British forts in the Mississippi Valley. His forces take Mobile and Pensacola in West Florida, at the time a British colony. Spanish forces defeat a combined British and Indian army at St. Louis and later invade Michigan. Gálvez commands an army of more than 7,000 soldiers — of both African and European descent — from Spain, Cuba, Puerto Rico, Mexico, Hispaniola and Venezuela. He is appointed governor of Cuba and then viceroy of New Spain. | | | | **1770**

through

1779 |
| | *FOR CLASSROOM USE* | *FOR CLASSROOM USE* | *FOR CLASSROOM USE* | |

**1770
through
1779**

1770

The Massachusetts Spy begins publication in Boston.

After the "Boston Massacre," in which Crispus Attucks and several others are killed, the British Parliament repeals the Townshend Acts, but retains the duty on tea.

Spanish forces drive the British out of the Falkland Islands. The Spanish remain in control until the area is abandoned in 1811.

1772

Colonists under Samuel Adams and Joseph Warren establish Committees of Correspondence as a network to keep people informed.

Relations between Britain and the colonies are further strained by the *Gaspee* incident. When colonists from Rhode Island board and burn the customs ship, *Gaspee*, officials in the colonial legislature indicate that any people suspected of participating in the affair will be sent to England for trial. The colonial governor of Massachusetts decides that he and the colony's judges will try the case but that judicial salaries shall be paid directly by Britain and not by the colonies. As a result, the Massachusetts Assembly threatens secession unless colonists are given their civil rights.

Salem College is founded at Winston-Salem, North Carolina.

1773

Britain passes the Tea Act, giving the British East India Company a virtual monopoly on the sale of tea in the colonies. This is a disruptive, forced subsidy by the crown to avoid the bankruptcy of the East India Company. Previously, tea was sold at auction. The Boston Tea Party takes place as a protest against the new import duty on tea. Angry colonists dress as Indians and toss the cargos of three tea ships into Boston Harbor, Massachusetts.

The Philadelphia Museum is established in Pennsylvania.

Dickinson College is founded at Carlisle, Pennsylvania.

Louisville, Kentucky, is initially planned and laid out; colonization takes place in 1778 and it is officially named in 1780.

Earthquakes destroy Guatemala's capital city of Antigua.

1774

The British Parliament passes the so-called Intolerable Acts to retaliate against the Boston Tea Party. One of these acts closes the Port of Boston in Massachusetts, and another greatly increases the powers of the royal governor.

Britain's Parliament passes the Quebec Act, which establishes French civil law and British criminal law in the North American colonies, decrees government by royally-appointed council rather than representative assembly as earlier announced, extends Quebec's borders to include the Ohio Valley and the Great Lakes, and grants religious freedom to Roman Catholics. The act ignores the claims of colonists in Connecticut, Massachusetts and Virginia to the Ohio Valley.

The First Continental Congress, the federal legislature of the 13 colonies (and then of the early United States), meets in Philadelphia and petitions the British government to repeal the Intolerable Acts, the Quebec Act and the duties imposed on colonists. A ban on the importation of British goods to the colonies is enacted.

Massachusetts establishes a military force known as the Minutemen.

The Connecticut and Rhode Island colonies prohibit the further importation of enslaved Africans.

Harrodsburg, the oldest European American city in Kentucky, is founded.

The Hudson's Bay Company takes over Fort Abitibi from the French.

Samuel Hearne builds Cumberland House, a Canadian fur-trading post near the Saskatchewan River. It becomes Hudson's Bay Company's first permanent community in that area.

Juan Perez leads an expedition commissioned by the Spanish crown to explore the west coast of North America; the group are the first Europeans to visit Prince of Wales Island, in southeastern Alaska.

Fifty women of Edenton, North Carolina, sign and send a petition denouncing British policy toward the colonies. This is the first time American women organize to defy the British government.

1775

The Continental Congress elects George Washington as commander of the Continental Army and approves the issuance of continental currency. The Continental Marines and the beginnings of the Navy are established by the Continental Congress.

Under the new Continental Congress, Benjamin Franklin is named the first Postmaster General; British postal service ends in America.

Ethan Allen, a New Hampshire land speculator, leads a band of New England colonists in the capture of Fort Ticonderoga from British forces. Fifty-nine cannons seized at the fort are hauled 175 miles overland to Boston to aid the army there.

Britain hires German mercenaries to fight in the colonies.

Richard Montgomery becomes commander of the American expedition to invade Quebec. Two armies set out on different routes to meet at Quebec. One, led by Benedict Arnold, arrives at Point Lévis across from Quebec. The other, led by Montgomery, travels up Lake Champlain to Montreal.

Guy Carleton, 1st Baron Dorchester and governor of Canada, evacuates Montreal and retreats to Quebec. American forces under Montgomery occupy Montreal, and all of Canada except for Quebec City is in American hands.

An American military force under new commander John Thomas attacks Quebec. Commander Montgomery is killed, and Benedict Arnold wounded. British relief troops arrive and American forces retreat. Thomas dies during a smallpox epidemic among the American soldiers.

Cherokee chiefs meet with Judge Richard Henderson of North Carolina and sign an agreement selling approximately 20 million acres of land in Kentucky and Tennessee for about 2.5 cents an acre. Henderson asks James Robertson and John Donelson to lead an expedition to colonize Middle Tennessee. Their community, Nashboro (now Nashville) is established over the next four years.

The Second Continental Congress votes to prohibit the importation of enslaved Africans.

For her valor in taking the place of her mortally wounded husband in battle, and for her wisdom, Nanye-he (Nancy Ward) is named "Beloved Woman," by the Cherokee and leads the Women's Council, with representatives from each clan. She also sits as a member of the Cherokee Council of Chiefs, and encourages economic independence, with reliance on commercial vegetable and livestock farming.

Shipbuilders at Portsmouth, New Hampshire begin work on the Continental Navy's *America, Raleigh,* and *Ranger.*

1775-1783

As a result of the American Revolutionary War, a wave of Loyalist migration to Canada takes place, especially to New Brunswick and Ontario.

1776

The British Parliament offers a 20,000-pound reward for discovery of a northwest passage across North America. Explorer James Cook takes up the challenge, sailing from Plymouth, England, in the *Resolution*.

The Continental Congress authorizes the term "United States," rather than "United Colonies," and adopts the Declaration of Independence as drafted by Thomas Jefferson of Virginia.

The making of rum from molasses is the largest manufacturing enterprise in New England at the outbreak of the Revolutionary War.

The first community of Shakers (United Society of Believers in Christ's Second Appearing, or Shaking Quakers) in the United States is founded at Watervliet, New York, under the leadership of Ann Lee (Mother Ann).

Hampton-Sydney College is founded in Virginia.

Delaware prohibits the further importation of enslaved Africans.

The oldest Greek letter organization in the United States, Phi Beta Kappa, is founded at the College of William and Mary, Williamsburg, Virginia. It becomes a national scholastic honor society.

The viceroyalty of La Plata is established, with jurisdiction over Argentina, Uruguay, Paraguay and Bolivia.

The Continental Congress decides against including the abolition of slavery in the Declaration of Independence.

Abigail Adams voices her concern for the rights of women to her husband John, who will later become president of the United States. She admonishes him that women will find it very difficult to support a new legal system in which they have no voice.

Mary Katherine Goddard is authorized by Congress to publish the first copies of the Declaration of Independence.

Thomas Paine's "Common Sense" is published, advocating the separation of the colonies from Great Britain.

The *presidio* (fort) of Tucson is established by Hugo O'Connor, an Irish mercenary working for Spain.

In Pennsylvania, Sara Franklin Bache and Ester De Berdt Reed organize a group of more than 2,000 women to raise money, buy supplies and make clothing for the Continental soldiers.

c. 1776

The site that later becomes San Francisco, California, is colonized by a Spanish expedition.

Esek Hopkins of Providence, Rhode Island, is the Continental Navy's first admiral and commander-in-chief.

1776-1777

Spain acquires Portuguese territory in Brazil.

1777

The American flag, designed and sewn by Betsy Ross, with 13 stars and stripes is formally adopted.

Lydia Darragh warns General Washington of a planned British attack led by General Howe. Sixteen-year-old Sybil Ludington rides through her New York town to call for fighters to aid the Connecticut troops. Deborah Champion rides for two days with an urgent message to General Washington in Boston. And in Virginia, a young enslaved African woman, whose name is not recorded, runs bullets for the Revolutionary Army. Despite her valor, she is still in bondage after the war; at 80 years of age, she finally escapes to Canada.

France recognizes America's independence.

John Burgoyne becomes field commander of British military operations in Canada. His plan is to divide the states at the Hudson River. Burgoyne's army, nearly 8,000 strong, drives United States forces from Fort Ticonderoga. Burgoyne and his men are later surrounded and outnumbered by United States troops, and are forced to surrender at Saratoga, New York.

1778-1783

During war between Spain and Britain, Guatemalan Captain General Matías de Gálvez thwarts British attempts to take Nicaragua.

1779

The United States Army Corps of Engineers is founded.

French forces take St. Vincent and Grenada in the West Indies.

Spain raises troops and money in its American colonies to support the United States' fight for independence from Britain.

British Canadian forces under command of Francis McLean build a military outpost at Castine, Maine, to protect loyalists and repel a possible United States attack on Nova Scotia. The fort is soon under attack, but British relief arrives and several United States ships are lost.

Nashville is founded in Tennessee.

1770

through

1779

THE WORLD	THE WORLD	THE WORLD	THE WORLD

1770 through 1779

1770

Austria begins a program of educational reform.

The Muslim holy city of Mecca is seized by the troops of Ali Bey, sultan of Egypt. Damascus is taken the following year.

Russian influence causes a revolt in the Peloponnesus, but the conflict is quickly suppressed.

The population of China exceeds 260 million.

The Industrial Revolution begins in Britain with the advent of steam power, a factory-based textile trade, a strong international commercial empire and the expansion of personal liberties.

Romanians migrate to Transylvania in large numbers.

Captain James Cook reaches Botany Bay and sails north to Cape York to claim eastern Australia for Britain.

1771

The Russian navy secures the Crimea and soundly defeats the Ottoman fleet.

Serfdom is abolished in Savoy.

Gustavus III becomes king of Sweden after the death of his father, Adolphus Frederick (1751). Gustavus III rules until 1792.

1772

The First Partition of Poland divides that country among Austria, Prussia and Russia and reduces its land area by one-third.

Britain passes the Royal Marriage Act to prohibit "undesirable" royal weddings.

The Somerset Case, decided by Chief Justice William Murray, the first earl of Mansfield, rules that a slave becomes a free person upon landing in England since England has no laws establishing slavery.

The revolt of Egyptian troops sends Ali Bey (1768) into exile.

In an attempt to increase his authority, King Gustavus III of Sweden reduces the power of the Diet and imposes a new constitution.

Warren Hastings becomes governor of Bengal after Robert Clive (1758). Hastings also serves as governor general of India from 1774 until 1784.

French explorer Louis Antoine de Bougainville visits New Zealand and Tasmania.

1772-1775

British explorer Captain James Cook crosses the Antarctic Circle, explores the New Hebrides and sights New Caledonia.

1773

The Regulating Act brings the political activities of the British East India Company under British government control, and provides for a British governor general for India.

Czechoslovakia's government takes control of the education system and establishes German as the official language.

Denmark cedes the duchy of Oldenburg (in present-day Germany) to Russia.

Jesuits are expelled from China; Pope Clement XIV dissolves the Jesuit order and Emperor Joseph II expels them from the Holy Roman Empire. Jesuits are expelled from Poland the following year.

Victor Amadeus III becomes king of Sardinia after the death of his father, Charles Emmanuel III (1730). Victor Amadeus III rules until 1796.

1773-1775

Yemelyan Ivanovich Pugachev, a Cossack claiming to be Peter III, leads a revolt of workers from Russia's lower classes in the lower and middle Volga and Ural regions and takes the eastern city of Kazan. The revolt is unsuccessful. Catherine II (the Great) has Pugachev captured, brought to Moscow and killed.

1773-1786

The kingdom of Champa is annexed by Vietnam. In the Tay Son Rebellion, revolutionaries overthrow the Le dynasty and take command.

1774

Russia forces the Treaty of Kuchuk-Kainardi (Kutchuk-Kaainardji) on the Turks at the end of the first Russo-Turkish war. The treaty forces the Turks to cede a number of Black Sea ports in the Crimea to Russia and declares independence for the rest of the region. Russia's right to intervene in Walachia and Moldavia is acknowledged by Turkey and Russia's commercial fleet obtains rights to sail in Turkish waters.

Siam (Thailand) and Luang Prabang enter into an alliance.

Trade in enslaved Africans increases dramatically from the following cultures: Ashanti (Asante), Yoruba, Ibo, Jelofe, Senegal, Dahomey, Angola, Guinea and Minas.

Abdul-Hamid I becomes Ottoman sultan after the death of his brother, Mustafa III (1757). Abdul-Hamid I rules until 1789.

Louis XVI becomes king of France after the death of his grandfather, Louis XV (1715). Louis XVI rules until 1792.

British Captain James Cook continues his Pacific explorations, which include the islands he calls Fiji.

1774-1775

Peasants in Austria and Bohemia revolt to protest their living conditions.

1775

The First Mahratta War against Britain begins.

The Portuguese surrender their oversight of the Chinese opium trade to the British.

Russia tightens control over its people and strengthens the institution of serfdom.

The British government suspends emigration at the outbreak of hostilities in the American colonies.

1776

During the next four years, British Captain James Cook explores the west coast of North America until he hits solid ice and ends hopes for a direct passage from the Arctic to the Atlantic Ocean.

The Treaty of Copenhagen is signed between Russia and Denmark.

Scottish economist Adam Smith's *Wealth of Nations* is published; it later becomes an influential text in the study of economics.

The first commercial steam engine is produced by Scottish inventor James Watt and British engineer Matthew Boulton.

c. 1776

The British are increasingly irritated by the Dutch Republic's refusal to lend support of any kind in suppressing the uprising in North America, and that anti-English sentiments in Holland are increasing.

1777

Maria I becomes queen of Portugal after the death of Joseph I (1750). She rules until 1816.

Charles Theodore becomes elector Palatine after the death of the elector of Bavaria. This leads to a dispute with Austria, Prussia and the German states and forms a reunion of Palatine and Bavaria, separated since 1294.

The Treaty of San Ildefonso remarks the Portuguese-Spanish boundaries in South America and confirms Spain's possession of the Banda Oriental and Portugal's possession of the Amazon basin. Portugal's foreign affairs minister, Pombal, is dismissed.

c. 1777

Thai forces under General Phya Tak (Taksin) expel the Burmese from Siam (Thailand). General Tak rules until 1782.

Vientiane (now part of Laos) is looted by Thai forces. The two Laotian regions, Vientiane and Luang Prabang, are made vassal states of Siam (Thailand).

France and the Netherlands officially recognize the independence of the United States.

1778

British Captain James Cook charts the Sandwich Islands (Hawaii) and names them for the British Earl of Sandwich.

THE WORLD	FOR CLASSROOM USE	FOR CLASSROOM USE	FOR CLASSROOM USE	
The War of the Bavarian Succession begins between Prussia and Austria. **1779** Britain begins a three-year war against the Mahrattas in India. The Peace of Teschen ends the bloodless War of the Bavarian Succession. Spain declares war on Britain, beginning a four-year siege of Gibraltar. The Boers begin a two-year war in Africa against the Xhosa (Kaffir) people, a Bantu tribe. Englishman Samuel Crompton invents the mule spinning frame for spinning yarn.				**1770** through **1779**
THE WORLD	FOR CLASSROOM USE	FOR CLASSROOM USE	FOR CLASSROOM USE	

NATIVE AMERICAN	AFRICAN AMERICAN	AFRICAN AMERICAN	ASIAN AMERICAN
1780-1800	**1780**	Absalom Jones and Richard Allen form the Free African Society in Philadelphia to give economic and moral support to African Americans.	**1784**
Smallpox and measles outbreaks decimate Native American tribes in Texas and New Mexico.	The Maryland legislature passes a law that enables both enslaved and free African Americans to serve in the Continental Army.		The *Empress of China* sails from New York Harbor for Canton to start United States-Chinese trade.
1781	**1781**	The New York African Free School is established, mainly through the efforts of the New York Manumission Society.	**1785**
The Yuma (Quechan) people of the lower Colorado River rebel against Spanish dominance and are generally successful in raids against Spanish forces.	Enslaved African Americans in Williamsburg, Virginia burn several buildings, including the capitol. One European American man is killed.	**c. 1787**	Three Chinese crewmen — Ashing, Achun and Accun — from the ship *Pallas* are the first recorded presence of Chinese people in the United States. They are stranded in Baltimore for about a year.
1783	**1783**	Lemuel Haynes becomes the first African American to minister to a European American congregation when he becomes pastor of a church in Torrington, Connecticut.	**1788**
Yuma uprisings isolate the Mexican provinces of Sonora and California from each other. The unrest and resulting separation continue for 40 years.	The African American regiment is deactivated at the end of the Revolutionary War.	**c. 1788**	Chinese crewmen and craftsmen hired by Captain John Meares are the first known Chinese people to visit Hawaii. They migrate north, and build and maintain a fort at Nootka Sound on Vancouver Island.
George Washington proposes a plan to the Committee on Indian Affairs to end all troubles with Native Americans. Indians should be told their land now belongs to the United States, and that they can be expelled from their territory. Washington advises, however, that the land should be bought through treaties.	A court decision in Massachusetts grants suffrage to African American males who pay taxes.	Dr. James Derham, born a slave in Philadelphia, establishes a lucrative private medical practice in New Orleans after purchasing his freedom from Dr. Robert Dove, from whom he learned many of his skills.	**1789**
	The Virginia legislature passes a law that enslaved Africans serving in the War — many as substitutes for their owners — cannot be reenslaved after returning from battle.	Gustavus Vassa, who arrived in America as an enslaved African in 1756, purchases his freedom, moves to England and becomes a prominent abolitionist. In his two-volume autobiography, *The Interesting Narrative of the Life of Olaudah Equiano, or Gustavas Vassa,* which used both his African and American names, he argues against the evils of slavery.	A Chinese man deserts from a passing ship, and becomes the first Chinese recorded to live in Hawaii. He serves King Kamehameha I and is seen by Captain George Vancouver when the latter's ship stops at Hawaii in 1794.
1786	**1784**		
The Continental Congress passes a measure reorganizing and centralizing the Indian Department in order to thwart manipulation and abuse of Indians by the states and by individual traders. The secretary of war is made responsible for Indian affairs.	Unemployed European American seamen protest the large numbers of African American bondsmen being hired as laborers and seamen. A law is passed limiting the number of African Americans on each ship's crew.		
1787	Barbados-born Prince Hall founds the first Masonic Lodge for African Americans when he obtains a charter from England for the establishment of African Lodge No. 459 in Boston, Massachusetts. Hall serves as the first Grand Master and is instrumental in organizing lodges in other states.		
The Northwest Ordinance declares that "the utmost good faith shall always be observed towards the Indians...."			
The United States Constitution gives Congress the authority "to regulate commerce with foreign nations ...and with the Indian tribes."	**1786**		
	The state of Virginia gives James, an enslaved African American, his freedom as a reward for his spying activities in 1781.		
1789-1850	**1787**		
During this time the United States negotiates and ratifies 245 treaties with Indian tribes. In these treaties the government acquires more than 450 million acres of land for less than $90 million.	In the Northwest Ordinance, Congress forbids the extension of slavery into the new territories, which become the states of Ohio, Indiana, Illinois, Michigan, Wisconsin and part of Minnesota.		

1780 through 1789

EUROPEAN AMERICAN	HISPANIC AMERICAN	HISPANIC AMERICAN	FOR CLASSROOM USE	

EUROPEAN AMERICAN

1782

The Continental Congress grants Feliks Milaszevicz of Boston, a Lithuanian immigrant, the right to run privateering operations against British shipping.

1784

Le Courrier de l'Amérique, established at Philadelphia, Pennsylvania, by Gaillard and Boinot, is the first French newspaper in the country.

Russian immigrants, including Ukranian Cossacks from Siberia, establish their first community in Alaska at Three Saints Bay on Kodiak Island. The group is under the leadership of Grigorii Shelikov. Population of the new community is just over 190, and includes one woman, Shelikov's wife, Natalia. She is the first Russian woman known to have come to America.

1785

Acadians who have been living in France for almost 30 years begin an exodus to Louisiana, on the first of seven passenger ships. More than 1,600 Acadians return to America on these seven ships, plus a handful of native French people.

1788

Marietta, the oldest permanent colony in Ohio, is established by New Englanders under the direction of Manassah Cutler and Revolutionary War General Rufus Putnam.

Losantiville is founded in Ohio. In 1790 it is renamed Cincinnati by Arthur St. Clair, the first governor of the Northwest Territory.

French Canadian Julien Dubuque obtains the right to work the lead mines of the Fox Indians at a site that later becomes Dubuque, Iowa. Dubuque is the first person to hold private lands in this territory when he obtains a land grant from the governor of Spanish Lousiana.

HISPANIC AMERICAN

1780

In Puerto Rico, coffee surpasses tobacco as the island's biggest cash crop.

1780-1800

Smallpox and measles outbreaks decimate Native American tribes in Texas and New Mexico.

1780s

A strike occurs at the Real de Monte mine in New Spain (Mexico).

1781

José Gabriel Condorcanqui, a descendant of Peru's early Inca rulers, leads a revolt against Spanish authority. He takes the name of his ancestor Tupac Amaru, raises an army of about 80,000 men and seizes control of southern Peru as well as parts of Bolivia and Argentina. The revolution is eventually defeated by Spanish forces and Condorcanqui and his family are executed.

A Yuma uprising cuts off communication between Alta California and Mexico.

A permanent Spanish community is established at Los Angeles (the Town of Our Lady the Queen of the Angels of Porciuncula), California.

1783

Spain regains Florida from Britain at the Peace of Paris. Spanish rule in Florida continues until 1821.

1784

The branding of enslaved people is prohibited in all Spanish dominions.

1785

The Royal Mercantile Company is established in Puerto Rico to export tobacco.

1787

The first public integrated school in the United States is founded in St. Augustine, Florida. The first teacher of this school is Father Francisco Traconis, who was born in Santiago, Cuba.

HISPANIC AMERICAN

1788

The people of Pecos Pueblo are almost completely destroyed by a smallpox epidemic. Only 180 survive.

1789

Alejandro Malaspina leads a scientific expedition through South America and Mexico, reaching Alaska in 1790. Malaspina, as other Spanish sailors, claims Alaska for Spain.

Count Revillagigedo the Younger is appointed viceroy of New Spain by King Charles IV. He institutes administrative reforms and improvements in finances, agriculture, industry, mining, education and the arts. The count consolidates Spanish authority in California and rules until 1794.

The viceroy of New Spain commissions Estéban Martínez to build a fort on Nootka Bay. Martínez and an expedition of two ships and almost 200 soldiers build Bastión de San Miguel de Nutka (St. Michael's Bastion of Nootka).

Puerto Rico recognizes the right of enslaved people to buy themselves out of slavery over time, according to their market value.

1780

through

1789

1780 through 1789

1780

Tupac Amaru's rebellion takes place against Spanish rule in Peru. The uprising lasts three years.

c. 1780

Charles Lynch, a member of the Virginia House of Burgesses, creates an extra legal court to try Tories suspected of conspiracy. This action clearly exceeds his authority and although the Loyalist punishment was flogging, the term "lynching" has come to symbolize severe punishment (hanging) imposed by a mob that illegally abducts and tries an individual.

European women who own property are allowed to vote in Massachusetts and some of the other colonies. However, once the state constitutions are in place, women are disenfranchised.

1780-1783

A growing number of Indian uprisings in the Andes culminates with the revolt of *mestizo* (a person of combined European and Indian ethnicity) José Gabriel Condorcanqui, who renames himself Tupac Amaru II. Nearly 100,000 people die before the revolt ends.

1780s

Caribbean plantations suffer economic crisis. The supply of enslaved Africans has become erratic, world crop prices are falling, and rebellion of enslaved Africans is frequent; these factors lead many owners to abandon their plantations.

Francisco de Miranda, a wealthy Latin American merchant, travels throughout the United States seeking assistance for a Latin American independence movement. He is warmly received.

1781

The Articles of Confederation are drawn up in the United States.

George Washington's Continental Army is bankrupt. The Comte de Rochambeau, Jean Baptiste Donatien de Vinear, gives the army gold worth $20,000 to continue their efforts.

Vermont functions for 10 years as a sovereign nation while claim to it is disputed by New York, Massachusetts and, briefly, even Canada.

Nancy Ward, "Beloved Woman," spies for European Americans against the Cherokees and carries peace messages to the United States government.

Two missions in Colorado are destroyed by Yuma Indians, essentially closing the major route to California.

Los Angeles is founded in California.

1782

The United States and Britain reach a peace agreement.

The Bank of North America, the first incorporated bank of the new nation, is opened in Philadelphia, Pennsylvania.

The Order of the Purple Heart is established by George Washington.

American privateers raid the coast of Nova Scotia, attacking Lunenburg and other towns.

1783

As a result of the Treaty of Paris, which ends the American Revolutionary War, the midwestern boundary between the newly independent colonies and British Canada is established, giving the United States the region lying between the Great Lakes and the Ohio River. The United States also receives rights to fishing off the coast of Newfoundland.

The last major Indian uprising in Peru is put down by Spanish forces.

Maryland prohibits the further importation of enslaved Africans.

African Americans are allowed to vote in Massachusetts.

1783-1787

Approximately 40,000 British loyalists, mostly Scots, leave the United States and flee north, relocating in Canada.

1784

The Empress of China sails from New York to Canton, China. This trade activity enables American commerce to recover from the British blockade during the Revolutionary War.

Water-powered looms begin to replace hand looms in the United States textile industry.

North Carolina cedes its western lands beyond the Appalachians to the new central government. Delegates from the counties that are now eastern Tennessee vote to establish the state of Franklin. For the next four years, the state of Franklin exists, though factionalism causes the establishment of two separate state governments.

Canada's census reports over 110,000 inhabitants.

New Brunswick separates from Nova Scotia.

Bermuda's first newspaper, *The Bermuda Gazette*, begins publication.

1785

The Ordinance of 1785 is passed by Congress. It establishes basic policy for the government's disposition of western lands by surveying and dividing the lands prior to their occupation. The ordinance is considered by some to be one of the most important pieces of legislation in American history.

The Virginia Act of 1785 authorizes the construction of the first American turnpike.

James Madison's Religious Freedom Act abolishes religious tests in Virginia.

Toypurina, a Native American woman and religious leader, helps lead the unsuccessful revolt against the San Gabriel, California, missions.

The University of Georgia is founded at Athens.

Russians build communities in the Aleutian Islands of the northern Pacific Ocean.

British law forbids the importation of United States goods into Canada.

Spain's Central American colonies are restructured. Separate governments are established for Chiapas, Honduras, Nicaragua (includes present-day Costa Rica) and San Salvador.

1786

Shays Rebellion, led by Daniel Shays, occurs in Massachusetts when impoverished farmers demand economic relief, disrupt local court proceedings and attack the arsenal at Springfield.

Captain James White leads in the establishment of a community on the site that is now Knoxville, Tennessee.

American inventor James Rumsey builds the first mechanically driven boat.

American inventor Ezekiel Reed produces a nail-making machine.

c. 1786

Syracuse is founded in New York.

1787

The United States establishes a federal government and the dollar is introduced as its official currency. The Constitution of the United States is signed, and Delaware (first), Pennsylvania (second) and New Jersey (third) ratify it.

The Northwest Ordinance provides that a governor, a secretary and three judges will administer the territory north of the Ohio River in the United States until a minimum of three or a maximum of five new states (with rights equal to the original 13) are created from the territory. Each new state may elect its own legislature when it has 5,000 voting citizens and becomes eligible for statehood when it reaches a population of more than 60,000 free inhabitants. The ordinance also provides that no man born in the territory will be a slave, that the rights of British liberty and freedom apply and that education should be available to all citizens.

Franklin and Marshall College is founded at Lancaster, and the University of Pittsburgh is founded at Pittsburgh, both in Pennsylvania.

American inventor John Fitch builds and sails the first practical steamboat on the Delaware River.

The first cotton mill in the United States opens at Beverly, Massachusetts.

1787-1788

All states except North Carolina and Rhode Island ratify the Constitution.

1788

Georgia (fourth), Connecticut (fifth), Massachusetts (sixth), Maryland (seventh), South Carolina (eighth), New Hampshire (ninth), Virginia (tenth) and New York (eleventh) ratify the United States Constitution.

New York City becomes the federal capital of the United States.

A great fire in New Orleans destroys more than 800 homes, about half of the town.

In East Tennessee, Bishop Francis Asbury leads the first Methodist Conference west of the Alleghenies.

Marietta and Cincinnati (originally called Losantiville) are founded in Ohio.

Dubuque is founded in the area that is now Iowa.

1789

The first United States Congress meets in New York City. George Washington is inaugurated as president, John Adams as vice president, Thomas Jefferson as secretary of state and Alexander Hamilton as secretary of the treasury.

The Constitution of the United States is ratified, and by the federal Judiciary Act, the government establishes a court system. John Jay becomes the first chief justice of the Supreme Court. He serves until 1795.

The federal Department of War is established by an act of Congress.

North Carolina becomes the twelfth state to join the Union.

Hudson's Bay Company sells to Canada a vast tract of land, which includes parts of what are now Ontario, Quebec and Alberta, as well as all of Manitoba and Saskatchewan.

A Spanish warship commanded by Estéban José Martínez sails to the area of Nootka Sound to protect Spain's claim to the area. Martínez and his men seize several British vessels, sparking what is called the Nootka Crisis, and bring Spain and Britain almost to war. The following year, Spanish officials apologize and offer to make reparations for damage to British ships. An agreement is reached and the Spanish government abandons its exclusive claim to the western coast of Canada.

The University of North Carolina is founded at Chapel Hill; Georgetown University is founded at Washington, D.C.

Boston explorer Robert Gray sails for Canton, China. On his return the following year, he becomes the first American to circumnavigate the globe. In 1792 Gray sights and enters the Columbia River and names it for his ship, the *Columbia*.

In the Brazilian town of Minas Gerais, a revolutionary movement for independence is suppressed. The rebel leader, Tiradentes, is executed.

Revolution breaks out in the western section of the island of Hispaniola (now Haiti) as a result of the French colonists' refusal to honor the commitment of equality for all citizens made during the French Revolution.

Civil war breaks out in Saint Domingue between European plantation owners, with British allies; *mulattoes* (people of combined African and European ethnicity) and European laborers, who are finally granted equality by the French Revolutionary government; and Africans, either indentured or enslaved, who seek help from Spanish Dominica. The war continues for 10 years.

c.1789

The Massachussetts legislature cites Deborah Sampson Gannett for "extraordinary heroism." Gannett disguised herself as a man and served in a Massachussetts regiment of the Continental Army.

1789-1850

The United States government and various American Indian tribes sign 245 treaties in which the government secures 450 million acres of land for less than $90 million.

1780

through

1789

1780 through 1789

1780

In the Second Mysore War, which lasts until 1784, the British are opposed by forces led by Hyder Ali and his son, Tippoo Sahib.

England declares war on the Netherlands in an attempt to prevent Dutch trade expansion with the United States. The West Indies trade port of St. Eustatius, which Dutch ships used as a port for trade with the United States, is seized and razed by British forces.

Anti-Catholic "No Popery" riots, led by George Gordon, take place in London.

Sikh ruler Ranjit Singh becomes *maharajah* (prince) of the Punjab. He rules until 1839.

Although he took the title of Holy Roman Emperor in 1765, Joseph II now exercises full authority only after the death of his mother, Maria Theresa (1740). He rules until 1790.

c. 1780

Bohemia, Hungary and Austria abolish serfdom.

1781

Emperor Joseph II issues the Edict of Toleration reducing the authority of the papacy in Austria and allowing for freedoms of the press and religion. More than 1,000 Protestant congregations are reestablished.

The Dutch colony at Negapatam, Madras, is captured by the British.

Hyder Ali of Mysore and his troops invade the Carnatic but are defeated near Madras by British troops under Sir Eyre Coote.

c. 1781

A severe famine exists in Japan.

1781-1784

During this period, peasant and Hui rebellions occur against Qing (Ch'ing) rule in China.

1782

The Treaty of Salbai ends the war between the British and the Mahrattas.

The Spanish siege of Gibraltar is ended by a British force under Admiral Richard (Earl) Howe.

A combined French and Spanish force retakes Minorca from the British. Spain retains possession by treaty in 1783.

Henry Grattan, a Catholic advocate for a free Irish Parliament, is a leader in the repeal of the Poynings Law of 1494, which made the parliament and laws of Ireland entirely subject to England's parliament.

The United States and the Netherlands make a formal treaty of friendship and trade.

Rama I (General Chao P'ya Chakri, Buddha Yodfa) becomes the ruler of Siam (Thailand). He establishes the new Chakra dynasty with its capital at Bangkok. Rama I rules until 1809.

Tippoo Sahib becomes sultan of Mysore after the death of his father, Hyder Ali (1764). Tippoo Sahib rules until 1799.

James Watt's rotary engine is an early version of the steam-powered machines that fuel the Industrial Revolution.

1782-Present

This is the time span generally ascribed to the Chakri dynasty that governs Siam (Thailand).

1783

An earthquake in Calabria, Italy, kills 30,000 people.

At the Peace of Paris (Versailles), Britain returns Minorca and Florida to Spain but retains control of Gibraltar.

Japan experiences a severe famine.

Russia's Czarina Catherine II (the Great) installs imperial governors in the Balkan provinces, thus strengthening her authority in the area. Russia annexes the Crimea and Catherine II makes Grigori Aleksandrovich Potemkin the area's ruling prince. Potemkin rules until 1791.

In Annonay, France, Joseph Michael and Jaques Etienne Montgolfier are the first people to fly in a hot air balloon; their brother, Charles, makes the first ascent in a hydrogen balloon in 1787.

1783-1785

Devastating volcanic eruptions occur in Iceland.

1784

In the Treaty of Constantinople, Turkey accepts Russia's annexation of the Crimea.

Emperor Joseph II's social reforms, especially his suspension of the Hungarian constitution, meet with resistance.

At the end of the Second Mysore War, Tippoo Sahib makes peace with Britain by the Treaty of Mangalore.

The British government takes control of India from the British East India Company.

English preacher John Wesley issues his Deed of Declaration, the founding document of Wesleyan Methodism.

James Watt produces the first double-action steam engine.

The Falkland Island sealing industry begins. Millions of seals are killed for their skins. Around 1800 the last seals disappear from this area.

1785

Russian colonists build communities in the Aleutian Islands, in the northern Pacific Ocean.

The United States begins trade relations with Prussia and sends the first American ambassadors to France and Britain.

The League of German Princes is formed by Frederick II (the Great) of Prussia against Holy Roman Emperor Joseph II.

The Treaty of Fontainbleau between France and the Dutch Estates is opposed by *Stadtholder* (governor) William V of Orange.

An imperial edict orders farmers to plant sweet potato crops in North China.

Frenchman François J. P. Blanchard and American-born Dr. John Jeffries cross the English Channel by balloon; Matthew Webb swims across later this year.

1786

By agreement with the prince of Kedah, the Malaysian island of Penang becomes the site of a British trading post.

William V of Orange suspends the Dutch Estates.

More than 1 million deaths caused by famine in Japan spark civil and political unrest.

The Austrian Netherlands (Belgium) is declared a province of the Hapsburg monarchy.

Frederick William II becomes king of Prussia after the death of his uncle, Frederick II (1740). Frederick William II rules until 1797.

Britain's Lord Charles Cornwallis becomes governor general of India. He rules until 1793.

As a child, Ienari becomes shogun of Japan after the reign of Ieharu (1761). Ienari gains maturity in 1793 and rules until 1837.

1787

Granville Sharp and other abolitionists establish Freetown in Sierra Leone to relocate Africans freed from slavery in England.

Fearing that Catherine II will seize the Caucasus, Turkey declares war on Russia. The two countries fight until 1792 and Russian troops capture and annex the southwestern part of the Ukraine.

The assembly of nobles is dissolved in France.

William V is returned to power as *stadtholder* of the Dutch Netherlands with the help of the Prussian army.

c. 1787-1980

This is the time span generally ascribed to Britain's colonial presence in Africa.

1788

In support of Russia, Austria declares war on Turkey.

The first British community in Australia is a penal colony at Fort Jackson (Sydney). The colony is 1,000 people strong, and is established under Captain Arthur Phillip.

Serfdom is abolished in Denmark.

THE WORLD	THE WORLD	THE WORLD	FOR CLASSROOM USE	

France's King Louis XVI receives a list of grievances from the parliament in Paris and recalls Jacques Necker as minister of finance.

The Times newspaper is founded in England.

Charles IV becomes king of Spain after the death of his father, Charles III (1759). Charles IV rules until 1808.

1788-1790

Russia and Sweden are at war with each other.

1789

Belgian independence from the Hapsburgs is announced, but the new government is too weak to withstand an Austrian takeover.

Austrian forces capture Belgrade and overrun Serbia.

An outbreak of smallpox among Australia's indigenous people reduces the population from approximately 250,000 to less than 15,000.

In Sweden, King Gustavus III abandons the constitutional monarchy form of government and rules with total authority.

Selim III becomes Ottoman sultan after the death of his uncle, Abdul-Hamid I (1774). Selim III rules until 1807.

Luft Ali Khan becomes shah of Persia. He rules until 1794.

1789-1799

The French Revolution begins when the Third Estate (commons) meets at Versailles, declares itself the National Assembly and its delegates refuse to disband until France has a constitution. At the time France is bankrupt from fighting in America and the French government attempts to tax the upper class. The three estates (nobles, clergy and commons) are now united. Louis XVI dismisses his minister of finance and a mob storms the Bastille, at that time a symbol of royal power. The National Assembly votes for a constitution, the Declaration of the Rights of Man, a limited monarchy, nationalization of church property, the abolition of the feudal system and other social reforms. Louis and his court move to Versailles from Paris and members of the nobility begin to leave France. In 1790 Louis XVI accepts the Constitution. In 1791 the French Assembly elects Honoré Gabriel Riquetti Mirabeau as president and Louis XVI and his family are captured at Varennes trying to escape from France and are returned to Paris. Massacres take place in Paris and Avignon. In 1792 the Revolutionary Commune is established and the First French Republic is proclaimed; the royal family is imprisoned and Louis XVI stands trial. The War of the First Coalition begins, continuing until 1797, an attempt by Austria, Britain, the Netherlands, Prussia and Spain to restore the power of the French nobility. This war is the beginning of more than two decades of battles between France and the other European powers.

In 1793 the Jacobins, an extreme political club led by Georges Jacques Danton and later François Marie Isidere de Robespierre, take power from the more moderate Girondist party and establish the Committee of Public Safety. They begin a reign of terror as a tactic to control the country. Louis XVI and his wife Marie Antoinette are executed; Charlotte Corday is executed for the assassination of Jean Paul Marat. In 1794 there are widespread killings between the various factions seeking power; Danton, Camille Desmoulins, Robespierre and Louis de Saint-Just are executed. The Jacobin party is destroyed; the Committee is replaced by Commissioners and the reign of terror stops. The third French Constitution is enacted in 1795 and sets up a Directory government with a ruling council of five directors; Napoleon Bonaparte is appointed commander-in-chief in Italy. In 1796 Paris is divided into 12 ruling districts. In 1797 Napoleon arrives in Paris. After a series of military encounters, the revolution ends when Napoleon returns from Egypt, overthrows the Directory, appoints Charles Maurice de Talleyrand as prime minister and declares himself first consul.

1780

through

1789

151

NATIVE AMERICAN	NATIVE AMERICAN	AFRICAN AMERICAN	AFRICAN AMERICAN

1790 through 1799

NATIVE AMERICAN (column 1)

1791-1794

Little Turtle, chief of the Miami, leads a coalition of midwestern tribes against European Americans. The coalition is victorious in fighting on the Upper Wabash River, Ohio; however, Little Turtle and his forces are ultimately defeated at the Battle of Fallen Timbers, Ohio, in 1794.

1792

Drought ruins the Creek corn crop and famine threatens. The United States government sends supplies and money.

1792-1827

Several persons of full- or part-Native American ancestry are freed from slavery in Virginia when they realize they were actually freed by laws passed in 1691 and 1703. Many more remain enslaved due to ignorance or inaccessibility to the courts.

1793

James Bradby, a European American, makes his home among the Chickahominy (Maryland and Virginia) and takes a Native American wife. By his influence many Chickahominy are converted to the Baptist faith.

1794

By the terms of the Treaty of Canadaigua, the Seneca Indians of northern New York state are granted the rights "in perpetuity" to their reservation lands.

1795

The Indian Treaty of Greenville, Ohio, is signed, ceding to the United States territory that today is Ohio and most of Indiana.

1795-1822

The federal government experiments with a "factory" system — factories being federal stores or trading houses — among Indian tribes. Twenty-eight such factories are established and run by agents. They are created to ensure that Native Americans get a good, fair price for furs, and to counteract British and Spanish influence in Native American lands.

NATIVE AMERICAN (column 2)

1796

Factory Superintendent Benjamin Hawkins inspects his jurisdiction south of the Ohio River. He finds the system working well and the Creek tribe pleased with their dealings with the factories. Hawkins has a reputation for being fair and honest in his treatment of Native Americans.

AFRICAN AMERICAN (column 3)

1790

The first United States census reports almost 60,000 free African Americans living in the United States; 13,000 in New England, 14,000 in the middle states (Pennsylvania, New York, New Jersey) and 33,000 in the South. In New England, the almost 4,000 enslaved Africans account for less than 1 percent of the region's population. But the southern states continue heavy economic reliance on the labor of enslaved people.

c. 1790

William Flora, a veteran of the Revolutionary War, becomes a successful businessman, operating a livery stable in Portsmouth, Virginia.

1791

By this year 24 percent of the population of Texas is African American.

Benjamin Banneker, the first acknowledged African American scientist, begins publication of his almanacs, which earn acclaim for him in the United States and in Europe.

When Vermont joins the Union, its constitution provides that no person, regardless of how they arrived in Vermont, should be "a servant, slave or apprentice after the age of twenty-one."

1794

Slavery is abolished in the French colonies.

The Reverend Richard Allen who, like thousands of enslaved African Americans, bought his own freedom, founds the African Methodist Episcopal denomination and establishes its first meetinghouse — Bethel — in Philadelphia.

1797

The first petition by African Americans to the United States Congress is presented by fugitive slaves in Philadelphia, asking that their freedom be protected. Congress declines even to receive the petition.

AFRICAN AMERICAN (column 4)

The state of Connecticut begins the emancipation of its enslaved Africans by passing a law that no one can be held in slavery after he or she reaches the age of 21.

Paul Cuffee, born to a manumitted father and a Native American mother, becomes a successful shipbuilder and entrepreneur. He purchases a farm for his family at Westport, Connecticut, and using his own funds, builds a school for African American children. He later becomes very active in the organization of the American Colonization Society.

1798

Georgia's constitution makes killing or maiming an enslaved African American an offense equal to killing or maiming a European American.

Peter Williams, a tobacconist, founds the African Methodist Episcopal (Zion) Church in New York City, and finances its first building at Church and Leonard Streets.

1799

In Connecticut Eli Whitney is awarded a federal government contract to produce muskets; over the next decade he develops a process of making and using interchangeable parts, an idea with broad industrial applications.

ASIAN AMERICAN	EUROPEAN AMERICAN	EUROPEAN AMERICAN	HISPANIC AMERICAN	

Although Chinese seamen have engaged in significant maritime activity from the middle of the seventh century, when Manchus conquer the Chinese people in 1644 and bring the Ming dynasty to an end, a major change in foreign policy occurs. Fearing that Ming loyalists will create a revolutionary force outside the country, officials of the new Qing (Ch'ing) dynasty pass edicts barring emigration. Though many Chinese people, especially from the southeastern provinces of Fujian (Fukien) and Guangdong (Kwangtung), continue to travel back and forth between China and the countries of southeast Asia, where sizeable Chinese colonies flourish, most of the Chinese people are isolated from the West until early in the nineteenth century.

Japan's location off the coast of the Asian mainland keeps its inhabitants relatively isolated from outside visitors. The Japanese people withstand attempted invasions by Kublai Khan in the 1200s, and first encounter Europeans when Portuguese traders arrive off the Asian mainland in the early 1500s. European missionaries follow but, fearing the examples seen in other Asian countries where missionaries were soon followed by military forces, the Tokugawa shogunate issues an effective anti-Christian decree. Japan remains isolated until a United States fleet under Commodore (later Admiral) Matthew Perry sails into Tokyo Bay in 1853.

1790

The United States census reports, among other groups, 54,900 native French and 44,000 native Irish residents in this country. Some historians argue that the actual figure for Irish-born Americans is actually much higher.

1790-1800

French refugees come to the United States in large numbers. An estimated figure is between 10,000 and 25,000.

1793

At Philadelphia, French-born J. P. F. Blanchard takes the first successful hot-air balloon ride in the United States.

Jacob Fahlstrom, a Swedish immigrant, becomes a woodsman and trapper in the Minnesota area, and is the first Swedish person known to make his home there.

Alexander Baranov opens a foundry near Sitka, Alaska. The foundry becomes known for the heavy bells it makes and sells to California's Franciscans.

1794

The first European community in the Dakota Territory is established by a French group under Jean Baptiste Trudeau.

Louisiana's first newspaper, *Le Moniteur de la Louisiane,* goes into production. Its publisher is Louis Duclot, a refugee from Santo Domingo.

1795

Demetrius Augustine Gallitzin from Lithuania is ordained as the first Roman Catholic priest educated in the United States.

The First Russian Orthodox Church is established at Kodiak, Alaska.

1796

Cleaveland is founded by General Moses Cleaveland on a surveying mission for the Connecticut Land Company, which has obtained a parcel of land in the Western Reserve section of Ohio. The spelling is changed to Cleveland in c. 1830.

Salina, the first European American community in Oklahoma, is established on the site of a trading post by French explorer Pierre Lacléde.

1798

A law allowing Frenchmen to own land in New York State is rescinded.

The immigration of Irish people to Canada begins. From there, many migrate south into the United States.

Hungarian merchant Benjamin Spitzer becomes a shopkeeper in New Orleans. He tries to establish trade relations between the United States and his native land, and is believed to be the first Hungarian immigrant in New Orleans.

1790

The population of New Mexico is just under 31,000.

1794

Spain cedes Nootka Bay and Quadra Island (now Vancouver) to Britain.

1795

The first anti-Spanish sentiment arises in Puerto Rico.

1795-1848

Twenty-two revolts of enslaved people are recorded during this period in Puerto Rico.

1797

A British naval fleet attempts and fails to capture San Juan, Puerto Rico.

A smallpox epidemic occurs among the Indian tribes of Mexico.

1799

Cuban-born Sebastián Calvo de la Puerta y O'Farrill, Marquis of Casa Calvo, becomes interim governor of Louisiana. He serves for two years.

1790

through

1799

1790

The first United States census records the country's population at 3.9 million, approximately 25 perecent in New England, 25 percent in the middle states and 50 percent in the South. People of English birth or descent account for 60 percent of the European American population or 49 percent of the total population. Other leading European groups are German, Scotch-Irish, Dutch, French and Spanish. The African American population totals 757,200, of which 92 percent are enslaved. More than 90 percent of the country's population is engaged in agriculture.

The United States Congress establishes a national Post Office and a Patent Office. Samuel Osgood is named the country's first Postmaster General; and the first patent is issued to Samuel Hopkins, for a new fertilizer ingredient.

Rhode Island becomes the 13th state to join the Union.

Although Philadelphia becomes the federal capital of the United States, plans are instituted to move it to Washington, District of Columbia (D.C.), which is founded this year.

The Supreme Court of the United States holds its first session.

The first United States Naturalization Act allows only "free white persons" to become American citizens.

Samuel Slater, using plans that he memorized while working for a British spinning mill, finds financial backing in Rhode Island and builds the first factory in America. A second mill is established in 1793.

The economy of Rhode Island begins a gradual transition from shipbuilding to industry, as the success of Samuel Slater's mill in Pawtucket becomes apparent. Major manufactured goods are textiles and metal products. Industrializing towns draw laborers away from agriculture, and as word of the labor market spreads, immigrants are attracted from Ireland and Canada.

1790

through

1799

British naval officer George Vancouver explores the northwest coast of America.

c. 1790

Kamehameha I becomes king of Hawaii. He rules until 1819.

1790-1800

During this 10-year period, the United States capital is Philadelphia, Pennsylvania.

1791

Britain's Parliament passes the Canada Act, also called the Constitutional Act, which divides Canada into two provinces, Upper and Lower Canada, and grants each province its own legislature and lieutenant governor. Britain's Parliament includes Michigan in its redefining of Canada's government.

After 10 years as a sovereign nation, Vermont becomes the 14th state to join the Union.

The Bill of Rights, the first 10 amendments to the United States Constitution, is ratified by the state legislatures.

The United States government sets up a national bank. This action opens a continuing debate on how the Constitution is to be interpreted, that of "loose construction" (implied powers) as advocated by Alexander Hamilton or "strict construction" (powers not delegated to Congress remain with the states) as argued by Thomas Jefferson.

In the Northwest Territory, warriors of the United Tribes of the Ohio Country (Shawnee, Delaware, Miami, Wyandot, Kickapoo and others) destroy the 3,000-man army of General Arthur St. Clair.

The University of Vermont is founded at Burlington.

Enslaved Africans on the island of Hispaniola revolt. François Dominique Toussaint L'Ouverture of Haiti emerges as their leader, and begins a fight for independence. The three-year revolt sends between 10,000 and 20,000 French residents fleeing for their safety to the United States.

1792

The United States government begins minting coins.

Kentucky becomes the 15th state to join the Union.

The Lancaster Turnpike in Pennsylvania is the first to be built and operated by a private company.

Two political parties are formed in the United States: the Republican under Thomas Jefferson and the Federalist under Alexander Hamilton and John Adams.

Under the ideology of "Republican Motherhood," education for women is beginning to become acceptable and necessary for women in order for them to be able to raise their sons to be responsible citizens.

Irish born James Hoban wins the competition to design a mansion for the president, later to be called the White House.

Captain George Vancouver explores the Pacific coast of Canada and circumnavigates Vancouver Island.

Russia's Catherine II grants a fur-trade monopoly in Alaska to Grigorii Shelikhov.

1793

George Washington begins his second term as president of the United States.

Postal service runs regularly between the United States and Canada.

Philadelphia experiences an epidemic of yellow fever.

Williams College is founded in Williamtown, Massachusetts.

Robert Baily Thomas publishes the first edition of the *Farmers Almanac*.

Eli Whitney introduces the cotton gin, which rapidly separates cotton seed from fiber. Cotton soon becomes the economic staple of the South and the main export product from the United States.

Canada prohibits the importation of people for enslavement.

Alexander Mackenzie and a nine-person Canadian expedition cross the Continental Divide and, continuing their journey, become the first Europeans to cross North America north of Mexico.

During its war with France, Britain invades Hispaniola. French resistance on the island is organized by Toussaint L'Ouverture and André Rigaud.

1794

The Jay Treaty between Britain and the United States provides that British forces will leave the Great Lakes region within one year and guarantees members of the Mohawk tribe unrestricted travel between the United States and Canada. This opens the area for American expansion as well as control over the fur trade.

The Battle of Fallen Timbers takes place in northwestern Ohio. Local Indian tribes are driven out of the area by the fledgling United States Army, commanded by Anthony Wayne. This fight demonstrates the strength and organization of the young army.

Congress enacts a law providing relief for French refugees who come to the United States from Santo Domingo.

In Pennsylvania, the Whiskey Insurrection occurs, in which farmers resist paying the whiskey tax.

Blount College is founded in Knoxville, Tennessee, as the first nonsectarian college in the country. It later becomes the University of Tennessee.

1795

Congress passes the Naturalization Act which requires declaration of intent, a five-year residency, an oath of allegiance to the Constitution, and satisfactory proof of good character and behavior as prerequisites for United States citizenship.

The Eleventh Amendment to the United States Constitution is ratified, providing limitations on the federal courts, and making the states immune from suits brought by individuals in national courts.

The Treaty of San Lorenzo, negotiated by Thomas Pinckney between the United States and Spain, establishes the boundaries of Louisiana and Florida, gives the United States the right to freely navigate the Mississippi River, provides for the right of deposit in New Orleans, and generally establishes trade relations between the two countries. Spain cedes Alabama and Mississippi to the United States.

John Rutledge is nominated to become chief justice of the United States Supreme Court. He serves only until the end of the year because his appointment is not ratified by the Senate.

Milwaukee is founded by the North West Company as a fur-trading post in Wisconsin.

Union College is founded at Schenectady, New York.

The first successful commercial sugar crop is harvested in Louisiana.

The Spanish fort at Nootka Sound is turned over to British forces.

Santo Domingo, the eastern part of the island of Hispaniola and approximately two-thirds of its total area, is ceded to France by Spain in the Treaty of Basel.

c. 1795

The islands of Hawaii are united under King Kamehameha I.

1795-1796

The territorial census of Tennessee indicates that the region is populated enough to apply for statehood. A constitutional convention is called at Knoxville, with Governor William Blount presiding. The convention draws up the first constitution, chooses Tennessee as its name and petitions the federal government for admission. President George Washington signs into law the legislation that makes Tennessee the sixteenth of the United States.

1795-1799

Enslaved Africans rebel in several parts of Spanish America, including Bahia (Baía), Brazil, and Maracaibo, Venezuela.

1796

President George Washington issues his farewell address and offers three pieces of advice: avoid political parties, especially if they are established along geographic lines; avoid permanent alliances with foreign powers, although temporary ones may be useful in emergency situations; and the United States should be prudent in repaying its debt obligations and maintaining good credit.

Congress enacts a protection law to limit European American encroachment onto Indian hunting lands. The act establishes fines or jail terms for violators.

Tennessee becomes the 16th state to join the Union.

Oliver Ellsworth becomes chief justice of the United States Supreme Court. He serves until 1800.

Cleaveland (later Cleveland) is founded in Ohio.

British troops evacuate Detroit and other Northwest forts.

Thirteen years after the Treaty of Paris ends the American Revolutionary War, United States Army troops under Lt. Colonel John F. Hamtramck enter Detroit and replace the British flag with the United States flag. British forces have been hesitant to relinquish this fur trading center.

1797

John Adams, a Federalist, takes office as the second president of the United States with Thomas Jefferson, a Democrat/Republican, as his vice president.

The XYZ Affair, a failed attempt at a treaty of friendship and commerce between the United States and France, fuels existing antagonism between the two countries and leads to a two-year, undeclared naval war. Peace is restored by the Convention of 1800.

A yellow fever outbreak occurs in the United States capital city of Philadelphia.

Charles Newbold patents a single-cast iron plow in the United States.

Earthquakes in Quito, Ecuador, and Cuzco, Peru, kill 41,000 people.

1797-1799

Spanish authorities open trade between the captaincy-general of Guatemala (Central America) and "neutral states," a trade arrangement which is favorable to the United States.

1798

The United States Marine Corps and the Department of the Navy are established by Congress.

Fear of increased foreign arrivals leads the United States Congress to amend the Naturalization Act with the passage of four laws known as the Alien and Sedition Acts. These acts increase the period of residency for citizenship from five to 14 years, establish new powers for the president to control all aliens he feels pose a danger to the country and restrict political opposition to national laws. The Sedition Act violates the right to freedom of expression and is soon rendered ineffective, not by an appeal to the Supreme Court, but by the election of a new government — the Republican administration of Thomas Jefferson — which opposes the issuance of the act.

The "Theory of Nullification" develops when Kentucky and Virginia oppose the Alien and Sedition Acts. This theory, when coupled with a strict interpretation of the Constitution, is the basis for the concept of states' rights in America.

Georgia prohibits the further importation of enslaved Africans but requires the consent of the owner for a person currently enslaved to become free.

The University of Louisville is founded in Kentucky.

A boundary commission sets the border between New Brunswick and Maine at the St. Croix River.

A revolt occurs in Bahia, Brazil, as people of European, African and mixed ethnicity unite to fight for freedom and equality.

c. 1798

During a brief period at the close of the century, women in New Jersey have the right to vote.

Toussaint L'Ouverture leads the slaves' revolt against the British (who had allied themselves with the Spanish) on French-controlled Hispaniola.

Peter Williams, a tobacconist, founds the African Methodist Episcopal (Zion) Church in New York City, and finances its first building at Church and Leonard Streets.

1799

The Russian government grants a monopoly of trade in Alaska to the Russian-American Company.

In Connecticut Eli Whitney is awarded a federal government contract to produce muskets; over the next decade he develops a process of making and using interchangeable parts, an idea with broad industrial applications.

1790

through

1799

1790 through 1799

1790

Mutineers from the HMS *Bounty* bring women from Tahiti and make a community on Pitcairn Island in the Pacific Ocean.

The Treaty of Varala ends the Russo-Swedish War.

The Third Mysore War begins after the British create an alliance with the local ruler of Hyderabad (a province of India). The war continues until 1792.

A devastating drought leads to famine in Bombay. Starvation is so imminent that some resort to cannibalism to survive. This period is known as the "Skull Famine."

The Turkish fleet is destroyed at Sebastopol (Sevastopol) by the Russians, who also capture the Izmail (Ismail) region of what is now Romania under Aleksandr Vasilyevich Suvarov.

The Convention of Reichenbach is held between Austria and Prussia.

Leopold II becomes Holy Roman Emperor after the death of his brother, Joseph II (1765, 1780). Leopold II rules until 1792.

Forces of Emperor Leopold II take control of the Austrian Netherlands (Belgium).

1790-1801

The Fulani tribe comes to prominence in what is now northern Nigeria.

1791

Despite the opposition of nobles in Russia and Prussia, Stanislaus II, supported by Leopold II, introduces reforms and a liberal constitution in Poland. This action leads to an additional partitioning of Poland in 1793.

The Gurkhas invade Tibet.

In Britain, William Wilberforce's motion for the abolition of the slave trade in the British West Indies is adversely affected by the riots in Haiti.

The United Irish Society (United Irishmen) is founded by Wolfe Tone at Belfast to support political independence for Ireland. The society becomes a secret organization in the mid-1790s and turns to leaders of the French Revolution for support.

French playwright Olympe de Gouge writes a pamphlet, "The Rights of Woman," which closely copies the French Declaration of the Rights of Man. In 1793, for her views and for her criticism of Robespierre, she dies on the guillotine.

1792

Coal-gas lighting is first produced by Scottish engineer William Murdock.

The Treaty of Jassy ends the Russo-Turkish War and confirms that the Crimea is a Russian territory.

The French declaration of war against the "First Coalition" alliance of Austria and Prussia leads to a French victory at the Battle of Valmy (northeastern France) and to the French conquest of the Austrian Netherlands.

Mary Wollstonecraft publishes "Vindication of the Rights of Women," the first major statement of feminist ideology. The modern women's rights movement is said to date from this time, as her work is widely read in Europe and America.

The Australian continent's first commercial sealhunt begins in New Zealand.

Russia invades Poland.

Denmark becomes the first nation to abolish the slave trade in its colonies.

Britain sends its first envoy to Peking.

Francis II becomes Holy Roman Emperor after the death of his father, Leopold II (1790). He also rules as the first Austrian emperor until 1835. Francis II's abdication in 1806 under pressure from Napoleon marks the end of the Holy Roman Empire.

Gustavus IV, a child, becomes king of Sweden after his father, Gustavus III, is assassinated (1771). His uncle, who later rules as Charles XIII, serves as regent. Gustavus IV comes of age in 1796 and rules until 1809.

English inventor Edmund Cartwright perfects the power loom — first patented in 1785 — and also creates a machine for making rope.

1792-1815

The Napoleonic Wars sweep over Europe, causing tremendous economic dislocation in several countries, especially lands held by the Hapsburgs, who see their rule weakening and their territories shrinking.

1793

The Second Partition of Poland divides that country between Prussia and Russia.

France declares war on Spain, the Netherlands and Britain.

Catholics gain the right to vote in Ireland.

With the help of Britain, Pasqale Paoli declares independence for Corsica. The independence lasts three years until Napoleon returns Corsica to French control.

Napoleon and his troops capture Toulon, a port city on France's southeastern coast, from British and Spanish forces.

1794

Frenchman Claude Chappe develops a semaphore long distance signalling system.

In Poland, peasants led by Thaddeus Kosciuszko revolt against Russian rule. The rebellion is suppressed and this leads to the third partitioning of Poland in 1795.

Britain suspends the Habeas Corpus Act, thereby denying people due process of law.

Corsica is taken from France by British forces.

1794-1925

This is the time span generally ascribed to the Kajar (Qajar) dynasty that rules Persia (Iran).

1795

British forces expel the Dutch from Ceylon (Sri Lanka). Britain also takes control of Cape Colony, South Africa for eight years.

France annexes the Belgian provinces and regains Luxembourg from Spain.

French forces invade the United Provinces and establish them as the Batavian Republic; *Stadtholder* William V (1751) flees.

Malacca (on Malay peninsula) is overrun by British forces.

French loyalists, aided by the British fleet, arrive in Quiberon (Brittany, northwest France) but are defeated by government troops under General Lazare Hoche.

Poland undergoes its Third Partition when it is divided among Russia, Prussia and Austria. Stanislaus II (1764) abdicates the throne. Russia annexes Courland (a region bordering the Baltic Sea) and takes the majority of the territory.

In western Africa, British explorer Mungo Park traces the flow of the Niger River upstream from Segu (Segou).

1796

An edict of the Qing (Ch'ing) emperor forbids the importation of opium into China and the planting of the opium poppy.

The population of China is approximately 275 million.

Napoleon and his forces march into northern Italy and institute political and social changes. His armies are also victorious in Sardinia and Austria.

Spain declares war on Britain.

English physician Edward Jenner's vaccine proves that cowpox provides immunity against smallpox. Jenner's work lays the foundation for the study of antibodies and the human immune system.

Paul I becomes czar of Russia after the death of his mother, Catherine II (the Great, 1762). He rules until 1801.

THE WORLD	THE WORLD	THE WORLD	FOR CLASSROOM USE	

Charles Emmanuel IV becomes king of Sardinia after the death of his father, Victor Amadeus III (1773). Charles Emmanuel IV rules until 1802.

Jia-qing (Chia-ch'ing) becomes emperor of China after the reign of his father, Qianlong (Ch'ien-lung, 1796). Jiaqing rules until 1820.

Aga Muhammad Khan becomes shah of Persia (Iran). He rules for one year.

1797

Napoleon creates the Cisalpine Republic after the French army conquers Austrian Lombardy and the Lombard Republic.

A mutiny of the British Royal Navy occurs at Spithead, England.

Merino sheep are introduced into Australia by John MacArthur.

France and Austria sign the Peace of Campo Formio.

French forces fail in an attempted invasion of Ireland.

Frederick William III becomes king of Prussia after the death of his father, Frederick William II (1786). Frederick William III rules until 1840.

Fath Ali becomes shah of Persia after the death of his uncle, Aga Muhammad Khan (1796). Fath Ali rules until c. 1834.

Baron Richard Colley Wellesley becomes governor general of India. He serves until 1805, holds various other posts and returns to India in 1833 for an additional year.

1798

Ceylon (Sri Lanka) becomes a British crown colony.

French troops under Louis Alexandre Berthier capture Rome, force Pope Pius VI to leave, and set up a new Roman Republic. The French invade Switzerland and set up the Helvetic Republic.

The Treaty of Hyderabad is signed in India between the British and Hyderabad's local ruler.

In Egypt, Napoleon's forces capture Malta and Alexandria and are victorious over the Mamelukes at the Battle of the Pyramids. In the Battle of the Nile, a British fleet under Horatio Nelson is victorious over the French at Aboukir (Abukir) Bay.

As soon as Napoleon's army captures Malta, a popular uprising begins. British forces join the rebel cause, and in 1800 the island is restored to its people.

Carnatic Wars resume and Tippoo Sahib of Mysore is attacked by a joint military force of British, Mahrattas and troops from Hyderabad.

An unsuccessful rebellion for an independent Ireland is led by Emmet and Wolfe Tone against British rule. After the rebellion is crushed, many rebel leaders flee to the United States.

Britain and Russia establish a new alliance, called the Second Coalition.

The operations of the East India Company come under Dutch government control.

After France seizes almost 1,000 United States ships, an undeclared naval war erupts between the two countries.

German printer Alois Senefelder invents lithography, the printing of an image from a flat stone plate based on the principle that ink (grease) and water do not mix.

1799

The French conquest of Naples leads to the establishment of the Parthenopean Republic.

Napoleon prevents a Ottoman invasion of Egypt by moving troops into Syria. His army is defeated at Acre but is victorious over Ottoman forces at Aboukir.

After the capture of Seringapatam by British troops under Arthur Wellesley, duke of Wellington, the kingdom of Mysore is partitioned between Britain and its allies. Tippoo Sahib (1782), the last sultan of Mysore, is killed in battle.

Austria declares war on France and overthrows the Cisalpine, Roman and Parthenopean Republics with the support of Britain, Russia, Naples and Portugal.

The Rosetta Stone, a piece of black basalt approximately $2\frac{1}{2} \times 3$ feet, is uncovered by the French in Egypt. It makes possible the deciphering of ancient Egyptian hieroglyphics.

Ireland's parliament, autonomous since 1782, is forced to disband.

1790

through

1799

NATIVE AMERICAN	NATIVE AMERICAN	AFRICAN AMERICAN	AFRICAN AMERICAN

1800 through 1809

NATIVE AMERICAN

c. 1800

Silversmithing is common among Native Americans of the Northeast and the Southwest.

1801

Secretary of War Dearborn appoints commissioners to press for land cessions from southern Indian tribes so that a road can be opened from cities and towns in the East to those in the West.

1802

The Tlingit tribe of southeastern Alaska captures the Russian fort at Sitka; Russians reconquer it in 1804.

Georgia cedes western lands to the United States government on the condition that land titles held by the Creek tribe in the state be nullified.

Federal law prohibits the sale of liquor to American Indians.

1802-1810

Separate treaties are signed between several American Indian tribes and the federal government in which the government acquires millions of acres of land for European Americans to move onto, and the tribes receive promises of smaller tracts of land, money and/or medicine and food. These treaties primarily involve tribes and land areas in Alabama, Mississippi, Georgia and Tennessee, although tribes in other areas are affected as well.

1803

President Thomas Jefferson, concerned about French acquisition of lands in Louisiana, persists in an attempt to acquire for the United States government all American Indian lands east of the Mississippi River, giving the native tribes the choice of assimilation or removal to lands west of the Mississippi River. After the Louisiana Purchase, Native American tribes in this region come under the jurisdiction of the United States.

1804

A Presbyterian school is opened in Tennessee by the Reverend Gideon Blackburn for the education of Cherokee Indians.

NATIVE AMERICAN

1804-1806

Sacajawea, a Shoshone woman, guides explorers Meriwether Lewis and William Clark to the Pacific Ocean.

1805

A band of Kickapoo Indians migrate to the lower Washita River in northeastern Texas. By 1815, they have many villages in the area and are allied with the Cherokee under Chief Bowles.

Tenskwatawa, the "Shawnee Prophet" and brother of Chief Tecumseh, calls for the rejection of alcohol and European customs and a return to native traditions.

1806

The United States Congress passes an act establishing trading houses beyond the Mississippi River and strictly controlling trade on American Indian land.

1809-1821

Sequoyah (Sogwali) creates the Cherokee Syllabary to record his people's language, and begins writing down tribal history.

AFRICAN AMERICAN

1800

The United States census reports 1 million African Americans in the United States, 18.9 percent of the total population.

Free African Americans in Philadelphia, led by the Reverend Absolom Jones, petition Congress for the gradual abolition of slavery; Congress votes to ignore the petition.

Gabriel Prosser of Virginia plans to enlist approximately 40,000 enslaved African Americans in a rebellion that has been planned secretly for months. The rebels' objective is to attack and capture Richmond and liberate its enslaved population. The plot is betrayed to Governor James Monroe, who declares martial law to defend the city. This action stops the rebellion and a violent storm prevents Prosser from escaping. He is captured and hanged, along with 35 of his men. Their courage and skill in planning the attack greatly strengthen antislavery sentiment in the South.

c. 1800

Using skills he learned during the Revolutionary War, James Forten develops an improved technique for handling boat sails and becomes one of the most prosperous African Americans in Philadelphia.

1801

James Varick and other African Americans obtain permission from the Methodist Episcopal Church to establish an African Methodist Episcopal (A.M.E.) Zion Church in New York.

1804

The Underground Railroad begins when General Thomas Boude refuses to return a fugitive African American woman to her mistress at Columbia, Pennsylvania.

New Jersey passes a law creating a policy of gradual emancipation.

Ohio passes "black laws" restricting the liberties of free African Americans.

AFRICAN AMERICAN

1807

Two boatloads of enslaved Africans arriving in Charleston, South Carolina, starve themselves to death rather than submit to slavery.

The antislavery group Friends of Humanity is created in Kentucky.

Southern manumission laws lead several northern states to disenfranchise or limit the voting rights of free African Americans. This is done in an effort to curtail the increasing migration of African Americans to the North.

1808

A federal law prohibits the importation of enslaved African Americans. The end of the importation of new slaves results in the forced migration throughout the country of at least 835,000 enslaved people, and many families are separated.

The community of Sierre Leone, Africa, becomes a British crown colony. Founded in 1787 as a refuge for former British slaves, it is managed by the African Institution in London and the British Sierre Leone Company.

1809

Reverend Thomas Paul of Boston, Massachusetts, establishes the African Baptist Church. Paul later plays a role in organizing the Abyssinian Baptist Church in New York City, which will become the largest Baptist congregation in the world.

ASIAN AMERICAN	EUROPEAN AMERICAN	HISPANIC AMERICAN	HISPANIC AMERICAN	

ASIAN AMERICAN

1802

Wong Tze-chun comes from China to Hawaii on a ship engaged in the sandalwood trade. He brings with him a vertical mill and is the first to make cane sugar in Hawaii.

1806

Eight shipwrecked sailors are picked up by an American ship and brought to Honolulu. They are the first Japanese to arrive in Hawaii.

1807

Merchant Punghua Wing Chong arrives in New York City from Canton to collect a debt for his father and stays for a year.

EUROPEAN AMERICAN

1803

The British Passenger Act puts so many limitations on passenger ships that it virtually stops the immigration of Scotch-Irish indentured servants to America.

Johan Georg Rapp, a German religious communitarian, purchases a 500-acre tract of land in Butler County, Pennsylvania. Two years later, 600 of his followers arrive and establish a community.

1804

John James Audubon, a Haitian born of French parents, arrives in the United States at the age of 19.

1805

German separationists, under the leadership of George Rapp, found the Harmony Society (Harmonists, Rappists). They believe in the common sharing of property and an austere life style. They construct the village of Harmony, Pennsylvania as an agricultural and industrial community based on their beliefs.

1806

Spaniards rebuild the community of Los Adaes in eastern Texas.

Spanish explorer Moraga advances to Mariposa, in California.

From a single glen in the Scottish highlands, 12 extended families travel together to America.

1807-1808

Russian colonists at Sitka, Alaska, build several commercial sailing ships.

1808

Joseph Carliss, an Irish immigrant, makes his home in St. Louis and begins publishing the *Missouri Gazette,* the first newspaper west of the Mississippi River.

1809

Jacob Henry of North Carolina is elected to the state legislature. He takes office after a challenge concerning whether he should be seated, on the grounds that he is a Jew.

HISPANIC AMERICAN

1800

Northern New Spain is now populated largely by native tribes and by people of mixed blood. This racial mixing results in Mexican Americans who might consider themselves Spanish, *mestizo* (people of combined Spanish and Indian ethnicity), Native American or *mejicano* (people of Spanish ethnicity born in Mexico).

1802

A Puerto Rican census of this year is the last to list native peoples ("Indians") as a separate category.

1804

Father Juan Alejo de Arizmendi becomes the first Puerto Rican to be named bishop of Puerto Rico.

A wave of Dominican and French refugees arrives on the western shores of Puerto Rico.

Alta and Baja California are made into separate provinces with their own governors.

1806

The native peoples of San Pedro Martir in Baja California stage a successful rebellion, causing the abandonment of the mission.

Puerto Rico has its first printing press. The official government organ, *La Gaceta,* begins publication in 1807.

1807

Puerto Rico's population is 183,000.

Sixteen families migrate from the area of modern-day Matamoros, Mexico, to San Marcos, Texas, as part of Mexico's strategy to prevent European American encroachment into Texas by moving Mexicans into the disputed territory.

Manuel Lisa leads in the construction of a fortified trading post, the first non-Indian community in the area that is now Montana.

1808

Spain's constitutional monarchy gives Puerto Ricans the right to choose a representative to the central governing council.

HISPANIC AMERICAN

1809

Ramón Power y Giralt, a Puerto Rican, is elected as the island's first delegate to the Spanish Cortes (Parliament).

1800

through

1809

1800 through 1809

1800

The United States census reports the country's population at 5.3 million.

The Convention of 1800 between the United States and France ends the two-year undeclared naval war created by the XYZ Affair and avoids a direct conflict.

The Indiana Territory, which includes Illinois, is formed when the Northwest Territory is broken up. Historically, the Indiana Territory is a part of the land ceded to the United States by Britain at the Treaty of Paris.

Washington, D.C., becomes the capital of the United States.

At this time, the United States Army has an official enlistment of about 4000 men.

Alexander Henry establishes a fur trading business at Park River, in the Dakota territory. He later moves his post to Pembrina where it becomes the foundation of the first European community in the area that is now North Dakota. Canadian fur traders visit the region frequently, and have established a regular trade route between Lake Winnepeg and the Indian communities to the south.

In what is now western New Mexico, vast copper and silver deposits are discovered at Santa Rita by José Carrasco.

c. 1800

John Chapman, better known as Johnny Appleseed, travels from Pennsylvania to the Ohio Valley planting apple trees along the way. He spends the next 40 years wandering in this area, helping colonists tend their own orchards and showing them how to develop new ones.

Eleuthère Irénée du Pont de Nemours establishes a gunpowder plant on the Brandywine River in Delaware. This event marks the beginning of the E.I. du Pont de Nemours & Company.

c. 1800-1803

Alexander Freiherr von Humboldt leads an expedition into Central and South America, during which time his group explores the Orinoco and Amazon Rivers and charts their courses.

Early 1800s

Cuba's economy is revolutionized with the growth of the sugar industry. The population of enslaved Africans and Indians rises from 40,000 in 1770 to 400,000 by 1840. Land and financial affairs are increasingly in the hands of foreign interests, mainly Spanish and United States investors.

1801

Thomas Jefferson becomes the third president of the United States. He was tied with Aaron Burr, and the final selection was made by the House of Representatives. Burr becomes vice president. Both are Democratic-Republicans.

War begins between the United States and the North African Barbary States (modern-day Algeria, Morocco, Tripoli and Tunisia) when pirates disrupt American shipping. The fighting ends in 1805 with a treaty between the United States and the *pasha* (governor) of Tripoli; however, tribute is still paid to some other North African states.

The Judiciary Act is passed by the United States Congress. It enables President Adams to pack the Supreme Court with Federalist judges.

John Marshall becomes chief justice of the United States Supreme Court. He serves until 1835.

Vincennes University in Indiana and the University of South Carolina at Columbia are founded.

The first building at the site that is now Grand Forks, North Dakota, is a trading establishment built by John Cameron.

François Dominique Toussaint l'Ouverture and rebels with him conquer most of Saint Domingue (Haiti) and call for full independence from France, which has controlled the island since 1795.

1801-1803

A secret agreement between France and Spain, through which France again takes possession of the Louisiana Territory, becomes public knowledge. United States officials, fearing a French stronghold at New Orleans, quickly decide to offer to buy the city and its environs. To the surprise of United States negotiators James Monroe and Robert R. Livingston, France's representative, Charles Maurice de Talleyrand, offers to sell all of the Louisiana Territory. A deal is struck; the treaty is signed and ratified by Congress in late 1803. By the Louisiana Purchase, the United States doubles its domain. For $15 million, the nation obtains almost 830,000 square miles of land, from the Mississippi River to the Rocky Mountains and from the Gulf of Mexico to Canada.

1802

The United States Military Academy is founded at West Point, New York.

French forces under Charles Victor Emmanuel Leclerc suppress a revolt of Africans in Santo Domingo.

1802-1804

French forces are sent to retake Saint Domingue; they kidnap Toussaint L'Ouverture and drive rebel forces from the eastern part of the island, but fail to destroy Haiti.

1803

Ohio becomes the 17th state to join the Union.

In *Marbury* v. *Madison*, the United States Supreme Court rules that courts can review the constitutionality of laws passed by Congress. In this case, the Court refuses to overrule President Madison's decision to cancel a commission awarded to William Marbury by outgoing President Adams. This case establishes the right of judicial review.

Fort Dearborn is founded by a group under the leadership of John Kinzie on Lake Michigan, Illinois. Although abandoned during the War of 1812, it is rebuilt in 1816 and from it the city of Chicago develops, becoming incorporated in 1837.

Colonists led by Joseph Elliott establish the village of Buffalo on Lake Erie and the Niagara River, New York. Almost destroyed in the War of 1812, it is rebuilt and is incorporated as a city in 1832.

The first Canadian paper mill is established near Lachute, Quebec.

1804

The Twelfth Amendment is added to the United States Constitution, requiring that electors vote for president and vice president on separate ballots.

Ohio University is founded at Athens.

In the United States, Alexander Hamilton is mortally wounded in a duel with Aaron Burr. Burr's anger results from Hamilton's support for Thomas Jefferson in the 1801 presidential election and for Hamilton's lack of support in Burr's run for governor of New York.

Haiti, the first predominantly African nation to gain freedom from European colonial rule, claims independence from France and expels Europeans from the island.

Jean Jacques Dessalines becomes governor for life of Haiti after independence is declared. He later takes the title of Emperor Jacques I and rules until 1806.

1804-1806

Meriwether Lewis and William Clark make their expedition across the United States with President Jefferson's instructions to explore the territory just purchased from France, and to scout as far as the West Coast. Their guide is a Shoshone Indian woman, Sacajawea, who is especially helpful in crossing the Rocky Mountains. Lewis and Clark bring back valuable information about the continent, and their expedition helps solidify the United States' claim to the Oregon Territory.

1805

Thomas Jefferson serves a second term as president of the United States; George Clinton is his vice president. Both are Democratic-Republicans.

A break in relations occurs between Britain and the United States over trade with the West Indies.

When the Northwest Territory is divided, Michigan is created as a territory, with Detroit as its capital.

Harmony, Pennsylvania, is established by German separatists under George Rapp.

Cattle from the Ohio Valley are driven to eastern markets for the first time.

Mercy Otis Warren's *History of the American Revolution,* published this year, provides later historians with the best accounts of the personalities and ideology of the fight for independence.

Zebulon M. Pike and his expedition reach the headwaters of the Mississippi River. This is the first time the Ojibwas of this area have seen Europeans. Pike's exploration in the Rocky Mountains results in the naming of Pikes Peak after him in 1806.

1806

Aaron Burr becomes involved in an unsuccessful attempt to either establish an independent country in the American Southwest or seize territory that is under Spanish rule. He is arrested and tried for treason but found innocent.

In Connecticut, Noah Webster publishes the first significant English dictionary in the country, his *Compendious Dictionary.*

English-born manufacturer and philanthropist William Colgate establishes a candle-making factory in New York City and begins making soap as well. This is the beginning of the Colgate-Palmolive-Peet Company.

The first gas streetlights in the United States are installed in Newport, Rhode Island, by David Melville.

Isaac Brock becomes the commander of British military forces in Upper Canada.

After the death of Jean Jacques Dessalines, a power struggle ensues between Henri Christophe and Alexander Pétion for control of Haiti. Unable to agree on sharing power, they divide the country into their respective spheres of influence.

1806-1807

Inventor Oliver Evans pioneers the development of high-pressure steam engines and conveyor belts, main components of mass production techniques.

British forces attempt several invasions in the viceroyalty of Rio de la Plata. They capture and hold the city of Montevideo for several months. However, an attempt by British troops to take Buenos Aires is repulsed by local militia. Britain is forced to surrender the territory, and Spanish government is reestablished.

1807

As a result of British seizures of American trade ships, impressment of American sailors in the *Chesapeake* and other incidents and additional naval violations, Congress passes the Embargo Act to restrict shipping. American shippers' resistance to the embargo and a lack of officials to enforce it produce widespread smuggling. Napoleon's French naval forces begin seizing American ships involved in smuggling.

The University of Maryland is founded at Baltimore.

Meriwether Lewis is made governor of the Louisiana Territory.

The first European community in the region that is now Montana is a fortified trading post built under the leadership of trader Manuel Lisa.

Robert Fulton makes the first successful steamboat trip on the *Clermont* between New York City and Albany.

Alexandre Pétion becomes president of southern Haiti (Republic of Haiti). He rules until 1818.

1808

The United States Congress bars the importation of people for slavery.

The American Fur Company is established in New York City by German-born John Jacob Astor.

When Napoleon's forces march into Lisbon, Portugal's royal family flees to Rio de Janeiro, and for a time this Brazilian city is the capital of the Portuguese Empire.

1809

James Madison becomes the fourth president of the United States; George Clinton is his vice president. Both are Democratic-Republicans. In 1812 Vice President Clinton dies in office.

In the United States, the federal Non-Intercourse Act lifts the Embargo Act of 1807; restrictions remain, however, on shipping to and from French and British ports. The rationale is that Britain and France need American goods more than the United States needs their trade.

Illinois, originally part of the Northwest Territory in 1787 and of the Indiana Territory in 1800, becomes a separate territory that also includes modern-day Wisconsin and part of Minnesota.

Canadian David Thompson establishes the first trading post in the Idaho Territory.

The first steamship line on the St. Lawrence River opens, with service between the Canadian cities of Montreal and Quebec.

France loses Martinique and Cayenne to Great Britain.

Spanish forces retake Santo Domingo from France.

An early attempt in South America to gain independence from Spain occurs when residents of Chuquisaca, in what is now Bolivia, stage a rebellion.

Ecuador becomes independent of Spain and part of the republic of Colombia.

1800

through

1809

1800 through 1809

Summary

The Napoleonic Wars devastate Europe, as nations are made and unmade according to Napoleon's conquests. France, Austria, Italy, the Netherlands, the Swiss Confederation and parts of Germany all suffer. As Francis II is forced to reject the title of Holy Roman Emperor, that empire comes to an end. In the Peninsular War, France fights a coalition of Britain, Portugal and Spain. Napoleon's army invades Spain, and Joseph Bonaparte is seated as king. The turning point comes as the French invasion of Russia fails. Prussia and Austria declare war, and France is defeated by the allied armies of Austria, Britain, Portugal, Prussia, Russia and Sweden. Napoleon is exiled, and the Bourbon monarchies are restored in France and Spain.

As a result of the Napoleonic Wars, Britain is recognized as a world power, the economies of many European countries are in ruins, and the Congress of Vienna redraws the map of Europe.

In India, British forces finally defeat the Mahrattas and end their resistance; the Sutlej River is established as the boundary between British holdings and the kingdom of Lahore in the Punjab; and Britain gains some influence in Nepal.

Dutch and British forces continue their fight for Africa. Cape Colony (Cape of Good Hope) changes hands several times. Sierra Leone and Gambia become British colonies. The sultanate of Sokoto is established by Fulani tribal leader Uthman dan Fodio; the Zulu kingdom experiences a brief flourishing under Shaka (Chaka); and Egyptian forces encroach into Nubia from the north. The Mahdi comes to power in the Sudan, raises an army, and fights British encroachment there; and the Ashanti (Asante) continue their effective resistance. By mid-century European explorers and missionaries have begun to make expeditions to Africa's interior.

In the Europe of the 1840s, continued economic depression, unemployment caused by industrialization, and major crop failures in Germany, Ireland and the Netherlands provide strong push factors for emigration. Most of the people who flee these hard times make their way to America.

By the end of the century, railroads are the primary means of overland travel in Europe and North America, and are growing rapidly in other areas. This industry boom creates new jobs for hungry laborers.

China's losses in the Opium War and the Taiping Rebellion open the country to foreign trade. Again, the rush of European traders is on, as British, Dutch and French groups establish posts in and near China. Singapore becomes a valuable stopover for trade ships. Commodore Perry's visits to Tokyo, and subsequent suppression of an anti-foreign movement, likewise open Japan to Western merchants.

As the 1800s draw to a close, skirmishes between British and Dutch expeditions in Africa have solidified into the Boer War.

1800

The population of the world is approximately 900 million: China, 300 million; India, 131 million; Europe, 200 million; United States, 5 million; and Japan, 15 million.

The Napoleonic Wars continue. The French army defeats Turkish troops at Heliopolis and takes Cairo. At the Battle of Marengo, Napoleon's army defeats Austrian forces, thus securing northern Italy for France.

Robert Owen begins his social reforms in Scotland when he moves to New Lanark and converts the community into a model industrial town.

Italian physicist Alessandro Volta makes the first battery, called "Volta's pile," using zinc and copper plates.

English inventor Richard Trevithick develops a high-pressure steam engine. In 1801 he builds and demonstrates his steam-powered coach.

1801

The governments of Ireland and Britain are consolidated by the Act of Union, producing one monarchy and one Parliament. Catholics are excluded from voting.

Austria makes a temporary peace with France in the Treaty of Lunéville. This agreement also marks the political end of the Holy Roman Empire, made official in 1806.

The Carnatic, a coastal region of India, is annexed by Britain.

The Tay Son faction in Vietnam is defeated by Nguyen Ahn and his forces. Nguyen declares himself emperor, and changes his name to Gia-Long.

Alexander I becomes czar of Russia after his father, Paul I (1796), is murdered. Alexander I rules until 1825.

Robert Fulton successfully operates his submarine, *Nautilus*, in France.

The paddle steamer *Charlotte Dundas* is built in Scotland. It is the first successful power-driven boat.

1801-1803

English navigator Matthew Flinders circumnavigates Australia and Tasmania, making valuable coastal maps and charts of the waters as he goes.

1802

France annexes Parma, Elba, Piedmont and Piacenza. Napoleon declares himself president of the Italian Republic.

The short-lived Treaty of Amiens is signed among France and Britain and their allies. France is to leave Naples and restore Egypt to Ottoman rule, and Britain is to return lands captured from France.

The Second Mahratta War begins in India. This war extends British control in the region.

Victor Emmanuel I becomes king of Sardinia after the reign of his brother, Charles Emmanuel IV (1796). Victor Emmanuel I rules until 1821.

Britain makes Ceylon a crown colony.

1803

Under Napoleon's Act of Mediation, the Helvetic Republic of 1798 is reorganized as the Swiss Confederation and is expanded to include Grisons.

Dutch forces regain Cape Colony (South Africa) from the British. Britain declares war on France.

After two years in France meeting with exiled members of the United Irish Society, Robert Emmet returns to Ireland and leads a march on Dublin. The uprising leads to violence and Emmet is caught and hanged.

British troops under Arthur Wellesley defeat the Mahratta forces of Sindhia and Nagpur at the Battle of Assaye in India. The British army captures Delhi, and reinstates the Mogul emperor, Shah Alam, as a figurehead ruler.

1804

Serbs led by Karageorge stage a successful revolt against Ottoman domination of Yugoslavia.

Napoleon proclaims himself emperor of France and systematizes French law under *Code Napoleon*. By securing property rights gained during the revolution, he has increased support from French peasants.

1805

At the Battle of Trafalgar, British ships under Admiral Horatio Nelson defeat a combined French and Spanish fleet under the command of Admiral Pierre de Villeneuve, thus establishing British naval superiority and curtailing Napoleon's plan to invade England. Nelson is killed in the battle.

Napoleon's army is victorious over Austrian and Russian forces at the Battle of Austerlitz in Moravia (now part of Czechoslovakia). The war ends with the Treaty of Pressburg in which Austria cedes Venetia, Istria and Dalmatia to Italy; Tyrol and Augsburg are ceded to Bavaria; Napoleon is acknowledged as king of Italy; and Bavaria and Württemberg become kingdoms. Austria retains control of Salzburg.

British explorer Mungo Park, sent by the crown to chart the Niger River, is killed during the expedition.

The Ottoman Empire recognizes Albanian military leader Muhammad (Mehemet) Ali as the new ruler of Egypt. Ali rules until 1849.

1806

Augsburg loses its municipal freedom and becomes part of Bavaria.

The first European women arrive in New Zealand.

British forces again seize Cape Colony (South Africa) from the Dutch and rename it Cape of Good Hope Colony.

The French coast is blockaded by British ships.

Following victories at Jena and Auerstädt (cities now in Germany), Napoleon and his army enter Berlin. The French fleet closes Continental ports to British vessels.

Under pressure from Napoleon's forces, Francis II (1792) renounces the title of Holy Roman Emperor, officially ending the empire. The Hapsburg Austrian title becomes "Emperor of Austria."

Napoleon creates the Confederation of the Rhine, uniting western Germany. He introduces reforms based on the French Revolution.

Liechtenstein attains a measure of sovereignty as a member of the Confederation of the Rhine.

Karageorge's Serbian forces take Belgrade from Turkish control and massacre Turkish residents of the city.

The Beaufort scale of wind measurement is devised by British sailor Francis Beaufort.

1807

By the Treaty of Finkenstein, Napoleon agrees to pressure Russia into returning Georgia to Persia but his failure to make this happen reduces French influence in Persia.

Napoleon appoints a *Sanhedrin* (a group of rabbis and laymen) to review the situation and conditions of Jews in France.

King John VI and his family flee to Brazil after Portugal refuses to support Napoleon's plan to weaken Britain economically. This leads to the Peninsular War (1808-1814), in which France fights a coalition of Britain, Portugal and Spain.

Serfdom is abolished in Prussia.

By an act of the British Parliament the trade in enslaved Africans is officially abolished, one year before the United States law goes into effect.

The Treaty of Tilsit is signed by France, Russia and Prussia.

The African regions of Sierra Leone and Gambia become British crown colonies.

Mustafa IV becomes Ottoman sultan after his cousin, Selim III (1789), is deposed by the Janissaries, an elite military service corps of the Ottoman Empire. Mustafa IV rules until 1808.

1808

Napoleon's army invades Spain and captures Barcelona and Madrid. Napoleon seats his brother, Joseph Bonaparte, as king of Spain. British forces led by Arthur Wellesley, the duke of Wellington, aid Spanish guerillas defeating the French army of General Andoche Junot at Vimeiro. The war ends in 1814.

Napoleon abolishes the Inquisition in Spain and Italy.

Mahmud II becomes sultan of Turkey after the death of his brother, Mustafa IV (1807). Mahmud II rules until 1839.

Frederick VI becomes king of Denmark and Norway after the death of his father, Christian VII (1766). Frederick VI rules Norway until 1814, and Denmark until 1839.

Although Joseph Bonaparte has been proclaimed king of Spain, Ferdinand VII ascends to the throne after the abdication of his father, Charles IV (1788). Ferdinand VII spends the first six years of his reign — until 1814 — in prison; he regains the throne and rules until 1833.

Karageorge becomes chief of the Serbs, a title that is made hereditary. He rules until 1817.

1809

Russia receives control of Finland from Sweden as a result of the Treaty of Hamina. Czar Alexander I allows the Finnish people a good deal of autonomy, thus allowing a sense of Finnish nationalism to form. Russia retains this territory until Finland gains its independence in 1917. The czar's forces also capture Izmail.

In the Punjab, the Treaty of Amritsar is made between Maharajah Ranjit Singh and the British, fixing the Sutlej River as the southern boundary of Lahore.

Napoleon annexes the Papal States; Pope Pius VII is taken prisoner and brought to France after excommunicating Napoleon.

The Peace of Schönbrunn, ending the war between France and Austria, requires Austria to leave the Tyrol. Austrian patriot Andreas Hofer, governor of the Tyrol, refuses and leads a peasant rebellion against French and Bavarian rule. Hofer is captured, tried and shot for his role in the rebellion.

Danish explorer Jörgen Jörgensen seizes power in Iceland.

Charles XIII becomes king of Sweden, gaining the throne after his nephew, Gustavus IV (1792), is deposed. He also becomes king of Norway in 1814 and adopts French Marshal Jean Baptiste Jules Bernadotte as his heir. Charles XIII rules Sweden and Norway until his death in 1818.

Maximilian I becomes king of Bavaria. He rules until 1825.

Rama II (Buddha Loetla) becomes king of Siam (Thailand) after the reign of Rama I (1782). Rama II rules until 1824.

French botanist Jean-Baptiste Lamarck offers a theory that living things evolve through inheritance of characteristics.

1800

through

1809

163

NATIVE AMERICAN	NATIVE AMERICAN	AFRICAN AMERICAN	AFRICAN AMERICAN

1810 through 1819

NATIVE AMERICAN

1810

Shawnee Chief Tecumseh warns European Americans encroaching on his tribe's territory that no more land will be ceded without unanimous tribal approval, and that all American Indians should unite.

1811-1813

Tecumseh tries to unify the midwestern and southeastern tribes against European Americans. Forces led by his brother Tenskwatawa are defeated at the Battle of Tippecanoe in 1811. Tecumseh then sides with the British in the War of 1812, but he is defeated and killed in the Battle of the Thames River in Ontario, Canada, in 1813.

1812

A British agent for the North West Fur Company encourages the Ojibwa (Chippewa) tribe to side against the United States in the War of 1812, but Chief KeeKeeshuv refuses.

1813-1814

In the Creek Indian War, Creek fighters are defeated by forces under General Andrew Jackson at the Battle of Horseshoe Bend, Alabama.

1815-1830s

Because of harassment from the United States government, many Native American groups migrate from the north and east into Texas. Chief Bowles leads Cherokees into the Kickapoo territory, and Shawnees and Delawares move in later. Together they form a loose confederacy in alliance with Mexicans in the area.

1816

General Andrew Jackson leads an attack on a fort in western Florida where hundreds of escaped African Americans live among the Creek and Seminole tribes. Three hundred forty-four Native and African Americans are killed.

1816-1819

In three separate treaties, the Cherokee Nation cedes all its land in South Carolina to the United States government.

NATIVE AMERICAN

1817-1819

The First Seminole War takes place in Florida, after Seminole chief Neamathla insists that federal soldiers stop trespassing on his tribe's land. The Seminoles are forewarned of two impending federal attacks, and flee into the Florida swamplands.

Thousands of Cherokees migrate beyond the Mississippi area into what is now Arkansas, thus forming a Cherokee Nation East and a Cherokee Nation West.

1818

A federal law is enacted giving the president and Senate authority over Indian affairs.

In separate treaties, Delawares, Miamis and Chippewas cede land in Indiana and Ohio to the United States for a promise of western land, supplies and annuities.

1819

Congress establishes a fund for the "civilization of the Indians."

AFRICAN AMERICAN

1810

The United States census reports more than 1.3 million African Americans, representing 19 percent of the country's population. More than 185,000 are free, but almost 1.2 million are enslaved. They work on plantations and farms. Their contributions are essential to economic growth in the early period.

Federal law excludes African Americans from carrying the mail.

In *Maryland* v. *Dolly Chapple,* a court rules that enslaved African Americans may testify in court regarding criminal acts in which enslaved people are victims.

Georgia law establishes trial by jury in cases in which enslaved African Americans are accused of capital crimes.

1812

Captain Paul Cuffee (Cuffe) of Massachusetts takes approximately 38 African Americans aboard his ship and sails to Sierra Leone in Africa, paying the expense of this repatriation out of his own pocket. Earlier (1797), when Cuffee lived in Westport, he built a much-needed public school on his property with his own funds after the town was unwilling to sponsor the school.

1814

Records indicate that more than 10 percent of the troops defending New Orleans are African Americans. Their bravery and determination draw praise from Commodore Stephen Decatur and General Andrew Jackson.

New York State calls for the assembling of two African American regiments to aid in the war with Britain. Two thousand enlist. An African American battalion is also formed in Philadelphia.

AFRICAN AMERICAN

1816

Hundreds of African Americans, who have escaped slavery and are living among the Creek and Seminole Indians in Florida, take over a fort abandoned by the British. On the orders of General Andrew Jackson, United States troops march in to destroy the fort, thus beginning the First Seminole War. This fighting is primarily a "slave-catching" expedition.

The American Colonization Society is formed by European Americans Elias B. Candwell, the Reverend Robert Finley, John C. Calhoun and Henry Clay to send African Americans to Africa. Free African Americans in large urban areas hold protest rallies against this effort.

Sixteen independent African Methodist congregations join together to form the African Methodist Episcopal Church. Richard Allen, ordained as deacon in 1799, becomes its bishop.

1817

In *Burrows* v. *Negro Anna,* a Maryland court rules that a gift of property by an owner to an enslaved person entitles the recipient to "freedom by implication," since enslaved people may not own property.

John Jones is the country's wealthiest African American. Born free in North Carolina, he teaches himself to read and write. He is twice elected Cook County Commissioner in Illinois, helps pass laws abolishing local school segregation, and operates an Underground Railroad station.

AFRICAN AMERICAN	ASIAN AMERICAN	EUROPEAN AMERICAN	FOR CLASSROOM USE	

AFRICAN AMERICAN

In Richmond, Virginia, opposition to the colonization movement is led by free African Americans William Bowler and Lenty Craw. They argue that colonization is potentially a sound idea, but one that should occur within the borders of the United States. James Forten, Richard Allen and Absalom Jones in Philadelphia agree that sending people outside the nation's borders places a stigma against African Americans. Some people who support colonization have other reasons. For example, Lott Cary's travels to Liberia in 1821-1828 are to extend his missionary work.

1818

John C. Stanley, an African American, is credited with purchasing the freedom of 23 enslaved people.

ASIAN AMERICAN

1815

In the War of 1812 Filipino soldiers from Louisiana serve under General Andrew Jackson in the Battle of New Orleans.

Three Japanese seamen are rescued off a drifting ship and brought to a community about 50 miles north of present-day Santa Barbara, California. These three are the first Japanese people to visit the American mainland.

The first Chinese immigrant known to make his home permanently in California, Ah Nam, serves as a cook for the governor of Monterey.

1818-1825

The first Chinese people known to have attended school in the United States are Wong Arce, Ah Lan, Ah Lum, Chop Ah See and Lieaou Ah See. They attend a foreign mission school at Cornwall, Connecticut.

EUROPEAN AMERICAN

c. 1811

The first Russian community in California is established at Bodega Bay, north of San Francisco. Called Fort Ross, it is built by a group of Russians and Aleuts sent from Sitka, Alaska to grow food for the Sitka colony.

1812

Captain Mordecai Myers, a Jewish American, leads a significant and successful battle against British forces outside Williamsburg, Virginia, during the War of 1812.

1813

By this time, Louisiana boasts three French-language newspapers.

1815

The first recorded Portuguese immigrant in California is António José Rocha, who jumps ship in Monterey.

The end of hostilities between the United States and Britain precipitates unprecedented immigration. British immigrants of this period are almost entirely self-financed.

1815-1835

Irish immigrants are a large percentage of the labor force building roads and canals during this period.

1817

After a lull of German immigration between 1775 and 1815, some 20,000 Germans, including many experienced farmers, come to America. A series of disastrous harvests in Germany is a major push factor.

1818

A fur-trading post is founded by colonists under Solomon Juneau. The community expands to incorporate as the city of Milwaukee, Wisconsin in 1846.

1819

New laws in the United States, including the Passenger Act, stop the immigration of German redemptioners, people who paid for their travel to America by a specified term of indentured service.

1810

through

1819

HISPANIC AMERICAN	HISPANIC AMERICAN	FOR CLASSROOM USE	FOR CLASSROOM USE
1810 Rafael Cordero y Molina, a Puerto Rican educator and pioneer who is also a *mulatto* (a person of combined African and European ethnicity), opens a school for underprivileged children. **1810-1812** Puerto Rican Delegate Ramón Power y Giralt is elected first vice president of the Spanish Cortes. **1811** Juan Bautista las Casas leads a rebellion against Spanish authority in San Francisco. The revolt is defeated after several months. **1812** José Bernardo Maximiliano Gutiérrez de Lara tries to drive Spanish Royalist forces out of Texas. With help from Americans who want to win Texas for the United States, Gutiérrez enters the area from Louisiana. After several victories, the expedition degenerates into factional bickering, and is soundly defeated by Royalist forces in 1813. Puerto Rican sugarcane is traded in the ports of Philadelphia, Boston and New York. The Spanish constitution of 1812 proclaims citizenship for all residents of Spain's American colonies, including Indians. The governor of Puerto Rico is given absolute power. **1812-1814** Puerto Rico is considered a province of Spain. **1813** The first newspaper in Texas, a bilingual paper called *El Mejicano,* is published by José Alvarez de Toledo. Alejandro Ramírez becomes officially responsible for economic development of the island of Puerto Rico.	**1815** General Andrew Jackson's troops at the Battle of New Orleans include a battalion of men born in the Canary Islands and other Hispanics from New Orleans. The "Real Cédula de Gracias" allows immigration to Puerto Rico from Catholic countries other than Spain, and from other Spanish colonies. It also regulates commerce. The San Diego mission in California has 50,000 acres of land, 1,250 horses, 10,000 cattle and 20,000 sheep. **1816** Spanish officials try to prohibit trade between the Chumash tribe of Mission Santa Barbara and the Colorado River Hamakhava natives. Cuban-born José Coppinger is appointed governor of Florida. He is the last Spanish governor, and serves until 1821 when Florida is acquired by the United States. **1818** A Philadelphia merchant notes the importance of trade with "the very valuable island of Puerto Rico..." and the "...growing industry of its population."		

1810

through

1819

THE AMERICAS	THE AMERICAS	THE AMERICAS	THE AMERICAS

1810

The United States census reports the country's population at just under 7.2 million, including 60,000 new immigrants and 1.2 million enslaved people.

Macon's Bill is a third attempt to stop French and British raids on American shipping. The bill lifts all embargoes, and threatens to reimpose an embargo on whichever of the two countries continues to disrupt American shipping. This bill brings the United States and Britain to the brink of war.

In the case of *Fletcher* v. *Peck*, the United States Supreme Court establishes the high court's right to decide on the constitutionality of legislation.

The Hawaiian Islands are united under King Kamehameha I who has defeated the local island kings.

The fight for independence begins in Mexico. In "El Grito de Dolores," Father Miguel Hidalgo y Costilla proclaims Mexico's independence from Spain. The revolt fails initially, and Father Hidalgo is captured and executed.

Argentina's victory in its fight for independence from Spain sparks South American battles for autonomy in Venezuela, New Granada, Rio de la Plata and Chile. The city council of Buenos Aires appoints a junta made up of Brazilian-born leaders and dismisses the Spanish viceroy. Argentina never returns to Spanish rule. Simón Bolívar and José de San Martin come to prominence as rebel leaders.

The city council in Caracas overthrows the Spanish captain-general of Venezuela and establishes a junta to govern the country. Francisco Miranda is appointed commander of the Venezuelan army. He later becomes dictator.

Britain now controls Guadeloupe, the last French colony in the West Indies.

1811

Contracts are awarded for the beginning of the Cumberland Road, the first section of the National Road, designed to run from Cumberland, Maryland, to St. Louis, Missouri. Actual construction is delayed until c. 1815 because of the War of 1812.

Lord Thomas Douglas Selkirk purchases land from Hudson's Bay Company for a colony in the area that is now Manitoba.

Henri Christophe establishes control of northern Haiti and, despite the presence of Alexander Pétion in the south, declares himself King Henri I. His death and that of his son during the rioting of 1820 bring an end to the royal line.

The city of Cartagena (in modern-day Bolivia) proclaims its independence from Spain.

In Chile, José Miguel Carrera and his brothers Juan José and Luis overthrow the government headed by Martínez de Rozas. José Carrera loses power to Bernardo O'Higgins in 1813 but takes control again the following year, and remains in a constant battle for leadership of the country. He is finally ousted when O'Higgins becomes dictator in 1817.

In a bloodless revolution, Paraguay declares its independence from Spain. José Gaspar Rodríguez de Francia becomes dictator in 1814 and rules Paraguay until 1840.

Colonists in Uruguay under José Gervasio Artigas revolt, seeking independence from Spain. Portuguese officials intervene at the request of the Spanish government.

Venezuela experiences a brief period of independence, but rebel leader Francisco de Miranda and his forces are soon defeated.

1812

Louisiana becomes the 18th state to join the Union.

The Missouri Territory is established.

West Florida is occupied and claimed by the United States.

When the Jeffersonians rearrange the voting districts into salamander-like shapes in an attempt to remain in political control of Massachusetts, the term "gerrymander" is born. It combines the name of then-Governor Elbridge Gerry with the amphibian.

Rochester is founded by Colonel Nathaniel Rochester in New York and the village is incorporated in 1817.

Detroit is taken from the French by a combined force of approximately 300 English troops under Isaac Brock and 600 Indians led by Shawnee chief Tecumseh.

Scottish immigrants arrive on the Red River in southern Manitoba, Canada, and build a community there.

In a naval battle off the coast of Nova Scotia, the British ship *Guerrilè* is defeated by the United States vessel *Constitution*, under the command of Isaac Hull.

The nationalist army in Venezuela is defeated by Spanish forces led by General Domingo de Monteverde. Miranda is turned over to Spanish authorities by Simón Bolívar and other nationalists who believe Miranda has deserted them.

1813

James Madison serves a second term as president of the United States; Elbridge Gerry is vice president. Both are Democratic-Republicans. In 1814, Vice President Gerry dies in office. He is not replaced.

An earthquake causes the formation of Reelfoot Lake in Tennessee.

British troops are forced to evacuate Detroit and retreat into Canada.

José María Morelos continues the revolution in Mexico following Miguel Hidalgo's execution. He declares independence from Spain in a congress held at Chilpancingo.

Mexican insurgents proclaim the Constitution of Apatzingán, which provides for universal male suffrage, the abolition of slavery and caste systems, and the elimination of judicial torture.

New Granada (Colombia) declares its independence from Spain.

1812-1815
The War of 1812

Continued British interference with American trade, impressment of United States seamen, incitement and support of Native American war parties and the American "War Hawks" desire for western expansion lead to war. United States forces capture and burn York (Toronto), but other American attacks on Canada are generally unsuccessful. For example, William Hull, governor of Michigan Territory, leads an abortive raid into Canada; his men are driven back by British troops, and are forced to surrender Detroit after only minimal resistance. The city is retaken by American regulars under William Henry Harrison the following year. Oliver Hazard Perry and his crew on the *Niagara* defeat British forces in 1813 on Lake Erie. Perry's battle report contains the statement, "We have met the enemy and they are ours." British forces are also defeated at the Battle of the Thames (southeastern Ontario province, Canada) and Tecumseh, the Shawnee chief fighting for the British, is killed. United States troops are thwarted in two attempts to take Montreal. In the Battle of Plattsburg, New York, a British flotilla is defeated on Lake Champlain. The British capture and burn Washington, D.C., in 1814 but fail to capture Fort McHenry in Baltimore. The Treaty of Ghent ends the war, but before news of the agreement arrives, United States forces defeat British troops at the Battle of New Orleans. In that battle, General Andrew Jackson and his men inflict heavy damage on the British army while only losing a few men. The war settles little but strengthens the position of the United States as an independent nation.

1810
through
1819

1810 through 1819

THE AMERICAS

The city of Bogotá (in modern-day Colombia) proclaims its independence from Spain and calls itself the Republic of Cundinamarca. Simón Bolívar is appointed general and leads his army into Venezuela. They capture Caracas in August, and Bolívar is given the title "Libertador." He becomes dictator of Venezuela's Second Republic. Bolívar's refusal to abolish slavery enrages enslaved Africans, who join the royalist resistance. Bolívar is driven into exile in 1815.

José Gaspar de Francia becomes dictator of Paraguay, and serves until his death in 1840.

1813-1816

A Creek Indian war party attacks Fort Mims, near Mobile, Alabama, and kills some 250 people, including European American and enslaved African American men, women and children. United States regulars under the command of General Andrew Jackson defeat Chief Weatherford's Creek forces at Horseshoe Bend; of 1,000 Indians involved in the fight, almost 900 are killed.

1814

United States Captain Stephen Decatur's expedition against Algiers ends the taking of tribute from American shippers by the Barbary States of North Africa.

The U.S.S. *Fulton* becomes the first steam-powered warship. The United States frigate *Essex* is captured by British ships in Valparaiso, Chile.

Francis Scott Key writes *The Star Spangled Banner* at Fort McHenry in Baltimore.

Irish-born James Hoban supervises the reconstruction of the White House in Washington, D.C., after it is burned by the British. Hoban is the original designer of the structure.

The Kimbrough mine is Tennessee's first commercial coal mine.

THE AMERICAS

King Ferdinand's VII's return to the Spanish throne sparks factionalism in Spanish America; ideological lines are drawn between royalists who support the monarchy, nationalists who seek independence, and moderates who seek reform within the existing system.

Brazil declares itself an independent empire.

Montevideo, Uruguay, is briefly overrun by Argentinian rebels. However, the insurgents are driven out, and Argentina's revolutionary government is forced to recognize Uruguayan sovereignty under José Gervasio Artigas. The struggle for independence continues with Brazil occupying Montevideo in c. 1820. After defeating Brazilian troops in 1828, Uruguay gains its independence under the leadership of Juan Antonio Lavalleja.

General José de San Martín is named commander of the army at Tucumán in Argentina.

1814-1815

The Federalist party holds a convention in Hartford, Connecticut, but the secrecy of its meetings causes widespread distrust and results in a weakening of the party.

c. 1814-1815

Harmonists under George Rapp move to Indiana and establish a new community called Harmony. It is sold in 1825 to social reformer Robert Owen and renamed New Harmony.

1815

British law prohibits the immigration of United States citizens to Canada.

Montreal becomes the first Canadian city to install street lights; these are fueled by whale oil.

Mexican rebel leader José María Morelos is captured and executed. His death marks the end of the first phase of organized Mexican revolution.

Spain's King Ferdinand sends a 10,000-man army to Spanish America in an attempt to quell the growing unrest.

THE AMERICAS

General Simón Bolívar is forced to leave Venezuela after the defeat of his army by Spanish forces.

1816

The United States institutes a protective tariff against Britain.

The American Colonization Society is formed in Washington, D.C., to assist the transportation of free African Americans back to Africa.

Indiana becomes the 19th state to join the Union.

Although Philadelphia has already tested street lights, Baltimore becomes the first United States city to light its streets with gas lamps.

Pittsburgh, established in the area around Fort Pitt, Pennsylvania, is incorporated as a city.

A revolt of enslaved Africans takes place in Barbados. Its leaders are an enslaved man named Bussa and a free *mulatto* (a person of combined African and European ethnicity), Washington Franklin.

Alexandre Pétion welcomes exiled South American leader Simón Bolívar to Haiti and offers to assist him in his liberation efforts.

The United Provinces of La Plata, an area made up of what is now Argentina, Uruguay, Bolivia and Paraguay, declares its independence from Spain. This union is short-lived, as the different regions seek separation and independence. Fighting continues as Spain attempts to regain control.

1817

James Monroe becomes the fifth president of the United States; Daniel D. Tompkins is vice president. Both are Democratic-Republicans.

With the appointment of John C. Calhoun as Secretary of War, the United States Army sees a dramatic improvement in modernization, organization and discipline. Under Calhoun's leadership, supply and purchase procedures are restructured, an artillery school is established, and the training and discipline of soldiers is standardized.

THE AMERICAS

Mississippi becomes the 20th state to join the Union.

Under the terms of the Treaty of Ghent, a group is established to study United States-Canada border issues. This committee awards most of the Passamaquoddy Bay islands (New Brunswick) to Britain. At the Rush-Bagot Convention, representatives of the United States and Canada agree to keep warships off the Great Lakes.

Construction begins on the Erie Canal, which connects Albany and Buffalo, New York.

At Hartford, Connecticut, Thomas Gallaudet founds a free school for deaf students, the first in the United States.

The University of Michigan is founded at Ann Arbor.

The use of the word "immigrant" becomes widespread in America. In earlier times, new colonists were called "emigrants," emphasizing that they migrated *from* somewhere. After 1817, colonists are perceived as migrating *to* a new nation.

Simón Bolívar establishes an independent Venezuela as Spain loses hold on its South American colonies.

Policarpa Salaverrieta (La Pola) is publicly executed by Spanish officials for her role in the revolutionary cause in Gran Colombia. Her execution results in a successful uprising against the official who ordered her death. In every country seeking independence female combatants like Policarpa appear. Women also preside over social occasions where revolutionary ideas against Spanish rule are discussed.

1817-1818

General José de San Martín and General Bernardo O'Higgins defeat the Spanish army at Chacabuco, Chile. San Martín's Andean army is almost 50 percent African and *mulatto*. O'Higgins is named supreme dictator of Chile; he rules until 1823.

1818

The London Convention is signed by the United States and Britain. Under its terms, the United States regains rights to catch and cure fish in the Newfoundland area, and the 49th parallel, as far west as the Rocky Mountains, is provisionally established as the border between British and United States territories.

Illinois becomes the 21st state to join the Union.

The Cumberland Road, the first section of the National Road, is opened between Cumberland, Maryland and Wheeling (in what is now West Virginia).

A fur-trading post is established by colonists under Soloman Juneau. This community expands and, in 1846, incorporates as the city of Milwaukee, Wisconsin.

The Black Ball Line begins regular shipping service between Liverpool, England, and New York City.

St. Louis University is founded in Missouri.

British arctic explorer (Sir) John Ross, in an unsuccessful attempt at finding Bolívar's forces defeat the Spanish army at the Battle of Boyacá.

1818-1819

General Andrew Jackson leads an invasion of eastern Florida, and Spain cedes the territory to the United States through the Adams-Onís Treaty. The treaty also provides for the assumption of more than $5,000,000 of Spanish debt to United States citizens by the United States government.

1819

The United States experiences a financial panic caused by the increase in land speculation created by westward expansion. This panic, and a congressional act requiring payment for land in coin rather than paper money, force prices up. Many farmers and colonists short on hard currency lose their homes to foreclosures.

A series of regulations, known as "Steerage Legislation" is approved for American shipping. This legislation sets minimum standards of transatlantic vessels, and requires ships' captains arriving from abroad to list, in addition to name and country, the age, sex and occupation of each passenger.

Alabama becomes the 22nd state to join the Union.

In *Dartmouth College* v. *New Hampshire,* the United States Supreme Court rules that private contracts, such as the royal charter obtained by Dartmouth College from Britain's King George III, are protected by the Constitution and cannot be overturned by actions of the states, as was attempted in this instance by the New Hampshire legislature.

The first antislavery paper in the United States is the *Manumission Intelligencer,* later renamed *Emancipator,* published at Jonesborough, Tennessee by Elihu Embree.

The city of Memphis, Tennessee, is planned on the site of a small fort built in 1797. Memphis is incorporated as a city in 1849.

Fort Snelling is established on the Mississippi River, at the Falls of St. Anthony, Minnesota. The building of a sawmill in 1821 initiates the development of Minneapolis, which is incorporated as a city in 1867.

The University of Cincinnati in Ohio and the University of Virginia at Charlottesville are founded.

Kamehameha II becomes king of Hawaii after the death of his father, Kamehameha I (c. 1790). Kamehameha II rules until his death in 1824.

The United States vessel *Savannah* becomes the first steamship to cross the Atlantic Ocean. The voyage takes 26 days.

American inventor Jethro Wood patents a cast-iron plow that improves his early design of 1814. Removable parts and the redesigned moldboard greatly increase the efficiency and ease of maintenance of the plow.

By the Congress of Angostura, Simón Bolívar is elected president of Gran (Great) Colombia, which is made up of present day Colombia, Venezuela, Ecuador and Panama.

1810

through

1819

THE WORLD	THE WORLD	THE WORLD	THE WORLD

1810 through 1819

THE WORLD

1810

British troops capture the French island of Mauritius in the Indian Ocean. However, French influence remains strong.

Napoleon orders the sale of seized United States ships, annexes Holland and the German cities of Hamburg and Bremen, and orders the confiscation of British goods.

An edict of the Qing emperor bans the import of opium to Peking.

1810-1812

Napoleon is at the peak of his political and military power.

1811

British forces under Lord Minto take Java from the Dutch.

1812

Russia annexes Bessarabia, a region of Moldavia; the Treaty of Bucharest, ending the Russo-Turkish war, guarantees Russia's control over Izmail.

The population of China is approximately 360 million.

In the Battle of Borodino, Napoleon's nearly exhausted troops push back a Russian force and advance on Moscow. Their entry into Moscow is fruitless, as retreating Russians have left the city almost entirely deserted and in flames. Napoleon's army withdraws.

Helsinki becomes Finland's capital city.

British prime minister Spencer Perceval is shot to death as he enters the House of Commons lobby. His assailant is a bankrupt London businessman.

Jews are emancipated in Russia and Prussia.

1813

Prussia and Austria declare war on France. Napoleon's forces are defeated in Germany at the Battle of Leipzig. French troops are expelled from the Netherlands.

Germany establishes the Iron Cross, a medal for distinguished military service.

Sweden abolishes the slave trade.

THE WORLD

1814

Denmark cedes Norway to Sweden in the Treaty of Kiel. Norway gains a measure of independence but accepts Sweden's Charles XIII (1809) as king. Russia gains control over Finland, previously under Swedish rule.

Holland abandons the slave trade.

France is defeated by the allied armies of Austria, Britain, Portugal, Prussia, Russia and Sweden in the War of Liberation. Napoleon is exiled to Elba, an island off the Italian coast. Bourbon King Louis XVIII takes the French throne and rules until 1824.

After the first abdication of Napoleon I, the Treaty of Paris is signed between France and an alliance that includes Britain, Russia, Austria and Prussia.

Pope Pius VII reestablishes the Jesuit order, the Inquisition and the Index — the Roman Catholic Church's list of forbidden books.

In Spain, the Bourbon kings are returned to power after Napoleon's defeat. Ferdinand VII regains the throne and rules until 1833.

Anglican clergyman Samuel Marsden of Britain heads the first missionary expedition to New Zealand. He introduces sheep to the island and fights for the rights of the native Maoris against European colonists.

Seychelles is established as a dependency of Mauritius.

English engineer George Stephenson builds the first practical steam locomotive.

THE WORLD

1814-1815

After Napoleon's defeat and exile, the Congress of Vienna redraws the map of Europe. The outcomes are as follows: Louis XVIII returns to the throne of France. Italy is divided into seven regions with no immediate hope of reunification. Poland is divided again among Russia, Prussia and Austria, though the cities of Cracow and Warsaw are granted some autonomy. Napoleon's Confederation of the Rhine is disbanded and the German states and Liechtenstein are loosely united into the German Confederation, in which Austria and Prussia come to vie for leadership. Prussia acquires Saxony and part of Westphalia and the Rhine province; West Pomerania also becomes part of Prussia. Britain regains Ceylon and Cape Colony, some territory in the West Indies, and also gains control over Malta, Mauritius and the Seychelles; Austria acquires the Venetian Republic, the duchy of Milan and partial control of Parma, Modena and Tuscany; Sardinia recovers Savoy, Nice, Genoa and Piedmont. The autonomy of the Papal States is restored and Naples and Sicily (the Kingdom of the Two Sicilies) are united under Bourbon rule. The former regions of the Austrian Netherlands and the United Provinces are joined under the House of Orange as the Kingdom of the Netherlands. Russia retains Finland, Sweden acquires Norway, Denmark receives the duchy of Lauenburg. The Swiss Confederation is reestablished, and its independence and neutrality are formally recognized.

William, son of *Stadtholder* William of Orange, becomes King William I of the Netherlands as a result of the Congress of Vienna.

1814-1816

The Anglo-Nepali war occurs as a territorial dispute between British and Gurkha residents of Nepal. Results of the war are that Nepali prime minister Jung Bahadur Rana makes his office hereditary, and Britain continues to be a strong influence in Nepal.

THE WORLD

1815

Napoleon returns to France from Elba; marches on Paris; issues a new, liberal constitution; and the "Hundred Days" begin. Napoleon is defeated by forces under Arthur Wellesley, the duke of Wellington, and Prussian General Gebhard Blücher at Waterloo (in Belgium) and is banished to St. Helena in the southern Atlantic Ocean. Louis XVIII returns to Paris.

Britain's victory over Napoleon establishes it as a major world power.

Under British control, Ceylon is united for the first time and annexes the kingdom of Kandy.

The Sumbawa volcano in Indonesia erupts, killing more than 50,000 people.

In India, Rammohan Roy begins a reformation of Hindu society and religious beliefs with the founding of the Atmiya Sabha, the "society of friends." In 1828 this society becomes the Brahmo Sabha, or "society for the worship of the one true god."

Scottish inventor John London McAdam pioneers the development of road building by the use of crushed stone, now commonly referred to as macadam paving.

1816

British colonists establish the town of Bathurst on Africa's Gambia River.

The British East India Company pursues the importation of opium into China.

The Dutch regain control of Java from the British.

John VI becomes king of Portugal after the death of his mother, Maria I (1777). He rules until 1826.

Ferdinand I becomes king of the Two Sicilies. He rules until 1825. He previously ruled Naples as Ferdinand IV, and Sicily as Ferdinand III.

Shaka (Chaka) creates the militarist Zulu kingdom in Natal, southeastern Africa. He rules until 1828.

THE WORLD	THE WORLD	FOR CLASSROOM USE	FOR CLASSROOM USE	

The colony of Liberia is established in Africa by the American Colonization Society; it is located in a region already inhabited by people from more than 20 different tribes.

French chemist Joseph Nicéphore Niepce originates the concept of photography. It is perfected by Louis Jacques Mandé Daguerre after Niepce's death in 1833.

English engineer Sir Humphrey Davy invents the miner's safety lamp, although some believe that George Stephenson produced the same device the year before.

Frenchman René Laennec invents the stethoscope.

1817

Sikkim becomes a British protectorate.

Germany has a series of disastrous harvests.

Serfdom is abolished in Estonia.

Milos (Milos Obrenovich) is named prince of Serbia after the death of Karageorge (1808). Milos rules until 1839 and again from 1858 to 1860.

1817-1819

After the final Mahratta War, Britain takes control of India.

1817-1842; 1858-1903

These are the time spans generally ascribed to the Obrenovich dynasty that rules Serbia and maintains a struggle for power against the Karageorgevich family, which regains control from 1842 to 1858.

1818

Prussia establishes open trade borders between its provinces.

Charles XIV (Jean Baptiste Jules Bernadotte) becomes king of Sweden and Norway after the death of his adopted father, Charles XIII (1809). Charles XIV rules until 1844.

1818-Present

This is the time span generally ascribed to the Bernadotte dynasty that rules Sweden.

1819

Sir Thomas Stamford Bingley Raffles establishes Singapore as a British trading post under the British East India Company. The island is nearly uninhabited before Raffles's arrival, but soon becomes an important base to challenge the Dutch post at Malacca for control of trade in the area.

In England, a meeting called to request the repeal of the corn laws, which severely limit the import and export of grains, results in many injuries and deaths. This event comes to be known as the Peterloo (Manchester) Massacre.

1810

through

1819

NATIVE AMERICAN	NATIVE AMERICAN	AFRICAN AMERICAN	AFRICAN AMERICAN

1820 through 1829

NATIVE AMERICAN

1820

Secretary of War John C. Calhoun advocates the breakup of tribal life and a "guardianship" status for Native Americans.

1822

Jedidiah Morse publishes *A Report to the Secretary of War — On Indian Affairs.*

The "factory system" established in 1795 is abolished; goods on hand are sold at public auction. Trade with Indians is subsequently handled by private traders.

1823

The Supreme Court, in *Johnson and Graham's Lessee* v. *McIntosh,* recognizes aboriginal property rights and the right of Indians to use their property "at their own discretion." However, Native Americans cannot sell land to anyone except the United States government.

1824

Secretary of War Calhoun creates a Bureau of Indian Affairs within the War Department.

The Chumash Indians revolt against Spanish rule in Santa Barbara, California.

1825

The Treaty of Prairie du Chien (in Wisconsin) is signed by representatives of the Sioux, Chippewa and other midwestern tribes. By the terms of this agreement, the tribes place themselves under the patronage of the United States, agree to peace among themselves, and accept new boundaries of their respective territories.

Congress adopts a policy of removal of eastern Native American tribes to lands west of the Mississippi River.

Alexis de Tocqueville, a French social philosopher visiting the United States, criticizes the Native American removal policy, saying, "They kindly take the Indian by the hand and lead them to a grave far from the lands of their fathers.... It is accomplished with felicity, tranquility, legality, philanthropy and all without the shedding of blood. It is impossible to destroy mankind with more respect for the laws of humanity."

NATIVE AMERICAN

1827

The Cherokee Nation, one of the Five Civilized Tribes, adopts its first constitution at New Echota, Georgia, and elects Chief John Ross as president. The Georgia state legislature nullifies the constitution.

Illinois law declares African Americans, Native Americans and *mulattos* (people of combined African and European ethnicity) incompetent to be witnesses in court against European Americans.

1828

The Cherokee Phoenix, the first Native American newspaper, is published at New Echota, Georgia, in English and Cherokee, using the characters of the syllabary created by Sequoyah.

1829

Gold is discovered on Cherokee land. Only licensed persons are technically allowed to enter, but unlicensed mining operations create a period of lawlessness.

AFRICAN AMERICAN

1820

The Missouri Compromise admits Missouri to the Union as a slave state, but provides for jury trials for enslaved African Americans; equal punishments for enslaved African Americans and free European Americans for the same offenses; and court-assigned counsel for enslaved people accused of crimes.

Maine's constitution gives all its male citizens the right to vote and the right to an education, regardless of race.

Much of the objection against slavery appears in local papers. Elihu Embree publishes *The Emancipator* in Jonesborough, Tennessee.

1821

The American Colonization Society founds the colony of Liberia, in West Africa.

Maine law forbids interracial marriages and nullifies such marriages already existing.

The African Company, the first all-African American theater group, begins performing in New York City.

Abolitionist Benjamin Lundy, a supporter of colonization, travels widely in hopes of finding an ideal location for freed African Americans. Lundy begins publication of the *Genius of Universal Emancipation*, which continues until 1835. In that year he founds a Philadelphia publication, later renamed the *Pennsylvania Freeman* under its new editor and antislavery proponent, John Greenleaf Whittier.

1822

A major slave insurrection is planned for more than five years in Charleston, South Carolina, by Denmark Vessey and his chief aide Peter Poyas. Recruits are organized into units and weapons and disguises are made and stored. Almost 9,000 enslaved Africans are organized to participate, but two weeks before the planned revolt the leaders are betrayed by an informer. Vessey and more than 30 of his organizers are captured. They refuse to reveal the names of the other planners and participators in the insurrection and are later hanged.

AFRICAN AMERICAN

James Varick is elected as bishop of the African Methodist Episcopal (A.M.E.) Zion Church.

The first public school for African Americans opens in Philadelphia.

1824

The city government of New York assumes the support of seven African free schools; this gives African American children in that city access to free education even before the same is available to European American students.

Dartmouth College in Hanover, New Hampshire, admits an African American to whom it had previously denied admission, after widespread student protest at the college. The admission of African American students soon becomes school policy.

1825

Scottish American reformer Frances (Fanny) Wright establishes Nashoba, a colony for free African Americans, near Memphis, Tennessee. Wright is influenced by the work of Robert Owen at New Harmony, Indiana. However, plagued by administrative problems and hampered by disease, Nashoba fails. In 1830 the African Americans remaining in the colony move to Haiti.

Explorer James Beckwourth travels with fur trader and mountain man William Henry Ashley in his expeditions to the Rocky Mountains. Married to a Native American, Beckwourth later becomes a chief of the Crow nation.

1826

John Russwurm graduates from Bowdoin College in Maine, becoming the first African American to graduate from a United States college.

A South Carolina court rules that free African Americans may own real estate.

In Maryland, free African Americans are given a small payment after release from prison, and are then banished from the state.

AFRICAN AMERICAN	ASIAN AMERICAN	EUROPEAN AMERICAN	FOR CLASSROOM USE	

AFRICAN AMERICAN

1827

Freedom's Journal, the first newspaper owned and edited by African Americans, begins publication in New York City. Its editors are Samuel E. Cornish and John Russwurm.

Illinois law states that African Americans, Native Americans and *mulattos* are incompetent to testify in court against European Americans.

1829

David Walker's book, *Walker's Appeal, in Four Articles, Together with a Preamble, to the Coloured Citizens of the World, but in Particular and Very Expressly to Those of the United States of America,* is published and widely circulated. His call for violence causes great concern. Walker was born free in North Carolina, migrated to Boston in 1827, opened a retail clothing store and spent his spare time studying slavery, from reading about ancient Egypt to observing his enslaved contemporaries. His mysterious death in 1830 fails to stop the book's popularity.

ASIAN AMERICAN

1828

The Hung Tai Company starts the first sugar mill in Hawaii, on the island of Maui.

EUROPEAN AMERICAN

1821

American employers offer to pay the passage for English calico-printers, urging these tradesmen to bring their machines with them.

1821-1830

During this decade, approximately 50,000 Irish people come to live in the United States.

1825

The first group of 52 Norwegian immigrants arrives in the United States. They are mostly religious dissenters.

British social reformer Robert Owen purchases an interest in New Harmony, Indiana, but is unsuccessful in building a model town and textile mill as he had done in Scotland.

1826

A new wave of Scotch-Irish immigration surges. Weavers and spinners find jobs in textile industries. Those who were farm hands work in cities as laborers, draymen and servants.

1827

Florida law restricts voting to European Americans.

The first Mardi Gras celebration is organized by French American students in New Orleans.

1828

Laws passed in the German states of Bavaria and Württemberg that discriminate against Jews create a mass exodus of German Jews to America.

Two Irish communities are established in Texas, which is a part of Mexico at the time. James Power and James Hewitson lead 200 families to Refugio. A second group, with Patric McGloin and John Mullen leading them, make their homes at San Patricio.

1820 through 1829

HISPANIC AMERICAN	HISPANIC AMERICAN	FOR CLASSROOM USE	FOR CLASSROOM USE

1820 through 1829

1820

A three-year liberal period begins in Spain; during this time several concessions are authorized for Puerto Rico. The island is considered a province of Spain. Demetrio O'Daly and later José M. Quinōnes represent Puerto Rico in the Spanish Cortes (Parliament).

1821

Mexico gains independence from Spain. New Mexico and Texas are provinces of Mexico, and California is a Mexican territory.

Spanish missions in the Southwest are secularized, and church land is ceded to the Mexican government.

A rebellion of enslaved Africans takes place in Bayamón, Puerto Rico.

Venezuelan and Dominican refugees come to Puerto Rico as a result of wars for independence in those countries.

Antonio Valero, a Puerto Rican general fighting for Simón Bolívar's army, proposes a plan to liberate Puerto Rico.

The Ducondray-Holstein expedition leaves New York City en route to liberate Puerto Rico from Spain. Spanish authorities discover the plot, and participants in Puerto Rico are executed. The expedition's ships and weapons are confiscated in Curazao.

Governor Melgares of New Mexico renews war against the Navajos.

William Becknell and a group of traders reach Santa Fe to open the Santa Fe Trail.

1822

Joseph Hernández becomes the first Florida territorial — and the first Hispanic — delegate to the United States Congress. Two years later he is elected president of Florida's territorial legislature.

1822-1837

Under the tyranny of Spanish Governor Miguel de la Torre, the lives of Puerto Ricans are strictly regulated.

1823

Puerto Rican pirate Roberto Cofresi, who allegedly stole from the rich and gave to the poor, is captured and executed by firing squad.

The Puerto Rican and Cuban delegates to the Spanish Cortes introduce a bill requesting autonomous powers for the islands.

Stephen Austin brings European families to Texas under the Empresario system.

A grant is secured by Martín de Léon to move Mexican families north into Texas. In the next year, de Léon establishes a community that will become Victoria, Texas.

1823-1824

All the missions around San Antonio are secularized and their lands are distributed to local citizens.

1825

Comanches peacefully occupy San Antonio.

1825-1827

Mexican tax assessors visit Yaqui lands to raise revenues. The Yaquis protest, and Mexican troops are sent in. The Yaquis, under Juan de la Banderas, defeat a 200-man Mexican force. Some Opata tribesmen join the rebellion until Mexican officials offer concessions, and peace is largely restored.

1826

The Mexican government passes legislation to maintain its system of *presidios* (forts) in the far northern frontier. This prompts Hayden Edwards in Texas to call for independence.

174

1820

The United States census reports the country's population at 9.6 million. More than 80 percent of those employed have jobs in agriculture.

Immigration to the United States totals 8,385, of which 7,690 come from Europe, 6 from Asia, 1 from Africa, 1 from Oceania, 387 from the Americas and 300 are not specifically identified.

By the terms of the Missouri Compromise, Maine, a free state, becomes the 23rd state to join the Union; Missouri is admitted as a slave state one year later. Slavery is barred in the rest of the Louisiana Purchase territory north of parallel 36° 30′.

New York City is the country's largest city, with a population of more than 123,500.

The city of Indianapolis, Indiana, is founded on the White River.

Indiana University is founded at Bloomington.

American sea captain and whaler Nathaniel Brown Palmer first sights a peninsula in Antarctica he calls Palmer Land. Later renamed Graham Land by the British, this peninsula is now referred to as either Palmer Peninsula or Antarctic Peninsula.

Colonists from the United Provinces of La Plata (specifically Argentina) remove Spanish rule from — and reinhabit — Soledad on the Falkland Islands.

After failing to fend off a Portuguese invasion, Montevideo is occupied and Uruguay is annexed to Brazil.

Pedro remains as regent of Brazil when his father, King John VI of Portugal, goes home.

c. 1820

Joseph Aspdin invents portland cement, which hardens under water.

1820-1822

The institution of slavery in South and Central America collapses as many enslaved Africans and Indians join the revolutionary movements, escape their bondage during the upheaval, and threaten rebellion. Moves toward emancipation are seen in the laws of several of the new governments.

1820s-1830s

Frances (Fanny) Wright, a brilliant and eccentric Scottish American woman, tours the United States speaking out for educational and legal rights for women.

1821

James Monroe serves a second term as president of the United States; Daniel D. Tompkins is vice president. Both are Democratic-Republicans.

Missouri becomes the 24th state to join the Union.

The United States acquires Florida from Spain.

The first free public high school, the English High School, is opened in Boston, Massachusetts. The New York state legislature requires all localities to pay for education with tax dollars.

The George Washington University is founded at Washington, D.C. The Female Seminary in Troy, New York, is established by Emma Willard following her opening of a smaller school at Waterford in 1819.

In Mexico, Agustín de Iturbide and Vicente Guerrero proclaim the Plan of Iguala; the Spanish army is defeated and Mexico wins independence from Spain with the Treaty of Córdoba.

The new Mexican government invites United States immigrants to move into northern Texas (a province of Mexico at the time), on the two conditions that they: 1) agree to convert to Catholicism; and 2) abide by Mexican law. By 1835 Americans outnumber Mexicans in Texas by a 10-to-1 ratio.

Connecticut-born Moses Austin receives from the Mexican commandant of Texas a grant for 200,000 acres of land and permission to move 200 European American families into the area. After his death, his work is completed by his son, Stephen F. Austin.

General José de San Martín lands in Peru. Lima declares independence.

Simón Bolívar and his troops defeat Spanish forces at the Battle of Carabobo, and free Venezuela from Spain permanently. The next year Bolívar's army captures Quito and Guayaquil (now in Ecuador) and annexes them to Gran Colombia. Panama also becomes part of Gran Colombia.

c. 1821

A second "Great Awakening" takes place in the United States, led by Charles G. Finney in New York. It leads to the formation of many revival religions and has a great appeal to women whose frontier and urban lives are very difficult.

1821-1830

Immigration to the United States totals 143,439, of which 98,797 come from Europe, 30 from Asia, 16 from Africa, 2 from Oceania, 11,564 from the Americas and 33,030 are not specifically identified.

1822

The Santa Fe Trail, which runs from Independence, Missouri, to Santa Fe, New Mexico, opens and remains active until 1880. At that time the Atchison, Topeka and Santa Fe Railroad begins operation along this same route.

Agustín de Iturbide declares himself emperor of Mexico. He rules for one year.

Brazil proclaims its independence from Portugal in the "Grito de Yipranga" (Yipranga Cry). In contrast to other South American countries, Brazilian independence is won without bloodshed.

Prince Pedro becomes Emperor Pedro I of Brazil. He rules until 1831.

Simón Bolívar and Antonio José de Sucre lead their forces to victory in the Battle of Pichincha and thereby free Ecuador from Spanish control. Bolívar and San Martin join forces in Guayaquil (now in Ecuador), to coordinate a final assault on Peru. San Martin retires after putting his troops under Bolívar's command.

On the island of Hispaniola, Santo Domingo is overrun and annexed by Haiti.

1822-1844

Repeated uprisings on Spanish Dominica lead to the country's declaration of independence from Spain; slavery is abolished and Dominica unites with Haiti until 1844. The redistribution of land makes landowners of formerly enslaved Africans and Indians.

1823

President James Monroe announces the Monroe Doctrine that defines the special relationship between Latin America and the United States. It provides that the American continents may no longer be colonized; that the American political system is different from that of Europe; and that the United States will not become involved with the internal affairs of European powers and expects the same from them. This doctrine interferes with Simon Bolívar's plan of a strong trade and defense alliance with Britain.

Nebraska's first permanent European American community is the village of Bellevue, on the Missouri River.

Washington College (now Trinity) is founded at Hartford, Connecticut.

In Mexico, military and civilian government officials under the leadership of Guadalupe Victoria and Antonio López de Santa Anna join together to overthrow Iturbide and establish a new constitution that creates a republican form of government. The constitution is enacted in 1824.

1820

through

1829

1820 through 1829

Initially, five small regions south of Mexico are a part of Mexico. When Agustin Iturbide is ousted in 1823, these southern regions (Costa Rica, Guatemala, Honduras, Nicaragua and San Salvador) unite to become the Federal Republic of Central America.

Grenada grants full citizenship to free Africans and Indians.

1823-1832

Non-European residents in the Caribbean countries continue to fight for their rights. Grenada grants full citizenship to non-Europeans in 1823; similar freedoms are in place in Jamaica and Barbados by 1832.

1824

The United States House of Representatives elects John Quincy Adams to the presidency over Andrew Jackson. This vote is necessary because, of the four candidates running in the national election (the other two being William Crawford and Henry Clay), none received a majority of the votes.

Congressman Henry Clay from Kentucky uses the term "American System" to explain his program of self-sufficiency, which includes the creation of a national bank, tariffs imposed on imported goods and federal financing of the construction of roads and canals in the West.

In *Gibbons* v. *Ogden*, the United States Supreme Court supports congressional power over commercial transactions within state borders when a federal license issued to Thomas Gibbons to operate a boat across the Hudson River interferes with a New York state license issued to Aaron Ogden, successor to Robert Fulton.

Explorer Jedediah Strong Smith finds an alternate southern passage across the Rocky Mountains into the Great Basin. Mountain man and guide Jim Bridger is the first European American to visit Great Salt Lake in Utah.

Two significant labor strikes occur in the Northeast during this time, both involving women workers. In the first strike organized entirely by and for women, weavers at a textile mill in Pawtucket Rhode Island protest their 12-and 14-hour work days. In the cotton mill at Dover, New York, women workers walk off the job in protest of a new regulation from the mill owner fining them the equivalent of a third of a day's pay if they are five minutes late for work.

Rensselaer School (Polytechnic Institute) is founded at Troy, New York. It is the first private engineering and technical school in the United States.

The first Canadian medical school, Montreal Medical Institute, opens at Montreal. Two years later it becomes part of the new McGill University.

The Brazilian constitution is proclaimed, providing for a constitutional monarchy and a bicameral legislature. This form of government continues until 1889.

Simón Bolívar becomes emperor of Peru. His victory at Ayachucho marks the final defeat of Spanish rule in South America.

Freedom is granted to enslaved people in the Federal Republic of Central America.

1824-1855

As westward migration begins in the United States, Canada's western regions see a similar, though smaller-scale movement. The Hudson's Bay Company builds a string of trading posts in Canada's Northwest, including four in territory that will later be part of the United States.

1825

John Quincy Adams becomes the sixth president of the United States; John C. Calhoun is vice president. Both are Democratic-Republicans.

The Erie Canal between Lake Erie and the Hudson River is opened, providing water access to the Great Lakes from the Atlantic Ocean. The opening of the canal draws a flood of immigrants to Michigan, especially from New York and New England.

As a child, Kamehameha III becomes king of Hawaii after the death of his half-brother, Kamehameha II (1819), in 1824. Kamehameha III comes of age in 1833 and rules until 1854.

Scottish American reformer Frances (Fanny) Wright establishes Nashoba, a colony for free African Americans, near Memphis, Tennessee. Wright is influenced by the work of Robert Owen at New Harmony. However, plagued by administrative problems and hampered by disease, the colony fails. In 1830 the remaining African Americans move to Haiti.

Omaha, Nebraska, is established as a trading station. It receives its first main colonization in 1854 and is incorporated as a city in 1857.

Akron, Ohio, a site first visited by Europeans in 1807, is established. It becomes a city in 1865.

Britain and Russia sign a treaty regarding territory in northwestern North America.

Upper Peru (now Bolivia), which has resisted independence for fear of a slave revolt, is forcibly liberated by General Antonio José de Sucre, and the nation of Bolivia is created with Sucre as president. Cuba and Puerto Rico are the only colonies in America that remain under Spanish control. These two countries, which have large enslaved populations, fear that slave uprisings will increase the bloodshed and chaos if a revolution were attempted.

1825-1828

Brazil and Argentina fight for control of the region that is now Uruguay. The two powers eventually agree to the establishment of the state of Uruguay.

1825-1827

The survey and marking of the Santa Fe Trail from Independence, Missouri, to Santa Fe, New Mexico, is completed. Nearly 800 miles long, the trail comes to serve as a major caravan route for colonists migrating to the West.

1826

Explorer Jedediah Smith makes his first expedition across the Sierra Nevada and into California.

Simón Bolívar calls the Congress of Panama in an attempt to establish a South American union. However, many people resent Bolívar's dictatorial tactics, and the union he sought never comes to pass.

1826-1860

A period of extreme political upheaval occurs in the Spanish American colonies as *caudillas* (strongmen) fight over dwindling public funds. Mining and export agriculture industries become dormant, and much of the Indian population returns to subsistence farming.

1827

The Democratic Party is organized in the United States.

Massachusetts becomes one of the first states to require towns to provide free high school educations for their residents.

The Third United States Regiment, newly assigned to Cantonment (now Fort) Leavenworth, builds barracks there, thus beginning the first permanent European American community in the area that will become Kansas.

The city of Bytown is founded by Colonel John By on the Rideau Canal, Canada. In 1854 its name is changed to Ottawa.

The last known member of the native Beothuk tribe, Nancy Shanawdithit, dies in St. John's, Newfoundland, Canada.

All Spaniards are ordered to leave Mexico.

THE AMERICAS	THE AMERICAS	FOR CLASSROOM USE	FOR CLASSROOM USE	

1828

The Tariff Act of 1828, which many southerners call the "Tariff of Abominations," is passed by Congress and signed into law by the president to reduce imports. Vice President John C. Calhoun, a staunch advocate of states' rights, writes the "South Carolina Exposition and Protest" against the new law, arguing for the states' right to nullify the law.

The Workingman's Party is established in the United States.

Construction begins on the Baltimore & Ohio, the first passenger railroad line in the United States, chartered to George Brown and partially financed by Charles Carroll. The first section between Baltimore and Ellicott Mills (now Ellicott City) in Maryland opens in 1830. Horses, which pull the first railroad cars, are soon replaced by the steam-driven locomotive, invented by Peter Cooper. One of the first trains built is called the *Tom Thumb*.

Noah Webster publishes the *American Dictionary of the English Language*.

The Society of Beneficence of Buenos Aires is created in Argentina to promote education for girls and women. Education for women is a symbol of progress and culture in many of the new republics, and Brazil and the Caribbean.

After defeating Brazilian forces, Uruguay gains its independence under the leadership of Juan Antonio Lavalleja. The Treaty of Rio de Janeiro confirms this.

1829

Andrew Jackson becomes the seventh president of the United States; John C. Calhoun is vice president. Both are Democrats.

Rochester Institute of Technology is founded in New York.

United States inventor William Austin Burt patents his typographer, the ancestor of the modern-day typewriter.

Slavery is abolished in Mexico.

Santa Anna leads Mexican forces in thwarting a Spanish attempt to retake Mexico.

A liberal revolt takes place in Mexico; Vicente Guerrero rules the country briefly. However, later this year he is overthrown in a revolt led by his vice president Anastasio Bustamante..

Juan José Flores comes to power in Ecuador as that country's first president and dictator.

Juan Manuel de Rosas comes to power as governor of Buenos Aires; he acts as dictator over the feuding regions of Argentina. He rules until 1832 and again from 1835 to 1852.

c. 1829

United States physicist Joseph Henry constructs an electromagnetic motor and invents the electromagnetic telegraph.

1829-1833

Arctic explorer (Sir) John Ross, under the financial support of Sir Felix Booth, begins explorations for a Northwest Passage. During his trip, he charts and names the Boothia Peninsula, near Baffin Bay, Canada, for his patron.

1820

through

1829

1820 through 1829

1820

Revolutions take place in Spain and Portugal over the need for liberal constitutional reform. In Spain, the Inquisition is abolished.

British colonists arrive in Cape Colony and Grahamstown, which was established in 1812 as a fort.

As mass production techniques become popular during Europe's Industrial Revolution, skilled artisans see widespread unemployment.

Britain annexes all of Australia.

Egyptian Muhammad Ali and his troops begin the conquest of Nubia (northern Sudan). Ali's primary objective is the trade in gold and slaves.

The Spanish monarchy essentially loses its ability to suppress the revolutions in South America after a military revolt in Cadíz in which Spanish troops refuse to fight in America.

John VI reluctantly accedes to demands of Portugal's nobility and returns to Portugal from Brazil.

Jesuits are forced to leave Rome.

George IV becomes king of Great Britain and Ireland after the death of his father, George III (1760). George IV rules until 1830.

1820s-1902

The Ashanti (Asante) resist conquest by British forces.

1820s

Russian navigator A. I. Krusenstern gives the Gilbert Islands their name in honor of British Captain Thomas Gilbert who visited the island group in 1788.

Two of King Shaka Zulu's generals, Mzilikazi and Soshangana, establish their own separate kingdoms, Ndebele in western Zimbabwe and Shangane to the east.

1821

The Hongi Hika's wars begin in New Zealand; more than 2,000 are killed at Tamaki.

Daoguang (Tao-Kuang) becomes emperor of China. Because of the importing of opium, China develops an unfavorable balance of trade. Daoguang rules until 1850.

Charles Felix becomes king of Sardinia after the abdication of his brother, Victor Emmanuel I (1802). Charles Felix rules until 1831.

An agreement is reached between members of the American Colonization Society and local African chiefs to establish a colony for Africans formerly held in slavery in the United States. Cape Mesurado is chosen for the site and it is set up in 1822. Although the names Liberia and Monrovia are suggested by Ralph Gurley, an early governor of the colony, missionary Iehudi Ashmun — also one of the first governors of the colony — is recognized as the real founder of Liberia.

English scientist Michael Faraday develops the electric motor.

1822

Greece draws up a liberal constitution and declares its independence from the Ottoman Empire. Turks seize the island of Chios, massacre most of the citizens and then invade mainland Greece.

British forces oppose the Ashanti people in western Africa in the first Anglo-Ashanti War. The war continues for nine years.

An earthquake hits Aleppa in Asia Minor.

British explorer Hugh Clapperton begins his expedition into Africa. In 1823 he becomes one of the first Europeans to reach Lake Chad.

Jean François Champollion deciphers Egyptian hieroglyphics using the Rosetta Stone.

c. 1822

French scientist Joseph N. Niepce, who created a photographic negative in c. 1816, produces a positive image directly from an exposed plate. This is a major advance in the development of modern photography, a process that is perfected by Louis Jacques Mandé Daguerre after Niepce's death.

1823

Switzerland reinforces its policy of neutrality and refuses asylum to any political refugee.

In Ireland, Daniel O'Connell leads in the establishment of the Catholic Association, to fight for political and civil rights of Ireland's Catholic people.

Ferdinand von Wrangel, an explorer under Russian financing, proves that Asia and North America are separate land masses.

c. 1823

The discovery of an indigenous tea plant in northern India begins a new industry whose effect is a reduction of the Chinese monopoly in this product.

William Wilberforce and Thomas Fowell Buxton form an antislavery society in Britain.

1824

In the First Burmese War, Britain begins the piecemeal annexation of Burma. This war continues until 1826. Britain seizes more territory in the Second and Third Burmese Wars.

The British establish a community in Natal (southeastern Africa).

The British Parliament repeals the Settlement Act of 1662.

Turks capture the island of Ipsara from the Greeks but are later defeated at Mitylene.

The sultan of Johor cedes Singapore to the British East India Company.

Britain trades Bencoolen, Sumatra, to the Netherlands in exchange for Malacca.

Charles X becomes king of France after the death of his brother, Louis XVIII (1814). Charles X rules until 1830.

Rama III (Nangklao) becomes king of Siam (Thailand) after the reign of Rama II (1809). Rama III until 1851.

1825

Great Britain repeals laws prohibiting emigration.

The Decembrist Revolt in Russia is suppressed.

The Stockton-Darlington Railway opens in Britain. Built by George Stephenson, it is the first operational railroad in the world.

Nicholas I becomes czar of Russia after the death of his father, Alexander I (1801). Nicholas I rules until 1855.

Louis I becomes king of Bavaria after the death of his father, Maximilian I (1809). Louis I rules until 1848.

Francis I becomes king of the Two Sicilies after the death of his father, Ferdinand I (1816). Francis I rules until 1830.

1825-1837

Railway lines open in the United States and several European countries. Railroads are in use worldwide by the late 1800s.

1826

Siam (Thailand) and Great Britain sign a commercial treaty.

The First Burmese War ends with the Treaty of Yandabu, through which Britain annexes Manipur, Arakan, Tenasserim and Assam.

An economic depression in the Irish textile trade causes severe distress to Belfast cotton spinners.

A cholera epidemic begins in India and spreads to other countries.

C. L. Force, originally from Boston, Massachusetts, begins publication of the *Liberia Herald*, the first newspaper to be printed in Africa.

Singapore is annexed to the Straits Settlements; the city remains a valuable trade port for British interests throughout the Malay Peninsula.

Portugal's King John VI (1816) dies. His son, Peter IV, abdicates the throne of Portugal, accepts the throne of Brazil as Pedro I and names his young daughter as Queen Maria II of Portugal. Maria's uncle, Miguel, serves as regent to the queen and later marries her. Miguel exercises sole and absolute authority until 1834, when Brazilian forces under Pedro I topple him and restore Maria II to the throne.

Dost Muhammad begins his reign as *emir* (Muslim prince or commander) of Afghanistan. He rules until 1863.

1827

After an unsuccessful revolt against its Thai overlords, the Laotian kingdom of Vientiane is abolished.

Turkey rejects the urging of European powers to end its war with Greece. Egyptian forces led by General Ibrahim capture Athens. In the Battle of Navarino, the Turkish and Egyptian fleets are destroyed by a combined British, French and Russian fleet under the command of British Admiral Edward Codrington.

German physicist Georg Simon Ohm discovers the law of electrical resistance that bears his name.

1828

Russia declares war on Turkey.

An earthquake hits Echigo in Japan and causes approximately 25,000 deaths.

In the Treaty of Turkmanchay, Persia (Iran) cedes Erivan (Armenia) to Russia, which also maintains a fleet on the Caspian Sea.

French explorer René Caillié becomes the first European to visit Timbuktu (western Africa) and return.

Bengali spiritual leader Rammohan Roy shows proof that the tradition of burning a widow on her husband's funeral pyre, is not supported by the Hindu scriptures. The following year, British governor-general Lord Bentinck orders an end to this practice.

1829

Through the Treaty of Adrianople between Russia and the Ottoman Turks, Serbia becomes an autonomous state with guarantees of religious freedom. The treaty also promises independence to Greece — a move sought by France and Britain; allows Russia temporary occupation of Moldavia and Walachia; and cedes territory along the Black Sea to Russia.

The Catholic Emancipation Act removes most civil restrictions on Catholics in England and Ireland.

The *Rocket*, a locomotive produced by George Stephenson, proves to be the fastest in the world.

French educator Louis Braille, blind since age three, develops his system of writing with raised points for sight-impaired people.

1820

through

1829

NATIVE AMERICAN	NATIVE AMERICAN	AFRICAN AMERICAN	AFRICAN AMERICAN

1830 through 1839

NATIVE AMERICAN

1830

Congress passes the Removal Act. Federal troops begin the forced march of five southeastern tribes to lands west of the Mississippi River.

An Alabama law extends state jurisdiction over Native Americans, but does not give them political or civil rights.

1831

In *Cherokee Nation* v. *Georgia,* the United States Supreme Court defines Native American tribes as "domestic dependent nations." The decision states that American Indians have "an unquestionable...right to the lands which they occupy, until that right shall be extinguished by a voluntary cession to our government...."

The Menominee, Six Nations, Ottawa and Shawnee tribes cede lands in Michigan, Wisconsin and Ohio to the United States government in exchange for western lands, goods, annuities and education.

1831-1832

The Black Hawk War is fought in Wisconsin, between Sauk and Fox Indians under Chief Black Hawk and the Illinois militia led by General Atkinson. After an agreement to abandon their ancestral home and move west, the Sauk suffer crop failure and starvation in their new lands. Chief Black Hawk leads his people back to Illinois. When an Indian with truce flag in hand is murdered by a European colonist, Black Hawk is enraged, and leads his band to massacre the colonists. The Sauk tribe is pursued and virtually destroyed at the mouth of the Bad Axe River by Atkinson's volunteers, aided by a Sioux war party. Black Hawk realizes he is trapped, and displays a truce flag, which is ignored. Most of the Sauk, including old men, women and children are killed. The chief and a handful of others escape. Black Hawk surrenders to the Winnebago Indians, who in turn surrender him to government authorities. He is released in 1833, and returns to the poorer lands that the Sauk remnant occupies in Iowa.

NATIVE AMERICAN

1834

The Indian Intercourse Act officially establishes Indian Territory in Oklahoma, Nebraska and Kansas.

By this time 60 schools are established for Native Americans by six religious organizations and by Native Americans themselves. One hundred thirty-seven teachers are employed and almost 2,000 children are enrolled.

1835-1842

The Second Seminole War takes place in Florida, with forces under Chief Osceola eventually being defeated by United States forces.

1836

When Texas declares its independence, the Texas Rangers are organized to ride against the Comanche tribe.

1836-1838

A smallpox epidemic spreads among the Tlingit, Tsimshian and other Northwest coast tribes, as well as tribes of the upper Missouri River.

1837

The Mandan Indian band living near Fort Clark in North Dakota is almost completely destroyed by smallpox.

1837-1851

Kennekuk, the Kickapoo prophet, teaches among the Indians of Kansas. Many Potawatomies become his followers and are incorporated into the northern Kickapoo group.

1838

Government troops forcibly move the Cherokee from Georgia to Indian Territory. This is the Cherokee Trail of Tears; almost one-third of the tribe perishes on the journey.

AFRICAN AMERICAN

1831

In Southampton County, Virginia, a revolt of enslaved African Americans is led by Nat Turner, an enslaved African American minister and evangelist. Declaring the coming of a day of judgement for slaveholders, Turner leads his followers from plantation to plantation and kills 55 European Americans in two days of terror. A general panic occurs in the South and more than 3,000 European Americans arrive in the county to suppress the revolt. More than 100 African Americans, both free and enslaved, who were not involved in the conspiracy are killed by militiamen pursuing Turner and his men. Turner hides in the Dismal Swamp for almost two months. He is finally apprehended and hanged with 16 of his followers. This insurrection is so serious that it highly influences the passage of the Black Codes, designed to prevent this type of activity from happening again.

William Lloyd Garrison begins publishing the abolitionist periodical *The Liberator* in Boston. He is active in the establishment of the New England Anti-Slavery Society and two years later, helps found the American Anti-Slavery Society, which he serves as president from 1843 to 1865.

In Philadelphia, Pennsylvania, free African Americans come together for the first Annual Convention of the People of Color. Among other things, the attendees decide to oppose Liberian colonization efforts by the American Colonization Society, study the possibility of relocating African Americans to Canada and raise funds for a proposed African American industrial school in the United States.

1832

The Shiloh Presbyterian Church is organized in New York City. Henry Highland Garnet later serves as minister.

AFRICAN AMERICAN

1833

Prudence Crandell, who opened a school for women in Canterbury, Connecticut two years earlier, extends the school's enrollment to provide for the education of African American women. She is arrested and placed on trial for violating a local law making that form of instruction illegal. Although she is acquitted on appeal, constant threats to the school and its students force its closing in 1834.

Lucretia Mott, whose home is a station on the Underground Railroad, is one of the organizers of the Philadelphia Female Anti-Slavery Society, after women are not allowed full participation in male anti-slavery societies.

The American Anti-Slavery Society is founded in Philadelphia. Arthur Tappan serves as its first president.

1834

Free African Americans in Philadelphia receive passports stating that they are citizens of the United States.

Racial unrest and riots occur in Philadelphia and Columbia, Pennsylvania; Palmyra and Utica, New York; and several New Jersey cities.

South Carolina enacts a law prohibiting the education of African American children.

1835

Michigan's constitution limits voting rights to European American males. North Carolina repeals by a narrow vote the section of its constitution that would have given the franchise to all free adult males who own property. The state thus denies African Americans the right to vote.

Kentucky-born abolitionist and lawyer James Gillespie Birney serves briefly with the American Colonization Society. Returning to his family home, he frees his enslaved African Americans and helps found the Kentucky Antislavery Society. A believer in political action, he becomes head of the Liberty Party and unsuccessfully runs for the presidency in 1840 and 1844.

AFRICAN AMERICAN	AFRICAN AMERICAN	ASIAN AMERICAN	EUROPEAN AMERICAN	

AFRICAN AMERICAN

1836

The United States House of Representatives institutes a "gag rule," prohibiting any discussion of the slavery issue in the chamber.

1837

In Alton, Illinois, a mob murders Elijah P. Lovejoy for advocating the abolition of slavery.

Evangelist and educator Charles Grandison Finney becomes a professor of theology at Oberlin College, Ohio. He is a convincing instructor and many of his students become the leading abolitionists of this era.

William Whipper successfully operates and later owns a lumber business developed by his family. His article "An Address on Non-Resistance to Offensive Aggression," published in *The Colored American,* credits him with being one of the nation's first proponents of nonviolent resistance. He was also one of the founders of the American Moral Reform Society, established at Philadelphia in 1835.

Abolitionist Charles B. Ray becomes general agent for the *Colored American* and serves as its editor from 1839 to 1842.

1838

The term "Jim Crow" first comes into use as a synonym for an African American.

Frederick Douglass escapes from slavery in Maryland disguised as a sailor.

African Americans in the South develop escape routes to the North called the Underground Railroad.

The first African American magazine, *Mirror of Freedom,* is published in New York City.

South Carolina businessman Robert Purvis, born free in Charleston, becomes a leading advocate for abolition. One of the founders of the American Anti-Slavery Society, he devotes much of his time and resources to the Underground Railroad.

AFRICAN AMERICAN

1839

Joseph Cinque and a group of kidnapped Africans, sold into slavery at Havana, Cuba, are transported on the *Amistad* toward the island of Principe (Gulf of Guinea). A severe storm distracts the crew and Cinque leads a mutiny, overpowers the sailors and directs the captain to pilot the ship to Africa. Instead, the ship is redirected to the United States and Cinque is captured off the coast of Connecticut. In 1841 former President John Quincy Adams defends Cinque's actions in front of the United States Supreme Court, winning the group's freedom. The following year, Adams helps to secure their return to Sierra Leone.

Theodore Dwight Weld, a disciple of Charles G. Finney, and his wife, Angelina Grimké, become outspoken antislavery abolitionist leaders. Weld serves as an editor on the *Emancipator.* His most successful work, *American Slavery As It Is,* is reported to have influenced the writings of Harriet Beecher Stowe.

Stephen Slade, an enslaved African American in North Carolina, develops a new process for curing bright leaf tobacco.

ASIAN AMERICAN

1837

Maria Seise is the first Chinese woman to come to Hawaii. She stays for six years and then returns to Macau. In 1848 she arrives at San Francisco on the brig *Eagle* as a servant to a man named Charles Gillespie.

EUROPEAN AMERICAN

1830

The first women's magazine in the United States, *Godey's Lady's Book,* is published by French American Louis Antoine Godey.

Mining employers in Carbondale, Pennsylvania, offer to pay passage for Welsh miners and their families to come to the United States. By year's end, 20 Welsh families have arrived.

As the New England states continue industrialization, particularly in textile and metals manufactures, thousands of British immigrants come to work in the factories.

A wave of mass immigration begins in which Irish and German newcomers dominate. The first exodus from Poland begins, with about 1,000 refugees coming directly to the United States. The influx of Catholic immigrants results in a surge of Protestant nativism.

c. 1830

A regular trade and immigration route develops between the Azores Islands (Portuguese) and New Bedford, Massachusetts. Whaling ships bring the first substantial numbers of Portuguese immigrants to New Bedford, at this time the East Coast's primary whaling port.

1831

In this year, German immigration to America is approximately 15,000 people.

A special British government office, the Commission on Emigration, is created as an information clearinghouse for English people planning to come to the United States.

Cyrus McCormick, a Scottish American, invents the reaping machine, which comes to revolutionize American farming.

1831-1840

Approximately 540,000 immigrants come to the United States in this decade; more than 40 percent of them are Irish.

1832

A Jewish community is established at Louisville, Kentucky.

1830 through 1839

EUROPEAN AMERICAN	HISPANIC AMERICAN	HISPANIC AMERICAN	HISPANIC AMERICAN
1833 A mining survey from this time indicates that the vast majority of workers in United States mines are English and Welsh; a small percentage of miners are Scottish. **1834** In anti-Catholic violence in Charlestown, Massachusetts, an Ursuline convent is destroyed by fire. Increasing nativism is fueled by large scale Irish immigration that creates fierce job competition. **1835** Thousands of English woolens workers make their homes in the Philadelphia area, as that city becomes a center of the industry. **1836** The Ancient Order of Hibernians is established in the United States. Originally a clandestine, and sometimes violent, organization, its membership is limited to native-born Irish men. **1837** A German emigrant boarding a ship bound for America can expect to pay approximately $16 for steerage-rate passage. **1837-1839** Jewish communities are founded in Chicago, St. Louis and Cleveland. **1838** By this year there are only two Catholic priests left in Texas. A German-language newspaper, *Summeytown Bauernfreund,* offers this nativist opinion: "If more Irish come into our country, the English and the Irish will rule over us Americans."	**1830** With passage of the Colonization Law, the Mexican government officially encourages Mexican migration into Texas. The United States is the second major export market for Puerto Rico. The Mexican government passes laws to discourage Anglo American immigration into Texas; General Mier y Terán is appointed to oversee the restriction of colonization. Spanish missions in Arizona are abandoned, and the last missions in Texas are secularized. The Mexican American population of Chicago is reported at 20,000. **1830-1833** Mexican officials attempt to subjugate the Yaqui tribe. Yaquis, Opatas, Seris and other tribes unite against Mexican forces. Yaqui leader Juan de la Banderas is executed, but the rebellion continues under Husakamea. In 1833 Mexican forces withdraw, leaving the Yaquis independent. **1831** The Mexican government resumes its war against the Comanches. **1833** Mexico passes the Secularization Act and all 21 California missions are seized by the government. This ends the mission period. Mexico repeals the anti-immigration clause of the 1830 law. **1834** More than 20,000 European Americans now live in Texas. **1834-1836** All the California missions are secularized and their lands purchased by local citizens. **1835** In San Antonio, confrontation takes place between Mexican troops and European Texans.	William Barrett Travis and other Anglo Americans attack the customs house at Anáhuac, Texas in the first battle of the Texas rebellion. Texas delegates at San Felipe de Austin issue a conditional declaration of independence. Full independence is proclaimed the next year. Battles take place at the Alamo and Goliad. In California, Padrés and Híjar are arrested by Governor Figueroa, because they are seen as a Spanish threat to Californians. **1836** In the Texas rebellion, the Alamo in San Antonio is besieged and overrun by Mexican General Santa Anna, with 4,000 soldiers. Captain Juan Seguín fights at the Alamo along with nine Hispanic Texans against General Santa Anna's troops. Seguín is sent to get help before the final assault. Santa Anna's forces are defeated at the Battle of San Jacinto in Texas, and Texas declares its independence. Lorenzo de Zavala signs the Texas Declaration of Independence and is elected vice president of the Republic of Texas. Anglo Americans first attempt to evacuate San Antonio, and then try to purchase all the land. The new constitution drafted by Mexican centralists reduces regional self-government on the northern frontier. Puerto Rico exports more than 5 million pounds of cotton. **1837** Details of a plot by Quechan tribesmen to burn Guadalupe Mission in Baja California are leaked and the plot is foiled, leading to two years of peace in the northern Baja. Governor López de Baños decrees that all landless laborers in Puerto Rico must work on local plantations and must register in city rolls. **1837-1840** Comanche bands raid the lower Rio Grande valley, and reach Zacatecas, Mexico. Proclamations of rebellion against the Mexican government are issued in Sonora.	**1838** The last 17 survivors at Pecos pueblo in New Mexico are forced to abandon the village. Vincente Córdova leads rebel forces against the new Texas government, partly to oppose slavery and partly to regain Texas for Mexico. Texan forces break up the disturbance and Córdova flees south. A conspiracy to liberate Puerto Rico from Spain fails. **1839** European Americans attack native villages in northeast Texas. Chief Bowles is killed, and most of the group move north to Indian Territory (Oklahoma). A group of Kickapoos, however, moves south across the Rio Grande. Their tribesmen serve in the Mexican army, and the tribe makes its new home at Coahuila.

1830

through

1839

THE AMERICAS | THE AMERICAS | THE AMERICAS

1830

The United States census reports the country's population at approximately 12.9 million.

The era of Jacksonian Democracy, the philosophy of greater popular involvement in government, begins in the United States. President Andrew Jackson also coins the term "Kitchen Cabinet" when he relies on the advice of his friends, often meeting around the kitchen table, rather than the heads of official government agencies on policy matters.

The Mormon Church, also known as the Church of Jesus Christ of Latter Day Saints, is formed in Fayette, New York, by Joseph Smith and his followers.

Six schools for African American children are in operation in New York City; this is especially significant because impoverished European American children do not attend school.

The first section of the Baltimore & Ohio Railroad, the nation's first public, commercial railroad, opens this year. The railroad was chartered in 1827 by a businessmen's group who sought to regain some of the transit trade they lost when the Erie Canal opened (1825).

The New England states have more than a hundred textile mills. As a growing number of women and girls go to work in these factories, long hours and harsh working conditions become commonplace and bring about the first signs of discontent. Unrest grows as new European immigrants — unskilled and desperately poor — flood the industrial cities.

Anastasio Bustamante becomes president of Mexico after his forces oust Vincente Guerrero (1829). Bustamante serves until 1832 and again from 1837 until 1840.

In an attempt to maintain control of its Texas Territory, Mexico passes laws prohibiting further colonization and the importation of enslaved Africans into the region.

The Republic of Gran Colombia disintegrates after the death of Simón Bolívar. Venezuela, Colombia and Ecuador become independent countries.

c. 1830

The "prairie schooner," a wagon with a white canvas cover, begins to appear as pioneers in the United States move west. The prairie schooner is a lighter modification of the Conestoga wagon and requires fewer horses to pull it.

1830-1839

Francisco Morazán is president of the Central American federation, El Salvador.

1830s

A sharp increase in immigration to the United States begins; Irish immigrants become the dominant new group.

Temperance societies begin to arise as drinking is recognized as a national problem; most of these societies are local and church related. Women find themselves discriminated against in temperance and abolition reform movements.

1831

The Southampton Insurrection, a revolt of enslaved African Americans in Virginia, is led by Nat Turner. More than 50 European Americans die, and panic spreads across the southern states. Turner is captured and hanged.

The University of Alabama at Tuscaloosa and New York University at New York City are founded.

The *Coburg Star* is first published. Now the *Coburg Sentinel Star,* it is Canada's oldest weekly newspaper.

As a child, Pedro II becomes emperor of Brazil after the abdication of his father, Pedro I (1822). Because Brazilian liberals dislike the regent, Pedro II is declared to be of age in 1840 and is crowned in 1841. Brazil sees an increase in immigration, wealth and internal peace during his reign. Pedro II rules until 1889.

In Barbados, free African men are granted full citizenship, including the vote.

British officials force the Brazilian government to sign a treaty ending the trade in enslaved Africans, but the treaty is not enforced in Brazil. The trade continues in Brazil until after 1850.

Samuel Sharpe leads a revolt of enslaved Africans in Jamaica. This rebellion is successful enough that it is the major impetus behind Jamaica's abolishing slavery in 1840.

As a child, Pedro II becomes emperor of Brazil after the abdication of his father, Peter IV. Pedro is declared to be of age in 1840, at age 15, and rules until 1889.

1831-1840

Immigration to the United States totals 599,125, of which 495,681 come from Europe, 55 from Asia, 54 from Africa, 9 from Oceania, 33,424 from the Americas and 69,902 are not specifically identified.

1832

In an attempt to appease the southern states, the United States Congress passes the Tariff Act of 1832, which lowers duties on imported goods; South Carolina responds with the Ordinance of Nullification. Congress also enacts a law to recharter the Bank of the United States under Nicholas Biddle but President Jackson vetoes the measure.

The Oregon Trail opens, running from Independence, Missouri, to Portland and Fort Vancouver, in Oregon Country, an area whose ownership is in dispute between Britain and the United States.

John C. Calhoun, vice president under Andrew Jackson, resigns to become a United States senator from South Carolina.

American statesman and senator from New York William Learned Marcy delivers a speech in which he defends the concept that "to the victor belongs the spoils of the enemy." This gives rise to the term "spoils system" in which favors and positions are granted to friends of winners of political elections.

1830

through

1839

1830 through 1839

A three-volume collection of information on outstanding women in American history is written by Lydia Maria Child.

American inventor Walter Hunt of New York devises an early version of the sewing machine. Its marketing, however, is negated by those who feel it will put seamstresses out of work.

The first fine crucible steel in the United States is produced in Cincinnati, Ohio, by English Americans William and John Garrard. The crucible process produces high quality steel for specialty purposes.

The *Carrick,* an Irish passenger vessel, makes stops at Montreal and Quebec, Canada, with cholera-carrying immigrants. The resultant epidemic kills almost 8,000 people in those two cities.

1833

Andrew Jackson serves a second term as president of the United States; Martin Van Buren is vice president. Both are Democrats.

In *Barron* v. *Baltimore*, the United States Supreme Court clarifies the meaning of the Fifth Amendment. Using its right of judicial review, the Court fails to support Barron, who claims he was damaged when Baltimore city employees altered the course of a stream that flowed under his wharf and failed to compensate him for his loss of revenue. The Court agrees that the Fifth Amendment does protect citizens' rights, but only against the federal government; and that Barron must use the provisions in his state constitution to gain satisfaction.

The Compromise Tariff, proposed by Senator Henry Clay of Kentucky, satisfies northern states by maintaining import duties but placates the South by agreeing to lower these tariffs each year for the next 10 years.

Tennessee communities suffer a serious outbreak of cholera.

The majority of the National Road is completed. When finished, it runs from Cumberland, Maryland to St. Louis, Missouri, and is paid for by government funds.

The University of Delaware at Newark and Stephens College at Columbia, Missouri, are founded. Oberlin Collegiate Institute in Ohio (later Oberlin College), becomes one of the first major educational institutions in the United States to admit women. It is also active in the abolitionist movement.

People of mixed race in Virginia can get "certificates" exempting them from the state's Black Codes.

Hardy Ivy builds a cabin in Georgia on land previously controlled by the Creek Indians. In 1837 the town of Terminus is established around this site. Incorporated in 1843 as Marthasville, it is renamed Atlanta in 1845 and reincorporated in 1847.

The *Royal William* becomes the first Canadian steamship to cross the Atlantic Ocean using steam power only. The trip takes 25 days.

A functional horse-drawn grain harvester is patented by Obed Hussey.

General Antonio López de Santa Anna becomes president of Mexico; his vice president, Valentín Gómez Farías attempts to raise funds by secularizing church property. The Secularization Act is passed and all 21 California missions are seized by the Mexican government. This ends Mexico's mission period. Santa Anna rules until 1836.

British forces drive Argentinian troops out of the Falkland Islands and seize control.

The Emancipation Act is passed by Britain's Parliament, to go into effect in 1834; it declares freedom for enslaved Africans and Indians in all British possessions. European plantation owners in the Caribbean ignore the declaration, but freed Africans begin to walk away from the fields.

c. 1833

Samuel F. B. Morse begins a decade of research into the development of the electric telegraph.

1833-1840

The Reverend Moses Merrill and his wife, Eliza Wilcox Merrill, perform missionary work among the Indians of Nebraska.

1834

Mississippi state law allows married women to own property.

Tulane University at New Orleans, Louisiana, and Wake Forest University at Winston-Salem, North Carolina, are founded.

Cyrus Hall McCormick patents his reaper, a harvesting machine, which was successfully demonstrated in 1831.

The city of Toronto is incorporated in Ontario province, Canada.

Mexican President Santa Anna responds to a popular outcry against the sale of church property and institutes changes in his government.

When slavery is abolished in the British Empire, plantation owners in Guyana seek to strengthen their labor force by importing indentured workers from China, India and Portugal.

1835

The United States has more than 1,000 miles of railroad tracks in use.

Outnumbering Mexicans by almost six to one, European Americans in the Mexican territory of Texas declare their independence from Mexico. The first battle for independence is fought at Gonzales and is won by the Texans.

Mexican President Santa Anna proclaims an end to federalism; several states, including Texas, revolt.

Juan Manuel de Rosas (1829-1832) returns to power and becomes dictator of Argentina. He rules until 1852.

c. 1835

The Texas Rangers are organized. Initially established to protect the frontier against Indian attacks, they become a strong force for controlling lawlessness in the region. In 1935 they are merged into the Texas highway patrol.

Samuel Colt patents a revolving breech pistol.

1835-1837

American and Mexican residents of Texas resist Mexico's constitutional reforms, including the emancipation of enslaved people, and declare Texas's independence. Revolutionary forces defeat the Mexican army in 1837, and the Lone Star Republic is established, with Anglo American Sam Houston as president, and Mexican Lorenzo Zavala as vice president.

1836

The United States Congress passes gag rules in an attempt to limit House debate on the issue of slavery. The rules are in effect until 1844.

Roger Brooke Taney becomes chief justice of the United States Supreme Court. He serves until 1864.

Arkansas becomes the 25th state to join the Union.

Texans are besieged at the Alamo by the Mexican army under Santa Anna. The entire garrison, including Davy Crockett, William Travis and Jim Bowie, is killed. The Mexican army also inflicts heavy casualties on the Texans at Goliad.

At the Battle of San Jacinto, the Texans prevail over Mexican forces, and Santa Anna is captured. The Texans gain independence from Mexico and form the Lone Star Republic with General Sam Houston as their first president.

Wesleyan College is founded at Macon, Georgia.

American missionaries Marcus and Narcissa Whitman travel west to the Oregon territory. Narcissa Whitman becomes one of the first European women to travel across the continent.

The first Canadian passenger railroad opens with service between Laprairie and St. John's.

Mexico adopts a new constitution, *Siete Leyes* (or Seven Laws), which provides for centralism and restricts voting rights.

Spain accepts the independence of Mexico and other Latin American countries.

THE AMERICAS	THE AMERICAS	THE AMERICAS	FOR CLASSROOM USE	

A rebellion of enslaved Africans and Indians in Martinique finally compels France to abolish slavery.

A 50-year period of turmoil begins in Uruguay.

1837

Martin Van Buren becomes the eighth president of the United States. Richard M. Johnson is vice president. Both are Democrats.

Financial and economic panic takes place in the United States, with inflated land values, wildcat banking and paper speculation. This panic is also fueled by President Jackson's issuance of the Specie Circular, requiring that payment for public land be made in coin rather than paper money.

Beginning in New England, leading male abolitionists refuse to allow women to speak before or to hold significant positions in their organizations. Religious leaders prevent women's participation in the New England Anti-Slavery Society. Female abolitionists eventually respond to this prejudice by forming their own societies; one of the first is the National Female Anti-Slavery Society.

Michigan becomes the 26th state to join the Union.

Marshall University at Huntington, West Virginia, and the Institute for Colored Youth (Cheney University of Pennsylvania) at Philadelphia are founded.

Horace Mann becomes a leader in educational reform and, after serving in the United States Congress, becomes the first president of Antioch College. Mary Lyon opens Mount Holyoke Female Seminary (later Mount Holyoke College), in South Hadley, Massachusetts.

In Alton, Illinois, Elijah P. Lovejoy, an abolitionist publisher of the *Observer* is killed by a mob while protecting his printing office.

American merchant Charles Lewis Tiffany founds his jewelry company in New York City.

A factory to manufacture reaping machines is opened in Chicago by Cyrus H. McCormick.

The first school in Idaho, a school for Native American children, opens at Lapwai. The first European American child born in Idaho is born at Lapwai this year as well.

A two-year rebellion of the Reform Party breaks out in Upper Canada. The U.S.S. *Caroline* is sunk by Canadian forces to prevent supplies from getting across the Niagara River to French Canadians rebelling against British rule. Rebel leader William Lyon Mackenzie is arrested in the United States.

Canadians of African descent are given the right to vote.

A severe cholera epidemic ravages Central America, particularly the plains communities of Guatemala.

1838

Canadian lumbermen and American farmers dispute the boundary between Maine and New Brunswick along the Aroostook River. An agreement is reached between Britain and the United States and the border is officially established by the Webster-Ashburton Treaty of 1842.

The town of Kansas, Missouri, is laid out. Its name is changed to the City of Kansas in 1853 and finally to Kansas City in 1889. Kansas City, Kansas, is colonized by Wyandot Indians in 1843, purchased by the federal government in 1855, developed in 1857 and incorporated in 1859. It consolidates a number of small towns around it in 1886 into the structure of today's city.

Judson College is founded at Marion, Alabama. The Union Institute is founded in Randolph County, North Carolina. This institute later evolves into Trinity College, and in 1924 is restructured as Duke University.

Angelina Grimké publishes the first feminist tract in response to clergy and press criticism of her anti-slavery activities. Grimké also testifies against slavery three times this year before the Massachusetts legislature.

Jamaican planters import Chinese and later East Indian indentured workers to replace the freed Africans and Indians who formerly worked the plantation fields.

The British government attempts to enforce emancipation in its Caribbean possessions. Emancipated Africans and Indians establish "free villages" on land purchased with money they hoarded while in bondage.

1838-1839

The Federal Republic of Central America separates, forming the five individual nations of Honduras, Nicaragua, El Salvador, Guatemala and Costa Rica.

1839

Religious freedom is granted in Hawaii by King Kamehameha III; constitutional monarchy is established the following year.

The vulcanization process to increase the strength and elasticity of rubber is discovered by Charles Goodyear. He patents the process in 1844.

Abner Doubleday is credited with the invention of modern baseball at Cooperstown, New York, although many claim that a children's game similar to this has existed for many years.

The United Provinces of Central America, joined since declaring its independence from Mexico in 1823, separates into the nations of Guatemala, El Salvador, Honduras, Nicaragua and Costa Rica.

Edward Jordon is the first person of African descent to be elected to the assembly in Jamaica.

Rafael Carrera comes to power in Guatemala. He is a strong, forceful military dictator closely allied to and supported by the Catholic church. Carrera rules until his death in 1865.

War breaks out between Uruguay and Argentina.

1830

through

1839

1830 through 1839

1830

Revolutions begin in France, Germany, Belgium and Poland. A popular Polish insurrection against the repressive anti-Polish measures of Russian Czar Nicholas I is suppressed.

When Belgium revolts against the Netherlands and declares its independence, the Belgian government claims Luxembourg. King William I of the Netherlands circumvents the claim by giving autonomy to Luxembourg.

The population of China is almost 400 million.

French forces begin their conquest of Algeria with the capture of Algiers. Resistance is led by Abdu-l-Kadir.

France's July Revolution forces the abdication of King Charles X (1824). Louis Philippe becomes king of France. He rules until 1848.

William IV becomes king of Great Britain and Ireland after the death of his brother, George IV (1820). William IV rules until 1837.

Ferdinand II becomes king of the Two Sicilies after the death of his father, Francis I (1825). Ferdinand II rules until 1859.

1831

The London Conference, convened to discuss Greece's claim for independence from the Ottoman Empire, also orders a truce between the Belgians and the Dutch.

Jews in France gain the freedom to worship.

Radical agitation, violence and workers' uprisings take place in France. King Louis Philippe and the legislature are unresponsive.

The Austrian army crushes uprisings in Modena, Parma and the Papal States but fails to suppress the nationalist movement in Italy.

Syria, part of the Ottoman Empire since 1516, is captured by Egyptian forces under Ibrahim.

Leopold I is elected king of newly independent Belgium after rejecting the throne of Greece. He rules until 1865.

Charles Albert I becomes king of Sardinia after the death of Charles Felix (1821). Charles Albert I rules until 1849.

British physicist Michael Faraday discovers the process of electromagnetic induction.

c. 1831

A devastating cholera epidemic spreads from Russia into central Europe and reaches England.

1832

An era of change begins in Britain with passage of the Reform Act, which redistricts parliamentary seats and extends the right to vote.

The French siege of Antwerp forces the Dutch out of power.

1832-1841

Two wars take place between the Ottoman Empire and Egypt.

1833

After Spain's King Ferdinand VII (1808, 1813) dies, the First Carlist War begins as a battle between Ferdinand's daughter, Isabella II, and his brother, Don Carlos, for the throne of Spain. Don Carlos is defeated. As a child, Isabella II becomes queen of Spain. Her mother, María Cristina, serves as regent until 1840 and is followed by General Baldomero Espartero. Isabella II comes of age in 1843 and rules until 1868.

The Treaty of Katahya, by which Egypt gains control over Syria, temporarily suspends the fighting between Turkey and Egypt.

British forces take control of the Falkland Islands.

Siam (Thailand) and the United States sign a commercial treaty.

Slavery is abolished in the British empire.

Parliament passes the first British Factory Act.

After two years of rejected treaties of separation, a truce is finally reached between Belgium and the Netherlands.

A three-year famine begins in Japan.

Otto I is chosen to become the first king of Greece. He rules until 1862.

1834

The German Customs Union is created. It becomes the foundation for Germany's development as an industrial and economic power.

Clashes take place between the Bantus (Xhosa) and Dutch colonists of the Cape of Good Hope Colony in Africa. Dutch farmers begin to migrate to the country north of the Orange River.

Sikh forces under Ranjit Singh capture the Muslim city of Peshawar in India.

Maria II is restored to the throne in Portugal after her regent and uncle, Miguel (1826), is overthrown. She rules until her death in 1853.

British statesman Edward Gibbon Wakefield receives a charter for the South Australian Association, which leads to the founding of the South Australian colony. Five years later, Wakefield assists in the colonization of a section of New Zealand. He believes that land should be sold, and not given, to colonists and that some form of self-rule is necessary for colonial success. He also opposes the use of criminals as colonists.

c. 1834

The Cape of Good Hope Colony (Southern Africa) begins to emancipate its enslaved people.

English mathematician Charles Babbage invents an "analytical engine," the precursor to the modern-day computer.

1835

Anti-Jewish legislation appears in Russia and the pale of settlement begins whereby Russian Jews are allowed permanent residence only in certain specified provinces of Russia.

Ferdinand I becomes emperor of Austria after the death of his father, Francis I (1804). Ferdinand I rules until 1848.

Kajar Muhammad becomes shah of Persia. He rules until 1848.

Methodists arrive in Fiji for missionary work.

1835-1929

This is the time span generally ascribed to the Barakzai Dynasty that rules Afghanistan.

c. 1835-c. 1839

To escape British control and Bantu uprisings, Dutch farmers (Boers) leave the Cape of Good Hope Colony and begin their "Great Trek." Known as *voortrekkers*, these Boers establish the colonies of Transvaal, Natal and the Orange Free State (South Africa).

1836

Louis Napoleon is unsuccessful in instigating a revolt in Strasbourg.

English housewife Caroline Norton, forced to flee an abusive husband, begins a reform campaign for improved child custody laws and legal protections for married women.

Danish archaeologist Christian J. Thomsen suggests that ancient civilizations can be classified and studied according to the materials used to make their tools and implements. Thomsen is credited with starting the practice of classifying cultures into the Stone, Bronze and Iron Ages.

1837

An earthquake hits Safed and Tiberias in Palestine.

A Jewish newspaper is published in Berlin.

Victoria becomes queen of Great Britain and Ireland after the death of her uncle, William IV (1830). She rules until 1901. She also is empress of India from 1876 to 1901.

Austria's first railway opens.

The crowns of England and Hanover separate after the death of William IV (1830) because succession to the crown in Hanover is restricted to the male heir. After Victoria becomes queen of Great Britain and Ireland, Ernest Augustus becomes king of Hanover. He rules until 1851.

(Sir) Charles Wheatstone and (Sir) William Cooke, English inventors, produce an electric telegraph.

Ieyoshi becomes shogun of Japan after the resignation of his father, Ienari (1786). Ieyoshi rules until 1853.

1838

Zulu Chief Dingaan ambushes and kills a number of Boers. This ambush begins a conflict that eventually results in the Zulus' defeat at Blood River by forces led by Andries Wilhelmus Jacobus Pretorius. The Boer victory opens the door for the establishment of the Boer Republic of Natal.

Free Africans who emigrated to Liberia unite to form a commonwealth government. Their governor is appointed by the American Colonization Society.

The New Zealand Company is founded in London.

The Irish Poor Law leads to mass emigration of cottiers and laborers.

The Anti-Corn Law League is founded in Manchester, England, to agitate for repeal of Britain's restrictive laws on grain imports and exports.

1838-1842

The First Afghan War between Britain and Afghanistan stems from Britain's desire to protect its holdings in India and to block Russian interference in its control of central Asia. Britain is successful despite a military setback at Kabul as the war ends.

1838-1848

The Chartism movement arises briefly in Great Britain. A working people's movement, it seeks equal rights and government representation for Britain's poorer inhabitants. The movement gradually declines in England due to factionalism and conflicting goals of its leaders. Welsh laborers retain Chartist doctrine for a longer period, and seek labor and social reforms.

1839

The Netherlands and Belgium officially become two separate countries and the Treaty of London guarantees the neutrality of Belgium.

Imperial Commissioner Lin Zexu (Lin Tse-hsü) prohibits the importation of opium. This ban leads to a three-year war with Britain. It is known as the first Opium War.

The Treaty of Vergara, negotiated by General Baldomero and Carlist General Maroto, ends the war in Spain and enables Isabella II to remain in control, although she is still under the direction of her regents.

The new boundaries of the German Confederation are established.

A report regarding discontent in the Canadian colonies causes Britain's Parliament to fear that Canada might take the United States's example and seek full independence. The report and its accompanying fears lead to the formation of the British Commonwealth.

In Turkey, Jews are granted citizenship but in Persia, the Jewish community of Meshed is forced to convert to Islam.

Abdu-l-Mejid becomes sultan of Turkey after the death of his father, Mahmud II (1808). Abdu-l-Mejid rules until 1861.

Christian VIII becomes king of Denmark after the death of his uncle, Frederick VI (1808). Christian VIII rules until 1848.

Milan (Milan Obrenovich) becomes prince of Serbia after the abdication of his father, Milos (Milos Obrenovich, 1817). Milan rules for less than one year and is succeeded by his brother, Michael (Michael Obrenovich). Michael is deposed in 1842 but returns to power in 1860 and rules until 1868.

c. 1839

In an appeasement compromise between Egyptian *khedive* (viceroy of Egypt under the Ottoman Empire) Muhammad (Mehemet) Ali and the Ottoman Empire, the governorship of Egypt is made a hereditary office in the lineage of Ali. This agreement establishes the dynasty that will rule Egypt until 1952. Muhammad Ali rules Egypt until 1849.

Louis Jacques Mandé Daguerre announces the invention of the daguerreotype which he developed with Joseph N. Niepce. This process produces a photograph on a silver-coated copper plate that has been treated with an iodine vapor.

1830

through

1839

NATIVE AMERICAN	NATIVE AMERICAN	AFRICAN AMERICAN	AFRICAN AMERICAN
1840 Under pressure from the federal government, Wisconsin's Winnebago Indians cede their lands and move west into Iowa. In 1848 and 1849 they are moved again, this time to a reservation in Minnesota. **1843** The first mission school in Alaska is established by the Russian-Greek Orthodox Church, to educate and convert Inuit (Eskimos). European Americans in Virginia attempt to have the Pamunkey Reservation dissolved on the grounds that members of the tribe have some African blood. **1846** A treaty is made with the federal government uniting several Potawatomie bands into the Potawatomie Nation and moving them together to land along the Kansas River. In three treaties the Potawatomie Reserve, an area of approximately 30 square miles, is set aside in Indian Territory (Kansas) for the tribe. The Winnebago tribe is compelled to sell to the federal government lands it previously occupied in Wisconsin in return for land in Indian Territory. **1847** Tiwas of the Taos Pueblo kill the first American governor of New Mexico. A smallpox epidemic devastates the Cayuse tribe in the Pacific Northwest (Washington). The tribe blames European Americans for the disease and retaliates, destroying the mission established by Marcus Whitman. He and other European Americans are killed. **1848** Much of the territory ceded to the United States by Mexico in the Treaty of Guadalupe Hidalgo has never actually been under Mexican control, but is populated by several Native American groups.	Sixteen manual labor schools and 87 boarding and other schools are in operation serving Creeks, Potawatomies, Chickasaws, Kansas and Miamis. The Indian commissioner reports that almost all the funds required to operate the schools are being furnished by Native Americans. **1849** The Bureau of Indian Affairs is transferred from the War Department to the newly established Department of the Interior. **1849-1850s** With the California gold rush, thousands of European American prospectors and colonists invade Indian lands; many local tribes are decimated by epidemics, war and dispossession.	**1840** The United States census reports almost 2,874,000 African Americans, of whom 386,000 are free. Born of free parents, Charles Lenox Remond is the first African American to serve as a regular lecturer for the Massachusetts Anti-Slavery Society. He is selected as a delegate to the World Anti-Slavery Society in London, where he remains for over one year soliciting Irish support for the abolitionist movement. **1841** The U.S.S. *Creole,* a ship carrying enslaved African Americans to Louisiana from Virginia, is overtaken by the passengers and sails to Nassau (Bahamas) where the Africans on board gain their freedom. **1843** Massachusetts repeals its law forbidding interracial marriage. Sojourner Truth, born in slavery in New York and emancipated by state law in 1829, begins to lecture against slavery and in favor of women's rights. The United States Attorney General declares that African Americans are neither aliens nor citizens, but somewhere in between. Radical abolitionist Henry Highland Garnet's address to the Convention of Free Colored People at Buffalo, New York is so powerful in its call for slave uprisings that Frederick Douglass's skill is required to keep peace at the meeting. Garnet, born into slavery in Maryland, is the editor of a Troy, New York paper, the *Clarion.* **c. 1843** Dr. James McCune Smith combines his talents as a physician with his beliefs in the abolitionist movement. A successful practitioner and owner of a pharmacy in New York City, he also authors many scholarly and scientific works on racial equality and the condition of African Americans in this country.	James Still, whose brothers Peter and William became prominent abolitionists, is a self-taught healer who begins to manufacture medicines for use by his patients in rural New Jersey. **Mid-1840s** Abolitionist Levi Coffin, operating from his home in Newport, Indiana, comes to be known as the "president" of the Underground Railroad. **1845** The gag rule is rescinded. It has prevented discussion of the slavery issue in the House of Representatives since 1836. Macon B. Allen, the first African American lawyer, is admitted to the bar in Worcester, Massachusetts. **1846** The Mexican War is denounced by antislavery forces as a war to extend slavery. **c. 1846** Millionaire William Alexander Leidesdorff, born in the Virgin Islands of a Danish planter and African mother, gains his initial wealth in the family's cotton business in New Orleans. He sailed for California in 1841 and obtained land grants from the Mexican authorities in San Francisco. Working with the Mexican authorities, he is able to secure additional property in San Francisco, some of which still bears his name. When United States troops capture the city, he serves on the liaison committee between the two powers and later becomes city treasurer. Norbert Rillieux, born into slavery in Louisiana and educated in France, returns to New Orleans and invents a method to speed up the refining of sugar. His new vacuum pan more efficiently uses heat during the evaporation process. It is not until the mid-1860s in the West Indies that this process becomes commercially viable.

1840

through

1849

AFRICAN AMERICAN	ASIAN AMERICAN	EUROPEAN AMERICAN	FOR CLASSROOM USE	
David Ruggles, an ardent abolitionist whose activities drained his health, receives relief from hydropathic treatment. Ruggles is so impressed with its value that he opens his own facility in Northampton, Massachusetts and becomes known as the "water-cure doctor."	**1843** A shipwrecked Japanese fisherman, Manjiro Naka-hama, is rescued at sea. **c. 1843** Three hundred Chinese contract workers are brought to Puerto Rico.	**1840** Father Innokenty (Ivan) Veniaminov becomes the first Russian Orthodox bishop of Alaska. He has the church's permission to conduct services in the native language.		**1840** **through** **1849**

AFRICAN AMERICAN

David Ruggles, an ardent abolitionist whose activities drained his health, receives relief from hydropathic treatment. Ruggles is so impressed with its value that he opens his own facility in Northampton, Massachusetts and becomes known as the "water-cure doctor."

1847

Frederick Douglass becomes president of the New England Anti-Slavery Society and, with the assistance of Martin R. Delany, establishes the weekly paper the *North Star.* Two years before, Douglass published the first edition of *Narrative of the Life of Frederick Douglass, an American Slave.*

A leading historian of the pre-Civil War period, William Wells Brown, is active on the Underground Railroad and as a proponent for women's suffrage. Born into slavery in Kentucky, Brown received his education in St. Louis, Missouri and worked for a time as an assistant to antislavery editor Elijah P. Lovejoy. Brown's autobiography, *Narrative of William Wells Brown, an American Slave,* is published by the Massachusetts Anti-Slavery Society.

1848

Blacksmith Lewis Temple invents a type of harpoon that becomes the standard for the whaling industry.

1849

Harriet Tubman becomes a fugitive and one of the most successful leaders of the Underground Railroad, bringing African Americans out of slavery into the North and Canada, sometimes forcing the fearful ahead with a pistol.

ASIAN AMERICAN

1843

A shipwrecked Japanese fisherman, Manjiro Naka-hama, is rescued at sea.

c. 1843

Three hundred Chinese contract workers are brought to Puerto Rico.

1844

The United States and China sign the Wangxia (Wanghia) Treaty. The United States is granted consular jurisdiction over Americans in China. China is not granted reciprocity.

1847

A group of Chinese students arrives in the United States. One of them, Yung Wing, later becomes the first naturalized American citizen of Chinese ancestry.

1848

Chinese miners begin to arrive in California due to the gold strike.

1849-1850s

Prefabricated houses are imported from China to California and contracted Chinese workmen are brought to America to erect them.

EUROPEAN AMERICAN

1840

Father Innokenty (Ivan) Veniaminov becomes the first Russian Orthodox bishop of Alaska. He has the church's permission to conduct services in the native language.

Because of their large numbers, the votes of German Americans in Pennsylvania are regarded as very important, and campaign biographies are issued in the German language.

American bank note makers import English tradespeople skilled in copperplate engraving as contract labor.

The linen industry in western Germany is in crisis because of the introduction of power looms. Entire families of linen tradespeople immigrate to the United States.

As a result of Mormon missionary activities in Britain, a sizable migration of British Mormons to the United States begins.

1840s-1850s

The first significant wave of Swedish immigration comes during this time, as the Swedish economy is depressed and the American economy is expanding.

1840-1849

Almost 800,000 Irish immigrants come to the United States. Total immigration for the decade is more than 4 million.

1841

Russian colonists at Fort Ross in California sell their holdings to Swiss colonist John Sutter and return to Sitka, Alaska.

The Pine Lake colony, led by the Reverend Gustav Unonius, is the first Swedish community in Wisconsin.

In this year, German immigration to America is approximately 43,000 people.

A group of unemployed potters in Staffordshire, England petitions the British government to finance their immigration to the United States. The government complies, supporting the travel of hundreds of potters.

1840

through

1849

EUROPEAN AMERICAN	EUROPEAN AMERICAN	EUROPEAN AMERICAN	HISPANIC AMERICAN

1840 through 1849

EUROPEAN AMERICAN

1842

A German newspaper, *Der Deutsche Courier,* begins publication in New Orleans.

More than 92,000 Irish immigrants come to America.

1843

German pietists at Buffalo, New York, draw up a constitution "approved by the Lord." Everything except clothing and household goods is shared. A council of elders governs the community, and a board of 16 trustees holds title to the property.

1844

The Russian American Company obtains its third charter. It gives the children of Russian fathers and Native American mothers the same rights as all Russian colonists.

Anti-Catholic, anti-Irish violence breaks out in Philadelphia. Fires, assaults and looting occur in the city's Irish neighborhoods, leaving 130 dead, more than 100 injured, and homes and churches destroyed by fire.

1844-1848

St. Michael's Cathedral in Sitka, Alaska, is constructed by Finnish carpenters. Built in the shape of a cross, of hand-hewn logs and planks, the church will stand until 1966, when it is destroyed by fire.

1845

Hundreds of thousands of Irish people come to America to flee starvation and disease. Nearly half of the immigrants die en route.

Swedish farmers and artisans and their families begin to arrive in the United States, some fleeing religious repression. Many homestead in the Midwest. Peter Cassel founds the first Swedish community in Iowa — New Sweden.

1845-1847

The phrase "manifest destiny" is coined by John L. O'Sullivan, embodying the idea that territorial expansion is the obvious destiny of the United States.

EUROPEAN AMERICAN

1845-1853

Most of the Dutch immigrants who come to America are Seceders — people who have seceded from the Dutch Reformed Church.

1846

Mass German immigration to the United States begins. By 1854 almost 900,000 Germans have arrived in America.

The *Adoptiv-Bürger* is the first German workers' newspaper in the United States. It is owned and operated by German communists.

During the Atlantic Dock Strike in Brooklyn, New York, striking Irish workers fight with a group of newly arrived Germans who are being used as strike-breaking labor.

The Netherlands Society for the Protection of Immigrants from Holland is formed in the United States, in an effort to protect naive arrivals from unscrupulous persons.

Norwegian immigrants pay between $25 and $38 apiece for passage to the United States, and supply their own food and bedding for the trip.

According to a Swedish-Norwegian consular report, more than 500 Norwegian and more than 900 Swedish sailors have deserted ship to remain in the United States.

1847

Irish immigration to America reaches 105,000 this year alone, due to the potato famine. German immigration also surges. Most German newcomers opt for the farmlands of the Midwest.

The first Scandinavian newspaper in the United States, *Skandinavia,* begins publication in New York City, serving the Danish, Norwegian and Swedish communities.

1848

More than 4,000 "American Letters" are sent back to Norway and are circulated from town to town. They tell of the benefits of moving to the United States, particularly of the availability of land.

EUROPEAN AMERICAN

A wave of German political refugees comes to the United States following the unrest in Germany. Friedrich Hecker, a law professor and leader of the rebel cause, is welcomed by a crowd of thousands in New York City.

Armed conflict breaks out in Ireland as a group called the Young Ireland movement seeks separation from Great Britain, and advocates the use of force to achieve its ends. The rebellion fails and several of its leaders flee to the United States.

HISPANIC AMERICAN

1840

The United States is the principal market for Puerto Rican sugar.

Richard Henry Dana's book *Two Years Before the Mast* is published; it popularizes California for Americans.

c. 1840

The majority of enslaved Africans arriving in Puerto Rico are from Nigeria, Ghana and what is now Zaïre.

1841

A planned rebellion of enslaved Africans is uncovered in Ponce, Puerto Rico.

1842

The first gold discovery documented in California is found by Francisco López at Placerita Canyon near Los Angeles.

c. 1843

Three hundred Chinese contract workers are brought to Puerto Rico.

The first Puerto Rican literary works appear: *El Aguinaldo Puertorriqueño* and *El Album Puertorriqueño.*

1844

A Mexican raiding party lands on Tiburon Island in the Gulf of California, kidnaps more than 350 Seri natives and takes them to Hermosillo. Most Seris gradually escape and return to Tiburon.

1844-1845

Californians rebel against Mexican rule. Mariano Guadalupe Vallejó helps write the first constitution of California. He favors union with the United States.

1845

Thousands of Mexicans living in Texas become United States citizens when Texas becomes a state.

Utes and Navajos war with Mexican communities in New Mexico.

1846

Puerto Rico has an enslaved population of 51,260, out of a total population of 443,130.

HISPANIC AMERICAN	HISPANIC AMERICAN	FOR CLASSROOM USE	FOR CLASSROOM USE	

When negotiations for the United States to purchase territory from Mexico fail, American troops move into the disputed area and defeat Mexican forces at Palo Alto, California. The United States formally declares war on Mexico and moves troops into Santa Fe.

Skirmishes occur in south Texas. New Mexico and California are occupied by Mexican forces; the Battle of San Pasqual in California results in a victory for Californians. Los Angeles and San Diego are recaptured by Mexicans; the Taos rebellion occurs against the American administration.

1847

The United States reconquers southern California and New Mexico; the United States army occupies Mexico City.

1847-1848

A revolt of enslaved people takes place in the town of Vega Baja, on the northern coast of Puerto Rico.

1848

United States forces capture Mexico City. The Treaty of Guadalupe Hidalgo ends the war with Mexico, and over a third of Mexico's territory is ceded to the United States. Most Mexicans in the ceded regions decide to stay and become American citizens.

Puerto Rico's Governor Juan Prim announces the *Código Negro* (Black Code), a measure to repress and control enslaved Africans.

The Treaty of Guadalupe Hidalgo is signed, ending the Mexican War. Mexico loses California, Nevada, Utah, and parts of New Mexico, Arizona, Wyoming and Colorado. The treaty guarantees property rights and the rights of citizenship to the Mexicans now living in the annexed lands. Over the next few years, many Mexican Americans lose their land.

1849

In Puerto Rico, Captain General Juan de la Pezuela imposes the "Libreta de Jornalero," which his detractors say are the regulations for "white slavery."

Manuel Alonso's *El Gibaro* is published in Puerto Rico.

Mexican Americans supply the technology for gold mining, but are paid less than half as much as European Americans. Mexican and Spanish rights guaranteed in the Treaty of Guadalupe Hidalgo are overridden and Mexican influence declines.

1840

through

1849

THE AMERICAS	THE AMERICAS	THE AMERICAS	THE AMERICAS

1840 through 1849

1840

The United States census reports the country's population at 17.1 million, including 2.87 million African Americans, of whom 2.5 million are enslaved. A great influx of Irish and German immigrants has created a wealth of laborers, reducing wages. This provides the climate for the growth of labor organizations.

Lucretia Mott attends the World Anti-Slavery Convention in London as an invited delegate. However, the majority of convention attendees vote to deny her a seat because she is a woman. She and her companion, Elizabeth Cady Stanton, are compelled to sit in an area that is curtained off from the main convention floor, and may not speak. On the resolve of these two women, the early women's rights movement is born. Mott and Stanton are instrumental in organizing the Seneca Falls Convention in New York in 1848.

Saint Mary-of-the-Woods College is founded in Indiana.

Lower and Upper Canada are united by an act of the British Parliament. This Act of Union also establishes an elected representative assembly for Canada, a legislative council and a governor-general appointed by the British monarchy.

Rafael Carrera becomes dictator of Guatemala. He rules until 1865.

After being awarded a contract by the British government to provide regular mail service between Halifax, Nova Scotia, and Liverpool, England, Sir Samuel Cunard, a prominent Nova Scotia merchant, establishes the transatlantic steamship line that bears his name.

Laws in Barbados allow free Africans to sit in the country's legislature.

c. 1840

Twenty-five percent of factory laborers are women.

1840-1849

The United States receives more than 200,000 British immigrants and almost 800,000 Irish immigrants.

1840-1857

The United States experiences rapid growth in industrialization, construction of railroads and export trade.

1840s-1850s

Large numbers of immigrant laborers, unskilled and desperate for work, pour into the eastern seaboard towns of the United States and flood the labor market, causing sharp competition for jobs.

The New England whaling industry, particularly out of Connecticut and Rhode Island port cities, is at its height.

1840s-1870s

Chinese laborers replace freed Africans on plantations in Central America, Mexico, Peru and the Caribbean.

1841

William Henry Harrison becomes the ninth president of the United States; John Tyler is vice president. Both are Whigs. When Harrison dies after only one month in office, Tyler becomes the first vice president to succeed to the presidency.

In response to the growing demand of people migrating westward, the United States Congress passes the Preemption Act, legitimizing "squatters' rights" by allowing a person or family to claim a piece of land and, after a brief period of occupancy, purchase the land before it goes to public auction.

A small colony is established as a fur-trading center on the Trinity River, Texas, possibly led by John Byran. It is incorporated as a town in 1856 and as a city in 1871. The city is named Dallas in honor of George Mifflin Dallas, later to become vice president and ambassador to Great Britain.

The first wagon train of colonists comes west across the Sierra Nevada to California and Oregon. Prominent on the trip are John Bidwell and Thomas Fitzpatrick. New York-born Bidwell, a former school teacher, organizes the trip. He becomes wealthy in the gold fields, establishes a large ranch in northern California (Chico) and serves in Congress. In 1892 Bidwell is the presidential candidate of the Prohibition Party. The guide for the expedition, Irish-born trapper Thomas Fitzpatrick, one of the most famous of the mountain men, leads the group as far as Fort Hall (south Idaho), where they divide into those going to California and those going into the Oregon Territory by horseback.

Oberlin Collegiate Institute in Ohio becomes the first major college in the nation to confer degrees on women.

Political journalist Horace Greeley produces the first issue of the New York *Tribune*, a paper he will edit for over 30 years.

Peru begins a four-year period of civil strife and unrest.

1841-1847

Brook Farm in West Roxbury, Massachusetts, is established as a model utopian community by Unitarians and Transcendentalists under the guidance of George and Sophia Ripley. It draws many literary leaders who wish to combine simple living with deep thinking. The farm proves unsuccessful, but the concept of sharing ideas remains an important one in the American literary tradition.

1841-1850

Immigration to the United States totals 1,713,231 of which 1,597,442 come from Europe, 141 from Asia, 55 from Africa, 9 from Oceania, 62,469 from the Americas and 53,115 are not specifically identified.

1842

The Webster-Ashburton Treaty between Great Britain and the United States confirms the location of the Canadian border, from Lake of the Woods to the St. Croix River, but the boundary of the Oregon Territory still remains undecided. Other provisions relate to the suppression of the slave trade and mutual extradition of criminals.

In Santa Feliciana Canyon near Los Angeles, gold is discovered by Francisco Lopez.

The University of Notre Dame in Indiana, Saint Mary's College at Raleigh, North Carolina; Villanova University in Pennsylvania; and Hollins College at Roanoke, Virginia, are founded.

Elijah White leads a large wagon train of colonists west into Oregon. The Oregon Trail becomes the route of massive westward migration, as thousands of people move into Oregon Territory.

Bavarian-born merchant Adam Gimbel establishes a small business in Vincennes, Indiana, that becomes the forerunner of his family's major department store chain.

Dorothea Lynde Dix, outraged by the imprisonment of the insane in criminal institutions, writes a paper for the Massachusetts legislature arguing for humane treatment of the insane. Her continuing work in this area results in the establishment of hospitals for the mentally ill in several states.

Crawford W. Long is the first to use general anesthetic (ether) in an operation at Jefferson, Georgia.

Francisco Morazán is assassinated by dissidents in his own camp after he tries to reunite Central America.

1843

In the United States the historic period of westward migration begins. Colonists travel in groups or wagon trains along the Oregon Trail, which stretches from the Missouri River to the Columbia River area (then known as Oregon). The journey of more than 2000 miles usually takes six months and is frequently led by the mountain men guides Thomas Fitzpatrick, James Bridger, Kit Carson and Joseph Meek.

A Connecticut state law passed this year gives Jewish people rights equal to Christians in forming and operating religious organizations.

Rhode Island's constitution of this year extends the franchise to certain classes of factory workers. The vote was formerly restricted to men who own property.

B'nai B'rith, one of the first international service organizations, is founded in the United States.

Mexico adopts a more restrictive constitution, *Las Bases Organicas*.

The population of enslaved Africans in Cuba is estimated at 436,000.

1844

The Democratic party convention calls for annexation of Texas and acquisition of Oregon.

The University of Mississippi at University and Moore College of Art and Design at Philadelphia, Pennsylvania, are founded.

Henry Wells joins with William G. Fargo to establish Wells & Company in Buffalo, New York. The following year, it becomes Livingston, Fargo & Company and by 1850, a series of mergers leads to the formation of the American Express Company. In 1852 Wells, Fargo & Company is established to handle the New York to San Francisco, California service that the gold rush stimulated as well as stagecoach service and banking on the West Coast. The American Express Company becomes the East Coast representative for Wells, Fargo.

In response to harsh conditions in the textile mills of Lowell, Massachusetts, Sara Bagley organizes the Lowell Female Labor Reform Association, which publishes pamphlets calling for reforms. In 1845, Bagley organizes and leads a strike, protesting a wage decrease and the 14-hour workday that has become common.

Samuel F. B. Morse patents the telegraph although some European countries, notably Germany, France and Britain, credit others with this invention.

Major iron deposits are discovered near Lake Superior.

Mormon leader Joseph Smith is arrested and imprisoned in Carthage, Illinois, on charges of treason and conspiracy. He is dragged out of jail and murdered by an angry mob.

Maine state law allows married women to own property.

The capital of Canada is moved from Kingston to Montreal, where it remains for five years.

Fighting erupts on Hispaniola as the eastern section seeks independence. The revolution is successful and the new country of the Dominican Republic is established. The new government is led by Pedro Santana, who serves as president until 1848.

Carlos Antonio Lopez becomes president of Paraguay. He serves until 1862.

1845

James K. Polk becomes the 11th president of the United States; George M. Dallas is vice president. Both are Democrats.

Florida and Texas become the 27th and 28th states, respectively, to join the Union. Texas surrenders its independent status as the Lone Star Republic after six years of financial and military difficulties.

The colony of Portland, Oregon, is laid out. It incorporates as a city in 1851.

The United States Naval School in Annapolis, Maryland, opens under the direction of Secretary of the Navy George Bancroft. It is later reorganized and renamed the United States Naval Academy. Baylor University is founded at Waco, Texas.

In her work *Woman In The 19th Century*, published this year, Margaret Fuller lays the foundation for America's feminist cause.

New England captains James Smith and Josiah Stevens both arrive at Baja California and begin to hunt for gray whales.

Massachusetts inventor Erastus B. Bigelow constructs the power loom for manufacturing carpets.

The Adventist Movement begins to develop in the United States. Organized as individual groups with a similar focus (the coming of the Day of Judgment), three of the best known are The Second Adventists (or Millerites), under William Miller, the Seventh-Day Adventists and the Church of God.

General Ramón Castilla becomes president of Peru. He serves until 1851 and returns to power from 1855 to 1862.

1846

Oregon Territory is ceded to the United States by Britain. The Oregon Boundary Treaty establishes the border between the United States and Canada, from the height of the Rockies to Vancouver Island, at the 49th parallel. All of Vancouver Island and lands north of the parallel are ceded to Britain.

As a result of Mexico's resistance to American immigration to California, the United States government, invoking the doctrine of "manifest destiny," declares war on Mexico.

1840

through

1849

THE AMERICAS	THE AMERICAS	THE AMERICAS	THE AMERICAS

1840 through 1849

The Wilmot Proviso proposed by United States Representative David Wilmot of Pennsylvania is an amendment to a bill to establish the border with Mexico. The amendment, stating that no territory obtained from Mexico will be open to slavery, passes the House but is defeated in the Senate.

Congress establishes the Smithsonian Institution in Washington, D.C. It is partially funded by a grant from the estate of British scientist James Smithson, who never visited the United States.

Iowa becomes the 29th state to join the Union.

New Mexico and California are annexed by the United States.

Inventor Elias Howe patents the sewing machine; however, finding little financial backing in the United States because garment makers feel resentment from workers, he sells development rights to William Thomas in England.

William Thomas Morton of Boston, Massachusetts, becomes the first to use a general anaesthetic (ether) in dental surgery.

Richard Marsh Hoe builds the first rotary press, more than tripling the speed at which paper can be printed.

In New Mexico, an abortive revolt against United States forces is led by Father Jose Martinez. Approximately 175 people who have barricaded themselves into a church in Taos are killed.

Canada's first telegraph company is established. By year's end, regular telegraph service is in operation between Toronto and Montreal.

Antonio López de Santa Anna (1833-1836) becomes president of Mexico for a second time and restores the federalist constitution of 1824. He serves until 1847.

1846-1847

After violent persecution from neighbors, Brigham Young leads the Mormons (Latter Day Saints) from Illinois to the Great Salt Lake in what is now Utah.

Late 1840s-Early 1850s

Immigration to the United States from Ireland and Germany is very heavy since both countries have suffered a series of crop failures.

1847

The United States Army under General Winfield Scott captures Mexico City and the forces of General Santa Anna.

The E. M. Holt textile mill is constructed in North Carolina. In 1853 this plant makes the South's first factory-dyed cotton fabric.

Adhesive postage stamps are introduced in the United States.

Pennsylvania enacts a law that jails in the state may not be used to detain African Americans fleeing slavery.

Maria Mitchell — school teacher, librarian and astronomer — wins fame when she discovers a new comet. She becomes the first woman elected to the American Academy of Arts and Sciences.

New Bedford, Massachusetts, incorporates as a city. Founded in the late 1700s, it has become one of the country's major whaling ports.

The University of Iowa at Iowa City and Midway College in Kentucky are founded.

The first United States governor of Mexico is killed by Tiwa Indians from the Taos pueblo.

1847-1853

The Caste War in Yucatán erupts when Maya indians revolt against Europeans. The rebellion is successful, and the Mayas regain most of Yucatán. Mayan resistance is not fully ended until the 1890s.

1848

The Treaty of Guadalupe Hidalgo is signed, ending the Mexican War. Mexico loses California, Nevada, Utah and parts of New Mexico, Arizona, Wyoming and Colorado to the United States. The treaty protects property rights and guarantees the rights of citizenship to the Mexicans living in the annexed lands. Over the next few years, however, many Mexican Americans lose their land.

The Free Soil Party is formally organized in Buffalo, New York. The party opposes the extension of slavery into the lands acquired from Mexico. Initial support for the organization comes from New York Democrats, antislavery Whigs and stalwarts of the Liberty Party.

Because of the unrest created when the 49th parallel established its northern boundary in 1846, the United States establishes the Oregon Territory to include those lands west of the Rockies and between the 42nd and 49th parallels.

Wisconsin becomes the 30th state to join the Union.

New York passes a law allowing married women to own property. Ernestine Rose, a Polish American, daughter of a rabbi, is forceful in urging the state legislature to pass this law.

Jane Grey Swisshelm initiates publication of *The Saturday Visitor,* a newspaper dealing with antislavery and women's rights issues. Her writings are instrumental in Pennsylvania's passage of laws allowing married women to own property.

The first American gold rush commences as gold is discovered at Sutter's Mill in the Sacramento Valley in California.

The first women's suffrage convention is held in Seneca Falls, New York. Elizabeth Cady Stanton and Lucretia Mott propose equal status for women in all areas, especially the right to vote. The meeting draws approximately 300 women.

The University of Wisconsin is founded at Madison.

The clause in Canada's Act of Union that makes English the country's official language is repealed.

The United States government offers to purchase Cuba from Spain. While many Cubans favor this so that they can continue benefitting from the labor of enslaved Africans, both Spain and the northern United States reject the idea.

Revolts by enslaved Africans on St. Croix convince the Danish government to end slavery.

c. 1848

Linus Yale invents a compact, pin-tumbler cylinder lock.

1849

Zachary Taylor becomes the 12th president of the United States; Millard Fillmore is vice president. Both are Whigs.

The Department of the Interior is established as part of the United States government.

The United States Supreme Court declares that state laws providing for head taxes on immigrants are unconstitutional.

A cholera epidemic ravages the midwestern United States; Scandinavian communities in Wisconsin and Illinois are especially hard hit.

As a result of the discovery of gold in the Sacramento Valley, California's population increases by 300 percent.

Central Connecticut State University is founded at New Britain, Connecticut.

The Associated Press is established through the combined efforts of several New York newspapers.

Elizabeth Blackwell becomes the first woman in the United States to graduate from medical school, when she receives her degree from Geneva Medical College (later Hobart College) in Geneva, New York.

New York inventor Walter Hunt patents the safety pin.

THE AMERICAS	*FOR CLASSROOM USE*	*FOR CLASSROOM USE*	*FOR CLASSROOM USE*	
Fifteen million bison still roam the American Plains, in two major herds. By 1880 the southern herd is gone and by 1885 the northern herd is decimated.

Toronto becomes the new capital of Canada.

Buenaventura Báez becomes president of the Dominican Republic. He serves until 1853. | | | | **1840**

through

1849 |
| THE AMERICAS | *FOR CLASSROOM USE* | *FOR CLASSROOM USE* | *FOR CLASSROOM USE* | |

1840 through 1849

1840

In New Zealand, the Treaty of Waitangi guarantees the Maoris their lands in exchange for becoming part of the British crown.

At the Conference of London, Austria, Britain, Prussia and Russia meet to resolve the conflict between Turkey and Egypt.

The World Anti-Slavery Convention meets in London. Although the attendees are deeply committed to the issue of abolishing slavery, the women delegates are not seated.

Britain stops sending convicts to New South Wales but continues the practice to Tasmania and South Australia.

Frederick William IV becomes king of Prussia after the death of his father, Frederick William III (1797). Frederick William IV rules until 1861.

William II becomes king of the Netherlands and grand duke of Luxembourg after the abdication of his father, William I (1815). William II rules until 1849.

c. 1840

German missionaries arrive in Togo (Gulf of Ghana, West Africa).

In Britain, a number of new factory acts are passed to restrict the hours of work and certain occupations for women and children.

1840s

English archaeologist Sir Austen Henry Layard leads in the excavation of the ancient Assyrian capital of Nineveh.

The Swazi people in Africa seek British assistance against their Zulu enemies.

1841

New Zealand gains its independence from New South Wales and becomes a British colony.

The Straits Convention closes the Dardanelles and Bosphorus Straits to everyone except Russia, Britain, France, Austria and Prussia.

The *Jewish Chronicle* is established in Berlin.

1842

The Treaty of Nanking is signed by Chinese and British officials after China's defeat in the Opium War. By its terms, Hong Kong is ceded to Britain; Canton, Shanghai and three other cities are opened to foreign trade and the importation of opium.

In Ethiopia, Theodore II (Ras Kasa or Lij Kasa) and his army seize Kawara during the civil war. Theodore II ultimately regains the throne.

Alexander (Alexander Karageorgevich) becomes prince of Serbia after Michael (Michael Obrenovich, 1839) is deposed. Alexander rules until 1858.

1843

Britain takes control over colonies in Ghana and makes them a protectorate in 1844 after the region is threatened by the Ashanti (Asante) kingdom. Britain annexes Natal, the Boer colony in southern Africa.

Gambia becomes a British colony.

The first Maori war breaks out in New Zealand with the Battle of Wairau after treaty violations. The Maoris fight increasing British colonization. The war lasts until 1848.

The Brahmo Samaj is established in Calcutta, India. It is formed to impede conversions to Christianity and to promote the ideology of a Hindu reformation as espoused by Rammohan Roy.

In India, Sind (Sindh) province comes under British control after the emirs are defeated at the Battles of Miani and Dabo.

Slavery is outlawed in Britain's Indian colonies.

The French annex Tahiti — over the objections of Tahitian Queen Pomare — and the Marquesas Islands.

1844

Greece has a constitution, granted reluctantly by King Otto I.

The United States and China sign the Wangxia (Wanghia) Treaty, which opens five Chinese ports to American trade ships.

Oscar I becomes king of Sweden and Norway after the death of his father, Charles XIV (1818). Oscar I rules until 1859.

The Young Men's Christian Association (YMCA) is founded in Britain by (Sir) George Williams.

1845

A complete failure of Ireland's potato crop marks the beginning of that country's "Great Famine," and creates a strong wave of immigration to the United States.

The *Great Britain* becomes the first propeller-driven ship to cross the Atlantic.

Russia passes laws to limit the hours of child labor but they are not enforced.

1845-1846

The First Anglo-Sikh War begins in India when the Sikh army, comprised of Sikhs, Punjabis, Muslims and Hindus under the overall command of Lal Singh and Tej Singh, crosses the Sutlej River and declares war on the British. British forces are victorious at Moodkee (Mudki), Ferozepore and Aliwal, and end the war with a victory at Sobraon. The Treaty of Lahore makes the Punjab a British protectorate and limits the size of the Sikh military strength.

1845-1848

Hostilities continue between European colonists and the native Maori in New Zealand.

1846

When a Polish peasant revolt against Russian domination is crushed, Polish nationalists outside the country intensify their pursuit of unification and independence for Poland.

Germany, Belgium and Holland suffer crop failures.

Elias Howe patents his sewing machine in the United States. Not having sufficient financial backing, he sells development rights to William Thomas in England.

Britain's Corn Laws are repealed; thus the last major barrier to free trade is removed.

1846-1951

This is the time span generally ascribed to the Rana dynasty that rules Nepal.

1847

The American colony of Liberia in West Africa becomes an independent republic under the leadership of Joseph Jenkins Roberts. The new country's constitution is modelled after that of the United States. Although most countries grant Liberia formal recognition in 1848, the United States does not do so until 1862.

Switzerland strengthens its central government after civil unrest in several provinces. A new constitution is drafted.

As a result of his participation in the unrest in Germany and his speeches calling for the overthrow of the governments of Poland and Russia, anarchist Mikhail Bakunin is expelled to Siberia.

In Scotland, Sir James Young Simpson introduces the use of chloroform as an anesthetic.

1848

A general unrest sweeps Europe with the following results: revolts in Vienna, Austria, lead to Foreign Minister Clemens Metternich's resignation and the expulsion of Emperor Ferdinand I; Italy's first war of liberation fails; Czech revolts against Hapsburg rule are suppressed; the revolt in France establishes the Second French Republic with Charles Louis Napoleon Bonaparte as president; and uprisings in Budapest, Venice, Berlin, Milan, Rome and Warsaw all require force to restore calm. The unrest in Germany is inspired by nationalist and democratic ideologies.

Vienna abolishes serfdom.

Switzerland's new constitution establishes a strong federal union.

The Netherlands revises its constitution to allow for greater democracy and claims jurisdiction over the colonization of Indonesia.

THE WORLD	THE WORLD	FOR CLASSROOM USE	FOR CLASSROOM USE	

The Magyars unite under Hungarian patriot Louis (Lajos) Kossuth and declare the union of Transylvania and Hungary, using the abolition of serfdom to seek Romanian support against Austria.

Andries Wilhelmus Jacobus Pretorius leads a group of Boers across the Drakensberg Mountains; they establish a colony which evolves into the Transvaal (now a province of the Republic of South Africa).

An earthquake hits Wellington, New Zealand.

Britain annexes the Orange Free State (in South Africa).

The Second Anglo-Sikh War begins in India with a Sikh attack on British colonists at Multan; British forces, after a series of skirmishes, end the conflict with a victory at Gujrat (Gujaret) and annex the Punjab.

Maximilian II becomes king of Bavaria after the reign of Louis I. He rules until 1864.

Frederick VII becomes king of Denmark after the death of his father, Christian VIII (1839). Frederick VII rules until 1863.

Francis Joseph (Franz Joseph) becomes emperor of Austria after the abdication of his uncle, Ferdinand I (1835). Francis Joseph rules until 1916.

Nasr-ed-Din becomes shah of Persia. He rules until 1896.

Armed conflict breaks out in Ireland as the Young Ireland movement seeks separation from Great Britain and advocates the use of force to achieve its ends. The rebellion fails and several of its leaders flee to the United States.

Charles Louis Napoleon Bonaparte becomes president of the Second French Republic after the abdication of Louis Philippe (1830). Bonaparte serves as president until 1852, when he proclaims himself Emperor Napoleon III. He rules as emperor until 1870.

Karl Marx and Friedrich Engels issue the *Communist Manifesto*.

Abbas I becomes *khedive* (viceroy) of Egypt. He rules until 1854.

c. 1848

Hajj Omar, leader of the Muslim Tukulor tribe, attempts to build a religious power in Senegal.

1849

Yemen (southwestern Arabian peninsula) is absorbed into the Ottoman Empire.

Britain annexes the Hindu states of Jaitpur and Sambalpar in India.

Hungarian revolutionary forces are successful in several spring battles against Hapsburg troops. Independence is declared, and Louis (Lajos) Kossuth is made president of Hungary. The Hapsburg court at Vienna asks for Russia's military assistance, and the combined forces crush the revolution. Kossuth resigns and goes into exile; 13 revolutionary generals are executed. Hungary and Transylvania are absorbed back into the Hapsburg's Austro-Hungarian Empire.

Austrian forces are victorious over King Charles Albert I of Sardinia at Novara (northwestern Italy). They also capture Venice.

William III becomes king of the Netherlands and grand duke of Luxembourg after the death of his father, William II (1840). William III rules until 1890.

Victor Emmanuel II becomes king of Sardinia after the abdication of his father, Charles Albert I (1831). Victor Emmanuel II rules until 1861. He then becomes the first king of a united Italy, and rules until 1878.

Scottish missionary David Livingstone reaches Lake Ngami in Africa.

German Heinrich Barth, working for Britain, begins exploring the Sudan. He sights the Benue River and makes expeditions into Chad.

1840

through

1849

NATIVE AMERICAN	NATIVE AMERICAN	NATIVE AMERICAN	AFRICAN AMERICAN
1850 A large number of bonds held for support of Native Americans are stolen from the Interior Department. Little is done to recover them. **1850-1860** Cholera breaks out among Native Americans of the Great Basin and the southern Plains. **1851** The Treaty of Fort Laramie (Wyoming) is signed by several Plains tribes including the Sioux, Cheyenne, Arapaho, Crow and Assiniboine. This agreement calls for peace among the signatory tribes and recognizes the federal government's right to establish roads and military posts on Indain lands in the northern Plains and in the Platte, Missouri and Yellowstone River drainage areas. It also establishes new tribal boundaries; promises $50,000 per year for the next 10 years to each of the signatory tribes; and threatens the suspension of these annuity payments to treaty violators. **1851-1852** A series of federal treaties establishes, on paper, reserves in California for several Native American groups, but either through the treaties not being signed or through their being ignored, these reserves are never created. **1851-1856** In the Rogue River War, the Takelma, Shasta and other Northwest tribes attempt unsuccessfully to stop the flood of European miners and immigrants. **1853-1857** The United States acquires 157 million acres from Native American tribes through 52 treaties that are subsequently ignored by the government. **1854** Kansas and Nebraska are organized as territories. As a result, the region known as Indian Territory is reduced to include only present-day Oklahoma.	In the Treaty of Wolf River (Wisconsin), the Menominee cede much of their tribal lands to the federal government and are granted the right to make their homes on Wolf River; the government agrees to compensate the Menominee with annuity payments. **1854-1855** In the Puget Sound Uprising, Nisqually Chief Leschi leads his tribe, the Puyallup, and their Sahaptin allies against European Americans. The coalition is defeated and Leschi is captured and hanged in 1857. **1855** A Tlingit revolt against Russian presence marks the last native uprising against Russian encroachment in the Alaska area. Many Winnebagos, dissatisfied with the western land they were given by treaties in 1846, move back to the Great Lakes area. European Americans force the Winnebagos to move out. By an act of Congress, the Klamath River Reserve, an area of 25,000 acres in California, is established. In 1892, this land is returned to the public domain. **1855-1858** The Third Seminole War takes place in Florida. At its conclusion, a portion of the Seminole tribe is removed to Indian Territory. The remaining Seminoles avoid removal by hiding in the Florida wilderness. **1856** Five Mesquakie Indians displaced in 1845 by the United States government return to their Iowa homeland. They raise enough money selling ponies to purchase an 80-acre parcel. Over the next 130 years, with land purchases by other Mesquakie, this reclaimed homeland grows to more than 2,000 acres. **1857** The Tonawanda Seneca sign a treaty with the United States government authorizing the tribe to buy back over 7,000 acres of their reservation in northern New York from the Ogden Land Company; the Seneca use money that Congress had set aside for their removal to Kansas.	Indian Commissioner James W. Denver advocates small reservations that will force Native Americans into farming, and where land will be allotted individually. **1858** Texas Rangers launch offensive attacks against the Comanche and Kickapoo tribes in Indian Territory. **1859** By an act of Congress and a presidential executive order, the Salt River and Gila River Reservations are established for Pima and Maricopa Indians in what is now Arizona.	**1850** The federal Fugitive Slave Act, passed by Congress as part of the Compromise of 1850, allows anyone claiming ownership of a runaway slave to take possession after establishing ownership before a federal commissioner. It also makes the harboring of a person fleeing slavery a crime, and gives owners the right to reclaim fugitives found in other states. In the United States, products of slave labor are valued at $136,505,435, mainly consisting of cotton (worth $98,603,720 alone), tobacco, cane sugar, rice and molasses. **c. 1850** Active in the cause against slavery, poetess Frances Ellen Watkins Harper is one of the most dynamic speakers on the Maine Anti-Slavery Society's lecturer tours. Harper was born free at Baltimore, Maryland. Josiah Henson emigrates to Canada after the passage of the Fugitive Slave Act and remains active in the Underground Railroad. He is reported to have helped more than 130 former enslaved African Americans to gain their freedom. His life story is said to have influenced the writing of *Uncle Tom's Cabin.* **1851** California law denies African Americans the right to testify in court against European Americans. Sojourner Truth presents her now-famous "Ain't I A Woman" speech at a women's rights meeting in Akron, Ohio. A school for African American girls, the first in the country, is opened at Wash ington, D.C., by Myrtilla Miner. **1852** Harriet Beecher Stowe's book, *Uncle Tom's Cabin,* is published. It portrays in emotional language the plight of enslaved African Americans.

The leftmost column of the page contains: **1850** through **1859**

AFRICAN AMERICAN	AFRICAN AMERICAN	AFRICAN AMERICAN	FOR CLASSROOM USE	

Frederick Douglass, in his famous oration in Rochester, New York, asks, "What, to the American slave, is your Fourth of July?"

Historian William C. Nell, an African American, publishes *Services of Colored Americans in the Wars of 1776 and 1812.*

New York-born educator and poet Charles L. Reason becomes director of the Institute for Colored Youth (now Cheyney University of Pennsylvania) at Philadelphia, a school initially developed by a Quaker grant in 1839.

1853

In Boston, Massachusetts, Sarah Parker Remond is forcibly removed from the Howard Athenaeum, even though she has a ticket, because she is an African American. Remond takes her case to court, and wins.

Lincoln University in Pennsylvania is established; it is the nation's first college for African Americans.

1854

Illinois lawyer Abraham Lincoln makes his first public statement against the extension of slavery: "Slavery is founded in the selfishness of men and nature."

In Norfolk, Virginia, Margaret Douglass is arrested and jailed for the crime of teaching African American children.

Elizabeth Jennings, a New York City school teacher on her way to church, is forcibly ejected from a streetcar reserved for European Americans. The African American community unites in her support, forming a committee to defend her. This committee hires a prestigious law firm, and the case is given to the young Chester A. Arthur. The court finds in Jennings's favor, and as a result, all streetcars in the city are desegregated.

1855

African Americans are mustered into military service in the South.

The Massachusetts legislature prohibits discrimination on the basis of race, color or religious preference in its public schools.

c. 1855

Berea College is founded in Kentucky under the direction of abolitionist leader Reverend John Gregg Fee.

1856

Under the direction of the Methodist Episcopal Church, Wilberforce University is established in Ohio with an interracial board.

Biddy Mason sues her owner under California law and wins her freedom.

1857

In *Dred Scott* v. *Sandford,* the Supreme Court allows slavery in federal territories and denies citizenship to African Americans.

New Hampshire enacts laws benefitting African Americans. One law declares that a person may not be excluded from citizenship or voting on account of African heritage, previous enslavement or color of skin. Another law frees any enslaved person brought into the state and makes forcing someone into slavery a felony.

1859

Connecticut-born farmer and abolitionist John Brown initiates his plan to end southern slavery by armed intervention. He leads a band of men, including five African Americans, on a raid against the United States arsenal at Harper's Ferry, Virginia (now West Virginia). The arsenal is retaken the next day by troops under Robert E. Lee. An African American, Dangerfield Newby, is killed in the attack. Earlier, Brown had been deeply moved by the Bible as he and his family travelled west. They assisted on the Underground Railroad wherever they could, and made their home in Kansas in 1856. Brown was involved in the massacre of proslavery activists at Pottawatamie Creek. He is later tried for his participation in the Harper's Ferry raid and hanged, as are two African Americans, John A. Copeland and Sheridan Leary, both from Oberlin, Ohio. Osborn Perry Anderson escapes and later writes of his experience at Harper's Ferry.

In Cincinnati, Ohio, a *mulatto* (a person of combined African and European ethnicity) woman is forcibly removed from a streetcar by the conductor. The woman institutes court action against the conductor on charges of assault, and wins her case.

1850
through
1859

ASIAN AMERICAN	ASIAN AMERICAN	EUROPEAN AMERICAN	EUROPEAN AMERICAN

1850 through 1859

ASIAN AMERICAN

1850

The United States census reports 725 Chinese on the United States mainland.

Ten thousand Chinese immigrants live in California by year's end. The Foreign Miner's License Tax is levied on Chinese and Mexican American miners.

The first Chinese American temple, to the Queen of Heaven (Tianhou), is founded in San Francisco, California.

Hikozo Hamada, also known as Joseph Heco, is rescued at sea by an American sailing ship. He studies in Baltimore, Maryland, and in 1858 becomes the first naturalized Japanese American citizen.

1850s

The first Chinese district associations are established in San Francisco to maintain order, settle disputes and provide protection against external threats.

A Chinese merchant guild is formed in San Francisco to settle disputes and to protect group interests. Other worker guilds are soon established.

1852

The arrival of 20,025 Chinese immigrants in California this year marks the beginning of large-scale immigration to the United States from China.

The governor of California advocates legislation to limit the entry of Chinese contract laborers and to exclude them from the mines.

Many mining areas in California expel Chinese miners.

Chinese masons are imported to erect the Parrott Building, the first granite edifice in San Francisco.

Presbyterians establish the first Protestant mission among Chinese Americans in San Francisco.

The Royal Hawaii Agricultural Society imports 280 Chinese contract laborers to work in the sugarcane industry.

1853

Commodore Matthew C. Perry and his fleet sail into Tokyo Bay, Japan. This first official visit from the United States leads to the opening of Japan to American traders.

ASIAN AMERICAN

1854

Political chaos and economic dislocation in southern China force many people to emigrate.

The California Supreme Court rules that laws prohibiting the testimony of Native and African Americans in cases involving European Americans also apply to Chinese Americans. This law is not repealed until 1872.

The first Chinese newspaper in the United States, the *Golden Hills News,* begins publication in San Francisco. It lasts for a few months.

Yung Wing becomes the first Chinese graduate of an American university when he receives his degree from Yale.

1855

California levies a $50 tax on the master, owner or consignee of a vessel for each person on board who is ineligible to be a citizen (that is, any Chinese person). This law is ruled unconstitutional in 1856 by the United States Supreme Court.

California laws ban non-European American students from public schools.

Chinese immigrants arrive in Gold Canyon, Nevada to work on a ditch. They later relocate to Chinatown (Dayton, Nevada) and engage in mining.

In San Francisco, the Reverend William Speer publishes the *Oriental,* the first bilingual Chinese-English newspaper. Speer's ill health causes the paper's closure in 1857.

1856

For two years, Ze Too Yune publishes the *Chinese Daily News,* the first Chinese daily in the world, in Sacramento, California.

1857

The first public school for Chinese students is established in San Francisco.

1858

The California Central Railroad and Pioneer Woolen Mills begin to employ Chinese workers.

EUROPEAN AMERICAN

1850

A German American ghetto known as "Kleindeutschland" (Little Germany) develops in New York City's 10th, 11th and 13th wards.

Heinrich Steinweg, founder of the piano company Steinway and Sons, immigrates to the United States from Germany. In 1855, his piano wins three prizes at the Crystal Palace Exhibition in New York City.

1850s

Violent encounters between nativist groups and recent German immigrants occur in several cities, including Louisville, Kentucky; Boston, Massachusetts; and Cincinnati, Ohio.

1851

Irish and French immigration sets record annual highs of 221,300 and 20,000, respectively. A high percentage of employed Irish women work as domestic servants, the rest in mills and factories.

Norwegian, Swedish and Danish colonists begin migrating into Minnesota in large numbers after the Indian Treaties of 1851 remove Native Americans from the land.

This is the all-time peak year for German immigration to the United States, with 221,253 persons arriving.

1851-1860

During this decade, more than 420,000 people from England and more than 910,000 from Ireland immigrate to the United States.

1852

Beth Hamidrash is established as the first Russian-Jewish congregation in the United States.

Many of the German immigrants to the United States are Jews, most of whom make their homes in urban areas of America.

Mormon overseas missions are established in all the Scandinavian countries. Several thousand Scandinavian Mormons immigrate to the United States under church supervision. Most migrate to the Salt Lake area of Utah.

EUROPEAN AMERICAN

1853

Austrian immigration begins to increase. Many Austrians were peasants and unemployed village laborers. They now work on farms on the agricultural frontier of the Great Plains.

Striking Irishmen on the Erie Railroad are replaced with armed African Americans.

A Norwegian newspaper is established in Chicago.

In Newark, New Jersey, 10,000 German Americans petition the city council to repeal "blue laws" that prohibit the sale of alcoholic beverages on Sunday. This becomes a recurrent point of contention between newer immigrants from Germany and the Scandinavian countries, where it is traditional to have a drink or two after church, and the older American communities where this is not done.

1854

Jewish Americans request that the United States government not ratify a treaty with Switzerland because that country denies certain rights to Jewish Americans traveling there.

The first Jewish Reform Congregation in the United States is established by Rabbi Isaac M. Wise in Cincinnati.

1855

The earliest significant Swedish newspaper printed in the United States, *Det Gamla Och Det Nya Hemlandet* (The Old and the New Homeland), begins publication in Illinois.

The optical company of Bausch and Lomb is founded by German Americans Henry Lomb and John J. Bausch.

Nearly one-third of New York City's 1,100 police officers are first-generation Irish immigrants.

Members of a German Pietist group led by Christian Metz migrate westward from the Buffalo, New York, area into what is now Iowa. They establish the Amana Communities, incorporated in 1859 as the Amana Society.

1856

A group of Norwegian religious dissenters called Haugeans leaves the Fox River colony in Illinois and establishes a new community in Iowa, which they call Palestine.

EUROPEAN AMERICAN	HISPANIC AMERICAN	HISPANIC AMERICAN	FOR CLASSROOM USE	

EUROPEAN AMERICAN	HISPANIC AMERICAN	HISPANIC AMERICAN		
Probably the most lasting German contribution to American education is the kindergarten. The first kindergarten in the United States is established in Watertown, Wisconsin, by Carl Schurz. An Irish Catholic colonization meeting is held at Buffalo, New York. **1856-1865** During this period, 11,000 Swedes and Norwegians desert ships to remain in the United States. After the Civil War, these numbers increase. **1857** An "American Sunday" versus "Continental Sunday" dispute arises in Madison, Wisconsin, where a large Norwegian population exists. Norwegian American clergy side with the older American community, which is outraged that many more recent Scandinavian and German immigrants prefer to drink beer before and/or after church on Sundays. **c. 1857** The Fenian Brotherhood, also called the Irish Republican Brotherhood, is established in New York City. An underground rebel organizaton, it seeks Irish independence by any means including violence. The group is led by John O'Mahoney, one of the organizers of the failed Young Ireland rebellion of 10 years earlier. **1858** Passenger ships of immigrants from Hamburg take as long as three months to make the journey across the Atlantic to America. One such vessel, the *Howard,* arrives in New York this year with more than 30 fatalities from cholera, a critical food shortage, and no drinkable water on board. Dr. Mary Anna Elson becomes the first Jewish American woman to graduate from Pennsylvania Women's Medical College. **1859** The German pietist community at Buffalo, New York, dwindling in numbers, moves to Amana, Iowa.	**1850** The United States census reports a Hispanic population of approximately 100,000. An estimated 60,000 Mexican Americans live in New Mexico, 7,500 in California, 20,000 in Texas and 1,000 in Arizona. The Foreign Miner's License Tax is levied on Mexican American and Chinese miners. **1851** Jean Baptiste Lamy is appointed New Mexico's first bishop. The Gwin Land Act, passed by Congress, challenges Mexican land claims in California. The federal land law, enacted to facilitate European Americans' acquisition of land from Mexican Americans, succeeds so well in California that in 1880 only 25 percent of the land owned by Californians at the time of the Treaty of Guadalupe Hidalgo is still in their hands. Colonel Covases of Fronteras (in Sonora province, Mexico) raids a peaceful Apache band camped at Janos, Chihuahua. He and his forces kill 20 and take more than 50 captives. **1853** Mexican immigrants arrive in Arizona to work the mines. **1854** Congress ratifies the Gadsden Purchase of southern Arizona and New Mexico from Mexico. This land acquisition makes possible a railroad route from El Paso to San Diego, and adds more Mexicans to the United States population. For years, Mexican Americans in Texas have been helping African Americans escape to freedom in Mexico. In an attempt to stop this, European American citizens of Seguin, Texas, pass resolutions prohibiting Mexican "peons" from entering the country. These resolutions also prohibit the association of African Americans and Mexican Americans, and call for prompt action against anyone consorting with enslaved African Americans without the permission of their masters.	**1855** A cholera epidemic in Puerto Rico kills an estimated 30,000 people. The African population is most affected. Dr. Ramón Emeterio Betances is later recognized for his efforts in aiding cholera victims. **1856** A planned slave rebellion in Texas is uncovered before it can be carried out. All Mexicans in the county are arrested and ordered to leave. Of the African Americans supposedly involved, two are hanged, 200 are whipped and two are whipped to death. **1857** The "Cart War" takes place in Texas, between European Americans and Mexican Americans over the business of transporting goods. European Americans resort to vandalism, destruction of convoys and murder to suppress the Mexican transport industry. The battle wanes when the Texas legislature and the secretary of state provide military escorts for cartmen. **1859** The "Cortina War" erupts in Brownsville, Texas, when Juan Nepomuceno Cortina shoots a city marshal after an insult. Cortina later enters the city and takes possession of it. He is a desperado, he says, because European Americans "blacken, deprecate, and load with insults" the Mexican residents of Texas. Cortina withdraws to Mexico, where he harasses Confederate troops during the Civil War.		**1850** **through** **1859**

201

1850 through 1859

1850

United States President Zachary Taylor dies of cholera while in office. Vice President Millard Fillmore succeeds him as the 13th president of the United States.

The United States census reports the country's population at 23.2 million, including approximately 3.2 million enslaved African Americans and 100,000 Hispanic Americans.

The Compromise of 1850, a series of bills to define the status of slavery in the new territories acquired from Mexico, becomes law. It prohibits the slave trade in Washington, D.C., but allows people there to keep existing enslaved Africans; it allows California to be admitted as a free state (the 31st state to join the Union); it enables the residents of New Mexico and Utah to decide on the slavery issue; and provides for a stronger Fugitive Slave Law. This compromise does little to quell the controversy over slavery in the United States.

The Clayton-Bulwer Treaty, named for Secretary of State John Clayton and Britain's Sir Henry Litton Bulwer, is approved by the United States and Britain. It provides for mutual access to a proposed canal that is to be built through Nicaragua to connect the Atlantic and Pacific Oceans. The treaty is nullified by the United States prior to the building of the Panama Canal.

The United States government releases to the Catholic Church missions in the Southwest that were seized during hostilities with Mexico.

The Michigan constitution gives the vote to all immigrants who have lived in the state for 2.5 years and have sworn their intention to become naturalized American citizens.

In the magazine, *Lily,* Amelia Jenks Bloomer castigates the Tennessee state legislature after that assembly declares that women may not own property because they have no souls.

Utah State University is founded at Salt Lake City.

A cholera epidemic in Jamaica kills 32,000 people.

1850-1851

North Carolina's first daily newspapers, the *Raleigh Register* and the *Wilmington Daily Journal,* begin publication.

1850s

In the United States, public elementary schools are established for both boys and girls.

Argentina, Colombia, Peru and Venezuela officially outlaw slavery.

Mid-1800s

George William Gordon, born on a Jamaican plantation to an enslaved African mother and a European planter father, is a leader in organizing newly emancipated African Jamaicans. He is assisted by Paul Bogle. Both men are executed in 1865, following a protest rally.

c. 1850-1900

Westward expansion in the United States is justified by the doctrine of manifest destiny.

1851

The colony of Seattle is founded in the Oregon Territory. It is incorporated as a city in 1869.

Santa Clara University and the University of the Pacific at Stockton, California and the University of Minnesota in Minneapolis are founded. The Female Medical College of Pennsylvania, the first women's medical college in the world, is founded in Philadelphia. In 1867, it is renamed the Woman's Medical College of Pennsylvania.

The community of San Luis is established in the area that is now Colorado. San Luis is generally considered to be the oldest permanent non-Indian community in Colorado.

Amelia Jenks Bloomer, an activist and the editor of *Lily,* a women's rights magazine, gets attention by wearing trousers, later called "bloomers."

Maine state law bans the sale and manufacture of liquor.

Tennessee's first successful commercial railroad, the Nashville and Chattanooga, goes into operation.

Isaac Merritt Singer invents a continuous stitching sewing machine.

Members of most of the Northern Plains Native American tribes meet and agree to allow European Americans traveling west to pass through Indian lands on the Oregon Trail.

The capital of Canada is moved from Toronto to Quebec.

Five hundred Cubans, joined by a handful of American soldiers, invade Cuba in an unsuccessful attempt to free the country from Spain. Narciso López, the expedition leader, is captured and executed.

1851-1852

The publication and serialization of Harriet Beecher Stowe's *Uncle Tom's Cabin* play a vital role in focusing people's antislavery attitudes in the northern United States.

1851-1860

Immigration to the United States totals 2,598,214 of which 2,452,577 come from Europe, 41,538 from Asia, 210 from Africa, 158 from Oceania, 74,720 from the Americas and 29,011 are not specifically identified.

1852

Ohio passes the first state labor law in the country, limiting women's workday to 10 hours.

Mills College is founded at Oakland, California.

Wells, Fargo & Company is founded as an express mail and package service from New York to California and other western points.

Working in Yonkers, New York, Elisha Graves Otis invents an automatic safety device to prevent machinery being hoisted from falling. In 1857 he invents the passenger elevator.

Canadian explorers find gold along the Pend Oreille River in Idaho.

Argentine dictator Juan Manuel de Rosas (1829, 1835) is overthrown after his defeat at the Battle of Caseros by troops under Justo de Urquiza.

The first of several French penal colonies is established in French Guiana. These colonies will develop a reputation for brutal treatment of prisoners.

1853

Franklin Pierce becomes the 14th president of the United States; William R. King is vice president. Both are Democrats. King dies in office, and the office remains vacant for the remainder of his term.

The Washington Territory is created out of lands formerly part of Oregon.

Dr. Elizabeth Blackwell, barred from public clinics because she is a woman, establishes her own one-room medical practice.

The Crystal Palace Exhibition is held in New York City to display and demonstrate new American inventions and advances in industry.

The University of Florida is founded at Gainesville.

William Walker, an adventurer from the United States, leads an invasion of Baja (Lower) California and declares himself president of the Republic of Sonora. He is arrested but is acquitted and returns to the United States.

In Cook Inlet, Alaska, Russian explorers see the first signs of oil seeping up through the ground.

Antoinette Brown Blackwell becomes the first female minister in the United States when she is ordained by the Congregational church.

Canada's Grand Trunk Railroad is completed, with service between Sherbrooke, in Quebec province, and the United States border.

Antonio López de Santa Anna returns to power in Mexico, declaring himself dictator. He rules until 1855.

Pedro Santana becomes president of the Dominican Republic after the term of Buenaventura Báez (1849). Santana serves until 1856.

THE AMERICAS	THE AMERICAS	THE AMERICAS	FOR CLASSROOM USE

Argentina adopts a new constitution. Justo José Urquiza becomes president. He serves until 1860.

1854

Congress ratifies the Gadsden Purchase (1853) whereby the United States buys from Mexico the area that is now southern New Mexico and Arizona south of the Gila River.

The Kansas-Nebraska Act is passed by Congress and signed into law, giving the two newly created United States territories the right to decide the slavery issue by popular sovereignty.

The Elgin-Marcy Treaty is signed by representatives of Britain and the United States; it reciprocally reduces or removes import duties on goods traded between the United States and Canada.

The Ostend Manifesto, drafted in Belgium, is designed to have the United States acquire Cuba as a slave state. Although it is a confidential document, it implies that the United States may attempt to take Cuba by force if Spain fails to sell. The manifesto becomes a political disaster and is hastily withdrawn.

The Republican Party is formed in Michigan as an antislavery party.

Tennessee's state legislature provides for taxation to support public education.

St. Paul, Minnesota, is incorporated as a city.

A colony is organized on the Missouri River. It incorporates as the city of Atchison, Kansas, in 1855.

An abolitionist society, the New England Emigrant Aid Company, under the direction of Charles Robinson, establishes the colony of Lawrence, Kansas, named for philanthropist Amos Adams Lawrence. The town serves as the center for Free Staters (antislavery colonists), and a proslavery attack on Lawrence provides the impetus for John Brown's attack at Pottawatamie in 1856.

A site used as a ferry dock on the Kansas River in the early 1840s is established by Free Staters from Lawrence, Kansas, as the city of Topeka.

Rhode Island College at Providence and Columbia College in South Carolina are founded.

Pirates led by Count Rousset de Bourbon attack the town of Guaymas, in Baja California, but are repulsed by General José Maria Yáñez and his forces.

The Plan of Ayutla, a reform program designed to remove Santa Anna from power in Mexico, is created.

1855

Armed factions for and against slavery clash in Kansas.

Kean College at Union and William Patterson College at Wayne, both in New Jersey, are founded.

David Edward Hughes invents an improved type-printing telegraph.

The first ship, the steamer *Illinois,* passes through the newly completed locks at Sault St. Marie, Michigan, marking the beginning of direct passage between Lakes Huron and Superior. Before this time, cargoes had to be unloaded and portaged around the rapids of the St. Mary's River connecting the two lakes.

The Western Union Telegraph Company is founded under the direction of financier Ezra Cornell.

French-born American explorer Paul Belloni du Chaillu makes his first trip to Africa, and brings back the first gorilla ever seen in the United States.

Approximately 30,000 people, most of them enslaved Africans, die during a cholera epidemic in Puerto Rico.

Toronto again becomes the capital of Canada.

The final defeat of Santa Anna leads to a period of change, called The Reform, in Mexican politics.

General Ramón Castilla (1845) again becomes president of Peru. He serves until 1862.

1856

Nativist activity leads to the formation of the American Know-Nothing Party, which calls for restricted immigration.

Wilberforce University is founded in Ohio. The University of Iowa in Iowa City becomes the first public college to accept women students.

Charlotte Forten Grimke graduates from normal school and becomes the first African American woman to officially instruct European American children. Grimke teaches in Salem, Massachusetts.

Abolitionist John Brown, declaring himself an instrument in God's hand, leads in the killing of five proslavery men in the Massacre of Potawatomie Creek, Kansas.

American merchant Marshall Field moves from his home in Pittsfield, Massachusetts, to become a clerk in a store in Chicago, Illinois. In 1865 he becomes a partner in a firm whose name is Field, Leiter and Company in 1867 and becomes Marshall Field and Company in 1881.

Buenaventura Báez (1849) becomes president of the Dominican Republic for the second time after the term of Pedro Santana (1853). Báez serves until 1858.

United States adventurer William Walker becomes president of Nicaragua after his private army captures Granada in 1855. He serves until 1857, when he is expelled by a combined Central American military force.

1857

James Buchanan becomes the 15th president of the United States; John C. Breckinridge is vice president. Both are Democrats.

In *Dred Scott* v. *Sanford*, the Supreme Court rules that neither free nor enslaved African Americans are United States citizens and therefore they cannot sue in federal court.

The Mountain Meadows Massacre occurs in Utah, when 120 European American colonists traveling west are killed by Indians. Mormon fanatic John D. Lee incited the Indians to act, supposedly in retaliation for Brigham Young's dismissal as governor of Utah.

A financial crisis hits the United States and Europe.

1850

through

1859

	THE AMERICAS	THE AMERICAS	THE AMERICAS	FOR CLASSROOM USE
1850 **through** **1859**	Illinois State University is founded at Normal. The first commercial oil well in North America opens at Oil Springs, Ontario. **1857-1861** Mexico adopts a liberal constitution, secularizing church property and reducing the privileges of the army. The reform leads to civil war between liberals and conservatives. When Acting President Ignacio Comonfort resigns in 1858, Benito Juárez becomes president and the liberals defeat the conservatives in the War of Reform. Juárez is Mexico's first full-blooded Indian president. **c. 1857** The Comstock Lode, a major silver deposit, is found in western Nevada. **1858** Minnesota becomes the 32nd state to join the Union. Fort Abercrombie is built as the first military post in what is now North Dakota. Auraria is established in present-day Colorado by gold prospectors. Joined by other small villages in 1860, it becomes Denver, which is incorporated as a city in 1861. A proslavery constitution is rejected in Kansas. Silver deposits are found in Nevada. Regular stagecoach service, carrying mail and passengers, begins from Missouri through Arizona to California. The Abraham Lincoln-Stephen Douglas debates take place during the campaign for Illinois's United States Senator seat. Abraham Lincoln makes a strong anti-slavery speech in Springfield: "...this Government cannot endure permanently half slave and half free." Although this campaign gains popularity for Lincoln, he loses the election. The Mormon community at Fort Lemhi, Idaho, is attacked by Bannock Indians. Two Mormons are killed; the rest flee back to Utah.	The first transatlantic telegraph cable is completed by Cyrus W. Field, although it breaks down after limited use. A more permanent and durable cable is installed in the mid-1860s. United States abolitionist John Brown conducts an anti-slavery convention in Chatham, Ontario, Canada. Pedro Santana (1853) again becomes president of the Dominican Republic after the term of Buenaventura Báez (1849, 1856). Santana serves until 1861. **c. 1858** Gold is discovered at Pikes Peak in Colorado, precipitating a rush of almost 100,000 people to the area by 1859. **1858-1859** The Colorado gold rush commences after William Green Russell, a Georgia miner, finds gold worth hundreds of dollars on a site that is now part of Denver. An estimated 50,000 people pour into the region. **1859** A border dispute arises between the United States and Canada over San Juan Island after a Canadian pig strays into an American potato patch on the island, and is shot by the landowner. Military forces from both countries occupy the island for several years. Germany's Kaiser Wilhelm is asked to arbitrate in 1873, and gives the disputed island to the United States. Oregon becomes the 33rd state to join the Union. One of the first commercial oil wells in the United States is drilled in Titusville, Pennsylvania. Arizona's first newspaper, the *Weekly Arizonian,* begins publication at Tubac.	Abolitionist John Brown initiates his plan to end southern slavery by armed intervention. He leads a band of men on a raid against the United States arsenal at Harper's Ferry, Virginia (now West Virginia). The arsenal is retaken the next day by troops under Robert E. Lee. Brown is later tried and hanged. George Mortimer Pullman begins converting railroad cars to accommodate long-distance passenger travel.	

| | |

1850

through

1859

| | |

1850 through 1859

1850

The population of China is approximately 430 million; India, 205 million; Japan, 33 million; Russia, 65 million; Ottoman Empire, 27 million; France, 36 million; the German states and independent cities, 35 million; the Italian states, 24 million and Britain, 21 million; Sweden's population is recorded at 3.5 million.

Ireland's Franchise Act increases voter rolls from 61,000 to 165,000 by lifting some franchise restrictions.

Missionaries from Germany explore the African interior, carefully detailing their travels in maps and charts. German groups are the first Europeans known to see Mounts Kenya and Kilimanjaro.

German scientist Robert Wilhelm Bunsen invents the gas burner that will bear his name.

1850-1864

The Taiping, or "Great Peace," Rebellion takes place, beginning in eastern Guangxi province, China. Led by Hong Xiuguan (Hung Hsiu-ch'üan), this is an uprising of predominantly poorer citizens against the Manchu dynasty. Women are a major force in this rebellion, fighting alongside the men. Many are from the Haka people, and are more agile fighters, as the Haka do not insist that women's feet be bound. The Taiping Rebellion continues for 14 years and results in the reduction of Manchu power; nearly 25 million people lose their lives.

1850-1880

Nine wars take place in South Africa between the native Bantu people and European colonists.

1851

France enters into a trade agreement with King Gezo of Dahomey.

Since the beginning of the potato famine in 1845, the Irish population has been reduced by about 2 million — half die from starvation and disease, half emigrate.

Prussia recognizes the German Confederation.

Gold is discovered in Victoria, Australia.

Dahomey (Benin) is under French control.

British officials place the administration of Singapore directly in the hands of the governor-general of India.

Jews gain religious freedom in Norway.

Rama IV (Mongkut) becomes king of Siam (Thailand) after the death of his half-brother, Rama III (1824). Rama IV rules until 1868.

George V becomes king of Hanover after the death of his father, Ernest Augustus (1837). George V rules until 1866 when Hanover is annexed to Prussia.

Scottish missionary and explorer David Livingstone becomes the first European to cross Africa. This year he reaches the Zambezi River; in 1855 he becomes the first European to see Victoria Falls.

1852

In New Zealand, gold is discovered at Coromandel.

Transvaal becomes the independent South African Republic.

The Second Anglo-Burmese War begins after King Pagan Min is deposed; when it ends, Britain annexes southern Burma.

The French government establishes a new constitution and begins the "Second Empire." President Charles Louis Napoleon Bonaparte proclaims himself Napoleon III, emperor of France. He rules until 1870.

Camillo Benso, the count of Cavour, becomes prime minister of Sardinia-Piedmont.

1853

Nanking becomes the capital of the Taiping under Hung Hsiu-ch'üan who has declared himself emperor of the new dynasty.

Women in China are sold into slavery to American men and sent to the United States.

United States Commodore Matthew C. Perry arrives in Tokyo Bay, Japan, with a fleet of four ships. He presents documents from President Millard Fillmore to the emperor requesting open trade between the countries and protection for seamen shipwrecked in the area.

The British annex Nagpur in India. They also annex Pegu in Burma at the end of the Second Burmese War.

Pedro V becomes king of Portugal after the death of his mother, Maria II (1826, 1834). He rules until 1861.

Iesada becomes shogun of Japan after the death of his brother, Ieyoshi (1837). Iesada rules until 1858.

English explorer (Sir) Richard Francis Burton, under a number of different disguises, visits the sacred forbidden Muslim cities of Mecca and Medina.

1853-1856

Russian Czar Nicholas I orders the occupation of the Turkish-controlled Danube regions. The Ottoman Empire declares war on Russia and the Crimean War begins. Major battles are fought at Alma, Balaklava, Inkerman and Sebastopol. The Ottomans are assisted by Britain, France and Sardinia — and their combined efforts thwart Russian attempts to encroach on Ottoman territory.

1854

United States Commodore Matthew C. Perry returns to Japan with a larger fleet and obtains an agreement, the Treaty of Kanagawa, with the Tokugawa shogunate for trade to begin between the two countries.

The Orange Free State in South Africa becomes a republic.

Shippers at Göteborg, Sweden, are swamped with requests for passage to the United States. Many prospective immigrants must travel by land to Hamburg, Germany or Liverpool, England and sail to America from these ports.

Said Pasha becomes *khedive* (viceroy) of Egypt after the death of his nephew, Abbas I (1848). Said Pasha rules until 1863.

English nurse Florence Nightingale organizes a unit of women nurses to serve Crimean War wounded. By the war's end, she and her corps are legendary. Nightingale has since come to be regarded as the originator of modern nursing techniques and service.

1854-1865

Senegal is occupied by French forces.

1855

A severe earthquake hits Wellington, New Zealand.

The Australian regions of New South Wales, Victoria, South Australia and Tasmania become self-governing colonies of Britain.

The Treaty of Peshawar creates an alliance between Britain and Afghanistan against Persia.

Alexander II becomes czar of Russia after the death of his father, Nicholas I (1825). Alexander II rules until 1881.

Theodore II (Ras Kassa, Lij Kasa) becomes emperor of Ethiopia after Ras Ali is deposed. Theodore II rules until 1868.

The Young Women's Christian Association (YWCA) is founded by Lady Kinnaird in London. It is officially named in 1877 when it merges with a similar organization operating as a prayer group in a different part of Britain.

Burton and John Speke explore previously uncharted sections of east central Africa. They visit Lakes Tanganyika and Victoria (the source of the Nile, also called Victoria Nyanza) in 1858.

Russian and Japanese officials sign a treaty that establishes their common border.

Madame Tinubu, a Nigerian Ibo, is expelled from Lagos for her opposition to British influence. A wealthy exporter of palm oil to Europe, she is representative of West African merchant women who achieve wealth and a measure of economic independence.

c. 1855

English inventor (Sir) Henry Bessemer discovers the process of manufacturing steel from pig iron. The process is patented in the United States in 1857.

1856

The Crimean War ends. The Congress of Paris negotiates the details of the end of hostilities. By its terms, Izmail reverts to Turkey from Russian control; the Black Sea is declared neutral; Moldavia and Walachia (later called Romania) and Serbia become partially independent but still under Turkish rule; Afghanistan's independence is recognized by Persia; the Russian-Turkish borders in Asia are restored to their prewar boundaries; and the Ottoman Empire is formally recognized by the European powers, though it must now honor Christianity within its borders. Russia's losses in the war weaken that country's standing as a world power; the advance of Russian forces into the Balkans is stopped as well.

In Africa, Britain makes Natal a crown colony; in India, Oudh is annexed to Britain.

British and French forces begin a siege of Canton, China.

Britain's Queen Victoria establishes the Victoria Cross to reward military acts of distinction.

1857

The great mutiny of native soldiers, known as the Sepoy Rebellion, begins in India. As a result, the East India Company is abolished and India is placed under British rule.

Russia begins a campaign to gain control over the Caucasus.

The French build a fort in Dakar, Senegal.

China's fleet is destroyed by the British navy that, with French assistance, captures Canton.

Europe, and especially Britain, experience financial panic due to speculation in United States railroads.

French chemist Louis Pasteur conducts studies showing that microorganisms cause fermentation; this work gives credence to the germ theory of infection, and lays the groundwork for the discipline of microbiology.

c. 1857

The Fenian Brotherhood (Irish Republican Brotherhood) is organized as a secret society whose desire is to free Ireland from British rule by military action.

1858

European powers begin trading with Japan.

Through the Treaty of Aigun, China cedes territory on the left bank of the Amur River to Russia.

The Treaty of Tientsin forces China to open many of its ports and begin foreign trade. The United States and China sign a new trade treaty.

The Government of India Act transfers the rule of India to the British monarchy.

Jews are admitted to the British Parliament.

Singapore is administered directly by the British crown.

One of the first successful oil wells in Europe is drilled at Wietze, Hanover.

Milos (Milos Obrenovich, 1817-1839) again becomes prince of Serbia after Alexander (Alexander Karageorgevich, 1842) is deposed. Milos rules until his death in 1860.

Iemochi becomes shogun of Japan after the death of Iesada (1853). Iemochi rules until 1866.

Felice Orsini is unsuccessful in the attempted assassination of Napoleon III.

1859

Unification of Italy starts under the leadership of Camillo Benso, count of Cavour, the prime minister of Sardinia-Piedmont. He drives the Austrians from northern Italy. France later joins Italy in its war with Austria, which ends with the Treaty of Zurich.

France begins its conquest of Indochina.

War erupts again between Britain and China.

Queensland (Australia) separates from New South Wales and becomes a self-governing British crown colony.

The German National Association is established to unite the German states under Prussian authority.

Alexander John I (Alexander John Cuza) is elected prince of both Moldavia and Walachia. He facilitates the union of the two regions into the nation of Romania in 1861. Alexander John I rules until 1866.

Charles (Karl) XV becomes king of Sweden and Norway after the death of his father, Oscar I (1844). Charles XV rules until 1872.

Francis II becomes king of the Two Sicilies (Sicily and Naples) after the death of his father, Ferdinand II (1830). Francis II rules until 1861.

English naturalist Charles Darwin puts forth his theory of the evolution of living things by natural selection in his work, *On the Origin of Species,* published this year.

1850

through

1859

NATIVE AMERICAN	NATIVE AMERICAN	NATIVE AMERICAN	AFRICAN AMERICAN
1860-1885

The Apaches of Arizona and New Mexico fight against European American squatters and United States troops.

1861

Of all the Native American tribes of eastern and central Indian Territory (Oklahoma), the Kickapoos alone refuse an alliance with the Confederacy.

By presidential executive order the Uintah Valley in what is now Utah is set aside for the Ute tribe. The remainder of the territory in this area claimed by Native Americans is taken by the federal government without formal purchase.

1861-1868

United States armed forces conduct a major campaign to subdue the Plains Indian tribes (Kiowa, Comanche, Cheyenne, Arapaho and Sioux). Battles are widespread from Wyoming to Texas, and the fighting continues north from 1865 to 1868.

1862

In a Sioux uprising in Minnesota, Chief Little Crow of the Mdawakanton band leads the Santee (Eastern Sioux) against encroaching colonists. The Sioux are defeated by Colonel Henry Sibley and his troops, and 38 Santee are hanged.

Kickapoo leader Machemanet moves 600 of his people from Kansas to Texas. They are attacked by Confederate troops at the Little Concho River in Texas, but repel the raid. The tribe then crosses the Rio Grande and moves into the Coahuila, Mexico, area, joining Kickapoos who migrated there in 1839. This scenario is virtually repeated by another Kickapoo group in 1864, and by 1865, all southern Kickapoo bands have relocated to Coahuila.

1863

The Treaty of Ruby Valley (in Nevada territory) is signed between the Western Shoshone and United States Superintendent James D. Doty; grazing rights defined by the treaty will remain a significant and unresolved issue into the 1990s. | **1863-1864**

After defeating the Mescalero Apache, the first New Mexican volunteers, organized and led by Christopher "Kit" Carson, force the Navajo to surrender and move to Fort Sumner (Bosque Redondo), New Mexico. This relocation is known as the Long Walk of the Navajo.

1864

Native Americans are considered competent by law to participate as witnesses in court proceedings.

More than 100 peaceful Cheyenne, mostly women and children, are killed in a surprise attack at Sand Creek, Colorado. The massacre is led by Colonel John Chivington.

By an act of Congress, the Hoopa Valley Reservation, an area of 155 square miles, is set aside in California for several Native American groups. In 1892 the United States government returns part of this reservation to the public domain.

1865

By an order of the United States Secretary of the Interior, land is to be set aside in Nevada and California for the Washoe tribe. No "suitable land" can be found, so no further action is taken.

1866

The Railway Enabling Act confiscates Native American lands for railroad use.

In the Fetterman Battle in Wyoming, Sioux forces ambush and destroy a small detachment of government troops on the Bozeman Trail. After this incident, the trail – a shortcut through Indian lands to gold fields in Colorado and Montana – is virtually abandoned.

1867

To obtain the Treaty of Medicine Lodge Creek, Kansas, representatives of the Kiowa, Comanche, Cheyenne and Arapaho meet with the Peace Commission established by Congress and agree to new reservations. | The federal Board of Indian Commissioners is established in response to the demand for a nonpartisan group to oversee the administration of Native American affairs. Staffed by reformers, it is often at odds with the Interior Department.

1868

In the second Fort Laramie Treaty, the northern bands of Cheyenne and Arapaho move to the Big Sioux Reservation in Dakota and relinquish all other land claims.

Navajos displaced by the troops of Colonel Kit Carson are allowed to return to a newly established reservation on the Arizona-New Mexico border.

In Arizona, captive Apaches are sold into slavery for $40 apiece.

At the Washita Massacre, Lieutenant Colonel George Custer and his forces attack Chief Black Kettle's peaceful Cheyenne village, killing more than 100 people, mostly women and children.

By an act of Congress, the Smith River and Mendocino Reservations in California are disbanded and the lands are returned to the public domain.

1869

President Ulysses S. Grant appoints Brigadier General Ely S. Parker as commissioner of the Bureau of Indian Affairs. A chief of the Seneca tribe, Parker is the first Native American to hold this position. He serves until 1871. | **1860**

The United States census reports 4,441,000 African Americans, representing just over 14 percent of the total population.

1861

William C. Nell is the first African American to hold a federal civilian position when he becomes a post office clerk in Boston.

Nathaniel Gordon is found guilty of violating the 1820 act that prohibits slave importation when his ship, the *Erie,* is captured with enslaved Africans aboard. Gordon is hanged the following year.

William Tillman, a cook on the *S. J. Waring*, is captured along with his ship's crew by a Confederate ship, *Jefferson Davis*. Tillman escapes, kills his captors and helps return the schooner to New York. As a reward for his service to his nation, he reportedly receives a stipend of more than $5000.

An experiment begun at Port Royal in the South Carolina Sea Islands demonstrates that African Americans are more productive as free, paid workers than they were as enslaved laborers. The effort is conducted by abolitionist Edward Philbrick, who sells parcels of land to his workers in 1864.

1861-1863

In the early years of the Civil War, President Lincoln and Union military officers refuse offers of help from African Americans who want to fight against slavery. However, African Americans are pressed into service in the southern states, forming several Confederate regiments. In early 1863 authorization is finally given for the muster of Union regiments of African American soldiers. In May the War Department organizes African American troops into the United States Colored Troops (USCT). By July, 30 African American regiments are under USCT command. |

1860 through 1869

208

African Americans serve with distinction during the war. Sergeant William Harvey Carney of the 54th Massachusetts Regiment performs with valor in the Union's unsuccessful attack on Fort Wagner near Charleston, South Carolina, in 1863. At the Battle of Port Hudson in Louisiana, Captain James Lewis, who began his participation in the war as a Confederate officer, leads his troops in battle. Martin R. Delany, the first African American field officer, serves as major of the 104th Regiment of Colored Troops. Robert Smalls, a sailor on the Confederate ship *Planter,* sails the vessel out of Charleston harbor and turns it over to the Union. Awarded the rank of captain, he serves the Union with distinction during the conflict. African American women also participate, many serving in hospitals and military camps. The total number of African Americans serving in the military during this war is estimated at 200,000, comprising approximately 10 percent of the Union fighting force; 38,000 of these lose their lives.

Eight African American physicians are appointed to the Army Medical Corps during the war. The most distinguished is Dr. Alexander T. Augustus, who is given the rank of major and placed in charge of Camp Barker, later organized as Freedmen's Hospital in Washington, D.C. Augustus thus becomes the first African American in the nation to head a major medical facility. The other seven physicians are Drs. Anderson Abbott, John V. De Grasse, William Ellis, William Powell, Charles Purvis, John Rapier and Alpheus Tucker.

Twenty-one African Americans receive the Congressional Medal of Honor, five for their service to the Navy and sixteen for valor in the Army. Of the Army awards, eleven are issued to soldiers exhibiting bravery and courage at the Battle of Chafin's Farm.

1862

President Lincoln's Emancipation Proclamation declares that all enslaved African Americans in the rebelling states are free. The proclamation goes into effect on January 1, 1863.

Mary Jane Patterson becomes the first African American woman to graduate from college in the United States, receiving a degree from Oberlin College.

1863

The Emancipation Proclamation goes into effect. Freed African Americans find themselves with very limited occupational opportunities. Many continue to work for their former owners. In cities, they face increased job competition and exclusion. Many African Americans enlist and fight in the Civil War.

Because of the war effort, rapid migration from south to north occurs. This migration, coupled with generally lower wages of the unstable Civil War economy, lead European American workers to fear that African Americans will replace them in the labor force and take all available new jobs. The result is a series of race riots, the most serious of which takes place in New York.

Bishop Daniel A. Payne, of the African Methodist Episcopal (AME) Church, heads a group that purchases Wilberforce University from the Methodist Episcopal Church. The school, which closed during the early years of the war, is reopened with Bishop Payne as its first African American president.

Henry MacNeal Turner, a minister (later bishop) in the AME Church, is appointed by President Abraham Lincoln as the first African American chaplain in the Union army. He later serves in the Georgia state legislature.

1864

Some Confederate officers vow to kill any African American Union soldiers captured. At the Battle of Fort Pillow, in Tennessee, African Americans surrender and nearly 300 are then massacred, including women and children.

A federal law is enacted freeing the wives and children of African American soldiers.

The National Equal Rights League is formed at Syracuse, New York, to promote the cause of African American suffrage and to lobby for equal rights. This is the first of a series of independent conventions that African Americans hold during the next six years to consolidate support for their newly won freedom.

The nation's first African American daily newspaper, the *New Orleans Tribune* is a bilingual publication, printed in French and English.

Mid-1860s

African Americans benefit from the $2,000,000 George Peabody Education Fund, established to promote education in the South. The funds are generally distributed on the basis of need.

1865

The Thirteenth Amendment to the United States Constitution abolishes slavery throughout the country.

Dr. John S. Rock becomes the first African American to practice law before the nation's Supreme Court. Rock, who gave up his medical practice due to ill health, was admitted to the Massachusetts bar in 1861.

The Chesapeake Marine Railroad and Dry Dock Company is established in Baltimore, Maryland, by Isaac Myers. The company employs hundreds of African American workers.

John Jones, a wealthy businessman, is instrumental in gaining the repeal of discriminatory laws in Chicago. In the early 1870s, he becomes commissioner of Cook County and the first African American to serve on the Chicago Board of Education.

Shaw University is founded at Raleigh, North Carolina.

The Freedmen's Bureau is formed within the War Department. It provides relief assistance and help in acquiring land for freed African Americans. The purpose of the Bureau is expanded by an amended act in 1866 to emphasize education. The Bureau is disbanded in 1872.

c. 1865-1866

After the Civil War, a number of states pass "black codes," designed to create legal restrictions on the rights granted by the Emancipation Proclamation. Although the wording and regulations of the codes vary in each state, they all serve the purpose of reducing the ability of newly emancipated African Americans to benefit from their freedom.

1866

Edward G. Walker and Charles L. Mitchell become the first African American state legislators when they are elected to the Massachusetts House of Representatives.

A civil rights act is passed by Congress, over President Johnson's veto. This act defines citizenship and prohibits discrimination based on race. Since it lacks support of either the president or the Supreme Court, the act has little practical effect.

James Milton Turner, one of the first African American teachers to be hired in Missouri, founds Lincoln University at Jefferson City. It succeeds a smaller school, Ashmun Institution, which was started in 1854.

Jonathan J. Wright becomes the first African American admitted to the bar in South Carolina. He later serves as an associate justice of the state Supreme Court.

Fisk University, named in honor of General Clinton B. Fisk, at Nashville, Tennessee, and Edward Waters College at Jacksonville, Florida, are founded.

The state of Rhode Island passes a statute ending segregated schools. The action is primarily the result of efforts by George T. Downing, a successful African American caterer and financier in Providence.

1860

through

1869

AFRICAN AMERICAN	AFRICAN AMERICAN	ASIAN AMERICAN	ASIAN AMERICAN

1867

Howard University, named in honor of General Oliver Otis Howard, is founded in Washington, D.C., by an act of Congress. Efforts of the American Missionary Association lead to the establishment of Atlanta University in Georgia and Talladega College in Alabama. Johnson C. Smith University at Charlotte and St. Augustine's College, both in North Carolina, and Morehouse College at Atlanta, Georgia, are also founded.

Although records are not entirely clear, it is believed that the first interracial jury convened on a federal level is the one empaneled to try Jefferson Davis for his participation in the Civil War.

1868

The Fourteenth Amendment to the United States Constitution grants citizenship to African Americans.

Hampton Institute, which grew out of a school begun in 1861 near Fort Monroe, Virginia, is founded. It becomes incorporated two years later. The medical school of Howard University opens to both African American and European American students. Initially operated as Camp Barker and then the Freedman's Bureau under the War Department, Freedman's Hospital in Washington, D.C., is organized on a permanent basis.

Jonathan Gibbs is elected as secretary of state in Florida. He serves until 1872.

Educated in England and Scotland, Francis L. Cardozo becomes South Carolina's secretary of state. He serves until 1872 when he begins a four-year term as state treasurer.

John Willis Menard is elected to the United States Congress from Louisiana. Although he is not granted his seat in the House, he is awarded full pay for the position.

1869

Jefferson F. Long, a Republican from Georgia, becomes the first African American to serve in the United States House of Representatives. He serves one term.

Fanny Jackson Coppin becomes president of the Institute for Colored Youth at Philadelphia after serving at the school as a teacher for four years. Her autobiography is entitled *Reminiscences of School Life and Hints on Teaching*.

The Colored National Labor Union is organized in Washington, D.C.

Ebenezer D. Bassett is appointed minister of Haiti by President Ulysses S. Grant. Bassett serves until 1877.

Tougaloo College in Mississippi is founded.

1860

The United States census reports 35,586 Chinese people on the United States mainland. Almost all live in California.

California levies a tax of $4 per month on each Chinese fisherman.

1860s-1870s

Chinese immigrants enter the garment industry. By the mid-1870s Chinese people comprise 20 to 25 percent of California's garment workers. For example, approximately 80 percent of shirtmakers are Chinese.

1862

A federal law prohibits the sale of enslaved Chinese people.

California levies a monthly capitation tax of $2.50 on every Chinese person. It is ruled unconstitutional.

Six Chinese district associations in San Francisco form a loose federation; they become the voice of the Chinese community.

Gold is discovered on the upper Columbia River in California. Chinese mining companies predominate in the area for the next four decades, and Chinese villages are established. The movement of miners to the gold fields, including Oregon, Washington, Idaho, Montana, South Dakota and Colorado, is the first major wave of Chinese migration throughout the United States.

1863

The earliest Chinese immigrants to Arizona arrive in this year.

1864

The first salmon cannery in the United States opens at Washington, California, and employs Filipino workers.

California's $4 per month tax on Chinese fishermen is repealed.

Mid-1860s

Farmers use Chinese labor to build levees and reclaim swampland in the Sacramento River delta near San Francisco, California.

1865-1869

About 12,000 Chinese immigrants are hired for construction of the Central Pacific portion of the transcontinental railroad. In the 1870s Chinese immigrants work on other United States and local railroads as well as roads. Movement of these workers is the second wave of migration of Chinese throughout the West.

1867

Two thousand Chinese American railroad workers strike for a week.

The Meiji government of Japan encourages Japanese students to study abroad.

1868

The United States and China sign the Burlingame Treaty recognizing the right of free immigration and emigration of citizens of both countries. The agreement also ensures a steady supply of cheap labor for the development of the West.

Approximately 170 contract laborers make up the first large group of Japanese people going to Hawaii. The Japanese government learns of their mistreatment at the hands of plantation owners and forbids further emigration.

1869

The first sizable group of Japanese immigrants to the mainland United States make their homes in Gold Hill, California, and establish the Wakamatsu Tea and Silk Farm colony.

With the completion of the transcontinental railroad, Chinese Americans migrate east and make homes in metropolitan centers.

1860

through

1869

EUROPEAN AMERICAN	EUROPEAN AMERICAN	HISPANIC AMERICAN	HISPANIC AMERICAN	

1860

The United States census reports 1.3 million people of German descent living in the United States.

For the first time, a rabbi opens a session of Congress with a prayer.

1861

The German American militia units in Texas are dissolved because they refuse to surrender their Union flags.

According to a census, the Russian communities in Alaska have 576 Russian men and 208 Russian women. There are nine Orthodox churches serving approximately 12,000 people. Church services are conducted in both the Russian and Aleut languages.

1861-1865

During the Civil War, all-Irish regiments of Union forces are raised in New York, Massachusetts, Michigan, Ohio, Indiana, Illinois and Iowa. At least 3,000 Swedish Americans serve in the Union army, nearly half of them from Illinois. About 177,000 German Americans are Union soldiers as well. Recent, poorer and jobless immigrants find army pay a strong inducement.

1862

Large numbers of Norwegians begin to arrive in the United States. At this time Norway is second only to Ireland in terms of the proportion of its population who come to America. New Norwegian immigrants usually seek out existing Norwegian communities, generally in the Midwest, and work on established farms, mines or lumber mills.

Swedish American inventor John Ericsson is responsible for the design and construction of the Union ironclad warship, *Monitor,* which sees action this year against the Confederate *Virginia (Merrimack).* Ericsson was urged to come to the United States after he patented his successful screw propeller in 1836.

Jews are allowed for the first time to serve as chaplains in the United States armed forces. Jacob Frankel becomes the first Jewish American chaplain.

1864

Labor recruiters for United States industries travel all over Europe as American demand for workers grows.

European migration to the United States increases to fill vacancies created by Americans either participating in the Civil War or moving west to avoid conscription. Passage of the United States Homestead Act also increases the flow of European farmers to America.

1865

Increasing numbers of Hungarians, primarily young men, come to the United States as "sojourners." They take hard, dirty, dangerous jobs and save their money so that they can return home with greater wealth.

The first woman college professor, Maria Mitchell, goes to work at Vassar College.

George Pomutz becomes the first Romanian American to attain the rank of United States brigadier general. He distinguishes himself in several Civil War battles.

1867

Maimonides College is established in Philadelphia, Pennsylvania, by Isaac Lesser. This is one of the earliest institutions for the rabbinate and other higher Hebrew learning.

1868

The first mass Swedish immigration occurs as 103,000 enter the United States. They are farm families in search of land and work.

The first Norwegian newspaper in Minnesota, the *Nordiske Folksblad,* begins publishing in Rochester.

1869

Several special newspapers are published in Sweden beginning this year. They promote immigration by reporting on the greater opportunities in the United States.

1860

Spanish Basque immigrants come to Nevada and begin the sheep raising industry there.

1861

Approximately 10,000 Hispanics fight in the American Civil War, most notable among them being Union naval officer (later Admiral) David Farragut and José Francisco Chaves, who attains the rank of lieutenant colonel.

A group of Mexican American soldiers in Zapata County, Texas, refuse to swear allegiance to the Confederacy and announce that they will obey only Union authorities. These soldiers march toward the county seat but are defeated by Confederate forces and suffer heavy losses.

During the Civil War, Havana-born Loretta Janet Velázquez disguises herself as a man and fights in the Confederate army. She participates in the Battles of Bull Run, Ball's Bluff and Fort Donelson. After she is discovered and dismissed, Velázquez becomes a spy for the Confederacy.

1863

Julio L. Vizcarrondo founds the Abolitionist Society in Spain to fight for the freedom of enslaved people in the Spanish colonies. The Society establishes an office in Puerto Rico.

Chipita Rodriguez, a Mexican American living in San Patricio, is the only woman ever sentenced to death and executed in Texas. She is convicted of killing a European American man, although the only evidence is that the man's body is found near her home.

1864

The first Puerto Rican newspaper in New York City is published, entitled *La Voz de Puerto Rico.*

1865

Cuban and Puerto Rican immigrants in New York City form the Republican Society to agitate for independence from Spain.

1867

Dr. Ramón Emeterio Betances and Segundo Ruiz Belvis are exiled from Puerto Rico for their political views. Ruiz Belvis goes to Chile and Betances travels to St. Thomas, the Dominican Republic, the United States and France seeking support for Puerto Rican independence.

La Borinqueña is written as a revolutionary song. With different lyrics, it later becomes the Puerto Rican national hymn.

1868

In Texas, seven Mexican Americans are executed, vigilante style, for possible implication in a murder. The European Americans who killed them are freed due to conflicting evidence.

Dr. Ramón Emeterio Betances, exiled to Santo Domingo, issues a "Provisional Constitution of the Puerto Rican Revolution."

The Lares Rebellion occurs, with rebel forces demanding Puerto Rico's independence from Spain. Nationalists in Lares declare a republic, and Mariana Bracetti sews the flag of Lares as a symbol of the revolution. However, the revolt is suppressed.

The Republican Societies of Cuba and Puerto Rico open offices in Philadelphia.

1869

The Spanish government authorizes the first Protestant religious services in Ponce, Puerto Rico, for foreigners. This begins the spread of Protestantism on the island.

1860

through

1869

THE AMERICAS	THE AMERICAS	THE AMERICAS	THE AMERICAS

1860

South Carolina protests Abraham Lincoln's election to the presidency by seceding from the Union.

The United States census reports the country's population at 31.4 million; this includes 4 million enslaved African Americans.

The United States has approximately 30,000 miles of railroad tracks in use.

By this time, one out of four teachers in the United States is a woman.

A handful of smaller rural United States medical colleges admit women students.

Pennsylvania has more than 200 textile factories.

Gold and silver deposits are discovered in Arizona.

Bartholomé Mitre becomes president of Argentina after the term of Justo José de Urquiza (1854). Mitre serves until 1868.

1860-1861

Mail in the United States between St. Joseph, Missouri, and Sacramento, California, is carried by the Pony Express. The service is gradually phased out after 1861 when the first telegram is transmitted over that distance.

1860-1863

Gold is discovered in the Clearwater, Salmon, Boise and Owyhee River areas in what later becomes the Idaho Territory.

1861

Abraham Lincoln becomes the 16th president of the United States; Hannibal Hamlin is vice president. Both are Republicans.

In separate legislative acts, Congress creates the territories of Colorado, Dakota and Nevada; adopts the income tax; and authorizes the Navy Medal of Honor.

Alexander Stephens, vice president of the Confederacy, says that the new government "rests upon the great truth that the Negro is not equal to the white man...."

Kansas becomes the 34th state to join the Union.

The Massachusetts Institute of Technology at Boston; Vassar College at Poughkeepsie, New York; and the University of Washington at Seattle are founded.

Mexican President Benito Juárez announces that Mexico will no longer pay its foreign debts. The following year, Spain, Britain and France invade Mexico seeking payment. Britain and Spain withdraw, but French forces remain.

In response to a threat of invasion by Haitian forces, leaders of Santo Domingo request and receive Spanish intervention.

1861-1865

Annie Wittenmyer gains a reputation for initiative, intelligence and humanity as she establishes a soldiers' aid society in support of Union troops. She visits western military camps and hospitals to ascertain needs, and then mobilizes women across her home state of Iowa to supply bandages, clothing and food. She works to have women nurses assigned to each Iowa regiment, and herself tends wounded soldiers on the battlefield. In 1862 Wittenmyer is appointed Iowa's first state sanitary agent. She pushes for the establishment of orphanages, sets up military hospital kitchens, and becomes a spokeswoman for several reform causes.

1861-1870

Immigration to the United States totals 2,314,824 people of which 2,065,141 come from Europe, 64,759 from Asia, 312 from Africa, 214 from Oceania, 166,607 from the Americas and 17,791 are not specifically identified.

1861-1865

The Civil War

The United States Civil War (the War Between the States or the War of Southern Rebellion) begins as attempts at compromise on the slavery issue fail. In addition to slavery, the Civil War arises out of the economic and political rivalry between an agrarian South and an industrial North, and the issue of the right of states to secede from the Union.

1861. Mississippi, Florida, Alabama, Georgia, Louisiana and Texas follow South Carolina's example and announce secession from the Union at the Congress of Montgomery. They form the Confederate States of America, with Jefferson Davis as president (January through March). War begins as Confederate soldiers fire on Fort Sumter and Charleston, South Carolina. President Lincoln calls for 75,000 volunteers. The Union's plan to win the war is based on their success in blockading the South to force starvation; dividing the South by first controlling the Mississippi River and then by marching to the sea through Georgia; and capturing the Confederate capital at Richmond. Southern ports are blockaded by superior Northern naval forces. Virginia, Arkansas, Tennessee and North Carolina secede to complete the 11-state Confederacy. The Union army, advancing on Richmond, is repulsed at the first Battle of Bull Run but two Confederate forts are captured. President Lincoln appoints General George McClellan to head the Union army. Indian Commissioner Albert Pike, a Confederate supporter, uses promises and gifts to urge Kiowa and Comanche bands to attack Union supply wagons along the Santa Fe Trail.

Women's participation in the war is extensive and varied. More than 400 women, on both sides of the war, put on men's clothing and go to the battlefields; Harriet Tubman serves the Union Army as a cook, nurse and scout; and women such as Clara Barton, Mary Bickerdyke and Annie Wittenmyer provide emergency

care to the wounded. Away from the battlefield, women replace men in factories, fields and classrooms and, after Civil Service restrictions are lifted in 1862, in certain government jobs as well. In many cities, women form soldiers' aid societies to help supply the front lines. For example, Mary Livermore organizes the Great Chicago Sanitary Faire which raises $70,000 to purchase food and medical supplies for the Union army.

1862. Edwin M. Stanton is named United States Secretary of War. Forces led by General Ulysses S. Grant win the first major Union victory, at Fort Donelson, Tennessee; Nashville falls to Union forces in February. Ironclad warships, the Union's *Monitor* and the Confederacy's *Virginia (Merrimack)* duel at Hampton Roads, Virginia. The Confederate army is defeated at Fort Henry, Roanoke Island, Fort Donelson and Jacksonville. Grant's army escapes defeat at Shiloh, Tennessee. New Orleans falls to the Union fleet under Admiral David Farragut, and the city is occupied. Memphis falls as Northern gunboats control the upper Mississippi. The Confederate army under General Robert E. Lee is victorious at the second Battle of Bull Run in August. At Antietam, Maryland, in the bloodiest battle of the war, the Union army under McClellan stops Lee's forces from advancing on Washington and into Maryland and Pennsylvania. President Lincoln removes McClellan for his lack of aggressiveness, and replaces him with General Ambrose E. Burnside. Burnside's drive on Richmond fails at Fredericksburg in December. Union forces under General William Starke Rosecrans chase General Braxton Bragg's Confederate troops through Tennessee; the Battle of Murfreesboro takes place from October through January 1863.

1863. President Lincoln signs the Emancipation Proclamation, freeing slaves in the rebelling states. Lee's Confederate forces are victorious at Chancellorsville, Virginia, though Thomas J. "Stonewall" Jackson, Confederate general, dies in battle. A Confederate invasion of Pennsylvania is stopped at

---

1860

through

1869

1862

In separate legislative acts, Congress authorizes the Army Medal of Honor, passes the National Bank Act and forms the Department of Agriculture.

A federal law provides that "any alien" honorably discharged from United States military service is eligible to apply for naturalization.

The United States Homestead Act provides 160 acres of surveyed public land on the Great Plains or in the Southwest free to anyone who will live on and farm the land for five years and who is or is willing to become a citizen.

The Pacific Railway Act authorizes construction of the transcontinental railroad across the United States.

Susan B. Anthony and Elizabeth Cady Stanton found the Women's National Loyalty League to gather petitions to force Congress and the president to act to abolish slavery. They deliver more than 300,000 signatures, mostly women's.

Arizona becomes a territory of the United States.

Idaho's first newspaper, *Golden Age,* is published at Lewiston.

The University of South Dakota is founded at Vermillion.

Richard J. Gatling invents the rapid-fire Gatling gun, forerunner of the modern machine gun.

On May 5 (Cinco de Mayo), Mexican forces of Benito Juárez are victorious over the French in Mexico. The war continues for five more years.

Francisco Solano López becomes dictator of Paraguay after the death of his father, Carlos Antonio López (1844). Francisco López rules until 1870.

British Honduras (Belize), inhabited by British lumbermen and traders and Africans from the West Indies, officially is made part of the British Empire.

1862-1865

Detailed diaries kept by Mary Chestnut provide an excellent firsthand account of Confederate leaders and Southern society during the war.

1863

West Virginia becomes the 35th state to join the Union.

The United States Congress passes the Morrill Act. This law, named for its sponsor, Vermont Republican Justin Smith Morrill, provides for the use of public lands for the establishment of educational institutions. These schools become known as "land-grant" colleges.

The Idaho Territory, formerly part of the Columbia River Country (Oregon Territory) and Washington Territory, is established for the influx of pioneers arriving in search of gold and silver.

Kansas State University is founded at Manhattan.

A four-day riot in New York City is sparked by a section of the draft law which allows people with enough money to buy their way out of service. Long-standing racism and southern sympathies erupt into violence, as most of the rioters are Irish Americans, and many casualties and much of the damage is done to the African American community. Approximately 1,000 people are killed before the police, the New York 7th Regiment (called back from Gettysburg) and West Point cadets are able to restore order.

Dorothea Dix is appointed superintendent of Union Army nurses.

Margaret Walker is the first female army surgeon. She receives a medal of honor for her work during the Civil War.

New Granada receives a new constitution and a new name — the United States of Colombia.

c. 1863

Abolitionist Cyrus K. Holliday leads a group in the formation of the Atchison, Topeka and Sante Fe Railroad.

1864

The United States Congress authorizes the creation of the Immigration Bureau in the State Department.

Salmon Portland Chase becomes chief justice of the United States Supreme Court. He serves until 1873.

Nevada becomes the 36th state to join the Union.

The Montana Territory is established. Originally part of the Louisiana Purchase of 1803, parts of it were formerly included in the Oregon country, Dakota and the Idaho Territory.

Swarthmore College in Pennsylvania, the University of Denver in Colorado, and the University of Nevada at Reno are founded.

Hawaiian plantation owners form the Planters' Society and establish a Bureau of Immigration.

The first salmon cannery in the United States is opened at Washington, California.

Philip Danforth Armour establishes the beginnings of his meat-packing company in Milwaukee, Wisconsin.

When French troops invade Mexico, President Juárez is forced to leave. Mexican conservatives and Napoleon III of France proclaim the empire of Mexico, and Maximilian, archduke of Austria, becomes emperor under French protection. Maximilian rules until 1867.

c. 1864-1870

The War of the Triple Alliance takes place with Argentina, Brazil and Uruguay opposing the Paraguayan dictatorship of Francisco Solano López. The war results from López's intervention in Uruguay's civil war and provides an opportunity for the allied nations to reduce his power. The war results in little territorial shifting, but Paraguay's economy and its male population are devastated. López, who foolishly led his country into this war, is overthrown, and Paraguay enters a time of unrest and rapid government turnovers.

1860

through

1869

Gettysburg by Union forces under the command of George Meade. Lee's army suffers the loss of 20,000 men. The Battle of Gettysburg in Pennsylvania and the Union victory at Vicksburg, Mississippi, mark the war's turning point. General George H. Thomas, the "Rock of Chickamauga," and his troops halt Braxton Bragg's forces at the Georgia-Tennessee border. William Tecumseh Sherman, Joseph Hooker and George Henry Thomas and their troops drive Bragg's forces back to Georgia. Tennessee is retaken by Union troops in November; Lincoln delivers the Gettysburg Address.

1864. General Ulysses S. Grant is named commander-in-chief of Union forces. In the Wilderness Campaign, Grant's troops force Lee's army of northern Virginia back toward Richmond. Union General Sherman and his army march from Chattanooga through Georgia. Confederate forces are defeated at Atlanta, and Sherman's men take Savannah, win the Atlanta campaign and continue their "march to the sea." A fleet under command of Union Admiral Farragut conquers Confederate forces in Mobile Bay, Alabama. The Confederate army under General John B. Hood is defeated at Nashville. Sherman's troops capture Savannah, Georgia.

1865. Congress passes the Thirteenth Amendment, ending slavery. The Union army under General Philip Henry Sheridan defeats Confederate troops at Five Forks, Virginia; Union forces capture Petersburg, Virginia; and the Confederate capital of Richmond is evacuated. On April 9, Confederate General Robert E. Lee surrenders to Ulysses S. Grant at Appomattox Court House. The Civil War ends with the surrender of Confederate troops after a skirmish at Shreveport, Louisiana. Reconstruction of the South begins.

1860 through 1869

1865

Abraham Lincoln, a Republican, begins a second term as president of the United States; Andrew Johnson, of the Union party, is vice president. After Lincoln is assassinated at Ford's Theater in Washington, D.C., by actor John Wilkes Booth, Johnson succeeds to the presidency and becomes the 17th president of the United States. Booth is caught and dies of gunshot wounds; four conspirators in Lincoln's death are hanged.

The Thirteenth Amendment to the United States Constitution is ratified by the states. It abolishes slavery and involuntary servitude except as punishment for a crime in which a conviction is received, in the United States or any place subject to its jurisdiction.

The United States Congress enacts a law establishing the Freedman's Bureau.

Russian immigrants bring Durum wheat to the Dakota territory.

The states of California and Illinois pass laws allowing African Americans to testify against European Americans in court.

The University of Maine at Orono and Shaw University at Raleigh, North Carolina, are founded.

Spanish forces withdraw from Santo Domingo.

Buenaventura Báez (1849, 1856) begins a third term as president of the Dominican Republic. He serves until 1866.

Mariano Ignacio Prado becomes president of Peru after the term of Ramón Castilla (1855). Prado serves until 1867 and again between 1878 and 1879.

In Jamaica the Morant Bay uprising is sparked by poverty and unfair political restrictions. Rebel leaders Paul Bogle and George William Gordon are executed.

c. 1865

As the United States becomes more industrialized, factories systematize their operations. Manufactured parts are standardized and tasks are divided to improve production output. American consumers have improved home heating furnaces, washtubs, ice and manufactured clothing available to them.

After the war, 9,000 women volunteer to teach freed African Americans. Many women who found employment during the war, especially in the federal government, lose their jobs to returning soldiers.

c. 1865-1879

A secret militant and mostly Irish American organization called the Molly Maguires is established in the Scranton coal mines of Pennsylvania to combat harsh conditions and the sometimes brutal private police forces of the mining companies. Some of its founders are members of the Ancient Order of Hibernians, an Irish American secret society established in 1836. Through violence, intimidation and murder, the Molly Maguires virtually control the Scranton mining area for 10 to 12 years. Around 1877 Pinkerton detective James McParlan is hired by the mining interests to infiltrate the organization. As a result of his efforts, several organization leaders are caught and hanged, and the group gradually disbands.

1866

The Civil Rights Act of 1866 is passed by the United States Congress over the veto of President Johnson. Because it lacks the support of either the president or the Supreme Court, the act has little practical effect.

In the United States, the National Labor Union is founded with the goal of limiting the workday to eight hours.

Tennessee is the first Confederate state to be restored to the Union.

The American Equal Rights Association is founded, with both men and women members, to support women's rights. The organization soon experiences conflicts over policy, and in 1869 divides into two groups. The National Women's Suffrage Association (NWSA) is led by Elizabeth Cady Stanton and Susan B. Anthony, whose singular purpose is see the Constitution amended to allow women to vote. They oppose passage of the 15th Amendment giving African American men the vote while *their* rights are still curtailed. The second suffrage group, the American Women's Suffrage Association (AWSA), is led by Lucy Stone and Julia Ward Howe. This organization takes a slightly more conservative approach by supporting African Americans' rights and by seeking local government support for women's suffrage.

Lincoln University at Jefferson City, Missouri; Edward Waters College at Jacksonville, Florida; the University of New Hampshire at Durham; and Fisk University at Nashville, Tennessee, are founded.

The Ku Klux Klan (KKK) is organized in Pulaski, Tennessee. A secret society opposed to Reconstruction, the group uses beatings, lynchings and terrorism to keep African Americans from voting or becoming educated. Local activity continues for a number of years, but the KKK is disbanded in 1869. However, it is reorganized in 1915.

Fenian forces, made up of Irish American Union Army veterans led by John O'Neill, begin an invasion of Canada with the intent of expelling the British. Though successful in one engagement with British forces, the Fenians disperse when the United States government intervenes.

The United States of Colombia receives a new constitution and a new name — the Republic of Colombia.

As a result of war with Peru, Spain withdraws from the Chincha Islands off Peru's west coast.

1867

In a transaction known as "Seward's Folly" arranged by Secretary of State William H. Seward, the United States buys Alaska from Russia for $7.2 million, or roughly two cents an acre. Half of the Russians there return home; many who remain later move to California. Alaska's fur seal population declines rapidly now that Russian restrictions are no longer in force.

The Reconstruction Act establishes United States military districts in the war-ravaged Southern states and makes military authority supreme.

A state law passed in Tennessee this year mandates state-funded schools for African Americans.

Nebraska becomes the 37th state to join the Union.

Talladega College in Alabama; Atlanta University and Morehouse College, both at Atlanta, Georgia; Johnson C. Smith University at Charlotte and St. Augustine's College at Raleigh, both in North Carolina; Howard University at Washington, D.C.; and Cedar Crest College at Allentown, Pennsylvania, are founded.

The first elevated railroad is opened to the public in New York City.

Oliver Hudson Kelley founds the Grange, or Patrons of Husbandry, as a social organization for farmers.

Christopher L. Sholes invents the first practical typewriter. He receives a patent in 1868 and the typewriter becomes a commercial product in 1874.

The British North America Act creates the Dominion of Canada; the provinces of Ontario, Quebec, New Brunswick and Nova Scotia are joined.

Sir John Alexander MacDonald, a Conservative, becomes the first prime minister of Canada. He serves until 1873.

After Napoleon III abandons Mexico by pulling out French troops, Maximilan (1864) and his forces are defeated by the troops of Benito Juárez and Porfirio Díaz. Maximilian is executed. Juárez restores order and is reelected president. He serves until his death in 1872.

1868

United States President Andrew Johnson is impeached for ignoring the Tenure of Office Act when he fired Secretary of War Edwin M. Stanton in 1867. The Senate, which acts as the tribunal in impeachment proceedings, fails by one vote to remove Johnson from office.

The Fourteenth Amendment to the United States Constitution is ratified, clarifying United States citizenship and enforcing the rights of "due process of law," "privileges and immunities" and "equal protection of the laws." This is the first time the Constitution has used the word "male" to describe citizens. The amendment also enables formerly enslaved African Americans to be counted in determining Congressional and electoral representation; prohibits Confederate leaders from holding public office unless approved by two-thirds of the Congress; and makes the South responsible for its share of the war debt.

The Burlingame Treaty is negotiated. It assures free migration between the United States and China, and thereby guarantees a steady supply of cheap labor for the development of the American West.

Georgia comes under military government after its legislature expels African Americans.

A bill in support of women's right to vote is first introduced in the United States Congress.

Dr. Elizabeth Blackwell expands her infirmary in New York to include a medical college to train women as doctors.

Hampton Institute in Virginia, Oregon State University at Corvallis, and Wells College at Aurora, New York, are founded.

One of America's first disaster relief campaigns is sponsored by B'nai B'rith for victims of the Baltimore flood.

The refrigerated railroad car is patented by William Davis.

George Westinghouse invents the railroad air brake and a number of railroad signaling devices.

Cuba's fight for independence from Spain, the Ten Years War, begins.

The immigration of Cuban tobacco workers to the United States increases as anti-Spanish conflicts devastate Cuban tobacco plantations.

Earthquakes hit regions of Peru and Ecuador and cause more than 25,000 deaths.

Buenaventura Báez (1849, 1856, 1865) again becomes president of the Dominican Republic. He serves until 1873.

Domingo Faustino Sarmiento becomes president of Argentina. An educated and well-traveled man, he encourages reforms in industry, education and foreign trade. Sarmiento serves until 1874.

1868-1878

Civil war rages in Cuba between small planters who favor independence, and owners of large sugar plantations, mostly Spaniards, who benefit from Cuba's colonial status. In the upheaval many enslaved Africans walk away from their servitude; slavery is formally abolished in 1886. Mariana Grajales, a free woman of African descent, organizes a jungle field hospital and urges her five sons to join the fight. Grajales is one of many Latin American women who, as spies, quartermasters to the armies, nurses and even fighters, help the independence movements.

1869

Ulysses S. Grant becomes the 18th president of the United States; Schuyler Colfax is vice president. Both are Republicans.

Central Pacific Railroad laborers, working east from Sacramento, California, and a Union Pacific Railroad crew, working west from Omaha, Nebraska, complete the first transcontinental railroad, which links the east and west coasts of the United States.

Probably for health considerations in the city of New Orleans, the Louisiana state legislature gives a 25-year monopoly to a single slaughterhouse. The protests of other operators turn this into a test of the Fourteenth Amendment's due process, equal protection, and privileges and immunities clauses. Known as the *Slaughter-House Cases*, the controversy reaches the United States Supreme Court in 1873.

When James Fisk and Jay Gould attempt to control the gold market, the "Black Friday" panic in the United States occurs.

Dillard University in New Orleans, Louisiana, Tougaloo College in Mississippi and the University of Nebraska in Lincoln are founded.

The National Woman Suffrage Association is formed in the United States, with Susan B. Anthony as its president. The American Woman Suffrage Association is formed, with Lucy Stone as the head, to work in local activities. These organizations unite in 1890.

Women gain the right to vote in local elections in the Wyoming Territory. This is the first suffrage attained by women in the United States.

The United States National Prohibition Party is founded in Chicago.

The Knights of Labor, an industrial union, is created by Uriah S. Stephens. The organization welcomes female workers and, by 1869, has a department dedicated to the concerns of its women members.

The New York Central Railroad Company is organized by Cornelius Vanderbilt.

The figure of Uncle Sam representing the United States is first used in *Harper's Weekly*.

Hudson Bay Territory (Rupert's Land) joins the Dominion of Canada.

A navigational device called an astrolabe, lost during one of de Champlain's 1613 expeditions, is recovered near Pembroke, Ontario, Canada.

Isabel Cousino of Santiago, Chile, is known as the "richest woman in the world." Her wealth comes from her acres of lands and coal, copper and silver mines.

1869-1870

A smallpox epidemic hits the Canadian Plains Indian tribes.

The first Riel Rebellion, also called the Red River Rebellion, takes place in Manitoba, Canada. Rebel leader Louis Riel, a Cree Indian, leads 10,000 Native Canadians to rebel after the Hudson's Bay Company transfers land it never owned to the Canadian government. The rebellion fails, and Riel flees the country.

The *Sitka Times,* Alaska's first newspaper, is published.

1860

through

1869

THE WORLD	THE WORLD	THE WORLD	THE WORLD

**1860
through
1869**

1860

The Swedish-Norwegian government ends passport regulation, thus removing the last serious obstacle to emigration.

The first official Japanese delegation visits the United States. Manjiro Nakahama serves as interpreter.

Italian unification continues as Giuseppe Garibaldi leads a 1,000-man volunteer army in the capture of Sicily and Naples. He unites them with Sardinia; Sardinians invade and conquer the Papal States. The Treaty of Turin cedes Nice and Savoy to France and unites Tuscany, Emilia, Bologna, Parma, Modena and Piacenza with Sardinia. The first Italian Parliament meets at Turin.

Michael (Michael Obrenovich) becomes prince of Serbia after the death of his father, Milos (Milos Obrenovich, 1858). Michael rules until 1868.

c. 1860s

Life for educated and skilled Jewish artisans improves in Russia and many are permitted to live outside the pale. However, this policy is reversed in the 1870s.

1861

Reforms instituted by Russian Czar Alexander II, especially the abolition of serfdom, improve the conditions of Russia's peasants.

Most of Italy, with the exception of Venetia, is united by this year, either through plebiscite or conquest. The region known as the Papal States is absorbed into the new Italy, and papal authority is limited to the Vatican. Victor Immanuel II, the king of Sardinia, becomes the first king of Italy. He rules until 1878.

Britain annexes Lagos (now part of Nigeria in Africa) to help prevent the continuance of the slave trade.

In India, codes of criminal and civil procedure are enacted, a unified judicial system is established and local citizens gain partial representation in some legislative offices.

In Africa, Muslim Tukulor tribal leader Hajj Omar and his forces conquer the Fulani of Massina.

Bahrain becomes a British protectorate.

Walachia and Moldavia formally join and become Romania. Alexander I (Alexander John Cuza, 1859), prince of both regions, facilitates the union.

The second Maori war breaks out in New Zealand. British forces led by Sir George Grey are victorious over the Maoris but the fighting continues for 10 years.

Gold is discovered in New Zealand at Gabriel's Gully, Otago (South Island), and in 1862, at Wakitipu. Over the next 20 years, New Zealand's population increases fivefold.

The Warsaw Massacre occurs when troops fire on demonstrators protesting Russian rule in Poland.

Abdu-l-Aziz becomes Ottoman sultan after the death of his brother, Abdu-l-Mejid (1839). Abdu-l-Aziz rules until 1876.

William I becomes king of Prussia after the death of his brother, Frederick William IV (1840). In 1871 William I becomes *kaiser* (emperor) of Germany. He rules both dominions until 1888.

Louis I becomes king of Portugal after the death of Pedro V (1853). Louis I rules until 1889.

1862

Otto von Bismarck becomes prime minister of Prussia, and advocates the unification of Germany under Prussian leadership.

French chemist Louis Pasteur's experiments with bacteria lead to his development of pasteurization, the process of partial sterilization of liquids.

An uprising against Ottoman rule occurs in Bulgaria.

1863

In Australia, the Northern Territory separates from New South Wales and becomes part of South Australia.

New Zealand's first railroad opens.

A major uprising in Russian Poland is defeated and a wave of Polish refugees flee to the United States.

Cambodia becomes a French protectorate.

Christian IX becomes king of Denmark after the death of Frederick VII (1848). Christian IX rules until 1906.

Ismail Pasha becomes *khedive* (viceroy) of Egypt after the reign of his uncle, Said Pasha (1854). Ismail Pasha rules until 1879.

Shere Ali becomes *emir* (Muslim prince or commander) of Afghanistan after the death of his father, Dost Muhammad (1826). Shere Ali rules until 1879.

George I is elected king of Greece after Otto I (1833) is forced to abdicate. George I rules until 1913.

As a child, Tongzhi (Tungchih) becomes emperor of China with Empress Cixi (Tz'u-hsi) as regent. Tongzhi rules until 1875.

1864

Fearing a loss of trade, European powers intervene in China and help the provincial armies defeat the Taipings.

A brief but devastating war against Prussia and Austria costs Denmark the provinces of Schleswig and Holstein, and thus makes German subjects of 20,000 Danes. The Peace of Vienna ends this conflict.

Romania ends serfdom and allows peasants to acquire land.

Combined forces of Britain, the Netherlands, France and the United States bombard Choshu forts at Shimonoseki, halting the antiforeign movement in Japan.

British troops occupy the southern part of Bhutan.

Russian troops crush revolts for independence in Poland and make the teaching of the Russian language a requirement in Polish schools.

A severe hurricane in Calcutta, India, causes almost 70,000 deaths.

The first Geneva Convention declares that military medical field facilities are neutral territory, and provides for the protection of sick or wounded soldiers and medical personnel. The convention, which is signed by representatives of 16 countries, also establishes the International Red Cross under the guidance of Jean Henry Dunant.

Financial panic and three years of crop failures hit Sweden, sending thousands of immigrants to the United States in search of economic opportunities. This causes the Swedish-Norwegian government to restrict emigration.

Louis II becomes king of Bavaria after the death of his father, Maximilian II (1848). Louis II rules until 1886.

Karl Marx is president of the First International Workingman's Association in London.

Sir Samuel White Baker leads an expedition along the Nile River from Cairo and explores Albert Nyanza (Lake Albert on the Congo/Uganda border). Baker returns to the area five years later to institute reforms against the slave trade and open the region to commerce.

1864-1913

Greece expands its territory, primarily by seizing Ottoman lands.

1865

A dual Austro-Hungarian monarchy is proclaimed by Emperor Francis Joseph. It becomes a reality in 1867.

Russia gains control over Tashkent (now the capital of Uzbekistan, formerly in the Soviet Union).

Labor recruiters for United States industries travel all over Europe as American demand for workers grows.

War breaks out between the Boers of the Orange Free State (South Africa) and the native Basuto people.

A military alliance between Prussia and Italy against Austria results in Austria's ceding more territory to Prussia. Napoleon III promises Bismarck at Biarritz that France will remain neutral if Austria and Prussia go to war against each other.

Leopold II becomes king of Belgium after the death of his father, Leopold I (1831). Leopold II rules until 1909.

The Salvation Army is founded in London, England, under the direction of William and Catherine Booth.

English surgeon Joseph Lister, influenced by Louis Pasteur's theories on bacteria, begins the process of making surgical procedures antiseptic.

1866

With military assistance from Italy, Prussia defeats Austria in the Seven Weeks' War. This victory solidifies Prussia's position as the strongest German state. The conflict was initiated by Bismarck to remove Austria from the German Confederation. By the Treaty of Prague, Austria is excluded from Prussian affairs and Venetia is ceded by Austria to Italy. Prussia makes peace with Saxony and annexes Hanover, Hesse, Nassau, Frankfurt, Schleswig and Holstein. The new North German Confederation, which replaces the former German Confederation, is made up of more than 25 member states and cities. The new alliance causes many Germans to immigrate to the United States to avoid compulsory military service.

Crete, with Greek support, gains partial self-government from the Ottoman Empire.

A severe epidemic, possibly cholera, is responsible for the deaths of almost 200,000 people in Austria and Prussia.

Hitotsubashi Keiki becomes the last Tokugawa shogun of Japan. He comes to power after the death of Iemochi (1858) and rules until 1867.

Land and labor reforms instituted by Prince Alexander John I anger Romania's nobility, the boyars, who force him to abdicate. Carol I (Charles of Hohenzollern-Sigmaringen) is elected prince of Romania after Alexander John I (1861) is deposed. Carol I rules as prince until 1881 and as the first king of Romania until 1914.

Dynamite is made by Swedish inventor Alfred Bernhard Nobel.

Austrian botanist Gregor Johann Mendel pioneers the study of genetic heredity. His work gets little recognition.

1867

The dual monarchy of Austria-Hungary is established with Francis Joseph I, emperor of Austria, as king. The monarchy takes control over Transylvania and lasts until 1918.

Diamond fields are discovered on the Orange River, near Hope Town, South Africa.

The Fenians lead riots in Ireland seeking home rule. The rioting is suppressed.

Midway Island is annexed by the United States.

An uprising against Ottoman rule occurs in Bulgaria.

In the New Zealand House of Representatives, four seats are reserved for delegates from the native Maori people.

1867-1868

With the victory of Mutsuhito (Meiji Tenno) and the resignation of Shogun Kekei after the death of Emperor Komei, the Tokugawa shogunate is overthrown, and direct authority is restored to the 16-year-old emperor. This period is called the Meiji Restoration. Reversing Japan's earlier isolationist policy, the emperor encourages greater contact with the West and begins the modernization of his country. Mutsuhito rules until 1912.

1868

Russia gains control over Samarkand and Bukhara (both now part of Uzbekistan).

Britain annexes Basutoland (Lesotho) and British forces enter Ethiopia, capturing Magdala.

The ruins of ancient Zimbabwe are first sighted by European explorers.

Celluloid, an early plastic, is first made.

The last British convicts are sent to Australia.

Queen Isabella II (1833) is deposed in the Spanish Revolution and flees to France. The new government abolishes religious orders, grants universal suffrage and allows a free press.

Johannes IV becomes emperor of Ethiopia after the death of Theodore II (1855). Johannes IV rules until his death, c. 1889.

Rama V (Chulalongkorn) becomes king of Siam (Thailand) after the death of his father, Rama IV (1851). Rama V rules until 1910.

As a child, Milan (Milan Obrenovich) becomes prince of Serbia after the death of his cousin, Michael (Michael Obrenovich, 1860). Milan comes of age in 1872, rules as prince until 1882 and as king of Serbia until 1889.

1869

The Suez Canal, designed by Ferdinand-Marie de Lesseps of France, is opened after a decade of construction. It connects the Gulf of Suez with the Red Sea.

As a result of the Sino-Japanese War, Taiwan is ceded to Japan.

Greek forces leave Crete to avoid a war with the Ottoman Empire.

Meiji Emperor Mutsuhito (Meiji Tenno) in Japan strengthens his power by gaining support and control over the four major clans, Choshu, Hizen, Satsuma and Tosa.

German explorer Gustav Nachtigal visits Bornu and the Sudan.

The periodic law of chemical elements, the basis for the modern Periodic Table of Elements, is developed by Russian chemist Dmitri Mendeleyev.

c. 1869

A severe famine in Sweden takes a heavy toll, with 22 deaths out of every 1,000 people.

1860

through

1869

NATIVE AMERICAN	NATIVE AMERICAN	NATIVE AMERICAN	AFRICAN AMERICAN

NATIVE AMERICAN

1870

Although the Fourteenth Amendment to the United States Constitution guarantees citizenship to "all persons born or naturalized in the United States," Native Americans — even if they reside off-reservation — are denied citizenship rights, except by special acts of Congress.

1870-1885

More than 10 million bison (buffalo) are slaughtered, mostly by European Americans, thus radically changing the existence of Indians on the Plains. This is done both for the money that the sale of buffalo hides brings and to deliberately destroy the Plains Indians' lifestyle.

1870-1879

The federal reservation policy is enforced by the military. The Native American land base is further reduced. The annuities and rationing system make Indians dependent on federal aid.

1871

The Indian Appropriation Act ends the negotiation of treaties with tribes as independent nations.

United States President Ulysses S. Grant declares that the Bitter Root Valley in Montana, which was set aside for the Flathead, Kutenai and Upper Pend d'Oreilles Indians by treaty in 1855, is not suitable. These tribes are forced to relocate farther north to the Joco (later Flathead) Reservation.

In the Camp Grant massacre in Arizona, more than 100 Apache Indians are killed by a combined force of Tucson vigilantes, Papago warriors (traditional enemies of the Apaches) and Mexican mercenaries; the slaughter is in retaliation for alleged Apache raids.

1872

By presidential executive order the Chiricahua Reservation in Arizona is established for the Apache tribe. This order is cancelled in 1876. The White Mountain Reservation in Arizona, also for Apaches, is enlarged; an executive order of 1876, however, returns part of this area to the public domain.

NATIVE AMERICAN

1872-1873

During the Modoc War, Chief Captain Jack refuses to move with his people to the Klamath Reservation in Oregon. He escapes to the lava beds of northern California but is eventually captured and hanged with other Modoc chiefs. The surviving Modocs are exiled to Indian Territory (Oklahoma).

1874

Gold is discovered in the Black Hills of Dakota Territory. Miners flocking into the area ignore Indian rights established by treaty.

1874-1875

United States forces finally defeat the Kiowa and Comanche Indians and drive them onto a reservation at Fort Sill, Oklahoma.

1875

By the president's executive order, the Camp Verde Reservation in Arizona, which was set aside for the Yavapai (or Mohave-Apache) tribe, is revoked. The Yavapai are forcibly relocated to the San Carlos Apache Reservation; more than 100 die during the 180-mile forced march.

1876

At the Battle of the Little Bighorn in Montana, a Sioux and Cheyenne coalition led by chiefs Sitting Bull, Crazy Horse, Gall and Two Moons wipes out General George Armstrong Custer and most of his 7th Cavalry. After the battle, Sitting Bull finds refuge in Canada.

When the federal government abolishes the Chiricahua Reservation, a few hundred (about one-third) of the displaced Indians are forcibly removed to San Carlos Reservation by their agent John Clum, a European American. Several hundred disaffected and displaced Chiricahuas follow Geronimo's escape to Hot Springs Reservation in New Mexico, but are eventually taken back to Arizona. Geronimo and other chiefs are arrested and taken to San Carlos in chains.

NATIVE AMERICAN

1877

Chief Joseph leads his Nez Perce across Idaho and Montana in a 1,000-mile attempt to escape to Canada. However, the group is forced to surrender less than 40 miles from the border. Like the Modocs, the surviving Nez Perce are exiled to Indian Territory.

1878

The United States Indian Police is established. Within three years the force is in operation on some 40 reservations. This paves the way for tribal units, instead of predominantly European American courts, to administer justice in all cases — except major crimes — involving Native Americans.

1879

Utes kill their newly assigned agent Nathan Meeker and other European Americans in retaliation for the loss of reservation land in Colorado.

Richard Pratt founds the Carlisle Indian School in Pennsylvania. The school's motto is "Kill the Indian, Save the Man."

The federal Bureau of Indian Affairs begins forcibly removing Indian children from their homes and sending them to boarding schools.

AFRICAN AMERICAN

1870

The Fifteenth Amendment to the Constitution is ratified, emphasizing the legal rights of African Americans to vote and prohibiting the interference of state and local governments.

Hiram R. Revels, a Republican, becomes the first African American in the United States Senate. He is appointed to replace Jefferson Davis. Revels serves until 1871.

Richard T. Greener becomes the first African American to graduate from Harvard University. A skilled attorney, he holds many academic and governmental positions during his career.

Benedict College at Columbia, South Carolina, is founded.

1870-1871

To enforce the provisions of the Fifteenth Amendment and to stem the activities of the emerging Ku Klux Klan (KKK), Congress passes the Force Act and two separate Enforcement Acts to protect African Americans' right to vote.

Four African Americans, all Republicans, are elected to the House of Representatives in the United States Congress. Joseph H. Rainey, Robert Brown Elliott and Robert C. DeLarge are elected from South Carolina. Rainey serves for four terms; DeLarge serves one term; and Elliott is elected for two terms, but resigns from each before the terms are completed. Benjamin S. Turner is elected from Alabama. He serves one term.

1872

Elijah McCoy develops many lubricating devices and holds 57 patents. The term "the real McCoy" is believed to come from his reputation.

Abolitionist leader William Still publishes *The Underground Railroad*.

Pioneer George Washington establishes a community in Centralia, Washington.

1873

Slavery is abolished in Puerto Rico.

AFRICAN AMERICAN	AFRICAN AMERICAN	ASIAN AMERICAN	FOR CLASSROOM USE	

Five African Americans, all southerners, are elected to the United States Congress. John R. Lynch is elected to the House from Mississippi. He serves two terms. James T. Rapier is elected to the House from Alabama for one term. Richard H. Caine is elected to the House from South Carolina. He serves two non-consecutive terms and is later elected Bishop of the African Methodist Episcopal (AME) Church. Joseph T. Walls is elected to the House from Florida. He serves one term. Pinckney Benton Steward Pinchback, a former lieutenant governor of Louisiana, is elected to the Senate but is not permitted to take his seat.

Patrick Francis Healy, a Jesuit priest, becomes president of Georgetown University, Washington, D.C. He serves until 1882.

Bennett College at Greensboro, North Carolina; Wiley College at Marshall, Texas; and Meharry Medical College for Negroes in Tennessee are founded.

1875

B. K. Bruce of Mississippi, a Republican, is the only duly elected African American to serve in the United States Senate during Reconstruction.

Edward A. Bouchet, a student at Yale University, is the first African American to receive a Ph.D.; physics is his field of study.

James Augustine Healy becomes the first Catholic African American bishop in the United States.

Knoxville College in Tennessee is founded.

1876

John H. Smythe, a graduate of Howard University Law School, becomes United States Minister to Liberia. He serves until 1886.

Stillman College at Tuscaloosa, Alabama and Huston-Tillotson College at Austin, Texas are founded.

1877

In *Hall* v. *DeCuir,* the United States Supreme Court rules that racial segregation on interstate public transportation is valid where state laws may vary on the legality of segregation.

Henry Ossian Flipper becomes the first African American to graduate from the United States Military Academy at West Point.

Philander Smith College is founded at Little Rock, Arkansas.

1878

Lewis H. Latimer is the only African American member of the Edison Pioneers, a group of scientists and inventors who work for Thomas Edison. In 1882 Latimer receives a patent for an improvement on the carbon filament used in Edison's electric lamps.

1879

The Knights of Labor organization recruits African Americans.

In the absence of the vice president, Republican B. K. Bruce presides briefly over the Senate and votes against a bill to restrict Chinese immigration.

United States General James Chalmers of Mississippi and a group of southern European Americans threaten to sink any boat on the Mississippi River carrying African Americans. Frightened ship owners abandon approximately 1,500 African Americans along the banks of the river. When the federal government threatens to intervene, the shipping companies resume operations.

Albion W. Tourgee, a judge in North Carolina, publishes *A Fools Errand,* which documents the activities of the KKK.

Joseph C. Price founds Livingstone College, Salisbury, North Carolina, under the sponsorship of the AME Zion Church.

1870

The United States census reports 63,199 Chinese Americans; 99 percent live in the West. The sex ratio is 1,284.1 males per 100 females.

The first mass anti-Chinese demonstrations and conventions are organized by labor unions in San Francisco.

An increasing number of Chinese Americans relocate to the eastern and southern United States.

Joseph Hardy Neesima is the first Japanese immigrant to receive a college degree in the United States, when he graduates from Amherst College in Massachusetts.

1870s

Chinese American workers are hired in quicksilver mines in California.

Chinese Americans are employed widely in vineyards in the raisin industry and in the harvesting of wheat. They also work in sugar beet fields, hopyards, cotton fields and citrus fruit orchards.

Chinese Americans develop shrimp and abalone fisheries in California.

1871

The San Francisco superintendent of schools closes the city's only public school for Chinese students.

A mob kills 21 Chinese people in Los Angeles.

Chinese workers are hired in West Coast seafood canneries and soon form the majority of the cannery work force.

1872

California bars Chinese Americans from owning land and from securing business licenses.

The Hawaiian Kingdom census reports 2,038 Chinese residents.

The first group of Chinese students sent by the Chinese Educational Mission arrives to study in New England. Three more groups, totaling more than 100 students, come in the next three years. After they complete middle school, the United States refuses to admit them to military academies. The Chinese imperial government recalls the students in 1881.

1870

through

1879

ASIAN AMERICAN	ASIAN AMERICAN	EUROPEAN AMERICAN	EUROPEAN AMERICAN
Kentaro Kaneko, a student from Japan, is admitted to Harvard University and studies law.	**1879** In its second state constitution, California prevents municipalities and corporations from employing Chinese workers. The state legislature passes a law requiring that all Chinese Americans be moved outside of city limits, but the Circuit Court declares this law unconstitutional.	**1870** Polish immigrants have come to America from Germany, Austria and Russian Poland and total more than 2 million people. Most of them are unskilled laborers employed in the lowest-paying positions in coal mines, meatpacking plants, textile and steel mills, oil refineries and garment factories.	Carl Schurz is the first German American to be appointed to a cabinet post, when President Rutherford B. Hayes names him secretary of the interior.
1874 Unionized European American cigarmakers in San Francisco urge a boycott of Chinese-made cigars.			The largest hotel in Saratoga, New York, refuses to admit Jewish American guests. This is the first open case of anti-Semitism in the United States since General Order No. 11 in 1862.
1875 Under federal law 1) the importation of Chinese or Japanese women for immoral purposes is prohibited; 2) the importation of consenting Chinese or Japanese people for the purpose of holding them to terms of service is punishable by imprisonment or heavy fines; and 3) the importation of enslaved Chinese labor is a felony.	Chun Afong becomes privy counsellor to Hawaii's King David Kalakahua; Afong is also appointed first consul for China in Hawaii.	The first Russian Orthodox parish is organized in New York City. *The Irish World*, is founded in New York City by Patric Ford. It grows to become one of the country's most powerful Irish American newspapers.	**c. 1877** German Jewish immigrants Max and Abe Idelman establish the liquor and tobacco trade in the Wyoming Territory.
The Union Pacific Railroad begins hiring Chinese coal miners at Rock Springs, Wyoming.		**1870s** A small Swedish community is established at New Sweden, Maine.	**1879-1893** As immigration from northern Europe peaks, more than 260,000 Norwegians, many of them peasants, arrive in the United States. The figure equals more than two-thirds of Norway's population increase in the period. Most of these Norwegians are artisans and laborers, often with seafaring skills. They work in the fishing, construction, shipbuilding and lumber industries.
1875-1876 Anti-Chinese riots take place in California. The anti-Chinese movement spreads to other states.		**1871** Fire destroys almost the entire Dutch American town of Holland, Michigan.	
1877 Irish immigrant Dennis Kearney founds the Workingmen's Party, which advocates Chinese exclusion.		**1875** The Union of American Hebrew Congregations is founded by Rabbi Isaac M. Wise. Rabbi Wise also establishes Hebrew Union College in Cincinnati, Ohio.	
The California Senate urges a ban on Chinese immigration.		**1876** Victor Lawson purchases the *Chicago Daily News* and becomes a leader in American journalism. A Norwegian American, he later leads the Associated Press out of a crisis and greatly influences the handling of international news.	
A joint congressional committee report recommends the restriction of Chinese immigration.			
Japanese Christians establish the Gospel Society in San Francisco, the first immigrant association formed by Japanese Americans.		The *Svenska Amerikanaren*, begins publication as a liberal response to the conservatism represented by other Swedish American newspapers, *Hemlandet* in particular. Through mergers and acquisitions, *Svenska Amerikanaren* becomes for a time the largest Swedish newspaper in the United States.	
1878 One Ah Yup is denied naturalization by the Circuit Court in San Francisco. This sets a precedent for denying citizenship to Chinese Americans.		**1877** The Workingmen's Party is founded, led by Irish immigrant Dennis Kearney. Among other things, it advocates Chinese exclusion.	
China's first permanent envoy to the United States arrives in Washington, D.C.			

1870

through

1879

HISPANIC AMERICAN	HISPANIC AMERICAN	FOR CLASSROOM USE	FOR CLASSROOM USE	

HISPANIC AMERICAN

1870

The Liberal Conservative Party and the Liberal Reformist Party are the first Puerto Rican political parties to be recognized by the Spanish government.

Puerto Rico exports the majority of its coffee crop to Europe.

By this year, Mexican Americans in California, including those who previously owned vast ranchos, are almost landless due to European American prejudice and harsh regulations.

1871

Puerto Ricans Julian Blanco and Manuel Cochado are elected as representatives to the Spanish Cortes (Parliament).

1873

United States troops invade Mexico and stage a devastating surprise attack against a Kickapoo band in Coahuila. Villages are burned, more than 30 prisoners are taken and many Kickapoo people die in the attack.

More than 300 Kickapoos move from Mexico to Indian Territory (Oklahoma) to join the prisoners taken earlier in the year. By this time, the Mexican Kickapoos are scattered west from Coahuila and south into Durango. Mexicans in Coahuila value the Kickapoos as fighters against the Apaches.

Slavery is abolished in Puerto Rico following revolts.

The Civil Institute of Secondary Education is founded in Puerto Rico by José Julián Acosta.

The first central sugar refinery in Puerto Rico is founded in Vega Baja.

1874

Juan Moya and his sons are lynched in Goliad County, Texas, for allegedly killing a European American couple. A few days later the real killers are caught and hanged, but the Moya murderers go free.

The Civil Guard is established in Puerto Rico to suppress political activity against the Spanish government.

HISPANIC AMERICAN

1875

Romualdo Pacheco, a Mexican American, is elected governor of California.

1876

El Ateneo Puertorriqueno is established. It becomes — and continues to be — a public hall where many historic events take place.

1877

The "Salt War" takes place in Texas, a series of disturbances between European Americans and Mexican Americans over the rights to salt deposits at the Guadalupe Salt Lakes.

1870

through

1879

1870 through 1879

1870

The Fifteenth Amendment to the United States Constitution provides that the right to vote shall not be denied to citizens on the basis of race, color or previous condition of servitude. Congress also passes legislation known as the Force Act to protect the rights granted by the Amendment, and specifically to curtail the activities of the Ku Klux Klan (KKK).

The United States census reports the country's population at 39.8 million. One-fourth of the nation's people live in urban areas.

The United States has more than 50,000 miles of railroad track in operation.

The California Foreign Miner's License Tax, levied against non-European American miners, is ruled unconstitutional.

Benedict College is founded at Columbia, South Carolina.

The Standard Oil Company of Ohio is organized as a trust, the first United States company to use this form of corporate structure on a large scale. It is organized by John D. Rockefeller, and later becomes Standard Oil of New Jersey.

Ada H. Kepley becomes the first American woman law graduate when she completes her studies at Union College of Law in Chicago.

Lucy Stone founds the *Woman's Journal*, the official publication of the American Woman's Suffrage Association.

German-born American businessman Frederick Weyerhaeuser, known as the "Lumber King," establishes the Mississippi River Boom and Logging Company.

By this time, sewing machines have become so popular in the United States that more than 200 different companies manufacture them.

The province of Manitoba, created out of Rupert's Land, joins the Dominion of Canada.

British Honduras (Belize) becomes a crown colony.

1870-1885

More than 10 million bison (buffalo) are slaughtered in the United States, mostly by European Americans, thus radically changing the existence of the Indians on the Plains.

1870s

Women in the United States begin to make careers as librarians.

In the United States education system, public secondary schools begin to replace private academies. Girls are regularly accepted into secondary schools.

In Brazil, Francisca S. da M. Diniz begins publication of *The Feminine Sex,* a newspaper supporting voting and education rights for women.

1870s-1914

Latin American countries enter an era of railroad building that spurs economic and population growth. Argentina exports wheat and meat; Chile, wheat and nitrates; Peru, sugar and copper; Brazil, Venezuela, Colombia, Costa Rica and Guatemala export coffee and fruits. Cities grow and population expands into frontier regions.

1871

The Treaty of Washington between Britain and the United States settles claims against Britain stemming from damage done to the Union's merchant marine by British-supported Confederate ships during the Civil War. An arbitration panel awards the United States more than $15 million based on the direct damage done by the ships *Alabama* and *Florida*, and most of the damage incurred by the *Shenandoah*.

Birmingham is established and incorporated as a city in Alabama.

The Great Chicago Fire causes 250 deaths and almost $200 million worth of damage.

The University of Arkansas in Fayetteville, Smith College at Northampton, Massachusetts and Ursuline College at Pepper Pike, Ohio are founded.

David Edward Hughes invents an early form of microphone.

A million of Elizabeth Butterick's innovative paper dress patterns have been sold in the United States.

Simon Ingersoll invents the pneumatic rock drill.

William H. (Boss) Tweed's corruption in New York City is exposed.

Victoria Woodhull states before the Judiciary Committee of the House of Representatives that under the provisions of the Fourteenth and Fifteenth Amendments, women are citizens and should be allowed to vote.

British Columbia joins the Dominion of Canada. The first official census of the new Dominion reports the population at almost 3.7 million.

Benito Juárez (1857-1861) is reelected president of Mexico. He remains in office until his death in 1872.

Brazil takes a first step in emancipation by passing its "Free Birth" law. Under this law, all children born to enslaved mothers are free.

1871-1880

Immigration to the United States totals 2,812,191 of which 2,271,925 come from Europe, 124,160 come from Asia, 358 from Africa, 10,914 from Oceania, 404,044 from the Americas and 790 are not specifically identified.

1872

Congress gives amnesty to most Confederate leaders and military personnel.

An investigation of the Crédit Mobilier of America company during the national election reveals that Oakes Ames sold or transferred shares in Crédit Mobilier to members of Congress at many times less than they were worth on the open market. Since the company incurred large debts in the completion of the Union Pacific Railroad, this activity creates a major scandal.

Susan B. Anthony is arrested for voting in her hometown of Rochester, New York.

Begun in 1864 near Fort Dodge as a trading post on the Arkansas River, Dodge City is established and incorporated as a city in 1875.

Yellowstone is named the United States' first national park.

The United States experiences a dramatic decline in foreign capital investment, especially from British investors.

Gold deposits are discovered near Sitka, Alaska, and in British Columbia.

Sebastian Lerdo de Tejada becomes president of Mexico after the death of Benito Juárez (1871). Sebastian Lerdo de Tejada serves until 1876.

1873

Despite public scandals, Ulysses S. Grant begins a second term as president of the United States; Henry Wilson is vice president. Both are Republicans. Vice President Henry Wilson dies in office in 1875.

The United States Supreme Court decides the *Slaughter-house Cases*, which stem from the issuance in Louisiana of a single 25-year operator's license to one slaughterhouse in New Orleans. Other operators object, claiming this monopoly deprives them of their property — that is, the right to function in this market — without compensation. They sue on the grounds that this violates the Fourteenth Amendment. The Court rules that the scope of the amendment is not to include such cases as this, and is intended to prevent discrimination against African Americans in the aftermath of the Civil War. The decision clearly draws the distinction between citizenship in a state and citizenship in the United States.

The United States Congress establishes gold as the only monetary standard and sets up the Bureau of the Mint.

The failure of Jay Cooke & Company, the firm handling large Civil War loans of the federal government, creates the Panic of 1873 in the United States. The failure is caused by overspeculation in an attempt to raise over $100 million for the Northern Pacific Railroad.

An economic depression in the United States this year is characterized by high unemployment due to the oversupply of unskilled immigrant labor. Many women are stirred to action, and seek reforms in relief for the destitute, job training, and the abolition of child labor.

The *Bismarck Tribune* begins publication under Colonel Clement A. Lounsberry. It continues publication to the present, and is North Dakota's oldest newspaper.

In *Bradwell* v. *Illinois,* the United States Supreme Court upholds a state law forbidding a married woman (Myra Colby Bradwell) from practicing law.

Bennett College at Greensboro, North Carolina; Wiley College at Marshall, Texas; and the College of Notre Dame of Maryland at Baltimore are founded.

The province of Prince Edward Island joins the Dominion of Canada.

Alexander MacKenzie, a Liberal, becomes prime minister of Canada after the term of Sir John Alexander Mac-Donald (1867). MacKenzie serves until 1878.

To maintain order in its far western territories that are now being colonized, the Canadian government establishes a temporary paramilitary force, called the North-West Mounted Police.

Construction is completed on Mexico's first railroad.

The ship *Virginius*, flying American colors, is seized in international waters by a Spanish warship and taken to Santiago de Cuba. The head of the primarily Cuban expedition, his aide, several Cubans and eight American volunteers are executed before a British official steps in and demands that the executions be stopped. The rest of the group is spared.

1873-1896

Canadians experience a prolonged economic depression.

1874

Morrison Remick Waite becomes chief justice of the United States Supreme Court. He serves until 1888.

The Woman's Christian Temperance Union is founded in Cleveland, Ohio, to promote physical and moral health, primarily through abstinence from alcohol. Francis Willard and Carrie Nation are its early leaders.

The first zoological gardens in the United States open in Philadelphia.

Mennonite immigrants from Russia introduce a new strain of wheat, Turkey Red, to the fields of Kansas. This hardy winter wheat proves to be an exceptional cash crop that earns Kansas the nickname of the Wheat State.

Congress sets the enlisted strength of the Regular Army at 25,000; it remains at this level until the start of the Spanish-American War in 1898.

Gold is discovered on Sioux Reservation land in the Black Hills of (South) Dakota. By 1877 miners have forced the Sioux off much of their lands.

Joseph Farwell Glidden perfects the design and production of barbed wire. It is initially used in the American West for fencing and later for military operations.

The Chautauqua movement begins, providing lectures, classes, camp meetings and entertainment as forms of adult education.

Tobacco processing plants are constructed in Winston and Durham, North Carolina, by R.J. Reynolds and Washington Duke.

An early typewriter, offering only capital letters, is manufactured for commercial use by E. Remington and Sons company.

1875

In *Minor* v. *Happersett,* the United States Supreme Court rules that suffrage is not inherent in citizenship as defined in the Fourteenth Amendment to the Constitution, and states have the right to allow or prohibit women's suffrage.

Congress passes and President Grant signs the Immigration Act, the first national exclusion law banning prostitutes and convicts. Before this time, American immigration policy was neutral, neither encouraging nor discouraging voluntary immigration; anyone wanting to immigrate to the United States could do so. This act marks the beginning of illegal or undocumented immigrants; laws that further restrict entry into the United States later multiply.

United States Secretary of the Treasury Benjamin Helm Bristow leads the investigation that breaks a major political scandal, the Whiskey Ring. The ring's purpose is to bribe officials to defraud the government of taxes on whiskey, and involves President Grant's private secretary, O. E. Babcock. Babcock is arrested but after the president's intervention he is acquitted.

A reciprocity treaty is signed between the United States and the Hawaiian Kingdom, which allows Hawaiian sugar to enter America duty-free. This treaty prompts the Hawaiian government to seek Chinese labor to take the place of the rapidly dying Hawaiian race.

David Kalakahua becomes king of Hawaii. He rules until 1891.

Wellesley College (for Women) at Wellesley, Massachusetts; Hebrew Union College at Cincinnati, Ohio; Knoxville College in Tennessee; Brigham Young University at Provo, Utah; and Mount Vernon College at Washington, D.C., are founded.

A French-American Union is formed to build the Statue of Liberty in New York City.

Pennsylvania coalfields suffer labor unrest.

The Supreme Court of Canada is established and William B. Richards becomes its first chief justice.

An earthquake hits regions of Venezuela and Colombia causing more than 15,000 deaths.

c. 1875

The first wave of Muslim immigrants comes to the United States from the regions that are now Syria and Jordan. Most are unskilled laborers who find jobs as migrant farmworkers.

1870

through

1879

1870 through 1879

1876

In the United States presidential election, Samuel J. Tilden (Democrat) receives 184 electoral votes and Rutherford B. Hayes (Republican) 165, with 20 votes in dispute. Although Tilden has received a majority of the popular vote, the Electoral Commission gives disputed Electoral College votes to Rutherford B. Hayes. Hayes becomes the 19th president. William A. Wheeler becomes vice president. Both are Republicans.

In the United States, the Civil Rights Act of 1876 proves to be ineffective because Congress fails to include enforcement procedures.

The United States Supreme Court declares that state immigration laws are unconstitutional, and that immigration is exclusively a federal responsibility. In the case of *Munn* v. *Illinois*, the Court upholds the policy of public regulation of private utilities that are for public use. The decision is overturned in 1886.

Gold deposits are discovered at Windham Bay, Alaska.

Colorado becomes the 38th state to join the Union.

Stillman College at Tuscaloosa, Alabama, and Huston-Tillotson College at Austin, Texas, are founded.

The Centennial Exposition is held in Philadelphia to mark the 100th anniversary of United States independence. Alexander Graham Bell demonstrates his invention of the telephone at the exhibition.

The carpet sweeper is patented by Melville R. Bissell in Grand Rapids, Michigan.

Porfirio Díaz becomes president of Mexico after he and his supporters overthrow Sebastian Lerdo de Tejada (1872). With the exception of the rule of Manuel González, 1880-1884, Díaz rules until 1911.

1877

During an economic depression in the United States, the first nationwide labor strike occurs as workers of first the Baltimore and Ohio, and then other railroad lines go on strike to protest reductions in wages. Riots occur in several major cities.

Reconstruction officially ends when the last federal troops are withdrawn from the southern United States.

Copper mining begins in Butte, Montana.

Philander Smith College is founded at Little Rock, Arkansas. The United States Revenue Cutter Service School of Instruction, established the year before, opens at New London, Connecticut. It is renamed the United States Coast Guard Academy in 1915.

Thomas A. Edison invents the carbon telephone transmitter, an early version of the modern-day microphone.

1877-1879

A textile workers' strike takes place in Paterson, New Jersey.

1878

Congress passes the Bland-Allison Act, named for its creators Richard P. Bland and William B. Allison. It requires the government to purchase between $2,000,000 and $4,000,000 of silver bullion each month for the purpose of making coinage that will serve as legal tender.

The United States attorney-general's report reveals that southern Democrats have stuffed ballot boxes and committed political murders in South Carolina, Louisiana, Texas and Virginia. President Hayes accuses the South of abrogating the rights of African Americans. A Senate committee is appointed to investigate.

The first commercial telephone exchange in the United States opens in New Haven, Connecticut.

The Knights of Labor becomes the first successful labor union in the United States, with membership open to both skilled and unskilled workers.

Thomas A. Edison patents his phonograph.

Joseph Pulitzer becomes publisher of the St. Louis *Post Dispatch*. In 1883 he acquires the *New York World* from Jay Gould.

Western Tennessee residents suffer a yellow fever epidemic.

Charles Taze Russell organizes his followers into the Russellites or Bible Students. In 1931 they become known as Jehovah's Witnesses.

Sir John Alexander MacDonald (1867), a Conservative, becomes prime minister of Canada for a second time after the term of Alexander MacKenzie (1873). MacDonald serves until his death in 1891.

Freed Africans in St. Croix, led by Queen Mary, a female canefield worker, revolt in protest against labor and land ownership restrictions. United States and French warships intervene, and the revolt is put down with help of troops from St. Thomas.

A French company with rights to dig a canal across Panama abandons the attempt after work crews are stricken with malaria and yellow fever.

Mariano Ignacio Prado (1865) again becomes president of Peru. He serves until 1879.

1879

California adopts a new constitution with a provision prohibiting the employment of Chinese workers.

Radcliffe College at Cambridge, Massachusetts; Livingstone College at Salisbury, North Carolina; and the Carlisle Training and Industrial School for Indians in Pennsylvania are founded.

Thomas A. Edison develops the first commercially successful incandescent light bulb, independent of the work of (Sir) Joseph Swan in England.

Special Congressional action allows Belva Lockwood to try a case before the Supreme Court. She is the first woman permitted to do so.

Frances Willard becomes head of the Woman's Christian Temperance Union. During her twenty-year tenure, she greatly expands the membership and areas of involvement of the organization.

Mary Baker Eddy founds the Church of Jesus Christ, Scientist, commonly called the Christian Science Church, in Boston, Massachusetts. She received a healing by reading a New Testament account of a healing Jesus performed, and came to believe that sickness is an illusion.

Frank Winfield Woolworth opens his first Five and Ten Cent stores in Utica, New York, and Lancaster, Pennsylvania.

Nicolás de Piérola becomes president of Peru after the term of Mariano Ignacio Prado (1865, 1878). He serves until 1881 and again from 1895 to 1899.

c. 1879-1884

In the War of the Pacific, Peru and Bolivia join forces against Chile for control of the Atacama Desert nitrate deposits in Chile. Nitrate is used for fertilizer and explosives. Both Peruvian and Bolivian armies are soundly defeated by Chilean troops. The conflict ends with two treaties. In the Treaty of Ancon, Chile is ceded the Peruvian province of Tarapacá and the right to occupy Tacna and Arica until their ownership is decided. In the Treaty of Valparaíso, Boliva is cut off from the sea when Chile gains control of the coastal region.

1870

through

1879

1870 through 1879

1870

Publication of the doctrine of papal infallibility is forbidden by the Austro-Hungarian Parliament.

The unification of Italy is complete when the Papal States are formally absorbed into the Italian Kingdom.

As a child in exile, Alfonso XII is declared king of Spain after the abdication of his mother, Isabella II (1833). At the same time, Amadeus of Savoy, son of Italy's King Victor Emmanuel II, reluctantly accepts the crown from the assembly in power in Spain led by Juan Prim. After Prim's death, Amadeus's support is weakened and when a new Carlist revolt takes place in 1873, Amadeus abdicates the throne and returns to Italy. Alfonso XII is crowned king in 1874 and rules until 1885.

c. 1870

The railroads of most major European countries are almost complete and industrialization intensifies.

1870-1871

France declares war on Prussia. After a series of military defeats, Napoleon III (1852) surrenders at Sedan, France; revolt occurs in Paris and the Third Republic is proclaimed. The Treaty of Frankfurt transfers Strasburg and Alsace-Lorraine from France to Germany. Germany is now unified and the German Empire is proclaimed at Versailles.

1870-1873

This is the time span generally ascribed to the House of Savoy that governs Spain.

1870-1940

This is the time span generally ascribed to France's Third Republic.

1871

William I becomes *kaiser* (emperor) of Germany and Otto von Bismarck becomes chancellor. Known as the Iron Chancellor, Bismarck dissolves Germany's parliament and levies illegal taxes to support the military, both at William I's request. Bismarck holds this office until 1890.

Feudalism is outlawed in Japan.

Britain annexes the diamond mines in the Kimberley region in South Africa and Britain's Cape Colony takes control over Basutoland.

Explorer and journalist (Sir) Henry Morton Stanley (John Rowlands) meets David Livingstone at the town of Ujiji on Lake Tanganyika in Africa.

1871-1918

This is the time span generally ascribed to the Hohenzollern dynasty that rules Germany.

1872

Japan gains control over the Ryukyu Islands, the southwest Pacific chain of islands that includes Okinawa. Japan's first railroad begins operation this year as well.

The British Parliament passes the Ballot Act; voting is now done by secret ballot.

The Three Emperors' League (Germany, Russia and Austria-Hungary) is formed.

Pago Pago, American Samoa, is selected as a potentially valuable harbor in the Pacific and is ceded to the United States in 1878.

Jesuits are expelled from Germany.

After Alexandra Kollontai visits a Russian textile mill and witnesses the appalling working conditions, she seeks out revolutionary groups and fights for change. At the close of the Russian Revolution, Kollontai becomes the first Soviet woman Commissar, and first female ambassador. Her liberated views on sex, marriage and the family ultimately are discredited by the Communist Party.

Oscar II becomes king of Sweden and Norway after the death of his brother, Charles XV (1859). Oscar II rules Norway until 1905 and Sweden until 1907.

Filipino patriots José Rizal, Marcelo H. del Pilar and Graciano Lopez Jaena lobby in Spain against corruption in the colonial government and for freedom, justice and racial equality.

1872-1876

The Second Carlist War takes place in Spain.

1873

Russia gains control over the Khiva region in Turkestan.

The Hui rebellion in Yunnan, China, is suppressed but the toll in lives and property damage is heavy.

An economic crisis begins in Europe.

The sale of enslaved people is abolished by Sultan Barghash Sayyid of Zanzibar under pressure from Britain.

Japanese Emperor Mutsuhito lifts the prohibition against Christianity.

The Hungarian towns of Buda, Pest and Óbuda are united as Budapest.

c. 1873

Sir Samuel White Baker completes the British conquest of the southern Sudan, instituting reforms against the slave trade.

1873-1874

A famine hits the Bihar region of India.

1874

Revisions to Switzerland's constitution serve to strengthen the nation's centralized government.

Britain annexes the Fiji Islands (southwestern Pacific Ocean).

France takes control of Annam (Vietnam).

Ghana is made a colony of the Gold Coast.

Fiji becomes a British colony.

Alfonso XII is crowned king of Spain after the abdication of Amadeus of Savoy (1870). Alfonso XII rules until 1885.

1874-1877

In Africa, British explorer and journalist Henry Morton Stanley identifies the Lualaba River with the Congo River during his first descent of the waterway system to Boma, near the Atlantic coast. In 1875 he explores Victoria Nyanza.

1874-1881

Charles George Gordon establishes British military installations on the upper Nile River (Sudan) and institutes reforms against the slave trade.

1875

Pierre Paul Brazza intervenes for France in Africa in an attempt to prevent Henry Morton Stanley from annexing the Congo region for Leopold II of Belgium.

The revolt of peasants in Herzegovina (Hercegovina) and Bosnia against Ottoman control is put down with military force.

Britain buys control of the Suez Canal from Ismail, *khedive* (viceroy) of Egypt.

Khama becomes chief of the Bamangwato people in what is now Botswana. During his reign, he makes an agreement with British officials that makes Beuchanaland, as it was then called, a British protectorate.

Guangxu (Kuang-hsü) becomes emperor of China after the death of Tongzhi (1863). Guangxu rules until 1908, although Empress Dowager seizes power in 1898.

1876

Russia gains control over Kokand (now part of Uzbekistan).

Belgian King Leopold II and Henry Morton Stanley establish the International Association for the Exploration and Civilization of the Congo.

By the Treaty of Jacobabad, the British army establishes forts on the Afghan border to monitor potential Russian advances into Afghanistan.

Japan recognizes Korea's independence from China. Korean ports are open to Japanese traders.

British workers construct the first railway in China.

Serbia and Montenegro declare war on Turkey; Serbian forces are defeated at Alexinatz and Bulgarians are massacred by Ottoman troops in retaliation for their declaration of war.

Murad V becomes Ottoman sultan after the death of his uncle, Abdu-l-Aziz (1861), who was overthrown by a liberal group known as the Young Turks. Abdu-l-Hamid II (the Great Assassin or the Red Sultan) becomes sultan of Turkey after his brother, Murad V, is declared insane. Abdu-l-Hamid II rules until 1909.

1876-1878

A three-year famine in India results in the deaths of 5 million people.

A severe drought in China destroys three years' wheat crops; nearly 1 million people die in the resulting famine.

1877

New Zealand's Education Act mandates free compulsory education.

Britain annexes the South African Republic (Transvaal).

Russia goes to war against the Ottoman Empire to support Serbia, and then invades Romania, proclaiming it an independent state.

The Japanese army defeats Samurai forces in the Satsuma Rebellion, further weakening the feudal system.

1878

Russian expansionist policy prompts Ottoman officials to make a pact with Britain. The Turks cede Cyprus to Britain in exchange for a commitment of military assistance if Russia attacks Ottoman border provinces.

The Treaty of San Stefano ends the conflict between Russia and Turkey. By its terms, Bulgaria receives the right to self-government, Turkey grants parts of Armenia to Russia, acknowledges independence for Romania, Serbia and Montenegro and institutes reforms for Bosnia and Herzegovina. This treaty greatly increases Russia's influence, which causes European powers to convene the Congress of Berlin.

The Congress of Berlin reduces the gains Russia extracted from Turkey at San Stefano. The Congress confirms Serbia, Montenegro and Romania as independent states although Romania exchanges certain lands with Russia; Bulgaria is divided into three jurisdictions; Bosnia and Herzegovina are placed under the control of Austria-Hungary; Russia gains additional territory from Turkey. Through a separate pact Cyprus is given to Britain and Crete is given the opportunity to establish a constitutional government.

Humbert I becomes king of Italy after the death of his father, Victor Emmanuel II (1849, 1861). Humbert I rules until 1900.

British physicist (Sir) Joseph Swan patents a successful filament electric lamp. Although Swan is acknowledged in Europe for his discovery of a carbon filament lamp c. 1860, he and American Thomas Edison are credited for the creation of a commercially viable lamp at about the same time.

1878-1879

Norwegian Nils Nordensköld is the first European to traverse the Northeast Passage.

1878-1880

In the Second Afghan War, *Emir* (Muslim prince or commander) Shere Ali (1863) seeks Russian support against Britain. By the Treaty of Gandamak, which ends this conflict, Afghanistan remains under British control and Shere Ali is removed from his position. The treaty recognizes Shere Ali's son Yakub Khan as *emir* of Afghanistan.

1879

Renewed famine occurs in Ireland.

Adult male suffrage is introduced in New Zealand.

Queensland (Australia) takes control of the islands of the Great Barrier Reef and the Torres Strait.

During the Meiji reform period, a handful of Japanese women begin a movement for women's rights. Through their lectures, publications and strikes, more and more women challenge the customary virtues that women are taught to obey. Some are jailed for their beliefs.

The Dual Alliance between Austria-Hungary and Germany is designed to contain Russia and assist Austria in gaining influence in the Balkans. It remains in effect until 1913.

Tewfik Pasha becomes *khedive* of Egypt after his father, Ismail Pasha (1863), is deposed. Tewfik Pasha rules until 1892.

Alexander I (Alexander of Battenburg) is elected prince of Bulgaria. He rules until 1886.

1879-1883

The British-Zulu War takes place. Zulus massacre British soldiers in Isandhlwana; British forces are successful at Rorke's Drift and Ulundi, and Zulu chief Cetewayo and his forces are defeated. The peace treaty divides up much of Zulu territory and a large portion of it ultimately becomes part of Natal.

1870

through

1879

NATIVE AMERICAN	NATIVE AMERICAN	NATIVE AMERICAN	AFRICAN AMERICAN
1880 The National Indian Defense Association is established by Dr. T. A. Bland, publisher of the *Council Fire.* The organization rejects the imposition of European American lifestyle on Native Americans. **1880-1889** The Bureau of Indian Affairs opens more than 20 off-reservation boarding schools. Strict discipline marks the forced acculturation of Native American children. **1881** Sioux Chief Sitting Bull returns from Canada and surrenders at Fort Buford, (North) Dakota. Helen Hunt Jackson's *A Century of Dishonor,* a nonfiction book about injustices toward Native Americans, is published. Sioux Chief Spotted Tail dies in (South) Dakota. One hundred six schools for Native Americans are in operation. **1884** Haskell Institute in Lawrence, Kansas, and Chilocco Indian School in Indian Territory (Oklahoma) open to provide vocational training for American Indians. Congress acknowledges the rights of the Inuit people (Eskimos) to Alaskan lands. Since that time, the Inuit have never sold, lost or ceded their land rights. The Supreme Court, in *Elk* v. *Wilkins,* states that a detribalized tax-paying Native American legally resident in Nebraska is not a citizen under the Fourteenth Amendment to the Constitution, because Native American tribes are "alien nations" and are not subject to United States jurisdiction. **Mid-1880s** The Sun Dance of the Sioux Indians is outlawed by the federal government because it involves elements of self-torture. **1885** The last great bison (buffalo) herd in the United States is exterminated.	A federal law is passed mandating the withdrawal of federal troops from the borders of Indian Territory, thus removing government protection of this land for Native Americans. The law goes into effect in 1889. Apache Chief Geronimo flees the San Carlos Reservation in Arizona and travels into southern New Mexico. **1886** Chiricahua Apache chiefs Geronimo and Naiche surrender to General Nelson Miles, ending years of Apache warfare in the Southwest. The Apaches are imprisoned at Fort Marion, Florida. Geronimo is relocated to Fort Sill, Oklahoma. The Apaches' status as prisoners of war is not lifted until 1913. The Supreme Court, in *United States* v. *Kagama,* rules that American Indians are "under the political control of the United States...." This directly contradicts the Court's 1884 decision in *Elk* v. *Wilkins.* **1887** The Dawes Allotment Act, sponsored by Henry Laurens Dawes and passed by the United States Congress, reverses the government's policy of confining Native Americans to reservations. The act breaks up the reservation system. Native Americans who accept grants of land are given citizenship. Tribal lands are allotted to individual Indians in 160-acre tracts. Surplus lands are distributed to European Americans for homesteading. This act is a serious blow to tribal corporate and social existence. As a result of the Dawes Allotment Act, the Native American land base drops from 130 million acres in 1887 to 49 million acres in 1933. In an effort to force acculturation, the Bureau of Indian Affairs forbids Native Americans from practicing their traditional ceremonies such as the Sun Dance. The commissioner of Indian Affairs forbids the use of native languages in American Indian schools.	**1888** Delegates of more than 20 tribes gather at Fort Gibson, Indian Territory, to discuss the creation of a Native American state. The plan fails. **1889** The commissioner of Indian Affairs advocates the elimination of reservations and tribes. He says that Native Americans are to be "individualized and conform to the white man's ways, peaceably if they will, forceably if they must...." At noon on April 22, the law rescinding federal protection of the borders of Indian Territory goes into effect. Thousands of European Americans who have been camped outside the borders cross them, and by nightfall they have established tent cities, banks and stores.	**1880** In *Strauder* v. *West Virginia,* the Supreme Court rules that exclusion of African Americans from jury duty is unconstitutional, under the equal protection clause of the Fourteenth Amendment. **1881** Rhode Island repeals its law banning interracial marriage. Dr. Charles B. Purvis is appointed chief surgeon of the Freedman's Hospital in Washington, D.C., thus becoming the first African American to head a major hospital under nonmilitary conditions. John P. Green becomes the first African American to serve in the Ohio state legislature. Tuskegee Institute, founded by Booker T. Washington in Alabama, and Spellman College and Morris Brown College, both at Atlanta, Georgia, are founded. **1882** Violette Johnson is the first African American woman lawyer permitted to present a case before the United States Supreme Court. **1883** The United States Supreme Court's decision that the Civil Rights Act of 1875 is unconstitutional sets in motion the doctrine of state action. Maine and Michigan repeal laws forbidding interracial marriage. African American inventor Jan E. Matzeliger builds and patents a lasting machine, which revolutionizes the manufacture of shoes. A top factory worker can turn out 50 pairs of shoes a day, while Matzeliger's machine increases that number to more than 200 pairs daily. Benjamin and Robert Pelham establish the newspaper *The Plaindealer* in Detroit, Michigan. George Lewis Ruffin becomes the first African American judge in the North when he is appointed by Massachusetts governor Benjamin Butler. He serves until his death in 1886.

1880

through

1889

AFRICAN AMERICAN	AFRICAN AMERICAN	ASIAN AMERICAN	FOR CLASSROOM USE	

AFRICAN AMERICAN

1884

Former Congressman John R. Lynch is elected temporary chairman of the Republican Convention, the first African American to preside over a national political party function.

Inventor Granville T. Woods patents the first of many inventions, a steam boiler furnace. Other major inventions are in the railroad and communication fields.

T. Thomas Fortune begins publication of *The New York Freeman,* which later changes its name to *The New York Age.*

The Medico-Chirurgical Society of the District of Columbia is organized with a biracial membership.

1885

Robert Smalls is elected to the United States Congress from South Carolina. He serves five terms.

1886

Augustus Tolton becomes the first African American to be ordained into the Catholic priesthood. He serves in Illinois.

Rust College at Holly Springs, Mississippi, is founded.

1887

John H. Alexander becomes the second African American to graduate from West Point.

1888

The transatlantic trade in enslaved Africans ends. Africa has lost between 50 and 100 million people. About 11 to 15 million landed in the Americas and the rest died in raids or crossing to the Americas.

The Louisville National Medical College is founded in Tennessee by Dr. Miles V. Lynk. It remains in operation until 1911.

AFRICAN AMERICAN

1889

Three African Americans, all Republicans, are elected to the United States House of Representatives. John M. Langston, former president of Virginia Normal and Collegiate Institute, becomes the first African American from Virginia to serve in the House. Because of a severe challenge, he obtains his seat at the end of 1890. Henry P. Cheatham from North Carolina serves two terms. Thomas E. Miller from South Carolina serves one term.

Charles Young becomes the third African American to graduate from West Point. He attains the rank of lieutenant colonel in 1916.

ASIAN AMERICAN

1880

The United States census reports 105,465 Chinese Americans in the mainland United States; 99 percent live in the West. The sex ratio is 2,107 males to 100 females. The census also reports 148 Japanese in the continental United States.

Chinese laborers represent more than 20 percent of California's total labor force.

Construction of the Southern Pacific Railroad brings to Tucson the largest Chinese community in Arizona.

A new treaty allows the United States government to regulate or suspend Chinese immigration, but not to prohibit it.

Mobs destroy Chinese homes and businesses in Denver, Colorado.

1880s

Guilds are formed among Chinese cigar workers, shoemakers and garment workers.

The first schools for Chinese living in Hawaii are established by missionaries.

1882

Chinese immigrants to America are excluded from many occupations and limited to service-type work. In the South, Chinese workers gravitate toward the grocery business.

The Chinese Exclusion Act bars all Chinese laborers for 10 years. The act does not ban Chinese ministers, businessmen, students and some of their relatives. Also, Chinese immigrants cannot be naturalized.

Anti-Chinese violence has been frequent since 1858, when the first lynching of a Chinese American took place.

In San Francisco, Chinese district associations unite and form the Chinese Consolidated Benevolent Association to fight the anti-Chinese movement.

1880

through

1889

	ASIAN AMERICAN	ASIAN AMERICAN	EUROPEAN AMERICAN	EUROPEAN AMERICAN
1880 **through** **1889**	**1883** The first test cases challenge the Chinese Exclusion Act in court. As Chinese immigrants win court decisions, new entrants begin to claim entry as family members of exempt classes and as citizens by derivation. The Hawaiian kingdom limits immigration of Chinese labor. **1884** Congress amends the Chinese Exclusion Act of 1882 to impose more restrictions on Chinese Americans. **1884-1885** A San Francisco superior court rules in *Tape* v. *Hurley* that Chinese American children must be allowed to enter public schools. The San Francisco Board of Education establishes a segregated Chinese primary school. **1885** In an anti-Chinese riot at Rock Springs, Wyoming, 43 Chinese Americans are killed or injured. Anti-Chinese riots spread throughout the West. Japan and Hawaii sign a treaty allowing Japanese contract laborers to go to Hawaii. The first group, 859 workers with women and children, arrives. Immigration from Korea to America begins, with a small number of students and political refugees. Chinese Americans are expelled from Tacoma and Puyallup, Washington. **1886** In Seattle, Washington, a mob forces several hundred Chinese people to board ships and leave the city. Troops are called in by the governor to restore order. After this incident, fewer than 300 Chinese residents remain in Seattle. **1888** Congress enacts a law specifying conditions for the return of Chinese laborers who left the United States temporarily.	In *Chae Chan Ping* v. *United States,* the Supreme Court rules that an entire race that the government deems difficult to assimilate may be barred from entry into the United States, and that the exercise of such power should be upheld in the lower courts regardless of prior treaties. The first school established by San Francisco's Chinese American community opens for enrollment. Several Japanese laborers immigrate to farms in Vaca Valley, California. **1889** The Japanese Methodist Church is established in Oakland, California.	**1880** The first electric lights in Chicago attract street crowds after they are installed in the shop of Norwegian American merchant Christian Nevje. The German American beer industry flourishes, with more than 20 breweries in operation in Cincinnati, Ohio, alone. **1880-1890** This peak decade for Swedish immigration to the United States results from agricultural failures, class divisions and compulsory military service in Sweden. **1880-1920** Mass immigration of Russians to America occurs. **1880s-1890s** Three Swedish American fraternal organizations, the Independent Order of Vikings, the Independent Order of Svithiod and the Vasa Order of America, are founded. In addition to providing health and old age benefits, they are social and cultural outlets for their members. **1881** Russian immigration to the United States increases. Czar Alexander III blames Russian Jews, and others, for his father's death; some of these new immigrants therefore carry anti-Semitism with them, thus introducing or increasing prejudice in areas where they make their homes. **1882** Almost 800,000 immigrants, of all nationalities, enter the United States, surpassing the previous record. Norwegian and Danish immigration to America also peaks this year, with the arrival of 29,000 Norwegians and 11,000 Danes. Most Norwegians seek the rugged farmlands of the upper Midwest. Many Danes are laborers and farmers who also migrate to the midwestern states. German immigration also reaches its post-Civil War peak, with 250,630 new immigrants arriving in the United States this year.	A significant number of Jewish immigrants from eastern Europe move to the United States — until restrictive American quotas cut the number dramatically. While earlier Jewish Americans spread out across the continent and work primarily as merchants, many of these new arrivals become industrial laborers or suppliers of consumer goods and services in the immigrant neighborhoods. The first Danish American fraternal organization, The Danish Brotherhood, is founded in Omaha, Nebraska. **1883** Thirty Spanish American families are expelled from Colorado. **1884** By opening its membership to all Roman Catholics of Irish lineage, the Ancient Order of Hibernians makes a move out of its secret origins and into the mainstream of the Irish American community. The organization restates its goals as: "agitation for Irish freedom, ardent support of the Church and the stimulation of interest in Irish history, culture and folklore." **1885** A large wave of immigration from eastern and southern Europe, known as the "New Immigration," begins. Many new arrivals to the United States are Russian Jews escaping persecution. Due to Germany's rapid progress in industrialization and to the success of German Chancellor Otto von Bismarck's "state socialism," the quality of life in Germany improves to the point where immigration to the United States drops sharply. Thomas F. Bayard becomes the first Scandinavian American to hold a cabinet post when President Grover Cleveland appoints him secretary of state.

EUROPEAN AMERICAN	HISPANIC AMERICAN	FOR CLASSROOM USE	FOR CLASSROOM USE	
1886 The radical German American newspaper *Arbeiter Zeitung,* published in Chicago, becomes a powerful voice of German American working people. It advocates using violence if necessary to bring about reform, and is considered to be a major contributor in the Haymarket Riot of this year. (*See* "The Americas, 1886.") **1887** *Arbeiter Zeitung* publisher August Spies, a German American, is one of those hanged in the aftermath of the 1886 Haymarket Riot in Chicago. Swedish Americans are the first of the farming population in the United States to install electric lighting on their farms and in their homes. **1888** British immigration peaks with about 108,000 new arrivals. Russian American businessman Peter Damianov founds the city of St. Petersburg, Florida. In Wisconsin, several European American groups unite and force the repeal of state laws requiring that all school instruction be given in the English language. Seven Latvian immigrants, led by master carpenter Jacob Sieberg, make their homes in Boston. This is considered the beginning of regular Latvian immigration to the United States. **1889** The Boston Latvian Benefit Society becomes the first Latvian American civic organization. The Semitic Museum is established as the nation's first Jewish museum, and is operated by Harvard University. The largest chair factory in the United States is established in Chicago by a Norwegian immigrant. The great terra cotta works at Perth Amboy, New Jersey, which is owned by two Danish Americans, attracts many newly arrived Danish immigrants as laborers.	**1880** Tobacco production in Puerto Rico is approximately 12 million pounds this year. The Unconditional Conservative Party is established in Puerto Rico. Writer José Martí begins a 15-year stay in New York City. He becomes a leader of the Cuban Revolutionary Party which brings the War of Independence to Cuba in 1895; Martí dies in battle that same year. **1880s** A land boom in California creates wealth for European Americans who have acquired Mexican Americans' lands. **1881** Dr. Carlos J. Finlay, a Cuban physician, first suggests that yellow fever is transmitted by mosquito bites. **1886** The Plan of Ponce advocates alternative autonomous measures as an answer to Puerto Rican government problems. A riot breaks out between European Americans and Mexican Americans at Murpheyville (now Alpine), Texas, with several lives lost from both groups. Vicente Martínez Ibor moves his tobacco factory and business from Key West to Tampa, Florida — thus the city of Tampa is founded. **1887** The Autonomous Party is founded by Ramón Baldorioty de Castro and former members of the Liberal Party in Puerto Rico. It approves a program calling for an autonomous government. This is known as the "Terrible Year" in Puerto Rico because of physical punishments and political persecution under the regime of Governor Romualdo Palacio. **1888** Four hundred forty-six sugar mills are operating in Puerto Rico; approximately one-third are steam-powered.			**1880** **through** **1889**

1880 through 1889

1880

An agreement with China allows the United States government to restrict the immigration of Chinese laborers.

The United States census reports the country's population at 50.16 million.

The nation has approximately 90,000 miles of railroad track in use. America's railroad building reaches its peak, with more than 70,000 miles of track added in this decade.

By this time, 65 percent of the nation's school teachers are women.

Richard Harris, Joseph Juneau and Kowee, a Tlingit chieftain, discover gold on Gastineau Channel in Alaska; the community of Juneau is established.

Inventor and philanthropist George Eastman opens a factory in Rochester, New York, for making photographic plates using his newly invented dry-plate process.

Canada's first woman doctor, Emily Howard Stowe, is admitted to practice in Ontario.

Manuel González becomes president of Mexico when Porfirio Díaz (1876) agrees to the policy of nonreelection. González serves until 1884.

1880-1889

The southern United States sees steady industrialization as more factories develop.

1880-1900s

Argentina's beef export industry expands rapidly as advances are made in refrigeration and transportation.

1880s

A period of "new immigration" to the United States begins, with the majority of people arriving from southern and eastern Europe.

Rebecca Johnson studies and experiments with improvements in poultry incubators. Eventually, she develops an incubator with a temperature warning alarm. Johnson is one of the first Iowa women to receive a patent for an invention.

1881

James A. Garfield becomes the 20th president of the United States; Chester A. Arthur is vice president. Both are Republicans. Garfield dies in September, two months after being shot by Charles J. Guiteau. Vice President Arthur succeeds him and becomes the 21st president of the United States.

The Atlantic & Pacific Railroad completes a line connecting San Francisco and the Pacific rail system with Tucson and the Arizona border, via the Laguna Indian pueblo and Fort Wingate. Many other smaller railroads complete connecting lines during the 1880s.

Russian immigration to the United States increases as a result of Czar Alexander III's actions to avenge the death of his father.

The American Red Cross is founded by Clara Barton.

A devastating Michigan forest fire leaves 300 people dead and gives the newly formed American Red Cross its first task in disaster relief.

Tuskegee Institute is established in Alabama, and Spelman College and Morris Brown College, both at Atlanta, Georgia, are founded.

Following victories in the war of the Pacific (c. 1879-1884), Miguel Iglesias, a military leader, assumes the presidency of Peru. He rules until his ouster by revolution in 1885.

1881-1890

Immigration to the United States totals 5,246,613 new arrivals, of which 4,735,484 come from Europe, 69,942 from Asia, 857 from Africa, 12,574 from Oceania, 426,967 from the Americas and 789 are not specifically identified.

1882

Congress adopts the Chinese Exclusion Act, banning Chinese workers from entering the United States for 10 years.

Julia Doak is appointed as Tennessee's Superintendent of Education, the first woman in the country to hold such a position.

The United States Navy bombs and then burns the Tlingit village of Angoon, Alaska.

Paine College at Augusta, Georgia and Lane College at Jackson, Tennessee are founded.

John D. Rockefeller's Standard Oil Trust is the first industrial monopoly in the United States, controlling over 90 percent of the domestic petroleum industry.

The electric iron is introduced in the United States.

1883

Congress creates the Civil Service Commission. The Pendleton Civil Service Act, requiring standardized competitive examinations for civil service jobs in the United States, is aimed at reducing jobs created by the "spoils system."

The Northern Pacific Railroad Line is completed.

The University of North Dakota is founded at Grand Forks. Columbia College of Columbia University in New York City offers the first course in the United States dealing with Latin American history.

New York's Brooklyn Bridge, designed by John A. Roebling, opens to traffic.

William Frederick "Buffalo Bill" Cody establishes his Wild West Show at Omaha, Nebraska, and begins touring the United States and Europe.

Large deposits of copper and nickel are discovered in Sudbury, Ontario, Canada.

1884

The United States recession of 1884 is precipitated by falling farm prices.

Mississippi University for Women is founded at Columbus.

American-born inventor Hiram Maxim makes the first true machine gun in England.

German-born inventor and watchmaker Ottmar Mergenthaler patents his invention of the linotype machine. It is put into general usage in 1886.

The Canadian government outlaws the Potlatch ceremony of the Northwest coastal Indian tribes.

In Canada, women are first allowed to vote in Ontario municipal elections.

Porfirio Díaz (1876) is again elected president of Mexico after the constitution is amended to allow reelection. Díaz becomes president after the term of Manuel González (1880) and serves until 1911.

1885

Grover Cleveland becomes the 22nd president of the United States; Thomas A. Hendricks becomes vice president. Both are Democrats. Vice President Hendricks dies in office.

Arizona State University at Tempe and University of Arizona at Tucson, both in Arizona, Stanford University at Palo Alto, California and Bryn Mawr College in Pennsylvania are founded.

Idaho's legislature passes the Test Oath Act, carefully worded to prohibit Mormons from voting or holding office.

The last great bison (buffalo) herd in the United States is exterminated.

American inventor Tolbert Lanston receives the first patent for his monotype machine. Over the next decade, he refines the machine, which sets type characters individually rather than in a connected line, and it becomes a commercial product in 1897.

The postal rate for a first class letter in the United States is two cents.

The second Riel Rebellion takes place in Canada. Louis Riel again leads Native Canadians and *Métis* (people in Canada of combined European and Indian ethnicity) in an attempt to secure land titles in Saskatchewan. The rebellion is put down and Riel is captured, tried and hanged.

Guatemalan President Justo Rufino Barrios tries unsuccessfully to unite Central America by force.

c. 1885

Inventor William Seward Burroughs embarks on a decade of research in St. Louis, Missouri, and obtains patents for the development of the adding machine. He eventually produces the first practical adding machine and later establishes the Burroughs Corporation.

1886

In the case of *Wabash, St. Louis & Pacific Railroad Co.* v. *Illinois*, the United States Supreme Court reverses the *Munn* v. *Illinois* decision and prohibits states from regulating interstate railroad rates. This decision leads to the creation of the Interstate Commerce Commission.

The Statue of Liberty is completed and dedicated in New York City.

Rust College at Holly Springs, Mississippi; Newcomb College, part of Tulane University, at New Orleans, Louisiana; and the University of Wyoming at Laramie are founded.

The American Federation of Labor is founded and Samuel Gompers is elected its first president.

The Haymarket Riot takes place in Chicago. Against the mayor's orders, police officers advance on a crowd of approximately 2,000 people who are protesting police actions that occurred at the McCormick Harvester Company strike the previous day. A bomb explodes, killing seven policemen and four bystanders; police open fire, killing several protesters. Four protest leaders, including the publisher of the German American *Arbeiter Zeitung,* are tried and executed; others receive prison sentences. This incident seriously hurts the growth of labor unions in the United States. In 1893 Illinois Governor John P. Altgeld, critical of the initial trial, pardons those in prison.

Canada's transcontinental railroad is completed.

Men of the Mohawk tribe on a reservation in Quebec receive training in high-steel construction and work on a bridge across the St. Lawrence River. In 1907, approximately 60 workers, many of them Indians, are killed when a section of the Quebec Bridge collapses.

José Manuel Balmaceda becomes president of Chile.

Cuba and Brazil abolish slavery.

Andrés Avelino Cáceres becomes president of Peru. Cáceres serves until 1890 and again in 1894.

1886-1887

This winter's severe blizzards on the Plains virtually stop open-range ranching.

1887

The Interstate Commerce Commission is established by Congress in response to public pressure to control railroad abuses, such as excessive and discriminatory practices in establishing rates.

The Standing Rock Indian Reservation in North Dakota is opened for homesteading by European Americans.

The Pratt Institute at Brooklyn, New York, and The Catholic University at Washington, D.C., are founded.

A normal school for Indians (now Pembroke State University) is established in Robeson County, North Carolina.

Congressman William Henry Hatch legislates for the act that bears his name. It provides for direct federal funding for scientific studies in agriculture.

The Canadian Pacific Railway, Canada's transcontinental railroad, officially opens, with almost 3,000 miles of track.

1887-1888

United States immigration laws are enacted as follows: the law of 1887 prohibits the admission of foreign contract workers, and the amendment of 1888 authorizes the deportation of violators if they are caught within one year of entry.

1888

After one of the most corrupt campaigns in history, Benjamin Harrison is elected president by the Electoral College, though Grover Cleveland wins the popular vote.

The historic March blizzard in the northeastern United States kills many people and causes property damage at a cost exceeding $25 million.

Melville Weston Fuller becomes chief justice of the United States Supreme Court. He serves until 1910.

Ricks College at Rexburg, Idaho and New Mexico State University at Las Cruces are founded.

The Washington Monument is opened to the public in Washington, D.C. The base was completed in 1880, the structure substantially completed in 1884 and it was dedicated in 1885.

George Eastman's box camera — the Kodak — and roll film are introduced.

Nikola Tesla, a naturalized American who immigrated to the United States from Croatia in 1884, invents the alternating current electric induction motor.

While Brazil's Emperor Pedro II is away, his daughter Isabel abolishes slavery without compensation in that country. Pedro II is forced to resign by reform-minded military officers who begin the transition to a republican form of government.

1889

Benjamin Harrison becomes the 23rd president of the United States; Levi P. Morton becomes vice president. Both are Republicans.

North Dakota, South Dakota, Montana and Washington join the Union as the 39th, 40th, 41st and 42nd states, respectively.

The United States Department of Agriculture is given cabinet-level status. The legislation is sponsored by Congressman William Henry Hatch and Jeremiah McLain Rusk becomes its first secretary.

The first conference of the American States takes place in Washington, D.C. Delegates from 18 countries participate in the conference, which establishes the Pan-American Union as an information bureau and will eventually bring about the creation of the Organization of American States (OAS).

Indian Territory (Oklahoma) is opened to European American colonization with the rescinding of federal protection of the borders. A land run occurs and those who leave early to cross the border are called "Sooners," which becomes the nickname for the territory.

More than 2,000 residents die in a Johnstown, Pennsylvania, flood caused by a break in the dam on the Conemaugh River.

Barnard College is founded in New York City, New York.

Andrew Carnegie delivers his "Gospel of Wealth" speech which justifies one's ability to accumulate wealth, become a "trustee" for that wealth and then use and control it during his or her lifetime for the good of others. Carnegie becomes a chief spokesman for the theory of Social Darwinism, which attempts to use Charles Darwin's theory of evolution in the economic sector.

Jane Addams and Ellen Gates Starr establish Hull House in Chicago, the first settlement house in the United States. They offer assistance and encouragement to poverty-stricken city residents.

A revolt of plantation owners forces Brazil's Emperor Pedro II (1831) to renounce the throne. The first Republic of Brazil is established under the leadership of General Manuel Deodoro da Fonseca.

1889-1892

Englishman Wilfred Grenfell explores arctic Canada and brings medical services to the Labrador Inuit (Eskimos).

1880

through

1889

1880 through 1889

1880

The first Anglo-Afrikaner war, the Boer Rebellion, begins after Transvaal Boers led by Paul Kruger declare their independence from Britain and establish a republic.

In France, the Jesuits, Benedictines, Carmelites and all other religious teaching bodies are dissolved and dispersed.

France annexes Tahiti.

At the Madrid Conference, the major European powers agree to the independence of Morocco from French control and maintain an open trade policy in the area.

Although explorer Pierre Paul François Camille Savorgnan de Brazza is unsuccessful in preventing Belgium's King Leopold II from annexing the Congo, France establishes a firm base in equatorial Africa when Brazza founds the cities of Brazzaville and Franceville.

Abdu-r-Rahman Khan becomes *emir* (Muslim prince or commander) of Afghanistan after his uncle, Shere Ali (1863), is forced into exile. Abdu-r-Rahman Khan rules until 1901.

Charles Stuart Parnell leads the predominantly Catholic Home Rule Party in Ireland.

The term boycott comes into common usage as a means of economic pressure when the tenant farmers of Irish land-owner Captain Charles Cunningham Boycott refuse to harvest their crops due to his ruthlessness.

c. 1880

The European powers begin their push for colonial expansion in Africa.

The Married Woman's Property Act becomes law in Great Britain, allowing married women to own property. This lays the foundation for additional legal protections for women.

1880-1890

This decade sees the peak of European colonial activity in Africa.

c. 1880-1898

In the Sudan, Muhammad Ahmad ibn Abdallah manages to unite several factions — including pro-slavery traders, groups who oppose Egypt's rule of the Sudan, and people who oppose corruption — into one warring force. Calling himself the Mahdi, or Savior, this Muslim fundamentalist declares a holy war against the Turkish rulers of Egypt, who also rule the Sudan. The Mahdi and his troops defeat the Egyptian army and capture Khartoum in 1885. For 13 years the Mahdi and his followers hold power in the Sudan. They are not subdued until 1898, when Britain launches a massive military assault.

1881

Irish nationalist Charles Steward Parnell leads the fight for reform in Irish land laws and improved conditions for tenant farmers. His actions as president of the Irish National Land League are instrumental in the passage of Prime Minister William E. Gladstone's Land Act, which alleviates the situation.

By the Treaty of Bardo, Tunisia becomes a French protectorate.

Boers in Transvaal defeat British forces, leading to the Treaty of Pretoria which recognizes the independent South African (Transvaal) Republic.

Anti-Jewish *pogroms* (organized attacks) break out in Russia and the enforcement of the pale compels Jews to live only in 15 provinces; Jews are expelled from Moscow a decade later.

Romania is proclaimed a kingdom, with Prince Carol I (1866) as king. He rules until 1914.

Alexander III becomes czar of Russia after the assassination of his father, Alexander II (1855). Alexander III rules until 1894.

German explorer Herman von Wissman explores the Zanzibar region of Africa. In 1883, working for Belgium's King Leopold II, he visits the Congo. Wissman serves as governor of German East Africa from 1885 to 1886.

c. 1881-1898

Forces led by Muslim leader Samory (Samori) fight French territorial expansion in Guiana and Ivory Coast. French forces prevail and Samory is exiled.

1882

The Dual Alliance of 1879 between Germany and Austria-Hungary becomes the Triple Alliance with the addition of Italy. It lasts until 1913.

Acts of violence, frequently led by the Fenians, continue to occur in Ireland after passage of land reform measures. In Phoenix Park, Dublin, British chief secretary Lord Frederick Cavendish and his undersecretary, Thomas H. Burke, are stabbed to death by the "Invincibles," a terrorist group that has separated from the Fenians.

British forces invade Egypt to protect their interest in the Suez Canal.

The first *aliyah* (large-scale Jewish migration) begins to Palestine (Eretz Israel). During the next decade, Jews arrive in large numbers from Russia, Persia, Romania and Yemen.

Milan (Milan Obrenovich), prince of Serbia since 1882, becomes that country's king.

Agricultural failure peaks in several European countries.

Frozen meat is successfully shipped from New Zealand to England, paving the way for the growth of New Zealand's beef industry.

Bacteriologist Robert Koch of Berlin announces his discovery of the tuberculosis germ.

1883

A third Reform Act takes effect in Great Britain, removing franchise restrictions so that nearly all men can vote.

The Krakatoa (Krakatau) volcano in the center of the Sunda Strait between Sumatra and Java, Indonesia, erupts. The volcanic ash and large tidal wave cause more than 35,000 deaths.

Papua New Guinea is annexed by Queensland; it becomes the Australian Territory of Papua.

Tunisia becomes a French protectorate.

Stephen John Paulus Kruger, who led the Boer Rebellion, becomes president of the South African (Transvaal) Republic. He retains the office through three subsequent elections, and governs until 1900.

1884

Annam (Vietnam) is made a French protectorate.

Germany annexes Togoland and the Cameroons (western Africa).

At the Convention of London, the autonomy of the South African (Transvaal) Republic is recognized.

German and British colonies are established in the region that is now Namibia.

Germany declares that coastal Namibia is its protectorate. This relationship is recognized by the Conference of Berlin.

Germany and Britain both claim parts of New Guinea.

Louis Pasteur develops a successful animal vaccine against rabies. The following year, he demonstrates that the vaccine can be used on humans as well.

The Japanese government legalizes emigration.

China declares war on France.

The first below-ground railway (subway) in the world begins operation in London.

(Sir) Hiram Maxim, an American-born inventor, creates the first contemporary automatic machine gun in England.

British clergyman Samuel Augustus Barnett establishes Toynbee Hall, the first settlement house in London, England.

1884-1885

The Conference of Berlin is convened to discuss changes in the territorial control of portions of Africa. Britain establishes its control over Nigeria, Belgium maintains authority over the Congo but France and Portugal have their historic claims to the areas rejected.

1885

The Mahdi's Sudanese army captures the city of Khartoum from the Egyptians. The garrison at Khartoum is under the command of British officer Charles George Gordon, former governor of the Sudan. Gordon is killed in the attack.

In Ireland, the Franchise Reform Act gives the Home Rule party 85 Parliament seats. Still, Parliament rejects a Home Rule Bill.

The French invade Madagascar (in the Indian Ocean).

China recognizes the French protectorate over Annam (Vietnam).

Great Britain establishes a protectorate over southern Nigeria and southern New Guinea and annexes Bechuanaland (Botswana).

Germany annexes Tanganyika and Zanzibar (Tanzania).

Both China and Japan agree to allow Korea to govern its own people.

The Indian National Congress meets for the first time in Bombay. It initially advocates economic reform, and later becomes the major voice for India's independence.

A brief war breaks out between Serbia and Bulgaria and ends with the Treaty of Bucharest; Alexander I (of Battenburg, 1879) of Bulgaria abdicates in 1886.

King Leopold II of Belgium takes the title of Head of the Congo Free State.

German inventor Gottlieb Daimler develops a successful lightweight gasoline-burning internal combustion engine, and attaches it to a bicycle, creating the first practical motorcycle. Daimler's compatriot, engineer Karl Benz has developed a similar engine, but fits his to a three-wheeled cart and thus pioneers the motorcar.

1886

In Transvaal, gold is found on the Witwatersrand.

Through the Convention of Peking, China recognizes British control of Burma and firmly establishes the Chinese-Burmese border.

Britain annexes Upper Burma at the end of the Third Burmese War.

As claimants to the throne, the Bonaparte and Orleans families are banished from France.

The unborn child of Alfonso XII (1870) is proclaimed monarch of Spain after Alfonso XII's death. Maria Christina, widow of the dead king, serves as regent until the child — a son, Alfonso XIII — comes of age in 1902. He rules until 1931.

Myanmar (now the Union of Myanmar) is united under British control and becomes a province of India.

Otto I becomes king of Bavaria after the death of his brother, Louis II (1864). Otto I rules until 1913.

1887

France's colonies and protectorates in Indochina are united into French Indochina. This union includes Annam, Cambodia, Cochin China and Tonkin. Laos and Kwangchowan join later.

Germany signs the Reinsurance Treaty with Russia after the Three Emperors' Alliance becomes void. The treaty is designed to avoid war over the Balkans.

China recognizes Portugal's right to Macao on the South China Sea.

Ferdinand (of Saxe-Coburg-Gotha) is elected prince of Bulgaria after the abdication of Alexander I (of Battenburg, 1879). Ferdinand rules as prince until 1908 and as czar of independent Bulgaria from 1908 to 1918.

Britain annexes Zululand (in South Africa), thus blocking Transvaal's access to the sea.

1888

Brunei, North Borneo and Sarawak, all part of Malaysia, become protectorates of Britain.

At the Convention of Constantinople, the Suez Canal is declared open to ships of all nations and free from blockade. Britain agrees to an orderly evacuation of its troops, provided that it can return to protect the canal against an invasion or internal strife. The Egyptian *khedive* (viceroy) Tewfit Pasha objects to the terms but lacks the power to change them.

Lobengula, king of the Matabele, acknowledges British protection and grants mining rights in his territory. Britain also gains influence in Mashonaland (now part of Zimbabwe).

This is the year of the "Three Emperors" in Germany. Frederick III begins a short reign as king of Prussia after the death of his father, William I (1861, 1870-1871). William II becomes *kaiser* (emperor) of Germany and king of Prussia after the death of his father, Frederick III. William II rules until 1918.

Northern and Southern Rhodesia (modern-day Zambia and Zimbabwe, respectively) are declared a British sphere of influence after Cecil Rhodes arranges mineral rights agreements with local chieftains.

Nauru, an inhabited atoll in the central Pacific Ocean near the Gilbert Islands, is claimed and annexed by Germany.

Scottish inventor John Boyd Dunlop invents a practical pneumatic bicycle tire.

1889

The first photographs of the Milky Way galaxy are taken by United States astronomer Edward E. Barnard.

The Second International, an organization of Socialist parties from many parts of Europe, is founded in Paris.

The Great London Dock Strike leads to the formation of new unions, especially among unskilled workers.

Gabon is annexed to the French Congo.

An agreement between France and Britain creates spheres of influence on Africa's Gold and Ivory Coasts and internally on the Senegal and Gambia Rivers.

In Spain, Filipino reformers found a newspaper, *La Solidaridad*.

Menelik II, king of Shoa (in central Ethiopia) becomes emperor of all Ethiopia after the death of Johannes IV (1868). He signs the Treaty of Uccialli (Acciali) with Italy but declares it invalid when he discovers that the Italian interpretation makes Ethiopia a protectorate. Menelik II unifies the country and rules until 1913.

As a child, Alexander I (Alexander Obrenovich) becomes king of Serbia after the abdication of his father, Milan (1868). Alexander I comes of age in 1893 and rules until 1903. His death marks the end of the Obrenovich dynasty.

Charles I becomes king of Portugal after the death of his father, Louis I (1861). Charles I rules until 1908.

1880

through

1889

NATIVE AMERICAN	AFRICAN AMERICAN	AFRICAN AMERICAN	AFRICAN AMERICAN

1890

The Ghost Dance religion, started by Paiute prophet Wovoka, spreads among the Plains tribes. It prophesies the end of European American expansion and the return of Native American lands.

Sioux Chief Sitting Bull, an advocate of the Ghost Dance, is killed by Indian police on the Standing Rock Reservation in South Dakota, reportedly for resisting arrest.

At the Wounded Knee Massacre on the Pine Ridge Reservation in South Dakota, some 300 Minneconju and Hunkpapa Sioux (including women and children) are killed by soldiers of the 7th Cavalry. The massacre is prompted by the alleged refusal of a Sioux Indian to surrender his weapon. Many Indians at Wounded Knee wear "ghost shirts," which they believe are bulletproof. After their tragic failure, the Ghost Dance declines.

The Curtis Act extends the allotment policy to the Five Civilized Tribes in Indian Territory (Oklahoma).

In this year alone, more than 17 million acres of land are taken from Native Americans by the United States government and distributed to European Americans.

1892

The Hoopa Valley and Klamath River Reservations in California are taken back from the Indians and returned to the public domain.

1894

United States troops forcibly gather Hopi children and place them in European American-type schools. Parents are punished for resistance.

1899

A monument is erected in Savannah, Georgia, by the Colonial Dames of America in memory of Creek Chief Tomochichi, who helped the first European colonists in Georgia.

1890

The United States census reports about 7,489,000 African Americans, representing 11.9 percent of the population.

The Supreme Court decision *In re Green* gives states authority over the choosing of presidential electors. This has the effect of legalizing possible disenfranchisement of African Americans.

Richard Robert Wright establishes Savannah State College in Georgia. He retires from the school in 1921 and continues a career in banking.

Although many have small circulations, there are more than 150 African American newspapers in the United States.

1891

Provident Hospital in Chicago opens the first training school for African American medical professionals. Dr. George Cleveland Hall, a skilled surgeon and administrator, becomes one of the founders of Provident Hospital.

1892

World champion bantamweight boxer George Dixon forces the integration of New Orleans' Olympia Club by refusing to fight there unless seats are set aside for African Americans. The club complies.

One hundred sixty African Americans are lynched this year. Since 1882, more than 1,400 African Americans have been lynched.

c. 1892

Ida B. Wells (Barnett) begins her activities opposing racial discrimination and acts of violence.

The *Afro-American* newspaper is established in Baltimore, Maryland by John Henry Murphy.

1893

Dr. Daniel Hale Williams, an African American surgeon, performs the country's first successful heart operation at Chicago's Provident Hospital.

George W. Murray, a Republican, is elected to the House of Representatives from South Carolina. He serves two terms.

1894

In Texas, the leadership of the African American political bloc shifts from the Republicans, headed by Norris Wright Cuney, to the Populists, led by John B. Rayner.

Mid-1890s

Cowboy Bill Pickett develops a technique to hold and throw a steer, popularly called "bull dogging."

1895

W. E. B. Du Bois receives his Ph.D. from Harvard University.

Booker T. Washington delivers his Atlanta Compromise speech which essentially condones political and social inequality in favor of economic and educational assistance.

The Frederick Douglass Memorial Hospital and Training School for Nurses is established at Philadelphia under the direction of Dr. Nathan F. Mossell.

Ida Wells Barnett's work, *The Red Record,* is published. The first comprehensive study of lynching in the United States using statistical data, it launches a nationwide anti-lynching campaign.

1896

In *Plessy* v. *Ferguson,* the Supreme Court rules that segregated "separate but equal" facilities are constitutional.

George Washington Carver becomes director of agriculture research at Tuskegee Institute in Alabama. During his lifetime, he develops more than 100 products from the sweet potato and more than 300 products from the peanut. A philanthropist in his later years, he leaves his life's savings to the establishment of a foundation in his name at Tuskegee to benefit young African American scientists.

Dr. Austin M. Curtis joins the staff of Cook County Hospital in Chicago, thus becoming the first African American to serve on the surgical staff in that facility.

The National Association of Colored Women (NACW) is founded, with more than 200 member clubs. Mary Church Terrell is elected president of the association.

Richard Henry Boys establishes the National Baptist Publishing House in Nashville, Tennessee.

Oakwood College at Huntsville, Alabama, is founded.

1897

George W. White, a Republican, is elected to the United States House of Representatives from North Carolina. He serves two terms and is the last African American to serve in Congress until the election of Oscar DePriest in 1928.

Voorhees College at Denmark, South Carolina, is founded.

1898

African American troops display valor in the Spanish-American war, especially units of the 9th and 10th Negro Cavalry that aid Colonel Theodore Roosevelt and his "Rough Riders" in their attack on San Juan Hill. The 25th Negro Cavalry captures a Spanish fort at the Battle of El Canay. Several men receive commendations for bravery. The first African American casualty is Elijah B. Tunnell, who dies on the U.S.S *Winslow*.

1899

Businessmen John Merrick and Dr. A. M. Moore form an insurance company that later becomes the North Carolina Mutual Life Insurance Company. C. C. Spaulding becomes the first manager of the enterprise.

1890

through

1899

ASIAN AMERICAN	ASIAN AMERICAN	ASIAN AMERICAN	FOR CLASSROOM USE	

1890

The United States census reports 107,488 Chinese people in the continental United States and 2,288 in Alaska. The Hawaiian Kingdom census reports 17,002 Chinese residents.

More than 12,000 Japanese immigrants have made their homes in Hawaii, and 3,000 in California.

1890-1920

Three hundred thousand Japanese, mostly young males, immigrate to the western United States. They are later joined by "picture brides," making the ratio of females to males more even.

1890s

Jujiro Wada receives honorary citizenship from the governor of the territory of Alaska for his daring rescue of an icebound ship. He journeyed alone over the ice to Nome for help.

1891

The Pacific Fruit Packing Company, one of the earliest Chinese American-owned canneries, is founded in San Francisco.

Railroads are among the first large industries to employ Japanese laborers.

1892

The Japanese Baptist Church opens an English-language night school in San Francisco.

The federal Geary Act extends Chinese exclusion for 10 more years. Chinese laborers are required to register. Chinese immigrants challenge the law in court and many do not register.

The first Japanese-language newspaper in Hawaii is started in Honolulu.

The Supreme Court hears the case of *Nishimura* v. *United States,* which challenges the right of the United States to bar a Japanese person from entering the country. This case is a determining factor in a treaty two years later between the United States and Japan to ensure the civil liberties of Japanese immigrants.

1893

The Supreme Court in *Fong Yue Ting* v. *United States* upholds the constitutionality of the registration requirement for Chinese laborers. Congress subsequently amends the Geary Act of 1892 to extend the registration deadline of Chinese laborers for six months.

1894

Sun Yat-sen and others found a revolutionary organization in Hawaii to overthrow the Chinese emperor. Sun travels to the United States mainland in 1896 and on later journeys to recruit supporters.

1895

American-born Chinese form the Native Sons of the Golden State in San Francisco to fight for the civil and political rights of Chinese Americans.

1896

The Hawaiian Kingdom census reports 21,616 Chinese residents.

The first Japanese-language school in Hawaii is started by the Reverend Takie Okumura at the Makiki Christian Church in Honolulu.

1898

Hawaii is annexed to the United States.

Seven crewmen of Japanese ancestry die in the sinking of the U.S.S. *Maine* in Havana harbor.

The United States Asiatic Squadron, under the command of Commodore George Dewey, enters Manila Bay and destroys the Spanish fleet. Approximately 5 percent of Dewey's crew is Chinese, some of them American-born.

The United States acquires the Philippines, Guam and Puerto Rico from Spain as a condition of the Treaty of Paris. A military government is established in the Philippines. Filipinos, having now become American nationals, have the right to travel on United States passports and enter the United States freely.

The first Japanese-language newspaper on the United States mainland is founded by Kyutaro Abiko in San Francisco. He later establishes the Yamato colony near Livingston, California.

The Supreme Court rules in *United States* v. *Wong Kim Ark* that a person born in the United States of Chinese parents is of American nationality by birth. This person cannot be considered Chinese under the Chinese Exclusion Act, due to Fourteenth Amendment protections.

Congress passes a joint resolution banning Chinese laborers from immigrating to Hawaii.

1899

More than 2,800 Japanese migrate to the United States mainland from Hawaii.

The Supreme Court rules that wives and children of Chinese merchants are entitled to enter the United States.

The Chinese Empire Reform Association is founded in Victoria, British Columbia. Branches soon spring up in Canada, the United States and Hawaii. This group advocates a constitutional monarchy in China.

The arrival of two Japanese Buddhist priests in the United States signals the beginning of the Buddhist Churches of America.

1899-1901

Filipinos stage an armed rebellion against United States military rule of the islands. The revolt is suppressed.

1899-1904

Sixty thousand Japanese immigrants come to the United States; most of these new arrivals make their homes in Hawaii.

1890

through

1899

EUROPEAN AMERICAN	EUROPEAN AMERICAN	HISPANIC AMERICAN	HISPANIC AMERICAN

1890 through 1899

EUROPEAN AMERICAN

1890

More than 12 percent of the residents of Minnesota are of Swedish descent. This percentage holds for the 1910 census as well.

In the city of Milwaukee, Wisconsin, this year, there are six daily German-language newspapers in publication.

1890s

Crop failures in the Dakotas and Montana result in the migration of many Dutch Americans to Washington state. This migration is encouraged by the Northern Pacific Railroad.

1892

The last major wave of German immigration to the United States takes place this year, with more than 119,000 Germans coming to this country.

William Goebel, a German American, becomes governor of Kentucky.

1893

The Latvian Workers' Association is founded in Boston. It is a welfare-oriented, socialistic organization that also sponsors a progressive amateur theater group.

The National Council of Jewish Women is founded by Hannah Solomon, to help newly-arrived Jewish women adjust to American culture.

1894

On the hardiness and endurance of Swedish American laborers, Great Northern Railroad President James H. Hill remarks, "Give me Swedes, . . . , and I'll build a railroad through hell."

1895

The Holy Ghost Russian Orthodox Church is built in Bridgeport, Connecticut. It is the first Russian Orthodox church in New England and the seventh in the nation.

The Russian Orthodox Society of Mutual Aid is founded to strengthen the Russian Orthodox church in America and to provide insurance for its members.

EUROPEAN AMERICAN

1896

"New immigration" from southern, eastern and central Europe constitutes the majority of total immigrants.

Lutheran Pastor Hans Rebane from Latvia immigrates to the United States to escape religious persecution.

Politicians in South Carolina adopt the "white primary," limiting the vote in the Democratic Party primary to European Americans.

Julegraven, an illustrated Christmas magazine written in the Danish language, begins publication at Cedar Falls, Iowa.

1897

A lumbering community of Latvians is established in Lincoln County, Wisconsin. The Heineman Lumber Company that employs these lumbermen donates a 40-acre site and building materials for the first Latvian Evangelical church erected in the United States.

1898

Admiral Winfield Schley, a German American, commands the forces that destroy the Spanish fleet at Santiago, Cuba during the Spanish-American War.

1899

Great numbers of Magyar-speaking people begin to leave Hungary. These Hungarians migrate from place to place in the United States where labor is needed in the coal mining and steel industries.

HISPANIC AMERICAN

1890

This year sees the birth of many strike movements in Puerto Rico.

The Mexican population of Los Angeles is down to 5 percent, and the group has lost all of its political strength.

1890s

In Texas, cattle ranching gives way to large-scale cotton farming. As cotton growing becomes big business in Texas, Mexicans come north to find work.

1891

Arturo Alfonso Schomburg immigrates from Puerto Rico to New York. Schomburg gradually accumulates a vast and significant collection of materials on African American cultures in the Americas.

Antonio Vélez de Alvarado creates the flag that in 1895 becomes the symbol of the Puerto Rican revolution. In 1952, this becomes the flag of the current government.

The federal Court of Private Land Claims is established in the United States, to hear and settle Spanish and Mexican land claims in the American Southwest.

1892

Puerto Rican autonomists Sotero Figueroa, Antonio Vélez de Alvarado and Francisco Gonzalo Marin come to New York City. Approximately 200 Puerto Ricans meet to combine their efforts for Puerto Rican independence, and the Borinquen Club is formed.

1893

A race riot breaks out in Beeville, Texas, between Mexican Americans and African Americans, primarily over economic and employment issues.

1895

The Puerto Rican section of the Cuban Revolutionary Party holds its first meeting in New York City, pledging the independence of both islands. Fifty-nine Puerto Ricans participate.

HISPANIC AMERICAN

The major Puerto Rican promoters of independence for the Antilles are Eugenio María de Hostos in South America and Dr. Ramón E. Betances, living in France.

A land grant claimed by J. Addison Reavis for 12.8 million acres in New Mexico and Arizona is declared fraudulent. Reavis goes to prison.

1897

The Catholic Diocese of Tucson, Arizona, is established.

The Spanish government grants the Autonomous Charter for Puerto Rican government. The charter grants significant self-rule in many areas.

Miguel A. Otero becomes governor of the territory of New Mexico. He serves until 1906.

1898

A small number of Puerto Ricans come to the United States, mostly to New York City.

Puerto Rican *independentistas* in the United States offer their collaboration with the United States government.

The Internal Autonomous cabinet is installed in Puerto Rico.

Dr. Ramón E. Betances voices his opposition to United States participation in the Puerto Rican and Cuban wars for independence.

President William McKinley asks for 340 volunteer cavalrymen from New Mexico to ride under Colonel Leonard Wood and Lieutenant Colonel Theodore Roosevelt in the Rough Riders in Cuba. The quota is mustered in eight days.

In action during the Spanish-American War, the United States naval fleet under the direction of Admiral Sampson shells San Juan Bay, Puerto Rico; and troops under the command of General Nelson Miles land on Guanica, on the south shore of the island.

Spain cedes Puerto Rico, Guam and the Philippines to the United States in the Treaty of Paris.

HISPANIC AMERICAN	FOR CLASSROOM USE	FOR CLASSROOM USE	FOR CLASSROOM USE	
Eugenio María de Hostos organizes the League of Patriots, which requests a plebiscite to decide whether Puerto Ricans want United States government rule or independence under American protection. The separation of church and state ends the payment of church expenses and salaries by the Puerto Rican treasury. The Federacion Libre de Trabajadores (FLT), the first modern labor union in Puerto Rico, is established. **1898-1900** Puerto Rico's Autonomous Charter is ended, and the United States establishes a military governorship. Puerto Rico undergoes a campaign by the United States to "Americanize," and a period of Protestant evangelism occurs. **1899** The Federalist Party led by Luis Muñoz Rivera and the Republican Party headed by José Celso Barbosa are formed in Puerto Rico. Hurricane San Ciriaco devastates Puerto Rico and ruins the coffee crop. The population of Puerto Rico is estimated at 933,243. General Guy V. Henry organizes a system of rural and graded schools in Puerto Rico. **1899-1901** Cases presented by Puerto Ricans in the federal court system begin to define the relationship between Puerto Rico and the United States.				**1890** through **1899**

1890

The United States Congress passes a number of legislative acts. The Sherman Antitrust Act, designed to regulate trusts that restrain trade or commerce, marks the first time the federal government has passed laws to control big business. The McKinley Tariff Act, sponsored by William McKinley, increases import duties substantially; it is well received as a benefit to the industrial powers in the United States but is opposed by farmers. Congress also passes the Sherman Silver Purchase Act, supported by John Sherman, which requires the goverment to increase its purchases of silver from the levels of the Bland-Allison Act of 1878. It also increases the amount of money in circulation. The act is repealed in 1893.

The United States census reports the country's population at 63 million, including American citizens living abroad.

The United States has more than 160,000 miles of railroad track in use.

Ellis Island, in New York harbor, is designated as an immigration station.

Idaho and Wyoming join the Union as the 43rd and 44th states respectively. Wyoming, which as a territory gave women the right to vote in 1869, becomes the first state to mandate local suffrage for women in its constitution.

The United Mine Workers union is formed in Columbus, Ohio, by merger of the National Progressive Union and mining locals affiliated with the Knights of Labor.

The National American Woman Suffrage Association is created with the merger of two groups, the National Woman Suffrage Association and the American Woman Suffrage Association, both founded in 1869. The *Woman's Journal* becomes the official publication of the National American Woman Suffrage Association.

The first hydroelectric dam in the United States is constructed at Great Falls, Montana.

Savannah State College in Georgia, Central State University at Edmond, Oklahoma State University at Stillwater, and the University of Oklahoma at Norman, all in Oklahoma, are founded.

John D. Rockefeller's Standard Oil Company controls almost all of the oil production/sales in the United States.

The Daughters of the American Revolution (DAR) is founded in Washington, D.C.

c. 1890

Brazil passes a law requiring that all purchases of land be made in cash; this has the effect of keeping immigrants from owning property and therefore forcing them to labor on other people's lands.

1890-1891

Chile experiences civil war, with opposition forces led by deposed president Jose Manuel Balmaceda. The rebels are defeated.

1890s

Large commmercial salmon canneries open in Alaska.

Gas cookstoves are first seen in the United States.

1891

The Forest Reserve Act becomes law in the United States providing for the conversion of public lands to a National Forest Reserve.

Bank failures occur in the United States.

A 900,000-acre tract of Indian land in Oklahoma is made available for homesteading by European Americans. The acreage was ceded to the United States by Sauk, Fox and Potawatomi Indians.

Miners at Briceville, Tennessee, call that state's first major labor strike.

Lydia (Lil) Liliuokalani becomes queen of Hawaii after the death of her brother, David Kalakahua (1875). She rules until 1893.

Basketball is invented at Springfield, Massachusetts, by Canadian-born Dr. James Naismith.

Reindeer are brought to Alaska from Siberia and Norway to provide an industry for the dwindling Inuit (Eskimo) tribe.

Sir John Joseph Caldwell Abbott, a Conservative, becomes prime minister of Canada after Sir John A. MacDonald (1878) dies in office. Abbott serves until 1892, when he resigns due to poor health.

Brazil adopts a federal republican constitution.

General Manuel Deodoro da Fonseca becomes the first president of Brazil. He serves for less than one year and is succeeded by Floriano Peixoto. Peixoto serves until 1894.

c. 1891

The Populist Party is formed in the United States with heavy support from farmers, who oppose high tariffs and "hard" money. The party platform consists of support for free and unlimited coinage of silver, government control of railroads, no national banks, graduated income tax, direct election of senators, an eight-hour workday, non-ownership of land by foreigners and reform of the immigration laws.

1891-1900

Immigration to the United States totals 3,684,564 of which 3,555,352 come from Europe, 74,862 from Asia, 350 from Africa, 3,965 from Oceania, 38,972 from the Americas and 11,063 are not specifically identified.

1892

The United States Congress passes the Geary Act, which extends Chinese exclusion for another 10 years and requires strict residency proof and identification for Chinese people in the country.

Ellis Island Immigration Station opens in New York harbor.

A major confrontation between striking steelworkers and Pinkerton guards erupts at Homestead, Pennsylvania; the union is defeated after the military intervenes. Silver mine strikers in Idaho fight against nonunion workers. Federal troops are required to intervene.

John Muir establishes the Sierra Club.

Mary Baker Eddy founds the First Church of Christ, Scientist in Boston, Massachusetts. This becomes the headquarters for all Christian Science churches.

Sir John Sparrow David Thompson, a Conservative, becomes prime minister of Canada after the resignation of Sir John Joseph Caldwell Abbott (1891). He serves until his death in 1894.

1893

Grover Cleveland becomes the 24th president of the United States; Adlai E. Stevenson is vice president. Both are Democrats. This is President Cleveland's second term; he is the only United States president to be elected to two nonconsecutive terms.

Congress repeals the Sherman Silver Purchase Act and returns to the gold standard.

The United States experiences an economic depression caused by a bank failure in Britain. United States banks become very conservative and call in loans, now payable only in gold. This puts a burden on farmers and small businesses. Lack of confidence and a stock market drop follow. The depression continues for four years.

Hawaii's Queen Liliuokalani (1891) is deposed in a coup assisted by the United States military. Hawaii becomes a republic. An annexation agreement with the United States is withdrawn from the United States Senate by President Cleveland.

The Ohio Anti-Saloon League is formed in Oberlin, Ohio, against the sale of alcoholic beverages. This organization becomes a major force in congressional passage of the Eighteenth Amendment to the Constitution (Prohibition).

The Cherokee Strip, 6 million acres of land purchased from the Cherokee in 1891, is opened for European American homesteading. More than 100,000 people rush into the area.

1890

through

1899

When African American women are excluded from most activities at the Chicago World's Fair, they begin to unite and form their own clubs. In 1896 the National Association of Colored Women (NACW) is founded, primarily through the efforts of Josephine Ruffin, and begins a program of assistance to the African American community. By 1915 the NACW has 50,000 members. Mary Church Terrell, its first president, works for the rights of African Americans.

Henry Street Settlement House is founded in New York City by Lillian Wald and Mary Brewster. It becomes one of the best known and most influential settlement houses in the country.

Montana State University at Bozeman and the University of Montana at Missoula are founded.

Working in his spare time in Detroit, Michigan, Henry Ford builds his first automobile.

Chicago surgeon Daniel Hale Williams performs the nation's first open-heart surgery. Dr. Williams, an African American, performs the operation at Provident Hospital.

1893-1907

The United States economy stagnates, resulting in high unemployment and depression.

1894

At its fourteenth convention, the American Federation of Labor again unanimously adopts a resolution affirming the unity of labor regardless of race.

Social reformer Jacob S. Coxey leads his "army" of approximately 500 unemployed men from Ohio to Washington, D.C., in a demonstration against government apathy regarding unemployment.

Socialist Eugene V. Debs calls a general strike of rail workers to support Pullman Company strikers in Chicago. When federal troops are called in to make sure the mail keeps moving, the strike is broken and Debs is jailed for six months.

The Immigration Restriction League is organized in the United States.

Thomas A. Edison's kinetoscope has its first public showing in New York City.

MacKenzie Bowell becomes prime minister of Canada after Thompson's (1892) death. He serves until 1896.

Andrés Avelino Cáceres (1886) again becomes president of Peru. His government is overthrown shortly after the election.

1895

Claiming jurisdiction under the Monroe Doctrine, United States President Cleveland intervenes to settle a territorial dispute between Venezuela and Britain over the border between Venezuela and British Guiana.

William Randolph Hearst, after a successful start as head of the San Francisco *Examiner*, establishes the *New York Morning Journal* and competes with Joseph Pulitzer for the New York market, developing the technique of sensationalism or "yellow" journalism to sell newspapers.

In *Pollock* v. *Farmers Loan and Trust Company,* the United States Supreme Court rules that federal income tax is unconstitutional.

Coal mining begins in Tennessee at Brushy Mountain Prison.

King Camp Gillette develops a safety razor with disposable blades.

Joshua Slocum of Annapolis, Nova Scotia, circumnavigates the globe alone. He is the first person to do so, in a voyage that lasts three years.

José Martí comes out of exile and returns to Cuba. He joins forces with General Antonio Maceo in an insurrection against Spanish rule. Martí is killed, but the fighting continues for three years.

Nicolás de Piérola (1879) again becomes president of Peru. He serves until 1899.

1896

In *Plessy* v. *Ferguson*, the United States Supreme Court upholds the constitutionality of the doctrine of "separate but equal." The case concerns the rights of Homer Plessy, an African American man who purchased a railroad ticket and tried to ride in the "all white" section of the train. For this, he was arrested and convicted; he eventually appealed his case to the High Court. Although the case specifically concerns only railroad accommodations, it is later used as a precedent for many other public areas, including education.

Utah becomes the 45th state to join the Union.

Although it was first sparsely colonized in the mid-1870s, Miami, Florida, incorporates as a city and becomes a main stop on the Florida railroad line. Its growth is stimulated by the interest and funding of financier Henry Morrison Flagler.

Idaho leads the country in lead production.

Oakwood College is founded in Huntsville, Alabama.

Gold is discovered in Bonanza Creek in the Klondike. During the next three years, the ensuing gold rush brings more than 30,000 people to Canada's Yukon Territory and to Alaska.

Politicians in South Carolina adopt the "white primary" limiting the vote in the Democratic party primary to European Americans.

William Jennings Bryan delivers his "Cross of Gold" speech at the Democratic Convention in Chicago. He says that cities depend upon the farms and that the nation's real wealth is generated by a base of successful farmers and laborers, not industrialists.

The will of Swedish chemist and inventor Alfred Nobel establishes prizes for peace, science and literature.

1890

through

1899

THE AMERICAS	THE AMERICAS	THE AMERICAS	FOR CLASSROOM USE

Sir Charles Tupper, a Conservative, becomes prime minister of Canada after MacKenzie Bowell (1894). Tupper's party, however, loses the election this year, and Sir Wilfred Laurier, a Liberal, becomes prime minister. Laurier serves until 1911.

1897

William McKinley becomes the 25th president of the United States. Garrett A. Hobert is vice president. Both are Republicans. In 1899 Vice President Garrett A. Hobert dies in office, and is not replaced.

Buildings and records at Ellis Island Immigration Station are destroyed by fire, but all people there escape safely.

The Dingley Act, sponsored by Congressman Nelson Dingley, places high protective duties on imported goods and places a high premium on Mexican American sugarbeet laborers by raising the tariff on imported sugar.

1890 through 1899

Fresh Alaskan halibut is shipped to the lower United States for the first time.

The National Congress of Parents and Teachers is founded in South Dakota; it spawns and sponsors local parent-teacher associations (PTAs).

Voorhees College is founded at Denmark, South Carolina.

Miguel A. Otero becomes governor of the United States territory of New Mexico. He serves until 1906.

Liberal leader Flavio Eloy Alfaro becomes president of Ecuador. He institutes reforms and serves until 1901. Alfaro serves again from 1907 to 1911.

1898

The United States battleship *Maine* explodes in Havana Harbor. As a result, the United States declares war on Spain. More than 17,000 soldiers invade Oriente province and, with the help of Cuban General Calixto García, defeat Spanish forces. When this, the Spanish American War, is over, the United States acquires Puerto Rico, the Philippines and Guam. (*See* "The World, 1898-1899.")

The United States annexes Hawaii; Chinese migration to Hawaii is barred.

Mother Jones, Irish American labor agitator, helps found the Social Democratic Party. She also is on hand in 1905 when the International Workers of the World is organized.

Almost all of Bismarck, North Dakota's business district is destroyed by fire.

The Christian Commercial Men's Association of America is founded at Boscobel, Wisconsin. Now an international Bible Society, it is commonly referred to as the Gideons and its mission is to place copies of the Bible in hotel rooms around the nation.

The Kensington Rune Stone, inscribed in runes of an ancient Germanic language from Scandinavia with a date of 1362, is found on a farm in Minnesota. If genuine, it shows that early Norse explorers penetrated the interior of North America. However, at the time the authenticity of the stone is subject to much question.

1899

The United States begins its "Open Door" Policy with China. Because the United States seeks direct trade with Asia after its acquisition of the Philippines, and the partitioning of China and Japan seem a reality, the United States wishes to maintain equal commercial rights within China.

The Rivers and Harbors Appropriations Act has a "Refuse Act" paragraph which forbids pollution of the nation's waterways. Chlorine is first used to purify public water supplies.

The United States and Britain reach a provisional boundary agreement establishing the Alaskan border.

The National Consumers League is founded by Florence Kelly. A major goal of the organization is to improve the lot of working women by buying only those goods made in factories that provide decent working conditions. The League establishes a labeling system to let consumers know what products qualify as "good" products.

The College of Saint Elizabeth is founded at Convent Station, New Jersey.

Cipriano Castro and troops under him march on Caracas, Venezuela. They overthrow the dictatorship of Antonio Gúzman Blanco and in 1901 Castro is proclaimed president. He serves until 1908.

1899-1902

Bloody civil war in Colombia leads to a series of bitter class struggles.

THE WORLD | THE WORLD | THE WORLD | THE WORLD

1890

Chancellor Otto von Bismarck is removed from power and Germany becomes an aggressive nation under *Kaiser* (Emperor) William (Wilhelm) II.

By the terms of the Zanzibar settlement, Tanganyika and Heligoland become German colonies, Germany agrees to leave the Upper Nile and Uganda and Zanzibar become British protectorates.

The House of Nassau comes to power as the ruling family of Luxembourg.

Britain recognizes French control over Madagascar.

Japan holds its first general election.

The first European colonists arrive in the area of modern-day Zimbabwe. They are sent by British agent Cecil Rhodes.

Severe influenza outbreaks occur in several parts of the world.

As a child, Wilhelmina becomes queen of the Netherlands after the death of her father, William III (1849). She rules until 1948. Though the crowns of the Netherlands and Luxembourg were united under William III, an agreement made in 1873 states that only males may rule Luxembourg. As a result, Adolph of Nassau becomes grand duke of Luxembourg, and the union with Netherlands is dissolved.

Japan's new emperor allows the enactment of a constitution, based in part on that of Prussia. Japan's government passes the Civil Code, transforming all of Japanese society into a legal model of the samurai family. For women, this is one of the most oppressive codes in their history.

Germany declares Namibia a crown colony.

Joseph Lister introduces antiseptic methods in his surgical practice in England.

1891

José Rizal establishes *La Liga Filipina* — the Philippine League — to promote social reforms in the Philippines. At about the same time Andres Bonifacio founds a secret revolutionary society, the Katipuman.

Germany, Austria-Hungary and Italy renew the Triple Alliance of 1882. Russia and France create the Dual Alliance, at the time a secret agreement.

Russia experiences widespread famine that continues into 1892.

J. Ballance, a Liberal, becomes prime minister of New Zealand.

The Young Turks, a group of Ottoman exiles, create an organization in Geneva, Switzerland.

French manufacturers René Panhard and Emile Levassor establish the precedent of assembling automobiles with the engine in the front.

1892

In Africa, French forces depose the king and annex Dahomey; they defeat the Fulani on the Upper Niger and capture Segu.

Gilbert and Ellice Islands are declared a British protectorate.

Abbas II (Abbas Hilmi) becomes *khedive* (viceroy) of Egypt after the death of his father, Tewfik Pasha (1879). Abbas II rules until 1914.

Prince Ito, one of the chief architects of the modernization of Japan, becomes that country's prime minister. He serves until 1896, regains the position in 1898 and again in 1900-1901.

German engineer Rudolf Diesel patents his internal combustion engine.

1893

In Southeast Asia, France assumes a protectorship over Laos, despite the objections of Siam (Thailand).

Transvaal annexes Swaziland.

Natal becomes self-governing.

R. J. Seddon, a Liberal, becomes New Zealand's prime minister.

The second Irish Home Rule Bill fails to pass in the British Parliament.

New Zealand becomes the first country to give women the right to vote. Elizabeth Yates of Onehunga is elected the first woman mayor in New Zealand.

France takes full control of the Ivory Coast after 23 years of conquest.

Britain takes control over the South Solomon and Gilbert Islands. Britain gets control of the North Solomons from Germany in 1900.

1893-1896

King Lobengula of the Ndebele leads uprisings against British encroachment in the area that is now Zimbabwe. Native inhabitants of Zimbabwe fight their first war for liberation. Uganda becomes a British protectorate when the crown takes control over the British East Africa Company. Rhodesia is named for Cecil Rhodes, who acquired the land for the British South Africa Company.

Norwegian explorer Fridtjof Nansen proves that the arctic cap is made up of ice, and not land, by letting his ship, the *Fram,* drift across the polar cap locked in the ice.

1894

Russia forms an alliance with France after Germany cancels the Reinsurance Treaty created by former German Chancellor Bismarck.

France annexes Madagascar.

The first European visitor to the area that is now Rwanda is Count von Goetzen, a German officer.

French army captain Alfred Dreyfus, an Alsatian Jew, is arrested, convicted of treason and sentenced to life in prison after allegedly leaking secret French documents to the German ambassador. Anti-Semitism is rife in the French community as well as the military at this time. This affair becomes a strong force in dividing the French people into rightist and leftist forces. Dreyfus is pardoned in 1906.

French president Marie François Carnot is assassinated by an Italian anarchist.

Nicholas II becomes czar of Russia after the death of his father, Alexander III (1881). Nicholas II rules until 1917; He is the last czar.

Abdu-l-Aziz IV becomes sultan of Morocco. He rules until 1908.

1894-1895

A Sino-Japanese war erupts over Korea. Japan defeats China with victories at the Yalu River and Port Arthur. By the Treaty of Shimonoseki Japan takes control of Formosa, the Pescadore Islands, Port Arthur and the Liaotung Peninsula. China also gives up control of Korea which now has nominal independence. The intervention of Russia, France and Germany forces Japan to return Port Arthur and the Liaotung Peninsula to China, but China pays an additional fee for their return.

1895

(Sir) Leander Starr Jameson leads a British raid into the Boer Republic to support the revolt of British and other foreign colonists. The intervention fails, and Jameson is captured and imprisoned. Germany's *Kaiser* William (Wilhelm) II sends congratulations to the Boers' S. J. Paulus Kruger, angering the British who interpret the message as an indication that Germany could become involved in the Transvaal.

Negeri Sembilan, Perak, Selangor and Pahang unite to form the Federated Malay States (FMS).

The first public cinema is opened in Paris by Louis Lumière.

German physicist Wilhelm Röentgen discovers the x-ray.

Austrian psychiatrist Sigmund Freud introduces the process of psychoanalysis.

Carsten Egeberg Borchgrevink participates in the first land expedition to explore Antarctica.

1896

In the Philippines, the identity of many of the Katipunan leaders, a secret society formed by Filipino nationalists to fight against Spanish control of the island, is discovered. This leads to a more open rebellion led by Andres Bonifacio and Emilo Aguinaldo. The Spanish government responds with a reign of terror and many are executed, including Dr. José Rizal, shot by a firing squad in Manila.

1890

through

1899

British forces seize control of Ghana, dethroning Ashanti (Asante) king Prempe and exiling him and his mother, Yaa Akyaa. The real power behind the throne, Yaa Akyaa, is a wealthy leader of royal birth who bribed politicians, waged war and directed campaigns to ensure that her son became king. Britain establishes a protectorate over Sierra Leone and East Africa.

An agreement between France and Britain acknowledges Siam's independence and its significance as a buffer state.

The first modern Olympic games are held in Athens, Greece.

The Italian invasion of Ethiopia ends in failure when forces of Ethiopian Emperor Menelik II defeat the Italians at Adowa; this leads to Ethiopia's declaration of independence, marking the beginning of the decline of European colonization in Africa.

Muzaffar-ed-Din becomes shah of Persia after the death of his father, Nasr-ed-Din (1848). Muzaffar-ed-Din rules until 1907.

Armenians are massacred by Turkish forces at Constantinople.

Guglielmo Marconi receives the first wireless patent in Britain.

The Nobel prizes for physics, physiology or medicine, chemistry, literature and the furtherance of the cause of peace, are established.

French scientist Henri Becquerel observes, with the use of uranium salts and a photographic plate, that some atoms emit energy in the form of rays.

1896-1898

A combined British and Egyptian military expedition led by Lord Kitchener defeats the Mahdi's army in the Sudan.

1897

Zululand becomes part of the British crown colony of Natal.

India experiences severe, widespread famine and an outbreak of bubonic plague. The joint effect is more than 1 million deaths.

The first Zionist World Congress is convened in Basle (Basel, Switzerland) by Theodor Herzl, a Hungarian Jew.

Viruses are discovered by Dutch botanist Martinus Beijerinck.

1897-1898

Crete unites with Greece; Turkey declares war on Greece and is defeated in Macedonia.

1897-1899

Germany, Britain and France lease territories from China. In 1898, for example, Britain leases Chinese territories around Hong Kong harbor for 99 years. Russia leases Port Arthur from China for 25 years.

1898

A joint British-Egyptian force under Horatio Herbert (Lord) Kitchener is victorious over the Mahdi at Omdurman, giving Britain control over the Sudan. Kitchener's army then forces French troops led by Major J. B. Marchand to leave the Upper Nile (the Fashoda Incident). Britain and Egypt agree the following year to the appointment of an Egyptian governor general approved by Britain.

A severe famine caused by drought and an outbreak of bubonic plague results in more than 1 million deaths in China.

Guam (in the western Pacific Ocean) is ceded to the United States by Spain.

The Boxer Rebellion begins in China, as a secret, anti-foreign group called "Boxers" stages uprisings against Europeans. The United States and other Western troops intervene to suppress the revolts. Empress Dowager Tz'u Hsi, a supporter of the Boxers, is successful in stopping the Western reform movement in China, but the unrest continues into 1900.

In this year 270,000 people leave Hungary.

French scientists Pierre and Marie Sklodowska Curie discover radium.

Wake Island (in the central Pacific Ocean) and American Samoa are annexed to the United States.

1898-1899

The Spanish-American War begins as many American people support Cuban rebels in their revolt against Spain. United States businesses see economic opportunity in unhindered trade with Cuba, and the United States government seeks to establish American power zones in Latin America. A submarine mine explodes the United States battleship *Maine* in Havana Harbor. Two hundred sixty are killed but responsibility is never fixed. Though it has no authority to do so, the United States Congress declares the independence of Cuba on April 19, and Spain declares war on the United States on April 25. Congress formally announces that the nation has been at war with Spain since April 21. Commodore George Dewey and his fleet win a seven-hour battle in Manila Bay against the Spanish fleet. In June General Emilio Aguinaldo, leader of Filipino revolutionary forces, declares the Philippines independent from Spain. At first, Filipinos and Americans collaborate in fighting the Spanish, but the collaboration ends in August with the capture of Manila, and the establishment of a United States military government which lasts until 1901. The Spanish fleet is destroyed off Santiago, Cuba, and the city surrenders. In September a Revolutionary Congress meets in the Philippines at the inland town of Malolos, Bulacan, out of the reach of American gunships. The assembly drafts the Malolos Constitution. The Treaty of Paris, ratified by the Senate in 1899, results in Spain's ceding the Philippines, Guam and Puerto Rico to the United States in consideration for over $20,000,000 in losses incurred by Spain during the war; Cuba gains its independence from Spain although it remains under United States military control until 1902.

1899

The First Philippine Republic, inaugurated at Malolos, becomes the first democracy to emerge in Asia. The Philippine War of Independence begins. After bitter guerrilla warfare resulting in the capture of most local leaders, United States troops capture Aguinaldo in 1901, marking the fall of the First Philippine Republic.

In an effort to retain firm control of Finland, Russia's Czar Nicholas II initiates a process of "Russification." This tactic is resisted by the Finnish people.

The Boer War begins in South Africa as a conflict between British colonists and Dutch Boers. Causes of the fighting are rooted in longstanding territorial disputes and in friction over political rights for English and other "suitlanders" following the 1886 discovery of vast gold deposits in the South African (Transvaal) Republic.

The United States annexes Eastern (American) Samoa and Germany gains control of Western Samoa.

Russia calls for the International Peace Conference (the First Hague Peace Conference) to meet.

Aspirin, developed by German doctors Felix Hoffman and Hermann Dreser, is widely used as medicine.

It is discovered that much of the evidence of treason against French captain Alfred Dreyfus was fabricated by Colonel Henry of French army intelligence. Henry commits suicide. Dreyfus is tried and again found guilty but his sentence is reduced to 10 years. A pardon is issued by President Emilé Loubet.

Kuwait becomes a British protectorate.

1899-1914

Western Samoa is a German protectorate during this time.

1890

through

1899

NATIVE AMERICAN	NATIVE AMERICAN	AFRICAN AMERICAN	AFRICAN AMERICAN
1900 The United States census reports the Native American population at 237,000, the lowest since contact with Europeans began. Over several hundred years, many Indians have died as a result of European-introduced diseases, conflicts with European Americans, intertribal warfare and the loss of lands and resources. **1901** Congress confers citizenship on all Native Americans living in Indian Territory. By this date, more than 30 tribes reside there permanently, including: the Five Civilized Tribes, Apache, Caddo, Cheyenne and Arapaho, Comanche, Delaware, Iowa, Kaw (Kansa), Kickapoo, Kiowa, Modoc, Miami, Osage, Otoe and Missouria, Ottawa, Pawnee, Peoria, Ponca, Potawatomi, Quapaw, Sac (Sauk) and Fox (Mesquakie), Seneca and Cayuga, Shawnee, Tonkawa, Wichita and Wyandotte. **1902** In *Lone Wolf* v. *Hitchcock*, the Supreme Court rules that Congress may ignore the provisions of treaties with American Indian tribes when it thinks such action is in the best interests of the United States and the Native Americans. **1906** Indian Territory and Oklahoma Territory are formally merged by the Congressional Enabling Act of this year. Approximately 50,000 acres of wilderness land in the New Mexico mountains is appropriated by the United States government as part of the Carson National Park. The area includes Blue Lake, which is revered by the Taos people. **1907** In the *Winters* decision, the Supreme Court recognizes American Indian water rights.	Oklahoma, which by this time includes Indian Territory, attains statehood; American Indians again lose lands to European American homesteaders. Charles Curtis, a Kansa Indian, is the first Native American elected to the United States Senate. He serves until 1913, is re-elected in 1915 and serves until 1929. Curtis resigns to become United States vice president under Herbert Hoover.	**1900** The United States census reports approximately 8.83 million African Americans, nearly 12 percent of the nation's total population. The National Negro Business League is founded at Boston by Booker T. Washington. Four African American banks are in operation in the United States. **1901** William Monroe Trotter begins publication of his militant newspaper, the *Boston Guardian*. Alabama initiates a new constitution which includes literacy tests, a grandfather clause and other technical provisions to disenfranchise its African American citizens. The voting rights cases of *Giles* v. *Harris* are not reversed by the United States Supreme Court in either 1903 or 1904; thus, such discriminatory provisions are permitted to remain in effect at this time. Robert H. Terrell is appointed judge of the Municipal Court for the District of Columbia by President Theodore Roosevelt. He is reappointed by Presidents Taft, Wilson and Harding and serves until his death in 1925. **1902** The state of Virginia adopts a new constitution that institutes a poll tax and a literacy test as requirements for voting, thus disenfranchising many African Americans. **1903** *The Souls of Black Folk,* by W. E. B. Du Bois, is published. The St. Lukes Penny Savings Bank is founded at Richmond, Virginia. It is organized by Maggie Lena Walker, secretary-treasurer of the Independent Order of St. Lukes. William H. Crogman becomes the first African American president of Clark University at Atlanta, Georgia. His major work, *Progress of a Race,* was issued the year before.	Christopher Payne is appointed by President Theodore Roosevelt as consul general of the Danish West Indies. Payne serves until 1917 when the islands are acquired by the United States and renamed the Virgin Islands. **1904** Bethune-Cookman College at Daytona, Florida, is founded by Mary McLeod Bethune. Mrs. Bethune later founds the National Council of Negro Women. **1905** A group of African American leaders, including W. E. B. Du Bois and William M. Trotter, meets at Niagara Falls, New York, and founds the Niagara Movement, an organization to fight for equal rights for African Americans. This group attracts little attention, but is a precursor to the National Association for the Advancement of Colored People, which is formed in 1909. Robert S. Abbott establishes the *Chicago Defender* newspaper. Sarah Breedlove "Madame C. J." Walker develops a hot iron or straightening comb to assist African American women in styling their hair. She becomes the first self-made woman millionaire in the United States. **1906** A race riot erupts at Brownsville, Texas, after units of the all-African American 25th Infantry Regiment arrive in the area to relieve a unit of the 16th Infantry. Brownsville already has experienced difficulty between the military and civilians; when citizens protest the African American replacements, an incident occurs in which one person is killed. The three African American units are blamed collectively for the death and are dishonorably discharged. Ohio Senator Joseph B. Foraker argues for years against the injustice of this discharge but it is never overturned.

1900

through

1909

AFRICAN AMERICAN	ASIAN AMERICAN	ASIAN AMERICAN	ASIAN AMERICAN	

Financier George Foster Peabody retires from his business activities and devotes much of his energies to improving educational opportunities for African Americans.

1908

A two-day riot occurs in Springfield, Ilinois, after an African American man is accused of raping a European American woman. Though the victim later changes her story and admits her assailant was European American, a mob still seeks to punish the man originally arrested. The governor calls in 4,200 troops. More than 2,000 African Americans flee the city. Before calm is restored, eight African Americans are killed, two by lynching; and 100 people are wounded.

Classical scholar William S. Scarborough is elected president of Wilberforce University.

1909

The National Medical Association begins publication of its *Journal.*

African American and European American leaders meet in New York City and form the National Association for the Advancement of Colored People (NAACP) to fight for the rights of African Americans. W. E. B. Du Bois becomes the editor of its journal, *The Crisis.*

Matthew A. Henson, an African American, accompanies Robert E. Peary in the discovery of the North Pole.

1900

The United States census reports the Chinese American population at just under 90,000 in the continental United States and approximately 3,100 and 25,700 in Alaska and Hawaii respectively. The sex ratio is 1,887 males to 100 females. Approximately 60,000 Japanese immigrants reside in Hawaii, while on the mainland there are only 24,000.

The Organic Act is passed by the United States Congress and goes into effect. It establishes Hawaii as an American territory and makes importation of contract laborers illegal.

The Japanese government discontinues passports to laborers bound for the mainland United States, but not for Hawaii. This is the first "Gentlemen's Agreement" between the two nations.

Contract laborers freed by the Organic Act and 12,635 Japanese men come from Hawaii to the West Coast of the United States. Between 1900 and 1905, nearly 20,000 Japanese come to California and Hawaii. They take the lowest paid jobs and have the poorest living quarters.

A federal law is enacted defining the status of Chinese people in Hawaii and providing for their registration.

An influential daily Chinese-language newspaper, *Chung Sai Yat Po,* is founded by Ng Poon Chew and others in San Francisco.

The United States territorial government of Hawaii refuses to recognize the citizenship of Japanese people who have become naturalized Hawaiians.

The Japanese Association of America is founded in San Francisco to counter racial discrimination.

c. 1900

Japanese immigrants convert California's barren interior lands into rich vineyards and truck farming areas.

1901

Dr. Jokichi Takamine isolates pure epinephrine (adrenaline) at the Johns Hopkins University. Dr. Takamine declines "honorary" citizenship until all immigrants of Japanese ancestry are allowed to become citizens.

The first of more than 1,000 United States civilian teachers begins arriving in the Philippines. Known in the islands as Thomasites, after one of the ships they arrived in, they teach English, introduce American culture and democracy, and begin teaching Filipinos through the widespread establishment of public schools.

1902

European American miners drive out Japanese immigrants employed at the Yukon Mining Company in Atkin, Alaska.

Congress extends Chinese exclusion laws indefinitely.

1903

Two thousand sugar beet workers of Japanese and Mexican ancestries strike in Oxnard, California, and form the first successful farm workers' union. The American Federation of Labor, however, refuses to recognize a non-European American union.

Seito Saibara, a former member of the Japanese legislature who came to the United States in 1902, migrates with his family to Houston, Texas, and begins a rice-growing industry.

The first group of Filipinos known as *pensionados* are subsidized by the United States government to study at American colleges and universities. Several of this first group are women. *Pensionados* continue to study in the United States up until the Great Depression of 1929.

Thousands of Koreans come to this country, mostly to Hawaii, and work for the Hawaiian Sugar Planters' Association (HSPA).

Chinese American Joe Shoong founds China Toggery in Vallejo, California, which he later moves to San Francisco and reorganizes as the National Dollar Stores. By the 1940s more than 30 branch stores are established in West Coast cities.

An anti-Chinese riot occurs at Tonopah, Nevada, when European Americans attempt to evict Chinese American families. One Chinese American is killed. None of the rioters is found guilty of the murder.

1904

Japanese military successes in the Russo-Japanese War that result in the seizure of Korea cause many people in the United States to regard Japan as the "Yellow Peril."

The St. Louis Louisiana Purchase Exposition is held as an American counterpart to the colonial expositions that are sweeping Europe. A special feature of the exposition is the "living anthropological exhibits." With a massive display of 1200 Filipinos and a large display of American Indians near the center of the fairgrounds, the United States government uses the exposition to announce its own imperial presence on the world stage. Several of the Filipinos die of maltreatment en route to the fair; at least three others die of pneumonia while camped on the fairgrounds.

1905

Articles against Japan appear in the *San Francisco Chronicle.*

The Oriental Exclusion League, claiming 78,000 members, launches a vigorous anti-Japanese campaign in California and other western states.

President Theodore Roosevelt refuses to exclude Japanese people from immigration.

The Shanghai, China, Chamber of Commerce conducts a boycott of American goods and services to protest the strict implementation of Chinese exclusion laws in the United States. President Roosevelt advises immigration officials to interpret the statutes more leniently and use discretion in enforcement.

1900

through

1909

ASIAN AMERICAN	ASIAN AMERICAN	ASIAN AMERICAN	EUROPEAN AMERICAN

<table>
<tr><td colspan="4"></td></tr>
</table>

1900 through 1909

ASIAN AMERICAN

1906

Mayor Eugene Schmitz of San Francisco and his political boss Abraham Reuf accuse Japanese Americans of taking jobs away from "native Americans."

California's antimiscegenation law is extended to cover Mongolians. Similar laws exist in many states banning marriages between European and non-European Americans.

A second wave of Filipino immigration to the United States occurs. These newcomers are mostly men.

The San Francisco School Board removes children of Japanese ancestry from regular schools and places them in a segregated school. Ninety-three children are affected, 25 of whom are American citizens.

After the San Francisco earthquake and the resulting fire, Japan contributes nearly $250,000 to relief, more than all other foreign nations combined. Ten thousand Japanese Americans move to previously European American neighborhoods, and many become victims of violence. Chinatown is destroyed by the quake, as are birth and immigration records. Many Chinese people can now claim American birth and not have their claims disputed. The city's Board of Supervisors considers moving Chinatown to Hunter's Point; however, the Chinese American community begins rebuilding on the existing site.

The Hawaiian Sugar Planters' Association, with government approval, encourages immigration of workers from the Philippines. About 20,000 Filipino laborers come to Hawaii over the next eight years.

ASIAN AMERICAN

1907

President Roosevelt pressures the San Francisco School Board into rescinding its segregation order. In exchange, Japan does not protest the Immigration Act of 1907, which prevents Japanese laborers from entering the United States via Hawaii, Mexico or Canada. Though this agreement relaxes segregationist treatment of Japanese American children, those of Chinese ancestry in San Francisco remain segregated.

Canton Bank, the first Chinese bank in the continental United States, is established. It remains open until 1926.

As Japanese immigration peaks with 30,200 arrivals, the United States enters into a second "Gentlemen's Agreement" with Japan, under which the Japanese government imposes quotas to limit emigration. As a result, Japanese immigration diminishes quickly, by one-third over the next seven years.

1907-1919

More than 28,000 Filipinos arrive in Hawaii as immigration from Japan, Korea (at this time a Japanese possession) and China is curtailed. Many Filipinos also come to the United States by enlisting in the navy as stewards.

1908

The "Gentlemen's Agreement" of 1907 goes into effect. The Japanese government agrees to cease issuing passports to all emigrating laborers except "former residents, parents, wives or children of residents."

United States Army veteran Buntaro Kumagai, a Japanese American, seeks citizenship under an 1862 law that provides citizenship to "any alien" who has served honorably in the armed forces. The district court in the state of Washington denies him naturalization on the grounds that the words "any alien" mean "free white persons or those of African descent."

ASIAN AMERICAN

1909

Eight thousand plantation workers of Japanese ancestry, led by Fred Kinzaburo Makino, strike for three months on the Hawaiian island of Oahu. Their efforts gain them a wage increase and improved working conditions.

Fong Yue becomes the first Chinese aviator in the world when he flies a plane of his own making for 20 minutes in Piedmont, California.

EUROPEAN AMERICAN

1900

The number of Italian immigrants to America grows rapidly. At least 100,000 arrive this year, most of them from southern Italy. More than 2 million Italians come to America in the first 14 years of the 1900s. In addition to working in agriculture, they are also hired as merchants, manufacturers, business professionals and industrial and construction workers. An estimated 75 percent of New York City's construction workers are Italian. During construction of the New York City subway, Italian workers struck several times and won shorter hours and better pay.

By this year, approximately 275,000 French Canadians have been hired by industries in the New England states.

The majority of mine workers in Montana, Utah and Nevada this year are of Cornish and Welsh descent.

1900-1910s

Immigration from Russia increases due to poor economic conditions and religious and political persecution in that country.

1900-1920s

The reform movement known as progressivism is embraced by Scandinavian Americans. Progressive government officials of Norwegian and Swedish descent are elected to various state offices, particularly in the Midwest.

1901

The St. Nicholas Russian Orthodox Cathedral is founded in New York City.

Robert Marion "Fighting Bob" La Follette is elected governor of Wisconsin. He is a French American and a progressive governor who opposes city bosses, supports the formation of a railroad commission, seeks to rid his government of corruption and establishes the first election primary.

EUROPEAN AMERICAN	EUROPEAN AMERICAN	HISPANIC AMERICAN	HISPANIC AMERICAN	

1901-1910

Mass immigration from Austria-Hungary begins, with about 28,000 people arriving in the United States each year throughout the decade. Most are young males who stay a few years and return home with their earnings.

1901-1920

About 350,000 people from Greece and 290,000 from Turkey arrive in the United States as Greeks, Armenians and Assyrians flee the persecution of the Turkish government. The majority of these new arrivals are unskilled males from rural areas.

1902

Corning, New York, becomes a major glass production area as the result of an influx of skilled Norwegian glassblowers.

1904

Steerage fare to the United States from British ports is approximately $15, lower than in several previous years. This creates a two-year increase in British immigration.

Amadeo Peter Giannini, an Italian American born in San Jose, California, helps newer Italian immigrants to the West Coast by opening a bank with Italian-speaking tellers and offering free assistance with naturalization papers.

1905

Large numbers of Russians, many of them poor peasants, arrive in the United States. The majority find work in coal mines, iron and steel mills, meatpacking and garment industries and the railroads.

At a demonstration in New York City, 125,000 Jewish Americans protest atrocities committed against Jews in Russia. Congress passes a joint resolution expressing sympathy.

1905-1907

Russians who belong to a religious group known as the Molokan sect suffer persecution in their homeland and immigrate to Los Angeles, California.

1906

Texas reports 40,000 Swedish Americans in its population, in several predominantly Swedish communities.

Henry Algernon du Pont, a French American from Delaware, is elected to the United States Senate. He serves from 1907 to 1917.

Oscar S. Straus is appointed as secretary of commerce, becoming the first Jewish American to hold a cabinet position.

St. Tikhon's Monastery is established in South Canaan, Pennsylvania. It is the first Russian Orthodox monastery in the United States.

1907

Ole Evinrude invents the outboard motor and goes on to become the president of a $4 million manufacturing corporation. Evinrude is a Norwegian American.

Austro-Hungarian immigration peaks with 338,000 people arriving in the United States this year.

Irish American educator and author Maurice F. Egan is appointed Minister to Denmark. In 1916 he is instrumental in arranging the purchase of the Danish West Indies (now the Virgin Islands) by the United States.

1907-1921

During this 14-year period, almost 70 percent of the Hungarians who come to America return to Hungary.

1908

Aram J. Pothier is elected governor of Rhode Island, the first French American governor in New England.

A study shows that 35 percent of German immigrants who arrive this year were helped by money or passenger tickets from relatives already in the United States.

1909

The first credit union association in New England, La Caisse Populaire Ste. Marie, is established, serving Massachusetts and New Hampshire. Nearly all of its depositors are French Americans.

1900

Congress passes the Foraker Act, which establishes a United States-controlled civilian government in Puerto Rico. Officials are appointed, except for the island's House of Representatives, which is elected by Puerto Rican voters. This type of government lasts until 1917, when Puerto Ricans are redefined as "nationals but not citizens" of the United States. This status is shared by Native Americans at the time. The Foraker Act also establishes a district court on the island to enforce United States laws.

1900-1919

Various organizations are founded in the United States by Cuban and Puerto Rican workers. Some are information and fundraising centers for the revolutionary cause in Puerto Rico. Other sectors in the community establish mutual aid, civic, social and labor organizations.

1901

Emigration of Puerto Ricans to Hawaii, Cuba, the Dominican Republic and other destinations begins. This movement continues until approximately 1915.

1902

Federico Degeteau is the first Puerto Rican delegate to serve in the United States House of Representatives.

Dr. Bailey K. Ashford discovers a tapeworm that causes the anemia from which many Puerto Ricans have suffered and died. He is assisted by Agustin Stahl, a Puerto Rican.

1903

Two thousand sugar beet workers of Mexican and Japanese ancestries strike in Oxnard, California, and form the first successful farm workers' union. The American Federation of Labor, however, refuses to recognize a non-European American union.

Eugenio María de Hostos, from Puerto Rico, is posthumously proclaimed "Citizen of the Americas" for his contributions to problem-solving in the Dominican Republic and other South American countries.

1904

Rosendo Matienzo Cintrón founds the Unionist party, which dominates Puerto Rico's political scene until 1920.

The United States Supreme Court rules in the *Isabel González* case that Puerto Ricans are not aliens and cannot be denied admission to the continental United States, but they are not classified as citizens.

Julio Larringa is elected resident commissioner of Puerto Rico.

1909

Puerto Rican legislators pressure for political reforms by vetoing the island's budget. President William H. Taft reinforces the sovereignty and authority of the governor of Puerto Rico.

1900

through

1909

THE AMERICAS	THE AMERICAS	THE AMERICAS	THE AMERICAS

1900

The United States census reports the country's population at 76.1 million, including American citizens living abroad.

Women have the right to vote in national elections in only four states: Colorado, Idaho, Utah and Wyoming.

Women make up approximately 20 percent of the labor force in the United States.

A 2,500-person military force is sent by the United States as part of the international force to help suppress China's Boxer Rebellion.

An anti-lynching bill is introduced in the United States Congress.

The new buildings of the Ellis Island Immigration Station in New York harbor, built after fire destroyed the original structures, are officially opened.

The International Ladies Garment Workers Union is founded in New York City when seven smaller local organizations consolidate.

Carnegie Institute of Technology is founded at Pittsburgh, Pennsylvania.

The Organic Act establishes Hawaii as a United States territory and declares contract laborers illegal.

A hurricane ravages Galveston, Texas, killing more than 6,000 people.

In Lansing, Michigan, Ransom E. Olds develops an engine that runs on gasoline, and establishes the country's first manufacturing plant specifically designed to produce automobiles.

John Phillip Holland and Simon Lake build the United States Navy's first submarine.

American Army surgeon Walter Reed builds on the work of Dr. Carlos J. Finlay (see "Hispanic Americans, 1869") and proves that yellow fever is transmitted by a bite from a disease-carrying mosquito.

Temperance activist Carrie Nation begins her campaign for prohibition of alcohol when she marches on the Carey Hotel in Wichita, Kansas.

Disease-resistant varieties of the cotton plant are developed by William Orton.

c. 1900

The San Francisco office of the Cigarmaker's International Union publishes flyers listing those manufacturers who employ Chinese workers. The flyers say that these employers are doing a great disservice to "our white working men and women."

The integrated town of Buxton, Iowa, is a true mill town, populated by mine workers of the Consolidated Coal Company. Homes, stores, schools and churches in the town are built by the mining company. Progressive and peaceful, the town at its height has approximately 5,000 residents, more than 50 percent of whom are African American. A newspaper in Des Moines calls Buxton "the colored man's mecca of Iowa." However, by 1923 Consolidated Coal virtually closes the Buxton coalfields, and the town gradually disappears. Present-day Buxton is a small collection of ruined buildings in a meadow in southern Iowa.

1901

William McKinley begins a second term as president of the United States; Theodore Roosevelt is vice president. Both are Republicans. President McKinley is fatally shot by anarchist Leon Czolgosz; Roosevelt succeeds him as the 26th president.

The Senate ratifies a treaty negotiated by John Hay and Julian Pauncefote that overrides the Clayton-Bulwer agreement and gives the United States permission to construct, fully control and manage a proposed canal connecting the Atlantic and Pacific Oceans, provided that the canal will be accessible to ships of all nations.

The Platt Amendment, sponsored by Senator Orville H. Platt as a rider to an army appropriations bill, authorizes United States intervention in Cuban affairs and establishes an American naval base in Cuba. Used often by the United States during the next three decades, it is finally abrogated in 1934.

The Currency Act makes gold the country's sole monetary standard.

Texas State College for Women is founded at Denton, Texas.

Captain Anthony Lucas discovers oil at Spindletop, Texas. Oil is also discovered near Jennings, Louisiana.

John Pierpont Morgan establishes the United States Steel Corporation in South Dakota.

1901-1906

During his term as governor of Wisconsin, Robert Marion "Fighting Bob" La Follette develops the "Wisconsin Idea," a series of reforms that includes the direct primary, tax reform legislation, voting by secret ballot and control of the fees charged by railroads.

1901-1910

Immigration to the United States totals more than 8.74 million. Eight million come from Europe, 324,500 from Asia, 7,400 from Africa, 13,000 from Oceania, 361,900 from the Americas and 33,500 are not specifically identified. This rapid immigration causes discontent to grow, and nativist groups increase their activities.

1902

The United States Congress passes the Newlands or Reclamation Act, named for Francis G. Newlands, to use federal funds to build dams and irrigation projects in Nevada.

The Chinese Exclusion Act is amended by Congress to extend exclusion indefinitely.

President Roosevelt adopts the slogan "Square Deal" to describe his domestic programs.

The average weekly wage for a British weaver in the United States is $11.

A five-month strike begins when almost 150,000 members of the United Mine Workers walk out of the anthracite coal pits in Pennsylvania. President Roosevelt is forced to intervene and appoints a commission, which grants higher wages but does not recognize the union as a rightful bargaining agent.

Twenty miners lose their lives and a dozen more are injured after coal dust explodes in a mine shaft in Lost Creek, Iowa. Fifty miners are trapped below ground by the explosion; rescue work is impeded by deadly gases in the mine. Among the casualties, both dead and injured, are boys as young as 12.

Argentina and Chile settle a major boundary dispute.

In Cuba, American military personnel are withdrawn and a republic is established.

Lava and ash from the volcanic eruption of Mount Pelée kill almost 30,000 people at St. Pierre, Martinique.

When Venezuela refuses to pay debt obligations, British and German warships blockade its harbors.

Tomás Estrada Palma becomes president of Cuba. He serves until 1906.

1903

Congress establishes the United States Department of Commerce and Labor at the cabinet level.

The Immigration Act increases the categories of people deemed inadmissible to the United States. The categories include people considered to have contagious diseases, polygamists, paupers and those guilty of moral turpitude.

In *Champion* v. *Ames,* the United States Supreme Court supports the federal government's right to regulate commerce; this case essentially establishes federal policing authority.

The United States and Canada establish the Alaskan border.

1900 through 1909

In the Militia Act passed this year, Congress recognizes the National Guard as an official military organization and establishes training and equipment guidelines comparable to those of the regular army.

Colombian officials reject a treaty with the United States to allow the construction of a trans-isthmus canal. Panamanians take this opportunity to secede and seek independence, and are supported by United States naval forces. Once Panama gains independence, the canal treaty is concluded, granting the United States permission to construct a canal in Panama on a piece of land 10 miles wide. Panama receives a cash payment of $10 million and will receive $250,000 rent each year.

A labor law in Oregon, one of the first in the country, limits the workday to 10 hours for women.

The Elkins Act, sponsored by Stephen Benton Elkins, ends the policy of railroad freight rebates.

Mary Harris "Mother" Jones organizes and leads a protest "March of Mill Children" to President Roosevelt's home to seek protection for child laborers.

The National Women's Trade Union League is formed to give working women some voice in wages and working conditions.

The University of Puerto Rico is founded at Rio Piedras (now part of San Juan), Puerto Rico.

Henry Ford organizes the Ford Motor Company in Detroit, Michigan.

Brothers Orville and Wilbur Wright fly the first powered, controlled, heavier-than-air plane 120 feet at Kitty Hawk, North Carolina.

Bolivia loses the Acre region to Brazil.

Britain and France sign a treaty with Venezuela and lift their blockade of Venezuelan harbors.

José Batlle y Ordóñez is elected president of Uruguay. He serves until 1907 and again from 1911 to 1915. Uruguay begins a period of stability and institutes social and economic reforms. This period continues until Batlle's death in 1929.

1904

President Roosevelt issues his corollary to the Monroe Doctrine of 1823 by stating that the United States will send troops if necessary to protect its interests in — and keep foreign intervention out of — the Western Hemisphere. This is an example of his "Big Stick" diplomacy.

Bethune-Cookman College is founded at Daytona Beach, Florida.

New York City's subway system opens.

Ida Tarbell, American writer and editor, releases *History of the Standard Oil Company,* which blasts the company for its cutthroat dealings with competitors and its waste of natural resources.

More than 130,000 immigrants enter Canada.

Argentina and Chile dedicate a symbol of their territorial cooperation, Christ of the Andes — a large statue on their common border high in the Andes Mountains.

William Crawford Gorgas arrives at the Isthmus of Panama and is instrumental in eliminating yellow fever from the canal zone. Construction on the Panama Canal begins.

Rafael Reyes becomes president of Colombia. He serves until 1909.

1904-1909

In a series of uprisings that come to be called the "Black Patch War," Kentucky's tobacco monopoly is broken after irate growers burn fields and storehouses.

1905

Theodore Roosevelt begins his second term (first elected term) as president of the United States; Charles W. Fairbanks is vice president. Both are Republicans.

One million people immigrate to the United States this year.

The College of Saint Catherine is founded at St. Paul, Minnesota.

Eugene Victor Debs founds the Industrial Workers of the World in Chicago, Illinois.

The H. J. Heinz Company opens its doors in Pennsylvania. Company founder Henry J. Heinz operates his processing plants with the progressive attitude that employees deserve a clean, safe and pleasant work environment and oportunities for advancement. Heinz also pushes for federal restriction of the use of chemicals and false labeling in the food processing industry.

The Japanese and Korean Exclusion League is formed in the United States.

The Olds Motor Works in Michigan manufactures 6,500 automobiles this year.

As a result of the abuse of the Chinese workers in America, the Shanghai, China, Chamber of Commerce begins an effective boycott of American merchants. An anti-missionary riot also takes place in China.

Alberta and Saskatchewan join the Dominion of Canada.

Simón Ituri Patiño begins excavations in Bolivia in what will become one of the world's largest tin mines.

When the Dominican Republic becomes bankrupt, President Roosevelt creates a receivership under the United States Customs office to prevent further disorder. United States Marines are sent in 1916 to maintain order.

1905-1914

During this decade 10.1 million people arrive in the United States. This is the highest immigration figure to date for a single decade.

1900

through

1909

1900 through 1909

1906

Congress passes the Hepburn Act, sponsored by William Peters Hepburn, which strengthens the powers of the Interstate Commerce Commission (ICC) by allowing it to establish ceilings on freight rates. Congress also passes the Meat Inspection Act and the Pure Food and Drug Act to protect the public interest in these areas.

President Roosevelt visits the Panama Canal Zone. This is the first time a president in office has made a trip outside the United States. Roosevelt also is awarded the Nobel Peace Prize this year, for his mediation efforts in ending the Russo-Japanese War (see "The World, 1904").

Many states, including California and Washington, pass alien land laws depriving persons who are ineligible to be citizens of the right to own land.

Diamonds are discovered in Murfreesboro, Arkansas. The area is mined from 1908 to 1925, and produces the only diamonds ever mined in the United States.

An earthquake and three-day fire in San Francisco, California, devastate the city; the death toll is estimated at more than 2,000. Records verifying birth dates are destroyed and many Chinese people residing in California who claim they were born in the United States cannot be disproven.

The Young Women's Christian Association (YWCA) is organized by Grace Dodge. An association dedicated to assisting young city girls, it is open to European Americans and African Americans alike.

American inventor Lee de Forest, a pioneer in the fields of sound transmission and television, invents the audion. He is often referred to as the "father of radio" and later makes a triode vacuum tube for the development of television.

Canadian American Reginald Aubrey Fessenden makes the first radio voice broadcast at Brant Rock, Massachusetts.

Norwegian navigator Roald Amundsen arrives at Nome, Alaska, after successfully navigating the Northwest Passage from east to west. He is the first person to complete this journey. Amundsen also determines the position of the magnetic North Pole.

When Tomás Estrada Palma is reelected president of Cuba, José Miguel Gómez leads a revolt. Palma eventually resigns under pressure.

1906-1909

President Roosevelt orders United States military forces to intervene in Cuba, and a reform-oriented provisional government, under the leadership of William Howard Taft and Charles Magoon, is established.

1907

The Immigration Act defines more inadmissible classes for entry into the United States, including people suffering from physical or mental defects affecting their ability to earn a living, those admitting crimes involving moral turpitude, women coming for immoral purposes and unaccompanied children under age 16. The 1.3 million new arrivals this year set an all-time annual record, and increase the domestic labor force by about 3 percent.

A financial panic, which starts on Wall Street in New York City, causes a run on the nation's banks. It is stopped when financier and industrialist John Pierpont Morgan imports millions of dollars in gold from Europe.

By the terms of their second "Gentlemen's Agreement," the United States agrees not to officially exclude Japanese immigrants and Japan agrees to tighten exit visa restrictions for those wanting to come to this country.

Oklahoma becomes the 46th state to join the Union.

The University of Hawaii is founded at Honolulu, Hawaii.

More than 350 miners die in an explosion at West Virginia's Mononga coal mine.

In the United States a clothes washing machine powered by electricity becomes available for home use.

Construction begins on the Quebec Bridge in Canada. More than 60 workers, many of them Iroquois Indians, are killed when part of the bridge collapses.

Jamaica suffers an earthquake that causes more than 1,000 deaths and millions of dollars in property damage.

George Washington Goethals heads the construction of the Panama Canal after the resignation of John F. Stevens, the chief engineer assigned to the project. Goethals later becomes governor of the Canal Zone.

United States troops are sent into Honduras to protect American lives and property.

1908

The United States Supreme Court, in the *Danbury Hatters'* case, outlaws secondary union boycotts and provides a precedent for the intervention of federal courts into the activities of labor unions.

In *Miller* v. *Oregon* the Supreme Court affirms a state's right to establish protective legislation for women. In this case, the court supports Oregon's new law limiting the workday of laundresses to 10 hours per day. The decision is later overturned.

Congress establishes the Bureau of Investigation as a division of the United States Department of Justice. It becomes the Federal Bureau of Investigation in 1935.

The White House convenes the Conference on Conservation to involve both business and state leaders in developing and protecting the nation's resources.

Henry Ford's Model T becomes the first automobile made with an assembly-line process. This model is nicknamed "Tin Lizzie" because the body is constructed of lightweight steel sheets. More than 15 million cars of this model are sold in the next 20 years.

General Motors is founded as a holding company by William C. Durant in Flint, Michigan.

The retail firm of Sears, Roebuck & Co. publishes its "Book of Modern Homes and Building Plans," which offers more than 20 styles of homes that can be mail-ordered at prices up to $2,500.

Augusto Bernardino Leguía becomes president of Peru. He serves until 1912 and again from 1919 to 1930.

General Juan Vicente Gómez comes to power in Venezuela. During his leadership, he encourages foreign oil interests, and the country gradually becomes the second largest exporter of petroleum in the world. Gómez serves until 1935.

1909

William Howard Taft becomes the 27th president of the United States; James S. Sherman is vice president. Both are Republicans. Sherman dies in office, and the vacancy is not filled.

The United States Congress passes the Payne-Aldrich Tariff Act, named for Congressman Sereno E. Payne and Senator Nelson W. Aldrich. Although less strict than the Dingley Act (1897), it is still considered a strong protectionist law. It helps the shoe industry by eliminating import duties on hides but maintains high duties on iron and steel and increases duties on cotton, silk and other items.

The National Association for the Advancement of Colored People (NAACP) is founded in New York City, as the direct result of the lynching of two African Americans in Springfield, Illinois, the previous year.

A major strike occurs among the garment workers of New York City, most of whom are women and recent immigrants. The strikers seek improved working conditions and the right to unionize. This strike is so widespread in the city that it comes to be called the Uprising of the 20,000, and effects changes in hundreds of garment shops.

THE AMERICAS	FOR CLASSROOM USE	FOR CLASSROOM USE	FOR CLASSROOM USE	

Nevada's state legislature bans gambling.

European American explorer Robert E. Peary, African American explorer Matthew A. Henson and four Inuit (Eskimo) people become the first expedition to reach the North Pole.

The formation of the Chilean Workers' Federation begins a period of social and political reform in Chile.

General José Miguel Gómez becomes president of Cuba following the resignation under pressure of Tomás Estrada Palma (1902). Gómez serves until 1913.

1909-1912

Cubans of African descent organize politically in the face of increased race restrictions that develop as the United States invests in Cuban industry. European Cubans react violently in what comes to be called the Race War of 1912, in which hundreds of African Cubans die.

1900

through

1909

1900 through 1909

Summary

The United States has gained a reputation as a world power by virtue of its strong stance in the Spanish-American War and its alliances with European powers to put down China's Boxer Rebellion.

Rivalries among European powers, including the expansionist ideology of Germany's Kaiser Wilhelm II, lead to World War I, the "Great War" in which the Central Powers (Austria-Hungary, Germany, Bulgaria and the Ottoman Empire) fight the Allies (Britain, France, Russia, The United States, Italy, Japan and others), on battlegrounds worldwide. More than 8 million people die and three empires — the Ottoman, Austro-Hungarian and czarist Russian — fall. Treaties ending the war limit Germany's military, place heavy war reparation debts on the German government, redistribute Ottoman lands and place former German colonies under League of Nations mandates.

In Russia, two successive revolutions put the Bolsheviks (Reds) in power; a communist government is formed and the Union of Soviet Socialist Republics is proclaimed.

Japan is recognized as a world power after its victory over Russia in Manchuria. China's government changes with the Nationalist revolution, but local warlords create turmoil that facilitates the rise of communism. Laos, Cambodia and Vietnam gain their independence as the French Union is dismantled.

The political climate of post-war Germany is one of turmoil and extremism; the economy suffers paralyzing inflation that is amplified by the Great Depression. In this atmosphere the Nazi party arises as a unifying force, with Adolf Hitler as its leader. In addition to savage nationalist and expansionist ideas, Hitler wants to solve the "Jewish question." Sporadic acts of oppression and violence against ethnic minorities, especially Jews, solidify into systematic genocide as Germany's war machine devastates a stunned Europe.

As the seriousness of Hitler's intent begins to dawn, nations again align themselves against Germany and gradually turn the war around. World War II, this war that *follows* the "War to End All Wars," results in more than 15 million military casualties and 35 million civilian deaths. An 11-month war crimes trial held at Nuremberg exposes the horrors of the Nazi death camps, where an estimated 6 million Jews died.

The Korean War puts the United States military in a leadership role, with American officers leading United Nations forces. As relations between the United States and the Soviet Union cool, terms such as "Iron Curtain" and "Cold War" come into use.

By the mid-1950s, European powers lose their hold on Africa as African countries gain their independence. Many of the fledgling nations experience years of strife before stable government can be maintained. In South Africa, *apartheid,* the strict separation of European Africans from native Africans, and the denial of native Africans' right to a voice in their own affairs is developed and perpetuated. In the United States, one African American woman refuses to move to the back of a segregated city bus; her action brings this country's civil rights movement to full bloom.

In the last half of the twentieth century, remarkable advances are made in communications. The space programs of the United States and the Soviet Union are exploring the uses of earth-orbiting satellites, and by the mid-1970s, the vast majority of American households have television sets. The Vietnam War, halfway around the world, is the first major conflict to receive extensive television news coverage; reactions to the violence take the form of peace marches and demonstrations throughout the United States. Finally, as the "space age" gives way to the "information age," the two letters, "PC" (personal computer) are becoming a household term.

1900

China's Boxer Rebellion is put down by a combined British, French, United States, German and Japanese force.

The Boer War continues in South Africa as British forces occupy Pretoria and other major cities, and eventually force the Boers (Dutch and French Huguenot residents) to capitulate. The 1902 Treaty of Vereeniging ends the hostilities.

Nationalist factions in Ireland unite and choose John E. Redmond as their leader.

Britain annexes the Orange Free State in southern Africa.

Nearly 50,000 Chinese people lose their lives as Russian forces occupy Manchuria.

Victor Emmanuel III becomes king of Italy after the assassination of his father, Humbert I (1878). Victor Emmanuel III rules until 1946. He also rules as emperor of Ethiopia from 1936 to 1943, and as king of Albania from 1939 to 1943.

Danish engineer Valdemar Poulsen invents the telegraphone, forerunner of the modern tape recorder.

Count Ferdinand Graf von Zeppelin invents the rigid airship in Germany.

Britain gains control over the North Solomon Islands, adding to their 1893 acquisition of the South Solomons and the Gilbert Islands.

c. 1900

The Irish nationalist movement known as Sinn Fein ("We, ourselves") emerges in Ireland. Its founder, Arthur Griffith, initially advocates passive resistance to all things English; he even encourages a revival of the Gaelic language.

1901

United States forces capture Aguinaldo in the Philippines, and the First Philippine Republic ends. The American military rules the island nation briefly, until a civilian government is formed with American William Howard Taft as governor-general.

The Commonwealth of Australia is formed by the union of the colonies of New South Wales, Victoria, Queensland, South Australia, Western Australia and Tasmania.

In India, British authorities establish the North West Frontier province between Afghanistan and the Punjab in an effort to maintain stability in the area.

Britain annexes the kingdom of Ashanti (Asante) in what is now Ghana.

The Italian government establishes passport requirements for emigrants. Previously, Italians needed no special papers or permission to leave the country.

Edward VII becomes king of Great Britain and Ireland after the death of his mother, Queen Victoria (1837). He rules until 1910.

(Sir) Edmund Barton becomes the first prime minister of Australia. He serves until 1903, when he is appointed to Australia's High Court.

Habibullah becomes ruler of Afghanistan after the death of his father, Abdu r-Rahman Khan (1880). Habibullah takes the title of king, and rules until 1919.

Italian physicist Guglielmo Marconi receives the first transatlantic wireless telegraph message at St. John's, Newfoundland. The message is sent from Poldau, Cornwall, England.

The first Nobel prizes are awarded. Established and endowed in 1896 by the will of Swedish chemist Alfred Nobel, the prizes are given in five (later six) categories: peace, chemistry, physics, physiology or medicine, literature and, added in 1969, economic science.

This year marks the beginning of the rule of the House of Windsor in England. Wettin, family name of Albert of Saxe-Coburg-Gotha, royal consort to Queen Victoria, is changed to Windsor by George V in 1917.

1902

The Treaty of Vereeniging ends the Boer War between British and Boer forces in southern Africa. The agreement acknowledges British commercial interests in the region, allows Boers to keep their own language, and continues to deny native Africans the right to vote.

France settles its disputes with Italy and the two countries create a new alliance to stop German expansion.

Ibn Saud and his forces seize the city of Riyadh, the capital of Nejd.

The Aswan Dam in Egypt is completed.

The first international organization for women's suffrage is established in Washington, D.C.

In Russia, unrest is triggered by the government's attempt to prevent students from organizing. The czar uses force to restore order and also puts down peasant uprisings caused by famine conditions.

The Pacific Cable is completed, running from Vancouver, British Columbia, Canada, to Brisbane, Australia.

Arthur James Balfour, a Liberal, becomes prime minister of Great Britain. He serves until 1905.

1903

The Russian Social Democratic Party splits into two factions at its second party Congress held in London: Mensheviks (members of the minority) led by Georgi Plekhanov and Bolsheviks (members of the majority) led by Vladimir Lenin and Leon Trotsky.

Denmark grants Iceland the right to self-rule.

Government reforms in Ireland enable peasants to own land.

In Africa, Sokoto falls to British forces, who now occupy all of northern Nigeria.

An anti-Jewish *pogrom* (an organized attack) results in 50 deaths and the destruction of more than 500 homes in Kishenev, Bessarabia, Russia.

Seychelles and Mauritius are divided administratively, with Seychelles becoming a separate British crown colony.

Peter I (Peter Karageorgevich) becomes king of Serbia after the assassination of Alexander I (Alexander Obrenovich, 1889), and Queen Draga. Peter rules until 1918. He then serves as king of the Serbs, Croats and Slovenes (later Yugoslavia) from 1918-1921.

Alfred Deakin becomes prime minister of Australia. He serves until 1904.

Emmeline Pankhurst founds the Women's Social and Political Union. By her personal strength, sound principles of organization and effective use of acts of civil disobedience, she gains a great deal of respect in Britain.

Marie Sklodowska Curie and her husband Pierre Curie receive this year's Nobel Prize for their work with radioactivity. In 1911 Marie S. Curie receives the Nobel Prize again, for her achievements in chemistry.

1903-1906

Norwegian explorer Roald Amundsen leads the first successful expedition through the Northwest Passage.

1904

Yemen is declared an independent kingdom by the *imam* (king) Yahya Muhammad Hamid.

In an action known as *Entente Cordiale,* Britain and France settle their international differences, and align to stop German expansion.

The second *aliyah* (a heavy wave of Jewish immigration) to Palestine begins. This mass relocation continues until 1916.

The Russo-Japanese War begins. This conflict is instigated by the advance of Russian forces into Manchuria, which leads to Russia's lease of Port Arthur and control of the Amur province. Japan breaks off diplomatic relations with Russia and suddenly, in 1905, successfully attacks and captures Port Arthur. Russian troops also suffer defeat at the Battle of Mukden and the loss of their Baltic fleet in the Tsushima Straits. United States President Theodore Roosevelt mediates the Treaty of Portsmouth, New Hampshire, ending the war. Russian advances into Korea (Chōsen) are stopped and Russia releases Korea and acknowledges Japanese interest in that land; Russia accepts Manchuria's return to Chinese sovereignty; Russian railroad lines in southern Manchuria are turned over to Japan along with the Liaotung Peninsula and the southern part of the island of Sakhalin. By virtue of its military victory, Japan is regarded as a world power.

John C. Watson serves for three months as prime minister of Australia. (Sir) George H. Reed then becomes prime minister. He serves until 1905.

English scientists Frederick Soddy and Sir Ernest Rutherford conduct early research into the field of radioactivity.

Charles Steward Rolls and Frederick Henry Royce form the automobile manufacturing firm of Rolls-Royce, Ltd. in England.

1904-1906

To help increase production in their mines, South African firms recruit more than 60,000 Chinese laborers during this time.

1904-1908

The Maji Maji (Khoikhoi) tribe, called Hottentots by European colonists, and the Herero tribe revolt against German control in what is now Namibia.

1900
through
1909

1900 through 1909

1905

Sinn Fein, loosely formed in Ireland c. 1900, begins to organize and become a political force.

The Russian Revolution begins with the "Bloody Sunday" massacre at St. Petersburg when Czar Nicholas II's troops fire on hundreds of workers seeking audience with the czar. Peasant revolts against landlords, mutiny of sailors on the *Potemkin* and a general workers' strike lead to the creation of the first workers' council, set up in St. Petersburg. Reforms including the first Imperial *Duma* (Parliament) and the granting of certain civil liberties are established by Nicholas II's "October Manifesto." A massive strike against Russian rule in Finland gains the region its own elected parliament.

The union of Sweden and Norway comes to an end as Norway's legislature votes to become an independent nation.

Revolution breaks out in Persia (Iran).

Haakon VII (Prince Charles of Denmark) is elected king of Norway after the reign of Oscar II (1872). Haakon VII rules until 1957.

Sir Henry Campbell-Bannerman, a Liberal, becomes prime minister of Great Britain after the term of James Balfour (1902). Campbell-Bannerman serves until 1908.

Alfred Deakin (1903) again becomes prime minister of Australia. He serves until 1908.

Albert Einstein's special theory of relativity and other key theories in physics are published in Germany.

Emmeline Pankhurst becomes a leader in the women's suffrage movement in England; along with her three daughters, she leads demonstrations and endures imprisonment. British women do not gain the right to vote until 1918.

1905-1906

Revolts and resulting violence in Russia cause more *pogroms* (organized attacks) and strikes and spur large-scale emigration, especially to the United States.

1906

Persia adopts its first constitution.

The All India Muslim League is founded by Aga Khan.

The Algeciras Conference is held in Morocco. After France has requested from the sultan that Morocco become a French protectorate, German forces land in Tangiers and call for full Moroccan independence. France and Spain win control over the territory with an agreement to respect Moroccan integrity but France and Germany remain estranged over the incident.

The original H.M.S. *Dreadnaught,* a heavily armored gunship, is launched as part of Great Britain's fleet.

British authorities grant self-government to the Boer Transvaal and Orange Free State (Orange River) colonies.

The Russian *Duma* meets and gains the right of suffrage, but Czar Nicholas II later dissolves the *Duma* and declares martial law.

Women in Finland receive the right to vote.

Frederick VIII becomes king of Denmark after the death of his father, Christian IX (1863). Frederick VIII rules until 1912.

W. Hall-Jones, a Liberal, becomes prime minister of New Zealand.

A submarine telegraph cable is installed between Iceland and Scotland.

1907

New Zealand becomes a self-governing dominion within the British Empire.

The Second Hague Peace Conference, called by Czar Nicholas II of Russia, is attended by 46 nations and adopts 10 conventions on the rules of war. The United States is unsuccessful in its attempt to create a world court.

Under pressure from Britain and France, Siam (Thailand) surrenders parts of Cambodia and all control over Kedah, Perlis, Kelantan and, in 1909, Tregganu (on the Malay Peninsula) to maintain its status as an independent country.

An Anglo-Russian reconciliation to stop German expansion is the final step in the formation of the Triple Entente of Russia, France and Britain. In separate negotiations, Russia settles its differences with Japan over territorial claims in China, while Britain agrees to divide Persia into two separate spheres of influence, one British and one Russian.

The second Russian *Duma* meets but is dissolved within a few months. The third *Duma* is elected; it exists for five years.

Gustavus V becomes king of Sweden after the death of his father, Oscar II (1872). Gustavus V rules until 1950.

Muhammad Ali becomes shah of Persia after the death of his father, Muzaffar-ed-Din (1896). Muhammad Ali rules until 1909.

With the help of British authorities, Ugyen Wangchuk, a powerful provincial ruler in Bhutan, becomes that country's first hereditary monarch.

In Hungary, 200,000 people are involved in a massive general strike in support of universal suffrage.

Italian physician and educator Maria Montessori, the first woman to receive a medical degree from an Italian school, opens her first school for children in Rome.

In South Africa, Indian attorney Mohandas Gandhi organizes his first *satyagraha* (a campaign of civil disobedience based on nonviolent opposition to laws that encourage racial discrimination).

A women's rights society in India holds its first meeting. Women in attendance must be accompanied by male relatives, since attacks on unescorted women are feared.

Belgium annexes the Congo Free State (now Zaïre).

1908

A rebellion in Turkey is led by the Young Turks who want the liberal constitution of 1876 restored. Although the rebellion fails, it further weakens the crumbling Ottoman Empire; Bulgaria declares its independence, and Austria-Hungary annexes Bosnia and Herzegovina, an act that draws support from Germany but angers Russia.

Indonesia's first nationalist organization, Budi Utimo, is established.

After King Leopold II cedes to Belgium his personal control of the Congo, the area becomes a part of the Belgian Congo.

In Africa, Italian forces take control of Somalia.

Oil is discovered in Persia.

A major earthquake in Messina, Italy, results in more than 82,000 deaths.

Pieces of a comet fall to earth near Tunguska, Siberia.

Herbert Henry Asquith, a Liberal, becomes prime minister of Great Britain after the term of Sir Henry Campbell-Bannerman (1905). Asquith serves until 1915, forms a coalition and serves another year.

Abdu-l-Hafid becomes sultan of Morocco after his brother, Abdu-l-Aziz IV (1894), is deposed. Abdu-l-Hafid rules until 1912.

Manuel II becomes king of Portugal after the death of his father, Charles I (1889). Manuel II rules until 1910.

Ruling Prince Ferdinand becomes czar of Bulgaria after independence from the Ottoman Empire is declared. Ferdinand rules until 1918.

Xuantong (Hsuan-tung) becomes emperor of China after the death of Guangxu (1875). Xuantong rules until 1911.

Andrew Fisher becomes prime minister of Australia after the term of Alfred Deakin (1903, 1905). Fisher serves until 1909.

The Boy Scouts is established in England by (Sir) Robert Baden-Powell.

THE WORLD				

1908-1916

China experiences unrest and political upheaval as the Manchu dynasty ends and Sun Yat-sen's Nationalist Revolution briefly gains power and then loses it to military dictator General Yuan Shikai (Yüan Shi-k'ai).

1909

Universal male suffrage is granted in Sweden. Women do not receive the vote until 1921.

Albert I becomes king of Belgium after the death of his uncle, Leopold II (1865). Albert I rules until 1934.

Muhammad V becomes Ottoman sultan after his brother, Abdu-l-Hamid II (1876), is deposed by the Young Turks. Muhammad V rules until 1918.

Ahmed becomes shah of Persia after his father, Muhammad Ali (1907), is deposed. The last of the Qajar dynasty, Ahmed rules until 1925.

Louis Blériot becomes the first pilot to fly across the English Channel from Calais, France, to Dover, England. The trip takes 37 minutes.

Alfred Deakin (1903, 1905) becomes prime minister of Australia for a third time after the term of Andrew Fisher (1908). Deakin serves until 1910.

1900

through

1909

NATIVE AMERICAN	NATIVE AMERICAN	AFRICAN AMERICAN	AFRICAN AMERICAN
1911 As a result of malnutrition, tuberculosis and trachoma, the Native American death rate is more than double the national average. The Bureau of Indian Affairs establishes a formal Indian health program. The United States Army forcibly enters Hotevilla, on the Navajo and Hopi reservation in Arizona, and captures more than 60 Hopi children to take them to government schools. "Surplus" lands on the Rosebud (Oglala Sioux) and Pine Ridge (Brulé Sioux) reservations in South Dakota are opened to European American homesteading. The Society of American Indians is founded by educated Native Americans including Charles Eastman (Sioux), Sherman Coolidge (Arapaho), Laura Cornelius (Oneida) and others. **1912** The first dictionary of the Navajo language is published by the Franciscan fathers of Arizona. **1914** In support of their country, the Six Nations of the Iroquois Confederacy declare war on Germany. **1915** The Alaska Native Sisterhood holds its first convention in Sitka, Alaska. **1916** The Supreme Court rules in *United States* v. *Rice* that American Indians may still be considered wards and have their affairs overseen by Congress, even if they have become citizens. In Chicago, Dr. Carlos Montezuma, a Yavapai Indian from Arizona and one of the first Native Americans to graduate from an American medical school, begins publication of *Wassaja,* this century's first militant Native American publication. Dr. Montezuma advocates the immediate dissolution of the Bureau of Indian Affairs and of the reservation system.	**1917-1918** More than 15,000 American Indian men see active duty in World War I. Many serve as "code talkers" contributing to Allied victories by communicating for United States forces in their native languages, which cannot be deciphered by the enemy. **1918** The First American (Indian) Church is established by Mack Hoag, a Cheyenne, and members from several other tribes, at El Reno, Oklahoma.	**1910** The United States census reports just over 9.83 million African Americans, 10.7 percent of the United States population. Attorney Robert L. Vann founds his newspaper, the *Pittsburgh Courier.* The Committee on Urban Conditions of Negroes is formed in New York under the leadership of George E. Haynes for the purpose of improving the employment and living conditions of urban African Americans. It merges the following year with the National League for the Protection of Colored Women, later becomes a biracial organization, and eventually changes its name to the National Urban League. Large numbers of African Americans begin to migrate to northern cities to avoid economic and racial difficulties in the South. **1911** Jane Edna Hunter organizes the Working Girls' Home Association (Phillis Wheatley Association) in Cleveland, Ohio, to assist African American women in finding employment. A news story of an African American being lynched appears in the nation's newspapers on an average of once every six days. Booker T. Washington is severely beaten in New York City, for allegedly approaching a European American woman. **1912** The National Association for the Advancement of Colored People (NAACP) desegregates New York theaters and the New Jersey Palisades Amusement Park. **c. 1912** In Jamaica, Marcus Garvey begins the Universal Negro Improvement Association to unite people of African descent, to improve living conditions, to establish states and communities in Africa and to promote African-owned business and industry.	**1913** Most African American federal employees are segregated in eating and rest room facilities by an executive order of President Woodrow Wilson. Dr. Daniel Hale Williams becomes a charter member of the American College of Surgeons. For years he remains the only African American member of the organization. **1914** The National Negro Business League reports that there are 40,000 African American-owned businesses in the country. Oscar Micheaux, of New York City, becomes the first African American film producer, and his production company is the first to employ only African Americans. The NAACP creates the Arthur B. Spingarn Award, to be given annually to an African American for achievement. Dr. Ernest E. Just receives the first award for his outstanding work in biological research. **1915** Almost all the southern states have "white primaries," in which only European Americans are allowed to vote. A South Carolina labor law prohibits textile factory owners from allowing African American and European American laborers to work in the same room, use the same entrances, stairs, pay windows, rest rooms, drinking cups or water buckets. Carter G. Woodson, Ph.D., organizes the Association for the Study of Negro Life History (ASNLH) in Chicago. William Augustus Hinton is appointed director of the Wasserman Laboratory of the Massachusetts Department of Health. His work in syphilis research produces tests that carry his name and demonstrates that the disease is a function of poverty and ignorance, not race.

1910

through

1919

AFRICAN AMERICAN	AFRICAN AMERICAN	AFRICAN AMERICAN	FOR CLASSROOM USE	

1916

The NAACP establishes an anti-lynching committee.

Dr. Ulysses Grant Dailey becomes president of the National Medical Association. In 1948 he becomes editor of the *Journal of the National Medical Association*.

The first issue of the *Journal of Negro History* is published by the ASNLH under the direction of Dr. Carter G. Woodson.

Marcus Garvey, champion of the "back to Africa" movement, arrives in New York and soon begins publication of the newspaper, *Negro World*.

1917

In *Buchanan* v. *Warley* the United States Supreme Court rules that a city segregation ordinance in Louisville, Kentucky, is unconstitutional because it violates the due process clause of the Fourteenth Amendment.

Almost 40 African Americans are killed in a July race riot in East St. Louis, Illinois. A silent protest parade is organized, and 10,000 people march through New York City.

In Houston, Texas, an African American Army battalion fights with European American residents; nearly 20 people are killed. The NAACP intervenes on behalf of the soldiers. President Wilson commutes 10 death sentences to life imprisonment. Some of the soldiers are released from prison four years later, and the last is released in 1938.

African American soldiers in Spartanburg, South Carolina, are refused service in local establishments, and beaten. To prevent further unrest, army officials send the regiment to Europe.

The literacy test that is part of the nation's new immigration law subsequently shows that newly arrived African immigrants are more literate than African Americans born in the United States.

During World War I, Mary B. Talbert is active in the nation's fund-raising effort and works with the troops as a Red Cross nurse in France. African Americans are not fully integrated into the fighting force; they train separately and are not afforded use of common facilities with other soldiers.

The Julius Rosenwald Fund is established in Chicago to provide a matching funds base for the construction of schools and the training of African American teachers in the South.

1918

A state civil rights law in New York expands equal accommodations provisions to include virtually all businesses and public places.

Henry Johnson and Needham Roberts, of the New York 15th Division, receive the croix de guerre from the French government for their courage in fighting off a German invasion against significant odds. The 369th Infantry is cited for bravery and the entire unit receives the croix de guerre. Other African American units serving with distinction in World War I are the 370th Infantry (8th Illinois) and the 372nd Infantry.

1919

During the last six months of this year, 76 African Americans are lynched, and 25 race riots occur.

The Tennessee legislature passes an anti-mob act to prevent lynching.

In *State* v. *Young,* the Supreme Court of West Virginia rules that a Mr. Young, sentenced to life in prison, was denied equal protection under the law by virtue of the fact that his jury had no African American members. The state subsequently admits African Americans to juries.

The federal government establishes a town exclusively for African Americans at Truxton, Virginia, near the Portsmouth naval station which employs most of the town's inhabitants.

The Associated Negro Press is organized in Chicago by Claude A. Barnett to serve as a clearing house of information on African Americans.

The first Pan African Congress is held in Paris. Organized by W. E. B. Du Bois, its purpose is to focus world attention on the plight of Africa and the exploitation of its citizens. Follow-up conferences are held in 1921, 1923, 1927 and 1945.

1910

through

1919

ASIAN AMERICAN	ASIAN AMERICAN	ASIAN AMERICAN	EUROPEAN AMERICAN

1910 through 1919

ASIAN AMERICAN

1910

The United States census reports that the Chinese population has dropped to approximately 71,500, 1,200 and 21,600 in the United States, Alaska and Hawaii, respectively. The sex ratio is more than 1,400 males to 100 females in the continental United States, and 380 to one in Hawaii.

Angel Island Immigration Station opens in San Francisco, California. Chinese immigrants are kept in detention barracks pending rulings on the validity of their claims for entry.

The first legal Filipino immigrants arrive at the California ports of San Francisco and Los Angeles.

Japanese "picture brides," begin arriving in the United States. Picture brides are generally selected long-distance by family and/or friends in Japan for Japanese Americans. This activity is necessitated because of anti-miscegenation laws in the United States, and the great disparity between numbers of Japanese American males and females. By 1920 more than 20,000 women will have come to the United States as picture brides.

Arthur K. Ozawa, born in Hawaii and a graduate of the University of Michigan Law School, is admitted to the bar in Michigan and Hawaii. He is believed to be the country's first Japanese American lawyer.

Tom Gunn of San Francisco is the first Chinese American to pass the licensing examination to become an aviator in the United States.

1913

By the terms of California's new Alien Land Act, also called the Webb Act, "aliens ineligible for citizenship" — that is, Asians — are prohibited from owning land and from leasing it for longer than three years. Similar laws are adopted in other states.

ASIAN AMERICAN

1914-1918

More than 800 Japanese Americans fight in World War I as Hawaii's all-Japanese Company D.

1915

The Native Sons of the Golden State reorganizes as the Chinese American Citizens Alliance. Lodges are established in other cities.

Chinese merchants led by Look Tin Eli found the China Mail Steamship Company as part of a boycott campaign against Japan for aggression in China. The company remains in business until 1923.

The Chinese American Bank is founded in Honolulu, the first of its kind in Hawaii. It remains in business until 1933.

1916

Chinese American K. C. Li founds the Wah Chang Corporation, providing tungsten to modern industries. By 1933 this corporation has become the world's largest tungsten refiner.

1917

Twenty-nine thousand *issei* (Japanese immigrant generation) and some *nisei* (first Japanese American generation born in the United States) register for the draft in Hawaii during World War I.

Largely because World War I produces a fear regarding the assimilability and loyalty of Asian immigrants, the Asiatic Barred Zone is created in United States immigration law. This law establishes a geographic area from which no immigrants will be admitted; it discriminates against all Asians except Filipinos, who are United States nationals.

1918

Effie Chew becomes the first Chinese American teacher in the California public school system.

Sing Kee, a Chinese American from San Jose, California, is awarded a Distinguished Service Cross for extraordinary heroism during World War I.

ASIAN AMERICAN

1919

First generation Japanese American farmers own more than 450,000 acres of California land and produce more than 10 percent of the state's vegetables.

Philippine Women's College is founded in Manila. It is the first women's college established in Asia by Asians. Its founders were educated in United States schools.

EUROPEAN AMERICAN

1910

The Republican Party begins nominating Swedish and Norwegian Americans to a variety of posts in an effort to secure the Scandinavian vote in the midwestern states.

The Russian American newspaper, *Novoye Russkoe Slovo,* begins publication in New York City.

1911

The Dillingham Commission on Immigration issues a report calling for restrictions on eastern and southern European immigration. The demand for large-scale restriction on immigration fails because of the continuing demand for labor and the growing political power of the new immigrant groups.

More than 140 women, many of them young Jewish Americans, are killed in a fire at the Triangle Shirtwaist Company factory in New York City. This incident spawns national legislation dealing with workplace safety and major reforms in the garment industry.

1912

French American surgeon and biologist Alexis Carrel wins the Nobel Prize for medicine.

1913

Nearly 300,000 Russian immigrants come to the United States in this year alone, the highest number in history.

School children in Pierre, South Dakota, discover a lead plate thought to have been left by French explorers two centuries earlier.

1914

The Anti-Defamation League is founded by the Independent Order of B'nai B'rith to combat derogatory literature and acts of hatred against Jews in America.

EUROPEAN AMERICAN	HISPANIC AMERICAN	HISPANIC AMERICAN	HISPANIC AMERICAN	

EUROPEAN AMERICAN

President Wilson presents the dedication speech at the unveiling of a statue of American Revolutionary naval hero John Barry. In his remarks, the president opens a long-standing controversy when he refers to Barry as "an Irishman whose heart crossed the Atlantic with him, unlike some Americans, who needed hyphens in their names, because only part of them has come over." At the time, many so-called "hyphenated" Americans, Irish American groups in particular, are angry at this comment which they feel seriously questions their loyalty to their new homeland.

1915

Italian immigration slows from more than 280,000 people in 1914 to fewer than 50,000 this year.

Moses Alexander is elected governor of Idaho. He is the first Jewish American to hold the office of governor.

Louis D. Brandeis is nominated as the first Jewish American associate justice to the United States Supreme Court. He takes his seat on the court in 1916, and serves until 1939.

Leo Frank, a Jew, is lynched in Georgia.

1917

As the United States declares war on Germany, German American communities become targets of fear and hatred. Americans of other ethnic backgrounds question the loyalty of German Americans: cultural and ethnic events are suspect; German place and street names in many cities are changed. In some places this attitude erupts into violence, as when a German American in Illinois is arrested, and then lynched by a mob, for reportedly making "disloyal" statements.

A group of Russian engineers and professionals establishes a technical school in New York City.

1918

Fewer than 2,500 Swedes come to America this year.

A second major wave of Russian immigration to the United States begins as a result of the Russian Revolution (1917).

HISPANIC AMERICAN

1910

The outbreak of the Mexican Revolution and resulting chaos drive thousands of Mexicans to the United States. Illegal Mexican immigrants take jobs in industry, in mines, on railroads and in agriculture.

There are approximately 30,000 Mexicans in Arizona, 32,500 in California, 11,000 in New Mexico, and 125,000 in Texas.

1911

Jovita Idár and Soledad Pena organize the Liga Feminil Mexicanista in Texas to support education for *Chicanas* (Mexican American women) and to protest Mexico-Texas border violence.

1911-1914

Mexican immigration to the United States during this time is 82,500.

1913

Ladislas Lázaro is elected as a Representative to the United States Congress from Louisiana. He serves until his death in 1927.

1914

La Liga Protectora, or the Protection League, is founded in Arizona to combat discriminatory treatment of Hispanic Americans.

The Spanish-language daily newspaper *La Prensa (The Press)* begins publication in New York City.

1914-1919

World War I increases the United States' demand for laborers. More than 91,000 Mexicans come north across the border, bringing the total for the decade to more than 173,000.

1915

In Washington, D.C., the resident commissioner of Puerto Rico is denied his request that a plebiscite be held on the island on the question of United States citizenship.

HISPANIC AMERICAN

1916

Francisco "Pancho" Villa leads a raid against the border town of Columbus, New Mexico, killing several American citizens. United States troops under General John J. Pershing cross the Mexican border in pursuit of Villa. The New Mexico National Guard is mobilized, but Villa eludes capture.

President Wilson adds a rider to the War Department Appropriations Act that provides for the elimination of elections in Puerto Rico. As a result, the Puerto Rican Unionist majority cannot vote against United States citizenship.

Ezequiel Cabeza de Baca becomes governor of New Mexico. He dies soon after taking office and Octaviano A. Larrazolo, originally from Chihuahua, Mexico, is elected to replace him.

1917

United States immigration laws expand the head tax and literacy test to include Mexican immigrants. The laws are virtually ignored by southwestern agriculture growers who need migrant Mexican labor.

The Jones Act gives Puerto Ricans American citizenship. Residents of the island may travel freely to and from the mainland United States. Puerto Ricans begin to migrate in larger numbers. The act also permits Puerto Ricans to elect their own senate.

Félix Córdova Dávila is elected resident commissioner of Puerto Rico. He serves until 1932.

Out of 18,000 Puerto Ricans drafted for World War I, only one is killed and five are wounded.

The Puerto Rican Feminist League, led by Ana Roque de Duprey, begins a campaign to obtain voting rights for literate women in Puerto Rico.

HISPANIC AMERICAN

The Mexican Constitution of 1917 is adopted under President Venustiano Carranza. It forbids foreign ownership of land near the borders or seacoasts and reserves all mineral rights for Mexico. This eventually deepens the conflict between Mexico and the United States, and increases demands for intervention from American property holders and oil and mining companies.

1918

Strong earthquakes and sea disturbances occur on Puerto Rico's northwest side.

1919

Ninety-three migrant Puerto Rican farm laborers die in Arkansas because of poor working and living conditions.

1910

through

1919

1910 through 1919

1910

The United States census reports the country's population at 92 million, including American citizens living abroad.

Congress passes the Mann-Elkins Act, which increases the power of the Interstate Commerce Commission to approve rates charged by the telephone, cable and telegraph companies; also passed is the Mann Act, named for sponsor James Robert Mann and known as the White Slavery Act, which prohibits the transportation of women from one state to another for immoral purposes.

Four out of five elementary and high school teachers in the United States are women. Approximately 6 percent of the doctors and 3 percent of the dentists in the nation are women.

Edward Douglass White becomes chief justice of the United States Supreme Court. He serves until his death in 1921.

The first major parade in support of women's suffrage is held in New York City. This year, the state of Washington grants the vote to its women citizens.

The Angel Island Immigration Station opens in San Francisco Bay, California.

The Boy Scouts of America is founded by illustrator and naturalist Daniel Carter "Uncle Dan" Beard.

The Camp Fire Girls of America is founded by Luther Halsey Gulick, a pioneer in the field of physical education.

American Elmer A. Sperry invents a successful gyrocompass and improvements in street lighting.

A dispute between Canadian and United States fishing fleets over fishing rights and boundaries in the Atlantic Ocean is decided by an international arbitration board.

A devastating forest fire sweeps through northern Idaho, destroying approximately 3 million acres of timber, or one-sixth of the state's forest land. More than 80 people lose their lives, most of them firefighters.

The Royal Canadian Navy is formed.

Revolution breaks out in Mexico after liberal reform leader Francisco Madero loses the fraudulent 1910 presidential election. Madero and his followers stage a revolt and oust Díaz and in 1911 Madero — well-intended but lacking in leadership abilities — becomes president of the country. However, Madero is assassinated in 1913 by one of his generals, Victoriano Huerta, who then seizes power. In 1914 military intervention by the United States forces Huerta's resignation, and Venustiano Carranza, a supporter of constitutional government, becomes president. Peasants are organized into revolutionary armies and demand land reform. Calm is gradually restored, though different opposition groups led by Pancho Villa and Emiliano Zapata continue to conduct isolated attacks for several years. In all the conflicts of the Mexican revolution, women are highly visible as cooks, nurses, scouts and fighters. During the 11 years of fighting, approximately 1 million Mexicans lose their lives.

A railroad across the Andes Mountains from Chile to Argentina is completed.

1910-1935

Investment by Americans in large Puerto Rican sugar plantations forces small farmers out of business. Ownership of land and refineries is increasingly in the hands of a small number of owners.

1911

In one of its earliest antitrust actions against corporate monopolies, the United States Supreme Court dissolves Standard Oil Company.

The National Progressive Republican League is formed. Its candidate in the presidental election of 1912 is Robert M. La Follette, but the decision of former President Theodore Roosevelt to run leads to the establishment of the new Progressive Party (the Bull Moose Party) in 1912, splitting the Republicans. The conservative Republican candidate is William Howard Taft.

The Angel Island immigration station receives direct telephone service from San Francisco, California, and the immigration service ferry, *Angel Island* is launched at Alameda.

The United States Joint Commission on Immigration, also called the Dillingham Commission after its chairman, Senator William P. Dillingham, issues a multi-volume report purporting to demonstrate the inferiority of immigrant "races" and blaming them for a variety of problems.

By this time, the Woman's Christian Temperance Union has 245,000 members in the United States. This makes it the largest women's organization in the country.

The women's suffrage movement sees a major victory as California state law gives women the right to vote.

Dr. Franz Boas, a professor of anthropology at Columbia University in New York City, denies the inherent superiority of any race in *The Mind of Primitive Man*.

A fire at the Triangle Shirtwaist Company in New York City kills almost 150 people, most of them seamstresses who are trapped in the building. This event brings national attention to the conditions of sweatshops in America and is an impetus for workplace reform.

Frank W. Woolworth incorporates the F. W. Woolworth Company, with more than 1,000 stores. The Woolworth building is finished in New York City two years later.

The Connecticut College for Women is founded at New London.

Charles F. Kettering invents the first practical electric self-starter for cars.

Sir Robert L. Borden, a Conservative/Unionist, becomes prime minister of Canada after the term of Sir Wilfred Laurier (1896). Borden serves until 1920.

A total of 350,000 immigrants enter Canada, including approximately 144,000 from Britain and 131,000 from the United States.

The federal Weeks Act names New Hampshire's White Mountains as a national forest.

After the Mexican Revolution, Porfirio Díaz (1876, 1884) is replaced by Francisco Madero as president of Mexico. Madero serves until 1913.

Spectacular remains of the ancient Incan community of Machu Picchu in Peru are found by an American expedition led by archaeologist Hiram Bingham.

Chile and Peru break off diplomatic relations because Chile has begun to colonize the Tacna and Arica areas in violation of the terms of the Treaty of Ancón.

José Batlle y Ordóñez (1903) is elected president of Uruguay. He serves until 1915.

1911-1920

Immigration to the United States totals more than 5.74 million, of which 4.32 million come from Europe, 247,200 from Asia, 8,400 from Africa, 13,400 from Oceania, 1.1 million from the Americas and 1,100 are not specifically identified.

1912

New Mexico and Arizona join the Union as the 47th and 48th states, respectively.

Hadassah, the Women's Zionist Organization of America, is founded by Henrietta Szold. Active in helping refugees relocate to Israel, this group's main activities in the United States are in education and related youth needs.

The "Bread and Roses" strike among East Coast textile workers is organized by Elizabeth Gurley Flynn.

Alaska becomes a territory of the United States.

Women's right to vote is granted by state laws in Arizona, Kansas and Oregon.

The Girl Scouts of America is founded at Savannah, Georgia, by Juliette Gordon Low. The headquarters moves to New York City the next year.

The volcano of Mount Katmai, in Alaska, erupts and creates the Valley of Ten Thousand Smokes.

American inventor Glen Hammond Curtiss develops a seaplane. He is known for his earlier speed flight from Albany to New York City in 150 minutes.

The Canadian provinces of Manitoba, Ontario and Quebec are extended to Hudson Bay, giving them their present shapes.

When the Nicaraguan government falls behind in its payments on bank loans, the United States sends troops to intervene, protecting the interests of the American banks, and averting a potential civil war.

The election of Eduardo Schaerer as president of Paraguay brings stability to that country's government.

Middle class protesters in Argentina unite and form the Civic Union, which demands more equitable government. This group's success marks the beginning of a series of political challenges from working class groups. Protest activities are a major factor in enactment of the Sáenz Peña Law of 1912, guaranteeing universal secret male suffrage.

c. 1912

Construction is completed on the Lincoln Highway, the United States' first transcontinental automobile highway, which runs from New York to San Francisco.

1913

Woodrow Wilson becomes the 28th president of the United States; Thomas R. Marshall is vice president. Both are Democrats.

The Sixteenth Amendment to the United States Constitution is ratified. It grants Congress the authority to levy and collect taxes on incomes, from whatever source derived, without apportionment among the states and without regard to any census or enumeration. The Seventeenth Amendment is also ratified, establishing direct popular election of United States senators.

Congress creates the Federal Reserve System to regulate the American banking industry. Congress also passes the Underwood Tariff Act, named for sponsor Oscar W. Underwood, which significantly reduces tariffs on many foreign imports.

Mount Mary College is founded at Milwaukee, Wisconsin.

The Moorish-American Science Temple in Newark, New Jersey is founded by Timothy Drew. He teaches Islamic principles as he understands them, and is the first to suggest that African Americans can unite under these principles. Drew changes his name to Noble Drew Ali.

Five thousand marchers and 20,000 bystanders assemble in Washington, D.C., for a women's suffrage parade organized by Alice Paul.

In their first state victory east of the Mississippi River, women gain the right to vote in Illinois.

Authorities in San Antonio, Texas, have the Alamo restored and designated as a historic monument.

Garment workers strike in New York City and Boston; they are successful in gaining pay raises and shorter workdays.

Henry Ford's automobile factory in Detroit, Michigan, enhances the assembly line manufacturing process with the addition of the moving conveyor belt.

Russian-born American Igor I. Sikorsky constructs and pilots the first multimotored plane and pioneers the development of helicopter flight.

The Squaw Man, the first full-length film produced in Hollywood, California, is released.

Forces of Victoriano Huerta stage a bloody coup in Mexico in which President Francisco Madero (1911) and his brother are murdered. Huerta seizes power and rules until 1914. In response to the violence, the United States government places a trade embargo against Mexico.

Felix Ortega and his followers wage a two-year war in the mountains of Baja against Mexican authorities. Although unsuccessful, the uprising helps pave the way for the Constitution of 1917 and a redefinition of civil liberties in Mexico.

Mario García Menocal becomes president of Cuba after the term of José Miguel Gómez (1909). Menocal is re-elected in 1916 and serves until 1921.

A permanent civil government is established in the Panama Canal Zone by executive order of United States President Woodrow Wilson.

1913-1914

Flooding in Ohio results in more than 350 deaths, prompting Congress to act on flood control measures.

1914

The United States Congress sets up the Federal Trade Commission and passes the Clayton Antitrust Act, both designed to help regulate the activities of large corporations. The Clayton Act authorizes peaceful picketing and prohibits exclusive sales contracts, intercorporate stock holdings and unfair price cutting to eliminate competition. Congress also passes the Smith-Lever Act to provide federal funds to state schools.

World War I begins (*see* "The World, 1914-1918, World War I").

The Six Nations of the Iroquois Confederacy in the United States declare war on Germany.

Women in Montana and Nevada gain the right to vote.

The Canadian passenger steamer *Empress of Ireland* is sunk in a collision with the Norwegian ship *Storstad* in the Gulf of St. Lawrence. More than 1,000 lives are lost.

As initial surveys begin for the Alaska Railroad, the town of Anchorage develops from a construction camp.

More than 75 percent of the automobiles in use in the United States are manufactured in Michigan.

The western section of Canada's Grand Trunk Pacific Railway is completed in British Columbia.

United States Marines occupy Vera Cruz, Mexico, intervening in the civil war to protect American interests. This incident forces President Huerta (1913) to resign. Venustiano Carranza becomes president of Mexico. He serves until 1920.

The Panama Canal officially opens. George Washington Goethals is governor of the Canal Zone until 1916.

Buenos Aires, Argentina, is host to a large European immigrant population, and reports say that 30 percent of the city's residents are foreign-born. European immigrants also make up a significant population group in São Paulo, Brazil.

1915

The United States population passes 100 million people.

The first American transcontinental telephone conversation is held, between Alexander Graham Bell in New York City and Dr. Thomas A. Watson in San Francisco, California.

The United States Revenue Cutter Service School of Instruction in New London, Connecticut, changes its name to the United States Coast Guard Academy.

The Ku Klux Klan (KKK), a new organization, is formed by William J. Simmons and holds its first meeting in Stone Mountain, Georgia. It is far more radical than its predecessor (1866) and its platform of "white supremacy" and extreme nativism gives it a wider base than just the South.

1910

through

1919

1910

through

1919

The National Birth Control League is founded in the United States. Also this year, Margaret Sanger leads in establishing the nation's first birth control clinic, in New York City. The police close the clinic and arrest Sanger, who receives a 30-day jail sentence.

The Ford Motor Company introduces a diesel version of the tractor, which will increase agricultural output. Ford also announces a policy of paying factory workers top scale under the theory that the workers will be more productive and will not turn to unions for support.

Alabama's cotton crop is severely damaged by boll weevils.

1915-1934

United States military forces occupy Haiti and establish an interim government until political and economic stability is achieved.

1916

The United States Congress expands the nation's armed forces; it also passes the Federal Farm Loan Act, which establishes new banks to provide loans to American farmers. The National Park Service is founded as a bureau of the United States Department of the Interior.

The National Defense Act goes into force in the United States, providing that the National Guard may be called into federal service to cover emergency situations.

The Federal Highway Act of this year initiates federal aid for highway construction.

Louis Dembitz Brandeis is sworn in as the first Jewish American justice on the United States Supreme Court. He serves until 1939.

United States forces led by General John J. Pershing enter Mexico in pursuit of Francisco "Pancho" Villa, who led a raid into New Mexico in retaliation for United States support of his rival, Carranza. Villa is not caught, but relations between the two countries are further damaged.

Jeanette Rankin, a Republican from Montana, becomes the first woman elected to the United States Congress. She serves from 1917 to 1919, and again from 1941 to 1943. A staunch advocate of peace, Rankin is the only member of Congress who votes against America's entry into both world wars.

An act of Congress gives United States railroad workers the eight-hour day.

An explosion at a munitions dock on Black Tom Island, off the coast of Jersey City, New Jersey, causes more than $20 million in damage. It is believed to have been triggered by German saboteurs.

Labor activist Thomas J. Mooney is arrested, tried and sentenced to death for his participation in bomb killings during the San Francisco Preparedness Day parade. Many feel his trial is unfair, and Mooney is pardoned by California Governor Culbert Olson in 1939.

The Passing of the Great Race in America, written by noted naturalist Madison Grant, is published. This book becomes popular, and fuels nativist sentiment in the United States.

Anarchist leader Emma Goldman is arrested in New York City for publicly advocating birth control.

The Canadian province of Manitoba grants women political equality, including the right to vote. Women also are enfranchised in Saskatchewan.

Mexico adopts a liberal constitution.

Hipólito Irigoyen, representing labor and working-class interests, becomes president of Argentina. He serves until 1922, and again from 1928 to 1930.

1916-1924

After several years of political and economic instability in the Dominican Republic, United States forces intervene and establish a provisional government.

1917

Woodrow Wilson begins a second term as president of the United States; Thomas R. Marshall is vice president. Both are Democrats. Wilson was re-elected with the slogan, "he kept us out of the war."

Congress passes the Selective Service Act. President Woodrow Wilson delivers his "peace without victory" speech and the United States declares war on Germany. The first American destroyers land at Queenstown, Ireland; and the American Expeditionary Force under General John J. Pershing arrives in Paris. United States entry into the war is justified by: Germany's failure to honor the rights of neutral countries; the sinking of neutral merchant and passenger ships, the most famous being the British oceanliner *Lusitania*; the closeness many Americans feel toward Britain and France; and reaction to the Zimmerman Note, a document sent by Germany to Mexico but intercepted by the United States. The note stated that if America enters the war, Mexico should attack the United States and Germany would help Mexico regain lost lands — specifically New Mexico, Arizona, Texas and parts of California.

Congress enacts a law, over President Wilson's veto, to require that prospective immigrants pass a literacy test as a basis of entry. The statute also increases the inadmissible classes by barring those coming for immoral purposes, chronic alcoholics, stowaways, vagrants, and those with at least one attack of insanity. The law also includes a provision excluding Asians and Pacific Islanders by creating an Asiatic Barred Zone — a geographic area from which no immigrants would be admitted. Filipinos, considered to be United States nationals, are exempt from this geographic restriction.

More than 200 women marchers are arrested in Washington, D.C., during a parade in support of the constitutional amendment that would give them the vote. When some of those arrested begin a fast, they are force-fed; this creates a lot of favorable and sympathetic publicity for them. At the gates of the White House, some of the marchers who were not arrested establish a "silent vigil" that continues for 18 months.

State laws give women the right to vote in Arkansas, Connecticut, Nebraska, New York and North Dakota.

American attitude in general is redefined in light of Russia's Bolshevik Revolution. Reform-oriented organizations are suspected of being anti-American, among them those that seek better protection for women in the form of birth control access and more equitable divorce laws.

The United States obtains the Virgin Islands, formerly part of the Danish West Indies, from Denmark for $25 million. The country's inhabitants are mostly of African descent, but also include more than 3,000 Danes.

Frank Little, an organizer of the Industrial Workers of the World (IWW), is lynched in Butte, Montana.

Postage for a first-class letter in the United States is three cents.

The National Hockey League is formed. Hockey probably originated in Canada, and was brought to the United States by immigrating French Canadians.

The University of Alaska is founded at Fairbanks.

Canada experiences its worst maritime disaster when a French munitions ship and a Belgian relief vessel collide in the narrowest part of Halifax Harbor, Nova Scotia. The resulting explosion causes over 1,800 deaths and the destruction of most of the city of Halifax.

Helen Emma MacGill is appointed as Canada's first woman judge.

THE AMERICAS	THE AMERICAS	THE AMERICAS	FOR CLASSROOM USE	

The Mexican Constitution of 1917 is adopted under the leadership of President Carranza. It forbids foreign ownership of land near the borders or seacoasts and reserves mineral rights for Mexico. This eventually leads to more United States-Mexico conflict and demands for intervention by American property holders and oil and mining companies. With the exception of the boom in Mexico's oil exports, the country's economy is slow to recover.

Brazil and Cuba side with the Allied forces in World War I.

Emiliano Chamorro becomes president of Nicaragua. He serves until 1920 and again in 1926.

1918

President Wilson publicly supports the women's suffrage amendment.

Congress passes the Espionage Act that forbids citizens from speaking out against the United States or the war effort. Eugene V. Debs is convicted of violating the act and is sentenced to 10 years in prison, a sentence later reduced by President Warren G. Harding.

The Passport Act becomes law. It prevents arrival in or departure from the United States without authorized documents; requires visiting foreigners to obtain visas; and begins overseas screening of aliens for visas. The federal Anarchist Act, providing for the deportation of alien radicals, becomes law and about 250 people are deported.

In an address to Congress, President Wilson outlines his "Fourteen Points" as a means of establishing a lasting peace.

A War Industries Board is established to supply United States military needs. It is headed by Bernard Mannes Baruch.

State laws in Michigan, Oklahoma, South Dakota and Texas give women the right to vote.

The participation of the United States in World War I increases nativist sentiment. Several states adopt "English only" regulations in their public schools.

A worldwide influenza epidemic strikes; it causes almost 500,000 deaths in the United States alone during the next two years.

The Alaska Agricultural College and School of Mines is established by Congress as a land grant college; it opens in 1922.

Douglass College, part of Rutgers University, is founded at New Brunswick, New Jersey.

The Canada Elections Act gives women the right to vote in national elections.

1919

The Eighteenth Amendment to the United States Constitution is ratified, prohibiting the manufacture, sale or transportation of intoxicating liquors. Although many citizens voted for this amendment for health reasons and a desire to use the grain to feed soldiers, this ban, which takes effect in 1920, creates extensive illegal manufacture and sale (bootlegging) of alcohol from Canada and the West Indies, the opening of private clubs (speakeasies), large scale home manufacture of alcoholic beverages and a new wave of criminals who specialize in the illegal alcohol market. The Volsted Act, enabling enforcement of prohibition, becomes law.

The Treaty of Versailles, the major agreement ending World War I (see "The World, 1919"), incorporates President Wilson's draft covenant for a League of Nations. However, opposition to the League of Nations, led by Senator Henry Cabot Lodge, is so strong that Congress does not ratify the treaty. Congress formally ends United States involvement in the war by declaration in 1921.

In preparation for passage of the women's suffrage amendment to the United States Constitution, the League of Women Voters is proposed by Carrie Chapman, to prepare and educate women for their new privilege and responsibility as voters. Chapman is president of the National American Woman Suffrage Association.

Grand Canyon National Park is established by the United States Congress.

The American Legion is founded in Paris, France. Its constitution is adopted later this year in St. Louis, Missouri.

More than 300,000 steelworkers walk off their jobs across the United States to protest their seven-day workweek and the owners' refusal to allow them to unionize. Other strikes occur in garment and textile, railroad, telegraph and telephone industries.

United States women professionals, a group slowly increasing in numbers, begin to form their own professional organizations, since they are barred from participation in many men's groups. In 1919 these women's groups unite to form the National Federation of Business and Professional Women's Clubs.

State laws give women the right to vote in Indiana, Iowa, Maine, Minnesota, Missouri, Ohio, Tennessee and Wisconsin.

A group of Boston policemen who joined the American Federation of Labor are fired by the police commissioner; the city's entire police force strikes. Calvin Coolidge, then governor of Massachusetts, calls in the National Guard to keep peace, and fires all striking officers.

Radio Corporation of America (RCA) is founded by Owen D. Young.

Anarchist Emma Goldman is deported from the United States despite her American citizenship. Goldman has lectured for the full emancipation of women.

Uruguay adopts a new constitution. Containing policies proposed by President José Batlle y Ordóñez, it limits the authority of the presidency.

Augusto Bernardino Leguía (1908) again becomes president of Peru. He serves until 1930.

1919-1933

The state of Maryland acquires the nickname, "the free state" by refusing to enforce prohibition.

THE AMERICAS	THE AMERICAS	THE AMERICAS		1910 through 1919

THE WORLD	THE WORLD	THE WORLD	THE WORLD

1910 through 1919

1910

The Union of South Africa is formed by the former British colonies of Cape of Good Hope and Natal and the Republics of the Orange Free State (Orange River colony) and the Transvaal. The new nation becomes a member of the British Commonwealth. The common law of Holland is still recognized, and Afrikaans and English are the official languages.

The resignation of Ito Hirobumi, Japan's first resident-general of the Protectorate of Korea (Chōsen), leads to Japan's annexation of Korea, a control that continues until 1945. Japan and Russia agree on the division of sections of northeast China into their respective spheres of influence.

The French Congo is reorganized and renamed French Equatorial Africa.

China abolishes slavery.

The Anglo-Bhutanese Treaty is signed; under its terms, Britain subsidizes Bhutan's economy in exchange for the right to control Bhutanese foreign affairs.

A revolution takes place in Portugal. King Manuel II (1908) abandons the throne, the nation is declared a republic, and Teófilo Braga becomes president. He serves until 1911.

George V becomes king of Great Britain and Ireland after the death of his father, Edward VII (1901). George V rules until 1936.

Rama VI becomes king of Siam (Thailand) after the reign of Rama V (1868). Rama VI rules until 1925.

Nicholas I declares himself king of the independent Balkan kingdom of Montenegro. He rules until 1918.

Louis Botha becomes the first prime minister of the Union of South Africa. He serves until 1919.

Andrew Fisher (1908) again becomes prime minister of Australia after the term of Alfred Deakins (1903, 1905, 1909). Fisher serves until 1913.

A team led by British archeologist Arthur Evans excavates the ancient ruins of Knossos on the island of Crete.

In Germany, the Socialist Women's International, under the leadership of Klara Zetkin, designates March 8 as International Women's Day.

French scientist Marie Sklodowska Curie, with the assistance of André Debierne, isolates metallic radium in France.

1911

The Agadir crisis is created by the arrival of the German gunboat, *Panther,* in Morocco's seaport of Agadir. At the Convention of Berlin, Germany agrees to French control over Morocco and is compensated with territory in French Equatorial Africa.

In China, the Manchu government is overthrown by the revolutionary movement of Dr. Sun Yat-sen. Emperor Xuantong (1908) abdicates and a new republic is formed.

Outer Mongolia becomes an autonomous region after Mongol chieftains overthrow the Chinese Manchu government controlling that territory. However, in 1919, Chinese forces reoccupy the region and impose Chinese rule.

The United States, Great Britain, Canada, Russia and Japan sign a joint agreement protecting sea otters and limiting the hunting of fur seals.

The Northern Territory separates from South Australia and comes under direct authority of the Commonwealth of Australia.

Widespread strikes occur in Britain due to famine and generally poor business conditions that result in layoffs.

During the Tripolitan War, Italy is the first nation to use aircraft as offensive weapons. Italian forces defeat the Turks and through the 1912 Treaty of Ouchy Italy gains control over Tripoli, Libya and Rhodes. Italian authorities reorganize the area into the colonies of Tripolitania and Cirenaica (now Libya).

Anton Herman Fokker, born in Java, constructs aircraft factories in Germany and begins work on bi- and triplanes. His planes will be used by the Germans in World War I. Fokker emigrates to the United States in 1922 and is later naturalized as an American citizen.

Norwegian explorer Roald Amundsen, with a two-dog sled and skis, is the first person to reach the South Pole.

1912

Sun Yat-sen becomes president of the new Chinese Republic and forms the Kuomintang (Nationalist Party). However, within a few weeks he transfers power to General Yuan Shikai (Yüan Shih-k'ai). Yuan Shikai serves until his death in 1916.

Albania declares its independence from the crumbling Ottoman Empire.

Morocco is divided between France and Spain, with France obtaining 90 percent of the region as a protectorate.

The SS *Titanic* of the White Star Line sinks after hitting an iceberg in the North Atlantic while on its maiden voyage to Europe. More than 1,500 people die, many because of a scarcity of lifeboats.

Tibetan troops remove Chinese forces from Lhasa, the country's "Forbidden City."

The South African Native National Congress (NNC) is formed. It later becomes the African National Congress (ANC).

The Third Home Rule Bill for Ireland is introduced in Britain's parliament. This bill would eventually place Irish police forces strictly in Ireland's control. Ulster residents — Protestants — fear domination by the country's Catholic majority, and raise a protest. The private police force, the Ulster Volunteers, is raised. This organization is soon followed by a parallel Catholic police force, the Irish Volunteers, in the south.

Christian X, brother of King Haakon VII (1905) of Norway, becomes king of Denmark after the death of his father, Frederick VIII (1906). Christian X rules until 1947. He also rules as king of Iceland until 1944.

Yoshihito becomes emperor of Japan after the death of his father, Mutsuhito (Meiji Tenno, 1867-1868). Yoshihito rules until 1926.

English biochemist Sir Frederick Hopkins is credited with the discovery of vitamins, which he calls "accessory food factors."

T. MacKenzie, a Liberal, becomes prime minister of New Zealand. W. F. Massey, of the Reform party, follows MacKenzie this same year.

1912-1913

The Balkan Wars result from territorial disputes over former Ottoman lands. In the first war, Turkish forces are defeated by those of the Balkan League, an alliance of Bulgaria, Serbia, Greece and Montenegro; the London peace treaty of 1913 partitions most of European Turkey among the victors. In the second war, Bulgarian troops attack Serbia and Greece and are defeated after Romania, Greece and Turkey intervene. The conflicts are resolved by the Treaty of Bucharest that partitions the Balkans and strips Bulgaria of most of its territorial gains, the Treaty of Constantinople between Bulgaria and Turkey and the Convention of Athens between Turkey and Greece. This fighting further weakens Turkey and heightens nationalism in eastern European countries.

1913

Crete is annexed by Greece.

The former Ottoman province of Macedonia is divided among Greece, Serbia and Bulgaria.

The Natives Land Act becomes law in South Africa, limiting land ownership by native Africans to territory in the outlying areas.

Women in Norway gain the right to vote.

THE WORLD	THE WORLD	THE WORLD	FOR CLASSROOM USE	

Constantine I becomes king of Greece after the death of his father, George I (1863). Constantine I rules until he is forced to abdicate in 1917. He again takes the throne in 1920, ruling until 1922.

Lij Yasu becomes emperor of Ethiopia after the death of Menelik II (1889). Lij Yasu rules until 1916.

(Sir) Joseph Cook becomes prime minister of Australia after the term of Andrew Fisher (1908, 1910). Cook serves until 1914.

Louis III becomes king of Bavaria after Otto I (1886) is deposed. Louis III, the last king of Bavaria, rules until 1918.

Mohandas Gandhi leads a group of Indians on a march into the Transvaal region of South Africa. Although arrested for his nonviolent protest, he forces the South African government to relax its discrimination against Hindus.

c. 1913

In Germany, Hans Geiger invents the radiation detector that now bears his name, the Geiger counter. An earlier, less reliable model was developed by English physicist Sir Ernest Rutherford c. 1906.

1914

Northern and southern Nigeria are united as a single colony of Britain, and Egypt becomes a British protectorate. Except for Ethiopia and Liberia, all of Africa is under European control.

New Zealand takes Western Samoa from German control.

Archduke Francis (Franz) Ferdinand, heir to the throne of Austria, is assassinated at Sarajevo, Bosnia, by Serbian nationalist Gavrilo Princip (Prinzip). This event begins World War I (see "The World, 1914-1918, World War I").

Irish Home Rule becomes law through the Government of Ireland Act, but Britain's House of Commons adds the provision that Ulster may be excluded from Home Rule for six years. In what comes to be called the Curragh Incident, many British troops in Ireland resign rather than have to enforce Home Rule in Protestant Ulster. Extensive gun-running operations are conducted by both Catholic groups and Protestant resistance factions. As World War I begins, the Home Rule issue is tabled.

Mohandas Gandhi returns to India from South Africa to practice law and promote his belief in nonviolent resistance to social injustices.

Kuwait's independence and sovereignty are acknowledged by Britain.

Australian forces occupy northeastern New Guinea.

Ferdinand becomes king of Romania after the death of his uncle, Carol I (1866, 1881). Ferdinand rules until 1927.

Hussein Kamil becomes *khedive* (viceroy) of Egypt after Abbas II (1892) is deposed. Hussein Kamil rules until 1917.

Andrew Fisher (1908, 1910) again becomes prime minister of Australia after the term of (Sir) Joseph Cook (1913). Fisher serves until 1915.

1915

Denmark's new constitution creates a two-house parliament elected by general vote of the people.

The United States government protests German submarine actions, specifically the sinking of the British oceanliner *Lusitania* off the coast of Ireland. Nearly 1,200 lives are lost, including 128 United States citizens. The incident adds to a growing sentiment that the United States should enter the war against Germany; as a result, America lends $500 million to France and Britain to aid their war efforts.

Japan presents China with a list of "21 Demands," among which are long-term leases on Japanese-controlled territory in Manchuria and Inner Mongolia, control over formerly German-dominated Shantung, interests in various Chinese industries and a promise by China not to lease or cede any part of her coast to foreign interests. China accepts the demands but refuses to become a full protectorate of Japan.

The first Women's Peace Congress meets in the Hague. As a result of this gathering, the Women's International League for Peace and Freedom is formed.

Chinese forces regain control of Mongolia.

In an unprecedented act of genocide, an estimated 600,000 Armenians are massacred by Turkish forces.

Nearly 30,000 people die as the result of an earthquake in Avezzano, Italy.

c. 1915

Albert Einstein formulates his "General Theory of Relativity" in Germany.

1916

The Easter Rebellion against British rule takes place in Dublin, Ireland. It is quickly suppressed by British troops, and many of the Irish leaders are eventually executed. However, the dispersed Irish nationalists gradually reunite and later form the Irish Republican Army (IRA) with Michael Collins as their leader. The IRA uses guerrilla warfare and terrorism to oppose British rule.

The death of China's Yuan Shikai (Yüan Shih-k'ai, 1911) marks the beginning of the rise to power of local warlords.

Husein ibn Ali, the chief magistrate of Mecca and Colonel T. E. Lawrence (Lawrence of Arabia) of Britain work together to expel Ottoman forces from Arabia and establish the independent territory of the Hejaz.

The Sykes-Picot Agreement, a secret plan by Britain and France to partition Turkey, is formulated.

1910

through

1919

1914-1918

World War I

Rivalries over control of lands in Africa, trade markets in Asia and China and protection of existing borders lead to the "Great War" between the Central Powers (Austria-Hungary, Germany, Bulgaria and Turkey) and the Allies (United States, Britain, France, Russia, Belgium, Serbia, Greece, Romania, Montenegro, Portugal, Italy and Japan).

1914, Europe. On June 28, 1914, Austrian Archduke Francis (Franz) Ferdinand, heir to the throne of the Austro-Hungarian Empire, and his wife are assassinated in Sarajevo, Bosnia, by Serbian nationalist Gavrilo Princip (Prinzip). Austria-Hungary declares war on Serbia on July 28. Within a few days, Germany declares war on Russia, and then France, and invades Belgium. Britain and Belgium declare war on Germany. Russian troops defeat German forces at Gumbinnen, Germany. French troops unsuccessfully attack Lorraine and then suffer heavy losses in mid-August at the Battle of the Frontiers. The German army under Field Marshal Paul von Hindenburg defeats Russian forces in the Battle of Tannenberg (then in Germany) on the Eastern Front in August. The German military strategy, the Schlieffen Plan, is designed to encircle France by cutting through neutral Belgium. The German army marches across Belgium and at the first Battle of the Marne in September, the German drive is stopped 25 miles from Paris. Germany's African colonial territories are under Allied control by mid-September. In November, Britain, France and Russia declare war on Turkey after the Turkish fleet has attacked Russian seaports. The Battle of Ypres (Ieper), which lasts almost the full month of November, halts the German advance. The Battle of Crakow, which begins in mid-November, produces heavy losses on both sides, but little strategic advantage. By year's end, the war on the Western Front (France) is "positional" trench warfare running from the English Channel to Switzerland.

1914, Africa, Asia and the Americas. On August 26, 1914, British and French troops defeat German colonial forces and partition Germany's African colonies. Japan declares war on Germany on August 23 and on Austria-Hungary two days later, seizing German interests in China. A German fleet defeats the British off the coast of Chile in early November but the British recover in December with a victory in the Falkland Islands.

1915, Europe. In 1915 Sir Douglas Haig takes command of British forces. The German submarine blockade of Great Britain begins in February. In the Dardanelles campaign British forces try unsuccessfully to run the strait and seize Constantinople. In April British forces land in Turkey for a second attempt, but are forced to withdraw from Gallipoli at the end of the year. The German military uses chlorine poison gas at the second Battle of Ypres. Italy enters the war in May with an attack on Austria. When nearly 1,200 people die, 128 of them United States citizens, in the sinking of the *Lusitania* ocean liner in May, America considers entering the war. Italy declares war on Turkey in August. On the Eastern Front (Russia), the German and Austro-Hungarian "great offensive" under Field Marshal August von Mackensen and Hindenburg conquers all of Poland and Lithuania; 1 million Russians die in the fighting by September 6. The "Great Fall Offensive" by the Allies during September and October results in little change from 1914. Bulgaria declares war and joins Austria-Hungary and Germany in a successful attack on Serbia; Britain, France, Russia and Italy then declare war on Bulgaria in October.

1915, Africa and Asia. South African troops attack German positions in Swakopmund in German South West Africa in January and by May, have taken control of Winhhoek, capital of the colony. By July all German forces have surrendered to the South African army commanded by Louis Botha. In September British forces attack Turkish troops in Mesopotamia.

1916, Europe. In early 1916 the Germans and French each lose approximately 350,000 men at the Battle of Verdun in France. Extensive submarine warfare begins in March. The sea battle of Jutland between Britain and Germany, started May 31, is considered a British victory although Britain suffers the heavier losses; however, the German fleet never ventures forth again. On the Eastern Front, the Brusilov offensive demoralizes the Russians and costs them 1 million people. At the Battle of the Somme (river in France), which lasts from July to November, the British lose more than 400,000 men; the French, 200,000; and the Germans, about 450,000; all with no strategic results. Romania declares war on Austria-Hungary in late August and the Greek fleet surrenders to the Allies at Athens in October. On November 16 Poland receives recognition from Germany and Austria-Hungary as an independent country; however, German forces occupy Poland. Bucharest, Romania, is captured by the Central Powers in December.

1916, Africa and Middle East. Allied forces complete their occupation of the German Cameroons in February 1916. In April Turkish forces capture Kut-el-Amara in Iraq from the British. In June Arab and British fighting units join forces to remove Turkish control from the area, and German positions in East Africa are attacked by troops under Jan Smuts. In September British troops capture Dar es Salaam (Tanganyika), at the time the capital of German East Africa.

1917, Europe. The Russian revolutions of March and October seriously demoralize the Russian army. On April 6 the United States declares war on Germany after Germany announces it will begin unrestricted submarine warfare. Submarine warfare is at its peak in April. On the Southern Front (Italy), Italian forces retreat from the Battle of Caporetto, losing 600,000 people as prisoners and deserters from October to December. On the Western Front, the Battles of Arras and Champagne (both in France) and the third Battle of Ypres take place. The first large British tank attack begins in November. On December 7 the United States declares war on Austria-Hungary. An armistice is negotiated between the transitional Russian government and Germany on December 15.

1917, Africa, Asia and Middle East. British troops capture Baghdad, Iraq, in March. Arab forces led by British Colonel T. E. Lawrence attack a Turkish garrison and capture sections of the Hejaz railroad, weakening communication lines for the Turkish army. In August China declares war on Germany and Austria-Hungary. In October, the German offensive in East Africa is successful and German forces are victorious at the Battle of Mahiwa. The British victory over Turkish forces at Gaza and Jerusalem leads to the Balfour Declaration to establish a Jewish homeland in Palestine.

1918, Europe. The Treaty of Brest-Litovsk on March 3, 1918, among Russia, Austria-Hungary and Germany, removes Russia from the war. In the spring of 1918 a great German offensive is led by Hindenburg and General Erich Ludendorff. At Château-Thierry in northern France, American troops engage in their first important fighting role, joining the French under Marshal Ferdinand Foch to stop the German advance. The second Battle of the Marne in July and August is followed by the successful Allied offensive in France, with fights at Amiens and St. Mihiel. The Battles of the Argonne and Ypres, also in France, panic German leadership, which then asks for an armistice in early October following mutinies and unrest in many major cities. German Kaiser Wilhelm II abdicates in November and hostilities cease on the Western Front.

1918, Asia and Middle East. Japanese troops move on Siberia in August. The British offensive against Turkish forces begins in Palestine in September. By October a united British and Arab force captures Damascus. Britain and Turkey sign an armistice in October. German forces surrender all positions in Northern Rhodesia in November.

Worldwide, more than 8 million people die during the war, including 112,000 Americans, and 2 million are wounded worldwide. Three empires — the Ottoman, the Austro-Hungarian and the Russian — are ended.

1910

through

1919

By the terms of the Lucknow Pact, the Indian National Congress and the All India Muslim League agree to cooperate on the issue of home rule in India.

Qatar becomes a British protectorate.

Belgian troops occupy Rwanda. By a League of Nations mandate, Belgium receives protectorship over the Territory of Rwanda-Urundi (now the separate nations of Rwanda and Burundi).

The state of Czechoslovakia, formed from the lands of Bohemia, Moravia and Slovakia and including 3 million ethnic Germans, declares its independence from the Austro-Hungarian Empire. Czech nationalists Tomáŝ G. Masaryk and Edvard Beneŝ, along with other Czech and Slovak leaders, come together in Paris and establish the Czechoslovak National Council. This group seeks Allied acknowledgement as the country's government in exile. In 1918 this provisional government is officially recognized. Masaryk assumes the presidency. He governs until 1935.

Romania declares war on Hungary and invades Transylvania. In late September Hungarian forces launch a counteroffensive, and Romania is defeated.

Charles I becomes emperor of Austria after the death of his great uncle, Francis Joseph I (1848). Charles I rules until 1918. He also rules Hungary as Charles IV.

Judith, daughter of Menelik II (1889), becomes empress of Ethiopia after Lij Yasu (1913) is deposed. She reigns until 1930.

David Lloyd George, a Liberal, forms a coalition government and becomes prime minister of Great Britain. He serves until 1922.

1917

William Morris Hughes becomes prime minister of Australia after the term of Andrew Fisher (1914). Hughes serves until 1924.

Czechoslovakia gains independence from Russia.

Finland takes advantage of the collapse of Russia's csarist government and declares its independence.

British Foreign Secretary Arthur Balfour issues a letter explaining that the British government favors the creation of a Jewish state in Palestine.

Alexander becomes king of Greece after his father, Constantine (1913), is forced to abdicate under Allied pressure. Alexander rules until 1920.

1917-1920

In the March Revolution in Russia, Czar Nicholas II (1894) is overthrown, ending a long period of unrest. A moderate provisional government is created and Aleksandr Kerensky becomes prime minister. His willingness to remain in World War I and inattention to economic conditions at home cause his government to weaken. In the October Revolution, the Bolsheviks seize power in an armed coup d'état led by Vladimir Ilyich Lenin and Leon Trotsky. Kerensky escapes to Paris. Civil war erupts in Russia between the Reds (Bolsheviks) and Whites (Mensheviks), and in 1918 Nicholas II and his family are executed. Due to superior organization, the Reds are victorious by 1920 and a new ruling council is established with Lenin as chairman.

1918

Women who are heads of households and over the age of 30 are given the right to vote in Britain.

A worldwide influenza epidemic strikes; by 1920, nearly 20 million people are dead.

The Treaty of Brest-Litovsk, negotiated among Leon Trotsky for Russia, Richard von Kühlmann for Germany and Count Ottokar Czernin for Austria-Hungary, ends the conflict between Russia and the Central Powers. Russia gives up all claims to Estonia, Latvia, Finland, Lithuania, Poland and the Ukraine. Once the war ends later this year, Germany and Russia both renounce this treaty.

The Kingdom of the Serbs (which includes Montenegro, Bosnia and Herzegovina), Croats and Slovenes comes into existence. Peter I, king of Serbia, is named king of the new country. He rules until 1921.

Iceland gains further independence from Denmark; Latvia declares its independence from Russia; Poland gains its independence, though its borders are still in dispute; Romania gains control of Izmail (Ismail) from the Russians; Armenia gains its independence but remains strongly influenced by Russia and Turkey.

In general elections in Northern Ireland, the Sinn Fein movement sweeps the board in areas outside Ulster.

A revolution overthrows the German monarchy. The socialist faction takes control and establishes the Weimar Republic.

Turkish forces withdraw from Yemen, and the country becomes independent.

French forces occupy Lebanon.

Strong opposition to Hapsburg rule in Hungary forces Emperor Charles I (1916) to renounce his throne. The independent countries of Hungary and Austria are formed. In Hungary a democratic revolution is victorious. The new republic has Mihály Károlyi as its head of state. New laws extend suffrage and establish freedom of the press.

Peasant women in Japan's countryside begin a series of uprisings. They loot and burn rice storehouses in reaction against greedy absentee landlords and rice vendors.

Polish independence is proclaimed. Jozef Pilsudski becomes the nation's leader.

Muhammad VI becomes Ottoman sultan after the death of his brother, Muhammad V (1909). Muhammad VI, the last sultan of the Ottoman lands, rules until 1922.

Boris III becomes czar of Bulgaria after the abdication of his father, Ferdinand I (1908). Boris III rules until 1943.

1910

through

1919

THE WORLD	THE WORLD	THE WORLD	FOR CLASSROOM USE

1910

through

1919

c. 1918

The government of the Netherlands begins plans to drain the Zuider Zee and create usable land, a program that will ultimately increase the country's size by almost 7 percent.

1918-1921

The Home Rule resistance movement in Ireland suffers a split over the issue of guerrilla warfare and terrorist strategy.

1919

At the Paris Peace Conference, negotiations for the end of World War I culminate in the Treaty of Versailles, one of the five treaties ending this war. Leaders at the conference include President Woodrow Wilson of the United States, Georges Clemenceau of France, Prime Minister David Lloyd George of Britain and Vittorio Emanuele Orlando of Italy. Incorporating President Wilson's draft Covenant of the League of Nations, the treaty is signed by the Allies (England, France and Italy) and Germany but is rejected by the United States Senate, which does not declare the war ended until 1921. At the talks, President Wilson does not wish to honor the secret treaties made during the war, and fights for his League of Nations concept. Territorially, Alsace and Lorraine are returned to France, as is control of the Saar region for 15 years; the former German colonies are to be governed by League mandates; Danzig becomes a free territory; Poland acquires most of West Prussia, which includes access to the Baltic Sea; and the Rhineland (region of Germany west of the Rhine River) is to be occupied for 15 years by an Allied force. The German army and navy are to be reduced in size and prohibited from constructing new weapons, and Germany is to pay reparations for war damages. Also, Albania's independence from Turkey is acknowledged.

The Treaty of Neuilly, France, another of the five treaties ending World War I, is signed between Bulgaria and the Allies. Bulgaria cedes territories to Greece and to the Kingdom of the Serbs, Croats and Slovenes. Bulgaria is also forced to reduce the size of its army.

The Treaty of Saint-Germain, France, the third of the five treaties ending World War I, is signed between the Allies and the newly created republic of Austria. It dissolves the Austro-Hungarian monarchy and recognizes the independent countries of Hungary; Czechoslovakia; Poland; and the Kingdom of the Serbs, Croats and Slovenes. Austria must reduce the size of its military force and may not enter into an alliance with Germany without permission of the League of Nations.

With assistance from British naval forces, Estonians overthrow their Soviet government; a democratic republic is declared.

After Afghan forces under *Emir* (Muslim prince or commander) Amanullah invade Britain's Indian holdings, Britain grants full independence to Afghanistan with the Treaty of Rawalpindi.

Vladimir Ilyich Lenin establishes the Third International (Comintern) in Moscow to further his revolutionary goals and to gain leadership in the socialist world.

The third *aliyah* (a heavy wave of Jewish immigration) to Palestine begins. It continues until 1923.

Finland adopts a new constitution by which the office of president is created.

In India, in an incident known as the Amritsar massacre, hundreds of Sikh nationalists are killed in an enclosed park by British troops under the command of General Reginald Dyer. The general is forced to resign his commission over the incident.

The Government of India Act passed by the British Parliament is designed to prepare India for self-rule. It places the government in the hands of a viceroy.

The Slovakian Soviet Republic is established, with its capital at Eperjes (today Prešov, Czech Republic).

Benito Mussolini is elected to Italy's Parliament. He begins to solidify his followers into the Fascist party.

The International Labor Organization (ILO) is created by the Versailles Treaty and is designed to improve labor conditions, social justice and a general standard of living. Originally affiliated with the League of Nations, in 1946 it becomes affiliated with the newly-established United Nations.

The May Fourth Movement, a student and teacher rebellion in Peking (Beijing), China, protests foreign interference and seeks greater democracy. The demonstrations grow into a movement which attacks the old political and moral system based on Confucianism, and advocates democracy, modern science, and equal rights for women.

A demonstration at the offices of Hungary's newspaper *Népszava* turns hostile. Béla Kun and other Communist Party leaders are arrested.

Jan Christian Smuts becomes prime minister of the Union of South Africa after the death of Louis Botha (1910). Smuts serves until 1924.

In China, after Zhao Wajie kills herself by slitting her throat while in the bridal chair on its way to her arranged wedding, Mao Zedong begins a vigorous campaign against such arranged marriages.

Amanullah becomes king of Afghanistan after the assassination of Habibullah (1901). Amanullah rules until 1929.

K. J. Stålberg becomes president of Finland. He serves until 1925.

Lady Nancy Witcher (Langhorne) Astor takes her seat as the first woman member of the British Parliament.

English pilots J. W. Alcock and A. Whitten Brown make the first nonstop airplane flight across the Atlantic Ocean, flying from Newfoundland to Ireland in under 17 hours.

FOR CLASSROOM USE	FOR CLASSROOM USE	FOR CLASSROOM USE	FOR CLASSROOM USE	
				1910 through **1919**
FOR CLASSROOM USE	FOR CLASSROOM USE	FOR CLASSROOM USE	FOR CLASSROOM USE	

NATIVE AMERICAN	NATIVE AMERICAN	AFRICAN AMERICAN	AFRICAN AMERICAN

1920 through 1929

NATIVE AMERICAN

1922

The controversial Bursum bill (named after its sponsor, Senator Holm O. Bursum of New Mexico), which would give European Americans homesteading rights on Pueblo lands in New Mexico, is the cause of the largest united opposition effort by the Pueblos in modern times. Public opinion turns to support the Indians, and the bill is never passed. One further result is that the Pueblo Land Board is established by Congress in 1924 to support Indian land rights.

Oil is discovered in the Hogback and Rattlesnake areas of the Navajo reservation in San Juan County, New Mexico.

1923

The reorganized Navajo Tribal Council holds its first meeting. Originally formed to ratify oil leases, the council continues to give Navajos a voice in their own affairs.

The secretary of the Interior creates a Committee of One Hundred to advise him on Indian policy.

1924

Congress passes and President Calvin Coolidge signs into law the bill giving Native Americans the rights of citizenship — including the right to vote — in their homeland.

1926

At Taos Pueblo in New Mexico, the Commissioner of Indian Affairs has all pueblo council members imprisoned for violating the bureau's religious crimes code.

Gertrude Simmons Bonnin, a Dakota Sioux, leads in the formation of the National Council of American Indians, which has as its purpose the protection of Native Americans in light of their new citizenship status.

NATIVE AMERICAN

1928

The *Lewis Meriam Associates Report,* published under the Herbert Hoover administration, calls for reforms in the Indian Office and changes in federal policy toward Native Americans. The BIA education system is exposed as grossly inadequate.

1929-1933

Reforms within the BIA somewhat improve Native American schools, partially stop the seizing of Native American land and begin to reduce the power of the bureau's agents on reservations.

AFRICAN AMERICAN

Early 1920s

Marcus Garvey establishes the Black Star Steamship Line with plans to sail from the United States to the West Indies and Africa. A stronger visionary and orator than businessman, Garvey sees his venture fail and is arrested on charges of mail fraud. He is convicted in 1925 and serves two years in prison before being released by a presidential commutation and deported to Jamaica.

1920s

An important African American cultural movement generally called the Harlem Renaissance begins. New York's Harlem district becomes a center for African American arts, music and literature.

1922

The Ku Klux Klan (KKK) reaches its peak. Increased Klan aggression results in many acts of violence against African Americans.

The National Association for the Advancement of Colored People (NAACP) voices its opposition to the United States' occupation of Haiti.

1923

A riot breaks out in Elaine, Arkansas, when African American farmers trying to unionize are shot at by European Americans. Twelve African Americans are sentenced to death and more than 60 receive prison terms in a trial marred by a mob scene and the mistreatment of witnesses. The decision is appealed by the NAACP, and goes to the United States Supreme Court as *Moore* v. *Dempsey.* The High Court rules that due process is violated if the trial is disorderly, a decision that is upheld in several later cases.

Inventor Garrett A. Morgan, whose first invention in 1901 was a belt fastener for sewing machines, patents the first automatic stop signal, the forerunner to the modern traffic light.

Xavier University at New Orleans, Louisiana, is founded.

AFRICAN AMERICAN

The Brotherhood of Sleeping Car Porters is organized at New York City by A. (Asa) Phillip Randolph, who becomes the union's president. It affiliates with the American Federation of Labor in 1929.

1926

In Chicago, African American women strike against wage cuts at the Morris Stuffed Date factory. The strikers are supported by food and money from the International Workers Aid.

Mobs of European Americans burn churches and attack African American families during riots in Carteret, New Jersey. As a result, all African Americans leave town.

Birmingham social worker Mrs. Indiana Little, and a group of women with her, are beaten by election officials while attempting to register to vote in Alabama.

1927

The NAACP begins a long legal fight against the Texas "white primary" law. As the test case of *Nixon* v. *Herndon,* the matter reaches the United States Supreme Court. Dr. L. A. Nixon, an African American, presents a certificate signed by election officials C. C. Herndon and Charles Porras stating that they did, in fact, deny him the right to vote in the Democratic primary. The Supreme Court rules that the "white primary" is a violation of the Fourteenth Amendment. The Texas legislature repeals the law, but puts voter qualification in the hands of local Democratic party committees.

Citizens of Toms River, New Jersey, demand the dismissal of the school principal because he discriminates against African American students. The dismissal is upheld by the state supreme court.

The Chicago Urban League initiates a boycott of European American-owned stores that refuse to hire African Americans even though the businesses are in African American neighborhoods.

AFRICAN AMERICAN	ASIAN AMERICAN	ASIAN AMERICAN	FOR CLASSROOM USE	

AFRICAN AMERICAN

1929

The NAACP begins a campaign against bus companies in Chicago that practice discrimination.

Oscar DePriest, a Republican from Illinois, is elected to the House of Representatives of the United States Congress. He serves three terms.

Educator John Hope, who shares W. E. B. Du Bois' objections to the compromise theories of Booker T. Washington, is instrumental in uniting the colleges of Atlanta into a cooperative system.

c. 1929

Dr. Theodore K. Lawless, a recognized expert in the field of dermatology, makes significant contributions to the treatment of leprosy and syphilis.

ASIAN AMERICAN

1920

The United States census reports approximately 61,600 Chinese Americans in the contiguous United States, 50 in Alaska and 23,500 in Hawaii. Ratio of males to females is 7 to 1. Slightly more than 50 percent of Chinese Americans in Hawaii were born there, as opposed to having been foreign-born. The census also reports 5,000 Filipinos in the United States, 3,000 of them in California.

Japanese American farmers' organizations are established for mutual aid and protection. These include the Japanese Agricultural Association of Southern California and the California Farmers Cooperative.

Three hundred fifty Japanese professionals, mostly women, enter the United States.

California's revised Alien Land Act prohibits Japanese immigrant parents from serving as guardians of property for their minor citizen children, or from buying property in their children's names.

The picture-bride custom is outlawed by the Japanese government.

In Hawaii, 8,700 plantation workers of Japanese and Filipino ancestry strike for six months.

1920s

Many Filipino contract laborers come to work on the sugarcane and pineapple plantations of Hawaii, in the vegetable fields of California, the lumber mills of Washington and Oregon and the salmon canneries of Alaska.

1921

Fifty-eight Japanese immigrant laborers are driven out of Turlock, California, and warned never to return.

Approximately 1,000 Japanese immigrants are mining coal in central Utah.

ASIAN AMERICAN

1922

In *Ozawa* v. *United States,* the Supreme Court declares Japanese immigrants ineligible for naturalization. The test case was filed in Honolulu in 1917 by Takao Ozawa, a man so dedicated to America that he insisted his family speak only English and eat only American food. Ozawa loses his bid to overturn the discriminatory exclusion laws.

Under the Cable Act, an Asian American who marries a foreign citizen is denied the right to regain United States citizenship when the marriage ends.

1923

Tokutaro Nishimura Slocum's citizenship is cancelled because he is an Asian American. Slocum was a sergeant major with the 82nd Division in France during World War I and was seriously wounded.

1924

The Immigration Act of this year refuses entry to aliens ineligible for citizenship, which includes everyone except Europeans and Africans. The act also establishes specific requirements for Chinese students to 1) have certificates of admission to American institutions, 2) have sufficient funds for education and 3) return to China upon completion of education. Filipinos are not affected by the new law. Their status as nationals of the United States gives them unlimited freedom to immigrate to America.

1925

An abrupt decline occurs in Filipino immigration to the United States. Anti-Filipino propaganda is spread by the American Federation of Labor because of economic fears.

A district court in Massachusetts approves naturalization for Hidemitsu Toyota, who served in the United States Coast Guard for 10 years. The court of appeals cancels his citizenship, and the Supreme Court upholds the cancellation.

1920

through

1929

	ASIAN AMERICAN	ASIAN AMERICAN	EUROPEAN AMERICAN	EUROPEAN AMERICAN
1920 through 1929	The United States Supreme Court rules that Filipinos are ineligible for citizenship unless they serve in the United States Navy for a period of three years. **1926** The first bilingual Chinese American newspaper in Honolulu, Hawaii, *Chinese News,* begins publication. Dai Yen Chang and Yew Char are elected to the Honolulu Board of Supervisors and Hawaii Territorial House of Representatives, respectively. These are the first Chinese Americans elected to office in the United States or its territories. **1927** The American Federation of Labor makes initial petitions to Congress to exclude Filipinos. The proposed act fails because it is in direct violation of the Immigration Act of 1924, which specifically provides that "citizens of the islands under the jurisdiction of the United States shall not be treated as aliens." The Supreme Court rules that the Hawaiian government acted unconstitutionally in depriving parents of the right to provide language instruction. This case resulted from a class action suit filed by scores of Japanese-language schools in Hawaii, to fight Hawaii's attempt to stop the teaching of Japanese. **1928** James Y. Sakamoto begins publishing the *Japanese American Courier* in Seattle, Washington. **1929** A sudden increase in Filipino immigration leads to lowered wages and, in some cases, starvation wages because of the surplus of workers. The Japanese American Citizens League (JACL) is founded as a national organization, headquartered in San Francisco.	The *San Francisco News* reports that the city has suffered more than 430 spinal meningitis cases resulting in 170 deaths. Filipinos are accused of bringing the disease to the United States. Increased Filipino immigration into San Francisco and Los Angeles occurs in anticipation of possible future exclusion. An anti-Filipino riot occurs in Exeter, California.	**1920s** As the northern states experience a period of industrial growth and prosperity, immigration of French Canadians to New England mill towns increases. **1920** More than 38,000 British immigrants come to the United States. The United States census reports that more than 10 percent of the British-born men in America have not started naturalization proceedings to become United States citizens. This suggests that British immigrants remain more strongly loyal to their homeland. More than 2 million people flee Russia. Thirty thousand come to the United States as refugees. These Russians usually have more education than previous Russian immigrants and are employed in skilled jobs. Italian immigrants Nicola Sacco and Bartolomeo Vanzetti are arrested for murder in connection with a payroll robbery near Boston. The pair are convicted, and later executed, although the evidence against them is weak. Many people at the time believe that Sacco and Vanzetti are harshly and unfairly dealt with because they are anarchists. These sentiments stimulate six years of worldwide protest and questioning. **1921** More than 95,000 Polish immigrants arrive in America, the highest number in any single year. **1921-1930** German immigration to the United States for this decade is just over 410,000.	**1922** In New York City, the American Friends of Lithuania, Latvia and Estonia come together and form the Baltic-American Society, with Robert J. Caldwell as president. Goals of the group include fostering friendship and communication between the Baltic Republics and the United States, increasing awareness of Baltic culture in this country, and maintaining economic and educational links between Baltic Americans and ethnic regions. Station WDAU in New Bedford, Massachusetts, broadcasts the country's first Portuguese-language radio program. **1923** Russian-born American Igor Sikorsky, an aeronautical engineer and pioneer in aircraft manufacture, forms the Sikorsky Aero Engineering Corporation, which builds 14-passenger S-29 twin-engine airplanes. **1924** Sweden suffers a severe economic depression, while a postwar boom takes place in the United States. As a result, Swedish immigration revives, with more than 18,000 Swedes entering the United States in the first part of the year. **1927** The *Szbadság* newspaper in Cleveland, Ohio, publishes the first known history of Hungarian Americans. The work is in the Hungarian language, and is entitled *Magyarok Amerikában, Az amerikao magyarság története 1583-1927 (Hungarians in America: The History of Hungarians in America, 1583-1927).* **1929** The *Vorposten,* a Nazi newspaper, begins publication in Chicago.

HISPANIC AMERICAN	HISPANIC AMERICAN	HISPANIC AMERICAN	FOR CLASSROOM USE	

1920

The first large wave of Puerto Rican migration to the United States is recorded. The census reports the Puerto Rican population in the United States at approximately 11,800.

Legal immigration from Mexico reaches a new high — about 500,000 enter the United States on permanent visas. This figure, representing 11 percent of the total United States immigration of the period, is spurred partly by the Cristero Revolution of 1926-1929 and by the continued growth of the American economy. These immigrants are welcomed by industries, agriculture and railroads, which need laborers.

1920-1930

Controversy arises in Puerto Rico over attempts to make English the official language. Student strikes support the use of Spanish.

Clubs representing specific Puerto Rican towns are established in New York. Other organizations are formed to support civic, social, cultural, legal, economic, political and athletic needs.

1922

The Campbell Project is proposed, which would create an *Estado Libre Associado* (Associated Free State) government for Puerto Rico. The bill is tabled in the United States House of Representatives in 1923.

Puerto Ricans under José Coll Cuchi pull away from the Unionist movement and establish the Nationalist party, which supports Puerto Rican independence.

1923

The League of United Latin American Citizens (LULAC) is founded in Corpus Christi, Texas.

1924

The Puerto Rican Alliance party is founded.

1924-1930

The State Department and southwestern industrialists unite to keep immigration from Mexico unrestricted.

1925

The Puerto Rican Women's Suffragist Association is created.

Casa de Puerto Rico (The Puerto Rico House) is established in New York City by professionals and intellectuals to promote Hispanic culture, customs and traditions.

The Border Patrol of the United States Immigration and Naturalization Service is given absolute search and seizure authority over Mexican immigrants.

1926

Attacks against Puerto Ricans provoke a riot on the east side of Harlem in New York City.

Ateneo Obrero is established by Puerto Rican workers for cultural and educational purposes and to address the needs of second generation Puerto Rican Americans in New York City.

La Milagrosa is opened by the New York Catholic Archdiocese as the first church for Puerto Ricans in New York City.

1927

La Liga Puertorriqueña e Hispana (The Puerto Rican and Hispanic League) is established in New York City to unite, educate and represent Spanish-speaking organizations to the authorities. The league also urges voter participation and improvement of conditions in the Hispanic community.

1927-1928

The first effective union of Mexican American agricultural workers is established in California. Called the Confederacion de Uniones Obreras Mexicanas (CUOM), it soon has 3,000 members in 20 locals. In 1928, CUOM's first strike, in California's Imperial Valley, is broken up by mass arrests and deportations.

1929

A law is enacted in Puerto Rico giving literate males and females age 21 or older the right to vote.

The Trade Union Unity League, a Communist party organization, helps Mexican workers to organize when the American Federation of Labor refuses to do so.

1920

through

1929

1920 through 1929

1920

The United States census reports the country's population at 105.8 million, including American citizens living abroad. The census figures show that the majority of Americans now live in urban areas and not on farms.

The Nineteenth Amendment to the United States Constitution is ratified. It provides that the rights of citizens to vote shall not be denied or abridged by the United States or any state on account of sex.

The United States is in a period of isolationism. An attitude known as the "Red Scare" results in nationwide raids led by United States Attorney General Alexander M. Palmer against labor and political leaders suspected of being communists or disloyal to the nation. The fear is based on the communist takeover of Russia in 1917 and results in mass arrests of "anarchists," communists and labor agitators. This activity leads to the founding of the American Civil Liberties Union to protect the rights of citizens.

The United States Women's Bureau is established in the Department of Labor.

The National League of Women Voters is formed in Chicago, Illinois, by Carrie Chapman Catt. In 1948 the name is changed to the League of Women Voters of the United States.

By this time, half of all women garment workers belong to one of two large labor organizations: either the Amalgamated Garment Workers Union or to the International Ladies Garment Workers Union (ILGWU).

After passage of the Nineteenth Amendment, several major women's organizations unite into the Women's Joint Congressional Committee (WJCC). By 1922 this group is respected in Washington as a strong lobbying unit. Two primary objectives of the WJCC are reached within a few years. First, the Sheppard-Towner Act of 1921 provides money for public health care for expectant mothers and infants. Second, a constitutional amendment prohibiting child labor is passed in Congress in 1924, though it is never ratified by the states.

More than 9 million automobiles are registered in the United States. The electrical age arrives: 3 million homes have radios; electrical lights are common in urban areas; and appliances such as vacuum cleaners, washing machines, refrigerators, stoves and dishwashers are available for home use. However, 85 percent of rural American homes do not yet have electricity.

Radio Station KDKA, in Pittsburgh, Pennsylvania, goes on the air as the country's first commercial broadcast station.

John Llewellyn Lewis becomes head of the United Mine Workers of America.

Arthur Meighen, a Conservative, becomes prime minister of Canada after ill health causes Sir Robert L. Borden (1911) to resign. Meighen serves until 1921.

Canada's Parliament passes a law giving Indians the right to vote.

The Royal North-West Mounted Police is officially renamed the Royal Canadian Mounted Police. Originally established as a temporary peace-keeping group as Canadians migrated westward, it is formally expanded into a permanent national police organization.

Adolfo de la Huerta becomes interim president of Mexico after the death of President Venustiano Carranza (1914). Huerta is followed by Álvaro Obregón, who rules until 1924.

1920-1930

President Augusto Bernardino Leguía institutes a new constitution and modernizes Peru. But his policies strain the country's resources and greatly increase the national debt. Leguna is able to establish his programs by strong suppression of his political opponents.

1920-1932

Paraguay experiences a period of social, educational and economic reforms.

1920-1950

Rose Schneiderman, a Polish American, serves as president of the National Women's Trade Union League. She comes to be a major activist for working people.

1921

Warren Gamaliel Harding becomes the 29th president of the United States; Calvin Coolidge is vice president. Both are Republicans.

William Howard Taft becomes chief justice of the United States Supreme Court. He serves until 1930.

The United States Congress passes the first National Origins Quota Act (Johnson Act). It limits immigration and reserves immigrant visas on the basis of American ethnic composition of European origin, favoring northern and western Europeans. This quota act permits an annual admittance of up to 3 percent of the foreign-born of each nationality as enumerated in the 1910 Census.

Arlington National Cemetery is dedicated as a memorial to Americans who served their country in the military.

A large portion of the cotton crops in Georgia and South Carolina is destroyed by boll weevils. A positive effect of this is that farmers in both states are forced to diversify.

Oil is discovered near El Dorado, Arkansas.

Italian-born anarchists Nicola Sacco and Bartolomeo Vanzetti are convicted of the 1920 armed robbery of a Massachusetts shoe company and the murder of a guard. The case stirs worldwide protests because the evidence against them is weak and many feel the two men's only crime is their political beliefs. In the early 1960s, using modern equipment, the gun that Sacco carried is confirmed to have fired the fatal shot, linking him to the crime, but also suggesting that Vanzetti was probably innocent.

William Lyon Mackenzie King, a Liberal, becomes prime minister of Canada after the term of Arthur Meighen (1920). King serves until 1926, loses his post briefly to Arthur Meighen, regains it and governs until 1930.

Voters elect the first female member of Canada's House of Commons, Agnes C. McPhail.

The United States and Colombia sign a treaty in which Colombia receives $25 million from the United States as compensation for its loss of Panama, with United States military help, in 1903; Colombia formally recognizes Panama's independence.

Alfredo Zayas becomes president of Cuba. He serves until 1925.

1921-1930

Immigration to the United States totals more than 4.1 million, of which 2.5 million come from Europe, 112,100 from Asia, 6,300 from Africa, 8,700 from Oceania, 1.5 million from the Americas and 230 are not specifically identified.

1922

Under the Cable Act, an Asian American who marries a foreign citizen is denied the right to regain United States citizenship when the marriage ends.

In Fresno, California, Mexican grape-pickers attempt to unionize, but are strongly opposed by growers.

Labor strikes temporarily close several textile mills on the Amoskeag River in New Hampshire.

The first formal airmail service to the South begins, with flights between Chicago, Illinois, and Nashville, Tennessee.

Readers Digest begins publication in the United States.

Oil is discovered in Venezuela.

Marcelo Torcuato de Alvear becomes president of Argentina after the term of Hipólito Irigoyen (1916). Alvear serves until 1928.

1923

Calvin Coolidge becomes the 30th president of the United States after the death of Warren G. Harding.

The United States Supreme Court rules that the state law limiting women's work hours is unconstitutional.

Widespread violence caused by the Ku Klux Klan (KKK) occurs in the United States.

The National Women's Party, led by Alice Paul, proposes a constitutional amendment: "Men and women shall have equal rights throughout the United States and in every place subject to its jurisdiction. Congress shall have power to enforce this article by appropriate legislation."

The College of Saint Mary (for women) is founded at Omaha, Nebraska.

Time magazine begins publication in the United States.

Margaret Sanger organizes the first American birth control conference, and forms the National Committee on Federal Legislation for Birth Control.

The "Halibut Treaty" is signed between the United States and Canada to protect Pacific coast halibut fisheries. This is the first treaty Canada enters into as a sovereign entity.

The United Church of Canada Act is passed by Canada's Parliament. It joins Congregationalists, Methodists and Presbyterians into a single Protestant church.

1924

Congress passes the Second Quota Act (the Johnson-Reed Act) which, until 1929, allows for an annual admittance of two percent of the foreign-born of each nationality as enumerated in the 1890 census. After 1929 the quota of a country stands in the same relation to 150,000 as inhabitants of the United States of that ethnic origin to the total United States inhabitants in the 1920 census, with a minimum quota of 100 persons. Western Hemisphere countries are exempted from the quota system as part of a Good Neighbor policy. Asians are declared ineligible for citizenship by the Second Quota Act; those ineligible for citizenship are barred from immigration by the same act, thus continuing the exclusion of Asians to the United States. This quota act also establishes the Border Patrol.

Congress passes the Citizenship Act which grants Native Americans the rights of full citizenship, especially the right to vote.

In *Radice* v. *New York,* the United States Supreme Court upholds a law prohibiting women from working certain jobs between 10:00 p.m. and 6:00 a.m.

United States Secretary of the Interior Albert B. Fall and oilmen Harry Sinclair and Edward L. Doheny are charged with conspiracy and bribery in the Teapot Dome Scandal, involving fraudulent leases on naval oil reserves in Teapot Dome, Wyoming. In 1931 Fall is sentenced to a year in prison; Doheny and Sinclair are acquitted of bribery.

Norman Mattoon Thomas becomes head of the Socialist Party in the United States.

Nathan Leopold and Richard Loeb are tried in the "thrill killing" of Bobby Franks in Chicago, Illinois. They are defended by Clarence Darrow, convicted and sentenced to life in prison. Loeb is killed by a fellow convict in 1936. Leopold, paroled in 1958, dies in 1971.

More than 2.5 million radios are being used in homes in the United States.

Walter Percy Chrysler produces his first car. He founds the Chrysler Motor Company the following year.

Clarence Birdseye experiments with a process for quick freezing of foods.

The Royal Canadian Air Force is founded.

Plutarco Elías Calles becomes president of Mexico after the term of Álvaro Obregón (1920). Calles serves until 1928.

Horacio Vásquez becomes president of the Dominican Republic when United States occupation ends. He serves until 1930.

In Peru, *Alianza Popular Revolucionaria Americana* (APRA) is founded under the leadership of Víctor Raúl Haya de la Torre. Also referred to as *Partido Aprista,* the organization advocates radical reform in areas of land and Indian rights. Its tactics of political disruption and terror cause it to be outlawed during its early existence. However, the party becomes somewhat more conservative, and remains influential for decades.

United States troops are sent to Venezuela to maintain order and protect American interests in that country.

1924-1927

During a military revolt in Brazil, junior army officials are forced to flee into the hill country, and there experience firsthand the crushing poverty and lack of services of their rural countrymen. This event draws these officials into the reform movement.

1925

Calvin Coolidge begins his first elected term as president of the United States; Charles G. Dawes is vice president. Both are Republicans.

Xavier University at New Orleans, Louisiana, and Trinity College of Vermont at Burlington are founded.

The most destructive tornado in history is recorded in the midwestern United States. The death toll is close to 700 people, more than 230 of them in Murphrysboro, Illinois.

1920

through

1929

1920 through 1929

John T. Scopes is arrested for teaching the evolutionary theory of man's origin in a public school science class in Dayton, Tennessee. The "Scopes Monkey Trial" attracts worldwide interest in the creationism vs. evolution controversy and pits lawyer Clarence Darrow and the American Civil Liberties Union in defense of Scopes against William Jennings Bryan and state prosecutors. Scopes is convicted and fined but the sentence is later set aside.

Nellie Taylor Ross becomes governor of Wyoming, the first woman governor in the country.

In Winslow, Arkansas, voters elect a woman mayor, Maud Duncan, and an all-woman city council. After two years the women all resign, saying they have proven that women are as capable at government as men.

In Arizona authorities seize more than 50 illegal stills operated by moonshiners.

Irish American labor organizer Mary Harris Jones (Mother Jones), at age 95, speaks out for the coal miners and rights of children. Her story, *The Autobiography of Mother Jones,* relates her spirit but is not regarded as a serious historical document.

Gerardo Machado is elected president of Cuba after the term of Alfredo Zayas (1921). Machado serves until he is overthrown in 1933.

1925-1948

The government of Ecuador experiences repeated turmoil; no president elected during this period is allowed to complete his term.

1926

American aviators and explorers Richard Evelyn Byrd and Floyd Bennett become the first men to fly to and from the North Pole.

At Auburn, Massachusetts, American physicist Robert H. Goddard produces and fires the first liquid fuel rocket.

United States swimmer Gertrude Ederle is the first woman to swim across the English Channel. Her feat takes over 14 hours.

The concept of a 40-hour workweek is instituted in Henry Ford's automotive manufacturing facility.

Labor organizer Ella Wiggins is murdered in North Carolina.

Arthur Meighen (1920), a Conservative, again becomes prime minister of Canada, but is defeated this same year by William Lyon MacKenzie King (1921), a Liberal. King serves until 1930.

United States marines intervene in Nicaragua to protect American interests and to maintain peace. Augusto César Sandino leads guerrilla activities against the marines until their departure in 1933.

Emiliano Chamorro (1917) again becomes president of Nicaragua. He serves only this year.

1926-1934

Liberal and conservative factions wage a civil war in Nicaragua. United States marines intervene, train a Nicaraguan national guard and establish election reforms; the marines then become entangled in guerrilla fighting against forces of Augusto César Sandino. The United States withdraws its forces in 1934.

1927

After the Massachusetts Supreme Court denies petitions for a new trial, Nicola Sacco and Bartolomeo Vanzetti are executed for the 1920 armed robbery of a Massachusetts shoe company and the murder of a guard. This case generates a lot of controversy since many people feel these two men's only crime was their political beliefs.

An estimated 100,000 people are homeless as a result of flooding of the Mississippi River. Twenty percent of the acreage of the state of Mississippi is under water.

Charles A. Lindbergh makes the first solo nonstop airplane flight from New York to Paris. His trip in the *Spirit of St. Louis* takes over 33 hours.

Texas inventor John Daniel Rust and his brother Mack Donald Rust invent the mechanical cotton picker. Because of its efficiency, it reduces the need for manual labor and becomes a significant factor in African American migration to the North.

Idaho sculptor Gutzon Borglum begins carving the faces of Mt. Rushmore National Memorial, in South Dakota. The project will take 14 years to complete.

The Jazz Singer starring Al Jolson becomes the first part-talking motion picture made in the United States.

After a long-standing territorial dispute between Newfoundland and Quebec provinces, Labrador becomes part of Newfoundland by order of the Imperial Privy Council.

Carlos Ibáñez del Campo becomes president of Chile. He serves until 1931.

1928

The Food Control Act establishes the United States Food and Drug Administration to oversee the safety, purity and accurate labeling of foodstuffs and pharmaceuticals.

The Ford Motor Company introduces the Model A automobile.

American aviator and explorer Richard E. Byrd leads a group on a journey to the Antarctic. The expedition, which returns in 1930, gathers a large amount of scientific information.

William S. Paley leaves his family's cigar business and purchases the United Independent Broadcasters, Inc. The following year, he changes the name to the Columbia Broadcasting System (CBS).

American Amelia Earhart becomes the first woman to fly across the Atlantic Ocean.

Canada's Supreme Court declares that women are not "qualified persons" and therefore may not sit in the Senate.

Mexican President-Elect Álvaro Obregón (1920) is killed before he can take office. Mexican politics is being controlled by former president Plutarco Elias Calles (1924), who appoints Emilo Portes Gil as the figurehead president. Gil serves until 1930.

Hipólito Irigoyen (1916) becomes president of Argentina again after the term of Marcelo Torcuato de Alvear (1922). Irigoyen serves until 1930.

1929

Herbert Clark Hoover becomes the 31st president of the United States. An Iowan, he is the first president born west of the Mississippi River. Charles Curtis becomes vice president. Both are Republicans.

Stock market prices collapse in the United States, with domestic securities losing more than $26 billion. Known as "Black Thursday," this action in October marks the beginning of the Great Depression. The oversupply of war goods with no real corresponding demand leads to plummeting prices, farm failures and mass unemployment. Because of loose monetary controls, many people borrowed money to purchase stocks (buying "on margin") and when they cannot repay the loans after the crash, banks are forced to close. The inhibiting effects of the Great Depression, combined with restrictive laws on immigration, are enormous. The percentage of foreign-born declines steadily.

The United States Congress establishes a Farm Board to buy up surplus agricultural production and hold it until prices go up. Tremendous surpluses created by the Great Depression make this plan impractical.

Severe drought conditions begin in North Dakota.

American aviator and explorer Richard E. Byrd flies to and from the South Pole. He is credited with the sighting of the Rockefeller Range and Marie Byrd Land in Antarctica.

THE AMERICAS	FOR CLASSROOM USE	FOR CLASSROOM USE	FOR CLASSROOM USE	
The St. Valentine's Day gangland massacre takes place in Chicago, Illinois. The Canadian merchant ship *I'm Alone,* carrying over 2,500 cases of liquor, is sunk by the United States Coast Guard 200 miles off the coast of Louisiana. Canadian Ambassador Vincent Massey files a protest. The ship's crew is released and the case goes to arbitration. Overturning the 1928 ruling of Canada's Supreme Court, the Imperial Privy Council officially declares that a woman is a "person" and may legally sit in the Senate of Canada. With the assistance of a proposal made by President Hoover, Chile and Peru resolve their border dispute. Chile retains control of Arica but constructs a free port for Peru at that site. Peru receives back the province of Tacna and all Chilean-owned buildings in the territory. The Peruvian Communist Party is formed under José Carlos Mariátegui, who proposes that the poverty of Peru's native people, the bulk of the country's population, can only be alleviated under a socialist economy.		279		**1920** through **1929**
	FOR CLASSROOM USE	FOR CLASSROOM USE	FOR CLASSROOM USE	

THE WORLD	THE WORLD	THE WORLD	THE WORLD
1920 The League of Nations, created in 1919 by the Treaty of Versailles in France, holds its first meeting in Geneva, Switzerland. The United States Senate votes not to join. The Treaty of Trianon, the fourth of five treaties ending World War I, is signed at the Grand Trianon Palace in Versailles, France. By its terms, Hungary formally cedes Transylvania to Romania and loses more than half of its total territory to its neighbors; the Kingdom of the Serbs, Croats and Slovenes obtains Croatia, Slavonia and part of the Banat; and Czechoslovakia obtains Slovakia and Ruthenia as well as access to the sea. The fifth treaty ending World War I, the Treaty of Sèvres, France, is signed by Turkey and the Allies. The treaty ends Turkish control over the lands of the former Ottoman Empire and limits Turkey's landholding to Anatolia. Although it is accepted by Sultan Muhammad VI at Constantinople, it is rejected by the rival government of Kemal Atatürk in Ankara. The Ottoman territory is divided as follows: Iraq and Palestine become British mandates, Syria (the territory of Syria/Lebanon) becomes a French mandate, Greece acquires some of the Aegean Islands and control of Smyrna and Azerbaijan, and Georgia and part of Armenia become part of Russia. Turkey's rival government under Kemal Atatürk attacks Greece and reclaims the disputed territory of Smyrna. Atatürk also establishes a separate treaty with Russia. These events lead to the renegotiation of Turkey's status through the 1923 Treaty of Lausanne. Poland invades Russia and becomes involved in the Russian civil war. Russia and Estonia agree to peace in the Treaty of Tartu. The Treaty of Riga in 1921 resolves the Russian-Polish conflict.	Under a League of Nations mandate, British South Africa (now Namibia) is administered by the government of South Africa. A League of Nations mandate places the islands of Western Samoa under New Zealand's protection. The first civil disobedience campaign begins in India. The "Little Entente" of Czechoslovakia, Romania and Yugoslavia is formed for mutual military and financial assistance. Yet another Home Rule Act incorporates Ulster into the United Kingdom of Great Britain and Northern Ireland. Tanganyika (formerly a German colony) is governed under a British mandate. Kenya becomes a British colony. Constantine I (1913) again becomes king of Greece after the death of his son, Alexander (1917). Constantine I rules until 1922. Nearly 100,000 people die as a result of an earthquake in Gansu, China. **c. 1920** The National Socialist Workers' party arises in Germany as a union of several radical factions discontented with the outcome of World War I. Adolf Hitler emerges as its leader. The term "Nazi" is coined by party opponents as a derogatory distortion of the organization's abbreviation. **1920s-1930s** Jews immigrate to Palestine in increasing numbers after the Balfour Declaration of 1917. Arab Palestinians fear being a minority in a Jewish state, and civil war erupts. **1921** A Paris conference of Allies establishes German reparation for damages during World War I at approximately $33 billion; inflation begins to increase in the German economy. The Chinese Communist party (CCP) is organized.	At Kronstadt naval station near Petrograd (St. Petersburg, Leningrad), Russia, sailors revolt against Vladimir Lenin's harsh wartime suppression policy. After several weeks of fighting the rebellion is put down, but this event causes some easing of Lenin's dictatorial tactics. The Irish Free State, under the direction of Sinn Fein leader Eamon De Valera, is formed in Southern Ireland as a self-governing dominion of the British Commonwealth. The six Ulster counties in Protestant Northern Ireland are not made part of the new state. The Permanent Court of International Justice (World Court) is established in The Hague, Netherlands. It lasts until 1945 when its functions are transferred to the International Court of Justice created by the United Nations. With Russian assistance, Mongolian forces overthrow their Chinese government. Outer Mongolia proclaims its independence from China and a monarchy is established. Jebtsun Damba Khutukhtu (the Living Buddha of Urga) rules until his death in 1924. A bloodless revolution occurs in Persia (Iran). Reza Khan Pahlevi, leader of the coup, comes to power, and arranges for the withdrawal of Russian troops from the country. He becomes prime minister in 1923 and arranges for British troops to leave. Iraq becomes a unified kingdom and Transjordan becomes an independent princedom; both are administered under British mandates. Martial law in British South Africa is replaced by a civilian colonial government. Charles IV attempts to restore the monarchy in Hungary, but is unsuccessful. The Hapsburg dynasty is abolished by statute. In Japan, Hirohito comes to power as regent when his father, Yoshihito (1912), is deemed unfit to rule. Hirohito becomes emperor in 1926.	Alexander I becomes king of Yugoslavia after the death of his father, Peter I (1903, 1918). Alexander rules until his assassination in 1934. Faisal I (Feisal I) becomes king of Iraq after a plebiscite confirms his nomination by British authorities. He rules until 1933. Paleobotanist Marie Carmichael Stopes and her husband, Humphrey Vernon Roe, found the first birth control clinic in the British Empire. **1921-1922** The Washington Naval Disarmament Conference is called by United States President Warren G. Harding, with representatives from Britain, France, Italy, Japan and the United States attending. The five powers agree to limit the number of warships each has, request the right to inspect each other's Pacific possessions, create a treaty outlawing poison gas as a weapon of war and respect the territorial integrity of China. **1921-1942** During this time, Papua New Guinea is a League of Nations mandate. Frederick Banting and Charles Best, Canadian scientists, develop the first insulin preparation suitable for use in humans. **1922** Benito Mussolini and his fascist forces march on Rome. When Italian King Victor Emmanuel III (1900) realizes that top-level government officials support Mussolini, he permits the formation of a new government. Mussolini gradually creates a dictatorship and opposes temporary emigration of Italians by attempting to provide employment at home. Victor Emmanuel III remains a figurehead king during the fascist regime. Polish leader Jozef Pilsudski refuses to run for president. The candidate he supports wins, but is assassinated within a few weeks.

1920 through 1929

THE WORLD	THE WORLD	THE WORLD	FOR CLASSROOM USE	

A treaty between Ireland and Britain solidifies the establishment of the Irish Free State. This agreement divides Ireland into two states and sparks civil war.

Kemal Atatürk and his army drive invading Greek forces out of Turkey and overthrow Muhammad VI (1918), the last Ottoman sultan. Atatürk establishes a new government and begins major reforms.

Russia's civil war ends and the Union of Soviet Socialist Republics (USSR or Soviet Union) is formally established.

By the Treaty of Rapallo, Germany recognizes the new Soviet Union. The two countries mutually cancel pre-war and war debts, and enter into a trade agreement.

Germany cedes Upper Silesia to Poland.

The League of Nations divides Togoland into two mandates, one British and one French.

Japan returns Shantung province to China.

Mohandas Gandhi is arrested and sentenced to six years in prison for his participation in civil disobedience that led to mob violence in the village of Chauri Chaura in India.

Cameroon is partitioned under British and French rule.

Sinn Fein leader Michael Collins is ambushed and killed between Banton and Macroom, Irish Free State.

The British Broadcasting Company (BBC) begins radio broadcast operations.

Egypt gains its independence from Britain and Sultan Fuad I (Ahmed Fuad Pasha) becomes king. Fuad I rules until 1936.

George II becomes king of Greece after the abdication of his father, Constantine I (1920). George II rules until 1923 and again from 1935 until 1947.

Andrew Boner Law, a Conservative, becomes prime minister of Great Britain after the term of David Lloyd George (1916). Law serves until 1923.

1922-1924

The economy of Germany suffers critical inflation that makes the German mark nearly worthless by 1924.

1923

Adolf Hitler's "Beer Hall Putsch" — an attempted nationalist coup in Munich, Germany, fails; in 1924 Hitler is sentenced to five years in prison, where he writes *Mein Kampf*. He is released after eight months, as the prevailing attitude in the country is one of unrest and extremism.

French and Belgian troops occupy Germany's Rühr district to enforce reparations payments; German inflation soars.

The Treaty of Lausanne, Switzerland, officially returns Smyrna to Turkey and recognizes the new Turkish republic as replacing the Ottoman rule of the region.

Severe earthquakes in Tokyo and Yokohama, Japan, leave more than 100,000 dead and 700,000 injured.

The Kuomintang (Nationalist Party, or KMT) is reorganized in China. Sun Yat-sen receives political and military support from the Soviet Communist party in exchange for allowing Chinese communists to have a voice in China's new government. Sun Yat-sen rules until his death in 1925.

Southern Rhodesia (Zimbabwe) becomes a self-governing British colony.

General Miguel Primo de Rivera comes to power in Spain with the approval of King Alfonso XIII. Primo de Rivera rules as dictator until 1930. Alfonzo XIII is figurehead king during Primo de Rivera's government.

Kemal Atatürk becomes the first president of Turkey. He serves until 1938.

Abdullah Ibn Husein, son of Husein Ibn Ali, king of Hejaz, becomes *emir* (Muslim prince or commander) of the independent country of Transjordan. He becomes king in 1946 and rules until 1951.

Stanley Baldwin, a Conservative, becomes prime minister of Great Britain after the term of Andrew Boner Law (1922). Baldwin serves until 1924.

On her return to Egypt from Europe, feminist leader Huda Sharawi throws her veil into the Mediterranean Sea. She is the first Egyptian woman to be seen unveiled. Sharawi later leads the Egyptian Feminist Union, working for civil rights for women.

1924

United States Vice President Charles G. Dawes offers his plan for the reduction of Germany's postwar reparations and the stabilization of the German economy.

The death of Outer Mongolia's ruling monarch, Jebtsun Damba Khutukhtu (the Living Buddha of Urga, 1921), makes possible the creation of the Communist-controlled Mongolian People's Republic.

The fourth *aliyah* (a heavy wave of Jewish immigration) to Palestine begins. It continues until 1932.

The Hashemites are driven from Arabia by Abdul-Aziz Ibn Saud, sultan of Nejd, who annexes the Hejaz to his lands. (Nejd and Hejaz are the kingdom of present-day Saudi Arabia.)

After the death of Vladimir Lenin (1917-1920), Joseph V. Stalin wins the ensuing power struggle. Stalin is dictator of the Soviet Union until his death in 1953.

Greece is proclaimed a republic after several years of unrest. The upheaval continues, however, until 1935, when the monarchy is restored.

Northern Rhodesia (Zambia) becomes a British protectorate.

Italian fascists murder socialist leader Giacomo Matteotti, an outspoken critic of Mussolini.

James B. M. Hertzog becomes prime minister of the Union of South Africa after the term of Jan Christian Smuts (1919). Hertzog serves until 1939.

Ramsey MacDonald, of the Labour party, becomes prime minister of Great Britain; however, he loses his position to Conservative leader and former prime minister Stanley Baldwin (1923) later this year. Baldwin serves until 1929.

1920

through

1929

1920 through 1929

Stanley M. Bruce becomes prime minister of Australia after the term of William Morris Hughes (1917). Bruce serves until 1929.

1925

Albania becomes a republic under the leadership of Ahmed Zogu.

Cyprus becomes a British crown colony; it obtains republic status in 1960.

The Locarno Pact is made by Germany, Great Britain, Italy, Belgium, Czechoslovakia, Poland and France at Locarno, Switzerland. The countries agree on postwar boundaries of several European nations. France, however, realizing that its eastern border with Germany is still unprotected by the agreement, begins building a series of border fortifications. Called the Maginot line after French statesman André Maginot, this defense system will later prove worthless against the German army.

Turkey's President Kemal Atatürk discourages veiling of women, and encourages their education. He opens schools for women and encourages female educator and writer Halide Edib to become politically active.

Volume I of Adolf Hitler's *Mein Kampf* is published; the Nazi party increases its power in Germany.

Belgian and French forces are withdrawn from Germany's Rühr district after Dawes Plan reparation modifications are accepted by the three countries.

In Japan, the Peace Preservation Law allows the government to suppress any political opinion it considers subversive.

Rama VII becomes king of Siam (Thailand) after the reign of Rama VI (1910). Rama VII is forced to grant a constitutional monarchy in 1932 and abdicates in 1934.

Paul von Hindenburg is elected president of Germany. He serves until 1934.

Reza Khan becomes shah of Persia after Ahmed (1909) is deposed. Reza Khan changes his name to Reza Shah Pahlevi, begins the Pahlevi dynasty and changes his country's name to Iran. He rules until 1941.

J. G. Coates, Reform party leader, becomes prime minister of New Zealand.

Lauri Kr. Relander becomes president of Finland after the term of K. J. Stålberg (1919). Relander serves until 1931.

1926

A two-week general strike in Britain, which began as a coal miner's dispute over hours and wages, brings the nation's activities to a halt.

Portugal's government is overthrown in a coup by the military. General Antonio Carmona comes to power.

After an attempted coup, Indonesia's Communist party is outlawed.

An alliance of nationalist and Chinese communist forces under Chiang Kai-shek begins the unification of China by eliminating or seriously reducing the power of local warlords.

Lebanon becomes a republic, but remains under the French mandate.

Muhammad Iqbal is elected president of India's Muslim League.

Women in India win the right to run for elective office. The All India Women's Conference is created. Years of women's activism follow.

Germany joins the League of Nations.

Hirohito becomes emperor of Japan after the death of his father, Yoshihito (1912). When Japan adopts a new constitution at the end of World War II, Hirohito remains in power as emperor.

After seven years of unrest under a parliamentary democracy, Poland's Jozef Pilsudski leads a coup. Although parliament continues to function, Pilsudski's authoritarian control of the country continues until his death in 1935.

Scottish inventor John Logie Baird develops an early form of television, one that is part mechanical and part electronic. He also invents the noctovisor, a device that uses infrared light to make objects visible in the dark.

1927

In China, the Kuomintang and the Communist party split. Chiang Kai-shek sets up the Nationalist Chinese government in Nanking (Nanjing), with himself as ruler. Troops under Chiang Kai-shek massacre Chinese communists and union leaders and expel Soviet forces from Shanghai. During this period, known as the "White Terror," women are especially targeted. Those thought to be communists, or associated with a "modern women's movement," are tortured and killed.

A severe earthquake at Nanshan, China, causes almost 200,000 deaths.

The Indonesian Nationalist party is established.

Socialists riot in Vienna, Austria, and a general strike follows the acquittal of Nazis accused of political murder.

Leon Trotsky is expelled from the Soviet Union's Communist party.

Australia's government seat is moved to the city of Canberra.

As a child, Michael I becomes king of Romania after the death of his grandfather, Ferdinand (1914). Michael I rules until 1930 and again from 1940 to 1947.

Muhammad V becomes sultan of Morocco. He later becomes king, and rules until 1961.

In England H. O. D. Segrave sets a land speed record of 203.79 miles per hour (327.89 kilometers per hour). He is the first to pass the 200-miles-per-hour mark.

Radioactive tracing is first used to diagnose heart disease by Herman Blumgart, a physician at Thorndike Laboratory, Boston.

1928

The Kellogg-Briand Pact, also called the Pact of Paris, is signed by 15 nations with the understanding that all conflicts should be settled by peaceful means and not by declaring war. It is ultimately ratified by 62 countries. However, because the pact lacks effective enforcement provisions, it proves ineffective.

After the interim government of Antonio Carmona (1926) in Portugal, a military dictatorship is established with Antonio de Oliveira Salazar as premier. Salazar governs until a massive stroke forces his retirement in 1968.

In India, a new constitution drawn up by Pandit Motilal Nehru calls for complete independence from Britain.

A severe earthquake hits the Mediterranean area. Smyrna, Turkey, is devastated. Corinth, Greece, rebuilt once after an 1858 earthquake, is again virtually destroyed.

All adult women gain suffrage in Britain. Previously, for a woman to vote, she had to be a head-of-household and at least 35 years old.

The National League of Filipino Women is formed as a women's suffrage organization. Together with the Women Citizens League, they begin to agitate for the right to vote.

Albania's President Ahmed Zogu (1925) announces the establishment of a monarchy, and proclaims himself King Zog I. He rules until 1939 when Italian forces occupy Albania. Zog I continues as figurerhead king in exile until 1943.

Joseph Stalin (1924) becomes the head of the Soviet Union's Communist party, and a series of programs intended to strengthen Soviet industry are set in motion. Stalin rules until 1953.

Joseph Ward, United party leader, becomes prime minister of New Zealand after the term of J. G. Coates (1925).

Scottish scientist (Sir) Alexander Fleming discovers penicillin. This discovery will prove itself invaluable during World War II.

THE WORLD	THE WORLD	*FOR CLASSROOM USE*	*FOR CLASSROOM USE*	
1929 Leon Trotsky is expelled from the Soviet Union; Stalin introduces rationing to increase the productivity of the work force. Under an agreement between the Vatican and the Italian government, church and state control over family law and practices is increased. Women are encouraged to have more children. However, during the Mussolini years, resistance to state control is strong, including resistance by women, and few families follow the dictate to increase their family size. Voters in Italy elect an all-fascist parliament. A series of disputes over Jewish access to Jerusalem's Wailing Wall leads to serious Arab-Jewish conflicts in Palestine. The Kingdom of the Serbs, Croats and Slovenes takes the name of Yugoslavia. The economy of Germany, already severely weakened by internal inflation and an unemployed population of more than 3 million, is esspecially devastated by the Great Depression. The airship *Graf Zeppelin* completes its first round-the-world flight. The trip takes over 21 days. Jawaharlal Nehru becomes president of the Lahore Congress. The first woman to hold a British cabinet post, Margaret Bondfield, becomes minister of labour. She serves until 1931. Afghan king Amanullah (1919) is deposed. Kabul is seized by forces under tribal leader Bacha-i Saqao, who then briefly rules the country. However, Bacha-i Saqao and his troops are defeated by an expedition led by Amanullah's cousin, Muhammad Nadir Khan, who takes the title of King Nadir Shah. He rules until 1933. Ramsey MacDonald, Labour party, becomes prime minister of Great Britain after the term of Stanley Baldwin (1924). MacDonald also becomes leader of the coalition National party. He serves as prime minister until 1935.	James H. Scullin becomes prime minister of Australia after the term of Stanley M. Bruce (1924). Scullin serves until 1932. In southeastern Nigeria, women attack sixteen native courts during the "Women's Wars," a series of protests against British colonial rule.			**1920** through **1929**

NATIVE AMERICAN	AFRICAN AMERICAN	AFRICAN AMERICAN	AFRICAN AMERICAN
1930 A Senate investigating comittee uncovers incidents in which Native American children have been forcibly removed from their families by officials of the Bureau of Indian Affairs (BIA). **1933-1950** The appointment of John Collier, a European American, as Commissioner of Indian Affairs by President Franklin D. Roosevelt marks the beginning of the "Indian New Deal." The BIA is administered by European American reformers, and generally becomes more supportive of American Indian cultural values and land rights, but fails to understand the desire for self-determination. **1934** Congress passes the Indian Reorganization Act (IRA). A reduced version of Collier's original proposal, the act is a turning point in Indian policy. The breakup of tribal lands into farm parcels and forced assimilation are replaced by the purchase of lands and promotion of tribal cultures. This act gives elected tribal councils the power to handle their own budgets, hire attorneys and incorporate. It does little, however, to soften the authority of the BIA. The Sun Dance, outlawed by the federal government since the mid-1880s because it involves elements of self-torture, is legalized. The ban is lifted by John Collier, Commissioner of Indian Affairs. Some sources believe that a few, small Sun Dances were celebrated in secret even during its prohibition. **1935-1939** Several Indian tribes incorporate and organize during this time under the terms of the Indian Reorganization Act. Santa Clara Pueblo in New Mexico is the first, drawing up its constitution after weeks of meetings, arguments and compromise. In the next few years, the Papagos, Pimas and Arizona Havasupai follow.	**1930** The United States census reports approximately 11.9 million African Americans, 9.7 percent of the total population. Farrad Muhammad establishes an organization in Detroit that is the precursor of the Black Muslim movement. **1931** The *Scottsboro Boys* case, in which nine African American boys are charged with raping two European American girls, is argued before the Supreme Court. Even though medical examination revealed no evidence of assault and one of the girls recanted her testimony, two lower court juries returned a guilty verdict, which carries a mandatory death penalty. In the Supreme Court, the convictions are overturned on the grounds that the youths were denied a fair trial because there were no African American jurors. A new trial is convened. The case becomes a rallying point for civil rights activists around the world, as American embassies in Europe and Latin America are picketed and stoned. After 6½ years of court proceedings, four defendants are released, one is condemned to death (his sentence later commuted to life in prison), and the remaining four to long prison terms. The last of the Scottsboro Boys is not released from prison until 1950. The Sharecroppers Union is organized in Tallapoosa, Alabama, to aid African American tenant farmers and sharecroppers. Roy Wilkins becomes editor of *Crisis,* the official publication of the National Association for the Advancement of Colored People (NAACP). He holds the position until 1949. Remaining in a leadership role, he becomes executive secretary in 1955 and executive director in 1964.	**1932** European American employees of the Illinois Central Railroad fight African American workers to keep them out of railroad jobs. Ten African American trainmen are killed. **1933** The NAACP files its first suit fighting segregation and discrimination in education, against the University of North Carolina. The case is lost on a technicality. Benny Goodman begins to hire African American musicians for his recording sessions. He later breaks the segregation lines in entertainment by including Teddy Wilson, an African American musician, in his performing band. **1935** A race riot in New York City's Harlem district is sparked by false rumors that a young African American boy caught shoplifting was beaten to death by police. Tension is already high in the community because of European American merchants' opposition to hiring African Americans. The riot results in the deaths of three African Americans and more than $100 million in damage as many businesses are broken into and looted. Arthur W. Mitchell, a Democrat from Illinois, is elected to the House of Representatives of the United States Congress. He serves four terms. The National Council of Negro Women is organized as an umbrella organization for several African American women's clubs. It becomes the most powerful organization of its kind, with Mary McLeod Bethune serving as president until 1949. **1936** Benjamin Oliver Davis, Jr., becomes the fourth African American to graduate from West Point. Like his father, General Benjamin Oliver Davis, Sr., he will attain the rank of general during his outstanding military career.	**1937** NAACP Lawyer Thurgood Marshall argues for equal salaries for public school teachers, regardless of race, before the Maryland Board of Education. The board orders salaries equalized. Benjamin O. Davis, Sr., becomes the first African American general in the history of the United States. Father John La Farge's *The Race Question and the Negro,* is published; it denounces segregation and the denial of equal economic and social opportunities to African Americans. William H. Hastie is appointed judge of the United States District Court for the Virgin Islands by President Roosevelt. He serves until 1939. **1938** Crystal Bird Fauset becomes the first African American woman legislator when she is elected to the Pennsylvania House of Representatives. The Supreme Court orders the admission of Lloyd Gaines, an African American, to the University of Missouri Law School. **1939** The Ku Klux Klan (KKK) in Greenville, South Carolina, warns: "The Klan will ride again if Greenville Negroes continue to register and vote." On Easter Sunday, singer Marian Anderson gives a performance at the Lincoln Memorial in Washington, D.C., after being denied the use of Constitution Hall. Though the Daughters of the American Revolution (DAR) state that the hall has already been booked, rumors of racial discrimination will persist for decades. In *Alston* v. *School Board of the City of Norfolk,* a federal court of appeals declares that under the Fourteenth Amendment, African American teachers cannot be denied equal pay with European American teachers.

1930

through

1939

AFRICAN AMERICAN	ASIAN AMERICAN	ASIAN AMERICAN	FOR CLASSROOM USE	

The underwriting manual of the Federal Housing Administration advocates the exclusion of African Americans and other minorities from federal housing and loans.

In Brownsville, Texas, several prominent African Americans are run out of town and an NAACP leader is murdered during a voter registration drive.

Jane M. Bolin is appointed as a judge of the Court of Domestic Relations in New York City, thus becoming the nation's first African American woman judge.

Herman Moore is appointed judge of the United States District Court for the Virgin Islands by President Roosevelt. He serves until 1957.

1930

The United States census reports 74,500 Chinese Americans living in the mainland United States, just under 30 in Alaska, and 27,700 in Hawaii. The census also reports 45,000 Filipinos in the United States, two-thirds of them in California.

The federal government allows entry of alien Chinese wives of Chinese American citizens who were married prior to enactment of the Immigration Act of 1924.

Japanese Americans gradually shift from rural to urban centers.

Twenty-one incidents of violence against Filipinos occur this year because of economic fears; competition between Filipinos and Mexicans for jobs on farms causes many of the disturbances. Filipino immigration to the United States begins to decline.

1930-1940

Nisei (first generation Japanese Americans born in this country) hold mutual aid meetings in Buddhist temples and Christian churches. Many have trouble finding jobs despite the sacrifices their families have made to educate them.

1931

Filipino men serving in the United States military become eligible for citizenship.

1934

The Tydings-McDuffie Act, also called the Philippine Independence Act, confers commonwealth status on the islands for 10 years, reclassifies Filipinos as aliens and restricts their immigration to 50 annually. This act is inspired partly by the independence movement in the Philippines, and partly by the Great Depression, which has made employment competition fierce in the United States.

Progressives in the American labor movement help Chinese Americans enter some of the more liberal unions. Craft unions continue to bar Chinese Americans and other non-European American workers.

1935

After 12 years of campaigning for the restoration of his naturalized United States citizenship, Takutaro Nishimura Slocum finally succeeds. The act restoring his citizenship also grants citizenship status to approximately 500 Asian Americans who served honorably with the United States military during World War I.

Thomas Chinn and Ching Wah Lee found the *Chinese Digest,* the first English language Chinese American newspaper in the continental United States.

The Commonwealth of the Philippines is inaugurated under President Manuel L. Quezon. The Philippine constitution is ratified. Quezon serves until 1944.

The Repatriation Act of this year, signed by President Roosevelt, offers free transportation to Filipinos who return to the Philippines.

1936

The Cable Act of 1922 is repealed. It forbade any Asian American who married a foreign citizen from regaining American citizenship when the marriage ended.

The Committee for Industrial Organization (later Congress of Industrial Organizations, or CIO) admits workers of Japanese ancestry and other non-European Americans into mainstream organized labor.

1937

Filipinos run into a unique problem with the Works Progress Administration, a New Deal program to provide construction employment on various building projects. Regulations specify that aliens are eligible only if they applied for citizenship prior to 1937. Most Filipinos have not bothered to apply because they were already American nationals.

During the Sino-Japanese War, Chinese Americans donate approximately $26 million for war relief and support of China's war effort.

1930

through

1939

ASIAN AMERICAN	EUROPEAN AMERICAN	EUROPEAN AMERICAN	HISPANIC AMERICAN
Philippine women gain the right to vote, the first women in Asia to do so. Twenty-four women are elected to municipal and provincial offices. In the pre-war national elections of 1941, the first Filipina is elected to the Philippine Congress. **1938** Hiram Fong, a Chinese American, becomes the first Asian member of the Hawaiian territorial legislature. He serves until 1954. Fong becomes a United States senator in 1959, when Hawaii becomes a state. **1939** Approximately 14,000 Filipinos are enrolled in colleges and universities in the United States. Many run out of money and drift into unskilled work.	**1930** The United States census reports nearly 168,000 foreign-born Portuguese Americans in the mainland United States, and another 27,500 in Hawaii. A total of 350,000 Americans claim Portuguese ethnicity. The census also reports that Minnesota has almost 268,000 Norwegian Americans; Wisconsin and North Dakota have approximately 125,000 each. Russian American sociologist Pitirim Sorokin establishes and heads a new department of sociology at Harvard University. This department becomes a major center of the social sciences during the 1930s. Jewish American scientist Karl Landsteiner wins the Nobel Prize in physiology and medicine for his discovery of human blood groups. **1931** Russian American Igor Sikorsky and his work crew design and build the S-40 aircraft, the first large American four-engine plane. **1931-1940** During this decade, more than 114,000 Germans come to the United States; many are fleeing Nazi brutality. **1932** Benjamin N. Cardozo is appointed as associate justice of the Supreme Court by President Herbert Hoover. Cardozo is a Jewish American, the second to serve on the Supreme Court. **1933** Although most German Americans strongly oppose the Nazi movement, several pro-Hitler events take place this year. In New York, 1,200 Germans demonstrate in support of Hitler; the Society of the Friends of Hitler movement begins weekly gatherings in several German communities in the United States, and in 1934 a branch of the Nazi Youth Corps is set up in New York City.	**c. 1934** The Steuben Society forms in forceful opposition to American Nazi activity. One study from this time period indicates that 70 percent of German Americans have no opinion on Nazism, 20 percent are strongly anti-Nazi; 9 percent are moderately pro-Nazi; and 1 percent are fanatically pro-Nazi. **1935-1940** Sweden experiences an economic boom with full employment, and Swedish immigration to the United States drops sharply. **1937** Many Austrian Jews come to America to escape the anti-Semitism that is sweeping their homeland. These new Jewish immigrants, most of them middle-class, take menial jobs in the United States until they meet the requirements to practice their professions. The American Nazi Party reports a membership of 200,000, with units or chapters existing in many major United States cities. **1938** In brutally strict support of national immigration quotas, Congress defeats a refugee bill to rescue 20,000 children from Nazi Germany. Russian American inventor Vladimir Zworykin develops an early television set. **1939** The Tolstoy Foundation is established in New York City to assist refugees from the Soviet Union and other communist countries with financial aid and employment.	**1930** Pedro Albizu Campos is elected president of Puerto Rico's militant Nationalist party. The Mexican American population in the United States is estimated at 3 million people. More than 1 million Mexicans immigrate to the United States this year alone. Competition between Filipinos and Mexicans for jobs on farms causes disturbances. **1931** Dr. José Padín is appointed commissioner of education for Puerto Rico by President Herbert Hoover. Dr. Padín believes Spanish should be the language of instruction in grades 1 through 8, and that English should be used in the high school grades. Antonio R. Barceló resigns from Puerto Rico's Alliance party and founds the Liberal party, which is pledged to seek independence. **1931-1934** Federal records indicate that approximately 300,000 Mexicans are deported during this time. **1932** Elections this year in Puerto Rico are the first in which women may vote. María Luisa Arcelay is the first woman elected to serve in the Puerto Rican legislature. **1933** President Franklin D. Roosevelt transfers jurisdiction over Puerto Rico from the War Department to the Interior Department. A federal emergency welfare program — the Puerto Rico Emergency Relief Administration (PRERA) — is created in response to the island's desperate poverty. President Roosevelt appoints Dr. José Gallardo as commissioner of education in Puerto Rico. Dr. Gallardo modifies the policies of his predecessor, Dr. José Padín (1931).

1930

through

1939

Illegal Mexican immigrants are repatriated from the southwestern United States. The number of legal immigrants is also sharply curtailed, through stricter patrol of the border by the United States. Among the victims of the repatriation process are naturalized and United States-born husbands, wives and children, who face the breakup of their families.

Santiago Iglesias is elected resident commissioner of Puerto Rico. He serves until 1939.

1934

President Franklin D. Roosevelt visits Puerto Rico and affirms support to rehabilitate the island's economy.

Casita Maria is established in New York City. It comes to play a significant role in service to Puerto Rican Americans in the city.

1935

At a Puerto Rican university, five people are killed in a confrontation between police and Nationalist party members.

Universal suffrage is established in Puerto Rico. Literacy is no longer a requirement for voting.

1936

Elías Beauchamp and Hirám Rosado, two young Nationalists, kill Puerto Rico's chief of police, Francis Riggs, and are later killed by the police who arrested them. Pedro Campos, head of the Nationalist party, and several of his followers are jailed for sedition. Campos is later sentenced and sent to prison.

The Tydings Project is presented to Congress, proposing Puerto Rican independence, but its terms are very negative for Puerto Ricans.

1937

On Palm Sunday, during a Nationalist party parade, the Ponce Massacre takes place. The majority of the approximately 20 who die are Nationalists; the police and government are held responsible for the deaths.

Oscar García Rivera is the first Puerto Rican American elected to the New York State House of Representatives. He represents the 14th district in Manhattan.

1938

The Popular Democratic party (PPD) is founded in Puerto Rico by Luis Muñoz Marín.

The Puerto Rican Migrant in New York City is published. It is the first comprehensive study of the experience of migrant Puerto Ricans coming to the mainland United States.

Nationalist party members open fire on the governor of Puerto Rico at a ceremony marking the island's 40th anniversary as an American possession. Two bodyguards are wounded, and several Nationalists are arrested.

Bolívar Pagan takes office as resident commissioner of Puerto Rico after the term of Santiago Iglesias (1933). Pagan serves until 1945.

1930

through

1939

1930 through 1939

1930

The United States census reports the country's population at 122.86 million, including American citizens living abroad.

Congress passes the Hawley-Smoot Tariff Act, which establishes the highest import tariffs to date and is designed to help United States manufacturers sell more products. Retaliatory tariffs by other countries severely curtail American foreign trade.

Charles Evans Hughes becomes chief justice of the United States Supreme Court. He serves until 1941.

The federal Veterans Administration is established to provide medical and educational assistance, loan guarantees and other services to veterans of the military.

More than 1,000 banks close in the United States as a result of the stock market crash of 1929.

Severe winds in drought-stricken North Dakota cause damage to more than 1,800 buildings.

Jacob Schick invents the electric razor. Production of it begins in Stamford, Connecticut, the following year.

The cyclotron is developed by Ernest O. Lawrence, an American physicist.

The planet Pluto is discovered by astronomers at the Lowell Observatory in Flagstaff, Arizona.

Richard Bedford Bennett, a Conservative, becomes prime minister of Canada after the term of William Lyon Mackenzie King (1926). Bennett serves until 1935.

Cairine Reay Wilson becomes the first woman appointed to Canada's Senate.

In Mexico, Plutarco Elías Calles (1924) supports the election of Pascual Ortiz Rubio as figurehead president, but Calles remains fully in control.

A group of Haitian women holds a public procession and demonstration to protest United States military occupation of Haiti. In addition to the women marchers, thousands of others line the streets in support. This action helps to convince the United States government to return Haiti to Haitian control.

Revolution in Argentina deposes President Hipólito Irigoyen (1916, 1928) and brings conservative leader General José Francisco Uriburu to power. He governs until 1932.

Getúlio Dornelles Vargas, governor of Rio Grande do Sul, comes to power as dictator of Brazil after being defeated in the presidental election. He claims fraud and leads a successful revolt to retain power. Vargas rules until the army removes him from office in 1945. He remains active in politics and regains the presidency in 1951, holding it for three years.

Rafael Leonidas Trujillo Molina becomes president of the Dominican Republic after the term of Horatio Vasquez (1924). Trujillo Molina serves until 1938 and is elected again in 1942.

Luis Sánchez Cerro ousts Augusto Bernardíno Leguía (1909) in a military coup and becomes president of Peru. Cerro serves until 1933.

1930s

As sugar prices plummet, depression in the Caribbean causes mass migrations to the United States from Haiti, the Dominican Republic, Puerto Rico and other islands. Riots break out in Jamaica, Barbados, St. Lucia, and Trinidad.

1930-1960

This period sees a decrease in women's college attendance in the United States.

1931

United States President Herbert Hoover proposes a one-year moratorium of war debts.

The Norris-La Guardia Act, named for its sponsors, George William Norris and Fiorello Henry La Guardia, prohibits the use of injunctions in most labor disputes and outlaws "yellow-dog" contracts, those that make the non-joining of a union a condition of hiring.

The Wickersham Commission issues its report stating that law enforcement of prohibition is inadequate.

Nevada's state legislature legalizes gambling.

The 102-story Empire State Building opens in New York City. It is the tallest building in the world at the time.

American chemist Harold Clayton Urey discovers heavy hydrogen.

The Nobel Peace Prize is awarded to American Jane Addams for her life-long anti-war activism.

Passenger air flights between New York and Miami are scheduled, with Raleigh, North Carolina, as a fueling stopover.

American gangster Al Capone is sentenced to 11 years in prison for tax evasion. However, he is freed in 1939.

Canada becomes a self-governing Dominion through the Statute of Westminster.

Arturo Araujo becomes president of El Salvador. He serves for one year.

General Jorge Ubico is chosen president of Guatemala in a special election. He serves until 1944.

Gabriel Terra becomes president of Uruguay. He serves until 1938.

1931-1940

Immigration to the United States totals 528,500, of which 347,600 come from Europe, 16,600 from Asia, 1,800 from Africa, 2,500 from Oceania and 160,000 from the Americas.

1932

The United States Congress sets up the Reconstruction Finance Corporation to stimulate the economy by loaning money to businesses, banks and railroads to help them maintain employees. When the country's unemployment rate exceeds 10 percent, the plan is extended to create state and local public works projects.

World War I veterans march on Washington, D.C., seeking early payment of cash bonuses approved for them in 1924 to be paid out in 1945. Most of this "Bonus Army" disperses after the Senate rejects their plan. The remaining protesters are removed by federal troops under Douglas MacArthur.

The United States Supreme Court overturns several convictions in the Scottsboro cases, and rules that all defendants have a right to counsel, even those charged with capital crimes. In this case, nine African American boys were charged, in Scottsboro, Alabama, with raping two European American girls on a railroad freight train. The case results in many court trials and draws nationwide and international protest. Several of the initial convictions are overturned, either because the defendants did not have proper representation or because the composition of the jury excluded African Americans. Five of the nine defendants serve time in prison, with the last "Scottsboro Boy" being freed in 1950.

The Brain Trust, a group of academic advisors to then-New York Governor Franklin D. Roosevelt, is organized.

Drought-plagued Nebraskan farmers are so determined to hold onto their farms that groups of them threaten violence at public foreclosure sales.

Saint Joseph College is founded at West Hartford, Connecticut.

Hattie Wyatt Caraway, a Democrat from Arkansas, is the first woman elected to the United States Senate. She serves until 1945.

Amelia Earhart becomes the first woman to make a solo airplane flight across the Atlantic Ocean. The trip takes less than 14 hours.

Women in Puerto Rico and Brazil receive the right to vote. In Puerto Rico, more than 100 women are elected to city councils in the next elections.

In Mexico, Plutarco Elías Calles (1924) supports the election of General Abelandr Luján Rodríguez as figurehead president; Calles, however, retains full control.

In Mexico, the Unique Front for the Rights of Women is formed. This organization is successful in unifying women throughout Mexico.

An ongoing border dispute precipitates Peru's invasion of Colombia. The League of Nations successfully arbitrates.

Agustín Pedro Justo takes office as president of Argentina, after an election marked by government suppression of liberal factions. Justo follows José Francisco Uriburu (1930) in office and serves until 1938.

El Salvador's President Arturo Araujo (1931) is ousted via a military coup led by General Maximiliano Hernández Martinez, who then takes control as dictator. Martinez rules until 1944.

1932-1935

Bolivia and Paraguay fight the Gran Chaco War. The war erupts when colonists from Paraguay refuse to vacate their farmlands to provide the Bolivians with access to the Paraguay River for their commercial transportation. The war is very costly in terms of lives lost on both sides, but it is won by Paraguay. By the provisions of the final agreement made in 1938, Bolivia gets access to the river and the right to construct a port, but Paraguay retains most of the land.

1933

Franklin D. Roosevelt becomes the 32nd president of the United States; John N. Gardner is vice president. Both are Democrats. Roosevelt proposes a "New Deal" program to bring the United States out of the Great Depression. His recovery plan is based on relief (jobs and money to the people), recovery (help for businesses and farmers) and reform (new legislation). Roosevelt also extends the concept of the Good Neighbor policy with Latin America. The government declares a moratorium on bank foreclosures of farms in the drought-stricken Midwest.

The Twentieth Amendment to the United States Constitution is ratified. It makes changes in the process of selecting or replacing a president or vice president and in congressional terms of office. The Twenty-first Amendment, which repeals the Eighteenth Amendment (Prohibition), is also ratified by the states. The manufacture, sale and transportation of intoxicating liquors becomes legal again, subject to local laws.

The Great Depression is at its worst. Approximately 25 percent of the United States labor force, between 12 and 14 million people, are unemployed. Programs instituted to help the country out of the depression are the Civilian Conservation Corps that creates new jobs for young people; the establishment of a National Bank Holiday allowing banks to reopen only when they have met new government regulations; the National Industrial Recovery Act to keep businesses from heavy price cutting and overproduction; the Tennessee Valley Authority instituting development of previously unusable land; the Agricultural Adjustment Act creating the Agricultural Adjustment Administration to slow down food production to raise prices; and the Federal Deposit Insurance Corporation to build public confidence in the banks.

Seven thousand Mexican American agricultural workers go out on strike in California.

Eleanor Roosevelt, a leading advocate of social reform, becomes the first president's wife to hold a press conference.

Frances Perkins is named United States Secretary of Labor, becoming the first woman to hold a cabinet post.

The Townsend Movement, a basic old-age pension plan sponsored by Francis Everett Townsend, is drafted. Although the plan fails to win support in the United States Congress, its consideration leads to the establishment of the Social Security system in 1935.

The United States recognizes the government of the Union of Soviet Socialist Republics (Soviet Union).

Nebraska's government declares a moratorium on bank foreclosures on farms, thereby protecting the state's farmers during the Depression.

Three hundred thousand acres of woodland are destroyed during the Tillamook Burn forest fire in Oregon.

Giuseppe Zangara is executed for the attempted assassination of President-elect Roosevelt in which Chicago Mayor Anton Joseph Cermak is fatally shot.

American newspaper columnist Heywood Campbell Broun is a founder of the American Newspaper Guild. He serves as its first president until his death in 1939.

Dorothy Day and Peter Maurin begin publishing *Catholic Worker,* a social activist newspaper.

Because of problems created by its World War I debts, Newfoundland loses its dominion status and reverts to being a British crown colony. With the help of British financial management, recovery is made and Newfoundland becomes a Canadian province in 1949.

Carlos Manuel de Céspedes becomes provisional president of Cuba when Gerardo Machado (1925) is overthrown. De Céspedes is immediately forced to resign and Ramón Grau San Martín takes office. Grau San Martín serves until 1934 and again from 1944 to 1948.

United States Marines leave Nicaragua.

Oscar Benevides becomes president of Peru after Luis Sánchez Cerro (1930).

1933-1939

Drought increases in the prairie states of the Midwest. High winds in the summer, particularly in 1934, pick the powder-dry soil up into enormous dust clouds. At its height in the late 1930s, the region referred to as the Dust Bowl encompasses approximately 25,000 square miles; a massive migration of desperate farm families from the area takes place. Though this dust bowl effect exists every summer into the present, modern irrigation and replanting have caused a steady decline in the acreage involved.

1934

The United States Congress passes the Tydings-McDuffie Act, also called the Philippine Independence Act, which reclassifies Filipinos as aliens and therefore subject to immigration control. The quota of immigrants from the Philippines is reduced to 50 a year. The Philippines gains its independence in 1946.

President Roosevelt initiates the Works Progress Administration (WPA) to encourage new construction and cultural programs to create jobs. The Federal Communications Commission (FCC) is established by the Federal Communications Act to grant, review and, if necessary, revoke radio broadcasting licenses. The Gold Reserve Act gives the president the power to adjust the value of the dollar. The Securities and Exchange Commission (SEC) is established to regulate the public issuance and sale of corporate securities and specifically to limit bank credit for speculative purposes in this industry.

Nebraska's state constitution is amended to establish a one-house legislature, the only one in the nation.

1930

through

1939

1930 through 1939

Mexican American agricultural workers call strikes in California, Michigan and Texas. These actions begin to weaken the stereotype of the docile Mexican who will submit to any conditions.

American scientist William Hallock Park pioneers research into a poliomyelitis vaccine.

The Dionne sisters, Annette, Emilie, Yvonne, Cécile and Marie, are born in Callandar, Ontario, Canada. They grow to become the first set of quintuplets in history to survive beyond infancy.

Lázaro Cárdenas is elected president of Mexico with the support of former president Plutarco Elías Calles (1924), who has ruled Mexican politics for several years. Cárdenas serves until 1940.

Grantley Adams, of African lineage, is elected to the House of Assembly in Barbados. This gives Barbados Africans their first real voice in the legislature in modern times.

Rising Cuban nationalism results in the abrogation of the Platt Amendment and supporting agreements between the United States and Cuba that justify American intervention in Cuban affairs.

United States military forces withdraw from Haiti after occupying it for 19 years.

Nicaraguan National Guard commander Anastasio Somoza comes to power in Nicaragua.

José María Velasco Ibarra becomes president of Ecuador. He serves until 1935 and again from 1944 to 1947, 1952 to 1956, 1960 to 1961 and 1968 to 1972. He is deposed by military coups in each of his first four terms.

1934-1940

Massive land and labor reforms culminate the social revolution in Mexico. Peasants and workers organize on local, state and national levels. Fifty million hectares of land are redistributed to peasants.

1935

President Roosevelt opens the second phase of his New Deal program in the United States with the Social Security Act that establishes unemployment and old-age insurance and the Wagner Act (named for its sponsor Senator Robert F. Wagner) to protect the interests of workers and labor unions.

The United States government establishes the Rural Electrification Administration (REA), which provides loans for the creation of local cooperatives to supply rural Americans with electricity.

Congress passes a series of Neutrality Acts—through 1937—to prohibit loans, the issuance of credit and sales of military supplies to those engaged in the conflict overseas. The laws also prohibit travel to reduce risks to American citizens.

John L. Lewis, head of the United Mine Workers of America, founds the Committee for Industrial Organization to represent the interests of unskilled workers in mass production industries in the United States. It is renamed the Congress of Industrial Organizations in 1938.

United States Senator and former Governor Huey Pierce "the Kingfish" Long is assassinated in Baton Rouge, Louisiana, by Dr. Carl A. Weiss.

The government of the United States officially apologizes to Canada for the 1929 sinking of the *I'm Alone,* with its cargo of liquor, and pays reparations of $50,000.

Jesus Palleres leads in the formation of the Liga Obrera de Habla Espanola (Spanish Speakers Workers League), a Mexican American mine workers' union that develops enough strength to force the Gallup-American Company in New Mexico to meet many of its demands.

Amelia Earhart makes the first-ever solo airplane trip from Hawaii to California.

Working for E. I. du Pont in Wilmington, Delaware, chemist Dr. Wallace H. Carothers develops nylon.

The Richter Scale, developed by seismologist Charles Richter, is used to measure ground motion.

William Lyon Mackenzie King, a Liberal, again becomes prime minister of Canada after the term of Richard Bedford Bennett (1930). King serves until 1948.

Ecuador's moderate government is deposed and a military junta is established.

José Luis Bustamante (Rivero) becomes president of Peru after the term of Oscar Benevides (1933). Bustamante serves until 1948.

Eleazar López Contreras becomes president of Venezuela after the dictatorship of Juan Vicente Gómez. Contreras serves until 1941.

1936

The United States Supreme Court declares invalid several significant parts of the Agricultural Adjustment Act of 1933, a major component of President Roosevelt's New Deal.

The United States Congress issues a charter to the Veterans of Foreign Wars, a group organized in 1899. Congress also establishes Fort Knox, a military base since 1932, as the official depository of United States gold bullion.

A rumor that jobs are being transferred to manufacturing plants with weak union ties is the spark that ignites a massive sit-down strike at General Motors Corporation (GMC) plants in Flint, Michigan. The strikers reject a court order that they leave the plant, and the National Guard is called in as a peacekeeping force. As the strike continues, the workers' wives organize to show their support and to keep the strikers fed. Larger issues in the strike include increasing unemployment, deteriorating working conditions, and GMC's refusal to recognize any single union's representation of workers. The Flint sit-down strike ends after a few months when GMC accepts several of the strikers' demands, the primary one being GMC's recognition of the United Auto Workers (UAW).

The Cable Act of 1922 is repealed. It forbade an Asian American who married a foreign citizen from regaining American citizenship when the marriage ended.

Hoover Dam, begun in 1931, is completed. Built on the Colorado River at the Arizona-Nevada border, it is a major source of power, flood control and irrigation support for the area. Much of its water is stored on man-made Lake Mead. The dam's name is changed to Boulder Dam in 1933, and changed back to Hoover Dam in 1947.

Miguel Mariano Gómez Arias becomes president of Cuba. He serves until the end of the year when a coup brings Vice President Federico Laredo Bru into power. Bru serves until 1940.

1937

Franklin D. Roosevelt begins his second term as president of the United States. John N. Gardner is vice president. Both are Democrats.

President Roosevelt attempts to create extra seats on the Supreme Court to ensure favorable rulings on his New Deal programs. Congress refuses approval of this "court-packing" plan but the High Court is more lenient with subsequent programs.

The United States government legalizes the distribution of information on birth control.

The Supreme Court overturns an earlier decision and upholds state minimum wage laws protecting women.

The Golden Gate Bridge, one of the world's longest suspension bridges, opens in San Francisco, California. More than 9,200 feet long, it connects that city with Marin County.

The Polaroid Corporation is founded in Cambridge, Massachusetts, by Edwin H. Land, inventor of the instant camera.

Japanese forces sink the American gunboat *Panay* on the Yangtze River in China. The United States cuts off oil shipments to Japan. Prejudice mounts against Japanese Americans, who are accused of being spies.

New Mexico officials participate in a highway conference held at Chihuahua, Mexico, on reopening the sixteenth-century highway from Mexico City to Santa Fe.

The plane carrying American flyers Amelia Earhart and Frederick J. Noonan is lost somewhere in the Pacific Ocean during their attempt to fly around the world.

Leon Trotsky is allowed to enter Mexico after the Soviet government has him expelled from Norway. He resides in a suburb of Mexico City until he is killed in 1940.

Anastasio Somoza becomes president of Nicaragua. He serves until 1947 and again between 1950 and 1956.

1938

The United States Congress passes the Fair Labor Standards Act, which establishes the minimum wage at 25 cents an hour, shortens the workweek and prohibits interstate shipment of goods made by young children. Congress also passes legislation giving the Agricultural Adjustment Administration power to store surplus crops and provide subsidies for farmers if they reduce production.

In the United States, the Committee for Industrial Organizations (CIO) changes its name to the Congress of Industrial Organizations and becomes a major challenger to the American Federation of Labor (AFL).

The House Un-American Activities Committee (HUAC), with Martin Dies as chairman, starts its work studying Nazi activities in the United States. The emphasis soon changes, however, to suspected communist activity. Most of the charges made by the committee are unfounded, based on insufficient evidence.

The Bartlett Dam, on the Verde River in the Salt River Indian Reservation, Arizona, is completed.

A hurricane and resultant flooding devastate Rhode Island and coastal regions of Connecticut.

Dr. Dorothy Anderson presents her research findings that identify cystic fibrosis.

After completing a flight from Los Angeles, California, to New York City, Douglas "Wrong-Way" Corrigan takes off for a return flight but, instead, flies from New York City, to Dublin, Ireland. Regardless of his intentions, he becomes a legend with his solo crossing, and adds the term "wrong-way" to popular slang.

Mexican President Lázaro Cárdenas seizes and nationalizes British and American oil companies in an effort to close long-standing disputes. Many American business interests demand intervention or retaliation, but the United States government, desirous of preserving a favorable relationship with Mexico, urges a peaceful resolution.

Worsening economic conditions in Jamaica lead to strikes and riots. Trade unions and political parties that support them gain acceptance. Alexander Bustamante and Norman Manley become prominent in supporting the working class.

Robert M. Ortiz becomes president of Argentina after the term of Agustín Pedro Justo (1932). However, Ortiz is forced to withdraw and Ramón S. Castillo takes the position. Castillo serves until 1943.

Alfredo Baldomir becomes president of Uruguay after the term of Gabriel Terra (1931).

1939

World War II begins in Europe (see "The World, 1939-1945, World War II").

Although President Roosevelt proclaims neutrality for the United States, he requests a large defense budget and declares that the nation is in a state of limited emergency. The general consensus in the United States is to remain isolated and out of the war effort because of America's own economic problems, and because of the belief that wars do not solve these issues, that the oceans will keep the war off of American soil and that the United Nations is responsible for solving these problems. Americans' confidence in the success of the United States' Good Neighbor policy in Latin America and a growing pacifist movement add to the general national consensus to remain neutral.

Defense manufacturers in the United States see an unprecedented economic boom. Not only are they building munitions and other war supplies for the United States Armed Forces, but this country becomes a supplier of military needs for the rest of the Allied countries. This boom and the accompanying shortage of manpower as military age men go to war suddenly open up new employment opportunities for women. They find work in fields not previously considered: engineering, transportation, chemistry and heavy manufacturing are a few examples.

The United States Congress modifies the Neutrality Acts by agreeing to sell war materials to any country paying cash and transporting the goods on their own ships. This directly helps Britain and France because both countries are in a position to meet these conditions.

The New York World's Fair opens in New York City.

Oil is discovered in Mississippi, at Tinsley and Vaughan.

The Civil Aeronautics Authority certifies its first woman airplane instructor, Evelyn Pinckert Kilgore.

Albert Einstein, who immigrated to the United States from Germany in 1933, writes to President Roosevelt about the feasibility of creating an atomic bomb.

Working on a budget of less than $700, John V. Atanasoff of Iowa creates a prototype electronic digital computer. His invention, however, is seen as a curiosity or a game rather than as a potentially functional tool; the project is shelved.

The Nobel Prize in physics is awarded to North Dakota scientist Ernest O. Lawrence for atomic research that included development of the cyclotron.

Russian American inventor Igor Sikorsky builds the first American-made helicopter.

Marshal Estigarriba becomes president of Paraguay. He serves until his death in an airplane crash in 1940.

Brazil and Chile suppress Nazi political activities and Brazil accepts 3,000 German Jewish refugees fleeing from Europe.

Approximately 28,000 people lose their lives in an earthquake in Chilian, Chile.

1930

through

1939

THE WORLD	THE WORLD	THE WORLD	THE WORLD

1930
through
1939

1930

At the London Naval Conference, Britain, the United States, Japan, France and Italy sign a disarmament treaty.

The last Allied troops leave Germany. The Nazi party gains strength in the national elections.

In India, Mohandas Gandhi's march from Ahmedabad to the seacoast begins the second civil disobedience campaign against British rule and discriminatory laws. Indian women, in support of Gandhi's campaign, openly protest British rule through demonstrations, boycotts of foreign cloth shops, and training themselves to make their own native clothing.

The Soviet Union establishes the Order of Lenin to honor individuals or groups that provide special service to the country.

The Colonial Statute of 1930 places Mozambique under the control of the Portuguese government.

Constantinople, Turkey, officially changes its name to Istanbul.

Haile Selassie (Ras Tafari Makonnen) becomes emperor of Ethiopia after the death of Empress Judith (1916). Selassie rules until 1974, though he is in exile during the Italian occupation from 1936 to 1941.

Carol II becomes king of Romania after removing his son, Michael I (1927), from the throne. Carol II rules until 1940.

English engineer (Sir) Frank Whittle patents the design for the jet engine.

British aviator Amy Johnson becomes the first woman to fly solo from London to Australia. The flight takes over 19 days.

United party leader G. W. Forbes becomes prime minister of New Zealand after the term of Joseph Ward (1928). Forbes serves until 1935.

1930-1932

A series of Round Table Conferences is held with Indian and British leaders in London, England, to discuss separate geographic entities for Muslims, Sikhs and untouchables, the release of political prisoners in exchange for stopping acts of civil disobedience and the development of an All-India Federation. The conferences produce very little in the way of positive action.

1931

German industrialists finance the development of the Nazi party.

In what becomes known as the Mukden or Manchuria Incident, a railroad explosion occurs near Mukden. Japanese officials capture the city and prepare for the occupation of Manchuria, then under Chinese control. This action violates the covenant of the League of Nations and Japan withdraws from the league in 1933.

The Statute of Westminster, passed by Britain's parliament, defines the dominions of the British Commonwealth as fully independent entities. The dominions include Australia, Canada, the Irish Free State, Newfoundland, New Zealand and South Africa.

Chinese civil code outlaws arranged marriages and the official keeping of concubines, as part of the communist strategy of giving women more voice and greater choices.

An earthquake hits Hawkes Bay, New Zealand.

Juan becomes king of Spain after the abdication of his father, Alfonso XIII (1886).

P. E. Svinhufvud becomes president of Finland after the term of Lauri Kr. Relander (1925). Svinhufvud until 1937.

1932

The Nazis become Germany's largest single political party but do not gain a majority in the *Reichstag* (the German Parliament).

Famine in the Soviet Union is worsened by peasant unrest and Joseph Stalin's actions to starve out those who oppose his rule.

Prime Minister Tsuyoshi Inukai of Japan is murdered in Tokyo by naval officers.

The Republic of Manchukuo (a state created by adding the Chinese province of Jehol to Manchuria) is proclaimed by the Japanese government. It lasts until 1945.

Siam (Thailand) becomes a constitutional monarchy when a coup forces Rama VII (1925) to grant a new constitution.

In Sweden, a socialist government comes to power.

A major earthquake in Gansu, China results in 70,000 deaths.

Arabian leader Abdul ibn Saud announces the union of the regions of Nejd and Hejaz into the new state of Saudi Arabia with himself as king. The region of Asir is annexed in 1933. Ibn Saud rules until 1953.

By the terms of the Poona Pact, the untouchable or lowest caste in India is given increased government representation.

Antonio de Oliveira Salazar becomes premier of Portugal. He rules until 1968.

Joseph A. Lyons becomes prime minister of Australia after the term of James H. Scullin (1929). Lyons serves until 1939.

1933-1945

The Holocaust

"Holocaust" is the term used to describe the Nazi annihilation of almost 6 million Jews (two-thirds of the pre-World War II European Jewish population), including 4.5 million from the Soviet Union, Poland and the Baltic states; 750,000 from Hungary and Romania; 290,000 from Germany and Austria; 105,000 from The Netherlands; 90,000 from France; 54,000 from Greece and the rest from other small countries.

In world history, the Holocaust is unique because it practices systematic genocide — the destruction of a people solely because of religion, race, ethnicity or nationality — on an unparalleled scale. Along with the Jews, another 9 to 10 million people — Gypsies, Slavs, Poles, Ukrainians and Belorussians — are killed. The only comparable act of genocide up to this point in modern times occurred in 1915 when an estimated 600,000 Armenians were massacred by Turkish forces.

In January 1933, Adolf Hitler is named German chancellor. Dachau, the first concentration camp, is established in the spring, and boycotts against Jews begin. In September 1935, the anti-Semitic Nuremberg Laws are passed by the German

Reichstag, outlawing marriage of Jews to non-Jews, and depriving Jewish citizens of their civil rights.

The Buchenwald concentration camp opens in the summer of 1937.

In the spring of 1938, anti-Semitic laws are extended to Austria after it is annexed by Germany. On November 9 a series of anti-Semitic riots known as *Kristallnacht,* or the Night of Broken Glass, occurs in Germany, Austria and Sudetenland (in the Czech Republic). Approximately 26,000 Jews are sent to concentration camps and Jewish children are expelled from schools. Widespread expropriation of Jewish property and businesses takes place. German authorities comply with a request from the Swiss government that passports of Jews be prominently marked so that immigration of Jews to Switzerland can be restricted.

As the war continues, Nazi acts against Jews are extended to all areas conquered by German forces.

In 1941 the deportation of German Jews begins; 175 Jews are killed, 1,000 are injured and 900 Jewish homes are destroyed in a *pogrom* (an organized attack) by the pro-Nazi regime in

THE WORLD	THE WORLD	THE WORLD	FOR CLASSROOM USE	

1933

Years of economic crisis in Germany have the effect of winning support for the Nazi party. Adolf Hitler is appointed chancellor of Germany. The *Reichstag* gives him absolute dictatorial power. Hitler and his Nazi party begin the systematic persecution and murder of European Jews and others that they feel oppose their ideals (*see* "The World, 1933-1945, The Holocaust").

In response to economic depression, growing unrest, and Nazi persecution, more than 100,000 people leave Europe. Many who cannot escape fall victim to Nazi persecution.

The fifth *aliyah* (a heavy wave of Jewish immigration) to Palestine begins. It continues until 1936.

Joseph Stalin begins a purge in the Union of Soviet Socialist Republics (Soviet Union). Many old Bolsheviks are arrested, imprisoned and executed.

The Soviet Union is formally recognized by the United States.

A world economic conference held in London fails to alleviate the Great Depression.

Germany and Japan announce their withdrawal from the League of Nations.

An earthquake in Japan results in nearly 3,000 deaths.

In New Zealand, Elizabeth McCombs becomes the first woman member of Parliament.

Romania's liberal prime minister Ion Duca is assassinated by the Iron Guard, a terrorist group within the popular Peasant party.

Ghazi becomes king of Iraq after the death of his father, Faisal I (1921). Ghazi rules until 1939.

Muhammad Zahir Shah becomes king of Afghanistan after his father, Nadir Shah (1929), is assassinated.

1934

In Germany, a neutrality treaty is signed with Poland.

Adolf Hitler (1933) takes the title *führer* (leader) after the death of Germany's President Paul von Hindenburg. Hitler rules until his death by suicide in 1945.

The Soviet Union is admitted to the League of Nations. The assassination of Communist party secretary Sergei M. Kirov leads to Stalin's "Treason Trials," and purges in the party.

During the Chinese civil war, Kuomintang defeat Mao Zedong (Mao Tse-tung) at Kiangsi and Chinese Communists begin the one-year "Long March" to Yenan, building peasant support along the way.

Dr. Engelbert Dollfuss, Austria's chancellor and virtual dictator of the country, is assassinated by members of the Austrian Nazi party. However, the attempted Nazi takeover of Austria is unsuccessful.

The Muslim League of India is reorganized by Mahomed Ali Jinnah. The organization's more concrete goal becomes the establishment of a seperate Muslim state in predominantly Hindu India. Jinnah later becomes known as the founder of Pakistan.

In a coup by fascist forces, Estonia's government is overthrown.

A major earthquake in Bihar-Nepal, India, results in 10,700 deaths.

Alexander (1921) of Yugoslavia is assassinated. Italian fascists or Croatian separatists are suspected. As a child, Alexander's son Peter II becomes king of Yugoslavia. He rules until 1945.

Leopold III becomes king of Belgium after the death of his father, Albert I (1909). Leopold III rules until 1951.

Henry Pu-Yi is made ruler of the Japanese-controlled state of Manchukuo. As Emperor Kangde (K'ang-te) he rules until 1945.

Scottish physicist (Sir) Robert Watson-West begins experiments that produce the first practical radar systems.

1935

The Saar, a hilly, mineral-rich region between Germany and France, administered by France through the League of Nations since 1919, is incorporated into Germany after the League conducts a plebiscite among the area's residents.

1930 through 1939

Baghdad, Iraq. More than 68,000 Jews are massacred in Odessa and Babi Yar (near Kiev); in Riga and Vilna, approximately 60,000 are killed. Nazi leaders select cyanide gas for the extermination camp "death showers" to implement their plans for a "final solution" to the existence of the Jewish population in Europe.

By early 1942 unified resistance in the Jewish ghettos begins, and resistance groups form in most of the conquered countries. They are organized to save Jewish people by hiding them or smuggling them to neutral countries, and to hinder the German war effort in any possible way. Most of Denmark's 8,000 Jews, for example, are smuggled to safety in Sweden — a neutral country. Swedish diplomat Raoul Wallenberg is said to have saved thousands of Jewish people in Budapest before his capture by Russian forces. Christians who help, hide or protect Jews face immediate punishment of death by firing squad.

In July 300,000 Jews from the Warsaw ghetto are deported to the Treblinka death camp in central Poland. During the German occupation of Libya, 2,000 Jews are deported and 400 are killed. The Warsaw, Poland, ghetto uprisings take place in January and April of 1943; the ghetto is ultimately overrun with German heavy artillery and destroyed, with more than 5,000

deaths recorded both inside and outside the ghetto. More than 20,000 Warsaw Jews are sent to the death camps at Auschwitz, Belzec and Maidenek.

In 1944, 476,000 Hungarian Jews are sent to Auschwitz. The family of Otto Frank, hiding from the *Gestapo* (Nazi secret police) in Amsterdam is betrayed and they are sent to Auschwitz. Their daughter, Anne, is transferred to Bergen-Belsen where she dies from disease. Her diaries, which reveal life in hiding under Nazi terror, are later discovered at the family's home in Amsterdam, now a museum. On D day, June 6, the Soviet army liberates Maidenek death camp. Late in the year, the Nazis try to hide evidence of their death camp activity.

In January 1945, Soviet troops liberate the Auschwitz death camp, but find few survivors in contrast to the more than 1 million who died in its gas chambers; Buchenwald, Bergen-Belsen and Dachau death camps are liberated by Allied forces in April 1945. Of the more than 500,000 survivors liberated from the camps, many die of disease and malnutrition within the coming year.

The Nuremberg war crimes trial is held, from November 1945 to October 1946 (*see* "The World, 1945-1946").

1930 through 1939

In Germany, Hitler and the Nazi regime repudiate the military restrictions of the 1919 Treaty of Versailles and introduce full conscription and military rearmament. Britain and France do not act to prevent the build-up of troops or armaments in Germany.

Czechoslovakia and the Soviet Union enter into an alliance to contain Nazi Germany.

Troops under Italian Premier Benito Mussolini invade Ethiopia. Despite a request from King Haile Selassie for help, the League of Nations invokes only ineffective sanctions against Italy.

In India, Jawaharlal Nehru objects to the Government of India Act but it is accepted by the Bombay Congress.

In China, Mao Zedong takes control of the Communist party.

The Philippines is granted internal self-government.

Rama VIII (Ananda Mahidol) is chosen king of Siam (Thailand) after the reign of his father, Rama VII. Rama VIII rules until 1946.

With the restoration of Greece's monarchy, George II (1922) again becomes king. He rules until 1947, though government by monarchy is regularly under attack in Greece.

Stanley Baldwin (1924), a Conservative, heads the coalition National party and again becomes prime minister of Great Britain. Baldwin serves until 1937.

Edvard Benes assumes the presidency of Czechoslovakia after Thomas Garrigue Masaryk (1918) retires.

M. J. Savage, a Labour party leader, becomes prime minister of New Zealand after the term of G. W. Forbes (1930). Savage serves until 1940.

More than 30,000 people die as the result of an earthquake in Quetta, India.

Irene Joliot-Curie and her husband, Frederic, are awarded the Nobel Prize for their work in creating artificial radioactive isotopes.

1935-1936

In a bloody rebellion, Japanese army officers try to take over the Japanese government. The rebels surrender only when Emperor Hirohito makes a personal appeal.

1936

German forces occupy the Rhineland, the demilitarized buffer zone between France and Germany previously under League of Nations control. Again, Britain and France fail to bring any pressure against Hitler.

A Rome-Berlin axis, or coalition, is proclaimed between Italy and Germany. In 1940 it is expanded to include Japan.

Japan and Germany sign an anti-Comintern pact against the Soviet Union; they are joined by Italy in 1937.

Azerbaijan becomes a republic of the Soviet Union.

Oil is discovered in Saudi Arabia.

Egypt and Britain sign an agreement whereby all British troops will leave Egypt except for those stationed at the Suez Canal.

Italy annexes Ethiopia and installs Victor Emmanuel III (1900) as emperor. Italy formally joins Ethiopia with Eritrea and Italian Somaliland to form Italian East Africa. Emperor Haile Selassie (1930) goes into exile. Victor Emmanuel III rules until 1943.

Edward VIII becomes king of Great Britain and Ireland after the death of his father, George V (1910). Edward VIII abdicates after a reign of 325 days to marry American-born divorcée Wallis Warfield Simpson. Edward VIII is the first British monarch ever to voluntarily surrender his crown. He is succeeded as king by his brother George VI. George VI rules until 1952.

Farouk I becomes king of Egypt after the death of his father, Fuad I (1922). Farouk I rules until 1952.

1936-1939

The Spanish Civil War takes place. Nationalist troops of General Francisco Franco are victorious over Loyalist forces, and Franco becomes Spain's dictator. After Barcelona and Madrid fall in 1939, the war ends. Italy and Germany support the Franco regime but Britain, France and the United States remain neutral. During the war, German planes bomb the unarmed town of Guernica, Spain.

1937

The Moscow "show trials" begin against former Trotsky followers who oppose the Stalin government in the Soviet Union.

Hitler repudiates the war guilt clause of the Versailles Treaty; he continues to build German military power but guarantees the neutrality of Belgium.

The government of the Irish Free State issues a new constitution that changes the country's name to Eire and asserts its right to the six northern counties.

Italy withdraws from the League of Nations.

Japanese forces invade China and conquer most of the coastal area. Chinese communists and nationalists fight together against the common enemy.

Japanese forces sink the American gunboat *Panay* in the Yangtze River in China. The United States cuts off oil shipments to Japan.

In an effort to circumvent import limits, Japanese exporting merchants reportedly are selling merchandise overseas with false "made in USA" labels.

Burma secedes from India. The Punjab becomes an autonomous province in India.

Aden (now in South Yemen) becomes a British crown colony.

The nonaggression pact of Saababad (suburb of Tehran, Iran) is signed by Afghanistan, Iran, Iraq and Turkey.

Neville Chamberlain, a Conservative, leads a coalition National party and becomes prime minister of Great Britain after the term of Stanley Baldwin (1935). Chamberlain serves until 1940.

Burma (Myanmar) becomes a British crown colony.

Kyösti Kallio becomes president of Finland after the term of P. E. Svinhufvud (1931). Kallio serves until 1940.

1938

Austria is invaded by Hitler's forces and is annexed by Germany, creating a political and geographical union of the two countries. Germany's anti-Semitic laws are promptly extended to Austria.

In the Munich Pact, Britain, France and Italy agree to allow Germany to partition Czechoslovakia, giving Hitler the German-speaking Sudetenland section. This act of appeasement is intended to prevent Hitler from further aggression in Europe.

Oil is discovered in Kuwait.

In Germany, *Kristallnacht* occurs. Gangs of Nazis burn synagogues and loot Jewish homes and businesses, killing or wounding many Jews and arresting thousands (*see* "The World, 1933-1945, The Holocaust").

The German automobile manufacturer Volkswagen begins production of its "people's car," the "beetle."

Ismet Inönü becomes president of Turkey after the death of Kemal Atatürk (1923). Ismet Inönü serves until 1950.

THE WORLD	THE WORLD	FOR CLASSROOM USE	FOR CLASSROOM USE	

1939

German forces occupy Bohemia and Moravia and threaten Danzig. The German government cancels agreements with Poland and Britain and concludes a secret, 10-year nonaggression pact with the Soviet Union, signed by German Foreign Minister Joachim von Ribbentrop and Russian Commissar of Foreign Affairs Vyacheslav M. Molotov. Called the Hitler-Stalin Pact, this agreement calls for Soviet control of Estonia, Lithuania, Latvia and Finland; forces Romania to relinquish territory; and details the partitioning of Poland if it is attacked. Poland is then invaded on the west by the German army while Soviet forces occupy the eastern section. The country is thus partitioned for a fourth time. Britain and France honor their support of Poland by renouncing the appeasement policy; they declare war on Germany. This invasion of Poland is considered the start of World War II (see "The World, 1939-1945, World War II.").

Led by former prime minister General Wladislaw Sikorski a Polish government-in-exile is formed in France. An "Underground State," meanwhile, is operating inside Poland during the harsh Nazi occupation. The secret government includes the Home Army, an underground press and educational, judicial and administrative systems. The Home Army gradually grows to be the fourth largest Allied army participating in World War II.

War begins between the Soviet Union and Finland; the Finns lose one-tenth of their territory in a 1940 peace treaty to end this conflict.

Japanese and Soviet troops fight on the Manchuria-Mongolia border; the Soviets are victorious.

Madrid falls to Franco's fascist troops and Spain becomes a dictatorship recognized by Britain, France and the United States.

Japanese troops occupy Indonesia.

Albania is occupied by Italian forces. King Zog I (Ahmed Zogu, 1928) flees after the invasion of his country. Italy's King Victor Emmanuel III is proclaimed king, but formally abdicates the Albanian throne in 1943.

Jan Christian Smuts (1919) again becomes prime minister of the Union of South Africa after the term of James B. M. Hertzog (1924). Smuts serves until 1948.

Siam officially adopts the name Thailand.

The United States Advisory Committee on Uranium recommends research and development of an atomic bomb. This program is later called the Manhattan Project.

Sir Earl C. G. Page serves for 20 days as prime minister of Australia after the term of Joseph A. Lyons (1932). Sir Robert Gordon Menzies succeeds Page. Menzies serves until 1941, and again from 1949 to 1966.

As a child, Faisal II becomes king of Iraq after the death of his father, Ghazi (1933). Faisal II rules until 1958.

Approximately 30,000 people die as a result of an earthquake in Erzincan, Turkey.

1930

through

1939

1930 through 1939

1939-1945

World War II

Before and during World War II, nations align themselves as follows: the Axis powers include Germany, Italy, Japan, Bulgaria, Hungary and Romania; the Allied powers, or the Allies, include the United States, Britain, France, the Soviet Union, Australia, Belgium, Brazil, Canada, China, Denmark, Greece, the Netherlands, New Zealand, Norway, Poland, South Africa and Yugoslavia. Sweden remains neutral during the war.

1939, Europe. Adolf Hitler's German forces occupy Czechoslovakia; in March Britain and France agree to support Poland. Italian troops invade Albania, and Hitler and Mussolini sign a mutual accord in May. Germany and the Soviet Union sign a nonaggression pact in August. On September 1, German forces begin a bombing attack on Poland, forcing Britain and France to give Hitler an ultimatum, followed by a declaration of war on Germany two days later. German forces invade Poland and annex Danzig. The Soviet Union invades Poland from the east; by the end of September, Poland is divided between the Soviet Union and Germany. British troop arrivals in France are complete by November and Soviet forces invade Finland the same month. The European Western Front sees limited activity ("Sitzkrieg").

1939, South America. In mid-December the Battle of the River Plate is fought, with the British cruisers H.M.S. *Exeter* and *Ajax* and New Zealand's *Achilles* against the German battleship *Admiral Graf Spee*. The German vessel is disabled off Montevideo, Uruguay, and Hitler orders it blown up on December 17 to prevent it from falling into British hands.

1940, Europe. In March the Soviet Union and Finland sign a peace treaty. In April and May, German forces invade Denmark, Norway, the Netherlands, Belgium, and Luxembourg. Several hundred Danish ships, outside their home ports at the time of the invasion, sail in Allied service throughout the war. Neville Chamberlain resigns as Britain's prime minister; Winston Churchill takes over. The German army crosses the French frontier, moving past the Maginot defensive line by using combined air, tank and infantry "Blitzkrieg" tactics. In the Dunkirk evacuation in late May and early June, 335,000 out of 400,000 British and French soldiers are rescued from Belgium by British civilian and naval craft. In June Italy declares war on France and Britain, and invades France. German forces enter Paris and the city is undefended. France, under Premier Henri Philippe Pétain, and Germany sign an armistice at Compiègne on June 22, and France is under German control. Soviet forces attack Estonia, Latvia and Lithuania in June and make them part of the Soviet Union. The Battle of Britain from July into October consists of almost daily airplane battles in British airspace. German armies capture Romanian oil fields in October and annex that country. The Italians' attempt to invade Greece in November fails because of British support. The Nazis bomb Coventry, England; the British Royal Air Force is victorious at the Battle of Britain; German losses are heavy enough that Hitler abandons his plan of conquering Britain.

1940, Africa and Asia. In July French ships of the pro-Nazi regime are sunk by the British navy at Oran, Algeria, in North Africa, causing the Vichy government to break diplomatic ties with Britain. General Charles de Gaulle escapes to Britain, signs an alliance with the British government, and forms a Free French government in exile. The Italian army invades the Sudan and follows with attacks on British Somaliland in August, but is severely beaten by the British by December. Japanese forces invade French Indochina in September.

1941, Europe. In April German troops launch attacks in the Balkans, occupy Estonia, and capture Albania and Macedonia. Yugoslavia surrenders but nationalist General Draja Mikhailovich continues guerrilla warfare; Marshal Tito leads left-wing guerrillas. German tanks enter Athens; remnants of the British army retreat from Greece late this month and from Crete in late May. In May, Rudolf Hess, Hitler's deputy führer, makes an unexplained trip to Scotland, where he is arrested. In a great naval battle, the H.M.S. *Hood* is sunk by the *Bismarck* which is then sunk by British air and naval fire — loss of life is heavy. In his Operation Barbarossa, Hitler attacks the Soviet Union on June 22. Finland declares war on the Soviet Union in hopes of regaining some of its conquered territory. After heavy fighting during the summer, German troops capture Smolensk. With the Atlantic Charter, United States President Roosevelt and British Prime Minister Churchill agree in August on war aims. German forces move to within 25 miles of Moscow and by September, Leningrad (formerly St. Petersburg) is under attack. The fighting around Moscow is a standoff during the winter months as the German army is unprepared for the cold. Germany and Italy declare war on the United States, thus ending United States neutrality in Europe. Hungary declares war on Britain, the Soviet Union and the United States. The United States Congress declares war on Germany and Italy on December 11.

1941, Africa and Asia. In January British forces enter East Africa and Haile Selassie returns to Ethiopia. German troops under Field Marshal Erwin Rommel cross north Africa in February and engage British troops, leading to a German counteroffensive in March. British forces arrive in Iraq in May and join Free French forces in their invasion of Syria and Lebanon in June to prevent a German takeover. By July Japanese forces have control of French Indochina and in late November Japan's carrier task force sails for Hawaii. The December 7 Japanese attack on Pearl Harbor cripples the United States Pacific fleet. Britain and the United States declare war on Japan. Japan declares war on the Allies and invades the Philippines and Guam the following week.

1942, Europe. In March the Royal Air Force begins "saturation bombing" of German targets; Cologne is struck at the end of May. The village of Lidice in Czechoslovakia is razed by German forces on June 10 in retaliation for the death of deputy Gestapo chief Reinhard Heydrich at the hands of Czech resistance fighters. Fighting continues in the Soviet Union. In July German forces capture Sebastopol in the Crimea. In August the German army begins an attack on Stalingrad. The siege of the city, which lasts until early February 1943, claims almost 1.5 million lives. In November the Vichy French scuttle most of their navy at Toulon, France, to prevent the ships from falling into Allied hands; additional German troops enter France.

1942, Africa and Asia. Manila, Philippines, falls to the Japanese in early 1942. On February 15 Britain surrenders Singapore to Japan. Allied forces are defeated in the Battle of the Java Sea and Japanese forces land on the Solomon Islands in March. In early spring Burma (Myanmar) is overrun by Japanese troops. United States troops on Bataan peninsula in the Philippines surrender, and on April 9 the infamous "Death March" begins. United States and Filipino troops on Corregidor Island in Manila Bay surrender to the Japanese on May 6. United States forces are victorious over Japanese troops in the Coral Sea, the first sea battle fought by aircraft from ships. Rommel prepares a German attack on Egypt from Libya. Americans are victorious over Japanese forces at Midway June 3-6. This victory marks the turning point of the Pacific campaign. In Syria, Tobruk falls to German forces in June. In August United States Marines under General Douglas MacArthur take Guadalcanal in the Solomon Islands. In late October and early November, British General Bernard L. Montgomery leads Britain's 8th Army in a successful defense of Egypt, with a resounding victory at El Alamein. Troops from the United States and Britain land in French North Africa on November 8. Rommel and his men are forced to retreat and lose Tobruk and Benghazi. MacArthur becomes Commander-in-Chief of the Allied forces in the Far East.

1943, Europe. General Dwight D. (Ike) Eisenhower is appointed supreme commander of the Allied Expeditionary Force. Soviet forces annihilate the Hungarian 2nd army near the Russian city of Voronezh; 100,000 Hungarian soldiers die. In early February an exhausted German 6th Army under Field Marshal Friedrich von Paulus surrenders at Stalingrad; this event marks the turning point of the war in the Soviet Union. Soviet forces drive the German army back to the Donets River. Germany's last major offensive campaign, at Kursk in July, is unsuccessful. Benito Mussolini is removed from power on the orders of Victor Emmanuel III on July 25, and Pietro Badoglio is named premier of Italy. Allied troops under General George Patton land on the Italian mainland in early September after the conquest of Sicily. The Italian government surrenders on September 8 but German troops in Italy continue to fight. Mussolini sets up a puppet "government-in-exile" in the German-controlled region. Allies land at Salerno with heavy casualties on September 9 and German forces seize Rome on September 10. Soviet forces retake Smolensk from the Germans on September 25. In October Italy declares war on Germany. At the Teheran Conference, November 28 through December 1, Roosevelt, Churchill and Stalin agree on plans to invade France.

1943, Africa and Asia. The British 8th Army enters Tripoli and defeats the Axis forces at the end of January. At the Casablanca Conference in mid-January, Churchill and Roosevelt agree on the goal of unconditional Japanese surrender. In March the Japanese are defeated at the Battle of the Bismarck Sea. On May 7 the Axis forces surrender in Tunisia. Remnants of the German army are trapped on Cape Bon, ending the war in Africa on May 12. In August, the Allied initiative against the Japanese in Burma begins. Allied forces land in the Solomon and Gilbert Islands in November. At the Cairo Conference in late November, Roosevelt, Churchill and Chiang Kai-shek of China pledge the defeat of Japan and the liberation of Korea.

1944, Europe. In January United States and British troops land at Anzio on the western coast of Italy. German U-boat activity in the Atlantic Ocean is brought to an end in March. The Allies take control of Monte Cassino, Italy, in May, after months of bombing. The Allied bombing of Berlin in March uses the highly secret Norden bombsight. Soviet troops invade German-occupied Bulgaria. The Crimea is liberated by the end of May with the recapture of Odessa and Sebastopol. Soviet forces also regain control of Estonia. German bombing of Britain uses new V-2 rockets designed by Wernher von Braun. United States and British forces enter Rome on June 4. On D day, June 6, Allies under the command of General Eisenhower launch an invasion of the Normandy peninsula. Hitler is wounded in a bomb attempt on July 20. Romania joins the Allied forces. Paris is liberated by Free French troops under General de Gaulle on August 25. British troops defend the Rhine bridges against German attack at the Battle of Arnhem, Netherlands, September 17-25. Athens is freed by the Allies on October 13. Ukrainians and Yugoslavs retake Belgrade on October 20. The Allies capture Strasbourg November 24 but on December 16 the Germans launch a counteroffensive in Belgium, the Battle of Bulge, which draws heavy casualties.

1944, The Pacific. In February Allied forces attack the Japanese base at Truk (an island group in the Western Pacific Ocean) and land on the Marshall Islands. Japanese forces abandon Rabaul in April and Allied forces land in New Guinea. United States planes control the skies in the Battle of the Philippine Sea in June, inflicting heavy losses on the Japanese air force. On July 9 United States forces capture Saipan on the Mariana Islands, giving the newly designed B-29 bombers a base to fly the 1,300 miles to bomb Tokyo. Americans invade the Philippines on October 20 and gain control by early January. American troops defeat the Japanese fleet in Leyte Gulf, October 25-26.

1945, Europe. In January Soviet forces begin an attack on East Prussia. The Yalta Agreement signed by Roosevelt, Churchill and Stalin establishes the basis for Allied occupation of Germany and returns some Soviet lands. The Soviet Union agrees to a friendship pact with China on February 11. Allied troops reach the Rhine in March and capture Cologne, Germany. Mussolini is killed at Lake Como on April 28, and Italy is surrendered the following day. Admiral Karl Doenitz takes command in Germany; Hitler's suicide is announced May 1. Berlin falls the next day. Germany signs unconditional surrender terms at Rheims on May 8, V-E Day. At the Potsdam Conference, which ends August 2, Truman, Stalin and Churchill (and later Atlee) establish a council of foreign ministers to prepare peace treaties and plan German postwar government and reparations. The Nuremberg trials of Nazi leaders, which will last almost one year, begin in Germany in November.

1945, Africa and Asia. United States marines attack Iwo Jima on February 19 and Okinawa in April and May. American air strikes devastate major Japanese cities beginning in March. United States troops capture Iwo Jima on March 16. Allied troops recapture Okinawa on June 21 after three months of intensive fighting. British forces drive the Japanese army out of Singapore. Atomic bombs are dropped on Hiroshima on August 6, and Nagasaki on August 9. The Soviet Union declares war on Japan on August 8 and immediately sends an occupation force into Manchuria. Soviet and United States troops invade Korea and force the Japanese to surrender. On V-J Day, August 14, Japan surrenders. Terms are signed on September 2, aboard the United States battleship *Missouri* in Tokyo Bay.

The war results in more than 15 million military casualties and 35 million civilian deaths, including approximately 20 million from the Soviet Union; more than 25 million people are left homeless.

1930

through

1939

NATIVE AMERICAN	NATIVE AMERICAN	AFRICAN AMERICAN	AFRICAN AMERICAN

NATIVE AMERICAN

1940

For the first time in history, American Indian men register for the draft. Seminoles, however, refuse to register because they are technically still at war with the United States.

1941

In *United States as Guardian of Hualapai* v. *Santa Fe Pacific Railroad Company* the Supreme Court restores more than 500,000 acres of land to Arizona's Hualapai (Walapai) Indians.

Relics of a pit dwelling community, c. 450, are discovered in Apache National Forest in New Mexico.

1941-1945

During World War II, approximately 25,000 Native Americans see active military duty. Choctaws, Navajos, Comanches and Kiowas again serve as "code talkers," as occurred in World War I. Ira Hayes, a Pima, is one of the Marines who raises the flag at Iwo Jima.

1942

Felix Cohen's *Handbook of Federal Indian Law* is published. It is the first consistent overview of federal policy toward Native Americans.

1944

Representatives of Native American tribes from 27 states meet in Denver, Colorado, and found the National Congress of American Indians (NCAI).

William G. Stigler, a Choctaw from Oklahoma, is elected to the United States Congress. He serves until his death in 1952.

1946

The Indian Claims Commission is established to hear cases regarding compensation to Indians for loss of land. This commission is viewed by many Indians as an attempt by the federal government to legitimize its prior seizure of their lands.

NATIVE AMERICAN

1948

The part of New Mexico's state constitution that denies Native Americans the right to vote is declared unconstitutional in federal court at Santa Fe. American Indians in the state are subsequently allowed to vote. A similar court case in Arizona gives Indians the franchise there.

1949

The Hoover Commission on the Reorganization of Government recommends the termination policy toward Native Americans.

AFRICAN AMERICAN

1940

Willard S. Townsend, president of the International Brotherhood of Redcaps, becomes the first African American to hold a national office in organized labor when he is made an international vice-president of the Congress of Industrial Organizations (CIO).

1941

When the U.S.S. *Arizona* is attacked at Pearl Harbor, messman Dorie Miller removes his wounded captain from the bridge and, although untrained on the weapon, mans an anti-aircraft gun, repelling the Japanese attack. For this act of bravery, Miller receives the Navy Cross.

Dr. Charles Drew, an African American, is recognized for innovations in blood preservation, surgical procedures and blood banks. These developments are especially significant during World War II.

1941-1945

Although segregation is still in practice, African Americans serve in every branch of the United States military. Many individuals and entire units win citations and medals of merit for their service during the war. A few examples are the 99th and 332nd Fighter Squadrons, the 614th Tank Destroyer Battalion and the 969th Field Artillery Battalion. Four Distinguished Service Crosses, four Navy Crosses and the Order of the Soviet Union are awarded to African American men. Four also receive France's croix de guerre.

1942

The Congress of Racial Equality is formed in Chicago and James Farmer, one of its organizers, becomes the first national director. Farmer serves until 1966. The organization favors the use of passive resistance and sit-ins to gain support for its goal of eliminating racial segregation and discrimination.

AFRICAN AMERICAN

The Johnson Publishing Company, formed under the direction of John Harold Johnson, begins publication of the *Negro Digest*.

The United States merchant ship *Booker T. Washington* is launched with an African American captain, Hugh Mulzac, and an interracial crew.

The first African American recruits are allowed in the United States Navy.

1943

William L. Dawson, a Democrat, is elected to the United States House of Representatives from Illinois. He serves 15 terms.

1943-1945

The 99th Pursuit Squadron, the first African American airborne unit, flies more than 1,500 combat missions. Members receive a commendation from the commanding general and a Distinguished Unit Citation for a long and grueling air attack on Berlin.

1944

The United Negro College Fund (UNCF) is established in New York City to provide financial support for African American colleges.

In *Smith* v. *Allwright,* the Supreme Court declares that the Fifteenth Amendment to the Constitution forbids the exclusion of African Americans from primary elections ("white primaries") conducted by the Democratic party of Texas.

1945

The Johnson Publishing Company begins publication of *Ebony*. The company follows in 1950 with *Tan* and in 1951 with *Jet*.

Adam Clayton Powell, Jr., a Democrat, is elected to the United States House of Representatives from New York. He serves 14 terms.

The first African American women members of the Navy Nurses Corps are sworn in.

1940 through 1949

AFRICAN AMERICAN	AFRICAN AMERICAN	ASIAN AMERICAN	FOR CLASSROOM USE	

1946

President Harry S Truman appoints European American and African American representatives to form the Presidential Committee on Civil Rights. In 1947 the committee issues a report recommending the creation of a permanent Fair Employment Practices Commission, the elevation of the Civil Rights Section of the Justice Department to division status, and the enactment of laws on a federal level to prevent lynching and promote equal legal treatment.

In *Morgan* v. *The Commonwealth of Virginia,* the Supreme Court rules that the state law requiring segregation on buses violates the commerce clause as it applies to interstate passengers.

Charles S. Johnson becomes the first African American president of Fisk University. He is also a founder of the magazine *Opportunity,* published by the National Urban League, and serves for a time as its editor.

1947

Jackie Robinson joins the Brooklyn (now Los Angeles) Dodgers baseball team as the first African American player in the major leagues.

1948

D. V. Carter, president of the National Association for the Advancement of Colored People (NAACP), is beaten by European Americans for escorting other African Americans to the polls in Montgomery, Alabama. In Vidalia, Georgia, Robert Mallard is lynched by a group of hooded men when he votes after being warned not to.

In Mississippi, the Reverend William Bender, educator and president of a local NAACP branch, is prevented from voting by three armed European American men.

President Truman issues Executive Order 9981 which bans racial segregation in the United States Armed Forces.

Edward R. Dudley is appointed ambassador to Liberia. He serves until 1953.

The United States Supreme Court rules in *Shelly* v. *Kraemer* and *Hurd* v. *Hodge* that agreements banning African Americans or any other racial group from owning or living on property are legally unenforceable.

1949

The country's first African American-owned radio station, WERD, goes on the air in Atlanta, Georgia.

Wesley A. Brown becomes the first African American to graduate from the United States Naval Academy at Annapolis, Maryland.

Dr. W. Montague Cobb becomes editor of the *Journal of the National Medical Association.* Dr. Cobb is instrumental in the creation of Imhotep, an organization whose purpose is to eliminate segregation in hospital services. He serves as president of the National Medical Association in 1964.

William Henry Hastie, who served as governor of the Virgin Islands since 1946, is appointed judge of the United States Circuit Court of Appeals by President Truman.

Congressman William Dawson is elected chairman of the House Committee on Government Operations.

Edward R. Dudley is appointed ambassador to Liberia. He serves until 1953.

1940

The United States census reports approximately 77,500 Chinese Americans in the mainland United States, 50 in Alaska and 28,700 in Hawaii. The sex ratio is 285 males to 100 females on the mainland.

There are 28 Chinatowns left in the United States, with the number decreasing as time passes. Some have already been integrated and others are involved in slum clearance projects.

Angel Island Immigration Station closes permanently after a fire destroys the administration building. The detention facilities are moved to San Francisco.

1941

Upon his arrival in the United States, Japanese Ambassador Admiral Kichisaburo Nomura exhorts all Japanese Americans to be loyal and true to the United States.

A government report states that Japanese Americans possess an extraordinary degree of loyalty to the United States, and that immigrant Japanese are of no danger to the nation. Secret surveillance by the Federal Bureau of Investigation (FBI) and Naval Intelligence supports these findings.

An Army intelligence school begins to teach the Japanese language in San Francisco, with four *nisei* (first generation Japanese American born in the United States) instructors and 60 students — 58 *nisei* and two European Americans.

On December 7, the Japanese bombing of Pearl Harbor draws the United States into World War II. Nearly 2,200 Japanese aliens are quickly arrested. Japan invades countries in Asia, including the Philippines. Thousands of Filipinos volunteer to serve in the United States Army as Philippine Scouts.

On December 9, the first of 160 *issei* (Japanese immigrant generation) community leaders from Hawaii are sent to the Sand Island (Honolulu) detention camp.

1940

through

1949

ASIAN AMERICAN	ASIAN AMERICAN	ASIAN AMERICAN	ASIAN AMERICAN

1941-1945

Many Filipinos get defense jobs, while others enlist or are drafted into the military and therefore acquire United States citizenship.

More than 33,000 Japanese American men and women serve in the United States military during World War II, 6,000 of them in the Pacific.

Wartime labor shortages open up job opportunities for Chinese in the United States, both immigrants and American-born.

1942

The War Department classifies Japanese American men of draft age as 4-C, enemy aliens. This designation stands until January 1943.

The Hearst newspapers on the West Coast attack Japanese Americans and begin the public outcry for mass exclusion.

General Delos C. Emmons, commander of the army, rejects a War Department order to fire all Japanese American civilians employed by the Army in Hawaii.

The War Department argues that it is necessary to remove Japanese Americans from the West Coast. President Roosevelt signs Executive Order 9066 which sets in motion the internment of all West Coast Japanese Americans.

Earl Warren, attorney general of California, testifies at public hearings in San Francisco that the very lack of anti-United States activities by Japanese Americans is confirmation that such actions are planned for the future.

The Wartime Civilian Control Administration (WCCA) is established to handle forced removal and interim detention. Japanese Americans are evacuated from the Pacific coast and placed in relocation camps behind barbed wire.

The Dies Committee (House Committee to investigate Un-American Activities) promises to release a "Yellow Paper" revealing a massive spy ring involving 150,000 Japanese Americans. No such paper is released, and no Japanese Americans are convicted of spying during the war.

Congressional bill H.R. 1844 enables Filipino residents of the United States to become naturalized citizens.

Western Defense Commander General John L. DeWitt issues the first of 108 military proclamations that result in the detention of more than 112,000 Japanese Americans from the West Coast. More than two-thirds of those interned are American citizens.

Minoru Yasui turns himself in at the Portland, Oregon, police station to test discriminatory curfew regulations issued by General DeWitt. In 1943 the United States Supreme Court upholds the government's position.

California Governor Culbert Olson fires all Japanese Americans in state civil service.

At the request of the United States government, 141 civilians of Japanese ancestry from South America arrive in San Francisco aboard a United States vessel. By the end of 1943, 2,100 persons of Japanese ancestry, mostly from Peru, are in custody for use as hostages for prisoner exchanges.

Japanese American Kanesaburo Oshima is shot and killed by a guard at the Fort Sill, Oklahoma, internment camp. Fred Korematsu is arrested in Oakland, California, for remaining in a "military area" and refusing to report for detention. Two Japanese American men, both invalids, are shot and killed by guards at the internment camp at Lordburg, New Mexico.

An all-*nisei* army battalion is formed in Hawaii. The soldiers are sent to the mainland for training and become the 100th Infantry Battalion.

By June 5, all persons of Japanese ancestry in the Pacific Coast region are now in temporary detention camps called assembly centers.

The Native Sons of the Golden West files a suit in San Francisco to strip Japanese Americans of their citizenship.

By the end of October, the army completes the transfer of all Japanese American internees from 15 temporary assembly centers to 10 permanent War Relocation Authority (WRA) detention camps, or relocation centers.

A mass strike and demonstration takes place at the Poston, Arizona, detention camp to protest the arrest of two inmates. During a similar demonstration at the Manzanar, California, camp, two men are killed when military police open fire.

1943

As China becomes a wartime ally against Japan, Chinese exclusion laws are repealed by Congress. The partial assimilation of Chinese Americans and their occupational specialties help to mitigate anti-Chinese feelings. The wartime labor shortage creates job opportunities for Chinese immigrants, who work in shipyards and other war-related industries or fill technical, professional and white-collar positions. Also about 8,000 serve in the American Armed Forces.

The all-Japanese American 442nd Regimental Combat Team assembles for training at Camp Shelby, Mississippi. *Nisei* combat units such as the 100th Infantry Battalion (the "Purple Heart Battalion") and the 442nd Regimental Combat Team give outstanding service throughout the war.

The Wyoming legislature enacts a law denying Japanese American citizens at the Heart Mountain, Wyoming, detention camp the right to vote. Similar laws are passed by other states.

A loyalty questionnaire is administered at all 10 detention camps to all Japanese American men and women over age 17.

The Congress of American Citizens is formed at the Heart Mountain, Wyoming, detention camp to protest the loyalty oath under the circumstances of imprisonment without due process.

The War Department announces the reinstatement of the draft for *nisei* men in detention camps.

The War Department insists that General DeWitt's *Final Report* be revised to conceal evidence that is damaging to the government in the pending *Hirabayashi* and *Yasui* cases.

At a mass meeting at Heart Mountain, 400 *nisei* vote unanimously to resist the draft until their constitutional rights are restored.

More than 100 *nisei* soldiers at Fort McClellan, Alabama, refuse to undergo combat training to protest the continued confinement of their families. Twenty-one are court-martialed and sentenced to prison. Others are assigned to the 1800th General Service Battalion.

In *Hirabayashi* v. *United States,* the Supreme Court upholds a conviction for violating curfew on the grounds that the federal government may take necessary measures to protect an area threatened by Japanese attack. The Court also rules in favor of the government in the *Yasui* case.

1944

Sixty-three young *nisei* men at Heart Mountain, Wyoming, are convicted of refusing to report for induction and are sentenced to three years in the federal penitentiary.

Seven leaders of the Heart Mountain Fair Play Committee in Wyoming are convicted of counseling others to resist the draft.

In anticipation of a Supreme Court decision, the War Department announces the revocation of the West Coast exclusion order against Japanese Americans effective January 2, 1945.

1940 through 1949

The Supreme Court rules that expulsion and detention are constitutional in *Korematsu* v. *United States*. In *Ex Parte Endo* the Court declares that the WRA can no longer detain admittedly loyal citizens against their will. This ruling opens the way for Japanese Americans to return to the West Coast.

1945

Much legislation restricting Asian Americans is overturned or repealed after the war. For example, the Western Defense Command issues a public proclamation revoking exclusion orders and military restrictions against persons of Japanese ancestry. Additionally, a court of appeals decision overturns the conviction of the Heart Mountain Fair Play Committee leaders accused of counseling others to resist the draft.

A California ruling enables Filipinos and others classified as Oriental to purchase land. Filipinos buy homes outside of "Little Manila" ghettos. Many buy small farms in the San Fernando Valley, Torrance and Gardena areas.

Many Filipinos in the United States who served in the military take civil service examinations and find employment in post offices, police forces and other agencies of federal, state and local governments. American citizenship is further extended for Filipinos, and the immigration quota is raised to 100 annually.

President Truman signs the War Brides Act, which allows Asian brides of American servicemen to enter the United States. About 6,000 Chinese women immigrate during the act's three-year operation.

1946

The United States provides aid to rebuild the Philippines.

The first Congressional Medal of Honor to a Japanese American is awarded posthumously to Pfc. Sadao S. Munemori, killed in action in Italy.

Congress passes the G.I. Fiancées Act facilitating admission of foreign-born fiancées engaged to members of the United States Armed Forces. Ninety-one Chinese people are admitted between 1947 and 1949.

The WRA program officially ends. The last of the 10 major detention camps, Tule Lake in California, closes.

The Philippines regains independence. Exchange students, workers and visitors overcome the rigid immigration quotas and remain in the United States by marrying United States citizens.

The combined 100th Infantry Battalion and 442nd Regimental Combat Team receive a Presidential Unit Citation, their eighth, from President Truman.

A law is enacted admitting Chinese alien wives and children of United States citizens on a nonquota basis.

Some Filipinos and immigrants from India are given naturalization privileges in recognition of their support and contributions during World War II.

Wing F. Ong becomes an Arizona state assemblyman, the first Chinese American in the continental United States to be elected to office.

Carlos Busolan's book *America Is In the Heart* is published, recounting the author's experiences as a young Filipino living and working in the United States during the 1930s.

1947

President Truman fully pardons all 267 Japanese American draft resisters.

1948

Congress passes the Displaced Persons Act, which grants permanent resident status to more than 3,500 Chinese people living in the United States since the outbreak of the civil war in China. This act begins the second large wave of emigration from China to the United States.

In *Oyama* v. *California,* the federal Supreme Court holds that a California statute violates the equal protection clause of the Fourteenth Amendment because the law creates a presumption that the title to land, conveyed to an eligible citizen but paid for by an ineligible alien, is held for the benefit of the alien.

California nullifies its anti-miscegenation law.

President Truman signs the Evacuation Claims Act, which pays less than 10 cents on the dollar for detainees' lost property. Many cannot file claims because required documents were lost or destroyed during their incarceration.

1949

As a result of the creation of the People's Republic of China (PRC), more than 3,400 Chinese visitors to the United States have their temporary status adjusted to permanent resident status under the provisions of the Displaced Persons Act of 1948. The victory of Communist forces leads to new emigration from China. Many who come to the United States are intellectuals, wealthy former officials and Nationalists.

Job horizons for Chinese Americans improve. Though the majority still work in restaurants, laundries, grocery stores, services and garment factories, a growing number are employed in professional and technical occupations.

Iva Toguri d'Aquino, a *nisei* woman trapped in wartime Japan, is found guilty of making propaganda broadcasts for Radio Tokyo. Her conviction is based on perjured statements of two *nisei* witnesses coached by United States government attorneys.

1940

through

1949

EUROPEAN AMERICAN	EUROPEAN AMERICAN	HISPANIC AMERICAN	HISPANIC AMERICAN

1940

Russian American inventor Vladimir Zworykin develops the electron microscope.

As German forces invade France during World War II, the United States becomes a refuge for French immigrants.

1941

The Tolstoy Foundation establishes the Reed Farm in upstate New York as a relocation center for European refugees.

1942

Archaeologist Philip Ainsworth Means examines an ancient cylindrical structure in Newport, Rhode Island, believed to have been built by Vikings in the 1300s. One theory is that this structure may be the oldest Christian church in the Western Hemisphere.

1946

Clinton P. Anderson, a Swedish American from New Mexico, is appointed secretary of the United States Department of Agriculture.

1947

Approximately 24,000 Hungarians seek admittance to the United States as refugees from Hungary's communist regime. They are part of a larger influx of central and eastern European refugees. Some are ardent nationalists or foes of communism; others seek economic opportunities.

A new wave of Soviet immigration to the United States begins. This group includes former war prisoners, slave laborers and refugees in Germany who refused to return to the Soviet Union after World War II.

1948

Thousands of Hungarians living in camps in West Germany at the end of World War II are classified by the United States Immigration and Naturalization Service as displaced persons. This designation enables them to immigrate to the United States in numbers greater than their standing quota, through the Displaced Persons Act of 1948. More than 13,000 Hungarians from these camps come to the United States.

1940

Popular Democratic party candidates win key offices in Puerto Rican elections. Luis Muñoz Marín presides over the Senate.

The United States census reports just under 70,000 Puerto Ricans living in the mainland United States and 1.88 million in Puerto Rico.

The Puerto Rican Industrial Development Corporation is established as an independent corporation furnishing credit and tax exemptions to assist private industry.

1941

Rexford Guy Tugwell, a European American, is named the last United States governor of Puerto Rico and joins Luis Muñoz Marín in an ambitious economic development program. Tugwell serves until 1946.

1941-1945

More than 400,000 Hispanic Americans serve in the United States military during World War II. Mexican Americans win more Medals of Honor than any other American ethnic group during this war. More than 65,000 Puerto Ricans participate in World War II; 23 are killed and 165 wounded.

1942

Bilateral agreements dealing with the *bracero* (temporary resident migrant worker) program are made with Mexico, British Honduras, Barbados and Jamaica for entry of temporary workers to relieve wartime labor shortages and to legalize and control the flow of agricultural workers into the United States. Under this program as many as 400,000 workers are admitted each year for seasonal agricultural labor.

Puerto Rico is virtually isolated from the United States for a time by Nazi submarines in Caribbean waters.

Hiram G. Bithorn is the first Puerto Rican to play professional baseball. He plays for the Chicago Cubs.

1943

In the summer, thousands of sailors and soldiers attack Mexican Americans in Los Angeles in what is known as the "zoot suit riot."

Antonio Manuel Fernández is elected as a representative to the United States Congress from New Mexico. He serves until his death in 1956.

1944

The Comité Méxicano Central el Racismo is created in Mexico to assist Mexicans in the United States in their fight against racism.

The Popular Democratic party wins the Puerto Rican election with 383,000 votes, compared to 208,000 of the combined opposition.

Jesús T. Piñero becomes Puerto Rico's resident commissioner. He serves until 1946, when he is named governor by President Truman.

Mid-1940s

An average of 20,000 Puerto Ricans come annually to the mainland as contract farm workers. Some stay on as permanent residents, mostly in the New York City area. They often work in menial or unskilled jobs.

1945

The Puerto Rican legislature prepares and submits the Tydings-Piñero Bill, which provides three alternatives for Puerto Ricans: independence, statehood or dominion status. The United States military opposes the bill for "national security reasons" and it is tabled.

1946

President Truman names Jesús T. Piñero, former resident commissioner, as the first Puerto Rican governor of the island.

Dr. Mariano Villaronga is appointed as Puerto Rico's commissioner of education by President Truman. Dr. Villaronga makes Spanish the primary language of instruction, with English required as a second language.

Gilberto Concepción de Gracia founds the Puerto Rican Independent party (PIP).

1940
through
1949

HISPANIC AMERICAN	FOR CLASSROOM USE	FOR CLASSROOM USE	FOR CLASSROOM USE	

The GI Forum is organized to assist Hispanic American war veterans.

Felisa Ricón de Gautier is elected mayor of San Juan, Puerto Rico. She serves until 1969. Antonio Fernos-Isern becomes resident commissioner; he serves until 1965.

1947

The Community Service Organization (CSO) is established to foster political activism and voter registration among Mexican Americans.

"Operation Bootstrap" is initiated in Puerto Rico as a plan for economic development. It is directed by "Fomento Económico," a government agency created to develop economic initiatives.

President Truman signs the Crawford-Butler Act, which gives Puerto Ricans the right to elect their own governor, instead of having one appointed by the president.

1948

The Popular Democratic Party wins in the Puerto Rican election. Luis Muñoz Marín becomes the first popularly elected governor of Puerto Rico. He serves until 1964.

The Puerto Rican Department of Labor sets up a Division of Migration in New York City.

1949

A Mayor's Committee for Puerto Rican Affairs is created to ease the adjustment of Puerto Ricans in New York City.

The Pan American Juridical Committee meets in Havana, Cuba, to study the problem of colonialism in America. One-third of its final report pertains to Puerto Rico, but the United States government convinces the committee that its purpose is to study the problem of colonies held by powers other than the United States.

1940

through

1949

1940
through
1949

1940

The United States census reports the country's population at 131.8 million, including American citizens living abroad.

The United States creates its first peacetime conscription with the passage of the Selective Training and Service Act.

In a 99-year lease agreement with Britain, the United States has use of approximately one-tenth of the land area of Bermuda for development of naval and air bases. The federal government also leases bases in Chile and Brazil.

The Nationality Act, which gives Chinese people the right to attain United States citizenship through naturalization, essentially repeals the Exclusion Law of 1882.

United States immigration services are transferred from the Department of Labor to the Department of Justice.

The Angel Island Immigration Station is closed after fire destroys the administration building.

The Smith Act requires registration and fingerprinting of aliens in the United States, makes it illegal to advocate the overthrow of the government or belong to any organization that does, and increases the grounds for deportation.

Margaret Chase Smith is elected to represent Maine in the United States House of Representatives. She will later become the first woman to serve in both the House and Senate.

The collision of a strong low-pressure system and a mass of arctic air over the Upper Mississippi area results in a storm that is best described as a winter hurricane, with Iowa the hardest hit. As the temperature drops 45 degrees in 16 hours, freezing rain is followed by deep blowing snow. More than 150 people lose their lives in this freak storm.

Former Russian Revolution leader Leon Trotsky is murdered in Mexico.

Manuel Ávila Camacho becomes president of Mexico after the term of Lázaro Cárdenas (1934). Camacho serves until 1946.

Fulgencio Batista y Zaldívar is elected president of Cuba after the term of Federico Laredo Bru (1936). Zaldívar serves until 1944.

1940-1941

The United States negotiates 99-year leases on formerly British military bases in Trinidad, Guyana, Antigua, St. Lucia, Jamaica and Bahamas.

1941

Franklin D. Roosevelt begins a historic third term as president of the United States; Henry A. Wallace is vice president. Both are Democrats. Roosevelt delivers his "Four Freedoms" speech to Congress, in which he sets out the goals for American policy: freedom of speech and expression, freedom of religion, freedom from want and freedom from fear.

Harlan Fiske Stone becomes chief justice of the United States Supreme Court. He serves until 1946.

President Roosevelt and British Prime Minister Winston Churchill agree to the Atlantic Charter, calling for the establishment of the United Nations after the end of the war. Roosevelt also signs the Lend-Lease Act creating a favored-nations structure for countries to receive military support. Those nations that cannot pay for the goods can either "borrow or rent" them.

President Roosevelt declares a national emergency and sets up the Office of Price Administration and Civilian Supply (OPA). In 1942 Congress gives the OPA authority to ration goods and set ceilings on consumer prices for many commodities.

President Roosevelt issues an executive order banning racial discrimination in defense industries. The President also orders the establishment of the Fair Employment Practices Committee (FECP) to eliminate federal employment discrimination.

The governor of the Territory of Hawaii places the islands under martial law; the state of emergency lasts until 1944.

In the United States, the Manhattan Project begins research on the creation of an atomic bomb.

In a surprise air raid, Japanese bombers attack Pearl Harbor, Honolulu, Hawaii. This action immobilizes the United States' Pacific fleet, destroys more than 340 aircraft, kills more than 2,400 Americans, and draws the United States into World War II. General Walter C. Short and Admiral Husband E. Kimmel, both held responsible for an "error of judgment" for not preparing for the Japanese attack, are forced to retire.

General Delos C. Emmons, commander of the army, rejects a suggestion by the joint chiefs of staff in Washington to intern all persons of Japanese ancestry residing in Hawaii. General John L. DeWitt, of the Western Defense Command, rejects the idea of interning Japanese Americans by stating, "An American citizen, after all, is an American citizen." He later changes his mind.

Jeannette Rankin is the only member of Congress to vote against the United States' declaration of war against Japan.

For her nursing work during the Pearl Harbor bombing, Captain Annie Fay receives a Purple Heart, the first awarded to a nurse.

Isaías Medina Angarita becomes president of Venezuela after the term of Eleazar López Contreras (1935). Angarita serves until 1945.

1941-1950

Immigration to the United States totals more than 1 million, of which 621,100 come from Europe, 37,100 from Asia, 7,400 from Africa, 14,600 from Oceania, 354,800 from the Americas and 140 are not specifically identified.

1942

The Roberts Commission issues its report on the Japanese air attack on Pearl Harbor. Based on rumors and innuendo, the report heightens the fear of sabotage on the West Coast. President Roosevelt signs Executive Order 9066, beginning the mass inland removal and detention of Japanese Americans. More than 120,000 Japanese Americans on the West Coast are eventually placed in detention camps for the duration of the war. Roosevelt also issues Executive Order 9102, which creates the War Relocation Authority (WRA). From 1942 to 1944, 18 European Americans are charged with spying for Japan; at least half are convicted. No Japanese American is ever charged with espionage and yet many lose their homes and businesses without compensation from the government.

By executive order, the War Production Board is set up to handle procurement of materials and move the United States to a wartime footing.

United States Navy Captain Joseph J. Rochefort breaks the Japanese naval code, which helps win the Battle of Midway.

Twenty-one Western nations meet in Rio de Janeiro, Brazil, to plan their defenses and to sever relations with Germany, Italy and Japan. Except for Argentina, all break diplomatic ties with the Axis powers.

Congress establishes the Medal of Merit to reward civilians and the nation's allies for their efforts during the war. Congress also authorizes the Women Accepted for Voluntary Emergency Services (WAVES) to support the navy. The organization is headed by (Captain) Mildred Helen McAfee, then president of Wellesley College, who runs the organization until 1946. Congress also establishes the Woman's Auxiliary Army Corps (WAAC). The organization is headed by (Colonel) Oveta Culp Hobby, then editor of the *Houston Post*.

Defense contractors begin actively recruiting women workers. More than 4 million women hold industrial positions by the end of the war.

The *bracero* (temporary resident migrant worker) program, initiated in the United States, results in thousands of Mexican farm workers crossing the border seeking employment.

The Grand Coulee Dam, a key component of the Columbia Basin Project, is completed in east central Washington state.

At the University of Chicago, a scientific team headed by Enrico Fermi produces the first self-sustaining nuclear reaction. This development is considered to be the beginning of the atomic age.

A Japanese submarine attacks Fort Stevens, near Astoria, Oregon. This is the only military site in the mainland United States to see enemy fire since the War of 1812.

A fire at the Coconut Grove nightclub in Boston, Massachusetts, kills almost 500 people and injures more than 250. This tragedy leads to the tightening of fire safety codes nationwide.

Japanese Canadians living on the coast of British Columbia are relocated to the interior, and their property is seized.

Rafael Leonidas Trujillo Molina (1930) again becomes president of the Dominican Republic. Women in the country receive the right to vote. Molina serves until 1961.

1943

President Roosevelt freezes prices, salaries and wages to curb inflation during the war; Congress introduces income tax withholding.

Attorney General Francis Biddle states in a memo to the president: "I shall not institute criminal proceedings [against Italian and German aliens] on exclusion orders which seem to me unconstitutional...It [Executive Order 9066] was never intended to apply to Italians and Germans."

The state of Connecticut establishes the Inter-Racial Commission, recognized as the first governmental civil rights agency in the country.

The Women's Army Auxiliary Corps is made a part of the United States Army; its name is changed to the Women's Army Corps (WAC).

A quota of 105 calculated under the Immigration Act of 1924 may be used by Chinese wishing to enter the United States. This policy change is instituted mainly to counter anti-United States propaganda directed at China by Japan.

The United States Army reaches a peak personnel strength of 8.3 million.

Georgia is the first state to lower the voting age to 18.

Development and testing of nuclear weapons begins at Oak Ridge, Tennessee; Hanford, Washington; and Los Alamos, New Mexico.

Seventy Montana coal miners die in the Smith Mine disaster.

In Mexico, the Paricutín volcano erupts suddenly out of a corn field, burying many towns, one of which provides its name. Eruptions continue until 1952.

In Argentina, Ramón S. Castillo (1938) is removed from power by a military coup.

1944

The United States Supreme Court rules that Democratic Party primaries in which only European Americans can vote are unconstitutional.

In the case of *Korematsu* v. *United States,* the United States Supreme Court rules that removal and detention orders against Japanese Americans are constitutional and represent a valid exercise of governmental war powers. In *Ex parte Endo* the Court rules that the government cannot detain loyal citizens against their will.

The G. I. Bill of Rights is enacted to assist returning veterans via low-interest housing loans, unemployment pay if needed and discharge or mustering out pay. Unemployment in the United States is reduced to 1 percent because of the war effort.

The Women Appointed for Voluntary Emergency Service (WAVES) begins accepting African American women.

The first Socialist government in North America is elected in Saskatchewan province, Canada, with Thomas C. Douglas as provincial prime minister.

A new constitution in Jamaica establishes universal adult suffrage. Women also gain the vote in Barbados, British Guiana, and Bermuda.

Ramón Grau San Martín is elected president of Cuba following the term of Fulgencio Batista y Zaldívar (1940). San Martín serves until 1948.

José María Velasco Ibarra (1934) becomes president of Ecuador for a second time. He serves until 1947, and from 1952 to 1956, 1960 to 1961 and 1968 to 1972. He is deposed by military coups in each of his first four terms.

Argentina severs diplomatic ties with the Axis powers.

Juan José Arévalo becomes president of Guatemala after Jorge Ubico (1931) is deposed. Arévalo serves until 1951.

1945

Franklin D. Roosevelt begins a fourth term as president of the United States; Harry S Truman is vice president. Both are Democrats. When Roosevelt dies in office, Truman becomes the 33rd president of the United States.

Congress establishes the Medal of Freedom to reward United States civilians and the nation's allies for their efforts during the war.

The United Nations charter is drafted and signed in San Francisco, California. The United Nations establishes its headquarters in New York City the following year.

Former first lady Eleanor Roosevelt is appointed to the United States delegation to the United Nations.

President Truman issues a directive to admit 40,000 war refugees.

The first atomic bomb is tested by the United States at Alamogordo, New Mexico. The test, code named Trinity, disintegrates the steel supporting structure.

1940

through

1949

1940 through 1949

Grand Rapids, Michigan, is the first city in the United States to add fluoride to the municipal water supply to prevent tooth decay.

The trend toward United States women working in industry begins to reverse. As men return from war, women return home and family size begins to increase.

Former United States Secretary of State Cordell Hull receives the Nobel Peace Prize for his diplomatic work during World War II.

African American women are first sworn in as navy nurses.

The first Canadian nuclear reactor, for experimental purposes, goes into operation at Chalk River, Ontario.

Rómulo Betancourt becomes president of Venezuela following a military coup. He serves until 1948 and again from 1959 to 1964.

1946

Congress establishes the Atomic Energy Commission by passage of the McMahon Act (named for Senator Brien McMahon, chairman of the Joint Committee on Atomic Energy). David Eli Lilienthal, former head of the TVA, serves as the new commission's first chairman. The Navy successfully tests atomic bombs at Bikini and Eniwetok Atolls in the Marshall Islands.

Fred Moore Vinson becomes chief justice of the United States Supreme Court. He serves until 1953.

In *Morgan* v. *the Commonwealth of Virginia* the United States Supreme Court rules that segregation on interstate buses places an unreasonable burden on interstate commerce and is therefore invalid. The case involves Irene Morgan, an African American woman who is arrested and convicted after refusing to move to the rear of a Greyhound bus.

Congress passes the War Brides Act, allowing admission to this country for foreign-born wives of American servicemen.

This year marks the beginning of the "baby boom," with almost 3.5 million babies born in the United States. Seventy-two million babies will be born over the following 20-year period, making this the largest generation in the nation's history.

Martinique and Guadeloupe become overseas departments of France; they are no longer considered colonies.

In a speech in Fulton, Missouri, Winston Churchill first uses the term "iron curtain" to describe the split that has divided Europe between the East Bloc and the western nations. He also warns of the dangers of Soviet expansion.

The United States grants independence to the Philippines; the island nation continues to lease military bases to the United States Navy.

A massive strike by several labor organizations, including the United Mine Workers, steelworkers, auto workers and trainmen, is in response to the deferral of raises and benefits during the war. Strikes over this year involve 4.6 million workers.

Senator James William Fulbright, a Rhodes scholar, sponsors an act that carries his name, which provides for an international exchange of students and teachers between the United States and other countries.

ENIAC (electronic numerical integrator and computer) is the world's first automatic electronic digital computer. It is built at Harvard University, Cambridge, Massachusetts, and reflects the work of a number of scientists and electrical engineers.

The first non-military use of reactor-produced radioisotopes is at Barnard Cancer Hospital, St. Louis, Missouri.

Construction begins on Garrison Dam, on the Missouri River in North Dakota. When completed in 1956, it will be one of the largest earth-filled dams in the world.

Felisa Rincon de Gautier becomes mayor of San Juan, Puerto Rico.

Mary Beard's *Women as a Force in History,* a primary work examining women's history, is published.

An army bomber airplane collides with the Empire State Building at the 79th floor. Fifteen people die, and fire damages 11 levels of the building.

The first drive-through banking window opens at the Exchange National Bank of Chicago, Illinois.

Canada passes the Canadian Citizenship Act, which for the first time establishes Canadian citizenship as being distinct and separate from that of Britain.

Miguel Alemán becomes president of Mexico after the term of Manuel Ávila Camacho (1940). Alemán serves until 1952.

Juan Domingo Perón, who gained popularity when Castillo was ousted in 1943, is elected president of Argentina. He serves until 1955.

Brazil experiences a new wave of democracy and creates a new constitution.

1947

President Truman announces the Truman Doctrine, the first significant attempt by the United States to "contain" communist expansion. The plan is specifically aimed at protecting Greece and Turkey, and pledges military support to enable countries under communism to regain their freedom.

Congress passes the Taft-Hartley Act over President Truman's veto. The act is designed to define and control the growing power of labor unions and to outlaw closed shops.

In *Fay* v. *New York,* the United States Supreme Court implies that women do not have the constitutional right to serve on juries because it is not "customary."

The state of Connecticut passes its Fair Employment Practices Act, which outlaws racial discrimination in employment.

In the United States, the Central Intelligence Agency (CIA) is established by the National Security Act as an independent government entity.

Texas City, Texas, is destroyed by fire after the French ship *Grandcamp* explodes in its harbor. Five hundred people are killed and 4,000 are injured.

A telephone strike involves 350,000 workers, 230,000 of them women. This strike involves the greatest number of women ever to walk off their jobs at one time.

The worst blizzard in the Northeast in more than 60 years drops 25.8 inches of snow in New York City in one day. Approximately 80 people lose their lives.

The carbon-14 method of radioactive dating of artifacts is first demonstrated.

First Lady Eva Perón incites Argentinian women to seek the franchise and to demand reform of divorce laws.

1948

The Truman administration initiates the four-year European Recovery Program—proposed in 1947 and also called the Marshall Plan—to help rebuild Europe so that these countries will not request communist aid. A key factor of the Marshall Plan is that monies approved for European assistance are to be spent on United States goods, thus helping both economies.

The Displaced Persons Act provides for entry into the United States of 341,000 refugees made homeless by World War II; 378,600 displaced persons—including Germans expelled from their homeland—arrive during the four-year program.

President Truman signs Executive Order 9981 directing "equality of treatment and opportunity in the Armed Forces."

The United States Supreme Court declares that prayer in public schools is unconstitutional as it violates the First Amendment.

The States' Rights Party, nicknamed the "Dixiecrats," is formed in the United States by disillusioned Southern Democrats who oppose the civil rights stance of the regular Democratic Party.

Former State Department official Alger Hiss is indicted on perjury charges in the United States after he denies passing secret documents to a communist spy ring. The jury in his first trial in 1949 cannot reach a decision but he is convicted in a second trial in 1950 and sentenced to a five-year prison term. Hiss is released in 1954, still claiming his innocence.

Margaret Chase Smith is elected to represent Maine in the United States Senate. She is the first woman to serve in both houses of Congress. Smith serves until 1973.

The National League of Women Voters changes its name to the League of Women Voters of the United States.

The California Supreme Court declares California's ban on interracial marriage unconstitutional because it unnecessarily limits a person's choice of a mate.

The state of Iowa leads the country in production of the following farm commodities: oats, corn, poultry, eggs, hogs and cattle.

In the heavily industrialized town of Donora, Pennsylvania, 20 people are killed when an air pressure inversion traps deadly smog over the city.

The invention of the transistor by John Bardeen, Walter H. Brittain and William Shockley is announced by the Bell Telephone Laboratories. This invention makes the miniaturization of electronics possible.

The xerographic photocopying process is first demonstrated by inventor Chester Carlson in New York City.

Louis Stephen St. Laurent, a Liberal, becomes prime minister of Canada after the final term of William Lyon Mackenzie King (1935). St. Laurent serves until 1957.

Carlos Prío Socarrás is elected president of Cuba after the term of Ramón Grau San Martín (1944). Socarrás serves until 1952.

The Organization of American States (OAS) charter is signed at Bogota, Colombia. The organization promotes peace and cooperation in the Americas and discourages intervention by other countries.

The Chilean government outlaws the Communist party.

Galo Plaza Leso becomes president of Ecuador. He serves until 1952.

Manuel Odría becomes president of Peru after the term of José Luis Bustamante (Rivero, 1935). Odría serves until 1956.

Rómulo Gallegos becomes president of Venezuela but a military coup removes him shortly after his election. General Marcos Pérez Jimémez comes to power; he rules until 1958.

1948-1958

In Colombia, the assassination of popular reformer José Eliecer Gaitán sparks a decade of violence, known as La Violencia, between Liberal and Conservative parties throughout Colombia. An estimated 250,000 people die in sectarian violence until the parties agree to alternate in power.

1949

Harry S Truman begins his first elected term as president of the United States; Alben W. Barkley is vice president. Both are Democrats.

Federal court restores American citizenship to three Japanese American women who were pressured as inmates in a relocation camp to reject their citizenship. The decision opens the door for the restoration of more than 4,300 other Japanese Americans in similar circumstances.

In his inaugural address President Truman proposes the Point Four Program, designed to provide the same type of assistance for Africa and Asia as the Marshall Plan has for Europe.

In signing the North Atlantic Treaty in Washington, D.C., the United States becomes a member of the North Atlantic Treaty Organization (NATO). Other charter members are Belgium, Canada, Denmark, France, Great Britain, Iceland, Italy, Luxembourg, Netherlands, Norway and Portugal. Greece and Turkey join NATO in 1952 and West Germany follows in 1955.

Leaders in a California cotton strike are arrested for forming carpools to inform pickers in the field that a strike has been called. One of these group leaders is young Cesar Chavez.

The Air Force B-50 bomber *Lucky Lady II* lands at Fort Worth, Texas, after the first ever nonstop flight around the world. The bomber has traveled 23,452 miles in 94 hours, one minute.

The average price of a gallon of gasoline in the United States is 25 cents.

Harvard Medical School graduates its first 12 women students, two of them with honors.

Newfoundland becomes the tenth province of the Dominion of Canada.

The Pan American Juridical Committee meets in Havana, Cuba, to study the problem of colonialism in America. One-third of its final report pertains to Puerto Rico, but the United States government convinces the committee that its purpose is to study the problem of colonies held by powers other than the United States.

Argentine President Juan Domingo Perón enacts a new constitution.

A major earthquake in Pefleo, Ecuador, results in 6,000 deaths.

1940

through

1949

1940 through 1949

1940

Italy attacks Greece from its bases in conquered Albania.

Estonia, Latvia, and Lithuania are annexed by the Soviet Union. Hungary declares war on the Soviet Union, and is quickly defeated. Romania cedes Ismail (Izmail) to the Soviet Union, and Ismail becomes part of the Ukranian territory.

Fifteen thousand Polish army officers who were imprisoned by the Soviets after Poland was invaded are taken from prison by Soviet security officers and are not seen alive again. In 1943 more than 4,000 of their bodies are found in a mass grave in the Katyn Forest.

British troops occupy Iceland.

Germany, Japan and Italy sign the Tripartite Pact, a mutual defense agreement.

After France falls to the German invasion, Japan signs a treaty with the German-controlled Vichy government in France to establish bases in Indochina. This causes the United States to freeze Japanese assets in America and virtually severs relations between the United States and Japan.

In central France, the discovery of the caves at Lascaux provides evidence of man at least 16,000 year ago in that area. The caves are explored more thoroughly during the next few years.

The United States trades 50 destroyers for leases on British bases in the Western Hemisphere.

In India, the Muslim League continues to lobby for an independent Pakistan. Following the pacifism of Gandhi, thousands of members of the Indian National Congress are arrested for their part in acts of civil disobedience.

The second highest British military honor, the George Cross, is established by King George VI.

In Romania, King Carol II (1930) is forced to abdicate after a military takeover assisted by the fascist Iron Guard. His son, Michael I (1927) takes the throne, but Ion Antonescu actually rules the country as dictator. Antonescu rules until 1944.

(Sir) Winston L. Churchill, a Conservative, leads a coalition to become prime minister of Great Britain following the term of Neville Chamberlain (1937). Churchill serves until 1945, and again from 1951 to 1955.

Peter Fraser, a member of the Labour party, becomes prime minister of New Zealand. He serves until 1949.

Risto Ryti becomes president of Finland after the term of Kyösti Kallio (1937). Ryti serves until 1944.

British pathologist (Sir) Howard Walter Florey continues the research of (Sir) Alexander Fleming (1928) and develops penicillin as an antibiotic.

1941

An embargo is placed on petroleum products to Japan by United States President Franklin D. Roosevelt. The British and Dutch governments impose similar embargoes.

The civilian government of Japan under Prince Fumimaro Konoye falls and is replaced by a military cabinet headed by General Hideki Tojo. The Japanese surprise attack at Pearl Harbor, Hawaii, brings the United States into World War II.

Romania retakes Ismail from the Soviet Union.

Ethiopia regains its independence from Italy and Haile Selassie (1930) returns from exile.

Muhammad Reza Shah Pahlevi becomes shah of Iran after his father, Reza Shah Pahlevi (1925), is deposed. Muhammad Reza Shah Pahlevi rules until 1979, when he is deposed by an Islamic coup.

Arthur W. Fadden serves for three months as prime minister of Australia. He is succeeded by John Curtin, who serves until 1945.

Norodom Sihanouk becomes king of Cambodia though he lives as a virtual prisoner during the Japanese occupation. He is restored to power in 1945 and rules until 1955.

1942

Although the term "united nations" was first used in 1941 by President Roosevelt to describe the countries fighting against the Axis Powers, the first official act of organization is a declaration by 26 countries, signed in Washington, D.C., to fight a joint war effort to its conclusion and not make separate peace treaties with Axis nations.

In India, the Congress rejects a British offer of dominion status after the end of the war; Mohandas Gandhi launches the "Quit India" campaign and is arrested.

In China and India, a serious famine is caused by a fungus that destroys most of the rice crop. It lasts for two years and causes an estimated 2 million deaths.

With the approval of Britain's war department, aviator Jacqueline Cochrane begins a tour to recruit 375 women for the British Air Transport Auxiliary during World War II.

1943

The Japanese establish a Central Advisory Council to rule Indonesia, with Sukarno in command.

At the Casablanca Conference in Morocco, President Roosevelt and Prime Minister Churchill agree that the war will end only with the unconditional surrender of the Axis Powers.

The Cairo Conference in Egypt, attended by Roosevelt, Churchill and Chiang Kai-shek of China, supports efforts of the three countries to press the war until Japan surrenders. A separate statement calls for Korean independence "in due course."

The Teheran Conference in Iran, attended by Roosevelt, Churchill and Soviet Premier Joseph Stalin, is held to fortify the relationship between the three countries and to plan their efforts against the Axis Powers, including the invasion of France. They also agree on the need for a strong United Nations and, in a separate document, to maintain the independence of Iran.

Comintern is dissolved by the Soviet Union to avert possible reprisals from its allies.

As a child, Simeon II becomes czar of Bulgaria after the mysterious death of his father, Boris III (1918). Simeon II rules until 1946 when the monarchy is abolished.

1944

The Bretton Woods Conference, held in New Hampshire, creates the International Monetary Fund and the International Bank for Reconstruction and Development (the World Bank).

The Dumbarton Oaks Conference attended by representatives from the United States, China, Britain and the Soviet Union discusses the establishment of a United Nations. This issue is further discussed at the Yalta Conference in 1945.

Ho Chi Minh, a former Comintern leader in China who has returned to his homeland of Vietnam, announces Vietnam's independence from France. The French government rejects this proclamation, however, and fights Ho Chi Minh's Viet Minh forces to retain the territory. The fighting continues until 1954, when French forces are finally defeated at Dienbienphu. Syria also declares its independence from France, but French troops remain in Syria until 1946.

The pro-Nazi Romanian government of Premier Ion Antonescu (1940) is toppled by forces of King Michael I (1927), whom Antonescu had thought was an easily controlled puppet king. Antonescu, who essentially handed Romania to Germany's Adolf Hitler, is arrested, tried, and later executed.

Albania has a provisional government established by the Congress of Permeti. Enver Hoxha is the country's new premier. He serves until 1954.

The Soviet army invades Hungary, and a provisional government is established.

Iceland gains full independence from Denmark. The country is declared the Icelandic Republic, with a new constitution and Svelnn Bjönsson as first president.

Carl Gustaf Mannerheim becomes president of Finland after the term of Risto Ryti (1940). Mannerheim serves until 1946.

The ninth Panchen Lama is installed in Tibet.

1944-1945

Greece is liberated from Axis control and enters into a brief civil war.

1945

Soviet and United States troops invade Korea and force the Japanese to surrender. The country is divided into North and South.

At the Yalta Conference held in the Crimea, Soviet Union, and attended by Roosevelt, Churchill and Stalin, agreement is reached that ending the war will be based on Germany's unconditional surrender. For security reasons, many of the agreements reached are kept secret for two years; they involve dividing Germany into four zones of occupation, collecting reparations for war damages, extending the war effort against Japan and fixing the status of countries that desire independence after the defeat of the Axis Powers. Churchill and Roosevelt both insist that the provisional Polish government be made up of representatives of both the exiled government of General Wladislaw Sikorski and the underground state that existed inside Poland during the War, and that free and democratic elections be held, with international observers. While outwardly agreeing to these conditions, Stalin covertly begins to deport Home Army troops, seize and imprison anti-communist leaders, and establish secret police. An agreement is also reached that the "big five" nations — China, Britain, France, the United States and the Soviet Union — would have veto power on United Nations Security Council resolutions.

The United Nations Conference is held in San Francisco, and the organization's founding charter is signed.

Functions of the Permanent Court of International Justice (World Court) are transferred to the International Court of Justice created by the United Nations.

The Potsdam Conference, attended by President Harry S Truman of the United States, Stalin and Churchill (replaced by Clement A. Attlee after the British electorate removes Churchill from office) establishes the basis of German reconstruction as decided upon at Yalta. Germany is divided into four zones, occupied respectively by Britain, France, the United States and the Soviet Union. The Allied military commanders are to supervise their zones of occupation. Germany will be demilitarized, the Nazi party abolished and an attempt made to rebuild the country based on democratic ideals. Poland and the Soviet Union are to maintain control of certain lands east of the Oder and Neisse Rivers. France is slighted by not being part of the "big four" and does not cooperate fully in the negotiations. This, added to the vague wording of many provisions, makes the conference relatively ineffective.

Germany surrenders to end the war in Europe.

The United States drops atomic bombs on Hiroshima and Nagasaki, Japan. Although the Japanese military plans to continue fighting, Emperor Hirohito forces a surrender for the safety of his country. World War II ends five days later.

After the end of World War II, Japanese forces are driven out of Vietnam; Cambodia declares its independence from France; Nationalists led by Sukarno and Muhammad Hatta proclaim Indonesian independence from Japan. Taiwan is taken from Japan by Chinese forces under Chiang Kai-shek; and Austria is reestablished as a republic. The Soviet Union gains control of East Germany; the Yugoslav assembly abolishes the monarchy, removes Peter II (1934) and declares a republic headed by Marshal Tito (Josip Broz); and Lebanon formally becomes an independent nation, although it was so declared by the Free French army in 1941. French and British troops remain in Lebanon until 1945.

The Japanese puppet-state of Manchukuo, an imposed union of Manchuria and the Chinese province of Jehol, returns to Chinese control.

The Arab League (League of Arab States) is formed as Egypt, Iraq, Transjordan, Lebanon, Saudi Arabia, Syria and Yemen join forces politically to attain their common goals of independence and improved economic status.

Francis M. Forde serves for eight days as prime minister of Australia. He is succeeded by Joseph B. Chifley, who serves until 1949.

Gheorghe Gheorghiu-Dej becomes secretary general of Romania's communist party. He holds various titles, including premier and head of state, until his death in 1965.

Sukarno becomes president of the Republic of Indonesia. After taking full dictatorial control in 1959, he declares himself president for life in 1963. He rules until 1966.

Clement Attlee, Labour, becomes prime minister of Great Britain after (Sir) Winston L. Churchill's (1940) first term. Attlee serves until 1951.

1945-1946

Judges from the United States, Britain, France and the Soviet Union hold an 11-month trial of Nazi war criminals. The results of the Nuremberg, Germany, war trial: 12 Nazi leaders, including one tried in absentia, are sentenced to hang, seven are imprisoned and three are acquitted. *Gestapo* (Nazi secret police) chief Hermann Wilhelm Goering commits suicide a few hours before the 10 other Nazis are executed.

1946

The first meeting of the United Nations General Assembly opens in London. The League of Nations is dissolved four months later and transfers all its assets to the United Nations. Norwegian diplomat Trygve Halvdan Lie becomes the first secretary general. He serves until 1953.

When the Soviet Union fails to honor its commitment to withdraw from Iran as dictated by the Teheran Conference, Iran appeals to the United Nations. In exchange for the withdrawal of Soviet troops, Iran agrees to allow Soviet oil drilling; however, the agreement is cancelled by Iran under advisement of the United States after the troops are withdrawn. This action adds to Cold War tensions between the Soviet Union and the United States.

The new constitution drafted for Japan provides for voting rights for women, a condemnation of war and a framework for democracy.

By the terms of the Malayan Union, Sarawak (ceded by Rajah Sir Charles Brooke), North Borneo and Singapore become British colonies. Malayans resent this plan, which reduces them from protectorate status to being part of a colony. In 1948 Britain replaces the union with a federation arrangement.

Violence in Calcutta, East Bengal, Bihar and Punjab results in almost half a million deaths as the borders are drawn between India and Pakistan.

A major earthquake in Honshu, Japan, results in 2,000 deaths.

1940

through

1949

1940

through

1949

The Dutch and Indonesians draft the Cheribon Agreement, which is designed to recognize the independence of the Indonesian countries as the United States of Indonesia, and their equal status with the Netherlands under the Dutch monarchy. This agreement is never successfully implemented.

The Philippines achieves independence following the Tydings-McDuffie Act, an agreement signed with the United States in 1934.

In Africa, the Ashanti (Asante) are incorporated into the British colony of the Gold Coast (Ghana).

In South Africa, a major strike of more than 75,000 gold mine workers necessitates the use of federal troops to maintain order. A proposal by South Africa to annex all of South West Africa (Namibia) is rejected by the United Nations.

Syria gains its independence from France.

The Albanian government is taken over by communist forces and is declared a people's republic; Hungary becomes a republic and adopts a new constitution; Yugoslavia proclaims itself independent and creates a constitution following the new Soviet model.

Bulgaria rejects the monarchy and establishes itself as a communist people's republic with Georgi Dimitrov as premier. He serves until 1949.

Hungary is declared a republic, under Soviet communist direction.

Edvard Benes is elected to continue as president in Czechoslovakia. Because Communists receive 38 percent of the vote, Benes asks Communist party leader Klement Gottwald to form a government.

As a child, American-born Rama IX (Phumipol Aduldej, Phumiphon Aduldet, Bhumibol Adulyadej) becomes king of Thailand after the death of his brother, Rama VIII (1935). Rama IX comes of age in 1950.

George II (1935) returns to Greece after a plebiscite favors the maintenance of the monarchy. He remains in power until 1947, although the restoration of the monarchy sparks another civil war.

Humbert II becomes the last king of Italy after the abdication of his father, Victor Emmanuel III (1922). The referendum following his father's abdication forms an Italian republic and forces Humbert II into exile in Portugal.

J. K. Paasikivi becomes president of Finland after the term of Carl Gustaf Mannerheim (1944). Paasikivi serves until 1956.

British officials establish the Malayan Union, which encompasses Malacca, Pulau Pinang and the nine Malay States.

Sarawak becomes a British colony.

Women gain the right to vote in Italy.

Transjordan becomes fully independent from Britain with Abdullah (Abdullah ibn Husein, 1923) as king. He rules until 1951.

British, United States and Soviet forces leave Iran.

Lebanon has full independence from French rule after British and French troops leave.

In a speech in Fulton, Missouri, Winston Churchill first uses the term "iron curtain" to describe the split that has divided Europe between the East Bloc and the Western nations. He also warns of the dangers of Soviet expansion.

1946-1958

This is the time span generally ascribed to the Fourth French Republic.

1947

The Paris Peace Conference is held and separate treaties are signed by the Allies and several of the Axis powers: Finland, Bulgaria, Hungary, Italy and Romania.

The first of the Dead Sea Scrolls are discovered by shepherds, in caves near the site of ancient Qumran (in northwest Jordan).

A new constitution is enacted in postwar Japan. Those who receive the biggest benefit under it are women, as five articles assure fundamental rights for women.

The Bulgarian government adopts a constitution modeled after that of the Soviet Union.

Malta is granted self-government.

Britain nationalizes its coal mines.

The Soviet Union rejects the United States' plan for a United Nations atomic energy control system.

The Marshall Plan for European recovery is proposed by United States Secretary of State George C. Marshall as a coordinated effort to help European nations rebuild their cities and their economies after World War II. By 1951 this "European Recovery Program" will cost more than $11 billion.

Cominform (Communist Information Bureau) is founded under Soviet auspices to rebuild contacts among European communist parties, missing since the dissolution of Comintern in 1943. Cominform is disbanded in 1956.

China's civil war between communists and nationalists ends. In 1949 the communist-led People's Republic of China is established, with Mao Tse-tung as chairman of the central governing committee.

Thailand's military seizes power in a coup.

Britain's former holdings in India are divided into the two independent states of India and Pakistan. These two states begin immediately to dispute which will retain the Kashmir region, a dispute that escalates into battle. More than 2 million Sikhs leave Pakistan. Over the next 20 years, many British colonial possessions gain their independence.

British forces pull out of Palestine and the nation's sovereignty issue is turned over to the United Nations, which votes to partition Palestine into Jewish and Arab states. Jerusalem would remain autonomous under international supervision. Jews accept the partitioning but the Arab League rejects the concept and announces it will use force to defy the plan.

The Great Synagogue in Damascus, Syria, is looted and Jewish prayerbooks are burned in the streets.

Poland becomes a communist-run state.

Russia regains control of Ismail (Izmail) from Romania.

Cambodia becomes a constitutional monarchy under King Norodom Sihanouk (1941). The country later becomes a state under the French Union, and gains full independence in 1953.

Belgium, Luxembourg and the Netherlands join to form the Benelux Union.

Under Mátyás Rákosi, a coalition government is formed in Hungary, with communists and socialists leading the country.

King Michael I (1927, 1940) abdicates the throne and Romania becomes a communist republic.

Francisco Franco (1936-1939) declares Spain a kingdom with a regency council, and names himself regent for life. Franco declares that the Spanish monarchy will be restored upon his death, and names Prince Juan Carlos as his successor.

Vincent Auriol becomes the first president of the Fourth French Republic. He serves until 1954.

Jawaharlal Nehru becomes prime minister of India. He serves until 1964.

Mahomed Ali Jinnah becomes governor general of Pakistan. He serves until 1948.

Frederick IX becomes king of Denmark after the death of his father, Christian X (1912). Frederick IX rules until 1972.

Paul becomes king of Greece after the death of his brother, George II (1922, 1935, 1946). Paul rules until 1964.

Norwegian explorer Thor Heyerdahl crosses the Pacific Ocean in a primitive raft, the *Kon Tiki,* from Peru to the Tuamotu (Paumotu, or Low) Archipelago in the southern Pacific Ocean.

1948

India's spiritual and political leader Mohandas Gandhi is assassinated in New Delhi, India, by a Hindu fanatic.

Finland and the Soviet Union sign a friendship and mutual aid pact.

A treaty of "friendship, collaboration and mutual assistance" is signed between Romania and the Soviet Union; this ushers in a period of Stalinist repression in Romania, including a purge of the Communist party.

In Czechoslovakia, the Communist party asserts that a Slovakian conspiracy against the Czechoslovak government has been uncovered; aided by a continued Soviet presence, the communists seize power. Benes resigns and Gottwald becomes president, serving until 1953.

With the end of the British mandate over Palestine, the United Nations creates the state of Israel with Chaim Weizmann as president and David Ben-Gurion as prime minister. One hundred thousand displaced Palestinians immigrate to Lebanon. Zionism, the movement to establish and recognize a Jewish homeland, is declared a crime in Iraq, and many affluent Jews there are arrested. Tensions run high and the Arab-Israeli War breaks out in the region. During the war, Syrian gunmen in the Golan Heights fire on Israeli communities. Approximately 20 percent of Israeli soldiers in this war are women. Israel is victorious and many displaced Arabs are forced to live in refugee camps in the Gaza Strip and West Bank.

Soviet leader Stalin and Tito of Yugoslavia sever diplomatic ties over their differing communist ideologies. Yugoslavia is expelled from Cominform.

The communist-controlled Democratic People's Republic of Korea (North Korea) is established. Three months later the Independent Republic of Korea (South Korea) is proclaimed following an election supervised by the United Nations. Syngman Rhee becomes South Korea's first president. Rhee serves until 1960.

In the Japanese war trials, Hideki Tojo and six others are sentenced to death and 18 are imprisoned.

Burma (Myanmar) leaves the British Commonwealth and achieves full independence. The Union of Burma is formed as a republic, with U Nu as prime minister. He serves until 1959 and again from 1960 until 1962.

Ceylon (Sri Lanka) gains its independence from Britain and dominion status in the Commonwealth.

The new government of India abolishes the age-old practice of discrimination against the untouchable class.

The Malayan Union disbands. Communists there conduct a campaign of terror to reverse the country's economic recovery.

The United Nations General Assembly adopts the Universal Declaration of Human Rights, which the general secretary calls the "Magna Carta of Mankind."

Although racial segregation has always existed in South Africa, the victory of the Afrikaner National party over Jan Smuts (1919, 1939) and the Union and Labor party helps to institute *apartheid* (strict racial segregation) as official government policy.

An earthquake in the Soviet Union results in 110,000 deaths.

The use of microwaves for cooking is developed.

Juliana becomes queen of the Netherlands after the abdication of her mother, Wilhelmina (1890).

1948-1949

The world faces its first Cold War crisis when the Soviet Union rejects a plan for a unified Berlin and Germany and the Allies object to Soviet currency being used throughout the area. The use of Soviet money is seen as a step in eliminating Western control. After the Allies issue their own currency, the Soviet Union cuts off all land and water communications between western Germany and West Berlin. The Allies respond with a successful airlift and the blockade is lifted 11 months later.

1948-1975

Australia sees an influx of 2 million new immigrants, mostly from central Europe.

1949

A cease-fire is declared in Palestine, and the following month, Israel signs an armistice with Egypt. As a result of the war, Israel increases its size by half and Jerusalem is divided between Transjordan and Israel, with Transjordan occupying the West Bank. Gaza becomes an Egyptian possession. Transjordan officially changes its name to Hashemite Kingdom of Jordan.

In Washington, D.C., the foreign ministers of Belgium, Canada, Denmark, France, Great Britain, Iceland, Italy, Luxembourg, the Netherlands, Norway, Portugal and the United States sign the treaty creating the North Atlantic Treaty Organization (NATO). NATO is established as an organization of mutual assistance in military matters that affect the North Atlantic area. Greece and Turkey join NATO in 1952 and West Germany follows in 1955.

The Council of Europe is formed by Belgium, Denmark, France, Great Britain, Ireland (Eire), Italy, Luxembourg, the Netherlands, Norway and Sweden. It later includes Greece, Iceland and Turkey.

The German Federal Republic (West Germany) is established with Konrad Adenauer as chancellor. Adenauer serves until 1963. The German Democratic Republic (East Germany) is established under Russian control with Otto Grotewohl as prime minister.

The People's Republic of China is formally proclaimed by Communist party Chairman Mao Tse-tung. Nationalist leader Chiang Kai-shek takes refuge on Taiwan after Chinese communists take control of the mainland.

Romania receives a new constitution, based on that of the Soviet Union.

Several former Dutch colonies in Indonesia receive their independence and unite under a federal republic form of government. Only New Guinea remains separate.

The Republic of Ireland (Eire) Act is passed declaring Ireland's complete independence from Britain.

United States military personnel are withdrawn from South Korea.

South West Africa's (Namibia's) bid for independence is referred to the International Court of Justice.

The United Nations enacts a cease-fire in Kashmir.

Laos becomes a semi-autonomous state within the French Union.

The Greek civil war ends with the defeat of communist rebel forces. The monarchy is reestablished with Paul (1947) as king.

The British North America Bill is amended by Britain's parliament. This gives Canada the authority to amend its own constitution.

The Soviet Union explodes its first atomic bomb.

The United Nations headquarters in New York opens.

Rainier III becomes king of Monaco.

Sir Robert Gordon Menzies (1939) becomes prime minister of Australia after the term of Joseph B. Chifley (1945). Menzies serves until 1966.

The Australian Service Medal is created to honor those who demonstrate distinguished military service.

Sidney George Holland, a Nationalist, becomes prime minister of New Zealand after the term of Peter Fraser (1940). Holland serves until 1957.

1940

through

1949

	NATIVE AMERICAN	NATIVE AMERICAN	AFRICAN AMERICAN	AFRICAN AMERICAN

1950 through 1959

NATIVE AMERICAN

1950

Dillon S. Myer, a European American, is appointed Commissioner of Indian Affairs. He furthers the policy of termination of the Indians' trustee status.

Approximately 56,000 Indians, or 16 percent of the total known Indian population, reside in urban areas.

Early 1950s

A revival of the Sun Dance occurs among the Sioux Indians.

1950s

The United States government implements its policy of termination of the federal trust relationship with American Indian tribes; 12 acts affect 12 tribes and many smaller Indian bands in Oregon and California. A federal law is also enacted to relocate American Indians from reservations to urban areas. More than 30,000 make this move before the program is terminated in the mid-1960s. Approximately 30 percent return to tribal lands within a year or two.

1953

In furtherance of the federal termination policy, Congress proposes giving individual Indians the same civil status as United States citizens, ending all limitations — and all government protections — on Native American tribes.

1954

The state of New York seizes St. Regis Mohawk tribal land. The Mohawks seek compensation. In 1959 the United States Supreme Court refuses to hear the case.

1954-1955

Under Public Law 568, Congress orders the Public Health Service to bring the level of health of Native Americans up to be consistent with the rest of the country. The Division of Indian Health is transferred from the Bureau of Indian Affairs (BIA) to the United States Public Health Service, in the Department of Health, Education and Welfare (now Health and Human Services). The motivation for this is that more funding is available in the newly created Department.

NATIVE AMERICAN

In *Tee-hit-ton Indians* v. *United States,* the Supreme Court rules that the government can seize American Indian property if it has not been specifically granted to the Indians by Congress.

1956

Plans are drawn up for the Kinzua Dam, to be built on the Allegheny Reservation in Pennsylvania. The dam would cause the flooding of 9,000 acres of habitable land and tribal gravesites on the Pennsylvania-New York border.

1957

A group of Mohawks under the leadership of Standing Arrow reoccupies European American lands on Schoharie Creek in New York State. The Indians' claim to the area is based on the terms of a 1784 treaty.

AFRICAN AMERICAN

1950

A conference of lawyers associated with the National Association for the Advancement of Colored People (NAACP) decides to mount a full-scale attack on educational segregation.

Ralph Bunche, acting United Nations mediator in Palestine, receives the Nobel Peace Prize for his work.

1951

An Oregon law forbids discrimination on account of race, color, religion or national origin at schools chartered or licensed by the state.

Florida NAACP Executive Secretary Harry Moore and his wife are killed by a bomb in their home. Both were active in voter registration and anti-lynching campaigns. No arrests are made.

1952

In *Gray* v. *University of Tennessee,* the university is ordered to admit African American students. The school complies. The University of North Carolina is also court-ordered to admit African Americans.

The time span of the Korean conflict is the first time that African American troops are officially integrated in the armed services. In fact, the first United States victory occurs when the African American 24th Infantry Regiment recaptures the city of Yech'on. The 24th wins numerous honors; two of its soldiers, Cornelius Charlton and William Thompson, posthumously receive the Congressional Medal of Honor.

Jessie D. Locker is appointed ambassador to Liberia. He serves until 1955.

AFRICAN AMERICAN

1954

In *Brown* v. *Board of Education,* the Supreme Court rules that school segregation is unconstitutional because "separate educational facilities are inherently unequal." This landmark decision overturns the *Plessy* v. *Ferguson* "separate but equal" ruling of 1896 and establishes the federal precedent for requiring school desegregation.

Benjamin O. Davis, Jr., becomes the first African American general in the United States Air Force.

1955

Roy Wilkins succeeds Walter White as the national executive secretary of the NAACP.

In Montgomery, Alabama, Rosa Parks, an African American, refuses to relinquish her bus seat to a European American man and is arrested. The African American community supports her, led by the Reverend Dr. Martin Luther King, Jr., and the first organized boycott for equal and desegregated public accommodations begins.

The Interstate Commerce Commission, in response to a suit filed by the NAACP, outlaws segregated buses and waiting rooms for interstate passengers.

Marian Anderson is the first African American to sing at the Metropolitan Opera House in New York City. She appears in Verdi's *The Masked Ball.*

Based on the 1954 ruling of *Brown* v. *Board of Education,* the United States Supreme Court rules that public facilities such as golf courses, swimming pools, etc., cannot remain segregated.

Charles C. Diggs, Jr., a Democrat, is the first African American to be elected to the House of Representatives of the United States Congress from Michigan.

Richard L. Jones is appointed ambassador to Liberia. He serves until 1959.

AFRICAN AMERICAN	AFRICAN AMERICAN	ASIAN AMERICAN	FOR CLASSROOM USE	

1956

The Civil Aeronautics Board bans the use of federal funds for building segregated airport facilities.

A hundred and one Southern congressmen sign the "Southern Manifesto" calling on the states to reject and resist the Supreme Court ruling against school segregation.

1957

The Southern Christian Leadership Conference is organized at Atlanta, Georgia, by Dr. King, Bayard Rustin and Stanley Levinson. King becomes its first president.

Federal troops, the 101st Airborne Division, are sent to Little Rock, Arkansas, after Governor Orval Faubus calls out the state National Guard to prevent nine African American students from entering Central High School. A mob of European Americans also has gathered outside the school for several days. The entry of the students, some 20 days after the beginning of the school year and under federal military escort, is a triumph for Daisy Gaston Bates, leader of the team that initiated legal action to integrate the high school. A small number of federal troops remain on guard at the school until the end of the year.

The NAACP Youth Council conducts a sit-down campaign in Oklahoma City, Oklahoma, that results in the desegregation of 39 lunch counters. In Wichita, Kansas, after four days of sit-ins, the Dockum Drugstore chain begins to serve African Americans.

Clifford R. Wharton is appointed United States minister to Romania. In 1961 he is appointed ambassador to Norway.

Congress passes the Civil Rights Act, the first federal action of this type since Reconstruction. Two primary thrusts of the Act are to establish a federal framework for civil rights issues and to protect the right to vote.

1958

Robert N. C. Nix, a Democrat, is elected from Pennsylvania to fill an unexpired term in the United States House of Representatives.

Walter Gordon is appointed judge of the United States District Court for the Virgin Islands by President Dwight D. Eisenhower. Gordon serves until 1964.

1959

The sit-in campaign grows among civil rights activists. College students desegregate eating facilities, mainly near college campuses in St. Louis, Chicago and Bloomington, Indiana.

Efforts to register African Americans to vote, which have been going on for many years despite heavy opposition from European Americans, begin to affect local politics, particularly in the southern states. Victories include the election of African American city officials in Nashville and Oak Ridge, Tennessee, and several North Carolina cities; the election of a moderate European American state senator in Virginia in spite of the powerful Byrd camp; and the defeat of staunch segregationists in Virginia local elections.

Brigadier General Benjamin O. Davis, Jr., is promoted to major general.

John Howard Morrow is appointed ambassador to Guinea. He serves until 1961.

1950s

As the Chinese government changes, students from Taiwan and Hong Kong come in increasing numbers to the United States. Most stay in this country after they complete their studies.

1950

The United States census reports approximately 117,600 Chinese Americans living in the mainland United States, 40 in Alaska and 32,350 in Hawaii.

The entry of the People's Republic of China (PRC) into the Korean War in late 1950 rekindles negative feelings against Chinese Americans. The United States government supports the Chinese Nationalist government on Taiwan and sends the 7th Fleet to prevent the PRC from attacking Taiwan. An embargo is imposed against the PRC. Students are prevented from returning to China. Many Chinese people in the United States sever ties with friends and relatives in the PRC.

Japanese Americans, including many World War II veterans, are called for active duty in the Korean War.

Congress passes the Internal Security Act. Citing the incarceration of Japanese Americans as a precedent, the act authorizes the president to intern any person on suspicion without evidence. Six detention camp sites are designated, one of which is Tule Lake, California.

1952

The California Supreme Court in *Fuji* v. *California* rules that alien land laws are unconstitutional.

A large number of Korean refugees, war brides and orphans are admitted to the United States.

1950
through
1959

ASIAN AMERICAN	ASIAN AMERICAN	EUROPEAN AMERICAN	EUROPEAN AMERICAN
With enactment of the Immigration and Nationality Act, also called the Walter-McCarran Act, the quota system is reaffirmed, and Asian exclusion is abolished. Japanese immigrants are finally eligible for naturalization. The practice of detaining immigrants for interrogation upon arrival is stopped. California voters repeal the anti-Chinese provisions in their state constitution. **1953** Congress passes the Refugee Relief Act, which admits more than 2,700 people from the People's Republic of China. John F. Aiso of Los Angeles, California, becomes the first mainland *nisei* (first Japanese American generation born in the United States) appointed to a judgeship. He is named by Governor Earl Warren. San Francisco merchants organize a Chinese New Year Festival to attract tourists to Chinatown. It is the first of its kind on the mainland. **1954** South Americans of Japanese ancestry held as hostages in United States detention camps since 1942 are allowed to apply for permanent resident status in the United States. Peru refuses them re-entry. **1955** The federal government begins investigating immigration fraud among Chinese people. The State Department issues a report by the United States consul general at Hong Kong, Everett Drumright, charging wholesale fraud. Some Chinese people are prosecuted. Only 16 cities in the United States still have Chinatowns, a decrease of 12 in 15 years. **1956** California voters repeal the state's alien land laws by a two-to-one margin. The overall effect of the repeal is that Chinese and Japanese immigrants may now own land.	The United States government begins a "confession" program in which Chinese immigrants may confess that they are aliens, and the government readjusts their immigration status. When the program is terminated in 1966, 13,895 Chinese have confessed, exposing 22,083 persons. **1957** Congress passes the Refugee Escapee Act. One of its provisions is suspension from deportation for anyone who has obtained a visa or documentation by fraud or misrepresentation, if he or she is the spouse, parent or child of a United States citizen. The National Conference of Chinese meets in Washington, D.C., and establishes the Chinese Welfare Council. It calls upon Congress to reform immigration laws. Chinese American professors Tsung Dao Lee and Chen Ning Yang win the Nobel Prize in physics. **1959** Delbert Wong becomes the first Chinese American judge in the continental United States when he is appointed as a Los Angeles municipal court judge. When Hawaii becomes a state, Daniel K. Inouye becomes the first Japanese American elected to the United States House of Representatives. Inouye was seriously wounded in World War II, and is a decorated veteran. He serves as representative until 1963, when he is elected to the Senate. Wilfred C. Tsukiyama, a Japanese American, becomes the first chief justice of Hawaii's Supreme Court. Hiram Fong is elected to the United States Senate from Hawaii. Fidel Castro's regime comes to power in Cuba and nationalizes many enterprises. Most of Cuba's 126,000 Chinese residents depart, many to the United States.	**1950** More than 2.3 million Scandinavians have immigrated to the United States since the first ones arrived in 1820. The Russian Orthodox Church in Exile establishes its own American synod and changes its name to the Russian Orthodox Church Outside Russia. **1951** The National Huguenot Society is founded in the United States, by and for Protestants who are descendants of French Huguenots. **1952** More than 104,000 Germans come to the United States this year. **1954** The American Hungarian Studies Foundation is formed in Illinois to foster appreciation of Hungarian culture and promote educational programs in Hungarian art, history, language and literature. The foundation later moves its headquarters to New Brunswick, New Jersey. **1955** Vincent du Vigneaud of Cornell Medical College wins the Nobel Prize in chemistry for isolating two hormones that aid in childbirth. **1956-1957** Two massive relief campaigns occur among Hungarian Americans, to provide financial assistance to refugees of the bloody Hungarian Revolution. More than 10,000 people assemble at New York City's Madison Square Garden and raise almost $1 million for Hungarian refugee assistance; more than 21,500 Hungarians come to the United States. In 1957 the American Hungarian Federation provides more than $510,000 and assists the entry into this country of more than 35,000 refugees.	**1958** Hungarian refugees are permitted to adjust their status to permanent resident aliens. Visas are made available to Dutch people displaced from Indonesia, and to Portuguese people unable to return to the Azores because of volcanic eruptions.

1950

through

1959

HISPANIC AMERICAN	HISPANIC AMERICAN	HISPANIC AMERICAN	FOR CLASSROOM USE	

HISPANIC AMERICAN

1950

The United States census reports 300,000 Puerto Ricans in the mainland United States and 2.2 million on the island.

Congress passes and the president signs the Puerto Rican Federal Relations Act, also known as Public Law 600, enabling Puerto Ricans to draft their own constitution.

Nationalist uprisings occur in Jayuya and other cities in Puerto Rico. An assassination attempt is made against Governor Luis Muñoz Marín. In the wake of the unrest in several locations, more than 25 people are killed, 90 wounded and thousands of independence sympathizers are jailed.

Two young Puerto Rican nationalists attack Blair House, the temporary residence of President Harry S Truman. One of the attackers and one federal security officer are killed. Pedro Albizu Campos and other nationalists are arrested for complicity. Campos is convicted and sentenced to a long prison term, from which he is pardoned in 1964.

c. 1950

The Hispanic Young Adult Association (HYAA), a group of Puerto Rican college students and young professionals, begins its own training sessions in leadership and initiates community projects in the United States.

1950-1960

In this decade, migration of Puerto Ricans to the United States totals 470,000, with the majority coming to the cities of New York, Chicago, Philadelphia, Cleveland and Buffalo, and the states of New Jersey and Indiana.

1951

The creation of a constitutional assembly is approved by referendum in Puerto Rico.

Operation Bootstrap is firmly established as the plan of economic development for Puerto Rico.

The *bracero* (temporary resident migrant worker) program that brings Mexican workers to the United States is renewed.

HISPANIC AMERICAN

1951-1954

Mexican American activists, particularly labor union organizers, are deported during the McCarthy era when any form of activism is viewed as dangerous and un-American.

1952

Puerto Rico becomes a commonwealth of the United States with a free and associated status. A new constitution defining this special relationship is ratified by ballot in Puerto Rico and by approval of the United States Congress.

The Immigration and Nationality Act, also called the Walter-McCarran Act, sets the tone and practice of Operation Wetback. Mexican and Mexican American residents of the United States are harassed and intimidated.

1953

The United Nations no longer lists Puerto Rico as a colonial country, and authorizes the United States to cease transmitting information on Puerto Rico since it is now a self-governing territory.

More than 61,000 Puerto Ricans participate in the Korean War, with approximately 730 killed and 3,000 wounded.

1953-1956

As Operation Wetback gets into full operation, more than 2 million Mexicans and Mexican Americans are repatriated, mostly from the southwestern states. The deportation program causes many civil liberties violations, as homes are illegally searched, peoples' civil rights are abused and some people are wrongly removed.

1954

Four Puerto Rican nationalists interrupt a session of the United States House of Representatives with gunfire. Five Congressmen are wounded.

Court action guarantees Mexican Americans the right to serve on juries.

Mid-1950s

El Barrio (the Neighborhood) on the east side of Manhattan becomes a vibrant Puerto Rican community in New York City.

HISPANIC AMERICAN

The Puerto Rican Institute of Culture is founded in Puerto Rico as an independent public corporation whose purpose is to study, preserve and foster Puerto Rican culture and heritage.

1956

The Catholic Archdiocese of Chicago organizes the Bishop's Committee for the Spanish Speaking in Chicago, which is concerned with the needs of Hispanic Americans.

The Council of Hometown Clubs (El Congreso del Pueblo), an affiliation of 80 clubs, is established. It considers Puerto Rican traditions important in the fight for civil rights; it also helps new Puerto Rican immigrants find shelter, housing and jobs.

Under the *bracero* program, 432,000 temporary workers are admitted to the United States in this year alone. Legal immigration and the *bracero* program cannot meet the United States' labor needs, particularly in agricultural, industrial and service jobs such as domestic employment. Many illegal Mexican immigrants come to fill the shortages.

The HYAA, established in c. 1950, becomes the Puerto Rican Association for Community Affairs (PRACA).

1957

The Puerto Rican Forum is founded in the United States to develop new Puerto Rican leadership and to address the problems of delinquency, housing, economic development and education.

Hernandez v. *Driscoll,* a district court decision challenges the Texas practice of requiring Mexican American children to spend two years in the first grade.

1958

Puerto Rico's Pro Independence movement is founded. It is a political organization that seeks complete independence for the island.

1959

Congress rejects the Fernos-Murray bill, which aims to amplify Puerto Rico's autonomy.

1950 through 1959

1950

The United States census reports the country's population at 151.2 million, including American citizens living abroad.

President Harry S Truman orders the development of the hydrogen bomb.

The Internal Security Act increases the grounds for exclusion and deportation from the United States of people considered to be subversive. Aliens are required to report their addresses annually.

Almost one-third of all women in the United States — 29 percent — are employed outside the home.

Senator Joseph McCarthy, chairman of the Senate's permanent investigations subcommittee, begins his "witch hunt," accusing United States government officials of being communists or communist sympathizers.

The first American military advisors are sent to Vietnam by President Truman; the communist-dominated Viet Minh wage a civil war against France's colonial army.

In order to avoid a strike, President Truman orders the army to seize control of the nation's railways.

The United States reports more than 33,000 cases of poliomyelitis.

The great Brink's robbery occurs in Boston, Massachusetts, when nine robbers wearing ski masks hold up the armored car service and take almost $3 million. This is the largest single cash heist in the country's history.

In Colombia, Laureano Gómez comes to power. He rules as dictator until 1953.

Anastasio Somoza (1937) becomes president of Nicaragua for a second time. He serves until 1956.

1951

The Twenty-second Amendment to the United States Constitution is ratified. It states that no person shall be elected to the office of president more than twice and that if a person has held the office of president more than two years of a term to which someone else has been elected, he or she may only be elected once.

President Truman removes General Douglas MacArthur from his command in the Far East after MacArthur proposes an invasion of China. Truman, in an effort to make peace, favors a policy of containment but MacArthur believes in force to restrain communism and threatens China with an atomic bomb.

A severe flood hits sections of Kansas and Missouri, leaving more than 200,000 homeless.

Julius and Ethel Rosenberg are sentenced to death for passing atomic secrets to spies from the Soviet Union. They are executed in 1953, becoming the first United States citizens to receive the death penalty for treason.

Color television is introduced in the United States. By 1960, more than 50 million sets will be in use.

The American Telephone and Telegraph Company reports more than 1 million stockholders — the first corporation in history to be able to say this.

Nuclear weapons testing by the Atomic Energy Commission begins at Yucca Flat, Nevada.

The first significant nuclear-produced electricity comes from an Idaho testing station.

Chrysler introduces power steering in its automobiles.

"Alert," an arctic weather station, is established as a joint project of the Canadian and United States governments. It is the northernmost permanent human community in the world.

The Mattachine Society, an early gay rights group, is founded in Los Angeles, California. The organization later establishes branches in several United States cities, publishes a magazine, and organizes annual national conventions.

Getúlio Dornelles Vargas is elected president of Brazil. He serves until 1954.

Juan José Jacobo Arbenz Guzmán becomes president of Guatemala after the term of Juan José Arévalo (1944). Guzmán serves until he is overthrown in 1954.

1951-1960

Immigration to the United States totals more than 2.52 million, of which 1.33 million come from Europe, 153,200 from Asia, 14,100 from Africa, 13,000 from Oceania, 996,900 from the Americas and 12,500 are not specifically identified.

1952

The Immigration and Nationality Act (McCarran-Walter Act) is passed over President Truman's veto. The act reaffirms the quota concept. Although Asian exclusion is dropped, would-be immigrants of Asian ancestry are treated differently from others. The ceiling of 150,000 for non-Western Hemisphere countries is maintained, and a preference system is included for the distribution of visas within each country's allotment. A section of this act enables the attorney general to admit for up to two years any person whose admission would be in the American interest. This serves as a justification for the admission of political refugees in the years that follow. The act also imposes fines and imprisonment for persons guilty of "harboring" illegal immigrants. But a "Texas Proviso" exempts Texas employers of undocumented workers from these penalties.

The United States tests the hydrogen bomb at Eniwetok Atoll in the Pacific Ocean.

The Tuskegee Institute reports that for the first time in 71 years, no lynchings occurred this year in the United States.

Adolfo Ruiz becomes president of Mexico after the term of Miguel Alemán (1946). Ruiz serves until 1958.

A military coup led by General Fulgencio Batista y Zaldívar (1940) overthrows the Cuban government of Carlos Prío Socarrás (1948). Zaldívar is elected to the presidency in 1954 but rules as a dictator until 1959.

In Bolivia the National Revolutionary Movement overthrows the government, institutes land and suffrage reforms and nationalizes certain mining ventures. Victor Paz Estenssoro comes to power. He rules until 1964, when the government is overthrown.

José María Velasco Ibarra (1944) again becomes president of Ecuador following the term of Galo Plaza Leso (1948). Ibarra serves until 1956 and again from 1960 to 1961 and 1968 to 1972. He is deposed by military coups in all but his final term.

1952-1967

In Uruguay the presidency is abolished, and the country is ruled by an executive commission.

1953

General Dwight David "Ike" Eisenhower becomes the 34th president of the United States; Richard Milhous Nixon is vice president. Both are Republicans.

Earl Warren becomes chief justice of the United States Supreme Court. He serves until 1969.

The United States Supreme Court reverses a court of appeals decision and declares that District of Columbia restaurants are legally required to serve "well-behaved and respectable" African American customers.

Oveta Culp Hobby, head of the Women's Army Corps, becomes the first secretary of the newly established United States Department of Health, Education and Welfare.

Congress passes the Refugee Relief Act, which admits more than 200,000 post-war European refugees above the existing quotas.

The first Alaskan oil well, near Eureka, marks the beginning of Alaska's oil production industry.

1950

through

1959

Fidel Castro leads an unsuccessful revolt in Cuba when his forces attack the Moncada army barracks in Oriente province.

The Treaty of Economic Unity is signed between Argentina and Chile.

A military coup led by Gustavo Rojas Pinilla takes control of Colombia. Pinilla rules until 1957.

Colonel Marcos Pérez Jímenez becomes president of Venezuela. He serves until 1958.

1954

The United States Supreme Court in *Brown* v. *Board of Education of Topeka, Kansas,* unanimously bans racial segregation in public schools by ruling against the 1896 doctrine of "separate but equal." The case was originated by Oliver Brown, an African American railroad worker, when a local elementary school would not admit his daughter, Linda.

A Senate subcommittee censures Senator Joseph McCarthy (1950) and orders him to end his "witch hunt" for suspected communists in the United States government. The censure stops "McCarthyism," a strong campaign against liberals and Marxists that often branded people as communists out of fear and without proof.

President Eisenhower offers his domino theory that if one country submits to communism, its neighbors are in danger as well.

A United States-Japan mutual defense treaty permits the gradual rearming of Japan.

The United States rejects a formal proposal from Israel for a mutual defense treaty.

Five congressmen are shot on the floor of the House of Representatives as Puerto Rican nationalists fire from the spectators' gallery above; all five victims recover.

The Communist Control Act is signed by President Eisenhower, banning the Communist party in the United States.

At Groton, Connecticut, the United States Navy launches its first atomic submarine, the *Nautilus.* Congress passes the Atomic Energy Act to build nuclear power plants.

Ellis Island Immigration Station in New York City's harbor is closed.

Hurricane Hazel strikes the North Carolina coast, causing severe damage and continuing inland.

In Pittsburgh, Pennsylvania, Dr. Jonas Edward Salk starts inoculating children against poliomyelitis with a killed-virus vaccine he has developed.

Linus Pauling, a native of Oregon, is awarded the Nobel Prize in chemistry.

The United States and Canada reach agreement on plans for a Distant Early Warning (DEW) missile detection radar system. It becomes operational in 1957.

More than 1 million illegal Mexican workers are deported from the United States this year.

An estimated three-fifths of United States households have television sets.

Fulgencia Batista y Zaldívar (1952) is elected president of Cuba. He serves until forces led by Fidel Castro overthrow his government in 1959.

João Cafe Filho becomes president of Brazil after the term of Getúlio Dornelles Vargas (1951).

A military coup in Guatemala is led by Colonel Carlos Castillo Armas and assisted by the United States Central Intelligence Agency (CIA). Guzmán (1951) is overthrown, and Armas becomes president. He serves until 1957.

General Alfredo Stroessner becomes president of Paraguay. Ruling as a dictator, he is "reelected" for his position several times. Stroessner rules until 1989, when his government is overthrown by the military.

1955

The American Federation of Labor and the Congress of Industrial Organizations merge into a single labor organization, the AFL-CIO.

After Rosa Parks, an African American woman, is arrested for refusing to give up her seat in the European American section of a city bus, the Reverend Dr. Martin Luther King, Jr., leads a successful one-year boycott of the Montgomery, Alabama, bus system.

The United States Air Force Academy begins instruction at Colorado Springs, Colorado.

The Presbyterian General Assembly accepts women as ministers; the Reverend Margaret Towner is the country's first ordained female Presbyterian minister.

The Daughters of Bilitis, the nation's first lesbian organization, is formed in San Francisco, California. The group later publishes *The Ladder,* a lesbian magazine, and forms chapters throughout the United States.

Hurricane Diane creates devastating floods in the northeastern United States, leaving 200 people dead.

Arco, Idaho, is the first town in the world to be lighted entirely by atomic power. Arco is the site of the United States' first nuclear power plant.

After being excommunicated by the Catholic church following his anti-clerical campaign in 1954, Argentina's dictator Juan Domingo Perón (1946) is overthrown by the military. Perón flees to Paraguay and then to Spain. The military, under General Pedro Aramburu seizes control of Argentina's government, and rules until 1958.

1956

Congress passes the Highway Act creating the highway trust fund to finance construction of an improved road system in the United States.

In its review of a Montgomery, Alabama, law, the United States Supreme Court rules that segregation on interstate buses is unconstitutional.

The parole authority of the Immigration and Nationality Act is invoked to allow Hungarian refugees to enter the United States.

1950

through

1959

THE AMERICAS	THE AMERICAS	THE AMERICAS	THE AMERICAS

1950 through 1959

A new vaccine using live virus against poliomyelitis is presented by Professor Albert B. Sabin of the University of Cincinnati, Ohio.

Guerillas of the 26th of July Movement, led by Fidel Castro, begin a rebellion in Cuba.

Juscelino Kubitschek becomes president of Brazil after the term of João Cafe Filho (1954). Kubitschek serves until 1961.

José María Lemus becomes president of El Salvador. He serves until 1960.

Luis Somoza Debayle becomes president of Nicaragua after the second term of his father, Anastasio Somoza (1950). Debayle serves until 1963.

Manuel Prado becomes president of Peru after the term of Manuel Odría (1948).

1957

Dwight D. Eisenhower begins a second term as president of the United States; Richard M. Nixon is vice president. Both are Republicans.

The United States Congress passes the Civil Rights Act of 1957. The first federal civil rights legislation since Reconstruction, it prohibits discrimination in public places based on race, color, religion or national origin. The Commission on Civil Rights is established to ensure that the voting process is not hampered.

Congress passes the Refugee Escapee Act, which defines a refugee as an alien who has fled from any communist area or from the Middle East because of persecution or the fear of persecution on account of race, religion or political opinion.

After African American students attempt to enter high school in Little Rock, Arkansas, Governor Orval Faubus activates the National Guard. President Eisenhower sends federal troops to Little Rock to quell mob action and to protect the program of school integration. In direct violation of the Supreme Court, Faubus closes all public schools in the states and reopens them as private, segregated institutions.

The Equal Rights Amendment pending in Congress receives verbal approval from President Eisenhower, but it is tabled in committee.

United States occupation forces leave Japan.

The Teamsters Union is expelled from the AFL-CIO for corruption.

The first large-scale nuclear power plant in the United States goes on-line at Shippingport, Pennsylvania.

Oil is discovered near Swanson River in southeastern Alaska.

John George Diefenbacker, a Progressive Conservative, becomes prime minister of Canada after the term of Louis Stephen St. Laurent (1948). Diefenbacker serves until 1963.

François "Papa Doc" Duvalier is elected president of Haiti. He changes the constitution to make the presidency a life term. His reign is marked by cruelty, repression and murder. Duvalier rules until his death in 1971.

Women in Colombia gain the right to vote.

1958

The United States Supreme Court rules in *NAACP* v. *Alabama* that freedom of association is protected by the First Amendment. The case arises when the State of Alabama orders the National Association for the Advancement of Colored People (NAACP) to reveal its membership list but the NAACP refuses, fearing that in this time of civil rights battles, publication of the list would cause problems for its members.

President Eisenhower orders the United States Marines into Lebanon at the request of President Chamoun, who fears his government will be overthrown by a rebellion. This act is in support of the Eisenhower Doctrine, which states that the United States will send its military forces to any Mideast country to fight international communism.

In the United States, the National Aeronautics and Space Administration (NASA) and the Federal Aviation Administration (FAA) are established. The nuclear submarine *Nautilus* travels under the arctic ice cap and the first Atlas intercontinental ballistic missile is tested.

The North American Air Defense Command (NORAD) is established.

The Army's Jupiter-C rocket fires the first United States earth satellite, *Explorer I,* into orbit.

Ethel Andrus is instrumental in founding the American Association of Retired Persons (AARP); she serves as its first president.

The John Birch Society is founded by Robert Welch at Belmont, Massachusetts. The organization favors repeal of the income tax and social security and the removal of all government officials sympathetic to communism.

The Supreme Court unanimously overturns the postal censorship of the gay magazine *One,* permitting the publication and distribution of lesbian and gay materials.

Postage for a first-class letter in the United States is four cents.

Women gain the vote in Mexico.

Adolfo López Mateos becomes president of Mexico after the term of Adolfo Ruiz (1952). Mateos serves until 1964.

The Federation of the West Indies is formed by 10 former British colonies: Antigua, Barbados, Dominica, Grenada, Jamaica, Montserrat, St. Kitts-Nevis-Anguilla, St. Lucia, St. Vincent and Trinidad and Tobago. The federation dissolves in 1962 because of disagreements that are made more acute by the different degrees of wealth on each island.

General Marcos Pérez Jiménez (1948) is removed from power in Venezuela; elections bring Rómulo Betancourt of the Democratic Action party to the presidency. A moderate, he supports limited land reforms and advocates the use of oil revenues for social programs. Betancourt's presidency begins a long period of elected governments in Venezuela.

In Argentina, a radical faction comes to power, and Arturo Frondizi is elected president. He serves until the military removes him from power in 1962.

Alberto Lleras Camargo becomes president of Colombia following the rule of Gustavo Rojas Pinilla (1953). Camargo serves until 1962.

Miguel Ydíoras Fuentes becomes president of Guatemala after the term of Colonel Carlos Castillo Armas (1954). He serves until 1963.

1959

The United States and the Union of Soviet Socialist Republics agree to end nuclear testing.

Alaska and Hawaii join the Union as the 49th and 50th states, respectively.

The Landrum-Griffin Act, the first major labor legislation since Taft-Hartley, requires unions to file annual financial statements.

The St. Lawrence Seaway, a man-made waterway built by the United States and Canada, is opened. It creates access from the Atlantic Ocean to Lake Ontario.

For the 11th year in a row, Eleanor Roosevelt is the Gallup poll's "Most Admired Woman in America."

As full-scale revolution breaks out in Cuba, three-quarters of the country's land is in the hands of foreign investors, as are 90 percent of Cuba's public utilities. After three years of guerilla fighting, Fidel Castro and his forces overthrow President Fulgencio Batista y Zaldívar (1952, 1954), and Castro seizes power with the support of peasants and laborers. He takes the title of premier and establishes a Marxist regime. Before the downfall of the Batista government, Cubans migrated to the United States at a rate of 10,000 to 15,000 a year. These immigrants were a mixed group, including out-of-favor elites and unemployed workers who came seeking jobs. Between 1959 and 1961, 1 million Cubans are exiled by the Castro government and the majority come to the Miami, Florida area.

FOR CLASSROOM USE	FOR CLASSROOM USE	FOR CLASSROOM USE	FOR CLASSROOM USE	
				1950 through **1959**
FOR CLASSROOM USE	FOR CLASSROOM USE	FOR CLASSROOM USE	FOR CLASSROOM USE	

1950 through 1959

1950

The Arab League formally begins a boycott of Israel.

The United States 7th Fleet assists Taiwan in resisting an invasion from the People's Republic of China (PRC).

India is made an independent republic within the British Commonwealth.

The Indian government issues a series of medals, the Param Vir Chakra, the Maha Vir Chakra and the Vir Chakra for courage on the field of battle.

The law of return grants automatic citizenship to Jewish people who immigrate to Israel.

China (PRC) and the Soviet Union sign a treaty of alliance and declare the United States and Japan common enemies.

In China (PRC), marriage laws are changed to give women more freedom. These changes are seen as a major step in transforming Chinese society, and as a way for women to work outside the home.

In attempts to end violence between Hindu and Muslim groups, the governments of India and Pakistan create a bill of rights, common to both regions, to protect religious minorities.

The first free elections are held in Turkey.

Forces from China (PRC) invade Tibet, after Tibet refuses to become a Chinese satellite, even with regional autonomy.

Medical evidence links cigarette smoking and lung cancer.

A United Nations report estimates that more than half of the world's 800 million children are undernourished.

1950-1953

The Korean War

1950. On June 25, in a surprise attack, communist forces from North Korea invade South Korea. The United Nations calls for a cease-fire and asks member nations to assist South Korea. President Truman orders American forces into Korea. Additionally, fighting units are sent from 15 other countries. North Koreans capture Seoul. The United Nations directs that all UN forces be placed under United States military command, and in July, General Douglas MacArthur is designated commander of the combined forces. After South Korean and a few American troops are driven into Pusan, the southern tip of the country, United Nations forces counterattack in late September; American troops make a daring landing at Inchon, and recapture Seoul, then take Pyongyang, the North Korean capital. This offensive pushes the North Korean army back almost to the Yalu River on North Korea's Chinese border. Chinese communists enter the war and in December force United Nations troops to retreat toward the 39th parallel.

1951. Communist forces reinvade South Korea. United Nations troops evacuate and then retake Seoul. Under President Truman's direction, General Matthew B. Ridgway replaces MacArthur as commander in chief of United States forces after MacArthur makes known his desire to invade China (PRC). Armistice negotiations begin in July.

1952. Chinese authorities accuse the United States of using germ warfare. General Mark W. Clark replaces Ridgway as commander in chief. A revolt of communist prisoners takes place on Koje Island. President-elect Dwight Eisenhower visits South Korea.

1953. A demilitarized zone is established between North and South Korea. The communists launch an offensive, mainly against South Korean forces. President Syngman Rhee of South Korea releases anti-communist prisoners. Peace talks resume and an armistice agreement is signed at Panmunjom on July 27. Chinese troops withdraw from North Korea but more than 200 violations of the armistice are recorded in the next six years.

1950-1975

The Vietnam War

South Vietnam, the United States and the Allies battle against North Vietnam and the National Liberation Front (Vietcong).

Background. In 1941 the United States warns Japan to stay out of Indochina after the fall of France. When Japanese forces take the island, friendly United States-Japanese relations end; this becomes one factor in the Japanese attack on Pearl Harbor. In World War II the United States supports Ho Chi Minh and the Vietnamese nationals against the Japanese.

1950. By this year Mao Zedong and his forces have gained control of mainland China. President Truman, to support his policy of containment, sends a 35-man advisory group to aid the French who are fighting to maintain their colonial power in Vietnam. This action angers former ally Ho Chi Minh, who wants an independent Vietnam. War soon erupts between France and the Viet Minh movement.

1954-1955. In July 1954, after the defeat of French forces at Dien Bien Phu, the Geneva Agreements provide for withdrawal of French and Viet Minh armies to either side of the demilitarized zone (DMZ) pending reunification elections. These elections are never held. North of the 17th parallel is ruled by Ho Chi Minh and South Vietnam is ruled by Ngo Dinh Diem. From 1954 onward, Presidents Eisenhower and Kennedy send first civilian advisors, then military personnel as well, to train the South Vietnamese army.

1956-1957. South Vietnamese leader Diem begins to assume dictatorial powers; this incites strong dissent. Opposition groups within South Vietnam are aided in 1959 by troops from the north.

1960-1961. Communists who oppose Diem form the National Liberation Front (Vietcong) in South Vietnam in 1960. The next year, the United States pledges further assistance to South Vietnam and increases its advisors there to 948. Later in 1961, 33 United States helicopters and 400 men land at Saigon.

1962. The United States Military Assistance Command (MAC) is established in South Vietnam.

1963. Diem, a Roman Catholic, does not have the support of his people; public opinion moves away from him when several Buddhist monks set themselves on fire in protest of his rule. Diem is slain in a coup on November 1, 1963. By this time, there are over 16,000 United States military advisors in Vietnam.

1964. North Vietnamese torpedo boats reportedly attack United States destroyers in the Gulf of Tonkin on August 2, 1964. President Lyndon B. Johnson orders retaliatory air strikes. Congress quickly approves the Gulf of Tonkin Resolution, which authorizes the President to take necessary steps to "maintain peace."

1965. Vietcong attack United States military barracks at Pleiku. President Johnson orders the bombing of North Vietnam. More than 3,500 marines land at Da Nang to guard the United States air base there. President Johnson offers unconditional peace talks. The bombing is stopped, but United States ground troops continue to fight. The Soviet Union admits it has supplied weapons to North Vietnam. A Christmas truce suspends the bombing. North Vietnamese President Ho Chi Minh rejects peace talks. United States military personnel in Vietnam number 184,300.

1966. Bombing of North Vietnam is resumed in early 1966. As Cambodia is considered to be a refuge for communist forces, that country is bombed as well. B-52s bomb the DMZ, which is reportedly used by North Vietnam for entry into the South. In August the United States experiences the highest monthly military draft since the Korean war. American troop strength in Vietnam now numbers more than 380,300. A 48-hour Christmas truce is observed.

1967. The "Iron Triangle" offensive begins. Thailand agrees to allow the United States to use Thai bases for B-52 bomber planes. The 500th United States airplane is lost over North Vietnam. Anti-war protests continue in the United States. A pro-GI parade is held in New York City. In May a record 2,929 United States casualties are reported. Chinese guns shoot down two straying Navy jets. In October South Vietnam's National Assembly approves the election of Nguyen Van Thieu as president.

1968. The United States has almost 525,000 troops in Vietnam. In the Tet Offensive in January and February, Viet Cong guerrillas attack Saigon, Hue and some provincial capitals. General William Westmoreland requests 206,000 new troops. The My Lai Massacre occurs, in which United States troops kill South Vietnamese civilians. On October 31, President Johnson orders a halt to the bombardment of North Vietnam. The siege of Khe Sanh is lifted after 67 days. Saigon and the National Liberation Front join the United States and North Vietnam in Paris for peace talks. General Clayton Abrams replaces Westmoreland as commander in chief.

1969. The Vietcong attack 105 towns. Selective bombing of Cambodia takes place. United States military strength reaches its peak of 543,400. United States combat deaths exceed the Korean War. Hamburger Hill is captured and then evacuated. President Richard M. Nixon announces a peace offer and begins troop withdrawals in June. The Vietcong form the Provisional Revolutionary Government. North Vietnamese President Ho Chi Minh dies at age 79; collective leadership is chosen. Some 6,000 United States troops are pulled back from Thailand and 1,000 marines are withdrawn from Vietnam. Massive demonstrations occur in the United States, expressing both sides of the war controversy.

1970. In April President Nixon announces he is sending troops to Cambodia to destroy North Vietnamese "sanctuaries." The last United States forces are removed from Cambodia at the end of June.

1971. On January 1 Congress bars the use of combat troops, but not air power, in Laos and Cambodia. South Vietnamese troops, with American air cover, fail in their attack on Laos. Many American ground forces are withdrawn from Vietnam. In June the *New York Times* publishes a specific classified Pentagon document that contains plans for the expansion of the war.

1972. President Nixon responds to the North Vietnamese drive across the DMZ by ordering mining of North Vietnam ports and heavy bombing of the Hanoi-Haiphong area. In December Nixon orders "Christmas bombing" of the north to force the North Vietnamese back to the conference table.

1973-1975. President Nixon orders a halt to offensive operations in North Vietnam on January 15, 1973. Representatives of North and South Vietnam, the United States and the National Liberation Front sign peace pacts in Paris on January 27, ending the longest war in United States history. The last American troops depart the area on March 29. However, in 1974, North and South Vietnam accuse each other of frequent violations of the cease-fire agreement, and in 1975, full-scale war resumes. Saigon falls and communist forces are victorious. South Vietnam's Premier Nguyen Van Thieu resigns on April 21. United States Marine embassy guards, American civilians and their dependents are evacuated. On May 15 the American merchant ship *Mayaguez*, seized by Cambodian forces, is rescued by United States Navy and Marines, 38 of whom are killed. More than 140,000 Vietnamese refugees leave by air and sea; many to come to the United States. The Provisional Revolutionary Government takes control of the area on June 6. South Vietnam, Cambodia and Laos are now under communist control. Election of a National Assembly in 1976 paves the way for reunification of North and South Vietnam.

War casualties are more than 1.5 million people dead — both military and civilian — and more than 1.7 million wounded.

A major earthquake in Assam, India, results in more than 1,500 deaths.

King Leopold III (1934) returns from exile following a referendum in Belgium. His arrival creates serious unrest, and he transfers power to his son, Baudouin. Leopold III formally abdicates in 1951.

Celai Bayar becomes president of Turkey after the term of Ismet Inönü (1938). Adnan Menderes becomes premier. They both serve until 1960.

Gustavus VI becomes king of Sweden after the death of his father, Gustavus V (1907). Gustavus VI rules until 1973.

Walter Ulbricht becomes first secretary of the East German Communist party. He serves until 1971.

1950s

The government of South Africa solidifies its policy of *apartheid* (strict racial segregation).

1951

Officials from Japan, the United States and 47 other nations sign a peace treaty by which Japan regains its independence. On the same day Japan agrees to a security treaty with the United States that continues American bases in Japan and commits the United States to defend Japan in case of need. This latter treaty is enacted in 1952.

The Colombo Plan for Cooperative Economic Development in South and Southeast Asia originates with the nations of the British Commonwealth aided by the United States. The plan is designed to provide aid, training, loans and equipment to nations needing assistance.

Australia, New Zealand and the United States enter into the ANZUS Treaty for mutual military security.

Chief Minister Kwame Nkrumah is the first native African to act as British governor of the Gold Coast.

A revolt led by Tribhuvan ends Nepal's Rana dynasty. A more liberal monarchy is established, with Tribhuvan as king.

Angola becomes a Portuguese territory.

1950

through

1959

1950 through 1959

Liaquat Ali Khan, prime minister of Pakistan, is assassinated by agitators who seek war with India.

General Ali Bazamari, the prime minister of Iran, is assassinated.

The Pathet Lao, a communist-controlled Laotian nationalist movement, is founded in North Vietnam.

The Egyptian government refuses to allow ships bound for Israel to pass through the Suez Canal and refutes the 1936 agreement with Britain.

Libya gains its independence from Italy and Idris I becomes king of the United Kingdom of Libya. Idris I rules until 1969.

Iran's oilfields are nationalized by order of Prime Minister Muhammad Mossadeq.

The sultanate of Muscat and Oman gains independence from Britain.

(Sir) Winston L. Churchill (1940), a Conservative, becomes prime minister of Great Britain for a second time, following Clement Attlee (1945). Churchill serves until 1955.

Baudouin becomes king of Belgium after the abdication of his father, Leopold III (1934, 1950).

Talal becomes king of Jordan after the assassination of his father, Abdullah (Abdullah ibn Husein, 1923, 1946). Talal rules for one year.

1951-1974

Cape Verde is a Portuguese territory.

1952

The NATO conference approves the formation of a European army.

The United States and Israel enter a formal military assistance relationship.

The United Nations establishes Eritrea as an autonomous region within Ethiopia.

Japan regains full sovereignty.

The European Coal and Steel Community, also called the Schuman Plan after French foreign minister Robert Schuman, is formed by Belgium, France, West Germany, Holland, Italy and Luxembourg. The member nations agree to consolidate their efforts to maximize production and sale of coal and steel.

The first hydrogen bomb is tested by the United States at Eniwetok Atoll in the Pacific Ocean.

The Mau Mau people in Kenya begin a series of bloody uprisings against Europeans.

A deadly smog in London, England, is blamed for approximately 4,000 deaths. As a result, in 1956, Great Britain becomes the first country to enact clean air standards.

Colonel Gamal Abdul Nassar and General Muhammad Naguib lead a military coup that takes control of Egypt and forces Farouk I (1936) to abdicate.

Nasser's Egyptian government tightens its blockade of Israeli ports and backs Arab guerrilla fighters in Gaza.

A power struggle in Romania's Communist party is won by the nationalist faction led by Gheorghe Gheorghiu-Dej.

Jigme Dorji Wangchuk becomes king of Bhutan. He rules until 1972.

Hussein I becomes king of the Hashemite Kingdom of Jordan following the short reign of his father, Talal (1951).

Elizabeth II becomes queen of Great Britain and Northern Ireland after the death of her father, George VI (1945).

1952-1954

In Iran, ongoing conflict over the nationalization of the British-controlled Anglo-Iranian Oil Company results in the creation of a nationalist government under Muhammad Mossadeq, who acts as dictator. Mossadeq is opposed by the shah and his forces, who regain control of the country.

1953

East Berliners rise against communist rule but the action is quelled by Soviet tanks.

Egypt becomes a republic ruled by military junta.

A new constitution is approved in Yugoslavia and Marshal Tito (1945) is elected president.

The Soviet Union announces the explosion of a hydrogen bomb.

The three colonies of Southern Rhodesia, Northern Rhodesia and Nyasaland form the Federation of Rhodesia and Nyasaland, still under British authority.

Bhutan's national assembly is established.

In Guyana, assembly elections give the leftist People's Progressive Party a majority. British officials who fear a communist takeover suspend the country's constitution and install a provisional government.

In Kenya, nationalist leader Jomo Kenyatta is imprisoned.

Nearly 2,000 people die in flooding in the Netherlands after several dikes collapse during a storm.

Biologists James Watson and Francis Crick report their findings on the molecular structure of deoxyribonucleic acid (DNA).

Cambodia gains its independence from France. Laos also gains its independence from France but the northeastern section is overrun and controlled by the Pathet Lao, with assistance from North Vietnamese communists. The Pathet Lao then establishes a rival government.

United States Marines intervene in Lebanon to help put down a rebellion.

Denmark has a new constitution that establishes a one-chamber parliament elected by the people.

The population of the People's Republic of China (PRC) exceeds 600 million.

Moshe Sharett becomes prime minister of Israel after the term of David Ben-Gurion (1948). Sharett serves until 1955.

Abdul-Aziz Al Saud becomes king of Saudi Arabia after the death of his father, Abdul ibn Saud (1932). Abdul-Aziz Al Saud rules until 1964.

After the death of Joseph Stalin (1924), Georgi M. Malenkov becomes Soviet premier. Malenkov rules until 1955. In 1961 he is expelled from the Communist party.

Czechoslovakia's Communist party leader Klement Gottwald (1946) dies. Antonin Novotny assumes control of the party. He rules until 1968.

Swedish diplomat Dag Hammarskjöld becomes secretary general of the United Nations. He serves until 1961.

René Coty is elected president of France. He serves until 1959.

New Zealand explorer (Sir) Edmund Hillary and Nepalese guide Tenzing Norkay are the first people to climb to the summit of Mount Everest, the world's tallest peak, on the Tibet-Nepal border.

1953-1954

Serious conficts begin in both Algeria and Morocco, as these countries seek liberation from French rule. Algeria's revolutionary National Liberation Front actively involves women as messengers and supply carriers. After independence, however, Algeria's new government again limits many of the freedoms women enjoyed during the fight.

1954

Dien Bien Phu, a French military outpost in Vietnam, falls to the Viet Minh army (see "The World, 1950-1975, The Vietnam War").

The eight-nation Southeast Asia Treaty Organization (SEATO) is established by representatives of Australia, Britain, France, New Zealand, Pakistan, the Philippines, Thailand and the United States, meeting in Manila.

China adopts a constitution modeled after that of the Soviet Union.

A conference of world powers meets at Geneva and divides Vietnam at the 17th parallel. Ho Chi Minh takes control of the communist North Vietnamese area. South Vietnam gains independence from France.

Laos gains full independence from France.

Todor Zhivkov becomes general secretary of Bulgaria's Communist party, and strengthens the country's ties as a satellite of the Soviet Union.

Egypt signs a new agreement with Britain calling for the removal of all British troops within the next two years. Although Britain gives up its bases at the Suez Canal, British forces may reenter the area to provide protection from an attack by a foreign power.

The Soviet Union opens one of the world's first nuclear power stations.

A mutual defense treaty signed by United States and Japanese officials permits the gradual rearming of Japan.

Scandinavian Airlines makes the first routine commercial flights over the shorter Arctic route.

The United States rejects a formal proposal from Israel for a mutual defense treaty.

The Algerian War of Independence against France begins; full independence is achieved in 1962.

Gamal Abdul Nassar (1952) arrests General Naguib and becomes premier and then president of Egypt. Nassar rules until 1970.

1954-1959

Tibetan forces rebel against Chinese rule.

1955

The Federal Republic of West Germany is granted full sovereignty, and joins NATO and the Brussels Treaty Organization.

Allied troops withdraw from Austria, and the country's independence is formally recognized.

The United States extends its military and financial assistance to Taiwan through a mutual defense pact.

Romania, Albania, Poland, Bulgaria, Czechoslovakia, East Germany, Hungary and the Soviet Union are aligned for mutual defense under the terms of the Warsaw Pact.

At the Bandung Conference in Indonesia, 29 African and Asian nations agree on plans to oppose colonialism and to work together for economic and cultural gains.

David Ben-Gurion becomes prime minister of Israel for a second time after the term of Moshe Sharett (1953). Ben-Gurion resigns in 1961 but is quickly re-elected. He serves until 1963.

The African National Congress (ANC) in South Africa announces its Freedom Charter.

After a three-year fight for independence, Tunisia is granted internal self-government.

Norodom Suramarit becomes king of Cambodia after the abdication of his son, Norodom Sihanouk (1941, 1947), who remains as prime minister. Suramarit rules until 1960.

Nikolai A. Bulganin becomes premier of the Soviet Union after the term of George M. Malenkov (1953). Bulganin serves until 1958, at which time he is expelled from the Central Committee of the Communist party.

Dom Mintoff of the Malta Labor Party (MLP) becomes prime minister of Malta.

Sir Anthony Eden, a Conservative, becomes prime minister of Great Britain after the term of Sir Winston L. Churchill (1940, 1951). Eden serves until 1957.

Constantine Karamanlis becomes premier of Greece. He serves until 1963.

1955-1956

Vietnam's Emperor Bao Dai is overthrown. South Vietnam becomes a republic with Ngo Dinh Diem as president. Vietnamese communist guerillas move into South Vietnam. Diem rules until 1963, when he is assassinated during a military takeover.

1955-1959

Civil war erupts in Cyprus. Cypriots generally seek to end British rule of the country; however, internal battles also take place between Turkish and Greek Cypriots, who have different aims.

1956

Nikita Khrushchev, first secretary of the Russian Communist party, denounces many of the policies of Stalin and creates a split with the People's Republic of China (PRC).

In Hungary, nationalists rise against Soviet rule under Ernö Gerö and János Kádár and establish a new government that will guarantee free elections. The Soviets respond with troops and tanks to crush the anti-communist rebellion and invoke tighter controls on the country, causing 190,000 refugees to flee.

Women gain the franchise in 22 countries, mainly as a result of nations gaining their independence from colonial rule.

At an international trade fair in Poznan, Poland, workers hold a demonstration, denouncing the government and demanding "bread and freedom." The protest is violently suppressed by the police. Government figures indicate 53 people are killed, but the actual figure is believed to be much higher. The election of Wladyslaw Gomulka as leader of the United Worker's party brings social and economic reforms to Poland. Gomulka rules until 1970.

Secretary of State John Foster Dulles withdraws the United States' offer of financial assistance to Egypt in building the Aswan Dam because Egyptian leader Nassar desires to remain neutral in the Cold War. In what comes to be called the Suez Crisis, Egypt then takes control of the Suez Canal. Israeli fighters launch an attack on Egypt's Sinai peninsula and drive toward the Suez Canal, while British and French forces invade Egypt at Port Said. A cease-fire is forced by the United States and all three countries withdraw when the United States and the Soviet Union intervene on behalf of Egyptian control of the canal.

1950

through

1959

1950 through 1959

Approximately 20,000 women march on South Africa's capital city of Pretoria to protest the new government policy of making women carry passes as do men. This march is only one of many demonstrations by women against the system of *apartheid*.

Sudan gains its independence from Egypt and Britain, and becomes a republic. Internal strife begins between the predominantly Muslim north and the mostly non-Muslim south.

Morocco gains its independence from France and Spain (with additional territory surrendered by Spain in 1958) and regains Tangiers from international control.

Queen Iffat, wife of King Faisal, uses her marriage anniversary as the occasion to open the first girls' school in Saudi Arabia. Originally established for orphans, the school gradually enrolls daughters of the country's elite. These become the first group of Saudi Arabian women professionals.

Angola's first independence movement, the People's Movement for the Liberation of Angola (MPLA), is created. The African Party for the Independence of Portuguese Guinea and Cape Verde (PAIGC) is also formed, to secure independence from Portugal.

The Mau Mau campaign in Kenya is suppressed; Jomo Kenyatta is released from prison.

One of the world's first full-scale nuclear power plants begins operating at Calder Hall, England.

Extensive and valuable mineral deposits are discovered in Siberia.

Pakistan's first constitution is enacted and the country becomes an independent Islamic republic within the British Commonwealth.

The first aerial hydrogen bomb is tested by the United States over Namu Islet, Bikini Atoll, in the Pacific Ocean. Its force is equal to 10 million tons of dynamite.

A major earthquake in northern Afghanistan results in 2,000 deaths.

Urho Kekkonen is elected president of Finland after the term of J. K. Paaskivi (1946).

Habib Bourguiba becomes prime minister of Tunisia. The following year the monarchy is abolished and Bourguiba becomes president.

1957

The Soviet space program launches *Sputnik 1,* the first earth-orbiting artificial satellite. One month later, *Sputnik 2* is launched with the dog Laika inside, making it the first inhabited space satellite. These events mark the beginning of the "space age."

The Federation of Malaya and the Gold Coast gain their independence from Britain. The Gold Coast merges with British Togoland and the two become the nation of Ghana, named in honor of the ancient kingdom. Kwame Nkrumah is the nation's first prime minister.

Tunisia becomes a republic.

Israeli forces withdraw from the captured Sinai; the Gaza Strip is returned to Egyptian control on the condition that the United Nations monitor the area and that access to the Gulf of Aqaba (Akaba, Elath) will remain open.

The quest for nuclear power produces an accident at Windscale, England, when a fire destroys the core of a reactor and sends deadly radioactive fumes into the air.

In Thailand, a military coup led by Field Marshal Sarit Thanarat takes control of the country and installs General Thonom Kittikachorn as president. The new government rules for one year.

Olaf V becomes king of Norway after the death of his father, Haakon VII (1905).

Harold MacMillan, a Conservative, becomes prime minister of Great Britain after the term of Sir Anthony Eden (1955). MacMillan serves until 1963.

Muhammad V (Sultan Sidi Muhammad II) becomes king of Morocco. The country, divided since 1912 between France and Spain, is reunited under Muhammad V. He rules until 1961.

United States occupation forces leave Japan.

Two separate earthquakes in Iran—one in July and one in December—result in more than 4,500 deaths.

Andre Marie Mbida becomes premier of Cameroon.

The European Economic Community (EEC, Common Market) is established by the treaty of Rome among France, Italy, Belgium, the Netherlands, Luxembourg and West Germany; its goal is the union of its members into one economic market through the eventual dissolution of import duties and tariffs, and the standardization of trade policies.

Olaf V becomes king of Norway after the death of his father, Haakon VII (1905). Olaf V rules until his death in 1991.

Keith Jacka Holyoake, a Nationalist, becomes prime minister of New Zealand. He is followed this same year by Walter Nash, of the Labour party. Nash serves until 1960.

1957-1958

In the Soviet Union, the "antiparty" faction is outlawed, and Premier Nikolai Bulganin is expelled from the Communist party's Central Committee for suspected antiparty sympathies.

1958

Egypt and Syria form the United Arab Republic; with the addition of Yemen, this union is called the United Arab States. The union ends in 1961 as Syria withdraws following a coup, and Yemen soon follows.

The United States submarine *Nautilus* crosses beneath the Arctic ice cap.

France's Fifth Republic begins as Charles De Gaulle is recalled from Algeria. The nation adopts a new constitution.

Japan becomes a member of the United Nations.

The Soviet Union withdraws its occupation forces from Romania.

United States Marines arrive in Lebanon to help suppress a revolt.

Women gain the right to vote in Egypt and Iran.

Oil is discovered in Libya.

Guinea leaves the French Community (formerly the French Union) and becomes an independent Marxist nation.

A military revolt ends the monarchy in Iraq; a republic is proclaimed. Faisal II (1939) and the royal family are killed.

Field Marshal Sarit Thanarat (1957) regains control of the Thai government. He rules under martial law for one year.

Dahomey, Upper Volta and the (French) Congo become self-governing dominions within the French Community.

Mutara II Rudahigwa becomes king of Ruanda (Rwanda) after the death of his half-brother, Kigeli V Ndahindurwa.

The All African People's Conference convenes at Accra, Ghana, with native African representatives from Ghana, Belgian Congo, Nyasaland (Malawi), Northern Rhodesia and Southern Rhodesia.

Ivory Coast gains self-government.

The South West African People's Organization (SWAPO) is established with the goals of full independence for South West Africa (Namibia) and full civil rights for native Africans.

After a military coup occurs in Sudan, the country is ruled by the Supreme Council of the Armed Forces.

Hendrik Frensch Verwoerd becomes prime minister of South Africa. Verwoerd serves until 1966.

Sékou Touré becomes the first president of Guinea. He survives several coup attempts during his long, occasionally harsh leadership. Touré is president until his death in 1984.

THE WORLD	THE WORLD			

General Muhammad Ayub Khan becomes president of Pakistan after a military coup. He serves until 1969.

General Abdul Karim Kassem becomes prime minister of Iraq. He serves until 1963.

Nikita S. Khrushchev becomes premier of the Soviet Union and first secretary of the Communist party after Nikolai A. Bulganin (1955) is expelled from the party's Central Committee. Khrushchev serves until 1964.

General U Ne Win stages a successful military coup and takes power in Burma from U Nu (1948). U Ne Win rules until 1960.

1958-1960

In the People's Republic of China (PRC), a communal experiment called The Great Leap Forward takes place, attempting to achieve "true communism." It is essentially a failure.

1959

The first deaths of United States military personnel in Vietnam occur as two advisors are killed by the Vietcong at Bien Hoa airport near Saigon.

The European Free Trade Association is founded by the "Outer Seven" nations: Austria, Britain, Denmark, Norway, Portugal, Sweden and Switzerland.

Revolution erupts in the Belgian Congo after riots against Belgian rule occur in the city of Leopoldville (now Kinshasa).

The British government grants autonomy to its Singapore colony. Singapore becomes part of the Federation of Malaysia in 1963 but drops out of that alliance in 1965.

The International Antarctic Treaty suspends all territorial claims to Antarctica and reserves an area for peaceful use.

The Central Treaty Organization (CENTO) is formed. CENTO members — Britain, Iran, Pakistan and Turkey with the support of the United States — work for economic and social cooperation in the Middle East.

Lebanese president Chamoun requests and receives military intervention from the United States. Chamoun fears rebellion and the overthrow of his government. In response to his request, President Eisenhower orders the marines into Lebanon.

Sudan joins Senegal to form the Federation of Mali, but the union falls apart the following year.

General Charles De Gaulle becomes president of the French Republic following the term of René Coty (1953). De Gaulle serves until 1969.

Field Marshal Sarit Thanarat (1957, 1958) becomes premier of Thailand when King Phumiphon approves an interim constitution.

Eamon de Valera becomes president of Ireland. He serves until 1973.

Lee Kuan Yew becomes prime minister of Singapore.

After four years of fighting, China formally annexes Tibet. Four thousand Tibetan refugees receive asylum in Bhutan, and the Dalai Lama flees to India.

Nepal's new constitution creates an elected legislative body.

Long-standing unrest between the Hutu and Tutsi ethnic groups erupts into open revolt in Ruanda (Rwanda). The Tutsi monarchy is overthrown, and more than 160,000 Tutsis seek refuge in neighboring nations.

Ceylon's (Sri Lanka's) prime minister Solomon W. R. D. Bandaranaike, is assassinated. His wife, Sirimavo Bandaranaike, succeeds him in 1960, becoming the world's first woman prime minister. She leads the country until 1965, and again from 1970 until 1977.

Egypt reinforces its refusal to allow Israeli trade vessels to travel through the Suez Canal.

1950

through

1959

NATIVE AMERICAN	NATIVE AMERICAN	NATIVE AMERICAN	NATIVE AMERICAN
1960 The United States census reports approximately 509,000 Native Americans, plus 43,000 "Alaskan Natives," identified as Indians, Aleuts and Eskimos. **1960s** Indian tribes in Washington State fight for their fishing rights. **1961** Representatives of more than 90 tribes meet at the American Indian Conference in Chicago and ratify a "declaration of Indian purpose," emphasizing fair treatment under law, and the right of self-determination. The National Indian Youth Council (NIYC) is founded in Gallup, New Mexico, by young Indian activists who feel the more established Native American organizations are not aggressive enough. Vine Deloria, Jr., is elected as the new executive director of the National Congress of American Indians. President John F. Kennedy appoints a Task Force on Indian Affairs. The group is headed by Phillips Petroleum Company vice president W. W. Keeler and has no Native American members. After months of study, the task force recommends that the termination policy be deemphasized. Allegheny Seneca President Basil Williams asks President Kennedy to stop the Kinzua Dam project in northern Pennsylvania. His request is ignored, and the resultant flooding of 9,000 acres of Native American lands violates the 1794 Treaty of Konondaigua (Canadaigua). **1962** The American Indian College Committee is formed in California and distributes a proposal for an American Indian university.	**1963** Members of the Omaha tribe stage a "war dance" in front of the Douglas County Courthouse in Omaha, Nebraska, to protest employment discrimination. The Wisconsin Supreme Court decides that exclusive hunting and fishing rights of the Menominee, granted by the 1854 Treaty of Wolf River, are essentially nullified by the 1954 Termination Act, and that the Menominee therefore no longer have exclusive rights. **1964** The Economic Opportunity Act, passed by Congress, extends to American Indian reservations. The Northern Cheyenne Tribe of Montana receives a $3.9 million land claim settlement from the federal government. The tribe makes available $1,000 to each tribal member. The American Indian Historical Society is formed in San Francisco with the primary goal of correcting textbook images of Native Americans. In Fairbanks, Alaska, Inuit artist Howard Rock establishes *The Tundra Times,* an activist Native American newspaper. **1966** President Lyndon B. Johnson appoints Robert L. Bennett of the Oneida tribe as Commissioner of the Bureau of Indian Affairs (BIA). Cherokee John Chewie is arrested for killing a deer out of season on Cherokee land. When hundreds of armed Cherokees surround the courthouse where his trial is held, the case is transferred to the federal courts. **1967** The first Native American state educational conference is held in California, with local and out-of-state American Indians in attendance. The event is sponsored by the newly formed California Indian Education Association, under the leadership of David Risling, Jr.	**1968** President-elect Richard Nixon announces his intention to reverse the termination policy of the two preceding decades and sets the stage for the new policy of Native American self-determination of the 1970s. The American Indian Movement (AIM) is founded by militant urban Native Americans in Minneapolis; AIM gains support among young Native Americans on reservations. The United Native Americans organization is founded in the San Francisco area to unite American Indians in a fight for control of Indian affairs. A coalition of American Indians in California succeeds in having the membership of a proposed state Commission on Indian Affairs changed from all European American to all American Indian. The court of claims overturns a Wisconsin court's 1963 ruling by declaring that the Termination Act of 1954 does not release the federal government from its obligation to grant exclusive hunting and fishing rights to the Menominee. The United States Supreme Court later upholds this claims court decision. Mohawks of the St. Regis reservation block traffic through their reservation at the United States-Canada border to reassert their legal authority over the area and to protest the Canadian government's refusal to honor the Jay Treaty of 1794. That treaty allowed the Mohawk unhindered travel back and forth across the border. **1969** BIA Commissioner Robert L. Bennett resigns. Eight months later, Louis R. Bruce, a Mohawk-Oglala from New York is appointed to fill the position.	Fairchild Semiconductors opens a plant at Shiprock, New Mexico. It is the largest manufacturing facility in the state, and soon grows to be the biggest employer of American Indians in the country. The plant is a joint venture of federal agencies, tribal authorities, industry and the non-Indian community. Navajo Community College in Arizona, the first American Indian-operated college in 400 years, opens its doors. Paiute Stanley Smart goes to court over a fine he incurred for shooting deer out of season on public land near the reservation in northern Nevada. He says, ". . . never have we given away or sold the land we used. . ." The case is dismissed on a technicality. American Indians representing 20 tribes occupy Alcatraz Island in San Francisco Bay to claim it as an Indian cultural center. *Custer Died for Your Sins: An Indian Manifesto,* written by Vine Deloria, Jr., is published.

1960

through

1969

AFRICAN AMERICAN	AFRICAN AMERICAN	AFRICAN AMERICAN	FOR CLASSROOM USE	

1960

The United States census reports more than 18.87 million African Americans, or 10.5 percent of the total population.

The Civil Rights Act of 1960 authorizes local judges to appoint overseers to assist African Americans in registering and voting, and establishes criminal penalties for mob action and bombings instigated to prevent enactment of court orders.

Elijah Muhammad, leader of the Nation of Islam, calls for the creation of an African American state. Malcolm X becomes a powerful orator for this organization.

In Greensboro, North Carolina, a lunch counter sit-in at the local Woolworth store by four African American college students begins a process that ends desegregation in the city's restaurants. The sit-in movement gains momentum in other southern states.

1961

The Freedom Riders' bus, organized by the biracial Congress of Racial Equality to help change segregation policies in the deep South, is bombed and burned outside Anniston, Alabama. Attorney General Robert Kennedy sends 400 United States Marshals to Montgomery to quell disturbances.

President Kennedy places three African Americans on federal benches: Thurgood Marshall to sit on the United States Court of Appeals, James B. Parsons (Illinois) and Wade McCree (Michigan) to the United States District Court. Marshall resigns in 1965 to become the first African American solicitor general of the United States. In 1967 he becomes an associate justice of the United States Supreme Court.

At the federal level, Congressman Adam Clayton Powell becomes chairman of the Education and Labor Committee and Robert Weaver becomes administrator of the Housing and Home Finance Agency.

Whitney M. Young, Jr., becomes executive director of the National Urban League.

Clifford R. Wharton, a foreign service officer, is appointed ambassador to Norway. In 1969 he becomes president of Michigan State University. Mercer Cook is appointed ambassador to Niger. He serves until 1964, when he is appointed ambassador to Senegal. He serves in that post until 1966.

1962

Escorted by federal marshals, James Meredith attempts to register at the University of Mississippi. In a riot led by white supremacists, two European American bystanders are killed. Order is restored when 12,000 federal soldiers are called in.

The Justice Department orders the courts to prohibit racial segregation in hospitals built with federal funds. President Kennedy signs Executive Order 11603 forbidding discrimination in sale or rental property that is involved with any form of federal spending.

Edith Spurlock Sampson is elected to the municipal court in Chicago, thus becoming the first African American woman judge in the United States.

Naval officer Samuel L. Gravely becomes the first African American to command a United States warship.

1963

Civil rights demonstrations occur throughout the country. Two hundred thousand march on Washington, D.C., where the Reverend Dr. Martin Luther King, Jr., delivers his famous "I Have a Dream" speech.

NAACP Field Secretary Medgar W. Evers is assassinated in front of his home in Jackson, Mississippi.

Four African American children are killed in the bombing of a church in Birmingham, Alabama.

Augustus F. Hawkins, a Democrat, is elected to the United States House of Representatives from California.

President Kennedy nominates A. Leon Higginbotham from Pennsylvania and Spottswood Robinson III from Washington, D.C., to sit on the United States District Court.

The first African American graduates of the United States Air Force Academy at Colorado Springs are Charles V. Bush, Isaac S. Payne and Roger Sims.

Carl T. Rowan is appointed as ambassador to Finland. He serves until 1964 when he becomes director of the United States Information Agency. Rowan serves until 1965.

1964

Race riots and demonstrations in support of civil rights occur in several large cities.

The bodies of three murdered civil rights workers, James Chaney, Andrew Goodman and Michael Schwerner, are found at Philadelphia, Mississippi, after a six-week search.

Atlanta restaurant owner Lester Maddox closes his facility rather than integrate the premises. He later uses his strong opposition to integration to gain the governorship of Georgia.

Clinton E. Knox is appointed ambassador to Dahomey. He serves until 1969.

1965

Malcolm X (Malcolm Little), a civil rights leader who mocked the noviolent stance of the Reverend Dr. Martin Luther King, Jr., is murdered in New York City.

In protest of the violence accompanying a Selma, Alabama, voter registration drive, Dr. King leads a massive civil rights march from Selma to Montgomery, Alabama. News coverage of the event brings thousands of people on both sides of the issue to Montgomery.

Dr. Alonzo Smythe Yerby is named commissioner of the New York City Department of Hospitals.

1960
through
1969

AFRICAN AMERICAN	AFRICAN AMERICAN	AFRICAN AMERICAN	ASIAN AMERICAN
A violent race riot, growing out of a minor traffic arrest, occurs in the Watts section of Los Angeles. In its wake are more than 30 deaths, 4000 arrests and property damage and lost business revenue in excess of $200 million. John Conyers, Jr., a Democrat, is elected to the United States House of Representatives from Michigan. Patricia R. Harris is appointed ambassador to Luxembourg. She is the first African American woman ambassador. She serves until 1967. Hugh Smythe is appointed ambassador to the Syrian Arab Republic. He serves until 1967 when he is appointed ambassador to Malta. He serves until 1969. Franklin H. Williams is appointed ambassador to Ghana. He serves until 1968. **1966** James Meredith is wounded by a gunshot on the second day of a voter registration march from Memphis to Jackson, Mississippi. The march is continued by Dr. King and other civil rights leaders. During the march Stokeley Carmichael launches the Black Power movement. Urban race riots occur in Atlanta, Chicago and Cleveland. Floyd B. McKissick becomes the national director of the Congress on Racial Equality (CORE). Constance Baker Motley is appointed judge of the federal circuit court of the southern district of New York. Robert C. Weaver is the first African American to hold a cabinet-level post when he becomes Secretary of Housing and Urban Development. Elliot P. Skinner is appointed ambassador to Upper Volta. He serves until 1969. Merle James Smith, Jr., is the first African American to graduate from the United States Coast Guard Academy. William Felton "Bill" Russell becomes the first African American coach of a professional sports team, basketball's Boston Celtics.	**1967** More than 100 cities are hit with race riots, the most severe being Detroit, Michigan, and Newark, New Jersey. In *Loving* v. *Virginia* the Supreme Court rules that antimiscegenation laws are unconstitutional. Boxer Muhammad Ali (Cassius Clay) is convicted in federal court of violating the Selective Service Act by refusing induction into the Armed Forces. Thurgood Marshall is confirmed as the first African American associate justice of the Supreme Court. Several African Americans are elected mayors, including Carl B. Stokes of Cleveland, Ohio, and Richard B. Hatcher of Gary, Indiana. Massachusetts voters send Edward William Brooke, a Republican, to the United States Congress, the first African American to sit in the Senate since Reconstruction. **1968** The Reverend Dr. Martin Luther King, Jr., is assassinated in Memphis, Tennessee. The murder triggers a national crisis as rioting occurs in more than 100 cities. President Johnson declares Sunday, April 6, 1968, a national day of mourning. The report of the National Advisory Committee on Civil Disorders states that white racism is a fundamental cause of riots in American cities. Shirley Chisholm of the Bedford-Stuyvesant section of Brooklyn, New York, is the first African American woman elected to Congress. In the same election, Harlem voters defy critics in Congress and re-elect Adam Clayton Powell, Jr., who was expelled in 1967. Samuel C. Adams is appointed ambassador to Niger. He serves until 1969. **1969** Representative Adam Clayton Powell, Jr., is seated by the United States House of Representatives. He serves one term.	William L. Clay of Missouri and Louis Stokes of Ohio, both Democrats, are elected to the United States House of Representatives. Terence A. Todman, a foreign service officer, is appointed ambassador to Chad. He serves until 1972. Samuel Z. Westerfield is appointed ambassador to Liberia. He serves until 1972.	**1960** The United States census reports approximately 237,000 Chinese Americans, about 60 percent native born. More than half live in four cities: Oakland, New York, Honolulu and San Francisco. The Chinese American family has a higher than average income. Census figures for Filipinos show the following occupational breakdown: men, 4 percent professional and technical, 3 percent farmers, 28 percent farm laborers and foremen; women, 34.9 percent clerical. A shift from rural to urban living is greater among Filipinos than any other group. **1960-1970** During Hawaii's first decade of statehood, numerous Japanese Americans are elected to public office. **1961** Most of California's Filipinos have become American citizens by this time. The first of thousands of Peace Corps volunteers arrive in the Philippines to work as teacher's aides in the elementary schools in the fields of English, math and science. Later groups work in high schools, colleges and community development projects. Hundreds of volunteers marry while in the Philippines and return to America with Filipino spouses. **1962** Daniel K. Inouye of Hawaii becomes the first Japanese American elected to the United States Senate. Seiji Horiuchi, a Japanese American, is elected to the Colorado state legislature. President John F. Kennedy signs an executive order permitting Hong Kong refugees to enter the United States. More than 15,000 are admitted up to June 30, 1965.

1960

through

1969

ASIAN AMERICAN	ASIAN AMERICAN	EUROPEAN AMERICAN	FOR CLASSROOM USE	

ASIAN AMERICAN

1964

Patsy Takemoto Mink, a Democrat from Hawaii, is the first Japanese American woman elected to the United States House of Representatives. She takes office in 1965.

1965

The Immigration Act of 1965, abolishing the National Origins Quota System, is signed into law. An equal immigration quota of 20,000 is allowed for each independent country. Hong Kong, as a British colony, has a quota of 200. The annual quota for Filipinos coming as permanent residents increases to 20,000. This initiates a third wave of Filipino immigration, which includes many white-collar workers and professionals and a more equal balance of men and women.

The Chinatown Planning Council is founded in New York City. It grows to be a multi-service social agency providing vocational training, English classes, housing management, legal advice, child care, translation and other services to Chinese Americans and immigrants.

1965-1976

More than 17,000 Vietnamese immigrants enter the United States. The percentage of all people admitted to the United States from southern Asia and the Far East increases from 5.6 percent in 1965 to 28.9 percent in 1974.

1967

Filipino immigration to the United States rises dramatically. Nearly 11,000 enter this year alone, and this figure doubles in two years. A big percentage of the Filipino immigrants are medical professionals. But those who come under the family preference allowance tend to lack education and have trouble finding skilled jobs.

ASIAN AMERICAN

1968

The Asian American Political Alliance is formed at the University of California-Berkeley and San Francisco State University, and promotes the use of the term "Asian" as opposed to "Oriental." This is the beginning of an organized Asian American movement for civil rights.

1969

Asian American studies programs are established at colleges and universities in response to student demands. Japanese American and Chinese American history is taught as an academic subject for the first time, at San Francisco State College.

San Francisco Chinese Americans found a civil rights organization, Chinese for Affirmative Action.

The first California pilgrimages to former mass detention camp sites take place — to Tule Lake and to Manzanar. The Manzanar pilgrimage becomes the most consistent, with people returning every year.

EUROPEAN AMERICAN

1960

The United States census reports that of the foreign-born residents of the country, 87,100 list Portuguese as their first language, and almost 277,500 declare Portuguese ethnicity.

John Fitzgerald Kennedy is elected the first Irish American and the first Catholic president in United States history.

1961-1975

More than 142,000 Greek immigrants come to the United States. This is the largest number in any 15-year period since before World War II. A large percentage of these new arrivals are professionals and skilled workers who, nevertheless, must take jobs in food-service industries, or as salesworkers and clerks. The unskilled work as domestics, farmers and cab drivers.

1967

Svetlana Alliluyeva, the daughter of Soviet dictator Joseph Stalin, defects to the United States. Her autobiographical book, *Twenty Letters to a Friend,* is published.

A group of Russian Orthodox Old Believers, a sect that practices an austere lifestyle and that has been persecuted for centuries, immigrates first to Oregon and then to Alaska, and establishes the community of Nikolaevsk.

1960

through

1969

1960 through 1969

1960

The United States census reports that the Puerto Rican population in the mainland United States is more than 892,000; in Puerto Rico, it is 2.36 million. Life expectancy on the island is 70 years, compared with 38 in 1910.

Mexican Americans in the United States number about 5 million, the majority of them living in the Southwest.

1961

Several members of the Puerto Rican Forum are appointed to top administrative posts in New York City.

Aspira of New York is founded by Dr. Antonia Pantoja. This bilingual agency provides Puerto Rican high school students with career and life counseling. By 1963 there are 52 Aspira clubs functioning throughout the city.

Henry B. González, a Democrat, becomes the first Mexican American from Texas to be elected to the United States House of Representatives.

1962

The Puerto Rican Family Institute is created in New York City to assist recent immigrant families.

Cesar Chavez leaves the Community Services Organization, forms the National Farm Workers Association (later renamed the United Farm Workers) and begins to organize migrant farm workers in California, most of whom are Mexican.

1964

Luis Muñoz Marín (1948) retires from the governorship of Puerto Rico. His hand-picked successor, Roberto Sánchez Vilella, becomes the Popular Democratic party candidate and easily wins the election.

The Puerto Rican Community Development Project (PRCDP) is developed in New York City. A comprehensive study, it proposes several self-help, community-based approaches to assist Puerto Ricans in the United States. Parts of this plan are later implemented.

The War on Poverty program, the civil rights movement and campus activity usher in an era of increased political awareness and activism among urban Mexican Americans.

In the face of public opposition to the miserable conditions of migrant workers and the influence of the civil rights movement, Congress ends the *bracero* (temporary resident migrant workers) program. This does not stop the flow of migrant workers. Denied the legal means of entry, they come illegally.

Joseph M. Montoya is elected to represent New Mexico in the United States Senate.

Eligio "Kika" de la Garza, a Mexican American, is elected to represent Texas in the United States Congress.

1965

The Civil Rights Act of this year abolishes literacy tests in English as a prerequisite to registering to vote. Puerto Ricans not English-literate may register by showing evidence of having completed six years of schooling.

Hermán Badillo becomes the first Puerto Rican president of the borough of the Bronx in New York City.

Raúl H. Castro is named United States ambassador to El Salvador.

Daniel Fernández is the first Mexican American to receive the Congressional Medal of Honor.

The Freedom Airlift begins bringing 4,000 Cubans to the United States each month. This airlift continues for several years.

1965-1975

The Vietnam War military draft is in effect. More than 48,000 Puerto Ricans participate in the United States Armed Forces; 270 are killed and 3,000 are wounded. Sixty percent of Puerto Ricans involved in the war are volunteers.

1966

The shooting of a Puerto Rican youth by a policeman in Chicago sets off two days of rioting in the Puerto Rican community there.

Rodolfo "Corky" González founds La Cruzada Para la Justicia (The Crusade for Justice) in Denver, Colorado, to encourage Mexican Americans to get involved in the political process.

A protest march 8,000 people strong takes place in Austin, Texas, in support of Cesar Chavez's efforts to improve working conditions for farm laborers.

The Schenley Corporation is the first to contract with Cesar Chavez's newly renamed United Farm Workers Organizing Committee (UFWOC). Several West Coast vineyards soon follow suit.

1967

A nationwide grape boycott is called by the United Farm Workers, in support of California grape pickers.

The New Progressive party (Partido Nuevo Progresista) is founded in Puerto Rico. It supports full statehood for the island.

A plebiscite over Puerto Rico's political status takes place. Commonwealth status receives 60 percent of the votes. Sectors of the independence and statehood movements abstain from participating.

A New York City conference about the Puerto Rican community takes place, the first of its kind. It makes recommendations to Mayor John Lindsey.

Efren Ramirez, the founder of a successful drug rehabilitation program in Puerto Rico, is brought to New York City by Mayor Lindsey to set up a similar program.

In San Juan, Puerto Rico, more than 5,000 demonstrators march for independence on the anniversary of the birth of patriot José de Diego.

The Mexican American Youth Organization (MAYO) is founded on the campus of St. Mary's College in San Antonio, Texas, by José Angel Gutierrez, Carlos Guerra and Mario Compean.

The Johnson administration holds committee hearings in El Paso, Texas, to study the concerns of Mexican Americans. Since no Mexican American leaders are invited to attend, activists boycott and demonstrate outside the conference building. Out of this demonstration, the Raza Unida is formed, the precursor to the Mexican American Raza Unida political party.

Land-rights activist Reies López Tijerina leads a raid on the Tierra Amarilla Courthouse in northern New Mexico. His flight after an unsuccessful attempt to make a citizen's arrest of the district attorney touches off a massive manhunt. Tijerina is eventually caught, tried and found innocent of all charges.

1968

A rift in Puerto Rico's Popular Democratic party causes Sánchez Vilella to leave, and he forms his own People's Party. Luis Negrón Lopez is the Popular candidate for governor. Luis A. Ferre and the pro-statehood New Progressive party win the governorship by a narrow margin, interrupting 28 years of Popular Democratic party rule.

Four Puerto Rican Americans are elected to the New York state senate and assembly: Roberto Garcia, Armando Montano, Luis Nine and Manuel Ramos.

Eugenio María de Hostos Community College is established in the Bronx, New York City. It is the first bilingual college in the country.

Luis Álvarez, a scientist from San Francisco, California, wins the Nobel Prize in physics for his discovery of subatomic particles that exist for fractions of a second.

The Mexican American Legal Defense and Education Fund (MALDEF) is organized in San Francisco to provide legal assistance to Hispanics.

HISPANIC AMERICAN	FOR CLASSROOM USE	FOR CLASSROOM USE	FOR CLASSROOM USE	

1969

The Young Lords party establishes a chapter in New York City. Originally a Chicago street gang comprised of Puerto Rican Americans and influenced by the Black Panther party, the organization supports the people's control of all community institutions and services. It establishes a free breakfast program for East Harlem children and initiates a preventive health care program.

Jorge Luis Córdova is elected resident commissioner of Puerto Rico after the term of Antonio Fernos-Isern (1946). He serves until 1973.

The Puerto Rican Planning Board reports a sharp decline in migration from Puerto Rico to the United States, with 7,000 more persons coming to the island than leaving it.

A special drive is undertaken in New York City to register Puerto Rican voters.

John Joseph Jova, a Cuban American, is appointed ambassador to the Organization of American States. He serves until 1974. He then serves as ambassador to Mexico from 1974 to 1977.

Puerto Rican studies programs are established at City University of New York and elsewhere in the United States.

El Museo del Barrio (The Community's Museum) is established. It is a full-service museum that represents the *barrio* (neighborhood) and exhibits the art of Puerto Rican and other Latino artists.

1960

through

1969

1960

The United States census reports the country's population at 180.1 million, including American citizens living abroad.

The United States Congress passes the Civil Rights Act of 1960 to stop the use of poll tax and literacy requirements as means of preventing African Americans from voting. Several Southern states have used these tactics since Reconstruction.

The Refugee Fair Share Act codifies various previous acts and provides an ongoing mechanism for the admission of refugees.

Nonviolent civil disobedience, generally in the form of sit-ins, becomes a major weapon in the integration battle in the United States. First demonstrated on a large scale in Greensboro, North Carolina, with four African American college students at a European Americans-only lunch counter, the concept spreads throughout the nation.

The United States launches *Tiros I,* its first weather satellite.

The nuclear submarine *Triton* completes an undersea round-the-world trip in 84 days.

Sixty percent of married women in the United States work outside the home.

The U.S.S. *Enterprise,* the world's first nuclear-powered aircraft carrier, is launched at Newport News, Virginia.

Jerrie Cobb is the first woman chosen to train as an astronaut in the United States space program.

The laser is developed at Hughes Research in Malibu, California.

Canada's Parliament unanimously approves that country's first Bill of Rights.

Fidel Castro orders that United States property in Cuba, valued at approximately $770 million, be confiscated. The Eisenhower administration responds by imposing an embargo on exports to Cuba. Cubans flee the country in large numbers. The Cuban refugee program is created in the United States in response to this influx.

1960 through 1969

The Federation of Cuban Women is founded in Cuba to give women a voice in that country's revolutionary process. However, difficulties remain in securing full social and political equality.

Brasília, a newly constructed inland city, becomes the new capital of Brazil and demonstrates the government's willingness to develop the country's interior. Rain forests begin to be cleared so the land can be used for agriculture.

c. 1960

As medical costs in the United States rise rapidly, health insurance becomes a necessity for most families.

1961

John Fitzgerald Kennedy becomes the 35th president of the United States; he is the first Catholic and the youngest man elected to the position. Lyndon Baines Johnson is vice president. Both are Democrats.

President Kennedy proposes the Alliance for Progress, a 10-year plan to raise Latin American living standards, and initiates the Peace Corps, an agency designed to offer training and other assistance through American volunteers going to developing countries. The Alliance is to operate under the structure of the Organization of American States (OAS).

The Twenty-third Amendment to the United States Constitution is ratified, giving residents of the District of Columbia the right to vote in presidental elections.

The Soviet Union violates its agreement with the United States not to perform any nuclear testing.

The Kennedy administration severs diplomatic relations with Cuba. Cuba is invaded at the Bay of Pigs by an estimated 1,200 anti-Castro exiles aided by the United States Central Intelligence Agency (CIA). The invasion is a failure and is crushed by the Cuban military. Castro consolidates his political control.

The first United States astronaut, Navy Commander Alan B. Shepard, Jr., rockets more than 116 miles up in a 302-mile trip into space. Two months later Virgil Grissom becomes the second American astronaut, making a 118-mile high, 303-mile-long rocket flight over the Atlantic Ocean.

The Commission on the Status of Women is established by United States President Kennedy; former first lady Eleanor Roosevelt is named to head the group. The Commission's report, released in 1963, states that women suffer discrimination in all arenas, of the same types and on the same scale as other minorities.

Two companies of United States Army helicopters arrive in Saigon (*see* "The World, 1950-1975, The Vietnam War").

The Congress on Racial Equality (CORE) begins a series of "freedom rides" through Alabama and Mississippi, testing the law that forbids discrimination on public transportation.

Three separatist organizations come into existence in Quebec province, seeking Quebec's independence from Canada.

Barbados achieves full self-government, with Errol Barrow as president.

The assassination of the Dominican Republic's dictator Rafael Leonidas Trujillo Molina (1930, 1942), sends the country into political turmoil. Democratic elections are held the following year.

Patria, Maria Teresa and Minerva, all Catholic nuns, are put to death for their part in the revolt against Dominican President Trujillo.

In Peru a military takeover puts General Ricardo Perez Godoy in charge of the country. Godoy cannot maintain power, and is deposed in 1963.

Lt. Colonel José Julio Rivera becomes president of El Salvador after the term of José María Lemus (1956).

Women in Paraguay receive the right to vote.

1961-1970

Immigration to the United States totals more than 3.32 million, of which 1.12 million come from Europe, 427,600 from Asia, 29,000 from Africa, 25,100 from Oceania, 1.72 million from the Americas and 90 are not specifically identified.

1962

The Cuban missile crisis erupts when American U-2 spy planes discover Russian missiles in Cuba aimed at the United States. President Kennedy orders Cuba blockaded. The crisis ends when Soviet Premier Nikita Khrushchev agrees to remove the missiles and nuclear weapons from Cuba and President Kennedy guarantees the sovereignty of Cuba and secretly agrees to remove United States missiles from Turkey. Cuba later releases 1,113 prisoners captured as part of the 1961 Bay of Pigs invasion attempt.

President Kennedy issues an executive order barring racial and religious discrimination in federally financed housing.

Astronaut Lieutenant Colonel John H. Glenn, Jr. is the first American to orbit the earth, completing three orbits in slightly less than five hours, in the space capsule *Friendship 7.*

The segregationist New Orleans Citizens' Council offers free one-way transportation to African Americans who want to migrate to northern cities. By October, more than 90 people have taken advantage of this offer.

An estimate from the Bureau of Labor Statistics predicts that for the next decade, between 200,000 and 300,000 employees annually will be replaced by machinery.

A total of 355,000 Cuban refugees have arrived in the United States since the Cuban revolution.

The United States launches *Telstar,* a communications satellite.

James Meredith, escorted by federal marshals, registers as the first African American student at the University of Mississippi.

THE AMERICAS

THE AMERICAS

The National Farm Workers Association (NFWA) is founded by Cesar Chavez in California. In 1972 the NFWA becomes part of the AFL-CIO.

Linus Pauling, an American who won the Nobel Prize for chemistry in 1954, takes the Nobel Peace Prize this year for his efforts in opposition to nuclear weapons.

Rachel Carson's book, *Silent Spring,* is published, exposing to the general public the dangers of the use of pesticides.

The world's longest highway, the Trans-Canada Highway, is completed, with 4,869 miles of roadway.

Commercial air flights between the United States and Cuba are halted.

Jamaica gains its independence and becomes a member of the British Commonwealth.

The Republic of Trinidad and Tobago becomes an independent state.

In Argentina, the military removes elected President Dr. Arturo Frondizi (1958) from power because of his support of Castro and the policies of Perón. José Maria Guido becomes president. He serves for one year.

In Colombia, Guillermo León Valencia is elected president after the term of Alberto Lleras Camargo (1958).

Victor Raúl Haya de la Torre is elected president of Peru with the support of APRA. A military coup prevents him from taking office.

1963

Lyndon Baines Johnson becomes the 36th president of the United States after John F. Kennedy is fatally shot in Dallas, Texas.

In *Gideon* v. *Wainright,* the United States Supreme Court rules that legal counsel must be made available for indigent defendants in criminal cases.

The Supreme Court rules that no locality may require recitation of the Lord's Prayer or other Bible verses in the nation's public schools. The Court also rules that racial segregation in courtrooms is unconstitutional.

THE AMERICAS

In the United States, the civil rights movement becomes more active, with sit-ins to protest segregation in public places and a major rally attended by 200,000 people, both African Americans and European Americans, in Washington, D.C. At the rally, Dr. Martin Luther King, Jr. delivers his famous "I Have a Dream" speech.

The Washington-to-Moscow "hotline," a direct telephone line from the president of the United States to the premier of the Soviet Union, opens. It is designed to reduce the risk of accidental nuclear war.

The Equal Pay Act goes into effect in the United States, forbidding pay inequity for people who perform essentially the same work for the same employer, regardless of race, nationality, religion, nation of origin, or sex.

Betty Freidan's *The Feminist Mystique* is published. It soon becomes a primary force in the modern feminist movement.

Bilingual instruction is initiated in Dade County, Florida, for Cuban children coming to Miami.

One hundred twenty-nine men lose their lives when the nuclear submarine *Thresher* is lost at sea. The sub's nuclear reactor is never recovered.

Postage for a first-class letter in the United States is five cents.

Lee Harvey Oswald, the accused assassin of President Kennedy, is shot and killed by Dallas nightclub owner Jack Ruby.

James Whittaker becomes the first American to reach the summit of Mt. Everest. He and a Nepalese guide climb the south side of the mountain.

THE AMERICAS

An army recruiting office in Montreal is the scene of a bomb explosion, the work of a new, radical separatist organization, Front de libération du Québec (FLQ). Several mail bombs explode in the English-speaking community of Westmount, in Montreal. The Quebec government offers a reward for information on terrorist activities, and an anti-terrorist squad is formed within the Montreal police department.

Lester Bowles Pearson, a Liberal, becomes prime minister of Canada after the term of John George Diefenbacker (1957). Pearson serves until 1968.

Castro pays an official visit to the Union of Soviet Socialist Republics (Soviet Union). In the second phase of his "revolution," Castro moves Cuba toward additional agrarian reform, and establishes compulsory military service. His attempts to "export revolution" to other Latin American countries fail.

Dr. Arturo Illia is chosen by Argentina's electoral committee as the country's new president after the one-year term of José Maria Guido (1962). Illia serves until 1966.

After a coup in Ecuador, Rear Admiral Ramon Castro Jijón becomes president. He leads the country until 1966.

Fernando Belaúnde Terry becomes president of Peru. He serves until 1968.

1964

The Twenty-fourth Amendment to the United States Constitution is ratified. It prohibits denying or abridging any citizen's right to vote for nonpayment of any poll tax or other tax. It also gives Congress the power to enforce the amendment by appropriate legislation.

The United States Supreme Court rules that congressional districts should be roughly equal in population.

1960

through

1969

1960 through 1969

The Civil Rights Act of 1964 creates the Equal Employment Opportunity Commission (EEOC) to combat racial discrimination in hiring, and also reinforces the policy that forbids discrimination in schools and businesses and instructs the United States government to withhold funds to any state that discriminates on the basis of sex or race.

President Johnson begins a campaign called the "War on Poverty": the Economic Opportunity Act provides job training for the unskilled, work-skills training for unemployed parents, and two school programs for children from low-income families — Project Headstart for pre-school training and Upward Bound for college students.

As a result of the civil rights movement, anti-Catholic, anti-Asian and anti-Semitic sentiments lessen in the United States.

Three civil rights workers — Michael Schwerner and Andrew Goodman, both European Americans, and African American James Chaney — are murdered in Mississippi.

Congress approves the Gulf of Tonkin Resolution which authorizes President Johnson to take necessary steps to "maintain peace" (see "The World, 1950-1975, The Vietnam War").

A devastating earthquake rocks Alaska, killing more than 110 people and destroying most of the town of Valdez.

Jack Ruby is convicted of murder in the slaying of Lee Harvey Oswald and is sentenced to death by a jury in Dallas, Texas. The conviction is reversed in 1966 but Ruby dies in 1967 before a second trial can be held. President Lyndon B. Johnson's Commission on the Assassination of President Kennedy (headed by Supreme Court Justice Earl Warren) issues the Warren Report, concluding that Lee Harvey Oswald acted alone.

The United States ends the *bracero* (temporary resident migrant worker) program; this increases substantially the number of illegal immigrants arriving from Mexico.

The first state lottery in the United States is conducted in New Hampshire.

The British Union Jack is left off Canada's new national flag.

Gustavo Díaz Ordaz is elected president of Mexico after the term of Adolfo López Mateos (1958). Ordaz serves until 1970.

The Bahamas gains independence from Britain.

After a period of civil unrest in Bolivia, President Victor Paz Estenssoro is removed from office.

A military coup brings General Humberto Castello Branco into power in Brazil.

Chile's President Montalva introduces a plan for financial and economic reform.

In Lima, Peru, more than 310 spectators die in a riot at a soccer game.

1964-1985

Brazil's military assumes control of the country, and brings General Humberto Castello Branco to power. Rapid economic development is advocated, creating an international debt of $100 billion. Urban and rural poverty grows unchecked. During the military rule, which continues until 1985, civil rights are limited.

1965

Lyndon Baines Johnson begins his first elected term as president of the United States; Hubert H. Humphrey is vice president. Both are Democrats.

Congress passes the Immigration Act of 1965, containing two innovations: a ceiling on visas for immigration from the Western Hemisphere and a requirement for all nonrelative and nonrefugee immigrants to obtain labor clearances. These clearances must state that American workers are not available for their intended jobs and that the immigrants will not lower prevailing wages and working conditions. The law abolishes the Asiatic Barred Zone as well as per-country quotas. It goes into effect in 1968.

Congress also passes the Voting Rights Act, which gives the federal government increased powers to fight discriminatory policies that prevent people — primarily African Americans — from voting. The "Great Society" reforms are continued with the Water Quality and Air Quality Acts, the establishment of the National Foundations for the Arts and Humanities and the Omnibus Housing Bill. The Social Security Amendments of 1965 establish Medicare and Medicaid health coverage for the elderly and impoverished, respectively. In addition, the Housing and Urban Development Department (HUD) is created.

The first nationwide antiwar demonstrations take place in the United States, the largest being in New York and Berkeley. In New York, the new federal law against burning one's draft-card is first enforced by arrest. In Berkeley, demonstrators are barred by police from entering Oakland. The marchers are then attacked by a group of Hell's Angels motorcyclists.

In *Griswold* v. *Connecticut*, the United States Supreme Court strikes down a state law forbidding the use of contraceptives by married persons.

A federal commission awards United States companies 75 cents on the dollar ($213 million) for properties damaged by American bombing raids on German-held territories during World War II.

The Reverend Dr. Martin Luther King, Jr., and more than 2,600 African American protesters are arrested in Selma, Alabama, during a three-day demonstration against voter registration rules.

Malcolm X, a leader of African American nationalism, is killed at a Harlem rally in New York City. African Americans riot for six days in the Watts section of Los Angeles, California. More than 30 people are killed, 1,000 injured and 4,000 arrested; the property damage due to fire exceeds $175 million. Two members of the Nation of Islam are later convicted of Malcolm X's murder.

Cesar Chavez leads in the formation of the National Farm Workers Association (NFWA), and calls the new group's first strike in support of the predominantly Filipino Agricultural Workers Organizing Committee (AWOC). NWFA and AWOC merge to form the United Farm Workers Organizing Committee and become charter members of the AFL-CIO. The grape pickers' strike begins in Delano, California.

Lesbian and gay activists first picket the White House and Philadelphia's Independence Hall to protest the federal government's discrimination against homosexuals.

Hurricane Betsy hits the Louisiana coast, resulting in more than 60 deaths and extensive property damage.

The United States space probe *Mariner 4* sends back the first photographs of the planet Mars. United States astronaut Col. Edward Higgens White, II, performs the first "walk in space" aboard *Gemini 4*.

Ralph Nader's book *Unsafe at Any Speed* is published in the United States. Resultant federal regulations force automobile manufacturers to improve the safety of their products.

The Royal Canadian Mounted Police seize $25 million worth of heroin in Montreal.

Abraham A. Okpik is the first Inuit (Eskimo) elected to the governing council of Canada's Northwest Territories.

The world's first processing plant for irradiation of food opens in Canada.

The Johnson administration signs a "Memorandum of Understanding" with Cuba, which establishes an airlift between Varadero, Cuba, and Miami, Florida. These daily flights bring a total of 257,000 Cubans to the United States by the time the airlift ends in 1973.

United States President Johnson sends the marines to the Dominican Republic as fighting persists between the deposed civilian government and the Dominican army. Joaquín Balaguer becomes president after a supervised election.

Political unrest in Uruguay prompts the National Council to proclaim that the country is in a state of siege.

1966

In *Miranda* v. *Arizona,* the United States Supreme Court overturns the conviction of a confessed rapist and establishes the requirement that arresting officers inform arrestees of their rights—the so-called Miranda warning.

The federal Department of Transportation is created in Washington, D.C.

A massive antiwar march takes place in Washington, D.C., as 63,000 demonstrators vow to vote only for antiwar candidates.

Robert Clifton Weaver, United States Secretary of Housing and Urban Development (HUD), becomes the first African American to serve in a president's cabinet. Weaver serves until 1968.

The United Farm Workers Organizing Committee, Cesar Chavez's new union, signs its first collective bargaining contract.

State laws enacted in California set acceptable automotive air pollution standards.

As the Third National Conference of Commissions on the Status of Women ends in Washington, D.C., Betty Friedan, Kathryn Clarenbach and other women recognize the need for a civil rights advocate group for women. The National Organization for Women (NOW) is founded out of this realization, with Friedan serving as its first president.

Dr. Michael E. DeBakey implants an artificial heart in a human for the first time at a Houston, Texas, hospital; the plastic device functions and the patient survives the operation.

Five major airlines in the United States are brought to a halt by a machinist's strike that lasts for several months.

Eighty people die in New York City in a deadly smog.

North Dakota residents suffer through that state's worst blizzard ever.

Barbados becomes an independent state of the British Commonwealth.

Joaquin Balaguer becomes president of the Dominican Republic. He is re-elected twice and serves until 1978.

A military coup in Ecuador deposes President Ramón Castro Jijón (1963) and reestablishes civilian government.

A military coup in Argentina forces the legislature to close. Student and labor organizations continue to strike in defiance of the military.

Guyana (formerly British Guiana) in South America gains its independence and becomes a member of the British Commonwealth.

1966-1970

Cuba reestablishes diplomatic relations with other Latin nations, and sends technicians, skilled personnel and troops to Latin American and African countries. Castro ends his attempts to spread revolution after Che Guevara is killed in Bolivia.

1967

The Twenty-fifth Amendment to the United States Constitution is ratified. It defines the responsibilities of the vice president in the event of the president's death, disability or inability to function in office.

Thurgood Marshall, formerly a lawyer for the National Association for the Advancement of Colored People (NAACP), is sworn in as the first African American justice of the United States Supreme Court.

During a test at Cape Kennedy, three United States astronauts—Virgil I. Grissom, Edward H. White II and Roger B. Chaffee—die in a flash fire aboard *Apollo*. This accident temporarily suspends the space exploration program in the United States.

In response to widespread racial unrest, President Johnson creates a panel on racial disorder and appoints Illinois Governor Otto Kerner, Jr., as its director.

President Johnson issues an executive order banning racial, sexual or religious discrimination by the federal government and its contractors and subcontractors.

Amendment of the Civil Rights Act extends the Bill of Rights to Indians living on reservations and allows for Indian consent in the transfer of jurisdiction from federal to state government.

Mass demonstrations are held in protest of United States military involvement in Vietnam.

A nationwide grape boycott is called in support of California grape pickers.

Racial violence takes place in Detroit, Michigan, and more than 7,000 National Guardsmen aid police after rioting breaks out in the African American community. More than 35 people are killed, 3,500 are arrested and 5,000 are left homeless. Similar riots occur in New York City's Spanish Harlem; Rochester, New York; Newark, New Jersey; Birmingham, Alabama; and New Britain, Connecticut.

The counterculture "flower-power" movement grows in the United States, with a major center in the Haight-Ashbury section of San Francisco, California. Focusing on communal living, the culture is based partially on the use of mind-expanding drugs to increase awareness and intellectual capacity.

Ernesto "Che" Guevara, a former leader of the Cuban guerilla movement and an effective revolutionary organizer in Latin America, is killed in Bolivia.

Anastasio Somoza Debayle becomes president of Nicaragua after the term of René Schick Gutiérrez. Debayle serves until 1972 and becomes president again in 1974.

1968

The population of the United States passes the 200 million mark.

The United States, the Soviet Union and 58 nations without nuclear weapons sign a treaty prohibiting the proliferation of such weapons.

Congress passes the Equal Employment Opportunities Act. President Johnson signs the Civil Rights Act of 1968, which bans racial discrimination in sale or lease of most of the nation's housing.

1960

through

1969

THE AMERICAS	THE AMERICAS	THE AMERICAS	FOR CLASSROOM USE
North Korea seizes the United States Navy intelligence ship *Pueblo* and holds 83 on board as spies.

The Reverend Dr. Martin Luther King, Jr., is killed in Memphis, Tennessee. Within hours of Dr. King's murder, riots begin in many cities. The rioting lasts for days, with more than 40 fatalities, 21,200 arrests, and 55,000 federal soldiers and national guardsmen called in for riot control. The most violent rioting takes place in Washington, D.C.; Chicago; Baltimore and Kansas City. James Earl Ray, indicted in the murder, is captured in London on June 8. In 1969 Ray pleads guilty and is sentenced to 99 years in prison.

Senator Robert F. Kennedy, brother of the late president John F. Kennedy, is shot and critically wounded in a Los Angeles, California, hotel after winning the state's presidential primary. He dies the following day. Sirhan B. Sirhan is convicted of the killing in 1969.

Shirley Anita Chisholm, a Democrat from New York, becomes the first African American woman to become an elected member of the United States House of Representatives. Her term begins in 1969.

Because of unusual circumstances that have increased the number of immigrants from Cuba, about 100,000 Cuban refugees have their resident status adjusted before the imposition of a 120,000-person ceiling on Western Hemisphere visa issuance. If this were not done, these refugees would completely absorb all available visas for that jurisdiction.

The National Advisory Commission on Civil Rights, headed by Illinois Governor Otto Kerner, issues a report warning the nation about the dangers of social inequalities between African Americans and European Americans in this nation. | More than 70 mine workers die in mine explosions at the Farmingham mines in West Virginia. This disaster prompts the United States Congress to enact new mine safety laws.

Postage for a first-class letter in the United States is six cents.

A combined Canadian-United States expedition reaches the North Pole by snowmobile. Their location is verified by a United States weather aircraft, so this becomes the first undisputed visit to the North Pole.

Two French Canadian separatist organizations unite at a convention in Quebec and form the Parti Québécois.

Pierre Elliott Trudeau, a Liberal, becomes prime minister of Canada following the term of Lester Bowles Pearson (1963).

José María Velasco Ibarra (1960) becomes president of Ecuador for a fifth time. He serves until 1972. He was deposed by military coups in each of his first four terms.

The meeting in Medellín, Colombia, of the Latin American Bishops Conference sets a new direction for the Catholic church in Latin America with discussion of liberation theology and a concern for economic equity.

Juan Velsaco Alvarado becomes president of Peru after a bloodless coup in which Fernando B. Terry (1963) is ousted. Alvarado serves until 1975.

1969

Richard M. Nixon becomes the 37th president of the United States; Spiro T. Agnew is vice president. Both are Republicans.

Warren Earl Burger becomes chief justice of the United States Supreme Court. The Court orders an end to school segregation "at once."

The United States, Denmark, the Soviet Union and Canada set up a joint council to study Inuit (Eskimo) issues.

In the largest antiwar demonstration in history, 250,000 people assemble in Washington, D.C., to protest United States involvement in Vietnam. This estimate of crowd size is considered conservative. | The first known American Acquired Immune Deficiency Syndrome (AIDS) casualty is a St. Louis teenager; however, this case is not identified or reported as AIDS until 1987.

United States *Apollo 11* astronauts Neil A. Armstrong and Edwin E. "Buzz" Aldrin, Jr., take man's first walk on the moon while their colleague Michael Collins waits in orbit.

The first accredited college course in the United States in women's studies is offered at Cornell University.

Hurricane Camille batters the United States Gulf coast with 170 mile-per-hour winds. More than 250 fatalities occur as people apparently ignore warnings about the storm's severity.

A police raid on the Stonewall Inn, a gay bar in New York's Greenwich Village, provokes the patrons to riot. Street protests continue for several nights. Stonewall becomes the symbolic origin of the gay rights movement.

The Woodstock Music and Art Fair, a weekend rock concert at Woodstock, New York, gathers 400,000 peaceful participants in one of the largest, and most famous, counterculture events of the 1960s.

Canada's Official Languages Act accepts the use of both French and English.

The St. Regis Reserve, outside Cornwall, Ontario, Canada is host to the North American Unity convention, which brings together American Indians from Canada, the United States and Central America.

Leaders of the Six Nations Confederacy declare that their reserve in Ontario, Canada, is a sovereign state and will not be governed by Ontario or Canada.

The so-called "Soccer War" breaks out as Salvadoran migrant workers are expelled from Honduras. The OAS intervenes in the dispute.

General Ovando becomes president of Bolivia. | |

1960

through

1969

1960

An American U-2 spy plane piloted by Francis G. Powers is shot down over the Soviet Union. Nikita Khrushchev cancels the Paris summit conference two weeks later because of the incident. Powers is sentenced to 10 years in prison but is freed in 1962 in exchange for Soviet spy Rudolf Abel.

One of the leaders of Nazi war crimes against the Jewish people, Adolf Eichmann, is captured in Argentina by Israeli forces. He is tried and convicted, and is executed in Israel in 1962.

A Soviet nuclear-powered icebreaker begins the regular task of maintaining an open 2,500 mile passage from Asia to Europe along the north coast of Siberia for 150 days a year.

China (PRC) and the Soviet Union split in a conflict over communist ideology.

A rightist organization seizes power in Laos.

Turkey's Prime Minister Adnan Menderes (1950) is executed following a military coup led by General Cemal Gürsel.

France explodes its first atomic bomb in the Sahara Desert in the Sudan.

The Organization of the Petroleum Exporting Countries (OPEC) is organized in Baghdad.

Many of France's African colonies and overseas territories gain their independence this year. Dahomey, Upper Volta (Burkina Faso), and French Cameroon gain their independence from France. Upper Volta's new president is Maurice Yameogo; the Republic of Cameroon is headed by President Ahmadou Ahidjo.

The Central African Republic, Chad, the (French) Congo and Ivory Coast also gain their independence from France. Chad's new president is François Tombalbaye. The new government of the Congo is headed by President Abbe Youlou.

Niger also achieves independence from France, with Hamani Diori as its first president. Togo gains independence from France; the Republic of Togo is declared, with Sylvanus Olympio as head of state. Mauritania also gains its independence as the Islamic Republic of Mauritania, with Moktar Ould Daddah as president.

The Belgian Congo gains full independence as the Republic of the Congo, under joint leadership of Joseph Kasavubu as president and Patrice E. Lumumba as prime minister. However, the immediate declaration of Katang province's independence under Moïse Tshombe opens a civil war that continues until United Nations intervention in 1963.

Gabon attains full independence from France. Leon M'Ba becomes president. He is ousted briefly by a coup in 1964, but soon returns to office. M'Ba serves until his death in 1967.

Senegal withdraws from the Federation of Mali; Sudan changes its name to the Republic of Mali and becomes fully independent. An agreement is signed with Ghana (now a republic) and Guinea to form the Union of African States.

Somalia (formerly Italian Somaliland) and Nigeria gain their independence from Britain.

Madagascar (formerly the Malagasy Republic) gains its independence from France and Philibert Tsiranana becomes its first president; the country changes its name in 1975 to the Democratic Republic of Madagascar.

Senegal becomes independent, with Léopold Sedar Senghor, leader of the Senegalese Progressive Union (UPS), as president. Senghor serves until 1980.

Laurian Rugambwa of Tanzania becomes the first black Roman Catholic cardinal.

In Sharpeville, South Africa, 70 native Africans are killed by police during a peaceful demonstration against the requirement that all South Africans of non-European descent must carry internal passports. The leading African protest groups, the African National Congress (ANC) and the Pan Africanist Congress (PAC), are outlawed. This incident comes to be called the Sharpeville massacre, and serves to make South African racist policies a focus of worldwide attention.

Keith Jacka Holyoake, a National party leader, becomes prime minister of New Zealand after the term of Walter Nash (1957). Holyoake serves until 1972.

The United States and Japan agree to a new security pact.

Cyprus becomes a republic. Archbishop Makarios becomes the country's first president. He is removed from office in 1974.

Norodom Sihanouk (1941, 1947) becomes head of state in Cambodia after the death of his father, Norodom Suramarit (1955). Sihanouk rules until 1970.

U Nu (1948) returns to power as prime minister of Burma. He serves until 1962.

Civil unrest in South Korea forces President Syngman Rhee's (1948) resignation.

Prime Minister Kwame Nkrumah is elected president of Ghana. He serves until 1966.

Félix Houphouét-Boigny becomes the first president of the Ivory Coast.

David Dacko becomes the first president of the Central African Republic. He serves until 1966.

1960-1961

Nepal's King Mahendra Bir Bikram Shah declares the dissolution of parliament and the outlawing of political parties.

1960-1970

Foreign-held oil firms in Iran are nationalized by order of Shah Muhammad Reza Pahlevi. Arab nations place an embargo against OPEC shipments to the United States, and an international energy crisis begins.

1960

through

1969

THE WORLD	THE WORLD	THE WORLD	THE WORLD

1960

through

1969

1960-1972

Dahomey (Benin) experiences a period of acute government upheaval.

1961

The Soviet Union's space program puts the first man in orbit around earth — Major Yuri A. Gagarin in *Vostok 1*.

In violation of the nuclear test ban agreement, the Soviet Union detonates a 50-megaton hydrogen bomb, at the time the biggest explosion in history.

East Germans intensify the conflict between the two Berlins by erecting the Berlin Wall to halt the flood of refugees between east and west. The wall will stand until 1989, when East Germany officially opens its borders.

Syria withdraws from the United Arab Republic and establishes its own government.

Nazi war criminal Adolf Eichmann is found guilty of crimes against humanity, war crimes and crimes against the Jewish people. He is sentenced to death and subsequently hanged.

The Islamic Republic of Mauritania elects acting president Makhtar Ould Daddah to continue as its first president.

Diplomatic ties are broken between Albania and the Soviet Union.

Sierra Leone achieves independence within the British Commonwealth, with Milton Margai, of the Sierra Leone People's Party (SLPP), as prime minister. Margai serves until 1964.

An unsuccessful revolt against Portuguese rule occurs in Angola.

British Cameroon is divided; the two parts are annexed, one by Nigeria to the north and the other by the Republic of Cameroon to the south.

After months of internal unrest in the Republic of the Congo (Zaïre), including major dissension between President Kasavubu and Prime Minister Lumumba, army commander Joseph-Désiré Mobutu temporarily takes over the government. Lumumba is imprisoned briefly, then released. His murder a short time later is blamed on Tsombe's mercenaries. Power is restored to President Kasavubu.

South Africa withdraws from the British Commonwealth and is declared a republic.

Tanganyika (Tanzania) becomes an independent member of the British Commonwealth, with Julius Nyerere as prime minister.

Kuwait achieves complete independence from Britain. Sheik Abdullah al-Salem al-Sabah rules as *emir* (Muslim prince or commander). Iraq claims Kuwait and threatens to invade. British and Arab League forces intervene, and Iraqi troops retreat.

South Korea's government is overthrown by a military junta, with Chung Hee Park as its chairman.

North Korea and China (PRC) enter into a mutual assistance pact.

United States President John F. Kennedy and Soviet Premier Nikita Khrushchev meet in Vienna, Austria, for a summit.

General Cemal Gürsel is elected president of Turkey. He serves until 1966, when failing health forces his resignation.

Hassan II becomes king of Morocco after the death of his father, Muhammad V (1957).

1962

France officially grants independence to Algeria. The new country adopts a republican form of government, with Ahmed Ben Bella at its first prime minister. Ben Bella serves until 1965.

Borg Olivier, of the Nationalist party, becomes prime minister of Malta. He serves until 1971.

Burmese diplomat U Thant becomes secretary general of the United Nations after serving since 1961 as acting secretary. He serves until 1972.

A United Nations resolution ends Belgium's trusteeship of Ruanda-Urundi. The two regions separate. Rwanda gains independence with Gregoire Kayibanda as president. He serves until 1973. Burundi gains independence and is ruled by a monarchy; Mwambutsa IV is king. He serves until 1966. Ethnic violence between Hutu and Tutsi peoples continues in both countries.

Eritrea is annexed by Ethiopia; the Eritrean resistance movement begins.

Nelson Mandela, leader of the African National Congress (ANC), is imprisoned in South Africa.

Tanganyika becomes a republic; Prime Minister Nyerere becomes president.

Imam Muhammad, king of North Yemen, is assassinated in a military takeover. North Yemen is formally declared the Arab Republic of Yemen, with Abdullah al-Sallal as president. Civil war erupts between those who favor a republic and those who want a monarchy. The fighting continues until 1967.

Uganda, a British protectorate since 1894, gains its independence within the Commonwealth. Milton Obote becomes prime minister. He serves until 1963, and again from 1966 until 1971.

Pakistan has a new constitution which allows, among other things, the formation of political parties. Muhammad Ayub Khan (1958) continues as president until 1969.

In Laos, a coalition government is established, representing several political opinions. Fourteen powers at a Geneva, Switzerland, meeting guarantee Laotian independence.

Conflict occurs as PRC forces attempt to seize lands along India's Himalayan border. Heavy fighting continues for 33 days, with little territorial consequence.

An earthquake in northwestern Iran results in 12,230 deaths.

General U Ne Win (1958) leads a second military coup in Burma and becomes that country's leader. He institutes strict isolationist policies that prohibit most outside contacts. He becomes president in 1974 when a new constitution is written.

Western Samoa gains its independence from New Zealand, with Fiame Mata'afa Mulinu'u as prime minister. Mulinu'u serves until 1970 and again from 1973 to 1975.

1963

Officials of France and West Germany sign a treaty of cooperation that ends four centuries of conflict.

The Moscow-to-Washington, D.C., "hot line," a direct telephone line from the Soviet premier to the president of the United States, opens. The telephones, designed to reduce the risk of accidental war, are staffed by both countries at all times.

The Soviet Union launches its space satellite *Vostok 6* and Valentina Tereshkova becomes the first woman to travel in space.

Dutch New Guinea, the last Dutch colony in Indonesia, becomes part of the Republic of Indonesia.

United Nations forces intervene in the Republic of the Congo and end the civil war there. Rebel leader Tshombe goes into exile.

Kenya gains its independence from Britain. It becomes a republic the following year, with Jomo Kenyatta as its first president. Independent Nigeria becomes a republic and B. N. Azikiwe becomes its first president.

Fighting in Laos between political factions resumes. A Paris conference in 1964 fails to end the battle.

South Vietnam's President Ngo Dihn Diem (1955-1956) is assassinated.

The Federation of Rhodesia and Nyasaland is disbanded; the two become the independent states of Zambia and Malawi, respectively.

Violent uprisings occur in Chad's northern Muslim sector under direction of the Chadian National Liberation Front (Frolinat), with Lybian support.

President Abbe Youlou of the Congo is forced to resign, and the nation gets a new constitution. Alphonse Massamba-Débat becomes president under the new framework. He serves until 1968.

Togo's President Sylvanus Olympio is murdered in a military takeover. Nicolas Grunitzky becomes president. He serves until 1967.

The Zimbabwe African National Union (ZANU) is founded in Southern Rhodesia, with Robert Mugabe as president. The goal of the group is to win for native Africans the right to govern their own affairs.

The Federation of Malaysia is formed by the union of Singapore, Sarawak, Saba (North Borneo) and Malaya. Tunku Abdul Rahman becomes Malaysia's first prime minister. Singapore leaves the federation in 1965. Rahman serves until 1969.

Uganda declares itself a federal republic with King Mutesa II as president. Mutesa II rules until 1966.

A Limited Nuclear Test Ban Treaty banning atmospheric nuclear weapons testing is signed by all major powers except France and China, who are still developing their own weapons.

French President Charles De Gaulle begins an independent, isolationist policy by vetoing Britain's admission to the European Common Market, opposing American plans for a NATO nuclear force, refusing to sign the Nuclear Test Ban Treaty, formally recognizing the PRC, opposing American participation in the Vietnam War and insisting that NATO bases in France be abandoned within four years.

An earthquake in Skopje, Macedonia, results in 1,100 deaths.

A submarine communications cable is laid between Canada and Iceland.

Ayatollah Ruhollah Khomeini is exiled from Iran for protesting the shah's policies.

Levi Eshkol becomes prime minister of Israel after the term of David Ben-Gurion (1955). Eshkol serves until 1969.

(Sir) Alec Douglas-Home, a Conservative, becomes prime minister of Great Britain after the term of Harold MacMillan (1957). Douglas-Home serves until 1964.

Chung Hee Park becomes president of South Korea. He serves until 1979.

Ludwig Erhard becomes chancellor of West Germany following the term of Konrad Adenauer (1949). Erhard serves until 1966.

1964

The merger of Tanganyika with newly independent Zanzibar forms the United Republic of Tanzania. Under President Julius Nyerere, Tanzania tries to weaken western influence in Africa and becomes a stronghold of African nationalism. Nyerere serves until 1985.

In South Africa, Nelson Mandela and other leaders of the African National Congress (ANC) are sentenced to life in prison for their fights for racial equality.

A new constitution gives Afghanistan citizens a bicameral legislature, an independent judicial system, and a prime minister chosen by the monarch.

The Soviet Union launches *Voskhod 1,* the first space satellite with a 3-man crew.

Chinese officials detonate that country's first atomic bomb.

Dorothy Hodgkin receives the Nobel Prize for chemistry. She is the first English woman to receive a Nobel Prize.

The Palestine Liberation Organization (PLO) is founded with the initial aim of dissolving the state of Israel. Gradually over the next three decades, its leaders adopt a more moderate stance.

Malta achieves independence within the British Commonwealth.

Jomo Kenyatta becomes the first president of Kenya. He serves until his death in 1978.

Albert Margai becomes prime minister of Sierra Leone after the term of his half-brother, Milton Margai (1961). Albert Margai serves until 1967.

Civilian government is restored in Sudan.

In the Soviet Union, Aleksei N. Kosygin becomes premier and Leonid I. Brezhnev becomes first secretary of the Communist party. The new leadership of the Soviet Union's Communist party removes Nikita Khrushchev from power.

Faisal becomes king of Saudi Arabia after his brother, Abdul-Aziz Al Saud (1953), is deposed. Faisal rules until 1975.

Shri Lal Bahadur Shastri becomes prime minister of India after the death of Jawaharlal Nehru (1947). Shastri serves until 1966.

Constantine II becomes king of Greece after the death of his father, Paul I (1947). Constantine rules until 1973, although he is forced into exile in 1967.

Harold Wilson, a member of the Labour party, becomes prime minister of Great Britain after the term of (Sir) Alec Douglas-Home (1963). Wilson serves until 1970.

1964-1965

Congolese rebel leader Tshombe (1961), who led the unsuccessful rebellion of Katanga province, returns from exile to the Republic of the Congo. In a conciliatory move, President Kasavubu appoints Tshombe interim prime minister. However, a power struggle soon develops between Kasavubu and Tshombe; again Mobutu (1961) and the military seize control. In late summer 1965 the country adds to its name to become the Democratic Republic of the Congo.

1965

Cambodia severs diplomatic ties with the United States.

Singapore announces its independence from the Federation of Malaysia.

Gambia gains its independence from Britain. It becomes a republic and a member of the British Commonwealth in 1970.

The Maldive Islands gain independence from British rule and are governed as a sultanate. They become a republic in 1968.

Southern Rhodesia's Prime Minister Ian Smith unilaterally declares the country's withdrawal and independence from the British Commonwealth. The native African organization ZANU is outlawed.

Algeria's president Ahmed Ben Bella (1962) is deposed in a military takeover led by Colonel Houari Boumédienne.

A military coup led by Jean-Bédel Bokassa in the Central African Republic ousts President David Dacko. Bokassa proclaims himself president and later takes the title of emperor for life.

Pakistan and India again fight over ownership of the Kashmir region.

French officials incite controversy in the European Common Market by opposing the policy of allowing EEC organizations to control sovereign powers.

Romanian leader Dej dies. Nicolae Ceauşescu is named first secretary of the Communist Party. The country is renamed the Socialist Republic of Romania.

Sheik Sabah becomes ruler of Kuwait after the death of his brother, Sheik Abdullah al-Salem al-Sabah (1961). He rules until his death in 1977.

Ferdinand Marcos is elected president of the Philippines. He rules until 1986, when he is driven into exile.

Singapore withdraws from the Federation of Malaysia and becomes an independent republic.

Suleyman Demirel becomes prime minister of Turkey.

1960

through

1969

1960 through 1969

1965-1966

In Indonesia, hundreds of thousands of people are massacred on orders of General Suharto as an attempted communist coup is brutally suppressed.

1966

The Cultural Revolution begins in China (PRC) under Mao Zedong, and the Red Guard begins to purge the country of revisionists.

In an effort to appease Sikhs demanding a separate state, authorities in India redraw the boundaries of the Punjab to give that state a Sikh majority.

NATO officially moves its headquarters from France to Belgium. French troops are withdrawn from NATO in protest over the large build-up of United States forces in Europe.

The kingdom of Lesotho (formerly Basutoland) gains its independence within the Commonwealth. Chief Leabua Jonathan becomes the new nation's first prime minister. He serves until 1986.

Uganda adopts a new constitution.

An earthquake in eastern Turkey results in more than 2,500 deaths.

Indira Gandhi, daughter of Jawaharlal Nehru (1947), becomes prime minister of India after the term of Shri Lal Bahadur Shastri (1964). She serves until 1977 and again from 1980 until her assassination in 1984.

Hastings Kamuzu Banda becomes president-for-life in Malawi.

Balthazar Johannes Vorster becomes prime minister of South Africa after the assassination of Hendrik Frensch Verwoerd (1958). Vorster serves as prime minister until 1978, and as president from 1978 until 1980.

Bechuanaland gains independence within the British Commonwealth, adopts a new constitution, and changes its name to Botswana. Sir Seretse Khama is elected the new nation's first president.

A military coup led by Colonel Sangoulé Lamizana takes place in Upper Volta. The constitution is suspended, political activities are banned and a military council is formed to govern the country.

Burundi's government is overthrown twice this year. Captain Michel Micombero comes to power, and declares Burundi a republic.

Ghana's President Kwame Nkrumah (1960) is deposed; General Joseph Ankrah rules the country.

The government of South Africa, which has administered South West Africa (Namibia) since 1920 under a League of Nations/United Nations mandate, extends its *apartheid* policies to the mandate region. The South West African People's Organization (SWAPO) announces and initiates an armed rebellion for Namibian independence.

Uganda's King Mutesa II (1963) is deposed, and Milton Obote again governs the country, this time as executive president. He holds this office until 1971.

Two coups occur in rapid succession in Nigeria. Much of the unrest is blamed on the northern Ibo tribe, and many Ibo members are indiscriminately slaughtered in retaliation.

Harold Holt becomes prime minister of Australia after the term of Sir Robert Gordon Menzies (1949). Holt serves until 1967.

Cavdet Sunay becomes president of Turkey following the resignation of Cemal Gürsel (1961). Sunay serves until 1973.

A military coup led by General Suharto, who prevented a communist takeover the year before, takes control of Indonesia from President Sukarno (1949). Suharto becomes acting president in 1967 and is formally elected in 1968.

Kurt George Kiesinger becomes chancellor of West Germany after the term of Ludwig Erhard (1963). Kiesinger serves until 1969.

1967

As a result of the Arab-Israeli Six-Day War, Israeli forces occupy the Sinai Peninsula, the Golan Heights, the Gaza Strip and the East Bank of the Suez Canal. Following the war, Israel annexes East Jerusalem. This more than quadruples the size of Israel. The victory is so swift, and Israeli presence in the occupied territories so uncompromising, that no peace treaty is signed.

By a unanimous vote, the United Nations General Assembly adopts a declaration calling for "equal rights for women in employment, politics and cultural life."

A popular referendum in Australia grants full citizenship to aboriginal peoples.

NATO withdraws all its troops from France.

Nicolae Ceaușescu becomes chairman of the Romanian Communist Party (RCP) state council.

China (PRC) explodes its first hydrogen bomb.

Indonesia, Malaysia, the Philippines, Thailand and Singapore form the Association of Southeast Asian Nations (ASEAN), in Bangkok, Thailand, to combine their efforts toward social and economic progress.

Russian cosmonaut Vladimir M. Komarov is the first known human fatality in space. He dies aboard *Soyuz 1* when a parachute malfunctions during reentry.

As British troops withdraw from Aden and the Federation of South Arabia, the two regions join and become the new nation of South Yemen. Qahtan al-Shaabi becomes the country's first president.

General Suharto, who took control of Indonesia in a coup in 1966, becomes acting president. He is elected president in 1968.

A military revolt in Greece, led by Colonel George Papadopoulos, sends King Constantine II (1964) into exile. Papadopoulos becomes premier. He rules until 1973.

The Democratic Republic of the Congo (Zaïre) adopts a new constitution.

Siaka Stevens becomes prime minister of Sierra Leone after the term of Albert Margai (1964). Although removed from office by a military coup, Stevens returns to power in 1968. He becomes president in 1971, and serves until 1985.

Albert-Bernard Bongo becomes president of Gabon after the death of Léon M'ba. Bongo was hand-picked for the presidency by M'Ba.

Lieutenant General Etienne Gnassingbé Eyadéma becomes president of Togo after Nicholas Grunitzky (1963) is deposed in a bloodless coup. Eyadéma serves until 1971.

John McEwen becomes prime minister of Australia. He serves until 1968.

Dr. Christian N. Barnard and a team of surgeons perform the world's first successful human heart transplant in Cape Town, South Africa. The patient survives for 18 days.

1967-1970

Disputes over oil revenues incite the Ibo people of Nigeria to begin a military bid for independence. The region of Biafra secedes under C. O. Ojukwu and a three-year civil war begins. The revolt fails.

1968

North Korean forces seize the United States Navy intelligence ship *Pueblo* and hold the 83 people on board as spies.

Representatives from the United States, the Soviet Union and more than 50 nations that do not have nuclear weapons sign a treaty agreeing to stop the creation of such weapons.

Most of the 70,000 Jews in Poland who survived the Nazi occupation are driven to leave the country by the intensified anti-Semitic activities of Communist party leader Wladislaw Gomulka.

The "Prague Spring"—a liberalization movement led by Czechoslovakia's first secretary of the Communist party, Alexander Dubček—is halted by an invasion of Soviet Union forces.

Swaziland gains its independence from Britain and becomes a constitutional monarchy under King Sobhuza II.

Members of the Arab Baath Socialist Party overthrow the government of Iraq.

Mauritius gains its independence within the British Commonwealth.

In response to a popular referendum, the sultanate of the Maldives is dissolved and the nation becomes a republic.

An earthquake in north-eastern Iran results in 12,000 deaths.

The Federation of Arab Emirates is formed by the union of Bahrain, Qatar and the Trucial States.

Bhutan's cabinet is formed by decree of King Jigme Dorji Wangchuk.

French troops are sent to intervene in Chad's political upheaval and assist in putting down a revolt.

By order of the United Nations, South West Africa's name is changed to Namibia.

A military coup led by Captain Marien Ngouabi ousts the Congo's President Alphonse Massamba-Débat. Ngouabi rules the country until his assassination in 1977.

Equatorial Guinea gains its independence from Spain, with Francisco Macias Nguema as the new country's first president. Nguema soon assumes absolute power as a dictator. He rules until he is overthrown in 1979.

Nauru gains its independence and is made a "special member" of the British Commonwealth. Hammer DeRoburt is elected president. Sobhuza II is king.

(Sir) John G. Gorton becomes prime minister of Australia. He serves until 1971.

Marcello Caetano becomes premier of Portugal after Antonio de Oliveira (1932) suffers a debilitating stroke. Caetano serves until 1974.

1969

Occasional anti-Soviet demonstrations continue in Czechoslovakia. Jan Palach, a student, dies after setting himself on fire. Alexander Dubĉek is replaced by Gustav Husak and harsh, Soviet-style rule is reestablished.

In Northern Ireland, Terence O'Neil and the Union party suffer election setbacks. Rioting continues between Protestants and Catholics. The Irish Republican Army divides into "official" and "provisional" factions. British troops are sent to Belfast and Londonderry.

Territorial conflict causes several armed clashes between Soviet and Chinese forces along the Ussuri River.

The supersonic airliner *Concorde* makes its maiden flight.

Strategic Arms Limitation Treaty (SALT) talks begin between the Soviet Union and the United States.

A military takeover occurs in Somalia, led by Major General Mohammad Siyad Barre. The country's constitution is suspended and a ruling military council is established. The Somali Democratic Republic is proclaimed.

A military coup takes place in Sudan under Colonel Gaafar Mohammed Nimeri. Sudan's name is changed to the Democratic Republic of Sudan. Nimeri rules until 1985.

Agha Muhammad Yahya Khan becomes president of Pakistan after the resignation of Muhammad Ayub Khan (1958). Yahya Khan serves until 1971.

Yasser (Yasir) Arafat, leader of the Al Fatah guerrilla organization, becomes the head of the Palestine Liberation Organization (PLO).

General Akwasi Afrifa replaces Joseph Ankrah as ruler of Ghana. Afrifa begins to return the country to civilian rule. He serves until 1970.

Moamer al Khaddhafi (Qaddafi, Gaddafi) leads a coup in Libya that overthrows King Idris I (1951).

Georges Pompidou becomes president of France following the term of Charles De Gaulle (1959). Pompidou serves until 1974.

Golda Meir becomes prime minister of Israel following the term of Levi Eshkol (1963). Meir serves until 1974.

Willy Brandt becomes chancellor of West Germany after the term of Kurt George Kiesinger (1966). Brandt serves until 1974.

Olof Palme becomes prime minister of Sweden. He serves until his assassination in 1986.

1960 through 1969

341

NATIVE AMERICAN	NATIVE AMERICAN	AFRICAN AMERICAN	AFRICAN AMERICAN

1970

The American Indian population in the United States nears 830,000.

President Richard M. Nixon calls for a new era of American Indian self-determination. Nixon also promises the return of the Blue Lake region of New Mexico to the Taos tribe. This promise becomes reality later this year when 48,000 acres of the Blue Lake area are returned.

American Indians occupy the Littleton, Colorado, office of the Bureau of Indian Affairs (BIA) to protest the bureau's discriminatory hiring practices. Similar protests take place at several other regional offices in western states.

1971

As compensation for lost lands, Alaska's Inuit, Indians and Aleuts receive 40 million acres and a payment of $962,500,000.

1972

By executive order of President Nixon, 21,000 acres on the Mount Rainier Forest Reserve, Washington, are restored to the Yakima tribe.

In a march called the Trail of Broken Treaties, members of the American Indian Movement (AIM) and their supporters demonstrate for their rights in Washington, D.C., and occupy the BIA offices. The demonstration and occupation gain publicity for Indian militants, but the federal government is unyielding to the Indians' demand for the right to renegotiate treaties.

1973

Approximately 14,000 American Indians are studying in off-reservation institutions of higher learning, almost triple the figure from 10 years ago. A small but growing number of Native Americans are taking employment off-reservation.

Armed members of AIM and Oglala Sioux occupy the village of Wounded Knee on the Pine Ridge Reservation, South Dakota. After a siege of more than two months, the government agrees to study its treaty obligations to the Sioux, and the Indians withdraw from Wounded Knee. Russell Means (Sioux), Clyde Bellecourt and Dennis Banks (both Chippewa) gain international recognition as AIM leaders.

Morris Thompson, an Athabascan from Alaska, is appointed as Commissioner of the BIA. His first official act is to name Shirley Plume, an Oglala Sioux, as the Bureau's first woman superintendent. She heads the Standing Rock office in North Dakota.

1974

In a landmark reversal of termination policy, BIA Commissioner Thompson announces that all federal services and trust relationship with the Menominee tribe of Wisconsin are restored. The Menominee lost their status during the government's termination campaign of the 1950s and 1960s.

Judge George H. Boldt reaffirms Native American fishing rights in Washington state. The suit in *United States* v. *State of Washington* resolves the controversy and asserts the western Washington tribes' fishing rights based on treaties.

1975

Congress passes the Indian Self-Determination and Education Assistance Act, which gives tribal leaders the authority to plan and carry out their own programs, under oversight of the federal government. Congress also recognizes native Hawaiians as a Native American group.

1970

The United States census reports more than 22.5 million African Americans, 11 percent of the total United States population.

Ronald V. Dellums of California, Ralph H. Metcalfe of Illinois, Parren H. Mitchell of Maryland, Charles B. Rangel of New York and Walter E. Fauntroy, a delegate from Washington, D.C., all Democrats, are elected to the United States House of Representatives.

Jerome H. Holland is appointed ambassador to Sweden. He serves until 1972. Clarence C. Ferguson Jr., is appointed ambassador to Uganda. He serves until 1972.

Joseph L. Searles becomes the first African American member of the New York Stock Exchange.

1971

The Congressional Black Caucus is organized.

The Supreme Court overturns the draft evasion conviction of boxer Muhammad Ali.

Operation PUSH (People United to Save Humanity) is organized in Chicago by the Reverend Jesse Jackson.

The United States Supreme Court upholds busing as a means of achieving racial balance in those schools where no other alternative exists. The busing issue remains a major controversy for years.

Samuel L. Gravely attains the rank of admiral in the United States Navy.

Charles J. Nelson is appointed ambassador to Botswana, Lesotho and Swaziland. He serves until 1974. John E. Reinhardt, a foreign service officer, is appointed ambassador to Nigeria. He serves until 1975.

1972

The National Black Political Convention is held in Gary, Indiana.

Andrew Young from Georgia and Barbara Jordan from Texas become the first African Americans elected to the House of Representatives from the South since the turn of the century. Both are Democrats. Jordan is the first African American woman from the South ever elected to the House. Yvonne B. Burke of California and Cardiss Collins of Illinois, both Democrats, are also elected to the United States House of Representatives.

African American Congresswoman Shirley Chisholm unsuccessfully seeks the Democratic nomination for president. She campaigns throughout the country and is on the ballot in 12 states. She is the first African American and the second woman to seek the presidential nomination.

W. Beverly Carter, a foreign service officer, is appointed ambassador to Tanzania. Carter serves until 1975. Terence A. Todman, a foreign service officer, is appointed ambassador to Guinea. He serves until 1975, at which time he is appointed ambassador to Costa Rica.

1973

Thomas Bradley is elected mayor of Los Angeles; Maynard Jackson is elected mayor of Atlanta.

O. Rudolf Aggrey, a foreign service officer, is appointed ambassador to Senegal and Gambia.

1974

Coleman A. Young becomes the first African American mayor of the city of Detroit, Michigan.

Frank Robinson is named manager of the Cleveland Indians, and becomes the first African American major league baseball manager.

David B. Bolen, a foreign service officer, is appointed ambassador to Botswana, Lesotho and Swaziland. He serves until 1976. Theodore Britten, Jr., is appointed ambassador to Barbados and Grenada.

1970

through

1976

AFRICAN AMERICAN	ASIAN AMERICAN	ASIAN AMERICAN	FOR CLASSROOM USE	

AFRICAN AMERICAN

1974-1975

Several incidents of racial violence occur in Boston as European Americans and African Americans clash over the issue of busing to achieve racial balance in schools.

1975

William T. Coleman is named Secretary of Transportation. Joseph Hatchett of Florida becomes the first African American state supreme court justice in the South since Reconstruction.

Harold E. Ford, a Democrat, is elected to the United States House of Representatives from Tennessee.

1976

In a landmark civil rights decision, the Supreme Court rules that African Americans who have been denied jobs in violation of the Civil Rights Act of 1964 must be awarded retroactive seniority. The decision also extends to sex, ethnic and religious discrimination.

Andrew Young is named ambassador and chief United States delegate to the United Nations.

W. Beverly Carter is appointed ambassador to Liberia. Ronald DeWayne Palmer, a foreign service officer, is appointed ambassador to Togo. Charles A. James, a foreign service officer, is appointed ambassador to Niger.

ASIAN AMERICAN

1970

More than 31,200 Filipinos immigrate to the United States this year, a greater number than any other nationality outside of the Western Hemisphere.

The Japanese American Citizens League (JACL) national convention held in Chicago passes the first of many resolutions to seek redress for World War II internment.

Japanese American employees of the state of California receive retirement credit for their time spent in detention camps. Eventually, credits are allowed for federal employees and for those eligible for Social Security benefits.

1972

Philippine President Ferdinand Marcos declares martial law and suspends the constitution and democratic freedoms. The number of skilled immigrants arriving in the United States from the Philippines is 8,500 — 30 times as many as in 1965.

Statistics indicate that almost 50 percent of the married Japanese Americans living in Los Angeles have non-Japanese spouses.

1973

More than 20,000 Koreans enter the United States. This wave of migration makes them one of the fastest growing ethnic groups in the country.

The former detention camp at Manzanar is designated a California state historical landmark. In subsequent years, many other former detention camp sites are given similar designations.

1974

Norman Y. Mineta, a Democrat from California, becomes the first mainland Japanese American elected to Congress.

George Ariyoshi is the first non-European American to be elected governor of Hawaii.

ASIAN AMERICAN

1975

More than 130,000 Vietnamese (including ethnic Chinese), 70,000 Laotian, 10,000 Mien and 60,000 Hmong people seek refuge in the United States as a direct result of the Vietnam War.

The Indochina Migration and Refugee Assistance Act is passed by Congress. Refugee centers for Indochinese people open at Fort Chaffee, Arkansas; Eglin Air Force Base, Florida; and Fort Indian Town Gap, Pennsylvania. All are closed by the end of the year.

Executive Order 9066, Inc. in Los Angeles and the Seattle JACL Redress Committee become the first groups to activate a redress campaign for Japanese Americans interned in camps during World War II.

1976

President Gerald R. Ford rescinds Executive Order 9066, the original internment order signed by President Franklin D. Roosevelt in 1942.

S. I. Hayakawa, a Republican from California, is elected to the United States Senate. He is a Japanese American.

1970

through

1976

1970 through 1976

EUROPEAN AMERICAN

1970

Only 770 Swedes, 540 Norwegians and 600 Danes immigrate to the United States this year.

Radio station WGCY in New Bedford, Massachusetts, becomes a full-time Portuguese-language station.

1972

Sally J. Priesand is ordained as a rabbi in Cincinnati. She is the first woman rabbi in the United States, and the second ever in Jewish history.

1973

To commemorate Spain's part in the history of Louisiana, the Spanish government establishes a fund of $587,000 toward the completion of a Spanish-style plaza in New Orleans.

1974

Abraham D. Beams becomes the first Jewish American governor of New York City.

The Rhode Island Department of Motor Vehicles issues the country's first Portuguese-language drivers' manual.

1975

Soviet author Alexander Solzhenitzin, a Nobel Prize winner in Literature, tours the United States extensively. His works are subsequently translated into and published in English, from *One Day in the Life of Ivan Denisovich* to *Gulag Archipelago.* In 1976 Solzhenitzin immigrates to the United States.

HISPANIC AMERICAN

1970

The United States census reports that approximately 1.5 million Puerto Rican people live in the mainland United States. The island's population is roughly twice this figure. Forty-eight percent of the mainland Puerto Ricans are under 20 years of age.

A Puerto Rican revolutionary pro-independence group, MIRA, admits it has performed 19 terrorist attacks since December 1969, seven of which were in New York City. It says the attacks will continue.

Hermán Badillo of New York City becomes the first Puerto Rican American elected to the United States House of Representatives.

Conflict deepens over the United States naval presence on the Puerto Rican islands of Culebra and Vieques.

The Mexican American independent political party, La Raza Unida, is formally established by José Angel Gutierrez and others.

The Reverend Patric Flores becomes the first Mexican American to be named a Roman Catholic bishop.

In California, Coachella and San Joaquin Valley growers sign contracts with the United Farm Workers Organizing Committee (UFWOC). By year's end, most of the table grape industry has signed contracts with the union. Leader Cesar Chavez then begins organizing lettuce workers.

c. 1970

The Puerto Rican Student Union in New York, influenced by the Young Lords party, plays an important role in open college admissions and the establishment of Puerto Rican studies programs in universities.

1970-1972

La Raza Unida party (LRUP) chapters are established throughout the Southwest. The party offers complete or partial slates of Mexican American candidates in Colorado, Texas, California, Arizona and New Mexico elections.

HISPANIC AMERICAN

1971

The Pro-Independence Movement party reorganizes into the Puerto Rican Socialist party and identifies itself with the Cuban government.

The United Farm Workers Organizing Committee signs a pact with the Teamsters giving the Teamsters jurisdiction over food-processing workers, and the United Farm Workers jurisdiction over field workers.

President Nixon names Ramona A. Bañuelos as the first Mexican American treasurer of the United States.

1972

The Popular Democratic party wins the elections in Puerto Rico. Rafael Hernández Colón becomes governor and begins a bipartisan system.

The United Nations Committee on Decolonization approves a resolution supporting self-determination and independence for Puerto Rico.

The Puerto Rican Legal Defense Fund (PRLDEF) is founded by a group of Puerto Rican lawyers in New York to challenge systemic discrimination. It files a class action suit against the New York City Board of Education, which results in the 1974 Aspira Consent Decree.

Approximately 4,000 Mexican American workers, most of them women, call a strike at three Farah slacks factories in Texas, seeking the right to unionize.

1973

Bishop Luis Aponte Martínez of San Juan, Puerto Rico, is elevated to the College of Cardinals by Pope Paul VI.

Centro d'Estudios Puertorriquenos (The Center for Puerto Rican Studies) is established as part of the City University of New York. Its library becomes the center in the United States for works on Puerto Rico and its people.

The United Farm Workers Organizing Committee officially changes its name to the United Farm Workers of America (UFW) and becomes fully accredited by the AFL-CIO.

HISPANIC AMERICAN

Lieutenant Colonel Mercedes Cubría retires after a lengthy career in the United States Army. She is the first Cuban-born woman to reach her rank, and the first to be inducted into the United States Army Intelligence Hall of Fame.

Jaime Benítez is elected resident commissioner of Puerto Rico following the term of Jorge Luis Córdova (1969). Benitez serves until 1977.

1974

As part of the Aspira Consent Decree, the New York City Board of Education agrees to provide bilingual education for all Limited English Proficient (LEP) students in the city schools. This decision is the result of a class action suit filed in 1972 by the Puerto Rican Legal Defense Fund.

Boricua College, a private, four-year bilingual college, is established in New York City.

Raul Castro, elected governor of Arizona, is the first Mexican American to hold this office.

Roberto Sánchez becomes the first Mexican American archbishop in the United States when he is named to this position in Santa Fe, New Mexico.

1975

Puerto Rico's economy reels under the impact of the United States recession; unemployment exceeds 18 percent, inflation is triple the mainland level, and the commonwealth government, for the first time, borrows millions to balance its budget.

United States Navy maneuvers on Culebra, Puerto Rico, are suspended and the occupied area is returned to the island's government.

The National Association of Latin Elected and Appointed Officials (NALEO) is formed in Washington, D.C., to promote Hispanic American representation in all levels of government.

1976

Carlos Romero Barceló of Puerto Rico's New Progressive party wins the next two elections.

HISPANIC AMERICAN				
President Gerald Ford publicly endorses statehood for Puerto Rico. The Congressional Hispanic Caucus is formed in Washington, D.C., as a forum for Hispanic members of the House and Senate.		345		**1970** through **1976**

1970

through

1976

1970

The United States census reports the country's population at 204.9 million, including American citizens living abroad.

Congress holds its first hearings on the subject of illegal aliens in the United States. Congress also establishes the Environmental Protection Agency and the Senate repeals the 1964 Gulf of Tonkin resolution.

United States President Richard Nixon secretly informs Central Intelligence Agency (CIA) Director Richard M. Helms that the Allende regime of Chile is not acceptable, and instructs the CIA to play a direct role in an overthrow. This information does not become known until the 1975 release of a Senate Intelligence Committee Report.

Four students at Kent State University in Ohio are shot and killed by National Guardsmen at a demonstration protesting President Nixon's bombing of Cambodia.

The first known interracial marriage in Mississippi's history takes place.

In New York City, 50,000 women assemble and march in celebration of the 50th anniversary of women's suffrage.

Nearly 40 mine workers die in a coal mine explosion near Wooton, Kentucky.

Earth Day is celebrated throughout the United States to demonstrate concern for the environment.

Terrorist attacks by the Front de Libération du Québec (FLQ) include the kidnapping of British Trade Commissioner James R. Cross, and the kidnapping and murder of Quebec Labor Minister Pierre Laporte. Militia are called into Ottawa to guard government buildings. The Canadian government invokes the War Measures Act, a limited form of martial law, to defend against terrorism.

Luis Echeverría Alvarez becomes president of Mexico following the term of Gustavo Díaz Ordaz (1964). Alvarez serves until 1976.

A severe earthquake strikes Peru near Chimbote and causes a section of Mt. Huascaran to fall on the cities below. More than 100,000 are either killed or injured and more than 150,000 buildings are destroyed.

Salvador Allende Gossens is elected president of Chile, the first democratically elected Marxist in the Americas. He serves until 1973.

1970s

Increased leftist guerrilla activity in Guatemala, El Salvador and Nicaragua results in increasing militarization and abuse of human rights. Urban guerrillas in Uruguay and Argentina undermine civilian government and provoke harsh military response.

1971

The Twenty-sixth Amendment to the United States Constitution is ratified, giving citizens 18 years of age and older the right to vote.

In the face of runaway inflation, President Nixon requests a wage and price freeze for the nation and temporarily suspends the conversion of dollars into gold.

The United States Supreme Court rules unanimously that busing of students may be ordered by the lower courts to achieve racial desegregation.

In *Phillips* v. *Martin Marietta Corporation,* the United States Supreme Court declares that private employers cannot refuse to hire women with pre-school children.

In *Reed* v. *Reed,* the Supreme Court declares that an Idaho state law giving automatic preference to males as administrators of wills is unconstitutional. This is a landmark decision, as it is the first case where the High Court strikes down a law treating women and men differently.

Antiwar protesters attempt to disrupt federal government business in Washington, D.C. Police and military units arrest as many as 12,000, although most are later released.

The National Women's Political Caucus is formed to support women's equality in the political arena.

An earthquake in California's San Fernando Valley results in 65 deaths.

Postage for a first-class letter in the United States is eight cents.

A riot breaks out at Attica Prison in New York. After four days of inmate control, the prison is retaken by 1,500 police officers and prison guards. Thirty-one prisoners and nine hostages die in the fighting.

Canada and the United States agree on specific terms for controlling pollution in the Great Lakes.

Jean-Claude "Baby Doc" Duvalier becomes president-for-life of Haiti after the death of his father, Francois "Papa Doc" Duvalier (1957).

1971-1980

Immigration to the United States totals more than 4.49 million new arrivals, of which 800,400 come from Europe, 1.59 million from Asia, 80,800 from Africa, 41,200 from Oceania, 1.98 million from the Americas and 12 are not specifically identified.

1972

The United States Congress passes the Equal Rights Amendment and requests state ratification. The amendment provides that equality of rights shall not be denied or abridged on account of sex. The states fail to ratify the amendment in the allotted 10-year period.

The United States Supreme Court rules that the death penalty is unconstitutional.

In *Eisenstadt* v. *Baird,* the United States Supreme Court strikes down a state law forbidding the use of contraceptives by unmarried persons.

President Nixon makes an unprecedented eight-day visit to Chinese Communist leader Mao Tse-tung in Peking, China, to attempt to end the Cold War with that nation.

Nixon signs the Strategic Arms Limitation Treaty (SALT I) with Soviet Communist party Secretary Leonid I. Brezhnev.

Five men later linked to President Nixon's reelection campaign are apprehended by police while attempting to bug the Democratic National Committee headquarters in Washington, D.C.'s Watergate hotel and office complex. This action marks the beginning of the "Watergate" scandal.

After several hijackings or attempted hijackings, United States airline officials begin mandatory inspections of passengers and luggage.

Title IX of the Educational Amendments makes sex discrimination illegal in all public undergraduate educational institutions and in most other schools receiving federal monies.

Alabama Governor George C. Wallace, a segregationist, is shot by Arthur H. Bremer at a political rally during his presidential campaign in Laurel, Maryland.

More than 90 miners die in a mine fire in Idaho.

Hurricane Agnes causes severe damage to the eastern United States. In Pennsylvania, the storm is responsible for the deaths of more than 50 people.

Floods in Rapid City, South Dakota, claim more than 200 lives. Mississippi is also hit with severe flooding that causes extensive damage to two-thirds of the state.

Canada officially condemns United States air raids on the North Vietnamese cities of Haiphong and Hanoi.

In Montreal, Dr. Henry Morgentaler is found innocent of performing an illegal abortion. His acquittal is overturned by the Quebec Appeal Court, and the second decision is upheld by Canada's Supreme Court. Morgentaler is sentenced to 18 months in jail, but a retrial is ordered after 10 months. Morgentaler is again acquitted, and the Quebec government drops charges.

Trinidad and Tobago gain their independence from Britain.

THE AMERICAS	THE AMERICAS	THE AMERICAS	FOR CLASSROOM USE	

An earthquake in Managua, Nicaragua, kills approximately 10,000 people.

1973

Richard M. Nixon begins his second term as president of the United States; Spiro T. Agnew is vice president. Both are Republicans. Agnew resigns as vice president and then, in a federal court in Baltimore, Maryland, pleads no contest to charges of income tax evasion on $29,500 he received as governor of Maryland in 1967. He is fined $10,000 and put on three years' probation. Under the provisions of the Twenty-fifth Amendment, Gerald R. Ford, the House minority leader, is selected and nominated by President Nixon to serve as vice president and is confirmed by Congress.

Congress passes the War Powers Act over the veto of President Nixon. This gives Congress, rather than the president, the authority to wage war.

United States troops are temporarily withdrawn from Vietnam.

President Nixon, on national television, accepts full responsibility — but not the blame — for the Watergate incident. Nixon accepts the resignations of advisers H. R. Haldeman and John D. Ehrlichman and fires John W. Dean, III, as counsel. Then, in the "Saturday Night Massacre," Nixon fires special Watergate Prosecutor Archibald Cox and accepts the resignation of Deputy Attorney General William D. Ruckelshaus. Following this, Attorney General Elliot L. Richardson resigns. Nixon then names Leon Jaworski as special prosecutor for "Watergate" and releases some audiotapes of the president's White House conversations, but gaps exist in the tapes.

The United States faces an oil embargo as the Arab oil producing countries, under the umbrella of the Organization of Petroleum Exporting Countries (OPEC), fail to provide all the oil that America needs. When the embargo ends in 1974, domestic oil prices have more than tripled, and inflation has risen approximately 11 percent. This prompts the United States government to look for alternative sources of fuel and to consider measures for full conservation of energy. Consumers switch to smaller, more fuel-efficient cars. Because the United States automobile industry is unprepared, new car buyers turn to imported cars from Japan and Europe.

The United States Supreme Court, in *Roe v. Wade*, removes state restrictions on a woman's right to have an abortion in the first three months of an unwanted pregnancy.

In its *Pittsburgh Press* decision, the Supreme Court rules that sex-specific help-wanted advertising violates equal employment opportunities provision of the 1964 Civil Rights Act.

In *Frontiero v. Richardson,* the Supreme Court strikes down the military regulations that deny women dependent benefits equal to those of men.

X-ray scanning devices are first mandated to check luggage contents at United States airports.

The Equal Rights Amendment is passed by both houses of the United States Congress. It is sent to the state legislatures for ratification.

Under pressure from lesbian and gay activists, the American Psychiatric Association removes homosexuality from its list of mental disorders.

The United States and Cuba sign an anti-hijacking pact.

As the Cuban Refugee Airlift program is terminated, immigration to the United States again becomes clandestine, or is carried on through a third country, such as Spain or Mexico.

The Bahamas become independent after three centuries of British colonial rule.

Juan Domingo Perón returns to Argentina and is again elected president. He serves until his death in 1974.

British Honduras is officially renamed Belize, and is granted limited autonomy in preparation for eventual full independence.

General Augusto Ugarte Pinochet becomes president of Chile after his military coup removes Salvadore Allende Gossens (1970) from office. Pinochet serves until 1990.

1974

The House Judiciary Committee adopts three articles of impeachment charging President Nixon with obstruction of justice, failure to uphold the laws and refusal to produce material (tapes of conversations in the White House) subpoenaed by the committee. The tapes are delivered to Congress and they show that Nixon did know about the break-in and had information about the cover-up.

Gerald R. Ford becomes the 38th president of the United States after the resignation of President Nixon; Nelson A. Rockefeller is nominated by President Ford and confirmed by Congress as the vice president. President Ford grants "full, free, and absolute pardon" to ex-president Nixon and limited amnesty to Vietnam War draft-dodgers and military deserters.

Congress approves $405 million to aid Southeast Asian refugees and the Indochinese Refugee Resettlement Program begins. More than 200,000 refugees enter the United States under parole authorization. About 90 percent are Vietnamese, and the rest are split equally between Laotians and Cambodians. Most of them find only low-paying, low-skilled jobs. Prior to this wave of refugees, there were few Indochinese immigrants to the United States. The total number of Vietnamese immigrants for the decade of 1966-1975 is just over 20,000. Vietnam War refugees are exempted from United States immigration quotas. Provisions are made to adjust them to permanent resident status.

1970 through 1976

1970

through

1976

Congress passes the Economic Credit Opportunity Act, which outlaws credit discrimination based on sex.

In *Lau* v. *Nichols,* the United States Supreme Court rules that children who do not speak English have a legal right to bilingual education as an "equal educational opportunity."

In *Cleveland Board of Education* v. *LaFleur,* the United States Supreme Court rules that mandatory unpaid maternity leave violates "due process" of pregnant women. In *Geduldig* v. *Aiello,* the High Court upholds California's denial of health insurance benefits for pregnancy-related disabilities.

A federal law is passed allowing women to enter United States military academies.

The United States space probe *Mariner 10* sends the first television pictures of Venus and Mercury to earth.

Ella Grasso is the first woman ever elected to serve as Connecticut's governor.

In September, postage for a first-class letter in the United States is 10 cents. By year's end it is increased to 13 cents.

Canada's National Assembly adopts French as the official language of Quebec province.

María Estela Martinez de Perón becomes president of Argentina after the death of her husband, Juan Perón (1946, 1973). She serves until 1976.

Grenada becomes an independent member of the British Commonwealth.

Eric M. Gairy becomes the first prime minister of Grenada.

Anastasio Somoza Debayle (1967) becomes president of Nicaragua.

1975

President Ford escapes two unrelated assassination attempts within a two-week period.

John N. Mitchell, H. R. Haldeman, John D. Ehrlichman and Robert C. Mardian are found guilty of participating in the cover-up of the Watergate scandal and receive jail sentences.

The United States satellite *Apollo 18*, with astronauts Thomas P. Stafford, Donald K. (Deke) Slayton and Vance D. Brand, meets in space with the Russian satellite *Soyuz 19*, manned by cosmonauts Aleksei Leonov and Valery N. Kubasov, to undertake joint experiments as part of the Apollo-Soyuz Test Project (ASTP).

The Organization of American States (OAS) allows its members to lift economic and diplomatic sanctions against Cuba.

General Francisco Morales Bermúdez becomes president of Peru after his military coup removes Juan Velasco Alvardo (1968) from office.

Surinam (Dutch Guiana), South America, gains its independence from the Netherlands.

1976

The United States Supreme Court rules that African Americans and other minorities are entitled to retroactive job seniority. It also rules that the death penalty is not inherently cruel or unusual and is a constitutionally acceptable form of punishment.

In *Planned Parenthood* v. *Danforth,* the United States Supreme Court rules that states cannot legislate a husband's authority to deny his wife an abortion; nor can parents of minor, unwed girls hold absolute authority over their daughters' abortion decisions.

The United States celebrates its bicentennial, the 200th anniversary of the signing of the Declaration of Independence, which occurred on July 4, 1776.

The United States Congress passes the Federal Election Campaign Act.

An arms purchase agreement is announced through which Iran will purchase $10 billion worth of weapons from the United States.

The Immigration and Nationality Act extends the per-country limitations of 20,000 immigrants to the United States and the preference system to the Western Hemisphere. The act retains two last vestiges of differential geographic treatment — the separate annual ceilings for the Eastern and Western Hemispheres.

Idaho's Teton Dam collapses, killing 11 people and forcing 300,000 to evacuate their homes.

The United States Census Bureau, in efforts to determine ethnicity, finds that the largest percentage of Americans, 14.4 percent, claim English ancestry, followed by German and Irish. However, the Census Bureau reveals that 8.5 percent of Americans do not know their ethnic origin.

Hurricane Belle hits the East Coast of the United States.

Inuit (Eskimos) file a claim asserting their right to more than 750,000 square miles of Canadian territory.

José Lopez Portillo becomes president of Mexico after the term of Luis Echeverriá Alvarez (1970).

An earthquake in Guatemala leaves more than 23,000 dead.

Lieutenant General Jorge Videla becomes president of Argentina after his military coup removes María Perón (1974) from office.

A coup in Ecuador brings a military junta to power.

Argentina's military begins its "Dirty War" with a coup against the government of Isabel Perón; the congress is dissolved, and massive detainment of civilians occurs. More than 9,000 people eventually lose their lives to government terror. Lieutenant General Jorge Videla becomes president of Argentina.

FOR CLASSROOM USE	FOR CLASSROOM USE	FOR CLASSROOM USE	FOR CLASSROOM USE	
				1970 through **1976**
FOR CLASSROOM USE	FOR CLASSROOM USE	FOR CLASSROOM USE	FOR CLASSROOM USE	

THE WORLD	THE WORLD	THE WORLD	THE WORLD

1970

Biafra surrenders after a 32-month fight for independence from Nigeria. It is estimated that more than 1 million civilians die from hunger during the war.

Polish officers open fire on striking workers at the Lenin Shipyards in Gdansk, Poland. The government officially claims that 30 people are killed, but other reports give a much higher figure.

Rhodesia severs its last tie with the British crown and declares itself a racially segregated republic.

The Khaddhafi regime in Libya confiscates all Jewish property without compensation.

Gambia becomes an independent member of the British Commonwealth.

General Joseph-Désiré Mobutu is elected president of the Democratic Republic of the Congo. Mobutu has been military ruler of the country since 1965.

By the Moscow Treaty, West Germany and the Soviet Union agree to renounce the use of force to solve disputes and recognize the sovereignty of existing European borders.

Civilian government is restored in Ghana. Edward Akufo-Addo becomes president. He serves until 1972.

Czechoslovakia's liberal reformers lose power and Alexander Dubĉek (1968) is expelled from the Communist party.

A cyclone and the resulting flooding in East Pakistan kill more than 400,000 people.

An earthquake in western Turkey results in more than 1,000 deaths.

Cambodia becomes the Khmer Republic.

Palestinian guerrillas hijack three airliners to Jordan, a country in the midst of civil war.

Egypt completes the Aswan High (Nile) Dam, located south of the smaller Aswan Dam, built in 1902.

A referendum in Upper Volta supports a new constitution, which initiates the return from military to civilian rule.

The Congo is declared a Marxist government, the People's Republic of the Congo.

Fiji achieves independence within the British Commonwealth; Ratu Sir Kamisese Mara serves as prime minister.

Qaboos bin Said becomes sultan of Muscat and Oman after his father, Said bin Taimur, is overthrown. The country's name is changed to the Sultanate of Oman.

After the Gdansk protest and riots claim the lives of 300 demonstrators, Poland's Wladyslaw Gomulka (1956) is replaced by Edward Gierek as leader of the Polish United Workers' [Communist] Party (PUWP). Gierek leads the party until 1980.

Anwar Sadat becomes president of Egypt after the sudden death of Gamal Abdul Nasser (1954). Sadat serves until his assassination in 1981.

Lon Nol becomes premier of Cambodia after he leads a military coup that deposes Norodom Sihanouk (1960) as head of state. Lon Nol rules until 1975.

Edward Heath, a Conservative, becomes prime minister of Great Britain after the term of Harold Wilson (1964). He serves until 1974.

Hafez al-Assad becomes president of Syria after a military coup ousts the civilian government.

Tun Abdul Razak bin Haji Hussein becomes prime minister of Malaysia after the resignation of Tunku Abdul Rahman. (1963).

Women fight along side men in the Angola, Mozambique and Guinea-Bissau wars of independence from Portugal.

1971

The United Nations seats the People's Republic of China (PRC) and expels Taiwan.

China enters the "space race" with the launching of its first satellite.

East Pakistan's declaration of the independent nation of Bangladesh sparks Pakistani civil war. With military assistance from India, Bangladesh gains its independence, and Sheik Mujibur Rahman is the new nation's first leader. He serves until 1975.

Syria, Libya and Egypt form the Federation of Arab Republics.

In Northern Ireland, the British policy of internment without trial leads to major disturbances, especially in Belfast.

Sweden's constitution is amended to place greater power in the *Riksdag* (the country's legislature).

Women in Switzerland receive the right to vote in national elections.

Turkish military leaders force the resignation of Prime Minister Suleyman Demirel.

Ugandan President Milton Obote (1966) is overthrown in a military takeover led by Idi Amin. Almost 49,000 Asian Ugandans are expelled. More than 300,000 of Amin's opponents are murdered.

Six Trucial States of Abu Dhabi, Dubai, Fujairah, Ajman, Sharja and Umm Al Qaiwain join to form the United Arab Emirates, with Sheik Zayed, *emir* (Muslim prince or commander) of Abu Dhabi, as the new nation's president.

The Democratic Republic of the Congo officially changes its name to Zaïre and makes the Popular Movement of the Revolution (MPR) the only legal political organization.

Conflict between Hindus and Muslims erupts into open warfare along the Indo-Pakistani border.

Bahrain gains its independence from Britain. The constitution adopted in 1973 grants women the right to vote.

Sierra Leone gains its independence from Britain. Siaka Stevens (1967) becomes the country's first president. He serves until 1985.

Zulfikar Ali Bhutto becomes president of Pakistan after Agha Muhammad Yahya (1969). Bhutto becomes prime minister in 1973.

(Sir) William McMahon becomes prime minister of Australia after the term of Sir John G. Gorton (1968). McMahon serves until 1972.

Todor Zhivkov becomes president of Bulgaria. He serves until 1989.

Erich Honecker becomes first secretary of the East German Communist party. He is named head of state in 1976, and rules until 1989.

1972

On "Bloody Sunday" in Londonderry, Northern Ireland, 13 demonstrators are killed by British troops. The resulting turmoil, which includes a national general strike and the destruction of the British Embassy in Dublin force Great Britain to take over direct rule of Northern Ireland in a bid for peace.

Eleven Israeli athletes at the Olympic Games in Munich are killed after eight members of an Arab terrorist group invade Olympic Village; five of the terrorists and one policeman are also killed.

The Ryukyu Islands, including Okinawa, are restored to Japan, ending America's 27-year occupation.

The use of germ warfare is banned by an international convention.

German-speaking Belgians are allowed to hold cabinet posts in their homeland for the first time.

Jigme Singye Wangchuk becomes king of Bhutan after the death of his father, Jigme Dorji Wangchuk (1952).

North Korea adopts a new constitution that establishes the office of president. North and South Korea begin discussion of possible reunification.

A strategic arms limitation treaty (SALT I) reached by the Soviet Union and the United States begins a warming of relations between the two countries.

THE WORLD	THE WORLD	THE WORLD	FOR CLASSROOM USE	

Sheik Khalifa becomes ruler of Qatar after a bloodless coup deposes his cousin, Emir Sheik Ahmad.

Thai military personnel withdraw from South Vietnam.

The sheikdom of Ras Al-Khaimah joins the United Arab Emirates.

Britain, Ireland and Denmark join the European Common Market.

For the first time since World War II, West Berliners are allowed to enter East Berlin.

Idi Amin expels all Asians and European missionaries from Uganda.

General Mathieu Kerekou comes to power in Dahomey (Benin) and establishes military rule, promising equal representation and a gradual return to civilian government. He leads the country until 1987.

An estimated 150,000 Hutu people are massacred by Tutsis in Burundi, after Hutus are suspected of the assassination of King Ntare V. Renewed intertribal fighting also occurs in Rwanda.

A military takeover in Ghana brings Colonel Acheampong to power.

Ceylon becomes a republic and changes its name to the Socialist Republic of Sri Lanka.

United States President Richard M. Nixon visits China; this action begins to reduce tensions between the two powers.

Austrian diplomat Kurt Waldheim becomes secretary general of the United Nations.

Pakistan leaves the British Commonwealth and Bangladesh becomes a member.

Norman Kirk, a Labour party leader, becomes prime minister of New Zealand. He serves until 1974.

Margaret II (Margrethe II) becomes queen of Denmark after the death of her father, Frederick IX (1947). She may legally take the throne since Denmark's constitutional amendment of 1953 allows female succession.

Edward G. Whitlam becomes prime minister of Australia after the term of (Sir) William McMahon (1971). Whitlam serves until 1975.

1973

After 40 years of majority strength in the Republic of Ireland, the Fianna Fáil party is defeated at the polls. Liam Cosgrave forms a coalition government; he serves as prime minister until 1977.

The United States bombing of Cambodia ends, marking an official halt to 12 years of combat activity in Southeast Asia.

Thailand's military regime is overthrown.

Civilian rule is restored in Turkey, with Bulent Ecevit leading the country. Ecevit serves until 1975 and again briefly in 1978 and 1979.

The fourth and largest Arab-Israeli war begins. Egyptian and Syrian forces attack Israel as Jews celebrate the holy Day of Atonement (Yom Kippur). Egypt and Israel sign a United States-sponsored cease-fire accord the following month.

In Afghanistan, with the assistance of an army-supported coup, Muhammad Daoud seizes power and abolishes the constitution. He remains in power until his assassination in 1978.

Diplomatic relations are resumed between East and West Germany.

Libya nationalizes United States oil interests. A seven year drought continues in West Africa and kindles the famine in Ethiopia that will be responsible for almost 100,000 deaths. The Kenyan government expels Asian traders and merchants.

The military seizes power in Rwanda, ousts President Gregoire Kayibanda (1962) and places Major General Juvenal Habyarimana in charge. Habyarimana abolishes the national assembly and bans all political parties and activities.

Bahrain has a new constitution which establishes an elected national assembly.

Captain Michel Micombero (1966) becomes president and prime minister of Burundi. He serves until 1976.

Albert-Bernard Bongo (1967) again becomes president of Gabon.

King Sobhuza II of Swaziland suspends that country's constitution and exercises absolute authority.

In Australia, aborigines gain the right to vote.

A military junta under Premier George Papadopoulos (1967) abolishes the monarchy and proclaims Greece a republic with Papadopoulos as president. Another coup follows and places General Phaedon Gizikis in office. Gizikis rules until 1974.

Charles XVI (Carl Gustaf) becomes king of Sweden after the death of his grandfather, Gustavus VI (1950).

1974

A coup takes place in Portugal and democratic reforms begin. This event also signals the end of Portuguese colonial possessions in Africa and Asia.

Guinea-Bissau (Portuguese Guinea) gains its independence.

A military coup led by General Teferi Benti removes Ethiopian Emperor Haile Selassie (1930) from power. The country is declared a socialist state.

General U Ne Win (1958, 1962) again becomes president of Burma. The government approves a new constitution that creates a one-party socialist republic. U Ne Win serves until 1981.

Japanese Prime Minister Kakuei Tanaka resigns amid accusations of financial misconduct in the Lockheed bribery scandal.

The world's deepest oil well, 31,440 feet (10,941 meters), is drilled in Oklahoma.

The Turkish military takes control of Cyprus and removes President Makarios from office.

Nicolae Ceauşescu (1965) becomes president of Romania. He rules until 1989, when his regime is overthrown and he is executed.

1970
through
1976

1970 through 1976

The failure in Northern Ireland of an attempt to "share power" between Catholics and Protestants is accompanied by an increase in Irish Republican Army terrorist activity. Several Britons are killed by bombs in Guildford and Birmingham, England.

In Niger, a military coup led by Seyni Kountché removes President Hamani Diori.

Zaïre's President Mobutu seizes foreign-owned companies and gives them out as political favors.

Ibrahim al-Hamadi seizes power in North Yemen and forms a military council to rule the country. He rules until his assassination in 1977.

In Zimbabwe, African nationalist leaders Joshua Nkomo and Secretary General Robert Mugabe are freed from prison.

The military government of Greece resigns because of their ineffective handling of the war over Cyprus.

Nine communities in Pakistan are devastated by an earthquake that claims 5,200 lives.

Constantine Karamanlis becomes premier of Greece. Late in the year, President Makarios returns to Greece.

Itzhak Rabin becomes prime minister of Israel after the term of Golda Meir (1969).

Valéry Giscard d'Estaing becomes president of France. He serves until 1981.

Harold Wilson, of the Labour party, becomes prime minister of Great Britain after the term of Edwin Heath (1970). Wilson serves until 1976.

Wallace Rowling, of the Labour party, becomes prime minister of New Zealand after the death of Norman Kirk (1972). Rowling serves until 1975.

Helmut Schmidt becomes chancellor of West Germany after the term of Willy Brandt (1969). He serves until 1983.

1975

Spain withdraws from Spanish Sahara after Moroccan forces invade the region to protect Moroccan inhabitants.

The United Nations proclaims "International Women's Year" and holds a conference in Mexico City. Attending delegates discuss methods and strategies for expanding women's rights and roles over the next decade.

Papua New Guinea becomes an independent nation within the British Commonwealth; Michael Somare is the new nation's prime minister. He serves until 1980, and again from 1982 to 1985.

In Bangladesh, Sheik Mujibur Rahman (1971) is assassinated, and martial law is imposed.

Greece adopts a new, republican constitution.

The Organization of Petroleum Exporting Countries (OPEC) increases oil prices by 10 percent.

Angola gains its independence from Portugal. A transitional government is formed with representatives of the existing political parties. Mozambique also gains its independence from Portugal after an 11-year war. A Marxist government is established, with Samora Machel as president. Machel serves until his death in 1986.

As the *emir* of Bahrain gradually assumes absolute authority, the prime minister resigns and the national assembly is disbanded.

Dahomey changes its name to Benin.

Cape Verde gains its independence from Portugal, with Aristides Pereira as first president.

Chad's President Tombalbaye (1960) is killed in a military coup led by Félix Malloum, who then rules as president of a military council. Malloum is forced to leave the country in 1979.

Comoros gains independence from France, with Ahmed Abdallah as president. The island of Mayotte, which has a Christian majority, votes to remain under French control.

The Pathet Lao, under Prince Souphanovong, takes control over Laos and abolishes the monarchy, forcing King Vatthana to abdicate.

The Suez Canal, closed since the 1967 Arab-Israeli war, is re-opened.

A civil war erupts in Lebanon between Christians and Muslims.

An earthquake in Turkey results in more than 2,300 deaths.

Sikkim abolishes its monarchy and becomes a state of India.

The space linkup of *Apollo*, with three American astronauts on board, and *Soyuz*, with two Soviet cosmonauts, marks a space policy shift from competition toward cooperation between the two nations.

Papua New Guinea becomes independent from Australian control.

Surinam gains its independence from the Netherlands with Dr. Johan Ferrier as president and Henck Arron as prime minister. Upon independence, nearly 40 percent of the country's population returns to the Netherlands.

Juan Carlos I, grandson of Alfonso XIII (1886), becomes king of Spain after the death of Francisco Franco (1947).

Two successive coups in Nigeria this year leave General Olusegun Obasanjo in power. He serves until civilian government is reestablished in 1979.

Habib Bourguiba is named president for life of Tunisia. He serves until he is overthrown in 1987.

Saigon falls to North Vietnamese forces.

Tupuola Taisi Efi becomes prime minister of Western Samoa after the death of Fiame Mata'afa Mulinu'u (1962). Efi is the country's first prime minister from outside the royal family; he serves until 1982.

Norodom Sihanouk (1960) becomes head of state of Cambodia after a Khmer Rouge revolt removes Lon Nol (1970) from office. Norodom Sihanouk serves until 1976.

In Taiwan, Chiang Ching-kuo assumes full leadership of the Kuomintang after the death of his father, Chiang Kai-shek.

John Malcolm Fraser becomes prime minister of Australia after the term of Edward G. Whitlam (1972).

Robert Muldoon, a National party leader, becomes prime minister of New Zealand. He serves until 1984.

Khalid ibn Abd al-Aziz al-Saud becomes king of Saudi Arabia after the death of his half-brother, Faisal (1964).

1976

Israeli airborne commandos attack Uganda's Entebbe Airport and free 103 hostages held by pro-Palestinian hijackers of an Air France plane; one Israeli and several Ugandan soldiers are killed in the rescue mission.

Khmer Rouge leader Pol Pot becomes prime minister of Democratic Kampuchea (Cambodia). At his instigation, communist leaders begin the systematic murder of intellectuals, dissidents, political enemies and other citizens accused of crimes against the state. An estimated 3 to 4 million people die in this massive attempt to purge the country of Western influence. Pol Pot rules until 1989.

Several areas of the world are devastated by major earthquakes, including Guatemala, Italy, the Philippines, New Guinea and eastern Turkey. By far the strongest, however, is in Tangshan, China, where 242,000 people die as a result of a quake that registers a magnitude of 8.2 on the Richter scale.

The Soviet Union and the United States sign a disarmament treaty to limit the underground testing of nuclear weapons.

President Jean-Bédel Bokassa changes the name of his country, the Central African Republic, to the Central African Empire and names himself Emperor Bokassa I. He rules until he is overthrown in 1979.

Western Sahara (formerly Spanish Sahara) declares its desire for independence but Spain's withdrawal has transferred the territory to both Moroccan and Mauritanian control. The Polisario Front, a nationalist group, fights for independence.

THE WORLD	THE WORLD	*FOR CLASSROOM USE*	*FOR CLASSROOM USE*	

Air France and British Airways begin regularly scheduled flights on the supersonic *Concorde*.

The Gilbert and Ellice islands separate into the states of Tuvalu and Kiribati.

A weapons purchase agreement between Iran and the United States is announced, whereby Iran will buy $10 billion worth of weapons.

Britain has its first woman ambassador in Anne Warburton.

Tun Husein Onn becomes prime minister of Malaysia after the death of Tun Abdul Razak (1970).

Burundi's President Micombero (1973) is overthrown in a military coup. Colonel Jean-Baptiste Bagaza is named president by the military regime. He rules until he is overthrown in 1984.

A student-led uprising against apartheid occurs in Soweto, South Africa. Approximately 600 young native Africans, of college age and younger, are killed by police and militia.

After the death of Mao Zedong (1949), an unsuccessful coup in the People's Republic of China is led by the Gang of Four, including Mao's widow. The four are arrested.

Iceland and Britain enter into a dispute over cod-fishing waters in the North Sea.

Indonesian forces invade and annex East Timor.

Guerrilla warfare occurs in the Sahara Desert, between Moroccan and Algerian forces. Diplomatic ties between the two countries are severed.

Bernard Dowiyogo becomes president of Nauru. He serves until 1978.

British ambassador Christopher Edward Biggs is assassinated in Dublin, Ireland.

Betty Williams and Mairead Corridan establish a peace movement in Northern Ireland.

Portugal adopts a new constitution that sets terms for a return to civilian rule. Mario Soares, a Socialist, heads the interim government. General António dos Santos Ramalho Eanes becomes president of Portugal this same year. He serves until 1986.

Seychelles gains independence within the British Commonwealth, with James Mancham as president.

Thorbjörn Fälldin, Centre Party leader, becomes prime minister of Sweden as head of a coalition government. Fälldin serves until 1978, and again from 1979 until 1982.

Military rule is reasserted in Thailand.

The Socialist Republic of Vietnam is proclaimed.

James Callaghan, of the Labour Party, becomes prime minister of Great Britain after the term of Harold Wilson (1974). Callaghan serves until 1979.

1970

through

1976

through				

_____

through

_____

355

through

FOR CLASSROOM USE	FOR CLASSROOM USE	FOR CLASSROOM USE	FOR CLASSROOM USE	
				――― **through** ―――
FOR CLASSROOM USE	FOR CLASSROOM USE	FOR CLASSROOM USE	FOR CLASSROOM USE	

_____ through _____				

FOR CLASSROOM USE	FOR CLASSROOM USE	FOR CLASSROOM USE	FOR CLASSROOM USE	
				_____ through _____
FOR CLASSROOM USE	FOR CLASSROOM USE	FOR CLASSROOM USE	FOR CLASSROOM USE	

	FOR CLASSROOM USE	FOR CLASSROOM USE	FOR CLASSROOM USE	FOR CLASSROOM USE
through				
	FOR CLASSROOM USE	FOR CLASSROOM USE	FOR CLASSROOM USE	FOR CLASSROOM USE

FOR CLASSROOM USE	*FOR CLASSROOM USE*	*FOR CLASSROOM USE*	*FOR CLASSROOM USE*	
				—— **through** ——
FOR CLASSROOM USE	*FOR CLASSROOM USE*	*FOR CLASSROOM USE*	*FOR CLASSROOM USE*	

Authors, Editors and Advisory Staff

The Americans All program is multifaceted. The developers have used interdisciplinary and multicultural resources to create this comprehensive approach. Experts in education, history, curriculum design, publications, human services, training, library science, public policy and multicultural issues have helped to develop these materials and this intervention strategy. The brief biographical profiles included here indicate the numerous individuals and areas of expertise that have been integrated in developing the Americans All resource materials.

- **Richard Eighme Ahlborn** has been curator of the National Museum of American History, Smithsonian Institution, since 1965. In 1978 he established the Division of Community Life to bring attention to American social, religious and ethnic groups. In graduate studies at Winterthur and Yale, and in dozens of publications, he has focused on Hispanic American material culture — architecture, furniture, saddlery and *santos* — especially in the Southwest.

- **Anthropology, Outreach and Public Information Office**, National Museum of Natural History, Smithsonian Institution. This office distributes free materials on anthropology, including Native Americans, in the form of information leaflets, bibliographies and resource packets for teachers, students and the general public.

- **Thomas J. Archdeacon,** professor of history at the University of Wisconsin-Madison, previously served as an assistant professor of history at the United States Military Academy, West Point. He received a doctorate in history from Columbia University. His works include *Becoming American: An Ethnic History* and *New York City, 1664-1710: Conquest and Change.* Dr. Archdeacon's research and teaching responsibilities focus on the history of immigration and ethnicity and on the application of computers and quantitative analysis to historical investigations.

- **Gloria Brooks-Bannister** brings 15 years of experience to the Americans All program as a professional social worker and former juvenile probation officer, as well as that of an internationally recognized vocalist who has performed throughout Europe. Her social work experience includes primarily race relations and educational projects. Ms. Bannister has been involved in the Americans All program since 1989. A member of the Americans All national training team, with experience in all five pilot cities, she has also worked as an Americans All program coordinator and community outreach worker in the Chicago area.

- **Jonathan C. Brown,** Ph.D., is a professor of history at the University of Texas, Austin. He served as director for the Texas Project in U.S. Studies for Latin American Scholars, the Lyndon Baines Johnson Presidential Library and the Eugene C. Barker Texas History Center. He has also served as publications chairman and associate director for the Institute of Latin American Studies at the University of Texas. He has authored *Oil and Revolution in Mexico* and *A Socioeconomic History of Argentina, 1776-1860,* and has written many articles on Latin American economics.

- **Roy Simon Bryce-Laporte,** director of Africana and Hispanic Studies at Colgate University, received his Ph.D. in sociology from the University of California, Los Angeles. He has served as director of the Yale University Afro-American Studies Program, the Smithsonian Institution's Research Institute on Immigration and Ethnic Studies and the Center for Immigration and Population Studies of the College of Staten Island, City University of New York. Born in Panama, he has written several publications on Caribbean immigration to the United States and Central America. He was the guest curator of *Give Me Your Tired, Your Poor—?,* a collection on black voluntary immigration to the United States shown at the Schomburg Center for the Study of Black Culture, New York Public Library, in 1986.

- **Paul Q. Chow** has been instrumental in the developmental and educational activities of the Angel Island Immigration Station Historical Advisory Committee since 1973. A prominent guest lecturer, he has been involved in many other civic and community activities. A Korean War veteran, he retired in 1988 after 35 years of service for the Department of Transportation, where he held the position of associate transportation engineer.

- **Douglas A. Conway** received a Master of Instruction in economics from the University of Delaware in Newark and an M.A. degree in secondary education from Arizona State University in Tempe. He is currently an instructor of microeconomics, macroeconomics and economic history of the United States at Mesa Community College in Mesa, Arizona.

- **Dorothy Laigo Cordova** is director of the Demonstration Project for Asian Americans and executive director of the Filipino American National Historical Society. She has been involved in the collection of oral histories of Filipino immigrants who came to the United States before 1940 and developed the photo exhibit, *Filipino Women in America/1870-1985,* that traveled throughout the country.

- **Fred Cordova** is a Seattle journalist and writer. The manager of news services at the University of Washington, he is founder of Filipino Youth Activities, Inc. A second-generation Pinoy Californian, he was a 1985 Smithsonian faculty fellow and the first president of the Filipino American National Historical Society.

- **Donald J. Crotteau,** a freelance illustrator and graphic designer located in the Washington, D.C., area, creates illustrated educational material for children. Mr. Crotteau also draws cartoons for magazines and newspapers in Virginia, Washington, D.C., and Chicago, Illinois.

- **Deidre H. Crumbley,** Ph.D., is a sociocultural anthropologist specializing in religious reformulation in Africa/African Diaspora. Her articles include "Even A Woman: Sex Roles and Mobility in an Aladura Hierarchy," "E Ku Idele Baba-o: The Celestial Church of Christ After the Death of Its Founder" and "Impurity and Power: Women in Aladura Churches." Currently teaching at the University of Florida, she was an assistant professor and coordinator of African and African American Studies at Rollins College, an assistant professor at the University of Ibadan and the recipient of several grants for her research in Africa and African diasporan studies.

- **Department of Puerto Rican Community Affairs in the United States** was created in 1989 for the purpose of making the rights of the Puerto Rican community valued and respected. The department offers such services as a political orientation and action program; social service programs; cultural promotion programs; a legal assistance program; and a migrant farm workers program.

- **Frank de Varona** is an educator with 25 years of experience in the Dade County Public Schools in Miami, Florida. The author of four biographies for elementary students, *Bernardo de Gálvez, Simón Bolívar, Benito Juárez* and *Miguel Hidalgo,* and a textbook, *Florida Government Activities*, he has also coauthored two textbooks, *Hispanics in U.S. History, Volume 1* and *Volume 2*. He has edited 20 books and has served as a consultant for United States History, World History, Government and Spanish textbooks for various publishers.

- **Loni Ding,** a filmmaker whose documentaries have won numerous awards, was executive producer for the video/curriculum series *On Location: Travels to California's Past,* winner of the 1988 National Educational Film Festival's Silver Apple award. She received the Pacific Mountain Network's

Best of the West award for the episode *Island of Secret Memories: The Angel Island Immigration Station.* She is a member of the faculty of the Asian American Studies Department, University of California, Berkeley.

- **Mary Agnes Dougherty**, Ph.D., and **Lyn Reese**, M.A., of New Directions Curriculum Developers, Berkeley, California, designed and directed the video/curriculum series *On Location: Travels to California's Past,* winner of the 1988 National Educational Film Festival's Silver Apple award and the Pacific Mountain Network's Best of the West award for the episode *Island of Secret Memories: The Angel Island Immigration Station.* They apply their training as professional historians and their wide experience as classroom teachers, administrators and authors to create social science curricula that engage the intellect and stimulate the imagination. Dr. Dougherty is a consultant to the Scholars in the Schools National Diffusion Humanities Network. Ms. Reese is on the board of the California Council of Social Studies Teachers and chairs the Gender/Social Justice Committee.

- **Robert R. Edgar**, Ph.D., an associate professor in the African Studies and Research Program at Howard University, Washington, D.C., has also taught at the University of California, Los Angeles, and lectured at the University of Lesotho and Georgetown University. Author of *Prophets With Honor: A Documentary History of Lekhotla la Bafo* and *An African American in South Africa: The Research Diary of Ralph J. Bunche, 1937,* he has also authored numerous articles on African and African American Studies.

- **Nila Modesta Salazar Fish**, executive director of The Council on U.S.-Philippine Relations, was formerly president of the Asian Pacific American Council on Culture and Education. A naturalized American citizen, she has lectured extensively on the Philippines.

- **Paula Richardson Fleming**, photograph archivist, National Anthropological Archives, Smithsonian Institution, has undertaken extensive research into nineteenth-century Native American photographs. She has organized a major exhibit for the Smithsonian and has contributed, to and coauthored, numerous publications on the subject.

- **Ronald C. Foreman, Jr.**, Ph.D., has a special interest in folklore and popular culture. During his tenure as an English professor and director of Afro-American Studies at the University of Florida, he has been chairman of the Folklife Council, Florida, and trustee, member and chairman of the American Folklife Center, Library of Congress. He proposed the Florida Folklife Heritage Award recognizing outstanding tradition bearers and edited *First Citizens and Other Florida Folks.*

- **Lawrence H. Fuchs** is the Meyer and Walter Jaffe Professor of American Civilization and Politics at Brandeis University, Waltham, Massachusetts. Dr. Fuchs' published work includes seven books on immigration and/or racial and ethnic diversity. His latest book is *The American Kaleidoscope: Race, Ethnicity, and the Civic Culture.* Dr. Fuchs, who received his doctorate from Harvard University, served as executive director of the United States Select Commission on Immigration and Refugee Policy from 1979 to 1981, and he testifies frequently before Congress on immigration policy.

- **Luvenia A. George** is a pioneer in the development of materials and techniques to incorporate ethnomusicology into music education curricula. Her primary interests are African American music and culture (1900-1930) and multicultural music education. She has taught general and choral music on all levels and serves as a clinician, consultant and lecturer for schools and professional organizations.

- **Richard Griswold del Castillo** is a professor of Mexican American Studies at San Diego State University. He received his doctorate in history from the University of California, Los Angeles, with an emphasis in Chicano and United States History. In his research and writing he has emphasized the community, family and international dimensions of the Mexican American experience. He has been a consultant for a variety of film and publication projects and actively promotes the inclusion of Mexican American history within the school curriculum.

- **Duane K. Hale**, Ph.D., a mixed-blood Creek, has developed a workshop series entitled "Researching and Writing Tribal Histories." He has served as cochair of the Navajo and Indian Studies Division of Navajo Community College and is currently at the American Indian Institute, The University of Oklahoma.

- **Nancy K. Harris** is a teacher trainer with the Interrelated ARTS Program in the Montgomery County Public Schools, Maryland. She develops and demonstrates strategies for teaching the curriculum through the arts. She has played a major role in adapting the "Being An Immigrant" materials that she has used to simulate the Ellis Island experience for more than 1,200 fifth and sixth grade students.

- **Walter B. Hill, Jr.**, Ph.D., is an archivist with the National Archives Records Administration and director of the Modern Archives Institute. He has served on the executive council for the Association for the Study of AfroAmerican Life and History, the Committee on Public History for the Organization of American History and numerous consultantships relative to African American life and culture.

- **The Hispanic Policy Development Project** is the nation's first Hispanic think tank dedicated to the encouragement of objective analyses of public policies that bear on the concerns of Hispanics in the United States. Founded in 1982, the project is especially concerned with the education and school-to-work problems of the nation's 3.4 million Hispanic young people. In response to a consensus among Hispanics that education is their top priority, the project's executive board has established a policy of focusing on problems faced by Hispanic students at the secondary level and in their transition from school to work.

- **Robert I. Holden**, a member of both the Choctaw and Chickasaw Nations, is a Washington, D.C.-based consultant on Native American environmental and cultural resource issues. Now a community scholar fellow with the Smithsonian Institution's National Museum of Natural History, he is writing a biography of Petaga Yuha Mani (Pete Catches, Sr.), an octogenarian Oglala Lakota medicine man and spiritual leader from the Pine Ridge Indian Reservation.

- **Crystal K. D. Huie** is a photographer deeply involved with programs of the Asian American community. An instructor at the Photography Center in San Francisco, his photographs have appeared in numerous publications and have been exhibited in galleries and museums throughout the country. He is the recipient of many fellowships in photography, museum education and community studies.

- **Janice Lee Jayes**, a graduate of The American University in Washington, D.C., specializing in U.S.-Latin American History will receive her Ph.D. in December 1993. She has been an instructor of history and foreign policy at Montgomery College, Maryland; U.S.D.A. Graduate School, Washington, D.C.; Gettysburg College, Pennsylvania; and The American University, Washington, D.C. She has also served as a researcher for the Smithsonian, Anthropology Archives; the Library of Congress, Hispanic Division; the U.S.-Mexican Business Group; and *Business Report.*

- **Charles B. Keely** is professor of demography at Georgetown University, Washington, D.C. He has been a Fulbright scholar in the Philippines, a research fellow at Brown University and the economics department of Jordan's Royal Scientific Society and a senior associate at the Population Council. He has also taught at Fordham University, Western Michigan University and Loyola College, and has presented testimony on immigration matters to Congress. His major research focused on labor migration in the Middle East, international refugee policy and United States immigration law. He is the author and editor of six books and more than 50 articles and book chapters on international migration and ethnic relations.

- **David Kelly** is a reference librarian in Washington, D.C. He holds an undergraduate degree in anthropology and his special fields of study include urban ethnicity and migration.

- **Paul J. Kinney**, a fundraising and public relations consultant for historic house museums, developed an abiding interest in the peoples of the world while serving as a Peace Corps volunteer in South Korea. From 1975 to 1986 he worked at the Statue of Liberty National Monument, first as registrar then as curator for the American Museum of Immigration, the Statue of Liberty and Ellis Island.

- **Marilyn Leiberman Klaban**, a drama specialist with the Interrelated ARTS Program in the Montgomery County Public Schools, Maryland, was instrumental in introducing, expanding and implementing many of the Ellis Island drama simulations.

- **Him Mark Lai** is a historian who has authored many books and articles on Chinese American history. He has served as past president of the Chinese Historical Society of America and the Chinese Culture Foundation of San Francisco, he has also served as archivist and consultant for the Asian American Studies Library, University of California at Berkeley.

- **Michael Lapp,** Ph.D., has taught United States history at the City College of New York. His thesis at Johns Hopkins University dealt with Puerto Rican migration to the United States mainland in the 1940s and 1950s, and he has conducted extensive archival research on Puerto Rican migration history.

- **Everette E. Larson,** Ph.D., is a supervisory librarian in Washington, D.C. Beginning his university studies in Spain, he later graduated from Georgetown University with a degree in Arabic. He also holds a master's degree in Spanish and another in library science. His doctorate is in Romance-Semitic studies from Catholic University. He has published a variety of bibliographies on Spanish and Latin American topics and recently served as an advisor to the *MLA International Bibliography.*

- **John Loughridge,** a reference librarian, received a bachelor's degree in art history at the University of Maryland. He then served as the university's Art Department photographer before studying at the Universita Internazionale del'Arte in Florence. He earned a master's degree in library science from the Catholic University of America in 1988. In 1989, while working as a reference librarian at Montgomery College, Rockville, Maryland, Mr. Loughridge won a Mellon Foundation Internship to the Library of Congress, Preservation Department.

- **Cesare Marino,** Ph.D., a Sicilian-born, American-trained anthropologist, became involved in Native American studies after researching Southern Italian folklore and ethnic and regional identities in Europe. He has visited numerous Native American reservations in the United States and Canada and has worked for the National Congress of American Indians and Americans for Indian Opportunity. Since 1983 he has been working on the *Handbook of North American Indians* at the Smithsonian Institution, Natural History Branch, as a researcher, and recently, as an author.

- **Elizabeth Martinez** is an instructor in the Department of Ethnic Studies at California State University, Hayward. She founded the Chicano Communications Center in New Mexico and served as the program director for Global Options, a research and advocacy center in San Francisco. She has lectured on Chicano studies at many colleges and universities and has written and edited a number of books in this field.

- **Gilbert Marzán** is a senior at the College of Staten Island, City University of New York. He is currently pursuing a bachelor's degree in sociology/anthropology.

- **William M. Mason,** history curator at the Los Angeles County Museum of Natural History, is a specialist on the early history of Los Angeles. He has served as a consultant for Asian American Studies at California State University and as a consultant for the Latino Museum in Los Angeles. He has published numerous articles and guides on the history of both Asians and Latinos.

- **Janet Brown McCracken,** M.Ed., an early childhood educator, specializes in drawing implications for developmentally appropriate practice from research and theory. She writes about and photographs young children and their teachers for several national projects and professional organizations. McCracken, who edited *Young Children* for more than 10 years, is an educational publishing consultant for Subjects and Predicates.

- **Lynda Cartagena Mobley,** a native of Louisiana, grew up in Rio Piedras, Puerto Rico, in a bilingual and bicultural atmosphere. An accomplished researcher in Latin American studies, she has provided material for use in many books and articles. She also has done commercial translations in both Spanish and English.

- **Joseph Monserrat,** former national director of the Migration Division of the Puerto Rican Department of Labor, has lectured extensively on education, labor, migration, farm workers and minority group problems. He has taught at the college level and has served as president of the New York City Board of Education. Active on many community and civic boards, he is currently working on a book tentatively titled *Hispanic, USA.*

- **The Montgomery County (Maryland) Interrelated ARTS (Arts Resource Teams in the Schools) Program** provides training and support to classroom teachers, giving them the information and background needed to integrate the arts into the curriculum. The program's goal is to give teachers the versatility to enhance student achievement at all levels by incorporating the arts throughout the curriculum. It is based on the philosophy that the arts are important to all human growth and development both as an impetus to appreciation and expression and as a means of viewing the human condition — the cultural heritage.

- **Carolyn Mulford** is a writer, editor and editorial consultant in the Washington, D.C., area. Formerly the editor of *Synergist,* a journal on service-learning, she is the author of a forthcoming young adult biography of Secretary of Labor Elizabeth Hanford Dole. She is also the coauthor/photographer of *Adventure Vacations in Five Mid-Atlantic States.* She writes and edits two national monthly newsletters, *Communications Concepts* and *Writing Concepts.* She has taught English in Ethiopia and continuing education classes at Georgetown University and The George Washington University.

- **National Women's History Project** develops curriculum materials, conducts teacher training workshops throughout the country and serves as a clearinghouse for women's history information and programming ideas. The project also markets books, posters, videos and kindergarten through grade 12 curriculum materials pertaining to women in American history for use by educators and community program planners.

- **Frank S. Odo,** Ph.D., is a *sansei,* a third-generation American of Japanese descent. He is currently director of the Ethnic Studies Program at the University of Hawaii but has held positions as curriculum coordinator, lecturer and professor in the same field. He has published numerous articles and books on Asian Americans with a special emphasis on Japanese history in both Japan and the United States.

- **Joseph Petulla,** professor of environmental science at the University of San Francisco, received his Ph.D. in 1971 from the University of California and the Graduate Theological Union, Berkeley. His published work includes four books in a Religion and Life textbook series and a three-book series on the history, philosophy and management of American environmental problems: *American Environmental History*; *American Environmentalism: Values, Tactics, Priorities*; and *Environmental Protection in the United States: Industry; Agencies; Environmentalists.*

- **Carol Brunson Phillips** is executive director of the Council for Early Childhood Professional Recognition, Child Development Associate National Credentialing Program in Washington, D.C. Dr. Phillips received her bachelor of arts degree in psychology from the University of Wisconsin, her masters in early childhood education from Erikson Institute and her Ph.D. in education from Claremont Graduate School. As a member of the human development faculty at Pacific Oaks College in Pasadena, she specialized in early childhood education and cultural influences on development for 13 years.

- **Michael Pietrzak** has worked as a teacher and administrator in a variety of public and Catholic school systems. He also holds adjunct positions at Northeastern Illinois University, St. Xavier University and DePaul University. He served on the founding faculty of the Teach for America Summer Institute, a national urban teacher preparation project. Mr. Pietrzak also provides consultant services to schools and districts throughout the country in reading/language arts, technology and general staff development.

- **Frances J. Powell,** Ph.D., professor of history and political science at Montgomery College, Maryland, received her Doctor of Arts in history from the Catholic University of America. As supervising director of social studies for the District of Columbia Public Schools, she provided leadership and direction in the design and development of social studies curriculum for grades K-12. As coordinator of the D.C. History Curriculum Project, she was involved in writing and publishing the textbook, *Washington, D.C.: City of Magnificent Intentions.*

- **Lyn Reese** (see **Mary Agnes Dougherty**)

- **Clara Rodríguez** is an associate professor in the Division of Social Sciences at Fordham University's College at Lincoln Center, New York. Previously

364

she was the dean of Fordham University's School of General Studies. Currently on sabbatical, she is a visiting scholar at the Massachusetts Institute of Technology and the recipient of grants from the Inter-University Program/Social Science Research Council, the Rockefeller Foundation and the Business and Professional Women's Association. She is the author of *Puerto Ricans: Born in the U.S.A.,* as well as numerous articles focusing on the Puerto Rican community in the United States.

• **Ricardo Romo** has been an associate professor of history at the University of Texas at Austin since 1980. From 1974 to 1979 Professor Romo taught at the University of California at San Diego. From 1989 to 1990 he was a Fellow at the Center for Advanced Studies in the Behavioral Studies at Stanford University. Professor Romo's principal teaching and research areas concern American twentieth century social and legal history. He has been named to International Authors and Writers Who's Who, Contemporary Authors, and *Hispanic Who's Who in America.*

• **Jo-Anne Rosen,** a member of the board of directors of the Angel Island Immigration Station Historical Advisory Committee, coauthored *A Teacher's Guide to the Angel Island Immigration Station.* She has taught English as a foreign language and college-level English composition. A short-story writer whose fiction has been published in several literary magazines, she operates a desktop publishing and computer software training service.

• **Jean Seley** provides consulting, writing, research and training services to nonprofit organizations. With 28 years of experience as a coordinator and manager of various nonprofit organizations, she specializes in education, training and counseling. After six years as an elementary school teacher, Seley went into the field of religious education. In 1968, she began working with low-income, minority youth as an education specialist for the Neighborhood Youth Corps and became assistant director of the Neighborhood House Youth Service Center, funded by the Criminal Justice System.

• **Jerry Silverman** has devoted more than 25 years to the art of bringing music to life through his pen, typewriter, teaching and the strings of an acoustic guitar. A formally trained music scholar, he has written more than 100 books dealing with various aspects of guitar, banjo, violin and fiddle techniques as well as numerous songbooks and arrangements for other instruments. In addition to writing, he teaches guitar to both children and adults and performs in folk concerts before audiences of all ages.

• **Richard Spottswood,** an active student and collector of early sound recordings, has produced numerous albums of jazz, blues and folk music. He is the author of a seven-volume discography, *Ethnic Music on Records*, and has served as chair of the National Council for Traditional Music. He is currently vice president of the Association for Recorded Sound Collections (ARSC). He hosts a weekly radio broadcast of traditional music and produces a syndicated program, *The Homegrown Music Hour.*

• **Eleanor Sreb,** founder of The Coordinating Committee for Ellis Island, Inc., currently serves as an organizational consultant in Washington, D.C. She worked in the Library of Congress for 22 years, and it was during her tenure as executive assistant to the director of the American Folklife Center that The Coordinating Committee, Inc., was formed.

• **Steven Sreb,** a management consultant, trainer and writer, specializes in career management systems and training development. Mr. Sreb has developed and delivered employee and manager training workshops, designed supporting information and human resource systems and forged linkages with performance appraisal and quality improvement programs. He is also a nationally recognized expert in self-directed job search training and program design. Approximately 38 states have implemented his program to assist the unemployed and welfare recipients in their transition to self-sufficient employment.

• **Margaret Sullivan,** recipient of the Commissioner's Distinguished Career Service award, served as a management analyst for the Immigration and Naturalization Service. She assisted in compiling the *Statistical Yearbook* and was responsible for preparing reports for Congress and the public. She retired in 1988 and now serves as a consultant in the Washington, D.C., area.

• **Andrea Temple,** a freelance writer and curator, served for five years at the American Museum of Immigration as exhibit technician and curator of exhibits, including the Sherman photographic collection. During her tenure, Ms. Temple exclusively handled the collection and photographed the originals as slides to be used in off-site talks.

• **Barbara A. Tenenbaum,** Ph.D., is the editor in chief of the *Encyclopedia of Latin American History.* Currently she serves as specialist in Mexican culture in the Hispanic Division at the Library of Congress, Washington, D.C. Previously she taught Latin American and Iberian history and served as director of Latin American studies at a number of colleges and universities. She is the author of several books and numerous articles on the history of Mexico and Mexican Americans in the nineteenth century.

• **Emory J. Tolbert** is a professor of history and chairman of the Department of History, Howard University, Washington, D.C. The author of several articles on the Garvey Movement, he is senior editor of the *Marcus Garvey Papers,* Volumes 2-4. His most recent work is a textbook on ethnic and racial minorities in the United States, *Race and Culture in America.* He has spent the past 20 years conducting oral history research in the areas of black nationalism and blacks in the American West. He is currently completing a book on the African American community in Los Angeles.

• **June F. Tyler,** Ph.D., coauthor of a number of guides in both social studies and general curriculum development, served as director of Educational and Editorial Services for The First Experience, Inc. She has taught at many different grade levels and has served as a consultant for the Connecticut Department of Education.

• **Clifford I. Uyeda,** M.D., is president of the National Japanese American Historical Society. A former captain in the United States Air Force, he has been active in both medical and community organizations, serving as national president of the Japanese American Citizens League, on the boards of many health organizations and as the editor of *Nikkei Heritage,* a quarterly journal.

• **Herman J. Viola,** Ph.D., former director of the National Anthropological Archives at the Smithsonian Institution, is director of the Quincentenary Programs for the National Museum of Natural History at the Smithsonian. During his federal career, Dr. Viola has been actively involved in exhibit work and has published numerous books, articles and reviews on topics related to Native Americans.

• **Gongli Xu** is currently at Brandeis University completing his Ph.D. studies in American Politics. Born in Beijing, China, he has studied English linguistics and literature at Beijing University. Formerly division director of the Chinese Association for International Exchanges, he has translated several current event articles and technical publications, published both in Chinese and English.

• **Ira W. Yellen,** a professional photographer and designer, is president of The First Experience, Inc., a Connecticut company specializing in the development and production of educational products. Mr. Yellen's work stresses the need for environmental preservation and he played a significant role in creating public awareness of the need for restoration of Ellis Island.

Biographical information was compiled at the time the individuals contributed to Americans All.

The AMERICANS ALL Resource Materials

Ethnic and Cultural Group Books

These books provide important background information for teachers at all grade levels. They can also be used by students in grades 10-12.

The Indian Nations: The First Americans

This resource book provides background information on the Indian nations that inhabited the United States about 500 years ago and discusses the impact indigenous and new populations had on one another. The culture and history of Native Americans is considered as well as the impact of European movement into their lands. United States governmental actions and policies, as well as Native American responses, are presented.

African Americans

This book is built around two historical perspectives of the African American experience. It discusses forced migration (slavery) as well as the voluntary immigration of African Americans to the United States and the migration from southern to northern states. The authors trace the African roots in this country that predate the slavery experience.

Asian Americans

The earliest Asian immigrants to our shores were Chinese, Japanese and Filipinos. Although the early Asian immigrants shared certain problems, including racial discrimination and an imbalance between the number of men

and women immigrants, each group had its own special difficulties and successes. United States immigration policies, both historical and current, are also discussed.

European Immigration From the Colonial Era to the 1920s

The earliest Europeans to come to this country, commonly called settlers, were actually immigrants. This book contains information on the history of European immigration to the United States and describes that experience in the context of early American history through its peak period at Ellis Island.

Mexican Americans

This resource book provides background information on the history of Mexican immigration to and migration within the United States. The issues of American migration as it affected the Mexican landowners is considered, particularly Mexican American resistance to dominance by the European American culture.

Puerto Ricans: Immigrants and Migrants

The history of Puerto Rican immigration to and migration within the United States is reviewed in this book. The issues that are unique to this Caribbean group are discussed, such as the status of Puerto Rican citizenship and the back-and-forth travel across open borders.

Teacher Resources

The Peopling of America: A Teacher's Manual for the Americans All Program

This teacher's manual introduces the conceptual framework, teaching philosophy and methodology of the Americans All program. It provides an overview of the program components, goals and objectives. A rationale for using the history of the peopling of the United States as a context for fostering multicultural development is addressed in this publication. The Americans All historical development and evaluation outcomes are included as well as biographical sketches of the program's national team of authors, educators and advisors.

American Immigration: The Continuing Tradition

This 72-page text on American immigration history and policy was developed for use by primary and secondary school teachers as they implement the Americans All program. The charts, graphs and statistical information describe how and why immigration laws were developed and explain immigration policy in relationship to some major events and trends in United States history.

An American Symbol: The Statue of Liberty

This resource book provides teachers and students in grades 10-12 with background information on the history and restoration of the Statue of Liberty.

Ellis Island

This resource book provides teachers and students in grades 10-12 with background information on the Ellis Island Immigration Station. Photographs by Augustus Sherman, William Williams and Lewis W. Hine are included. Their photographs depict the images of various groups that entered through Ellis Island.

Angel Island

This resource book provides teachers and students in grades 10-12 with background information on the Angel Island Immigration Station and discusses the experience of detention on the island.

Student Materials

Background Essays

These student essays provide background information on Native Americans, African Americans, Asian Americans, European Americans, Mexican Americans and Puerto Rican Americans, as well as Angel Island, Ellis Island and the Statue of Liberty. Adapted from the Americans All Ethnic and Cultural Group Books, the essays have been created to meet both the language and social studies requirements of grades 3-4, 5-6 and 7-9. These essays are in blackline master format and appear in their respective teacher's guide. Learning activities found in each teacher's guide encourage the use of these student essays both in the classroom and at home.

People Moving: A Teacher's Guide for Americans All Learning Activities That Foster Geographic Literacy

This book's activities link the Americans All classroom resources and geographic literacy, with masters of maps and learning aids.

The Peopling of America: A Timeline of Events That Helped Shape Our Nation

This book provides a comparative presentation of important events as they occurred in the history of the world and the Americas, and represents the six diverse groups emphasized in the Americans All program.

Teacher Guides

A Teacher's Guide to Learning Activities

There are separate teacher's guides for grades K-2, 3-4, 5-6, 7-9 and 10-12. Each teacher's guide contains two sets of learning activities to assist the teacher in using the Americans All resource materials. The first are generic activities that use the context of the peopling of the United States to introduce and reinforce concepts of self-esteem, stress management, motivation and multicultural development. The second are activities using the movement of people and cultural diversity as underlying themes. These activities are tailored to meet grade-specific social studies curriculum objectives whenever state, local and American history is taught. Each teacher's guide also contains

blackline masters of student resource material that is used with the learning activities.

A Simulation: The Peopling of America

This resource book contains instructions for conducting a simulation of one form of the immigration process. Also included are blackline masters to be used with this activity. Follow-up activities focus on the immigration, migration (forced and voluntary) and slavery experiences of the diverse groups that peopled this nation.

Audio and Visual Materials

Music Cassette and Guide: *Music of America's Peoples*

The Americans All music cassette contains 21 original recordings of historic songs representing diverse cultural and ethnic groups. The accompanying guide contains the recordings' scores and lyrics as well as background information and suggested activities that include the use of other Americans All resources.

Slides, Photographs and Guide: *The Americans All Photograph Collection*

This is a collection of more than 250 slides and photographs that portray a cross-section of the people who became Americans. It includes photographs of Native Americans, African Americans, Asian Americans, European Americans, Mexican Americans and Puerto Rican Americans. These are augmented by authentic, period-specific photographs of the Statue of Liberty and the major ports of entry, Angel Island and Ellis Island. The companion guide contains general and specific learning activity suggestions that start with basic learning skills, such as identification, classification and sequencing, and move onto higher levels of reasoning and interpretation skills.

Poster Collection

This collection of seven posters is designed for classroom and building display. The topics covered are Angel Island, Ellis Island, the Statue of Liberty and the Peopling of America (three different photographic collages). A poster of the Americans All logo is also provided.

Instructional In-Service Video

This in-service video explains the core concepts and philosophy that underlie the Americans All program. It also describes the individual components and demonstrates ways in which they can be effectively used in the classroom.

A NATIONAL EDUCATION PROGRAM

AMERICANS ALL